CONFLICT

IN WORLD POLITICS

EDITED BY

STEVEN L. SPIEGEL

University of California, Los Angeles

AND

KENNETH N. WALTZ

Brandeis University

WINTHROP PUBLISHERS, INC.
Cambridge, Massachusetts

© 1971 by Winthrop Publishers, Inc., 17 Dunster Street,
Harvard Square, Cambridge, Massachusetts 02138

P 87626-398-8
C 87626-399-6

Library of Congress Catalog Card Number 77-143584

Printed in the United States of America
Current printing (last number): 10   9   8   7   6   5   4   3   2   1

Contents

Part Four

Muted Conflicts

Part Five

Policy Conflicts

Preface

This book contains 22 original essays that deal with conflict in world politics by examining disputes occurring within the current international system. These conflicts, which vary in intensity, duration, scope, and type of issues over which contention arises, provide information and insights about many major confrontations of contemporary world politics. The book also provides a framework for examining the causes and consequences of various types of conflict.

The choice of conflict situations, beyond those that would obviously have to be included in any book of this sort, was necessarily arbitrary, but not accidental. Within the limits of 22 articles arranged in 11 chapters, we sought to include the most important conflict situations and to represent the greatest possible variety of confrontations and factors involved in them. We asked contributors to prepare essays for this book on the basis of their expert knowledge and close familiarity with the subject matter about which they would write. We did not shy away from people who might have developed preferences on some of the issues at hand. We simply sought those whose positions would be based on the fullest knowledge and the most careful consideration. A few contributors are citizens of one of the countries in the situation being examined; most are not. Collectively, the authors represent a wide range of intellectual style, political experience, age, nationality, and present geographic location.

As in any venture of this type, many people contributed to the successful completion of the book. James J. Murray, president of Winthrop Publishers, not only encouraged us to initiate the effort and assisted us in our tasks, but also placed the full facilities of Winthrop at our disposal. Miss Sarah Blackmun served as a devoted and perceptive editor; her counsel was invaluable throughout the preparation of the book. Finally, we want to express our gratitude to the 22 authors who prepared essays. Their diligent efforts enabled us to complete the book close to the original schedule, and in many cases this achievement required personal sacrifice. We acknowledge their dedication.

Steven L. Spiegel, Los Angeles, California
Kenneth N. Waltz, Waltham, Massachusetts

Conflict in World Politics

Chapter 1: Introduction

Steven L. Spiegel

This book provides a view of the range of conflicts in contemporary international politics. Most of the essays that follow tell the "story" of a conflict, but the story is not told merely for the sake of the tale or simply to indicate who did what to whom. Individually and collectively, the essays seek instead to explain why conflicts unfold as they do. The attention of the various authors centers on the origins of conflicts, on their scope, on the issues in dispute, on the methods, instruments, and strategies by which they are conducted, and on their outcomes. The degree of stress on each of these subjects is determined, of course, by the conditions of the particular dispute under discussion.

In each essay, the origins and evolution of a particular conflict are treated analytically. The question is not what happened when, but rather why it happened. Did a conflict emerge and become sharper and more intense even though no one really intended to produce such a result? In bilateral confrontations, did third parties play a role? What about the role of great powers? Why did a conflict broaden and become more general, or how was it narrowed and confined? Similarly, questions are posed about such matters as dampening effects, increase or decrease of bitterness, the choice and the effects of certain methods and instruments, movements toward or away from the use of force, and the advantages and disadvantages of the weak and the strong.

To study the occurrence and development of conflict requires examination of (1) the environment or context of conflict, (2) the participants or units in conflict, and (3) the causes and consequences of conflict.

Throughout this book, emphasis falls on the situation in which competitors find themselves and on the substantive issues that divide them. Our goal is to understand the life-cycle of conflicts. We have therefore rejected cross-cultural or cross-national approaches to the study of conflict. The essays in this volume examine the full scope of a conflict; they do not compare the origins, outcomes, or instruments of two or more conflicts. We have, for example, included a chapter on the Arab-Israeli conflict and one on the Indian-Pakistani conflict; we have not included a chapter comparing the origins of these two disputes or one comparing the military balance in the two confrontations.

Conflict is produced by a clash of cultures, a disharmony of interests, a disparity of perceptions—all of which result in the inability of the parties to accept separately and together the environment they live in. The immediate context of any conflict is created by the attributes and the interactions of the parties. The weaker the parties, the less consequential their fates will be for others. Outside intrusions then may well be negligible, and the local arena of struggle can be studied almost in isolation. Countries of greater capability will have wider and more varied interests, and conflict between them will have regional or even global significance. The global political environment is formed ultimately by the interacting attributes and capabilities of the United States and the Soviet Union. Always potentially, and often in fact, one or both of those countries will intrude in the conflicts of less powerful states.

How widely the environment's boundaries will have to be drawn is a question to be answered for each case. In some cases, an extended environment—a series of overlapping contexts, so to speak—will have to be considered in order to understand what has happened. The traumatic American experience in Vietnam provides an unfortunately apt illustration. The United States began its Indochinese intervention more than two decades ago under the impression that Moscow's domination of the Communist world would continue indefinitely and that any extension of Communism would therefore add to the strength of a single world movement. Intervention continued and increased apparently without sufficient American consideration of the fact that tensions and cleavage between Russia and China altered the global environment and especially the regional context. Once Russia and China were divided, any increase of Chinese strength that might follow from the extension of her influence in southeast Asia became first and foremost a worry for the Soviet Union, not for the United States. A redefinition of dangers and interests was called for, not because

Vietnamese were behaving differently, but because old problems took on a different meaning because of the change of the context.

Finally, American policy-makers understood but poorly the conditions within the arena of immediate struggle. They did not pay enough attention either to ethnic and religious differences within South Vietnam or to antipathies among Cambodia, Thailand, Laos, and the two Vietnams. Because the area was viewed largely in terms of American objectives and great-power contention, policies were formulated that did not take into account the likely effects upon the local balance of enmities. The projection of great power into an area populated by politically and militarily weak peoples may easily destroy their political integrity and undermine the conditions for political stability upon which the attainment of the great powers' own objectives in part depends.

The dynamics of a conflict are most clearly revealed by examining its immediate context. To appreciate the larger issues often requires looking to more distant horizons. In this book, some essays give the reader a sense of the wider context in which other struggles take place—the essays on the United States and China and the Soviet Union and China, for example, in relation to the situation in Vietnam.

The Units in Conflict

Conflicts may be precipitated, intensified, or resolved by changes in the environment or by changes in the attributes of the participants. The two types of change are closely related. The environment may be altered by an increase or a decrease in the number of participants in the conflict or through modification of the capabilities of the parties. In a given set of states, changes in the attributes of some may change the environment for all. Cultures and societies are formed over centuries; the basic capabilities of states do not change in the short run. But regimes, or at least their leading personalities, may suddenly be replaced, and military capability may be quite rapidly increased by mobilization or outside assistance, or lowered by military defeat or the squandering of resources through ineptitude and corruption. Capabilities themselves affect the enthusiasm of governments for active roles in international politics as well as their abilities to play them.

Whether one seeks to mute conflict by changing leaders or policies, by increasing military capabilities, or by altering the number of participants, formulas that look effective on paper may prove to be inoperative because they cannot alter the incentives and capabilities of participants enough to produce changes in their relations. In com-

Steven L. Spiegel: Introduction

plex relations, moreover, it is extremely difficult to predict how a change in one or a few variables will affect others. Knowing what to do in order to produce a desired result may be even more difficult than doing it.

International conflict arises from the aims and activities of independent states. Like the origins of conflicts, their alleviation depends primarily upon national efforts. On these assumptions the present book rests, and some will question their adequacy. A popular notion about current international politics is the assumption that nations are becoming closely interdependent and pervasively subjected to supranational organizations and forces. This position suggests that social, economic, and political barriers are declining as states become economically more dependent on each other and as their citizens and especially their elites come increasingly into more intense contact. In the process presumably their governments become politically more alike. In this conception, international organizations and multinational corporations are forces for unification through participating bureaucrats' experiences of cooperation and through their gradual assimilation of compatible procedures and methods of operation.

This book does not deal explicitly with questions of political unification and supranationalism. Indeed, we have rejected any preoccupation with international organization or cross-national consolidation. We have done so simply because in most parts of the world the conflict of states has overwhelmed whatever forces may be working toward the social and institutional unification of nations. We focus instead on disputes between states or among groups within them. They are the constituent elements of conflict, and such bodies as the United Nations, the European Economic Community, the Organization of African Unity, or the Organization of American States are considered only when they become factors in disputes or when they are able to affect conflicts between the contending parties. International organizations, even when they have some effect, reflect mainly the preferences and policies of their leading members.

The Causes and
Consequences of Conflict

The wide disparity between the acknowledged importance of international conflict and the amount of careful analysis of conflict situations is striking. The endless variety of states and the infinite variations in their relations make any given situation appear to be unique. If all situations are unique, studying any of them only generates knowledge that cannot be applied elsewhere. To reduce these impediments to the comparative study of conflict we have divided 22 case studies into eleven pairs. The two parts of each pair are linked by a clear element of similarity, whether in the context of conflict, in the capabilities of the parties, in their historical experiences, aims, and motivations, or in the kind of issue involved. The similarities do not eliminate the differences, of course, and may not even dominate them. For each pair, however, one can at least consider whether some common qualities of the outcomes are accounted for by similarities of conditions and experiences—and, of course, one can ask what difference the differences may make.

Both the Sino-Soviet and the Sino-American cases, for example, involve a challenge to a superpower. Unlike the United States and China, however, the Soviet Union and China share a common border, a similar ideology, and a long history of conflict. Both the Korean and the German cases involve formerly unified states that have been divided by the policies and acts of outsiders. Koreans, however, had lived for centuries in a politically united country and had formed a socially homogeneous people; Germans had known political unity for less than a century during which political, religious, and other divisions continued to mark their affairs.

By providing material for comparison, this book encourages exploration of the causes of conflict and its consequences. Why do some conflicts continue as if in perpetuity, while others simply wither away? Why do some conflicts result in extreme violence, while others simmer in crisis without issuing in open warfare? Why do conflicts that have lasted for generations finally come to an end? Is conflict necessarily malignant and destructive, or may the processes of conflict, even of violent conflict, be in some ways constructive in their results whether within or among states? Possible answers to such questions are suggested in the pages that follow.   .

Twenty-two Cases of Conflict

Part One deals with conflicts among great powers. The authors of essays on the United States and the Soviet Union identify the elements of conflict and cooperation within the superpowers' antagonistic relations, and they examine the reasons for the waxing and waning of hostility over time and in different places. Each essay investigates Soviet and American notions of national interests and international obligations and their respective images of conflict. The next chapter examines the challenge that the United States and the Soviet Union have perceived in the presence and policies of China. The two essays reassess common assumptions of the cold war and indicate how frequently fixed images of China have caused the superpowers to construe conciliatory and defensive Chinese policies as representing insolent defiance and aggressive intentions.

Part Two concentrates on the effect of great-power hegemonies in particular areas. The two major interventions of the late 1960s—in the Dominican Republic and Czechoslovakia—are taken as occasions for analyzing the complex relations inherent in the hegemony of a great power over a group of sovereign states. Each essay examines the effect of the intervention on the state in which the superpower intervened, on the superpower itself, and on the superpower's position in the entire region. The chapter on conflicts muted by hegemony assesses the contest for influence and prominence between leading states under conditions in which a hegemonic power is able to limit the scope and outcome of conflict. The essays on France and Germany and on Argentina and Chile examine the dialectic of collaboration and contention, and they also explore the effect of American involvement on the dynamics of each competition.

Part Three deals with conflicts among neighboring peoples—conflicts that are often intense, that involve occasional or even frequent violence, and that appear to continue without end, short of one side's conquering the other.

In Germany and Korea conflict between the two divided states is determined by their proximity and the similarity of their respective backgrounds. The issue of reunification between two ideologically divergent political entities is created and deepened by their common histories. The ethnonational confrontations of Arabs and Israelis and of Indians and Pakistanis represent conflicts between peoples who previously lived under the same colonial flags and have now become neighboring but hostile sovereign states. In each case, the division is primarily religious and social but progressively involves more complex political, economic, and military factors as well. The authors of these articles depict the intricate interplay between the conditions within communities and the conflict between them.

South Vietnam and Nigeria are both cases of internal conflict with international implications. In South Vietnam, political differences between the Viet Cong and the government overlapped with traditional antagonisms between villagers and city-dwellers and between members of various tribal and religious groups. In Nigeria, tribal antagonisms were projected onto administrative divisions, and tensions reached the breaking point when the army divided along similar lines. In both states, the internal conflict revolved around the problem of political unification, but the internal conflicts developed in opposite directions. In the case of South Vietnam, the key issues have been possible reunification with the north and the question of which factions would control the country politically. In Nigeria, the ability of Biafra to secede was the major question to be resolved in the struggle.

Part Four contains cases in which important elements of cooperation and conflict intermingle. The three-sided conflicts among Malaysia, Indonesia, and the Philippines, on the one hand, and Somalia, Ethiopia, and Kenya, on the other, demonstrate the greater complexity and variety of political antagonisms in a trilateral as opposed to a bilateral relation. In each triangle, communal conflicts exist within each state, especially between the indigenous peoples and the overseas Chinese in the Malay area and among various tribal groupings (including Somalis) in Ethiopia and Kenya. In addition, major territorial claims have disrupted relations among the parties: claims of Indonesia and the Philippines against Malaysia, and of Somalia against Ethiopia and Kenya. The complexities of three-way relations are also demonstrated by the mixture of conflicts within each set, some of them intense and some of them muted, with cooperative action by two parties against the third always a possibility.

The American-Japanese and Portuguese-South African cases have been linked because each pair is composed of distant states that have unusually close ties for historical, economic, and security reasons, but that nonetheless could well come into conflict in the future. As the authors of these essays suggest, the rising power of Japan and of the Union of South Africa, and regional strains in east Asia and southern Africa, may well give rise to serious conflicts.

The Canadian-American and Franco-British cases deal with neighboring and friendly states whose relations occasionally are marred by tensions generated, usually, by economic problems that are intertwined with political and military issues. Even though in both cases hostility was intense in past centuries, rivalry is now largely confined to economic competition and lingering social antagonisms.

The two chapters of Part Five deal with policy issues. The nuclear nonproliferation treaty and the war in Indochina are considered largely from the American standpoint. Even successful policies give rise to a series of conflicts in the dual sense that a price has to be paid for the achievement of one's aims and that some ends can only be achieved at the expense of others. The authors of these two essays vividly illustrate the costs of policies and the conflicts within them.

Steven L. Spiegel: Introduction

The organization of this book is designed to open vistas rather than to close them. The grouping and regrouping of essays according to criteria different from ours is a game that can be played with profit. The reader may wish to group essays according to conflicts that turn largely on questions of security and military power (interventions, for example, and conflicts between superpowers) or he may wish to analyze separately conflicts in which ideological factors strongly affect relations (China and the two superpowers; South Africa and Portugal; the divided countries). Special attention could be paid to conflicts that are deeply rooted in ethnic, religious, or communal factors (India and Pakistan; Malaysia, Indonesia, and the Philippines; Nigeria and Biafra). This book also provides an opportunity to examine one of the classic questions in international conflict: the role of capacity. The reader may wish to compare conflicts among parties of nearly equal strength (US and USSR; South Africa and Portugal; France and Germany) with those of grossly unequal capability (the superpowers and nations like Canada, the Dominican Republic, and Czechoslovakia).

The regrouping of essays can also point to important conclusions about present-day international conflict. On the one hand, this book corroborates conventional notions about world politics. The cases confirm, for example, the traditional view that great-power intervention in local conflicts tends to intensify contention (the divided countries; Vietnam; Israel and the Arab world), whereas conflicts that are isolated by the actions of one great power or are removed from great-power vital concerns are more easily muted (the three-sided conflicts; Argentina and Chile; Britain and France). This book also verifies the notion that distance tends to diffuse relations and make it easier to resolve contention (South Africa and Portugal), but proximity intensifies both cooperation (US and Canada) and conflict (internal conflicts; Israel and the Arab world; USSR and China).

On the other hand, the essays raise questions about familiar themes. Scholars and journalists tend to view international politics after 1945 as a conflict between two world-views—one Marxian and Russian, the other irrationally Lockean and American. Most conflicts described in this book are waged over ethnic, military, and even ideological issues for which the confrontation between American capitalism and Russian communism is largely peripheral and partly irrelevant. Similarly, one frequently hears it said that states no longer fight for territory, that territorial issues, forming the very substance of international politics in previous eras, have now virtually disappeared. This parochial view indicates only that in the bipolar relation of America and Russia, such issues have not been at stake. In nine of the essays that follow, territorial issues loom large: Israel and the Arab world; India and Pakistan; Chile and Argentina; the US and China; the USSR and China; the two Germanies; the two Koreas, and the tripolar conflicts of Africa and southeast Asia.

For the analysis of international politics, the 22 essays have wider and more varied uses than can be specifically described here. In general, this book should enable its readers to analyze conflicts that are not examined here in a more incisive and discerning manner. It should facilitate the comparison of conflicts with one another, leading to greater concentration in discussions and in writing, of the causes and consequences of international conflict. Finally, as the book's conclusion suggests, the essays presented here provide greater understanding of the meaning and function of conflict in world politics. It is with these objectives in mind that we invite the reader to explore the 22 essays that follow.

Part One

Great Power Conflicts

Chapter 2

Superpowers

The United States

ROBERT W. TUCKER

What are the prospects for significant change in American foreign policy? What form would this change take? And if American foreign policy is to undergo significant change, must not it be attended by equally significant change in the nation's conception of its position in the world? Are the American people now disposed to accept, if not indeed to insist upon, a more modest role for the nation?

These questions have been insistently raised in recent years. Clearly, they have been prompted very largely by the experience in Vietnam. Yet the meaning of this experience for American foreign policy remains unclear. It remains so when judged in terms of its more immediate effects upon policy. The general principles for American policy in Asia laid down by the Nixon administration during its first year in office are substantially the same principles that presumably were to have guided the Asian policy of preceding administrations. From Truman to Nixon each administration has looked to Asian states to assume primary responsibility for defending themselves against non-nuclear aggression, and particularly against internal subversion.

Nor is the significance of Vietnam apparent when judged in terms of the limits public opinion may impose on the future use of American power. It is apparent that the public wants no more Vietnams and that future administrations will ignore this public disposition only at their peril. Given the distinctive characteristics of the war, however, the reaction "no more Vietnams" may afford little indication of what the public can or cannot be expected to support, or at least to tolerate. Moreover, the characteristics that set this war apart from previous wars the nation has fought cannot alone account for the growing public conviction that it was a mistake ever to have intervened in Vietnam. That conviction came to prevail only when the demands imposed by the war reached an unexpectedly high level though the prospects for achieving military victory remained, at best, uncertain. In the light of these considerations the reaction "no more Vietnams" affords little indication of public reaction to future intervention in areas of more traditional interest than Southeast Asia. It may even give little indication of how the public will react to future intervention in Southeast Asia, provided the cost of intervention—always a critical determinant of public tolerance or opposition—can be kept modest and the apparent effectiveness of intervention can soon be made obvious.

Opposition to Vietnam, it is true, has not been based simply upon the cost and the seemingly inconclusive character of the war. Other and broader grounds must also account for it. Indeed, if the cost of the war appeared exorbitant to an ever increasing number, it did so largely because the reasons for which the war allegedly was being fought became increasingly suspect. Vietnam could not plausibly be represented either as a vindication of the principles of freedom and self-determination or, more important, as a measure indispensable to American security. But if the war and the ensuing debate revealed differences over the conditions and even the very meaning of American security, as well as over other interests the vindication of which would justify the use of American military power, there are few indications that these differences will soon be resolved. It would be rash to conclude that the failure to effectively employ the security argument in the case of Vietnam must mean that the same argument would fail elsewhere, including elsewhere in Asia, quite apart from the merits with which it might be made.

Thus, the more lasting effects of the debate and opposition that have attended the war remain unclear. In the case of conventional critics of the war, their defection can scarcely be equated with anti-interventionism as such, even in Asia, when many among them did not oppose the war in its earlier and less costly stages, and when others, although always opposing the Vietnam intervention, have advocated intervention in Asia, if it was necessary to meet and contain direct Chinese military expansion. Given this checkered record, the only conclusion that may safely be drawn is that conventional critics are opposed to intervening in the kind of conflict America has encountered in Vietnam. This qualified anti-interventionism need not point to a more fundamental disagreement over the interests and purposes of American foreign policy. Indeed, a great many conventional critics clearly continue to endorse in varying degree the expansive view of America's role and interests in the world that has characterized American policy in the past. While their opposition to the war led to a break in the foreign policy consensus of the past generation, the limited nature of that break leaves open the prospect of building a new consensus, or, more accurately perhaps, of rebuilding the old consensus once the war has been settled.[1]

If the meaning of Vietnam for future American foreign policy remains unclear, this is only to say that the effects of the war remain indeterminate. It is not to say that the war will have no effects on policy or that these effects will be insignificant. At any rate, the view that we may expect far-reaching change in American foreign policy need not rest simply upon the reaction to Vietnam. It may rest instead upon a number of important developments that have long been in the making and that Vietnam has illuminated and brought to the fore.

Vietnam and the ensuing debate have shown that many of America's present interests and commitments are largely the result of a concept of security that can no longer satisfactorily account for these same interests and commitments. This concept of American security was formed more than a generation ago in circumstances that bear only a remote resemblance to those of the present. In the 1940s it was still entirely possible, if not entirely plausible, to imagine an imbalance of military power that would threaten the physical security of America. Today, this contingency is no longer a meaningful possibility. If in the extreme situation America is indeed absolutely vulnerable vis-à-vis its great nuclear adversary, in other than the extreme situation it presently enjoys a degree of physical security that great powers seldom, if ever, enjoyed in the past. For the first time the prospect arises, if it has not already materialized, of a physical security no longer dependent on time-honored calculations of a balance of power and, consequently, no longer dependent on what transpires outside the North American continent.

Nor is the change in the structure of American security limited to physical security. In the 1940s it was still entirely possible, and altogether plausible, to imagine an imbalance of military power resulting in a security problem the solution of which would severely strain the nation's resources and jeopardize its democratic institutions. Today, this contingency is at best very remote. For the developments of the past 20 years have resulted in a Eurasia that bears no more than a

[1] The position of the radical critics of the war is another matter. For the radical critics, condemnation of an imperialistic foreign policy is of a piece with condemnation of American society. Both are found to need thoroughgoing reform, if not revolution. It is not the character of the radical critique that is unclear but the political impact of this critique, particularly in the period following a settlement of the conflict in Vietnam.

faint resemblance to the Eurasia of that earlier period. The great fear once entertained by American strategists, that a hostile power or combination of powers might succeed in uniting Eurasia and turning its immense resources against the western hemisphere, can no longer be seriously entertained.

If Vietnam has revealed the change that has occurred in the structure of American security in the years since the cold war began, it has also made clear the difficulties of finding a satisfactory substitute to replace this compelling incentive to sustained activism—and interventionism—abroad. To be sure, the attempt that has been made to identify, if not to replace, a narrower concept of security with one indistinguishable from the American vision of a desirable world order is in itself without novelty. It was already apparent in the Truman Doctrine, which in turn reflected a tradition that has deep roots in the American past. But although there is nothing new in this insistence upon identifying America's security with her purpose, the lengths to which this identification have been carried in recent years are novel. Equally novel is the skepticism shown toward this identification.

The lengths to which the identification of security and purpose have been carried in the context of Vietnam testify to the continued need to sanction the costs of war in terms of the nation's security. However great the emphasis placed on the larger purpose presumably informing American foreign policy, it still cannot alone bear the burden of justifying the blood and treasure required by war. It can do so only if the nation's purpose is effectively equated with its security. The domestic dissent over Vietnam testifies to the relative failure in making this equation effective.

The domestic dissent that has arisen in the course of the war also indicates the extent to which purpose itself has been called into question. Not only has purpose not been effectively equated with security; the very meaning and relevance of America's purpose in the world have become matters of increasing skepticism. To some—the more radical critics—America's purpose is suspect because it is seen as little more than a thin disguise for an imperialistic policy, a policy that has grown out of repressive domestic institutions and necessarily reflects them. To others—the more conventional critics—the continued relevance of America's purpose is suspect because the world is seen as increasingly resistant to this purpose. What only a few years ago was no more than an esoteric view—that America is not going to serve as an example for the underdeveloped states—has now become almost a commonplace. If these two groups start from quite different assumptions about the American purpose, they may nevertheless arrive at conclusions that are mutually supporting in terms of their policy implications.

Finally, Vietnam has shown that the nation retains a basic distaste for performing those acts which its present role and interests in an increasingly recalcitrant and unmanageable world commit it to perform. That distaste is attested even by revisionist historians of American foreign policy. While finding in expansion *the* principle of our institutions, they nevertheless emphasize that at least until recently this principle has been implemented, on the whole, through indirect methods of control. The revisionist argument may be granted that a preference for indirect methods of control reflected the rather obvious strategy of a nation possessed of preponderant economic power. The point remains that this preference also reflected a deep-rooted aversion to the methods required by direct control. The aversion has not disappeared any more than has the belief that America came to save the world, not to rule over it, and to save it through the power of her example, not through the power of her arms. One rules the world, if only in order to police it, because men and nations are recalcitrant, because they have conflicting aspirations, and because they are influenced more by arms than by example. And even if the nation were willing indefinitely to play the role of policeman to the world, Vietnam has demonstrated that the policeman's lot in this world has become very onerous and frustrating. For the world is not only more recalcitrant than ever, it is also more unmanageable than ever because the restraints on the use of power by the would-be guardians of order are greater than they have ever been.

A decline of insecurity that coincides with a rise in frustration over a world that seems less and less amenable to American power and example could form a powerful impetus for a far-reaching reappraisal of America's role and interests in the world. This is particularly so at a time when the world's most affluent society is in the throes of a revolution of rising expectations. It must remain a matter of conjecture whether affluent societies that no longer have a serious security problem will become progressively disinterested in the traditional stakes of foreign policy, particularly when those stakes seem more elusive and problematic than ever. What is not a matter of conjecture is the emergence of potentially powerful constraints on American foreign policy. These constraints are not simply a function of the consumer's desire for more. They are also a function of a sudden change in men's definition of what constitutes a tolerably just society and an awareness of the striking disparity between this definition and the realities of domestic life.

Thus, even if the meaning of Vietnam for future American foreign policy remains indeterminate, the war has illuminated developments that cannot but eventually affect that policy. The war has shown as perhaps no other event could that the still current conception of America's role and interests in the world was largely shaped by and resulted from a complex of circumstances that have changed radically in the course of two decades. These changes lay bare the essence of the contemporary American dilemma in foreign policy. To appreciate that dilemma more fully we must go back to the beginning of the cold war in order to see how and why America's present role and interests were formed, as well as how that role and those interests evolved in the course of the conflict that has dominated the American experience in the world since 1945.

The Cold War: An Interpretation

In the orthodox historiography of the cold war, America entered the postwar period with no clear and consistent view of the world or America's role and interests in it. Bemused by expectations that traditional forms of statecraft could be replaced, that victory over the Axis powers would mark the triumph of universalism and community of interests over spheres of influence and balances of power, America for a brief period—though a critically important one—hesitated to break clearly with its isolationist past and to acknowledge the position of world leadership that history had thrust upon it. A vision of harmony joined to a reluctance to accept the responsibilities inherent in the American position explain the well-meaning, though misguided, effort to compromise conflicting interests with the Soviet Union. That effort failed, and was bound to fail, because of the Soviet regime's morbid suspicions of and implacable hostility toward the West, which made even modest forms of postwar collaboration impossible, and because of Soviet determination to expand its power and influence wherever the opportunity presented, which made a defensive American response essential.

One need not accept the revisionist view of the cold war to find this orthodox position less than adequate. It neglects—or underestimates—the systemic causes of the cold war. Yet the greater the distance that separates us from the events in question, the greater appears the importance of the circumstances in which America and Russia found themselves at the end of the war. What before the war had been the center of the international system had suddenly collapsed. By destroying the prewar balance of power, by creating a vacuum in the heart of Europe, the war resulted in a situation that could not but give rise to Soviet–American rivalry. The vacuum thereby created in Europe not only attracted power, its continuing potential importance required each side to contest its succession by the other. For reasons of security alone, each side felt compelled to respond to this situation in a way that could scarcely avoid raising the suspicions and fears of the other side. In the past, similar circumstances had invariably led to rivalry, often intense, even between states that understood each other because they possessed many similarities of outlook and shared a common diplomatic tradition. Why should there be any mystery in the fact that these circumstances led to intense rivalry between states which did not understand each other, which entertained markedly divergent outlooks and shared no common diplomatic tradition?

If the orthodox position is inadequate because it neglects the systemic causes of the cold war, it is also inadequate in its portrayal of the American view of the postwar world. The common contention of orthodox historiography—both old and new—is that the cold war must be understood largely in terms of two quite different views of how the postwar world was to be organized: the universalist view and the spheres-of-influence view. As described in a recent essay on the origins of the cold war,[2] the universalist view assumed that "all nations shared a common interest in all the affairs of the world" and that "national security would be guaranteed by an international organization." By contrast, the spheres-of-influence view assumed that "each great power would be assured by the other great powers of an acknowledged predominance in its own area of special interest...and that national security would be guaranteed by the balance of power." No problem arises in identifying the Soviet Union with the spheres-of-influence view. The consistency with which the Russians made their view known during the course of the war and the persistence with which they applied it to eastern Europe are matters even the revisionists do not seriously dispute. What the revisionists do dispute is that the initial Soviet view equated a sphere of influence with a sphere of domination. If the Russians came in time to make eastern Europe into a sphere of domination, the revisionist argument is that American policy brought about this result by its reluctance to concede what were initially quite modest Soviet claims in eastern Europe, by its refusal to afford the Soviets with any reliable assurance against a renascent Germany, and finally by its active challenge to the entire Soviet postwar position in Europe.

[2] Arthur Schlesinger, Jr., "Origins of the Cold War," *Foreign Affairs*, 46, No. 1 (October 1967), pp. 26–52.

Robert W. Tucker: The United States

The revisionists may well be right in contending that American policy gave rise to Russian apprehensions that their principal wartime ally sought to deny them what the Russians regarded as no more than the legitimate fruits of victory. They are almost certainly wrong in contending that this was the principal, if not the only, reason for the eventual Soviet assertion of complete control over eastern Europe. That contention must assume that despite the ideological outlook of the Soviet regime, the political psychology of its rulers, and the circumstances in which power was exercised, the external behavior of Stalin's Russia could be considered in the same terms as the external behavior of any traditional state. If that assumption cannot bear critical examination, as it evidently cannot, neither can the argument that it was only Soviet apprehensions over their external security in the face of Western hostility that drove them to assert complete control over eastern Europe. A generation later, in 1968, the Soviet position in Europe and in the world at large had changed radically. Yet despite this change in the Soviet Union's world power position, despite the fact of Soviet control over eastern Europe for more than two decades, despite the changes that had occurred within the Soviet Union, and despite the now almost complete passivity of America, Soviet leaders concluded that in the case of Czechoslovakia they still could not risk making the distinction between a sphere of influence and one of domination. In large measure, they could not do so now for the same reason they could not do so in an earlier period: the fear that the twin virus of liberalization and national independence might spread to the Soviet Union, threatening the structure of Soviet power and the very integrity of the Soviet state.[3]

The question of primary concern here, however, is not what the Soviet view implied but what American professions of universalism implied. Clearly, universalism could not mean a literal opposition to any and all spheres of influence, for that would have had to include the American sphere of influence in the western hemisphere, particularly in the Caribbean and Central America where the distinction

---

[3] It may be argued, of course, that to the extent this fear prompted the Czech intervention it only serves to strengthen the view that Soviet control over eastern Europe has been based throughout on considerations of security. But if this argument is granted, it must also be acknowledged that Soviet security needs are indeed distinctive and that this distinctiveness, a result of the character of the regime, explains why the Soviets have been driven to equate a sphere of influence with one of complete control. It is another matter to argue that the United States would have opposed a Soviet sphere of influence in eastern Europe even if exercised in a manner more moderate than was in fact the case. Even if this point is well taken, as it probably is, the question remains whether the nature of the opposition would have been the same.

between a sphere of influence and one of domination had not always been clear. At the end of the war, it is true, the United States had sought to give institutional form to a multilateral version of the Monroe Doctrine. But this evolution of the Monroe Doctrine obviously did not mean, and was not interpreted to mean, an abandoment of the claim to hemispheric hegemony. If universalism meant opposition to spheres of influence, it was to spheres of influence beyond the hemisphere.

If the American commitment to universalism can scarcely be interpreted to mean a literal opposition to any and all spheres of influence, still less can it be interpreted to mean the commitment to multilateralism as a means for guaranteeing American security. It is vain to point to the United Nations charter, and to American support of the charter, as evidence of this commitment. The charter did not commit the great powers to multilateralism as a means for guaranteeing their security. The charter's design of order was made dependent on the condition that the great powers retain a basic identity of interests (a design which in itself can scarcely be considered as precluding acknowledgment of great power spheres of influence). But this design of order did not deal with the one contingency that could seriously threaten the security of a great power—conflict between the great powers. It merely assumed that in this contingency each great power would seek its protection in its own way and that the security system of the charter would become inoperative. This was certainly the American understanding of the charter. In joining the organization America retained, and insisted upon retaining, very nearly the same freedom of action it had enjoyed in the past. The American tradition in diplomacy had always been, par excellence, one of the "free hand"—that is, unilateralism—and there is in this early postwar period little evidence to suggest that it was prepared to abandon this tradition. Indeed, what evidence we have points rather to the conclusion that the methods for achieving American security were to remain essentially what they had been. The war and America's dramatic rise to world preeminence had not changed these methods, though they had changed, and markedly strengthened, the bases of American security. Nor was the nation to abandon its deeply rooted disposition to unilateralism once it decided to abandon its aversion to formal territorial commitments—alliances— outside the western hemisphere. Given America's vast power and the weakness—indeed, the almost complete impotence—of her allies, not only were America's commitments for all practical purposes unilateral in character but so were her relations generally.

What, then, did America's universalism mean? Clearly, it meant that we were opposed to certain kinds of spheres of influence— precisely the kind the Russians were establishing in eastern Europe.

But what did it mean in terms of a Soviet policy that would not have incurred our opposition? It will not do to answer that the question itself is meaningless. Even if it is granted that the Russians were compelled to pursue the policy they did in fact pursue, given the outlook and character of the Soviet regime, the question remains relevant unless it is assumed that the American outlook and character gave rise to no "compulsions" for American policy. More pointedly, what policy might the Russians have followed in the circumstances of the immediate postwar years, without arousing American opposition, that would have given them a degree of security at least roughly comparable to that enjoyed by the United States while leaving that security in Russian hands (for that exclusive control was no more than America claimed and enjoyed)? It is, in fact, very difficult to imagine what that policy might have been. But if this is so, the conclusion is difficult to avoid that the only policy the Russians could have pursued which would not have incurred American hostility was one that placed Russian security—and not only security—largely at the mercy of the good intentions of others—above all, America. There is no reason for assuming that America would have accepted such an arrangement in her own case. Why should it have appeared unreasonable and threatening that the Soviets refused a similar arrangement?

These considerations have prompted the revisionists to conclude that American universalism was little more than a euphemism for an outlook and policy which sought a world that would evolve in a "pro-American equilibrium."[4] Apart from a degree of exaggeration perhaps pardonable if only because of the intense opposition to it, the revisionist claim is surely true. Nor is it easy to understand why this claim has so often generated surprise and indignation. It is scarcely startling. What state that achieved the eminence and power America achieved by the end of World War II has not wanted the world to evolve in an equilibrium favorable to it? In America's case the desire is all the more understandable, given the nation's messianism and the conviction that the American experiment in freedom can continue to flourish only in a congenial environment. Of course, much of the opposition to a claim that might otherwise seem almost unexceptionable may be attributed to the assumption that to concede this claim is to concede still more specific claims. Yet it does not follow that if American leaders sought a world that would evolve in a pro-American equilibrium, they also were willing to employ any and all methods to achieve this goal, and did in fact employ them. This issue is one of historical evidence,

[4] William Appleman Williams, *The Tragedy of American Diplomacy* (New York: Delta Books, 1962), p. 202.

not of logical deduction. And if the evidence does clearly support the contention that we sought, however ineffectively, to exploit our economic strength and Russia's economic need to the end of making Russia more tractable in Europe, it does not support the contention that we seriously tried to use America's atomic monopoly for the same end. Indeed, even if American leaders in 1945–1946 had been intent on pursuing a policy that went beyond diplomatic protest and economic inducement, and even if the American public had been willing to support such a policy, there would probably have been no need to rely upon the atomic bomb. But the intent was not there, and even if it had been, it would not have elicited public support. Instead, the time-honored methods of American diplomacy were employed, with almost entirely negative results.

The essence of the revisionist case, however, does not concern the means American leaders were allegedly intent upon employing to ensure that the world evolved in a pro-American equilibrium. It is rather that in view of the limited aims of Soviet policy in Europe and, still more important, the vast superiority of power America enjoyed in the years following the war, this nation had no serious security problem. Given this power preponderance, America was in a position to explore alternatives and even to make concessions that the Soviet Union, from its relatively weak and still insecure position, was not. In refusing to do so, the revisionists conclude that America was simply acting consistently with the premises of the Open Door Policy. That policy went back at least as far as the turn of the century and sprang from the conviction that American freedom and prosperity were dependent upon an ever expanding American system. The Soviet Union was seen as a challenge to that policy and the vision informing it of a world recast in the American image. It was in response to this challenge, not in response to a meaningful security threat, that the United States, confident in its position of preponderant power, undertook a course of action that crystalized the cold war.

Only with the passage of time, and the many changes time has wrought, can this critique have the impact it presently enjoys. Only for a generation that does not know, and apparently cannot believe in, the problem of insecurity—at least, in the conventional sense—can this critique seem not only plausible but persuasive. At the time, however, no one knew, or could know, the extent of Soviet aims in Europe. It is altogether possible that the Russians themselves did not know, in any immediate policy-relevant sense, and that they adjusted their aims according to circumstance and opportunity. And even assuming that the Russians never seriously contemplated expanding into western Europe by conventional military means, conditions in western Europe in the

Robert W. Tucker: The United States

late 1940s appeared to hold out ample opportunities for expansion by other means. One need not subscribe to the position that ideology and the circumstances in which he exercised power compelled Stalin to constant expansion in order to argue that western Europe's weakness and instability nevertheless provided considerable temptation to expand. In comparable circumstances, most great states have sought to expand, particularly when they could do so without seriously risking war. Why should the Soviets, whose hostility toward and fear of the West were not in doubt, have been expected to refrain from expansion if it could be undertaken without serious risk of war?

In part, then, the answer to the revisionist argument is not that American leaders opposed Soviet policy in eastern Europe simply because they regarded as illegitimate the security interests that policy sought to achieve, or even because they regarded as illegitimate the methods by which the Soviets sought to achieve them (though this they surely did), but because the circumstances in which those interests were sought meant that achieving them would endanger American interests. Despite America's power preponderance, it was assumed that the domination of western Europe by the Soviet Union might shift the world balance of power decisively against the United States and thus in time create a direct threat to America's physical security. At the very least, it was assumed that domination of western Europe by the Soviet Union would result in a security problem the solution of which would severely strain the nation's resources and jeopardize its democratic institutions. In retrospect, a case can be made that these assumptions about the conditions of American security were exaggerated, particularly the first; it is now apparent that by the late 1940s the structure and bases of power had already changed in ways that made the security of America much less dependent upon a European balance of power than it had been only a decade before.

It is neither surprising nor unreasonable, however, that a persuasive case to this effect was not made at the time. If security policies necessarily point to the future, the standards they erect are largely anchored in the past. For America of the middle to late forties, the most relevant experience was the period before and during World War II, an experience seen to demonstrate convincingly the threat to American security that would result from a hostile power in control of Europe, or, still worse, of a hostile power or combination of powers in control of Eurasia. Nor was this experience confined to the threat held out by a victory of the Axis powers. It was also seen in terms of the period 1939–1941, when the prospect of a Eurasia partitioned and jointly controlled by Germany, Russia, and Japan could not be lightly dismissed. A revival of that prospect, though now with the Soviet Union as its sole architect and director, was widely considered to pose a serious threat even to a then preponderant America.

The revisionist view either neglects or dismisses these considerations. There is little justification for doing so. Security was the principal motive of American policy in the period in which the cold war was joined. Under the circumstances, apprehensions over American security were not unreasonable, though perhaps they were exaggerated. At the same time, other factors must help to account for the American response. Containment in Europe was not undertaken solely for reasons of security, narrowly construed, and no one contended so at the time. Considerations of political and cultural affinity were evidently very important. Moreover, the security motive itself was not clearly separated from other, broader considerations, as, indeed, it has seldom been separated in American diplomacy. In the historic expression of the policy of containment, the Truman Doctrine, President Truman declared that a willingness "to help free people to maintain their free institutions and their national integrity against aggressive movements that seek to impose upon them totalitarian regimes...is no more than a frank recognition that totalitarian regimes imposed on free peoples, by direct or indirect aggression, undermine the foundations of international peace and hence the security of the United States." Thus, preserving values and institutions identified with the life of the nation was seen to require an external environment whose characteristics extended considerably beyond the requirements of a balance of power. In insisting that preserving the institutions of freedom in America depended on preserving them—or realizing them—elsewhere, security was interpreted as a function not only of a balance of power between states but of the internal order maintained by states.

In emphasizing the need to employ American power and leadership to create and maintain a stable world order, an order which would enable "free peoples to work out their destinies in their own way" and which would "ensure the peaceful development of nations, free from coercion," the Truman Doctrine put forth a very expansive notion of American security. That expression cannot be dismissed as mere rhetoric, designed at the time only to mobilize public opinion in support of limited policy actions, though rhetoric taken seriously by succeeding administrations. For America came to the postwar period with a very expansive notion of the nation's security requirements, a notion that was the inheritance of a long period of geographical detachment and of a distinctive, even overweening sense of mission. The Truman Doctrine, in equating American security with interests that

Robert W. Tucker: The United States

went far beyond conventional security requirements, was a faithful response to this inheritance. It broke from the past not in the expansive notion of security it expressed but in the means it foreshadowed for achieving a congenial international environment.

It is important to emphasize these considerations, for they indicate the magnitude of America's conception of its role and interests in the world from the very inception of the cold war. If they are kept in mind, American policy in the fifties and sixties appears, not as a perversion of the conception of role and interests that dominated the early period of the cold war, but as its logical expression. It is quite true, however, that this conception was not immediately translated into policy. In the early policy of containment a narrower and more traditional conception of security received the greater emphasis. Whereas the Truman Doctrine was unlimited in geographic scope, was directed against communism itself, and proclaimed the objective of assisting all peoples to work out their destinies in freedom, the early policy of containment was centered in Europe, directed primarily against the expansion of Soviet power, and designed to ensure a favorable balance of power. This primacy of a narrower and more traditional security interest was not only of critical importance in eliciting public support for the Marshall plan and the North Atlantic alliance, the grand design for restoring Western Europe; it was also important in neutralizing criticism made at the time against the larger implications of American policy. Similarly, the relative absence of dissent to the intervention in Korea, and to other measures taken in Asia concomitantly with that intervention—measures which laid the basis of American containment policy in Asia—may be explained by the primacy of a security interest that centered in Europe. For the attack on South Korea was seen not only as a threat to Japanese security but—following as it did the Berlin blockade, the first Soviet explosion of an atomic device, and the Chinese communist accession to power—as a mounting communist offensive that was increasingly taking a military form and that if left unopposed, might well end in an armed attack against western Europe.

Once begun, the cold war followed a course broadly characteristic of hegemonial conflicts, save that in this instance the conflict did not result in war, but proved to be a substitute for it. All great conflicts gather a momentum of their own which persists and grows even after the causes that initially provoked the conflict have at least abated, if not disappeared. The cold war conformed to this experience. Not only did it arouse fears that could not readily be quieted once the threats that provoked them had begun to recede, its inner dynamic provoked new fears and created new objects of contention. The cold war had originated in Europe over what was considered to be the serious threat to the security of western Europe. That threat began to recede markedly by the early 1950s, only to be replaced by new fears and new objects of contention. Spreading first to Asia, the conflict soon became coextensive with what was for the first time a universal international system. The ubiquity of the cold war was matched by its intensity. A characteristic feature of the conflict was the tendency, common to hegemonial struggles, to make almost any discrete issue into a symbol of the whole and to relate almost any conflict of interest to the underlying and ultimate conflict of interest. Where survival itself is the issue increasingly seen to be at stake, specific conflicts of interest will be invested with a significance they would not otherwise have, for each confrontation is looked upon as a test of the will to resist and ultimately, therefore, to survive. The new weapons, and the appalling consequences of ever using them, appeared to exaggerate this characteristic feature of hegemonial rivalry.

These weapons may well have been the most important factor in preventing war between the United States and the Soviet Union. But even if they were, these weapons clearly exacerbated conflicts of interest that held out no more than the possibility of resorting to force. For the advent of nuclear weapons did not change the conviction that a meaningful and necessary relation must exist between the measures threatened and the interests for which the threat is made. If anything, this belief appeared more compelling than ever, given the prospect that any overt resort to force directly involving the superpowers might quickly lead to the use of nuclear weapons. In these circumstances, even the threat of non-nuclear force hardly seemed justified if the interests at stake were not made to appear somehow commensurate to the consequences that might follow a failure of the threat.

The course of the cold war cannot be understood, however, simply in terms of the dynamics of hegemonial conflicts. It must also be understood in terms of the character of the protagonists and, of course, the contingent events marking the conflict. Not only were the protagonists new to their postwar roles, but each invested its role with a distinctive sense of mission which the other saw as a supreme threat to its own vision of the world. It is pointless to retrace once again the argument between those who find in the cold war little more than a traditional power struggle and those who see primarily a conflict of ideology, that is, a conflict over the manner in which domestic societies and international society are to be organized. The cold war could scarcely have achieved its peculiar intensity and intractability had it not encompassed both these elements. No doubt America would have reacted to a noncommunist Russia which, in similar circumstances, sought to impose its control over eastern Europe and by doing so threatened the security and independence of western Europe. Even so, the nature of the American reaction was clearly influenced by the fact that the threat took the particular form it did, that it was attended by an ideology at once antithetical to the American commitment yet equally universal in character. Moreover, until the 1950s the Soviet example was one that continued to have considerable appeal in western Europe. These considerations must be set against the experience at that time with totalitarian regimes. None had moderated in character. None had been removed, save through war. In retrospect, it is easy enough to find in the western reaction, and particularly in the American reaction, to Stalin's Russia an almost hysterical exaggeration of the devil's strengths. But the face of Stalinism was at once frightening and awe-inspiring—so much so, in fact, that subsequent Soviet gains in material power have never quite compensated for the loss of these qualities in the post-Stalin period.

In the decade or so following the initiation of the cold war, Korea stands out as the decisive event in the evolution of the conflict and of American policy. Korea extended the cold war to Asia and intensified it everywhere. It may be argued that this extension and intensification would have occurred without Korea. Even so, in the absence of Korea these effects might have taken a different form. The dynamic of hegemonial conflicts determines general tendencies; how and to what extent these tendencies are realized in any given conflict still depend upon contingent events. To this extent, Korea was important. At the outbreak of the war, it was uncertain whether America would extend its alliance commitments beyond the western Hemisphere, the North Atlantic region, and the Pacific defense perimeter. Even within the area of commitment, the means by which America would implement its commitment to western Europe remained uncertain. Korea put an end to these uncertainties. In Europe, the war prompted the reestablishment of American forces, the establishment of an integrated command structure, and the decision to proceed with German rearmament. In Asia, the Korean conflict led to American intervention in the Chinese civil conflict and prompted the conclusion of a series of bilateral and multilateral alliances that continue today roughly to define the extent of the American commitment in that area.

In thus extending and intensifying the cold war, Korea altered the character of the struggle and of American policy. Within America, the general effects of Korea were manifested by a hardening of attitudes and by an increasingly ideological view of the cold war. In these effects, it has been argued, Korea facilitated the triumph of the Truman Doctrine over the early policy of containment. For Korea led to a policy of ever broadening commitment; it accentuated the sense of universal crisis, of a fateful confrontation in which every nation must choose between alternative ways of life; and it reinforced the conviction that America's security—indeed, her very survival—depended upon the outcome of this global confrontation. These were surely the salient features of the Truman Doctrine, and the Korean war provided a powerful stimulus for translating them into policy.

At the same time, Korea may be seen as facilitating the triumph of a particular version of containment. The Truman Doctrine apart, the assumptions that informed the early policy of containment had never been altogether clear. Thus, it was never clear whether containment was to be directed against Soviet power, or Communism, or both. So long as containment was confined to Europe, and so long as the Communist movement remained monolithic and subordinated to Russian interests, this was not an issue of practical importance. It was to become so when these conditions no longer obtained. But the policy of containment had always been ambiguous on this issue, just as it had always been ambiguous on the purpose of containment. Was containment intended to produce those conditions, those situations of strength, in which meaningful negotiations with the Soviets could take place? Or was it intended to give rise to a situation in which the Soviets would have to adjust their interests and behavior to American views? Or, finally, was containment intended primarily to induce change within the Soviet Union which, having taken place, would presumably be reflected in Russia's international position? The early policy of containment afforded no clear answer to these questions.

Korea may therefore be seen as facilitating the triumph not only of the Truman Doctrine but also of a particular view of containment—a view that never restricted containment to Europe, that never clearly distinguished between Soviet imperialism (or Chinese imperialism) and communism, and that never placed any confidence in the resolution of Soviet-American differences through the normal processes of diplomacy. In Europe, this view led to measures that confirmed the division of the continent and rendered negligible for the foreseeable future the prospects of a negotiated settlement. In Asia, it prompted a series of alliances with governments that all too often had little, if any, popular support. More generally, it fostered a policy that had as its guiding objective opposition to the expansion of communism, an objective roughly identified with world order.

The equation, by now all too familiar, of containing communism, maintaining world order, and preserving American security was firmly established by the middle 1950s and given the institutional expression it still bears. Moreover, it was firmly established at a time when change in the postwar configuration, which had given rise to containment, was

Robert W. Tucker: The United States

already well advanced. By the middle fifties the revival of western Europe and the recession of the threat that had stimulated American intervention were becoming accomplished facts. In the communist world, although the emerging schism between the two major states was not yet apparent, the attempt by eastern European states to assert a measure of independence from Soviet control was all too apparent. Yet, despite these and other changes, the equation mentioned above was not seriously questioned until almost a decade later. Why?

In part, the answer may be found in the fact that although the policy expressing this equation enjoyed no striking success, neither did it suffer any marked failure. This is true, above all, of American policy in Asia; it was supported for over a decade by what may be termed a negative consensus. If this policy evoked little enthusiasm, it also evoked little opposition so long as it did not entail a serious price.

In part, the answer is to be found in the momentum the cold war had built up after a number of years. One effect of that momentum was to blind men to change that was taking place before their eyes. And even when they did perceive change, under the influence of the cold war they often misread its import. Thus an awareness of the culmination of the colonial revolution and the growing importance of the new states prompted the conclusion that the cold war would be decided in the underdeveloped world. Instead of diffusing and dampening the cold war, the sudden emergence of the underdeveloped states in the international system only served to exacerbate the conflict. Given this built-up momentum of the cold war, in the absence of some spectacular and costly failure in foreign policy, serious opposition could scarcely be expected. Then, too, contrary to the Vietnam experience, which has retarded or frustrated social reform by creating a fierce budgetary competition between foreign and domestic expenditures and by siphoning off mental and moral resources, in an earlier period the cold war often appeared to be a stimulus for domestic change that otherwise would not have been undertaken.

For the most part, however, the answer to the question posed above must be found in the coincidence of change in the postwar configuration with the last great crisis in Soviet-American relations. The years from late 1958 to late 1962 mark the climactic phase of the cold war. In retrospect, it is still difficult to determine whether the critical events of this period betoken an aggressive or a defensive policy on the part of the Soviet Union. The Soviet demand for a change in the status of Berlin may have been prompted more by the desire to shore up a dangerously weak East Germany than by the intent to change the status quo in central Europe to the Soviets' advantage. Similarly, the abortive Soviet move to place strategic weapons in Cuba may have been prompted more by the desire to reduce the growing disparity between Soviet and American strategic military power (a disparity which, had it continued, could have placed the Soviets in a highly vulnerable position) than by the desire to force the West out of Berlin and to break America's hegemonial position in the western hemisphere. Whatever the correct interpretation of these moves,[5] they provoked a kind of return to the earlier atmosphere, and even the conditions, of the cold war. They did so not only because their meaning was commonly interpreted as a frontal challenge to American predominance and to the status quo, but also because they occurred at a time of declining American confidence that in the competition with the communist world, time was on the western side, that events were moving in a manner favorable to American interests.

American confidence was to be restored only with the passing of the Cuban missile crisis. In the aftermath of the crisis the fears that had beset America since 1958 seemed suddenly to dissipate. Whereas in the late fifties the conditions of competition seemed increasingly to favor the Soviet Union, now they appeared to have been dramatically reversed. Not only did America emerge in the period following Cuba in a position of marked economic and military preponderance, it did so at a time when the last semblance of any pretense to unity between the major communist powers was dropped and intense rivalry openly acknowledged. Even the prospects in the underdeveloped world appeared suddenly to have changed. Whereas a few years before the Soviets and the Chinese were considered to enjoy most of the advantages in the competition for influence among the new states, now the judgment was reversed and the conditions marking the crucial transitional process were considered to favor an outcome congenial to American views and interests.

In these circumstances, the cold war abated. Without doubt, the lessening of tensions resulted largely from the mutual realization of the dangers inherent in direct confrontation between the superpowers. Yet if these dangers were dramatically illustrated by Cuba, a common awareness of them surely antedated the last great crisis of the cold war. The Cuban missile crisis did not, in and. of itself, transform skeptics into true believers. If the stakes no longer seemed proportionate to the risks of confrontation, thus giving rise to a new restraint and prudence, it was not simply because the risks were suddenly seen in a new light but also because the stakes themselves had changed.

---

[5] These two interpretations are not mutually exclusive. Even if the interpretation suggested above is correct, it does not follow that the Soviets would have refrained, in the event of American submission, from further exploiting a move initially taken for defensive reasons.

Robert W. Tucker: The United States

One important reason they had changed was that the superpowers had partially and almost imperceptibly turned away from a view of their rivalry which heretofore had given it an almost completely hegemonic cast. They did so partly out of a sense of fatigue—perhaps even of boredom—over a contest that could no longer have a decisive outcome, if it ever could have had one. In part, however, they did so because a world that could no longer be defined in bipolar terms forced them to consider their interests in terms other than those of hegemonic rivalry. Once the period of intense hegemonic competition had passed, it was almost inevitable that they should begin to develop a parallel—even a common—interest in opposing change they did not initiate and could not readily control.

At the same time, the détente did not substantially affect the conception America had formed of her role and interests in the world. It did not prompt even a reappraisal of the equation of containing communism, maintaining world order, and preserving American security, let alone a change in that equation. Although the détente rested largely on the assumption that the Soviet Union would increasingly become, along with the United States, a status quo power, outside Europe the status quo was still defined in essentially the same terms in which it had been defined in an earlier period. It is true that President Kennedy found a new way of articulating the American commitment. There is little basis, however, for the view that in proposing "to make the world safe for diversity," Kennedy marked a break from the outlook of the Truman Doctrine. Given a world in which America was preponderant, diversity represented not so much a departure from a traditional aspiration as an expedient and felicitous formulation of that aspiration. Even a diverse world was still expected to be a world moving steadily in the direction marked out by the Truman Doctrine. To ensure this outcome, essentially the same policies would have to be pursued in the case of Asian revolutionary communist movements as had been pursued in the case of the Soviet Union.

Thus the rationale for the American commitment in Vietnam has had no novel elements distinguishing it from the views set forth by earlier administrations. The problem of Vietnam, the all too familiar argument runs, is a problem of how the peace of the world is to be organized and maintained. Is that order, and the peace it implies, to be one of consent or one of coercion, one that safeguards the right of self-determination or one that destroys this right, one that provides an environment favorable to the growth of free institutions or one that encourages the spread of arbitrary and irresponsible power? This is the ultimate issue that three administrations have found at stake in Vietnam. It is an issue that is seen to transcend Vietnam and southeast

Asia. It is presumably the same fundamental issue to which the Truman Doctrine responded a generation ago.

The Foreign Future of American Policy

We return, in conclusion, to the questions posed at the beginning of this chapter. What are the prospects for significant change in American foreign policy? Very small, obviously, if it is assumed that the nation's security remains dependent upon the purposes and objectives of the Truman Doctrine and the successive policies of containment. If that assumption is maintained, if the equation of world order and American security is to remain central to any foreseeable projection of American policy, then in the absence of fundamental change in the international environment the future imperatives of policy will prove to be much the same as past imperatives. Given that assumption, and barring a substantially more favorable international structure of power, the nation has no choice but to maintain intact its present commitments. It has no choice because the need for order will remain and, depending upon the final outcome in Vietnam, may even increase.

Is the equation of world order and American security valid? The answer depends upon the meanings we give to the terms of the equation. If world order is roughly synonymous with opposition to the expansion of communism, and security is defined as physical security, the equation no longer appears valid. It no longer appears valid even though it remains the case that America would risk nuclear war to prevent the loss of interests deemed vital in Europe and Asia—for the loss of these interests as such would not threaten the nation's physical security. What would still probably involve this nation in a nuclear war is by no means synonymous with what would threaten America's physical security. Nor is the case for equating world order and American security appreciably strengthened by the likelihood that a greater degree of disorder would stimulate nuclear proliferation. We have no persuasive reason for believing a nuclear peace to be indivisible. Indeed, given the consequences of nuclear war, a nuclear peace may well prove to be more divisible than any previous peace.

Clearly, the plausibility of equating world order and American security must rest upon a broader and even a transcendent meaning of security in which necessity becomes indistinguishable from desirability. The root issue this equation must raise does not concern the nation's physical existence but the integrity of its institutions, the quality of its domestic life, and, ultimately, the vision of itself in history. It is the latter interests that would presumably be jeopardized if

Robert W. Tucker: The United States

we were substantially to modify our present role in the world. For a substantial modification of our role, it is argued, could only mean in the present circumstances a marked reduction of American influence, a greater degree of disorder and instability, and an improved prospect for communist movements in the developing world.

It will not do to reply to this argument by refusing to acknowledge that these are the probable consequences of a substantive change in policy. Critics who call for the abandonment of "globalism" and "interventionism," without acknowledging the probable effects if this prescription is taken seriously, are deceiving themselves either about the methods required to vindicate America's present interests or about the nature of those interests. Yet it is the nature of American interests and the nature of the world in which these interests are pursued that require an interventionist policy. The methods of American policy can be seriously altered only to the extent the interests of policy are also altered. The abandonment of an interventionist policy cannot be seriously entertained without incurring the substantial risk of consequences already noted.

It is, of course, another question whether the occurrence of those consequences would jeopardize the quality of the nation's domestic life. The experience of Vietnam cannot provide a definitive answer. Vietnam has clearly proven seriously debilitating in its domestic effects. It does not follow, however, that the domestic effects of future interventions will prove more debilitating than the external consequences resulting from a more modest role in the world. Much would depend upon the circumstances attending future interventions. In this respect, as in so many others, the experience of Vietnam remains unclear. The tendencies in the domestic environment that Vietnam has revealed remain only tendencies.

But even if it is plausible to conclude that a substantially reduced role for America in the world would not, of itself, jeopardize the quality of the nation's domestic life, such change does not appear likely in the foreseeable future, if only because imperial powers have always been reluctant to let go of what they have. When they have done so, it has been in response to a decline in power that made a more modest role inevitable. Given America's material strength relative to others, the prospect of a decline in power can arise only from novel restraints imposed by the international environment. Although the restraints on the use of power—above all, military power—do indeed appear greater today than they have ever been, they have yet to change the traditional meaning of statecraft.

The prospects for significant change in American foreign policy must therefore depend largely on the public response to a policy that has increasingly lost its principal justification (security), to a world that is increasingly resistant to American power and example, and to domestic problems that depend for amelioration at least partly on resources heretofore devoted to external concerns. It is this combination of circumstances that has prompted many observers to conclude that significant change is not only likely but inevitable. Yet security has seldom, if ever, satisfied great nations. Whether it will do so in the future is, at the very least, problematic. Equally problematic are the effects of a rising frustration over a world that seems less and less amenable to American power and example. The deeper lesson of Vietnam may well be that the American purpose cannot be actively sought in today's world save through methods which, in the end, threaten the denial of this purpose. But even if true, this does not mean that the nation will readily abandon these methods, let alone that it will soon reconcile itself to the irrelevance of the American example for much of the world. Nations, like individuals, must suffer a great deal before they are ready to abandon the vision—or illusion—they entertain of themselves.

In sum, while the present conjuncture of circumstances is likely to result in widespread and continuing unease over American foreign policy, it is not likely to result in significant change of that policy. Although domestic criticism of the American role and interests in the world probably will persist, the nation's role and interests are not likely to change substantially. The prospect is for an uneasy compromise—a delicate balancing act—that may change much of the outward forms but not much of the substance of policy and that seeks to appease the most pressing of domestic demands while maintaining intact the structure of the nation's external interests and commitments.

The Soviet Union

WILLIAM ZIMMERMAN

For Americans whose basic attitudes toward world
politics have been shaped by events such as the Berlin
blockade, the Czechoslovak coup, the Korean war, the
Berlin wall, and the Cuban missile crisis, the words
"crisis" and "Soviet Union" are naturally associated.
Indeed, the association of "conflict" with "Soviet
Union" represents an automatic, almost visceral response
for most adult Americans accustomed to a reality
epitomized by phrases such as "cold war" and
"protracted conflict." Soviet-American relations for
a quarter century now—literally since the onset of
the nuclear age—have constituted the locus of major
tension in the world, the relationship that serves to
define the context of virtually all other interstate
relations.

Not only has the nature of Soviet-American relations
served to conjoin the terms "conflict" and "Soviet
Union"; beyond this, the terms have been inextricably
linked, because to plain Americans, policy-makers,
and academicians alike it has seemed that Soviet
decision-makers have had a unique belief system of
which a distinctive approach to conflict was an integral
part. That belief system, furthermore, it was widely
assumed, was especially suitable to the conflict-ridden
world of politics in the absence of government,
especially in a decolonizing, revolutionary,
thermonuclear, and bipolar era.

Soviet beliefs were seen, moreover, to contrast sharply
with the traditional expectations about politics held
by American elites. At the core of Soviet beliefs, it
was asserted, was a preoccupation with violence,

The author wishes to thank the International Organization
Program of the University of Michigan for typing
and other financial assistance in the preparation of
this essay.

conflict, and qualitative change and an assumption that the interaction of nation-states was merely a partial and possibly unimportant part of the overall world historical process. The beliefs of American decision-makers, by contrast, derived from a philosophic tradition that was legalistic and ahistorical and that tended to assume the existence of a natural harmony of interests, to view stability rather than conflict as the norm (in the sense both of the expected and of the desired) and to believe in the efficacy of incremental and intrasystemic change.

It is therefore readily understandable that an essay dealing with the Soviet Union should be included in a book about international conflict. This chapter does not, however, pretend to rehearse the history of the cold war or to explain its origins—tasks that others have performed many times.[1] It does not even attempt to provide the reader with a detailed examination of the evolution of Soviet beliefs about international politics in the atomic age—also a job that has been attempted elsewhere.[2] Rather, this chapter summarizes the changes that have occurred over time in Soviet perspectives on conflict in international relations, especially as they bear on the Soviet assessment of Soviet-American relations. In addition, it assesses the impact of Soviet experience *with* conflict on Soviet thinking *about* conflict and in turn on Soviet motives and modes of behavior. Finally, in light of the transformation in Soviet goals and behavior modes, the chapter hazards some projections about alternative patterns of Soviet-American relations in the 1970s.

International Conflict:
The Traditional Soviet Assessment

At the outset it should be noted that the traditional Western image of the Soviet world-view was fundamentally correct. The conventional Soviet wisdom adapted Marxist-Leninist doctrine, with its class and economic concepts, to account for a basically international and political arena. Politics, and international politics in particular, was conceived as a zero-sum game (that is, one in which the gains of one side are the losses of the other) and the configuration of political relations as rigidly hierarchical. States, classes, and individuals, except for histor-

---

[1] For a brief treatment see Robert W. Tucker's essay in this book. Among the many other materials one might consult, see especially Marshall D. Shulman, *Beyond the Cold War* (New Haven: Yale University Press, 1966) and Harold K. Jacobson (ed.), *America's Foreign Policy* (New York: Random House, 1965) pp. 245–419.

[2] William Zimmerman, *Soviet Perspectives on International Relations 1956–1967* (Princeton: Princeton University Press, 1969).

William Zimmerman: The Soviet Union

ically brief periods in which an actor supplanted another, were either on top not, and values were allocated accordingly. In such a world the key question of politics was *kto-kogo,* who [eliminates] whom. Would "socialism" as embodied in the proletariat in power (the Soviet Union) triumph over the forces of "capitalism" (after World War II headed by the United States)? Conflict in such a conception naturally enough was seen as the norm rather than the exception, an integral part of the political process. Conflict, moreover, was considered functional: world war facilitated the acceleration of the historical process. World War I had brought about the first stage in capitalism's general crisis and with it the triumph of socialism in one country. World War II similarly had produced the second stage in capitalism's general crisis and with it what Jan Triska has aptly called socialism in one bloc.

Such a world was divided between those who objectively or subjectively were allied with the main enemy—and those who were objectively or subjectively allied with the forces of socialism. Policy disputes in Moscow thus tended to center on the extent to which groups located along intermediary points of an enmity-amity continuum might serve as temporary allies against the United States. Leftist postures were ones highly chary of the political effectiveness of appeals to non-Communists of any stripe. For these exclusivists the watchword was "he who is not with us is against us." Rightist stances, on the other hand, emphasized the universalist appeals of Communism and were adopted by persons who at a particular time were prone to consider large numbers of non-Communists as available for mobilization against the main enemy. Common to both strands of communist thought, however, was the notion that there was a single key antagonist, the major imperialist power, and that it was the main enemy—with all that that phrase conveyed.

To these doctrinally generated attitudes toward conflict Stalin added a generous infusion of attitudes derived from two senses of the word "mobilization." One was military; the rhetoric of armed conflict (struggle, front, rear, detachment, etc.) permeated Stalinist vocabulary. Throughout the early postwar years, Stalin doggedly replicated the generals' penchant for preparing to wage the last war. The strategic implications of the atomic era (especially with regard to surprise) produced no alteration in Soviet military doctrine before Stalin's death. The mobilization war, with its emphasis on "permanently operating factors" and war potential (rather than forces-in-being) which World War II—the Great Patriotic War—had been, continued to serve as the model for future general war.

The second sense of "mobilization" that had relevance for Stalinist conceptions of conflict was political. The postulate of an implacably hostile international environment was crucial to the legitimation of the Stalinist mobilization system. In doctrinal terms the Stalinist proposition that domestic class contradictions intensify as the Soviet Union advances historically—the rationale for the institutionalized mutual suspicion that characterized Stalinist Russia—was tied directly to "capitalist encirclement," a term coined to depict the Soviet Union's isolation in a world of hostile capitalist states. Moreover for Stalin capitalist encirclement was a political and not a geographical conception—by which he meant that the increase of the domain of Soviet power brought on by the formation of the socialist camp, while desirable, had not mitigated the prospects for conflict with the West nor enhanced appreciably the security of the Soviet Union. The liquidation of capitalist encirclement would only occur with the elimination of capitalism in the principal capitalist countries.

Even while Stalin lived, in all probability, Georgy Malenkov and other prominent Soviet leaders differed with Stalin's conceptions of East-West conflict. We know, for instance, that in 1952 Stalin went to great pains to refute the arguments of "some comrades" that wars between capitalist countries were no longer inevitable. We know too that in 1949 Malenkov had expressed great enthusiasm that "never before in all its history has our country been surrounded with neighboring countries so friendly to our state"[3]—a view strikingly at variance with the aggressive insecurity inherent in the doctrine of continued capitalist encirclement. We know, finally, that in the ominous context of the "doctors' plot" there were Soviet citizens, presumably in key positions, who believed that changes in Soviet policy could bring about a reduction of East-West tension. For in January 1953 one of Stalin's mouthpieces attacked as appeasers "various liberals who have broken with the theory of class struggle and descended into right-wing opportunism" for advocating major and minor concessions to the imperialists.[4]

Perspectives on International Conflict: Developments After Stalin

In any event, important changes in nuance occurred soon after Stalin's death. Military theorists such as General Nikolai Talenskii

[3] As cited in Robert C. Tucker, *The Soviet Political Mind* (New York: Praeger, 1963) p. 28.

[4] *Ibid.*, p. 30. The above paragraph draws heavily on Tucker's account.

began to come to grips with the strategic implications of nuclear weapons and high-speed, long-range delivery systems. The overt complacency about the consequences of a new general war began to be replaced. First Malenkov and Anastas Mikoyan and then Nikita Khrushchev (after politically discrediting Malenkov for mouthing such heresies) publicly expressed concern about the losses each side would suffer in a general war. By 1956 authoritative Soviet spokesmen were declaring that war between socialism and capitalism was no longer "fatalistically inevitable"—a doctrinally insignificant amendment to the corpus of Leninism-Stalinism. (There never was a Leninist theory of inevitable war between socialist and capitalist states, only of inevitable war *among* capitalist states. What true Leninist in any event believed anything to be "fatalistically" inevitable?) But this amendment served as the starting point for a wholesale rethinking not only of Stalinist but even of Leninist perspectives on conflict at the international-system level in the atomic age.

Contrary to some accounts, however, it was not the Twentieth CPSU Congress in 1956 that witnessed the major Soviet reassessment of traditional Leninist perspectives on international conflict. Only during the late 1950s and especially in the early 1960s did such a fundamental reappraisal occur. Three major events provided the impetus for much of the reassessment: the launching of the first sputnik and the related development of the intercontinental ballistic missile, the Cuban missile crisis, and the Sino-Soviet split. There were many facets to that reappraisal. For our purposes the most important probably had to do with the notion of capitalist encirclement, the rupturing of the linkage between capitalism and war, the similar rupturing of the linkage between revolution and war, the reappraisal of world order and the reassessment of the motives of American decision-makers.

As we have seen, even before Stalin's death, voices in Moscow had called into question the notion of capitalist encirclement. It remained for Khrushchev in 1958 and 1959 to put to rest the notion of capitalist encirclement—since it was "no longer certain who encircles whom"—and to reduce symbolically the image of Soviet power under threat by affirming that imperialism was no longer capable of destroying Communist rule in the Soviet Union by force. By so doing, Khrushchev weakened the argument for a mobilized Soviet populace and in effect indicated a willingness to accept compliance rather than affirmation as the norm for the Soviet citizenry. At the same time, the prospect that conflict between East and West would occur simply because the Soviet regime needed to maintain high international tension in order to retain revolutionary élan at home was greatly reduced. (Indeed, one of the key points at issue between Mao—and Molotov—and the dominant faction in Moscow was precisely whether international tension should or should not be encouraged.)

The abandonment of the doctrine of capitalist encirclement might have been anticipated, in view of previous adumbrations of a reassessment. Moreover, the extension of capitalist encirclement to cover a period in which the Soviet Union was no longer isolated could easily be dismissed as a Stalinist distortion engendered by Stalin's obsessive (even in contrast with others in the Bolshevik tradition) preoccupation with enemies and his corollary preoccupation with control rather than influence. To tamper, as Khrushchev and others did in the late 1950s, with the linkage of war and capitalism was another thing. On some occasions Soviet commentators virtually acknowledged that war among the major capitalist powers under present conditions was no longer a possibility. At other times, the doctrinally safer stance that war among the capitalist states was unlikely was adopted. As for relations between the United States and the Soviet Union, here too it was doubtful whether the superpower relationship, in the dominant Soviet conception, was considered one in which the expectations of violence were high. Quite the contrary; the usual Soviet assessment was that, while not nil, the prospects of a general Soviet-American war were modest. What was most striking was the Soviet posture with respect to a disarmed world: whereas traditionally Leninists had looked on disarmament as a symbol to be invoked manipulatively, Moscow in the late 1950s and early 1960s adopted the stance that under conditions of general and complete disarmament, war as a social phenomenon could be eliminated even while capitalism continued to exist. A major consideration underlying the Soviet reformulations of the nexus between war and capitalism involved an awareness of the implications of war in the atomic age to human progress and revolution. To maintain revolutionary optimism, it had to be shown that war could be prevented even while capitalism existed. For the same reason it had also to be shown that world war and revolution could be separated. Because world war would "halt progress and throw humanity back tens or perhaps hundreds of years,"[5] and because "nowadays people ask not only *what* will the future be like, but *will* there be a future,"[6] it was difficult seriously to entertain the traditional Marxist-Leninist (and, before Marx, Clausewitzian) doctrine that war was the continuation of policy by other means. Khrushchev's way out of the dilemma was to relegate

[5] "The Policy of Peaceful Coexistence Proves Its Worth," *World Marxist Review*, Vol. 5 December 1962, p. 3.

[6] Y. Karyakin, "Allen Dulles Instead of Karl Marx," *World Marxist Review*, Vol. 5 April 1962, p. 87; italics in original.

Leninism and Lenin's *Imperialism, the Highest Stage of Capitalism* to the preatomic age by announcing the onset of a "new, third stage of capitalism's general crisis." By introducing a new stage, Khrushchev created the doctrinal basis for asserting that one must not "mechanically repeat now...what Vladimir Il'ich Lenin said many decades ago on imperialism."[7] He also strengthened his case, in the words of a *Pravda* editorial, against those, "Communists and especially Communists who are statesmen and political figures" who "rehash old truths from past centuries"[8] by insisting that ours was an "epoch of imperialism, wars, and proletarian revolutions" and who fail to see that "the world socialist system is becoming the decisive factor in the development of society."

Briefly put, Khrushchev's argument was that the kind of qualitative change in the global distribution of power which had been brought about by the two world wars of this century had been accomplished by the Soviet development of the intercontinental ballistic missile (reinforced by the decolonization process and the fissiparous tendencies in the Western camp). The Soviet development of an ICBM, it was affirmed, had put an end to the geographically based strategic invulnerability that had permitted the United States "to export counterrevolution"—that is, to provide arms, material, *and manpower* to deter and or prevent Communist seizures of power in the non-Communist world. Soviet deterrent capability, in other words, would prevent the outbreak of general war. Meanwhile, the revolution would be advanced through domestic social changes. To sever the linkage with world war and revolution, Khrushchev in effect returned to the Marxist conception of revolution as a phenomenon taking place within a state. The contemporary international system would be undermined and a communist international system created through the cumulative impacts of changes in the political structure of the participant units.

At the same time the notion of a third stage of capitalism's general crisis conveyed with it a radically novel conception (by Bolshevik standards) of the contemporary international order. Traditionally, Soviet commentary had pictured capitalist international relations as "a rigid hierarchy, secured by the distribution of power," with a configuration resembling a "pyramid." At the apex of the pyramid stood a single dominant power which utilized its resources to preserve or secure its position in the international order by carefully playing off the lesser

[7] N. S. Khrushchev, *O vneshnei politike Sovetskogo Souiza* (Moscow, 1961) II, 62.

[8] *Pravda*, January 7, 1963. For a more detailed discussion of the ramifications of the "third stage of capitalism's general crisis" see Zimmerman, *Soviet Perspectives*, pp. 131–52.

great powers and choosing the opportune moment to back the winning coalition of great powers. Shifts in the distribution of power produced shifts in the ranking of the great powers. The configuration, however, remained essentially constant over time. In the Khrushchevian calculus, the development by the Soviet Union of an operational ICBM, by eliminating the United States's geographically based invulnerability, had changed not only the distribution of power but also the shape of the international order. The passing of United States invulnerability had eliminated the dominant power *category*. Instead, the global order was headed by two powers, the United States and the Soviet Union, the leaders of which had to accustom themselves to operating in a world in which they were obliged to treat the other power more or less equally.

Moreover, Soviet commentary in the 1960s made it known that Moscow's expectation was that this condition would continue for the duration of the century. Despite a brief burst of enthusiasm in the years 1957–1961 about the prospects for a world Communist system, Soviet statements at no time questioned the United States's status as a world power. Equally significant, Soviet analysis revealed an implicit assumption that the US would maintain its world-power status throughout the remainder of the century and that during that time "it is quite clear that no single state will predominate."[9] In particular Soviet analysis: (1) lent little credence to the prospects for revolution in the United States; (2) considered unlikely an economic or social catastrophe (on the scale of the Great Depression) great enough to alter drastically the United States' international position; and (3) estimated the growth rate of the United States to the year 2000 at only a somewhat lower pace than that projected by American economists.

The cognition of the international political order as one characterized by long-term relative equality between the world powers was, however, only one facet of the Soviet reassessment of the international order. It became evident during the 1960s that Soviet affect for the contemporary international system was becoming increasingly positive. One major impetus for the more benign view of the present international system was the Sino-Soviet split, which produced overt misgivings in Moscow about the desirability of a future world of Communist states. Thus one spokesman wondered if the new world system of socialist states would be "a truly fraternal alliance of the nations, completely free of hostility and mistrust, or a system of states still tainted with mistrust between peoples, without real fraternal mutual assistance and help for each other, a system with trends to isolation

9 Karyakin, "Dulles Instead of Marx," p. 85.

and autarchy?"[10] Another hinted at a realization that the creation of multiple mobilization systems might produce "international relations of a new type" even more hazardous than those of the contemporary international system.[11]

The steady elongation of revolutionary expectations produced further evidence of the reduced relevance of a Communist tomorrow to Soviet decision-makers. At the onset of the decade Khrushchev had asserted a vision of revolutionary advance that was framed in generations. His successors' time-frame measured to the hundreds of years; they took comfort that "ultimate victory on a world scale belongs to Socialism as the most progressive social system," but emphasized that "the operative world is *ultimate*. Meanwhile it is the ups and downs of the struggle that in the main constitutes the content of international affairs."[12]

Moscow, moreover, was finding itself increasingly embroiled in the same dilemma in which German socialists had found themselves at the turn of the century. How does a group, class, or state overturn an order, domestic or international, in which it has a stake? In Marxian analysis the proletariat had been revolutionary because it had no stake in society. Lacking a stake, it alone had no ideology in the special sense that Marx meant by that term—namely, a situationally distorted perspective on events—and could therefore realize the nature of the social order. Moreover, the workers of the world could act on that realization because they had "nothing to lose but [their] chains."

The Soviet Union's position in the world in the 1960s was markedly at variance with the place conventionally allotted to the proletariat in the social order, a fact brought home dramatically to Soviet observers by the Cuban missile crisis. So vividly was the missile crisis etched in Soviet minds that after it had ended, an unsigned, authoritative editorial in *World Marxist Review* repudiated explicitly the most famous phrase in Marxist rhetoric:

Gone are the days when the working men rising in struggle against capitalism had indeed nothing to lose but their chains. Through selfless, heroic struggle, the masses have won immense material, political, and cultural gains, gains that are embodied in the socialist world system. Tomorrow the whole world and the civilization created by their labor will belong to the working people.[13]

[10] V. G. Korionov, "Proletarian Internationalism: Our Victorious Weapon," *International Affairs*, August 1963, p. 13.
[11] B. Ponomarev, "Proletarian Internationalism: A Powerful Force...," *World Marxist Review*, Vol. 7 (August 1964), p. 66.
[12] S. Sanakoyev, "The World Socialist System and the Future of Mankind," *International Affairs*, October 1966, p. 62; italics in original.
[13] "The Policy of Peaceful Coexistence," p. 6.

Still another facet of the more benign attitude to the contemporary international order was the new tone adopted toward the United States, the main actor in the international system. In earlier years, a modest familiarity with Leninism would have sufficed to anticipate Soviet declarations about American foreign policy. During the Khrushchev era a major evolution took place in Soviet perspectives on American foreign policy. Soviet commentary tended to focus more on the political system than the economy as the locus of decision-making. Rather than depicting the US as "the tool of monopoly capital for class rule," Soviet commentary, to Peking's consternation, frequently depicted the president as acting independently of "monopoly capital" and the Pentagon as independent of the White House. Soviet descriptions of American capabilities acquired a growing specificity; in the early 1960s Soviet citizens without access to classified data could obtain a reasonably accurate—and for those few with knowledge of Soviet capabilities, sobering—account of US strategic might. For our purposes, however, it was the Soviet reappraisal of American motives that was most revealing of the evolution in Soviet thinking about conflict in the nuclear age. Rather than providing a world-view in which the United States was located at the enmity pole of an enmity-amity continuum, the Khrushchevian imagery was more analogous to the perspectives of the minority leader in a two-party national system. To Khrushchev, the dominant, reasonable forces within the American "ruling circles" constituted the leading forces in the dominant opposition party and as such were the major adversary. They did not, however, constitute the main enemy. The greatest threat to Soviet values derived from the radicals of both sides—the Maos and the Goldwaters; in Khrushchev's imagery, "it is truly said, if you go left, you come out right." Unlike the lunatic fringe on both sides, men of reason in the United States were people with whom "struggle and cooperation" were necessary, desirable, and possible.

Soviet depictions of American motives during Khrushchev's last two years in power (especially after the Cuban missile crisis) clearly indicated an assumption that the successful pursuit of some American interests was compatible with an improvement in Soviet-American relations. The gains of the one country, in other words, were not necessarily the losses of the other. Indeed, at least one Soviet source specifically linked Khrushchev's conception of the new content of peaceful coexistence (involving *both* struggle and cooperation) with a conception of international relations as a non-zero-sum game—a conception which contrasted strikingly with the zero-sum implications of the traditional Bolshevik *kto-kogo*.

The last years of Khrushchev's tenure were the apogee of favorable

Soviet assertions about American foreign policy. The early months of 1965, however, were as replete with modestly charitable assessments of the prudence and reasonableness of leading American policy-makers as the years 1961–1964 had been. Indeed, some evidence indicated that Soviet commentators during the first few months after Khrushchev's ouster were preparing the Soviet public for a major improvement in Soviet-American relations. In any event, movement away from the peak years of the Khrushchev era was soon forthcoming. In late 1965, after the consequences of the American bombing of North Vietnam had been completely assimilated, old themes in the Bolshevik repertory began to be replayed. After the fall in 1965 the tendency was to emphasize the essential homogeneity of views within the American ruling group and to mute the distinction between the "two tendencies" that Khrushchev had professed to detect among the American ruling group. Khrushchev and those who thought as he did were criticized for assuming that in capitalist states the forces of reason would automatically be in the majority. American moves in Vietnam, the Dominican Republic, and elsewhere were seen as part of a single piece—as "not accidental." The United States, it was noted repeatedly, had by no means abandoned its goal of world domination or its role as global policemen.

New tunes were also heard. In particular, explanations of US foreign policy in cynical, narrow, national-interest terms that generally disregarded transnational class ties gained considerable prominence. Partly as a result of projection, Soviet observers began to speculate on American interest in exploiting "contradictions" within the socialist camp by playing to the Peoples' Republic of China. *Red Star,* for instance, in 1967 purported to detect "a Red China lobby" in the United States and "open talk" in Washington that "the ruling circles of the United States are interested in the retention of power by Mao Tse-Tung," while a Soviet specialist on American-Chinese relations speculated about a time when the United States would sacrifice the Chinese Nationalists in order to secure a rapprochement with Communist China.

US-Soviet
Relations Since 1964

The resurgence of traditionalist phrases notwithstanding, Soviet behavior in the six years since Khrushchev's ouster suggests that Chinese assertions that the views of United States foreign policy expressed by Soviet specialists immediately after October 1964 were "the very ones the new leaders of the CPSU would make themselves" were not too far off the mark. Repeatedly, Moscow has acted as though the ruling group agrees that even while the Vietnam war goes on, peaceful coexistence in Khrushchev's sense of the term—a limited adversary relationship entailing conflict and cooperation—is a necessity in the nuclear age.

At the same time, it should be stressed that evidently the "imperatives" of the nuclear age are not perceived with equal clarity by all policy-makers in Moscow. For every Soviet observer, the United States bombing of North Vietnam probably cast doubt on new hypotheses and rekindled old fears. For some, however, the bombing merely served to confirm their hostility to the United States and emphasized once again how basically hostile the United States is to Soviet goals. (Partly, of course, the divergence about American motives derives from differences in Moscow about Soviet goals and priorities.)

As a result the image of Soviet-American relations in the 1970s is unclear. Why it is unclear, however, bears significantly on the question of the impact of conflict on Soviet attitudes to conflict. Out of the experience of the cold war a conception of Soviet foreign policy emerged which until recently enjoyed considerable vogue. In that conception, Soviet behavior internationally was a product of a political system whose leadership was unaffected by domestic and international environmental influences—except to the extent, for example, it adjusted tactically to changes in the global power configuration. Soviet decision-makers, in this calculus, were seen to react to the external environment. What was missing was the extent do which they were socialized, either in that they were conditioned by the changing role and status of the USSR in the international system or in that they consciously acquired new attitudes as they assimilated the consequences of events (including moves by other states) in the international environment. The evolution of Soviet perspectives on conflict, however, illustrates that social learning has taken place, that the minds of Soviet decision-makers have proven more penetrable than was assumed. Indeed, the evolution of Soviet perspectives suggest that the usual metaphor of ideology-erosion leaves much to be desired as a term to describe the transformation in Soviet attitudes. Rather than a gradual process of encroachment on cherished beliefs, it has been the politically relevant core beliefs that have typically been subject to alteration and disavowal. The experience of extended participation in a system key elements of which have neither conformed to Soviet expectations nor been subject to Moscow's control has been an instructive one for

Soviet decision-makers. (It is not accidental that relations with eastern Europe have been most colored by ideological concerns. There, Soviet leaders are more able to coerce the reality of a conflict-ridden world of socialist states to conform to the doctrinal precepts of a qualitatively new international relations.) The knowledge that in all likelihood international reality will for the policy-relevant future continue to fail to jibe with basic Bolshevik assumptions about politics is probably equally salutary. Under these circumstances, the likely options in the potential shape of Soviet-American relations are constrained by the fact that the role and the stature of the USSR in the international system have changed. Whether Soviet spokesmen acknowledge it or not, the days are gone when the workers of the world have nothing to lose but their chains. In fact, Soviet decision-makers of nearly every stripe give every indication of realizing that in the nuclear age the Soviet Union is committed to a policy of maintaining and enhancing its position *within* the contemporary international system and that a modicum of cooperation, tacit or explicit, with the United States is essential to the task.

Since the USSR's role and status have changed, moreover, the possible range of Soviet-American relationships is further constrained: in the 1970s a reactive conception of Soviet foreign policy is likely to provide a better description of Soviet behavior than it did in the early years of the Soviet regime. Lacking an operative, all-encompassing goal and having been disabused of a unique perspective on conflict, Moscow is less likely than it was in the past to initiate radically new forms of conflict (such as, in its time, the Comintern had been). Moreover, it is probably the case that the United States (being more generously endowed with resources) will set the tone for American-Soviet relations in the 1970s. Already in the 1960s it made some sense to view Soviet behavior as an attempt to adopt American modes in order to compete effectively. Numerous instances might be cited. Thus Moscow's strategic policy of the early 1960s, sometimes termed one of "greater rubble for the ruble," followed in time Eisenhower's "bigger bang for the buck." After Khrushchev's ouster, the Soviet "missile gap" has been succeeded by an emulation of the Kennedy-McNamara doctrine. As a result, the United States and the Soviet Union now have almost identical weapons systems as Moscow has built an immense strategic arsenal and acquired a limited-war capability. Similarly, Soviet interest in the systematic study of international relations may be directly related to a judgment by some Soviet observers that game theory, simulation, and other techniques may have helped American policy-makers in their competition with the Soviet Union. It even turns out that the Soviet Ministry of Foreign Affairs, in imitation of the

US Department of State, has experimented with a policy planning staff! What is good for General Motors may not be good for the country, but it may be good enough for the Ford Motor Company.

At the same time, the limits in the patterns of Soviet-American interaction in the 1970s are also constrained in the other direction. Khrushchev and the modernist specialists in the Soviet Academy of Sciences' Institute of World Economy and International Relations overstated the case (perhaps to discredit the traditionalist perspective) when they declared that "a community of national interests" exists between the United States and the Soviet Union, that "at the present time there exist no territorial [or] economic disputes and conflicts" between the two countries, and that "their national interests do not collide either globally or regionally." As perceived by key elites within the two countries, the interests of the United States and the Soviet Union do and will clash. The possibility that peace will break out, that the relationship in the 1970s will be one of cooperation without enmity, can be safely excluded.

Within these limits, however, the range of options remains quite broad for several reasons. Naturally enough, one is that the attitudes of Soviet decision-makers toward Soviet-American relations under conditions of mutual deterrence are not shaped merely by the conditioning produced by the changed role and status of the Soviet Union or by the "realities of the atomic age." They are shaped by the moves of other major actors—especially China and, as I have suggested, the United States—the range of which in the past has been and in the future may be very broad indeed. Should we expect those who act in the name of the Soviet Union to have highly stable expectations about the policies toward the Soviet Union likely to be pursued by a peace-loving socialist country which is on record as claiming as its own a million square miles of Soviet territory? What policies are Soviet observers likely to expect of the United States on the basis of their experience in the 1960s—having witnessed one US president who handled the Cuban missile crisis in a way that permitted the Soviet Union to back down with grace, a second who was so insensitive to Soviet interests that he escalated the war in Vietnam by bombing North Vietnam while Alexei Kosygin was in Hanoi, and a third who, having made a career of anti-Communism, has since 1968 been at pains to stress his receptiveness to businesslike relations (to use a phrase much favored by Moscow) with the Soviet Union?

Beyond the major actors, moreover, are the smaller states. Soviet commentary explicitly recognizes that these actors have become increasingly able to maneuver in the world arena, independent of, and by implication sometimes contrary to, the interests of either superpower.

The wide variety of actions that will be forthcoming from these states during the 1970s will provide numerous occasions on which decision-makers in Moscow will have to make choices. Time and again Moscow is likely to be confronted with situations in which it has to choose between stability in a particular situation—with its implication of continued American influence and rather small prospects of Soviet-American conflict—and radical change—which may produce reduced American influence (frequently not coupled with a concomitant enhancement in Soviet influence) and relatively higher risk of Soviet-American confrontation over issues of tertiary import to the superpowers.

Changes in the external environment are not the only major reason for the breadth and range of scenarios that might characterize Soviet-American relations. Soviet perceptions and consequently Soviet behavior may vary because of changes in the cast of characters who constitute "Moscow," as a result of the changing constellation of political forces in the Soviet Union. (Mutatis mutandis, of course, the same point applies to the United States. If anything, it is even more analytically insufficient to project American foreign policy in the 1970s without regard to internal political outcomes.) The configuration taken by that constellation during the next decade will go a long way toward explaining what kind of reaction to external stimuli will be forthcoming from Moscow. Moreover, attention to the dynamics of Soviet politics should serve as an important reminder that in the Soviet Union, as elsewhere, organizational politics have a life of their own. These processes generate policy outputs which are in turn perceived by decision-makers abroad (accustomed to treating states—other than their own, of course—as unitary, rational decision-makers) as being moves from which one can judge an adversary's intentions and as requiring some kind of response.

Indeed, many Soviet and American decision-makers may ultimately act on a recognition that the United States and the Soviet Union have one mutual interest that did not exist in the heyday of bipolarity and internal consensus in each superpower. They may seek to achieve sufficient control over events so that once again, as in the years just after World War II, the outcomes of the global political process will be primarily a product of the interplay of conscious Soviet and American decisions. They may seek to achieve jointly through cooperation that which will not occur spontaneously. It is safe to assume, therefore, that the United Nations Security Council will play a far greater role in the 1970s than it did in the fifties and early sixties. Cooperation to reduce *unintended* conflict may thus produce a situation in which central political decision-makers of the two states in effect conspire to reduce internally generated pressures for certain kinds of actions the implementation of which adversely affects the interactive pattern of relationships between the United States and the Soviet Union. It is conceivable, for instance, that the cynics in Moscow (and Washington) may see the present strategic arms limitation talks (SALT) in just this light. Each side may feel that an explicit international agreement will reduce the political costs of denying internally generated pressures for development of weapons systems. It may even prove possible for persons acting in the names of the two countries to bring about a simultaneous reordering of priorities in each country by negotiating a series of self-enforcing, self-denying ordinances that would permit both countries to allocate more attention and resources to the domestic ailments of the respective societies. Such a prospect seemed almost in the offing in 1964–1965, when it appeared that the United States might address itself to building a "Great Society"—whatever that meant—and the Soviet Union might turn its energies to the "full-scale building of Communism"—whatever that meant. Similarly, it is not inconceivable that the United States and the Soviet Union may in effect conspire against their allies in order to prevent their respective "friends"—having made good their threat to collapse—from dragging down the superpowers with them—here the Middle East comes immediately to mind.

The experience of the 1960s, however, would tend to indicate that such a meeting of minds is likely only in the aftermath of a conflict of the magnitude of the Cuban missile crisis. In the short run, before the recurrence of such a searing event, decision-makers in both the Soviet Union and the United States will probably be disinclined to pay the political costs necessary to reassert greater control over the dynamics of their limited adversary relationship.

Chapter 3

Superpowers and Challenger

The United States and China

EDWARD FRIEDMAN

Almost since its establishment, the People's Republic of China has presented a challenge to the superpower policies of the United States. When America acts in Asia as a superpower—that is, when it tries to impose its will as far as its gargantuan might permits, even right up to China's frontiers—it finds itself confronted by a Chinese government willing to take significant military risks to secure those frontiers. The three major confrontations between America as superpower and China as challenger to the continuing extension of that American power occurred in Korea, in the Formosa Straits, and in Laos and Vietnam the successor states to French Indochina. Rather than attempt an exhaustive historical examination of Peking-Washington relations, we will analyze these three crucial instances as indicative of the interests and possibilities inherent in the relationship. In addition, rather than treat the foreign policy decisions of either state as emerging from inherent cultural traits or singular national interests, we will stress the larger political forces that shape and limit the options open to decision-makers.

Korea

Before America fought China in Korea from 1950 to 1953, the new government of China saw the United States as a potential enemy and potential friend. Although President Truman had helped Chiang Kai-shek's side in China's civil war with billions in aid, equipment, and advisers, the President had not committed massive American ground troops to the war. The President's military advisers saw little gain in involving American resources in a land war in continental Asia. While Truman would help nonradical nationalists or colonialists against revolutionaries

55

in the areas neighboring China to its south and southeast, the collapse of Chiang Kai-shek, despite similar American aid, suggested to Chinese leaders that such aid could not prove fruitful. By early 1950 China was demobilizing its army, directing her energies toward domestic reconstruction, state-to-state relations, and membership in the United Nations. After 100 years of war, weakness, and disunity, Chinese could proudly look forward to assuming a dignified role in international councils.

The euphoria of victory may for the moment have made the optimistic vision of China's young generation[1] the vision of the leadership in general. The paper-tiger generation, formed in the last years of China's revolutionary civil war and subsequently taking minor commanding positions in new military and political bureaucracies and lesser posts in established groupings such as foreign affairs and communications, badly underestimated America's capabilities. This generation was formed in the fiery experience following on Mao Tse-tung's 1946 announcement that "the atomic bomb is a paper tiger." In 1946 the Soviet Union would not help Mao win, and America, the only nation in the world with atomic bombs, was giving large-scale aid to Chiang Kai-shek's side. Mao was well aware "the atom bomb is a weapon of mass slaughter." He knew "we have only millet and rifles to rely on" against "Chiang Kai-shek's airplanes plus tanks." Given such seemingly hopeless odds, many in the revolutionary movement favored diplomatic surrender over military suicide. Mao could not promise his colleagues and supporters ready victory. Renewed warfare promised only "difficulties" and "hardships." Yet, whatever the odds, Mao could not quit the cause to which he had given his life. He offered his people a faith that, no matter what their individual fates, their cause would some day win. Other seemingly weak but just causes had prevailed in history. "From a long-range point of view," Mao believed, history was redemptive; good would ultimately triumph. To call reactionaries and atomic bombs "paper tigers" was a way of acknowledging one's weakness while insisting that the values and valuables at stake made it morally and politically impossible not to fight on.

As it turned out, Mao was wrong about that long, hard road. The enemy was decaying, split, without morale. In a couple of years the

---

1 Useful material on this vision of the paper-tiger generation may be found in Franklin Houn, "The Principles and Operational Code of Communist China's International Conduct," *Journal of Asian Studies,* XXVII (November 1967), 21–40; John Gittings, *The Role of the Chinese Army* (Cambridge: Oxford University Press, 1967), pp. 12–17, 234–241; Arthur Cohen, *The Communism of Mao Tse-tung* (Chicago: University of Chicago Press, 1964), pp. 59–71.

rural-based revolutionaries overwhelmed their armed opponents. Paper tigers no longer seemed tigers at all. The revolutionary fighters who had risked all could now believe—as Mao had not—that human will could more than compensate for diplomatic isolation and weakness in weaponry. Thus was born what we call the paper-tiger generation, a group increasingly persuaded that just as America did not use the bomb to help Chiang Kai-shek, so imperialism confronted by a united people would not resort to atomic warfare.

Another group of leaders placed at the commanding heights of the diplomatic and state bureaucracies learned their lessons of history and developed their policy prescriptions in the 1937–1945 resistance movement against Japanese invaders. The experience of this group, the united-front generation,[2] showed that success for the weak lay in forging the broadest possible patriotic united front in order to pinpoint, isolate, and destroy the major enemy. That was how Japan was defeated. After victory, the united-front generation feared that the Japan which America began to rebuild in 1948 might involve America in a war with China. Other nations that had fought Japan—Australia, the Philippines, and Burma—had similar fears about Japan, as France and Russia had about Germany. Chinese leaders worried that vengeful elements might reemerge in Japan and repeat the history of Germany after World War I. The security of China demanded alliance with and protection by the USSR, the only world power capable of deterring a Japan backed by the US.

But Stalin was wary of Mao. Tito had just turned on the Russians in Yugoslavia. What would prevent the Chinese from doing the same? The bargaining between Chinese and Russians was drawn out and bitter. Finally, in return for some economic aid and an agreement "jointly to prevent the rebirth of Japanese imperialism and the resumption of Japanese aggression or any form of aggressive act by any nation in collaboration with Japan," China had to make tremendous concessions to the Soviets, allowing Russia to use Chinese ports and railroads and to exploit Chinese natural resources. Even if the addi-

---

[2] The approach of the united-front generation to politics is most carefully delineated in Lyman Van Slyke, *Enemies and Friends: The United Front in Chinese Communist History* (Stanford: Stanford University Press, 1967). Its implications for Chinese diplomacy can be pieced together from the writings of C. P. Fitzgerald on the Bandung period (*Nation*, April 2, 1955, pp. 228–229; June 11, 1955, pp. 502–504; September 10, 1955, pp. 220–221; *Far Eastern Survey* [August 1955], 113–119; *Spectator*, September 16, 1955, pp. 355–356) and in Arthur Lall, *How Communist China Negotiates* (New York: Columbia University Press, 1968). It is not far different from that outlined in M. Halperin and T. Tsou, "Mao Tse-tung's Revolutionary Strategy and Peking's International Behavior," *American Political Science Review* (March 1965), 88–99.

tional rumors about Russian efforts to pit a northeast Chinese contingent against Mao and to place Russian troops on Chinese soil are not true, the established facts make clear that Chinese-Russian relations were very strained and tense just before the Korean war.

That is not how the world looked from Washington. In America it seemed that Russian imperialist aggression was on the march. Eastern Europe had fallen to the Kremlin's armies. In 1948 a coup subverted Czechoslovakia. In 1949 Communism won in China. Worse yet, by 1950 Russia was swallowing the northeastern part of China. And North Korea had fallen. China would soon be absorbed.

When civil strife exploded in Korea in June 1950, it was difficult for Americans to see it as other than a probe in international Communist aggression. The experience of not responding to Hilter, of Munich and World War II, led American leaders to see an armed act possibly related to a major hostile power as an aggression which, if not met, would result in world war. Those in Washington who suggested that this war was essentially a local, Korean affair were brushed aside. They had to be. Not to act would have been political suicide for the Truman administration in a domestic political world of Munich lessons, cold war, and McCarthyism.

Truman acted to save himself and, as he saw it, to save the world. Militarily it was necessary for him to send ammunition to south Korea. Politically he found it desirable to silence conservative critics by giving them what they wanted—American military protection for Chiang Kai-shek's defeated remnant holding out on the island of Formosa. Truman could concede to these conservative, cold-war concerns in Asia precisely because they were inconsequential in his scheme of priorities. With war a reality and the conservatives mollified, Truman also got what his security advisers insisted was necessary, a huge increase in the military budget from $13 to $50 billion. The new funds would permit Truman to build up the European defense forces he felt would safeguard world peace against an aggressive Russia.

The American commitment in Korea grew. General MacArthur ignored orders and sent bombers north of the 38th parallel. He asked for American troops and got them. He asked for reinforcements and reinforcements were sent. Once his plan for a landing behind the lines of his Korean opponent succeeded, he could not be stopped. For the first time it seemed that America had the "Communists" on the run. The original desire to protect south Korea turned into a dream of uniting all Korea. MacArthur crashed across the 38th parallel and headed north. As a march south led to an armed American intervention, so China had warned Washington that an American march north would provoke a Chinese response.

Even less than America subsequently would tolerate Russian missiles in Cuba could China afford to tolerate a powerful American force led by an out-of-control general marching toward its borders. The issue was not Korea. China could live with any outcome in a civil war in one of the small states on its periphery. None of those weak nations could harm China no matter the system of government. American military might was another matter. Chinese foreign policy spokesman Chou En-lai explained that "the south Koreans did not matter but American intrusion into north Korea would encounter Chinese resistance."

China had no desire to fight America. War would divert the Chinese from building their country. After long years of war Chinese longed for peace. To defend against the Americans would be costly. The Russians promised little aid. To defend against the Americans could be dangerous. MacArthur threatened to carry the war into China.

MacArthur ignored directives from Washington that he halt at particular points. Washington did not take him to task for insubordination. With great reluctance the Chinese finally committed their troops to Korea in October 1950 to stop MacArthur's advance. Peking understood that its willingness to stand up to the American thrust might well mean not merely war with America in Korea but an American nuclear attack on China.

The Chinese government began to prepare its people for the worst. Civil-defense measures were instituted in the area near Korea to reduce the physical impact of an American attack. The psychological impact was reduced, it was hoped, by stories of how the bomb wasn't as dreadful as people might think. An alleged eye-witness account from Hiroshima told how in no time life returned to normal in that bombed-out city. A Chinese military spokesman, eventually to head China's atomic bomb project, explained that he knew America might bomb China.

They might even drop bombs on us. What then? They may kill a few million people. Without sacrifice a nation's independence cannot be upheld. After all, China lives on the farms. What can atom bombs do then? Yes, our economic development will be put back. We may have to wait for it.

Perhaps to show Washington that China wasn't bluffing, Chinese troops fought in Korea from October 24 to November 8 and then pulled back. It was understood in Washington that granting China a buffer might well end the Chinese intervention because it would assure China that MacArthur finally was being restrained. Britain tried to serve as an intermediary to establish the buffer and dampen the conflict.

Instead MacArthur demanded that Chinese territory be attacked. Washington kept conceding to the General's demands. The popularity of his military successes made it politically impossible to halt him. The priority of domestic politics over reasoned policy in Asia was leading America to war with China. American policy, as China saw, was initiated by the General in the field and not by the President in the United States. When the Joint Chiefs asked MacArthur to halt his advance and permit a buffer to be established, the General denounced the suggestion as "appeasement of Communist aggression." He insisted on "complete victory" and ordered his troops to press northward. Despite a lack of paper-tiger or united-front conditions, Chinese leaders saw no choice but a new and very reluctant policy of counterattack, war on foreign soil, and war with America.

A new generation of leaders was formed for China by the new experience of the Korean war. These men, many of whom served in the upper and middle levels of military and party bureaucracies, came to place primary value on association with a major military backer. They believed that without the backing of the Soviet Union, which sent modern weapons to the Chinese and had the atomic potential to deter American strikes against China, the US would have attacked China and done much worse damage to the Chinese army in Korea. This group found in the Korean war that in international conflict with a major foreign power—unlike the experience of defense on one's own soil or revolutionary civil war—the sine quo non was modern weapons, modern training, and the backing of a major industrialized military power. That was how America was stopped in Korea.[3]

American strategists and leaders also learned lessons. They learned that "Communism" was prepared to use naked aggression, that it could be stopped only by force, and that this force was most legitimately applied in unity with other nations. (Oddly, the Chinese learned similar lessons: only force stopped America; only alliance with other nations stopped America.) And more force does better than less. That is, if America had early threatened China with a direct atomic attack, China probably would not have intervened. Peace was only wrung out of the Chinese in 1953 by Dwight Eisenhower when

---

3 People holding this view are usually referred to as the pragmatists or realists in most western literature on the subject. The major commentaries on their military-diplomatic outlook can be found in the writings of John Gittings, Alice Hsieh, Ellis Joffe, John Lewis, Ralph Powell, and Donald Zazoria. The general vision developed for Chinese foreign policy by Davis Bobrow, "The Chinese Communist Conflict System," *Orbis,* Winter 1966, pp. 930–952 is largely the one that I apply to this Korean war generation. The notion of major backer is Bobrow's.

America threatened China with the possibility of escalating to nuclear attack.

Of course, the lessons were false, as the attempt to apply them in Vietnam was to show. But what was important that was overlooked was not so much that even in 1953 neither Mao nor Stalin blinked before the American nuclear brinksmanship as that a large area of mutual interest existed between Washington and Peking. A major question raised by these missed opportunities is how much either was the master of its own fate.

China did not want the war, yet was pushed into it, thus delaying a desperately desired domestic development and deepening an unwanted dependence on the Soviet Union. From the time it entered the war, China moved to achieve a negotiating basis that would swiftly end the fighting. The Chinese did not pursue their early advantage. They let the American troops escape south and did not chase them beyond the Han river, the first natural, defensive barrier south of the 38th parallel. By the middle of 1951 politicians on both sides saw the wisdom in moving toward peace talks. Those peace talks dragged on because neither Stalin nor the American military did much to help them along. In addition, although it had nothing to do with national security considerations on either side, the issue of exchange of prisoners of war became a sensitive and explosive political issue for both China and America. The war made America and China enemies. The American government instituted an economic embargo against China, got the United Nations to brand China an aggressor, and committed itself to the defeated leader of the old order, Chiang Kai-shek, in exile on Formosa. In addition, the image of the Chinese as a people who don't value human life, who attack in endless hordes to kill Americans, became a fact of American politics although it was not a fact of the war, in which for the most part Chinese attacks were based on small units, three groups of three men. During the bloody war in Korea, China, in American politics, became the great orange threat, a combination of red menace and yellow peril.

Peace finally became possible as Stalin died and China held the American military to a stalemate, thus permitting politicians on both sides to reassert control of the situation. The Chinese were offered a compromise on the prisoner issue. They accepted it. Finally, all that stood between China, America, and peace was the south Korean patriotic tyrant, Syngman Rhee, and his desires to prolong the war. Rhee tried to sabotage the prisoner exchange. American military men who did not like the compromise peace did not stop Rhee. The war-minded south Korean leader threatened to fight on alone. Washington tried to control him with stick and carrot by limiting supplies sent to his troops and buying him off by promising him hundreds of millions of dollars in aid, an enlarged army, and a security pact with the US. At the same time, Chinese troops attacked and ripped apart the elite divisions of Rhee's troops. Instead of seeing the subsequent cessation of fighting as largely related to an overlap of American and Chinese interests, Chinese leaders saw it as a victory for their soldiers who finally brought America to its senses, and American leaders saw it as a victory for an implied threat of nuclear attack if China did not settle. The dangerous lessons learned by the two sides portended a future relationship in which American nuclear blackmail and Chinese willingness to stand up against it, protected by the Russian nuclear shield, would be matters of the utmost significance.

Formosa

The next major challenge of China to American superpower took place late in the summer of 1958 around the tiny Quemoy islands just off the east coast of China near the important port of Amoy.[4] The Chinese seem to have experienced a new threat from that superpower which the established policies of the united-front generation and the Korean war generation could not deal with. This opened the way for the paper-tiger generation to assert its policy prescriptions.

Under the Eisenhower administration, with its conservative and budgetary concerns, no major military initiatives were undertaken in Asia. By 1958 American liberal leaders worried that this fiscal conservatism was producing a dangerous gap between Communist (the Russian bloc) missile power and American weaponry. The liberals wanted America to leap ahead in new military spending. Instead the Eisenhower administration continued its policy of small military increases each year based on a level of spending that, though lower than during the Korean war, nevertheless amounted to 2½ times the Truman budgets of the later 1940s. From the viewpoint of a very weak and poor China, the military deployments resulting from that supposedly limited American spending already seemed overthreatening.

In 1957 America began to move missiles capable of carrying nuclear weapons into Korea, Formosa, and the island chain of Japan. The American government probably saw the initiative as essentially defen-

---

[4] American analysts differ on the nature of this confrontation. Some see it as China doing it in opposition to the wishes of the Soviet Union. Others insist that Peking and Moscow coordinated their efforts. My own understanding is that there were attempts at coordination but that a conflict of interest between Russia and China led to a difference between them of the issue. The evidence for any of these views is fragmentary. Honest differences of opinion are unavoidable.

sive and precautionary—but Washington's reaction in October 1962 to Russian missiles in Cuba should indicate how Peking might have felt about the new American nuclear threat. Superpower America risked nuclear war in 1962 to remove those missiles from off its shores. But what could a weak China do in 1958? It necessarily had to listen to the major-backer, Korean war generation with its insistence on the overwhelming importance of the Russian alliance and the Russian nuclear shield.

The united-front generation was in trouble. Its attempts to ally with everyone who could be allied with, to help neutral and independent governments in southeast Asia, to negotiate a peaceful resolution of the Formosa problem, to improve relations with America and Japan had all been brutally rebuffed. At Geneva in 1954 united-front generation leaders joined with Russia, France, and Britain to impose a settlement on the Viet Minh. For China the key to the settlement was the neutralization, the removal of foreign military might, from Laos, a state bordering China's southwest frontier. By 1958 the neutral government in Laos had been subverted with generous CIA help. In addition a military coup in Thailand had turned that government away from neutralism and toward integration with American military policies. In south Vietnam the CIA was helping Diem undermine the Geneva accords and build up his army. And early in 1958 the CIA, working from bases in Formosa and the Philippines, tried to engineer a military insurrection against the neutralist government in Indonesia. From China's vantage point, America, finding its air bases overseas negated by Russian missile gains, was attempting a general push in Asia backed by the threat of massive retalliation against any aid to those under attack. To make matters worse, not only was Taiwan integrated into this forward thrust as it turned down offers for talks, accepted nuclear missiles, and in May 1957 reinstituted a blockade on the port of Amoy, but in addition the Japanese government of the new premier, Kishi, who had served in Japan's war cabinet and been arrested as a war criminal, brushed aside China's diplomatic initiatives, welcomed American missiles, embraced Chiang Kai-shek, moved for a Japanese missile corps trained by Americans, made concessions to America to get its help in opening southeast Asia to Japanese business, and asked for a revision of Japan's constitution "because at present we can't send troops overseas." Kishi made clear to China that he intended to make Japan an integral part of America's militantly hostile anti-China policy in Asia and then confront China from a position of strength "when we are healthy enough.... But our first effort must be to attain such a state of health." The prescriptions of China's united front generation did not speak to this situation.

People of China's paper-tiger generation took more power in 1958 as the Great Leap Forward devolved power from the governmental bureaucracies to local party people. They may have taken advantage of this gain while united-front people lost—Chou En-lai stopped being foreign minister, and the foreign affairs bureaucracy was reorganized with more control given to party people concerned with other Communist states—to make much of insults to the Chinese flag and to Chinese diplomats in Japan. A perusal of how patriots are moved by public stress on such insults in most countries may be an index of how these Communist party people manipulated events and information to press their views. Similarly, the seizure, arrest, and trial of Japanese sailors on spying missions in Chinese territorial waters—there is little reason to believe that these were the first such missions—may further be an indication of how the paper-tiger generation tried to impose its prescription for standing up in armed defense. Perhaps in the turnover of journals and editorial staffs that followed a turn away from the liberalization policy of 1956–1957, the paper-tiger people were able to have many of their people promoted. As Chiang Kai-shek and the reactionaries could not be reasoned with in 1946, so America and the imperialists could not be reasoned with in 1958. Mao's writings were reedited and published in a collection headed IMPERIALISTS AND ALL REACTIONARIES ARE PAPER TIGERS.

The paper-tiger generation retaliated against Japan's hostile policies by stopping official Chinese visits, suspending trade agreements, and not extending fisheries agreement. In southeast Asia, China tried to undersell Japan.[5] And China used its military to challenge America's forward position on the offshore island of Quemoy.

The actual attempt to isolate and blockade Quemoy[6] during the typhoon season seems to have represented a compromise between generations, factions, and prescriptions. The Russians were trying to use their new breakthrough in intercontinental ballistic missiles to impose their will on the United States in Europe and the Middle East. They could not afford a breakdown in their diplomatic thrust against America. Consequently the still powerful Korean war, major-backer generation moved to avoid losing necessary Russian military backing, including the Russian nuclear shield (American threats to unleash atomic warfare against China in the Vietnam crisis of 1953–1954 and the offshore island crisis of 1954–1955 had not brought such

[5] Again the evidence is not conclusive. Economic reasons may have been more important than the general political response to the new threat.

[6] The facts on this attempt are developed in great detail in an unpublished manuscript by Morton Halperin.

bombings while the possibility of a Russian response existed[7]); it minimized the risk involved in the attempt on Quemoy by limiting the attack to a blockade in typhoon season with a political purpose, not a military one. That is, America's relations with the Chiang Kai-shek clique deteriorated in the mid-1950s. In May 1957 the militaristic youth corps of Chiang's son attacked the American embassy in Chiang's capital of Taipei on Formosa. Washington had been unsuccessfully pressuring Chiang to remove troops from the tiny island of Quemoy and Matsu just off China's shores. Chiang's government believed it needed America's commitment to that forward position to preserve its rationale for continuing military rule over the Formosan people. The American Government, as both Peking and Taipei knew, became involved with various anti-Chiang forces. Peking hoped that the minimal-risk blockade of Quemoy would bring Taipei-Washington tensions to a breaking point since America's major European allies would prevent Washington from risking war with Peking over such a minor matter while Chiang Kai-shek would insist on major American military support to hold the provocative islands and to counterattack. Thus, at little cost, new possibilities for big diplomatic gains would emerge for China.

The Korean war generation—and the more militant paper-tiger generation—miscalculated. Verbally, America backed Chiang to the hilt. Washington let it be known that an attack on Quemoy involved not just Quemoy, not only Formosa, but the fate of the entire western Pacific. America therefore might well use all means against the minimal Chinese attempt to blockade Quemoy. The US navy convoyed ships to the islands. Chiang's air force was provided with sidewinder missiles to win air battles over the area. Cannons capable of firing atomic missiles were brought in. So once again China was confronted with American nuclear blackmail. Was it an empty bluff or a credible deterrent? China's leaders could not afford to probe and find out. They lacked any Russian backing for any risk-taking. Instead, they hastily backed off, would not even risk attacking the US naval convoys sitting off Quemoy, and moved to the conference table.

Apparently the carefully controlled attempt at blockade had not been controlled enough. Russia was wary that China might try to disrupt its diplomatic gains vis-à-vis the US. Despite the Korean war generation's effort not to lose its major military backer, Russia found it

---

[7] Dulles said that if China tried to seize the islands of Quemoy and Matsu, "we'll have to use atomic weapons." President Eisenhower agreed on atomic weapons. "I see no reason why they shouldn't be used just exactly as you would a bullet or anything else."

had prior interests in dealing with America even to the point of trying to ease America out of the thorns of its rosy embrace with Chiang Kai-shek and his forward claims. Moscow and Washington began to find mutual interests in preventing Peking and Taipei from dragging them into a major conflict.

The head of the Korean war, major-backer generation went to Moscow to try to reestablish proper nuclear and military relations with the Soviet Union. Moscow, however, would not provide the desired weaponry unless it maintained control of it. In addition to doubts about Chinese reliability, such a policy was also desirable, from a Russian standpoint, as a counter to trade off to keep America from providing nuclear weapons to West Germany. In 1959 Moscow reversed its earlier decision about providing aid to China in developing nuclear weapons. Suddenly the Korean war generation was without a viable policy.

Most of the Chinese leadership seems to have believed that Dulles was bluffing over Quemoy in 1958. Their understanding of Dulles's diplomacy accepted his explanation as published by Life magazine in January 1956 in an article titled "Three Times at Brink of War: How Dulles Gambled and Won." Threats of unleashing an atomic war supposedly led to the Korean armistice, settlement of the war in formerly French Indochina, and conclusion of the Formosa Straits crisis in 1955. China believed you had to stand up to the bully. That's how they prevailed in Korea. Moscow couldn't see the point of calling America's bluff on what the Kremlin considered a minor issue. American intelligence analysts saw that Russia refused to play out the hand of bluff poker. The Chinese folded instead of raising the ante. According to Edgar Snow, Mao has "not trusted Khrushchev as a political strategist since he had unnecessarily betrayed his hand during Mr. Dulles's bluff in the Quemoy-Matsu crisis of 1958." Not trusting Russia's military judgments where vital Chinese interests were at stake, China could not accept a Russian offer for military cooperation under Russian hegemony which removed too much of the international and military initiative from China's hands.

The paper-tiger generation had no useful prescription. The retreat from the economic difficulties brought on by the Great Leap Forward forced China to swallow its pride and begin private trade with Kishi's hostile Japan, moving toward negotiations for larger, more regularized trade. The initiative should have passed back to the united-front generation. In part it did. China moved toward a new third-world policy of unity with major industrial nations other than the US: France, Britain, Canada, Germany, Italy, and Japan. But the Quemoy fiasco of 1958 left China with no nuclear shield. It thus had to try to maintain at least a façade of good relations with the USSR while hastening the development of its own nuclear deterrent. But this still left China open to American nuclear blackmail or American nuclear attack. It made China less likely for the time being to protect her frontiers, as in Korea, through forward defense. The Chinese Foreign Minister expalined that

US military bases in Taiwan, Okinawa, Japan, south Korea, south Vietnam, and the Philippines are all directed against China. How can we escape fear? The US has nuclear weapons. We have none. We have our fears. They are always in our minds. We cannot sleep easily at night.

With her vulnerability made manifest by the Quemoy debacle, Chinese leaders were prepared to compromise much to decrease massive American military activities on her periphery. In 1961–1962 at Geneva China actively aided another settlement for neutralization in Laos. The Japanese were told that China was ready for a general improvement in relations with America if the US would begin to move its military might away from the Formosa area. (Apparently some symbolic retreat by Washington in the Formosa area was needed so that Chinese political leaders would not be clobbered in Peking for being oversoft on American imperialism.) Pakistan, which was a member of SEATO, served as an intermediary to carry China's message of working to improve relations back to the United States. Other intermediaries and other public pronouncements by Chinese leaders made this renewed Chinese desire for negotiations, compromise, and peace quite clear.

The election of a new American president helped rationalize the new Chinese policies. John Kennedy was ready to insist that China should resume its sovereignty over Quemoy and Matsu, islands a couple of miles from China provocatively occupied by troops from Taiwan, 100 miles distant. This military occupation by hostile troops symbolized an armed unwillingness to accept the reality of the government of China. Kennedy clearly was abandoning the MacArthur-Dulles policy of trying to isolate and undermine that government. Kennedy was also open to diplomatic relations with Mongolia despite Chiang Kai-shek's objections. Chiang insisted that Mongolia was part of China. Here American and Chinese interests seemed to coincide. China too wished to make Mongolia less wholly dependent on Russia. Kennedy also was willing to consider a wheat deal with China. Again American and Chinese interests overlapped. Russia was trying to use China's economic difficulties to pressure China into line, into Moscow's international line. American aid permitted China to be more indepen-

dent of Moscow and helped keep Russia and China apart. It made
sense for China to approach the new American President.

But the American President couldn't deliver the goods. Back in
1958, after the Quemoy crisis, Dulles could not get Chiang Kai-shek
to remove his troops from their provocative deployments. Whatever
reductions in their size, removal of the blockade of Amoy, and decrease in forays on the coast Dulles won were won only at the cost
of other political and military concessions to the Chiang Kai-shek
leadership group.[8] The flak shot up by conservatives in opposition to
Kennedy's suggestion to defuse the time bomb of the occupied offshore
islands was so thick that Kennedy quickly backed down. The American President lacked the power and the will to make policy with
regard to China based on his understanding of US interest and of a
more peaceful Pacific. The foolhardly adventure at the Bay of Pigs
in April 1961 led the President to feel that he should shelve foreign
policy initiatives toward China that might be interpreted at home as
softness on communism. Despite dangerous confrontations with Moscow over Berlin in 1961, Cuba in 1962, and Laos from December
1960 to 1962, the President could not act on mutual interests with a
China that also was feeling fearful of deteriorating relations with the
Soviet Union. The will of the military ruler of Formosa, Chiang Kai-
shek, and his powerful friends in the US Congress and Pentagon was
strong enough, in a domestic atmosphere where presidents felt their
policies and prestige rested on a need to be tough on the "reds," to
check any wise change in American policy. The threat of future
confrontations between America and China was intensified by the
inability of the American Chief Executive to act upon his notion of
America's international interests.

Vietnam

In April 1965, for the first time since the Korean war, American and
Chinese military men fought, this time high over China's Hainan
island near the Gulf of Tonkin. Starting in 1964 growing, large-scale
American escalation to impose its will in Laos and Vietnam increasingly threatened a direct clash with China. This radical change temporarily undercut the policies of Mao Tse-tung and the united-front
people, which were predicated on the unlikelihood of war with America. It brought to the fore once again men of the Korean war genera-

[8] Tantalizing threads of evidence tentatively indicate that Washington withdrew
its support for anti-Chiang factions and gave its support to Chiang's son as his
successor in partial return for Chiang's concessions.

tion who insisted on the need for good relations with the Soviet Union to neutralize American nuclear blackmail of China, in case China, as in the Korean war, was called upon to protect itself by stopping an American army marching toward its borders. The crux of the debate was to understand the role Russia desired in Asia.

The Korean war generation could argue that without a Russian nuclear shield, China would be placed in a passive position. Its own territory would be endangered since any direct intervention on behalf of the revolutionaries to the south might serve as a pretext for America to bomb China's nuclear installations. Powerful individuals at the top of the Lyndon Johnson administration pressed for such a policy.

Between mid-1962 and mid-1963 Russia and America had worked out a treaty to ban further atmospheric testing of nuclear weapons and to preclude the proliferation of nuclear weapons. America's purpose, negotiator Averell Harriman said, was "to prevent China from getting a nuclear capacity." John Kennedy was willing to risk much to achieve that purpose. By the middle of 1963 President Kennedy was pushing Khrushchev on stopping China from manufacturing nuclear weapons. Harriman asked the Russians, "Can you deliver China?" "Suppose their rockets are targeted against you?" Washington inside-dopester Stewart Alsop finds that "before his death President Kennedy considered using A-11's to eliminate the nuclear plants then being completed by the Chinese. . . ." Secretary of State Rusk subsequently revealed, "We considered this but decided against it." Why not give in to what former CIA analyst Donald Zagoria called, "a great temptation to adopt a bolder policy toward China and to eliminate or seriously damage her extremely vulnerable nuclear plant"? According to the Secretary of State, because "in effect, such a decision, in all probability, would not be merely to take out a bomb or a plant, but to go to war with China—and perhaps ultimately with Russia." Why didn't the Soviet Union in 1964 go along with this American-programed Pearl Harbor in reverse? Perhaps because the struggle over the policies and eventual ouster of Khrushchev in 1963–1964 involved the Russian political elite in a reconsideration of foreign policy which at first excluded new adventures. In Laos, for example, the Russians stopped supplying the neutrals in 1963. This permitted American-backed rightists and neutralists to try to win everything. Laos, as in 1961, was becoming an area in which war between America and China was possible.

The new leadership in Moscow tried to improve relations with Peking in early 1965. Mao and his paper-tiger and united-front colleagues didn't trust the Russians. (Peking's preferred course was to have Japanese serve as intermediaries between China and America.)

Russian leader Kosygin went to Peking and asked the Chinese to help him work out a peaceful solution of the war in Vietnam by helping to save face for America. Peking refused. Mao Tse-tung was confident that the popular struggle in Vietnam would achieve victory and would not lead to larger-scale war with America. He would only negotiate leading to American military withdrawal from Vietnam. After the American bombing attack on north Vietnam in August 1964, which used the pretext of alleged incidents in the Gulf of Tonkin, China sent jet fighters to Hanoi to help repel further US attacks. China also began to build airfields just north of Vietnam to help deter further US attacks. The Chinese wanted to know why Kosygin would not offer similar, solid support to the people bombed by America intsead of selling out the rebels on the verge of complete victory.

Everything began to change in February 1965 when Washington bombed north Vietnam while Kosygin was in Hanoi on a peace mission. Russia would now have to help the Vietnamese revolutionaries. Washington had decided it could not achieve its superpower purpose of preventing a neutral or unified Vietnam at the bargaining table. Hordes of US troops poured into Vietnam while numerous American jets "accidentally" flew over Chinese air space. Although one US jet was shot down, Peking insisted that the Americans accidentally shot down their own plane. Such passive responses by China, according to sources close to the Pentagon, led to a judgment "that the Chinese wanted no part of a wider war—at least at the moment." Consequently, America could freely escalate in Vietnam without fear of a serious Chinese response.

Mao Tse-tung and his supporters from the united-front and paper-tiger generations had been wrong about the nonexistent nature of the American threat. Caution and security-consciousness now dictated that China act as if America might well carry its escalation into China. Therefore the Chief of Staff and many others of the Korean war generation insisted that China cooperate with Russia to fight America in Vietnam.[9] Strategy should be coordinated; Russia should have access to the south China airfields and to Chinese air space. Starting in the fall of 1965 China sent troops into north Vietnam to man anti-aircraft units against American planes, build jungle base-camps, and rebuild bombed-out railroads. Had America invaded north Vietnam, this Chinese trip-wire might have spelled war between America and China and success for Mao's anti-American, Korean war generation opponents. (Mao and his colleagues would fight only if America further

[9] For an introduction to this foreign policy debate see the articles by Uri Ra'anan and Donald Zagoria in Tang Tsou (ed.), *China in Crisis*, (Chicago: University of Chicago Press), 1968, vol. 2.

endangered China.) In 1965 Washington warned Peking that it could hit China with nuclear weapons if China intervened in Vietnam. Washington believed that this threat, predicated on the false lesson of the Korean war, kept China out. But the paper tiger generation answered that threat with counterthreat, pointing out that the Chinese now had the atom bomb, which "we did not possess in the past." Blinded by ignorant lessons of history, Washington did not see how close China's powerful anti-Mao leaders came to risking that larger war, as China had in Korea. Had the paper tiger or Korean war generation won the 1965–1966 struggle that exploded in the Cultural Revolution, America's escalation might have produced war with China,[10] or reconciliation with Russia of the major-backer, Korean war generation in China.

For Mao Tse-tung a continuing commitment to an earlier domestic political vision defined now in anti-Russian terms precluded close collaboration with the Soviet Union in foreign affairs. That is, Mao insisted that China's first order of business was to create a more egalitarian, communitarian, and selfless society where elite bureaucratic rule would not emerge as it had in the Soviet Union. No foreign policy prescription followed from that commitment. Perhaps for domestic reasons Mao had to turn temporarily to the second-rank paper-tiger generation to win backing for a policy of defense against America and Russia. Such people would attack both the united-front generation in the foreign affairs bureaucracy and military and political leaders of the Korean war generation. Mao and his colleagues rejected the advice of Asian Communist parties to join with Moscow on aid to Vietnam. Mao argued that revolutionaries must win largely on their own in long and protracted wars. Reliance on foreign aid undermines the revolution. A popular force in Vietnam which depended on outsiders would no longer be the popular nationalist force. This politically self-serving paean to self-reliance, embodied in Lin Piao's essay on people's war, was damned by the American Secretary of Defense, who called it "a program of aggression...that ranks with Hitler's Mein Kampf. We should take the Chinese Communists at their word and develop improved means of coping with their threat." So enamored was Washington with the notion that it was fighting a proxy Chinese aggression in Vietnam that it did not understand at all what was happening in China in late 1965 and early 1966. The beginnings of the vast power struggle inaugurating the Cultural Revolution went unseen because of American ideological blinders.

[10] For some further indication of how close the two sides were to war, see Allen Whiting, "How We Almost Went to War with China," *Look*, April 29, 1969, pp. 76–79.

The emerging preeminence of Mao in conjunction with united-front generation leaders led in 1966 to a retreat from the notion of America and Russia as major enemies and a concentration on one enemy at a time, this time Russia. The Soviet Union was seen as having emerged for the first time since 1905 as a major anti-Chinese Asian power. Already in 1962, the Soviet Union had monopolistically incorporated Mongolia into its economic sphere despite prior promises to China to maintain the area as a buffer. This increased China's felt insecurity to its north. At the same time, on its western borders, fighting exploded in Sinkiang province, which was the base of China's nuclear experimentation. The central Asian specialist of the *New York Times*, Harrison Salisbury, finds that

between 50,000 and 60,000 Uighurs and Kazakhs fled Sinkiang for Soviet Kazakhstan, often fighting their way across the frontier. Soviet border forces came to their assistance and provided trucks for fleeing families. Repeated armed clashes occurred between Russian and Chinese frontier forces. There were riots in Kuldja and Tcheng and other cities and villages of Sinkiang.

Among those who fled in 1962 was Zunum Taipov, a Chinese Communist general and former deputy military commander in Sinkiang. He has since emerged as a major spokesman for anti-Chinese propaganda emanating from Soviet radio transmitters beamed to Sinkiang. This year [1969] he has been calling upon his compatriots to rise in revolution against Mao Tse-tung.

At the same time India threatened China's southwestern border when Nehru ordered the Indian army to march north. Although former ambassador Edwin O. Reischauer describes the controlled Chinese response, followed by a Chinese withdrawal and a Chinese request for a cease-fire, a no-man's zone, and negotiations as a "military action [which] amounted to a small correction of the border," there probably was a bit more involved. China seems to have wanted to stop these Russian-backed probes into strategic Chinese border regions. The Russians subsequently claimed that it was their movement of troops which kept China from extending its counterattack against the routed Indian army. Similarly, the Russians claimed that they had checked China in a 1959 border clash with India by dispatching Russian military officers and engineers to strategic points on the China-Indian border. The Chinese could contrast this Russian support for an expansive Indian military policy with the efforts in autumn 1962 of the American ambassador to India to keep the Indians from using their air force to bomb China. They could contrast it with Ambassador Averell Harriman's trip to Laos in 1962 to halt the rightist forces seeking to further involve America on an anti-Chinese pretext. They could contrast it with the June 1962 assurances in Warsaw that America would halt Chiang Kai-shek's attacks on the China coast. China's Foreign Minister explained that

During the conversations between the ambassadors of China and the United States in Warsaw, the United States gave its assurance that it would not approve an invasion of the mainland by Chiang Kai-shek. To a certain degree we appreciate this gesture on the part of the United States. . . . However, verbal assurances are of no use. They cannot reduce tension in any fundamental way. The United States ought to withdraw the Seventh Fleet from the Taiwan Straits. In this way it could achieve a radical reduction in tension and make a contribution to peace. . . .

Instead America had committed itself to increasing Japan's role in Korea, Formosa, and southeast Asia while devoting its own resources, made possible by increased military spending and concentration on matters Asian, to war in southeast Asia. By mid-1966 America was bogged down in Vietnam, and China and America had reached some tacit agreement on the limits of their mutual involvement in Vietnam. The Chinese Foreign Minister said:

America is afraid of China and China is somewhat afraid of America. I do not believe the United States would invade present-day China. . . . I do not take a particularly pessimistic view of relations between the United States and China.

The Russians, witnessing this Chinese desire for horse-trading negotiations with America, busily engaged themselves in Asia trying to put together an anti-Chinese alliance. The Chinese saw Russia repeating the course of John Foster Dulles. It was the Russians who brought Pakistani and Indian leaders together at Tashkent to get them to stop their fighting and cooperate against China. The Russians made new overtures to the Japanese which led the Russians to feel secure enough in their new relations with Japan to move troops from positions opposite Japan to new positions on China's northeast borders. Russia continued to aid the Indonesian military, which was very anti-Chinese. Russia also began to build new military positions on China's borders in Mongolia, brought in new reinforcements from Europe, and used the radio to try to incite minority peoples of China's far western province, Sinkiang, to act against Mao's government. In the autumn of 1966 a member of Japan's conservative ruling party reported, after conversations with top officials in Peking, that "the real target of Chinese antagonism is not the United States so much as the Soviet Union." Yet not until the end of 1969 would President Richard Nixon announce that America was decreasing its naval patrols in the Formosa area. That gesture signified the possibility that Washington was reconsidering the costs of maintaining a superpower posture in Asia against China. Consequently it opened the possibilities for a new, less hostile relationship between America and China, at the same time that it called into question the basis of almost 20 years of American policy in Asia.

The Future

If the dynamics underlying America's attempt as a superpower to impose its will in Asia were the consequence of accident or error, one could be optimistic that Washington could now readily reassess the high costs and minimal gains of such a policy and then choose a wiser policy. But there may be deep societal roots to the American commitments. Some people have suggested that the willingness to play with nuclear threats or to deploy hundreds of thousands of men in continental Asia stems from the push to an ever more westerly frontier that led to American expansion into Hawaii, Guam, and the Philippines in the nineteenth century. Others have suggested that it flows from a global strategy of economic imperium in which successes by revolutionary or anti-imperialist forces anywhere are seen as endangering investments, markets, and resources everywhere; Vietnam threatens Venezuela. My own feeling, however, is that while there is some truth to both these views, what must be explained is not a historical continuity or an economic seamless cloth but new political and military initiatives which began after World War II. In the wake of the retreat of colonial Europe and of the defeat of militarist Japan, America had the might to move in and impose its will in many places in Asia. There were many rationales for this exercise of American power—stop Communism, stop China, stop Russian imperialism, preserve peace, maintain the area for democratic India or Japan, prove economic evolution works expand the economic area of the free world, and so on—but what they did was rationalize the expansion of American power. Rhee or Chiang or Diem or Ky, in conjunction with particular American military, bureaucratic, and political interests, won their parochial way in the name of one or another of these rationales because superpower America had the power.

Today that post-World War II world is fast vanishing. Russia has emerged as a major Asian power. Japan, now the world's third mightiest industrial state, is emerging, according to military strategist Herman Kahn, "in the 1970s as the true colossus of Asia," a formidable nuclear power. For superpower America to continue to act against a weak and poor China in disregard of the developing pattern of relations in Asia will fritter away time and resources. It may continue to serve particular parochial interests even of rulers in Moscow and Tokyo, but it will not serve any larger American purposes.

Mao Tse-tung will die. He may be replaced by Korean war, major-backer army men who in 1959, in 1965, and again in the future may be willing to sacrifice some Chinese sovereignty to gain armed Chinese-Russian cooperation against what they see as expansionist American imperialism. War could explode again in Korea and lead Japan to rearm in a fuller manner to intervene to prevent that so-called dagger pointed at its heart from falling further into powerful and unfriendly hands. And Russia, as in 1904, would be in Asia to meet the threat. Trying to impose one's super power in such powder-keg but unimportant areas is an explosive policy. Using that power to defuse the area by finding some basis for cooperation among the four major northeast Asian powers would be more productive, less dangerous.

After Mao's death or his passage into senility, younger men of the paper-tiger generation, ready to stand up to both America and Russia, might take power in China. They might find a Japan forced by economic need and American tariff policies, or by Russo-American détente, ready to join with them, as Japan suggested in the 1930s, to prevent Asian hegemony by the rich, white, western powers. Other scenarios which do not serve American interests and which may produce larger wars are easily conceivable in this new world. Significantly making such international dramas more likely is the continuing willingness from the end of World War II on to use the new power, the super power of the United States to impose its will anywhere and everywhere it can in Asia, even if it must go it alone. Only by facing up to the uniqueness of postwar conditions that led to America's emergence as a superpower can America recognize the new conditions which make certain that continued attempts to make policy on a projection of the normalcy and rightness of that postwar situation condemns America to frustrations and more wars.

China does challenge America as a superpower. It was the success of Chinese deterrence in Korea in the 1950s that made America a bit more cautious about its escalation into north Vietnam in the 1960s.

China has a trip-wire of troops in Laos and may respond to large-scale American intervention there. India is less likely to bomb Tibet because of China's nuclear deterrent. Southeast Asian nations are more likely to caution America against attacking China for fear of a Chinese counterattack on Bangkok or Kuala Lumpor. Chinese nuclear diplomacy does constrain the nuclear hegemony and blackmail of America as a super power.

In addition, efforts by American presidents in the last 20 years to act on some mutual-interest basis with China have readily been sabotaged by other powerful interests in America acting in cooperation with America's Asian allies. Richard Nixon's overtures at the end of 1969 have been met, if not stymied, by Chiang Kai-shek's offer to have Formosa serve as a military base and nuclear warehouse replacement for Okinawa, by the Pentagon's insistence that it can send new jet planes to Chiang and that the President can't stop them, by congressional attempts to write new military aid to Formosa into the foreign-aid bill against the will of the President. Yet these forces seem a bit weaker now than a few years earlier.

More important, China is not alone in its challenge to American superpower supremacy. Many Asian nationalists perfer to maneuver for maximum independence rather than accept an allegedly benevolent, American-sponsored hegemony. Just as east Europe prefers to play off relations with the United States to gain some independence from the Soviet Union, and just as Havana needs Moscow to stay independent of Washington, so Nepal, Cambodia, north Vietnam, north Korea, and Pakistan have needed a lever in China to maximize their independence. In addition, the independent interests of Russia, India, Indonesia, and Japan have not always been coincident with the American superpower. They too at times have turned to China. Such turnings can be expected to continue in the future so long as America goes on acting as the hegemon, the Asian superpower. Resources will be wasted. Plans will be frustrated. Dangerous wars will explode. Only by understanding the unnecessary difficulties of trying to impose America's will in the new world of Asia, only by understanding the mistakes of the past and the misconceptions of the present, can America learn in the future to desire less and thus achieve more. It would be nice to be optimistic about such accommodations with reality. It would also be unwise. Indications are that powerful Americans are still enamored of the role of superpower. Anything less is denounced as appeasment of aggression, another Munich, a factor which America's Asian allies have continually manipulated to their benefit. Unless America can open its eyes to what is happening, it may continue to strike out wildly at weak opponents. Unfortunately, a giant, blinded cyclops in pursuit of his smaller, seeing, fleeing adversaries can destroy much, including himself.[11]

[11] The best analyses of the real capabilities and interests of America in this Asian world are found in the writings of David Mozingo. See especially Mozingo's, "The Maoist Imprint on Chinese Foreign Policy," in Tang Tsou (ed.), *China Briefing* (Chicago: University of Chicago Press, 1968), pp. 23–51 and "Containment in Asia Reconsidered," *World Politics,* XVIII, (April 1967).

The Soviet Union and China

HERBERT S. DINERSTEIN

Alliances in which ideological community of interest plays a significant role have been exceptional and generally short-lived. The efforts of Christian rulers to liberate the Holy Land and Jerusalem were mounted only intermittently, over several centuries, and were characterized by sharp conflicts of interests among Christian rulers, including the papacy. The contest between Christian and Turk from the sixteenth to the twentieth century might be designated as ideological, but disunity was the salient feature of the Christian agglomeration. In fact, the Ottoman Empire owed the last century of its existence to the circumstance that the Christian states found it easier to accept its continuation than to agree on the division of its parts. In the sixteenth and seventeenth centuries one could talk in a very general way of a "Protestant" bloc and a "Catholic" bloc, but the consequence of the Thirty Years' War was to separate the Austrian and the Spanish Hapsburgs and to reshuffle the diplomatic alignments. A case exists for the general proposition that ideology is the solvent of alliances, not the cement. For the Sino-Soviet alliance, at any rate, the proposition seems to apply, as the following pages will seek to demonstrate.

The Development of the International Communist System

In the first decades after the Russian Revolution, the insistence on ideological unity was not so costly because only one of the Communist parties in the association was the effective ruler of a state and a large state at that. Until 1944 or 1945 the Communist party of the Soviet Union, (CPSU), although technically only one among equals, as the only ruling party dominated the others. The prestige of the Russian Revolution, the presence of the Communist International (Comintern) in Moscow and the financial support of the Soviet Union combined to make the CPSU the hegemonial party.

The official theory that all parties were equal, and that each party had the right to criticize and participate in the decisions of every other party was largely honored in the breach. Centralism, democratic or not, characterized the conduct of affairs within the Comintern as within the CPSU. The CPSU dominated the other parties, stifling attempts to assert independence; the means to discipline insubordination were numerous, varied and effective. In countries where the Communist party was illegal, a denunciation to the police frequently produced incarceration and sometimes execution. In the late 1930s the purge in the CPSU was attended by purges in the non-ruling parties, the investigation and the execution following upon an invitation to the seat of the Comintern, Moscow. The readiness of the NKVD to perform this rough prophylactic surgery produced subservience and conformity and as a consequence purges of the non-ruling parties came to reflect Moscow's overheated suspicions rather than to represent a response to lack of discipline.

But to be fair, much of the loyalty of the other communist parties to the Soviet Union derived from a genuine, albeit eroding, respect for the party which had made the first and only socialist revolution. Moreover, in the period before World War II, the Nazis threatened the existence of many European states, and of the Communist parties in those states. These threatened parties accepted much of Soviet behavior without understanding it because the Nazi danger left them no alternative. Many familiar circumstances have been alluded to in order to suggest that long experience had accustomed the Soviet leaders to expect subservience from other Communists. Within the Soviet Union itself, the hierarchically structured system provided the weak with few remedies against the arbitrary behavior of the strong. In the postwar period Soviet expectations from other Communist parties continued substantially unchanged although the power relationship had been radically altered.

The Development of the Sino-Soviet Relationship

Relations between the Communist party of the Soviet Union and the Commuinst party of China (CPC) had not been particularly good, and perhaps worse than average. In 1926, the necessities of the factional struggle between Trotsky and Stalin were reflected in pressures upon the CPC. First, Stalin urged continued collaboration with the Kuomintang and Chiang Kai-shek first in Canton and later in Shanghai. The consequences for the CPC were disastrous; Chiang arranged for the murder of large numbers of the party's members. The next year when Stalin revised his estimate of his internal factional necessities, his agents urged the CPC to rise up in Canton, again with disastrous results. Later, when some of the Chinese Communists, Mao Tse-tung among them, had moved into Kiangsi province to pursue the struggle from an agrarian base, Russian agents tried to make CPC tactics toward the peasants conform with the shifts in Stalin's policies toward the *kulaks* and middle peasants in the collectivization struggle in the Soviet Union. The two situations were hardly comparable: Stalin was forcing the peasants into collective farms almost a decade after conclusive victory in the Civil War; the CPC was seeking peasant support in order to survive the attacks of Chiang Kai-shek's armies. A quarter of a century later, when factional fighting in the Soviet Union furnished an opportunity for Chinese intervention in Soviet politics, ample precedents existed. Some old scores could be settled, too, because one of Stalin's henchmen, Molotov, was now a contender for power in the Soviet party.

The Communist party of China, unlike all others, had the experience, before assuming power over the whole country, of administering part of it for years. By 1945 an army of more than a million had been organized, and valuable experience in enlisting peasant support had been gathered.

Earlier developments in east Asia and Europe, however, had impelled the Soviet Union to make common cause with the Chinese government led by Chiang Kai-shek. After the Manchurian incident of 1931 and Hitler's assumption of power in 1933, Soviet foreign policy more than ever became a policy of playing for time during which the Soviet Union could augment its industrial and military strength. In China time could best be employed to encourage the Kuomintang, led by Marshal Chiang Kai-shek, to oppose the advance of the Japanese. Soviet policy, like Russian policy, had always sought to prevent the domination of China by a single, strong power. Given that understandable preference, the Soviets had little choice but to support Chiang Kai-shek. Support of Chiang Kai-shek meant subordination of the interests of the Chinese Communist party to the larger interests of world revolution, which in the Soviet conception was virtually identical with that of the Russian revolution. The Soviets, therefore, pushed the Chinese Communists into a United Front with the Kuomintang, but the two parties in this forced marriage parleyed without disarming and often engaged in open conflict.

The Soviet distaste for the Chinese Communists was little understood in the West, although Stalin and Molotov voiced it unmistakably on occasion. References by leading Soviet figures to the Chinese Communists as "margarine communists" puzzled American listeners. Similarly, Americans were rather startled to hear suggestions from the Soviet leaders that perhaps Tito was not the hero of Yugoslavia and that more attention should be paid to Mihajlovic and to the opportunities for restoring the monarchy. But now, 25 years later, we can accept those unflattering remarks as genuine and prescient reflections of Stalin's concern that independent Communist parties could damage the interests of the Soviet Union. Milovan Djilas' report that Stalin discouraged the Chinese Communists from proceeding rapidly with the revolution in China fits the pattern.

In the years between the end of World War II and the assumption of power by the Chinese Communists, the Soviet Union pursued a policy seemingly based on the assumption of an extended civil war in China or the partition of China along ideological lines, paralleling respective Russian and American spheres of influence. In their negotiations with Chiang Kai-shek's government, the Soviet Union retained imperial rights in China—namely, a special sphere in Sinkiang, co-ownership of the Chinese Eastern Railway in Manchuria, and a special regime in Port Arthur and Dairen. China's other allies almost completely abandoned their special rights; her enemies were forced to relinquish them. The United States acquiesced in the anachronistic retention of Soviet imperial rights because it believed, incorrectly, that Soviet participation in the war against Japan was necessary to its rapid conclusion. The Kuomintang acquiesced because it had no choice. Chiang Kai-shek, however, seemed to make a virtue of necessity and to use the Soviet presence, in the traditional Chinese style, to balance off the predominant US influence in China.

Although it seems very strange now, in the middle 1940s the United States seemed more threatening to the independence of China than to the Soviet Union. Relations between the United States and the Kuomintang had been deplorable. The United States insistently and unceasingly exhorted the Chinese to reform, end corruption, and govern properly. The Chinese swallowed their pride, accepted the lectures and a good deal of money, much of which ended up in private hands. Quite humanly, the Chinese leaders despised the Americans who had "forced" them to behave so shamefully. On the other hand, Soviet policy was correct and consistent, maintaining always that at that stage of Chinese history, Chiang Kai-shek was the proper leader of a coalition government into which Chinese Communists should enter as junior partners.

Meanwhile, the United States was trying to force the two Chinese factions into shotgun marriage. The US seemingly had more in common with the Chinese Communists than with the Kuomintang, and the Soviet Union seemingly had more in common with the Kuomintang than with the Communist party of China. Although such a formulation overstates the case, CPSU-Kuomintang relations were correct, while Kuomintang-United States relations were never comfortable. Whatever Chiang's ultimate aims, the Soviet Union had a vested interest in maintaining his regime. As long as the Chiang Kai-shek regime retained power in some parts of China, the Soviet Union could maintain its special rights and could anticipate that Kuomintang resentment of the United States would contribute to the withdrawal of the United States from the eastern extremity of the Eurasian land mass.[1] No nation on the western extremity of the Eurasian continent could be expected to resent the United States so deeply that the United States would withdraw support in frustration. This suggests once again how deep and desperate was Chinese hatred of Europeans. The Soviets, who at one point sought to exploit the outraged pride and xenophobia of the Kuomintang Chinese, were later to find the Chinese Communists directing the same emotions at the USSR.

The propensity of groups within the Kuomintang to play the Soviet card can be exaggerated, but in any case it was obvious to all, and obnoxious to the Chinese Communists, that the Soviet Union found it easy to treat with two claimants to the heritage of the Manchus. The Soviets may have argued and even believed that the first order of business was to speed the US departure and that an early defeat of the Kuomintang would cause the United States to revise the decision to depart. (Such a reversal of direction had occurred in Europe.) Therefore prudence dictated that the civil war be concluded after the United States had withdrawn from China. Stalin was nothing but prudent when he had to choose between the security of the Soviet Union and the ambitions of a Communist party to take power. One can readily understand the suspicion with which the Chinese Communists accepted any such rationale for holding back.

By 1949 when the Chinese revolution had been successfully completed, the Soviets had much relevant experience behind them in Europe. They had enlarged their own territory at the expense of their new, largely involuntary, postwar allies. Czechoslovakia was forced to cede the Carpatho-Ukraine to the Soviet Ukraine. East Germany had

---

[1] As a matter of fact, strained US-Kuomintang relations made it psychologically easier for US officials to accept the defeat of the Kuomintang as unavoidable: "They wouldn't listen to our good advice, and they got what they deserved."

to cede to the Russian Republic and to Poland territories which had been in German possession for hundreds of years. Poland, in turn, had to cede its western Ukrainian territories to the Soviet Ukraine; Romania had to give up Bessarabia. In the Far East the Soviets at first treated their new allies on their eastern borders as they had treated their western allies and retained the territorial concessions they had wrung out of a Kuomintang that had tried to maneuver among the pressures of the United States, the Chinese Communists, and the Soviet Union.

By the time the Chinese revolution had consolidated power on the mainland, Tito had been ejected from the Communist camp for a year. He had insisted on a measure of independence in the conduct of his internal and external affairs. His claim to autonomy was unacceptable to Stalin even though Tito was the most anti-American of all the satellite leaders. Indeed, Stalin viewed his anti-Americanism as excessive. After Tito's expulsion from the Cominform (the European rump of the Comintern), the other east European states, willingly in some cases, reluctantly in others, organized trials to prove that Tito had been an agent of the United States. Evidently Stalin came to believe the verdict of the trials he had commanded to be staged.

Although Stalin may well have feared that Mao Tse-tung would become a super-Tito, it was unwise to anathematize him and expect that the CPC would dismiss him in an expression of loyalty to the CPSU. Mao had led the Chinese much longer than Tito had led the Yugoslavs, and Mao had ejected all foreigners from Chinese soil in a single stroke. In Yugoslavia the process of freeing the country from foreigners had taken more than a century and had been completed a quarter of a century before Tito came to power. Very soon, the Korean war changed the balance of forces between China and the Soviet Union, putting the Chinese in a much stronger bargaining position.

The Consequences of the Korean War

The origins of the Korean war are still unclear. It is one piece of dirty linen that the Soviets and the Chinese have not yet chosen to wash in public. In addition to the generally accepted explanation that the Soviet Union deceived itself into believing that the United States no longer cared to maintain its position in South Korea and decided to pick up what was lying around loose, another, supplementary explanation can be proffered. The Soviets had succeeded in dominating the Communist party of North Korea, and this success, together with their extraterritorial rights in Manchuria, Port Arthur, and Dairen, gave them a base in northeast Asia from which they could exercise control over Mao. The three-month visit of high Chinese dignitaries to Moscow in 1950 has generally been interpreted as a planning session for the North Korean attack on South Korea, but it now seems that the Chinese had difficulty in persuading Stalin to sign a treaty of alliance obligating each party to come to the defense of the other in the event of a Japanese attack.

Whatever the genesis of the Korean war, its outcome was a disaster for the Soviet Union and a victory for China. When the United States recovered from its initial defeats and expanded its objectives from the restoration of the status quo to the reunification of Korea, Mao Tsetung, not Stalin, saved the day by bold and risky action. Consequently, the Korean Communist party became a client of China rather than of the Soviet Union; the recently established Chinese regime had fought the United States to a standstill while the Soviet Union had confined itself to verbal protests and the provision of arms. The Soviet Union charged the Chinese Communists for the war matériel they supplied. What appear to have been Soviet intrigues with Chinese regional leaders, especially Kao Kang in Manchuria, support the hypothesis that the USSR initiated the Korean war in pursuit of the traditional Russian policy of carving out spheres of influence in northeast Asia. The Chinese, by snatching victory from defeat in Korea and by disposing of Kao Kang, frustrated the Soviet scheme to play a dominating role in the area. The triumphant Chinese, however, maintained a public posture of deference to Stalin and continued to receive some Soviet assistance until 1957.

After Stalin's death the relationship between the two parties changed radically because the Soviet party was openly divided in a succession struggle and the Chinese party was, at least superficially, unified. For the first time since the twenties, when the German Communist party had intervened in a Soviet succession crisis, another party, and a ruling party at that, had its finger in the Soviet pie. Now foreigners could influence Soviet internal politics at the very pinnacle of power. Although this must have been very galling to the Soviet leadership as a whole, individual Soviet leaders sought to gain factional advantage by enlisting Chinese support in the bitter internecine struggle. Thus Khrushchev journeyed to Peking in 1954 to restore to the Chinese most of the territory which Stalin refused to release from his grasp. Khrushchev was opposed on the "left" by Molotov, who was loath to relax Soviet control over other socialist states, and on the "right" by Malenkov, who favored a dangerously radical policy (from the Chinese point of view) of improving relations with the West.

Khrushchev for all his shortcomings seemed to meet Chinese necessities better than any other Soviet leader.

Khrushchev had permitted a relaxation of Soviet controls in eastern Europe. During the Korean war Stalin very much feared that the United States might use its greatly improved nuclear capacities to strike at the Soviet Union, and he mercilessly forced industrialization in the Soviet Union and in the east European socialist states. He died leaving behind sorely strained economies in eastern Europe and in the Soviet Union. When his successors took over, they greatly reduced the power of the security police, for all feared that one of their number, by establishing control over that dread instrument, would employ it to eliminate the others. When first Beria was eliminated and then lesser security figures were executed, the secret police in the satellite countries quickly curtailed their activities because no one knew which of today's actions would be labeled a capital crime on the morrow. In this uncertain atmosphere, nationalistically oriented elements in the Communist parties of Poland and Hungary challenged the authority of the incumbent party leaders and of the Soviet Union.

Although the roots of the difficulties in eastern Europe lay very deep, Khrushchev had to answer for the crisis. At this critical juncture, the Chinese helped smooth over the Polish crisis and supported the Soviet Union in its forcible repression of the Hungarian revolution. In December 1956 and January 1957 Khrushchev's political hold on the Soviet Union was threatened. The Chinese support of Khrushchev during the East European crisis suggests that support was also offered in the struggle within the CPSU through the party and military leaders who favored strengthening the ties with China.

The Basic Differences Between the USSR and China

During these difficult years for the Soviet leadership the Chinese began to occupy the center of the stage in world affairs. The Bandung conference of 1955 was inspired by the Indonesian Prime Minister Ali Sastroamidjojo and Nehru, of whom the latter feared that he would need Chinese support against Soviet pressure in the future. (Nehru was correct in believing that India would benefit from Sino-Soviet differences, but was mistaken in believing that threat would be Soviet rather than Chinese.) The Chinese readily lent themselves to Indian and Indonesian purposes and the Bandung conference became an Asian combination against the West. The failure to invite the Soviet Union, in effect, lumped the USSR with the colonial powers. "Coexistence" as explained by the Chinese at Bandung referred essentially to China's relations with its neighbors, who were urged not to join a Western alliance on the ground that no Chinese threat existed to seek aid against.

The Chinese initiative challenged the Soviet Union on two counts. First, the Soviet Union had pretensions of its own to leadership of the underdeveloped world. Soon after the Bandung conference, Khrushchev and Bulganin, the chairman of the Council of Ministers, journeyed to India, Burma, and Afghanistan. The only other trips abroad by the head of the state and the party were Stalin's to Teheran and Potsdam. Khrushchev's choice of Southeast Asia for the first of what was to become a series of journeys was a striking demonstration of the importance of competition with the Chinese.

Second, the Chinese version of coexistence cut across Khrushchev's grand scheme. Khrushchev needed an improvement in relations with the United States in order to maintain his domestic position. In his struggle to undermine Malenkov, Khrushchev had argued that Malenkov was reckless with the security of the Soviet Union and that if war should come the Soviet Union could and would emerge victorious. By this attack Khrushchev won the support of the Soviet "hard-liners." But when he became first secretary of the CPSU, Khrushchev began to move toward Malenkov's position that nuclear weapons make war impossible to contemplate and necessary to avoid.

The hoped-for consequence of reaching an agreement with the United States, tacit or negotiated, on the basis of what later came to be known as mutual deterrence was a reduction of the arms burden and greater allocations to the civilian sector. It was anticipated that this shift in the allocation of domestic resources would strengthen weak groups or create new constituencies that would make Khrushchev less beholden to the "hard-liners." In his public and secret speeches at the twentieth Congress of the CPSU in 1956 Khrushchev burned the bridges back to Stalin's harsh policies by denouncing him as a bungler and a criminal. By enunciating the doctrine that wars were no longer fatalistically inevitable and the slogan of coexistence, Khrushchev was contradicting the Chinese formula of coexistence, for he was talking about nuclear coexistence—which meant coexistence with the United States. The basic contradictions between the Chinese and Soviet positions could be discerned in 1956, but Khrushchev continued to treat the Chinese in a gingerly fashion until he had consolidated his internal political position.

At the 1957 world meeting of the Communist parties, the Soviet Union agreed to help the Chinese with new military technology; the agreement included some imprecise provisions, later disputed, on nuclear weaponry. The Chinese entered a dissent on the feasibility of peaceful transitions to socialism, a necessity for Khrushchev's coexistence formula. Khrushchev could hardly have expected détente with the West if the Communist parties of those countries retained violent revolution as a likely policy. But the Chinese were willing at that juncture to let their dissent remain within the Communist family. In June 1957, however, Khrushchev triumphed over his opposition, which had exploited the Hungarian fiasco, and bested the antiparty group presumably by appealing to the Central Committee, which up to that point had been politically inert. Several months later Khrushchev disposed of Marshal Zhukov, whose support had helped him overthrow the antiparty group. At that point the relationship between China and USSR began to deteriorate sharply. Now Khrushchev no longer needed Chinese assistance, or his domestic position was strong enough to make their opposition manageable.

Khrushchev's consolidation of power coincided with a change in China that was to have fateful consequences. Mao had been in a state of semiretirement, symbolized in 1956 by changes in the Chinese constitution which effaced all references to the thought of Mao Tsetung and which restored the preeminence of Marxism-Leninism. Toward the end of 1956, and especially after the failure of the Hundred Flowers campaign in China, Mao moved to a counterattack against his opponents whose position and policies required reasonably good relations with the Soviet Union. The army professionals who wanted to modernize the Chinese army required Soviet weaponry; the economic planners who wanted to industrialize depended on Soviet economic assistance. Mao rejected their strategies and placed his reliance on élan and enthusiasm, which were to be found among former guerrilla leaders and the less educated members of the Communist party. In shunting the "experts" aside, Mao retired those elements that had a vested interest in more or less normal relations with the Soviet Union. Mao, in a sense, needed a Soviet enemy to make a domestic comeback.[2]

Khrushchev's domestic necessities in turn caused him to pursue foreign policies inimical to China. He needed successes in foreign policy to hold his shaky coalition together. He hoped that moderate improvement of the Soviet military position, together with a program of missile rattling, could force some concessions from the United States. Khrushchev tried to gain US agreement to a change in the status of West Berlin as a prelude to a settlement in Europe based on

[2] I am indebted to Professor David P. Mozingo for much of the material on Chinese politics, but he, of course, has no responsibility for my formulations.

two Germanies. Presumably a general standoff agreement with the United States on the nuclear balance would follow, but the situation in the underdeveloped areas would remain fluid. Khrushchev tried to carry out this scheme "on the cheap," expanding the Soviet intercontinental capability rather slowly and hoping that his menacing speeches would frighten the United States into concessions, or frighten its European allies so that they would urge concessions on the United States. This program which was calculated to serve Soviet foreign policy interests, and Khrushchev's domestic political fortunes did not suit Chinese needs—or, more accurately, Mao's needs.

The Chinese wanted international recognition of their revolution. That the US continued to recognize Chiang Kai-shek as the legitimate ruler of China frustrated that purpose. As I have indicated, the Chinese were willing to maintain good relations with neutral Asian states and, in the case of countries allied to the United States, like Thailand, to deny support to subversive movements as long as these countries did not provide military bases or other military services to the United States. When a country ceased to meet these standards, however, the Chinese treated them as enemies.

Sometime in the late fifties India fell into the category of relapsed neutrals. The immediate issue was Tibet, which the Chinese, both Nationalist and Communist, had considered an integral part of China. The disputed border areas between India and China provided an access route to Tibet, vital for the suppression of the Khampa rebellion in that country. Under pressure from his internal opposition Premier Nehru reluctantly had to take note of the Chinese activity in the disputed areas. In the ensuing controversy the Chinese accused Nehru of having served as a conduit for American assistance to the rebels in Tibet. Whatever the facts in this murky matter, the Chinese felt that the Indians were lending themselves to an assault on the integrity of China. In the Sino-Indian crisis of 1959 the Soviet Union adopted a neutral position. In the socialist state system, for a socialist state to remain neutral in a conflict between another socialist state and a nonsocialist state is the equivalent of outright hostility.

In the Taiwan Straits crisis a year earlier, the verbal support offered the Chinese by the Soviet Union was so tentative and belated that John Foster Dulles proceeded, convinced that he need reckon only with the Chinese. With each passing year, the Chinese were increasingly disappointed in Soviet support of their foreign policy goals. In cases where Chinese and Soviet policies were in conflict, the Soviet Union always decided that common alliance interests would best be served by pursuing Soviet goals. In such situations the weaker party acquiesces if the benefits received are unavailable elsewhere, particularly if the benefit is deterrence of a powerful enemy. But the Taiwan Straits crisis, after which the US Secretary of State boasted of having gone to the brink, made it clear that China need not fear attack unless she went beyond shelling the offshore islands. Clearly, self-restraint, not the deterrent power of the Soviet Union, was the key to Chinese security.

The Soviet Union, moreover, whittled down the other services offered by the alliance. No economic aid was forthcoming after 1957, and in 1960 the Soviet Union suddenly withdrew all its technicians in the belief that shock therapy would bring the Chinese to heel. The Soviet behavioral style, in both internal and external policy, is for the superordinate promptly to punish the subordinate who presumes beyond his station. But such behavior in China only consolidated Mao's position because he could represent the Soviet Union as China's external enemy against whom he led the resistance. As a result, by the end of 1960 Sino-Soviet meetings and wider party conferences had become confrontations.

In the 1960 meeting of the 81 Communist parties, the Chinese exploited the Soviet differences with other Communist parties, especially the powerful Italian Communist party, to force concessions from the Soviet Union, which wanted to maintain a façade of unity. If one compares the program of the 81 Communist parties published in December 1960 with Khrushchev's speech on the same general subjects on January 6, 1961, the great gulf between them becomes apparent. On every major issue they disagreed: the inevitability of war; the nature of coexistence; the future of the national liberation movement. These differences were couched in ideological terms, but the divergent interests of the Soviet Union and China were just beneath these formulations. For the Soviet Union, military balance with the United States was a salient feature of the international scene, one that was to be regulated by competition and by agreements, tacit and otherwise, with the United States. The enormous cost of modern weapons made arms expenditures a major item in decisions on allocating resources, which in the Soviet Union as elsewhere were the occasion for bitter political struggles. Khrushchev's desire to reduce or to halt the increase in military expenditures caused continuous conflict with his opponents. Khrushchev genuinely believed that nuclear war had to be avoided, and the economic consequence of that belief widened Khrushchev's domestic political base. If the United States shared this view of nuclear warfare, each side could be satisfied with a force adequate to deter attack; preparation to fight a war to a successful conclusion was unnecessary. Deterrent forces could be purchased much more cheaply than war-winning forces, and the Soviet political scene did not lack candidates for the use of the resources thus saved.

The Chinese could not possibly compete with the United States in nuclear weapons and could conserve no resources by agreements, formal or informal. China could not hope to deter the United States by the possession of a comparable military force. She could only avoid provoking the United States to the point of engaging in what all expected would be a difficult struggle. This genuine difference between the Soviet and the Chinese relationship with the United States was expressed in ideological terms. The Soviets said that the main task was coexistence, meaning that the US-USSR relationship must be sufficiently harmonious, at a minimum, to exclude the kind of crisis that could lead to a nuclear conflict and, at a maximum, to lead to mutual reduction of forces.

For the Chinese, the main task was the national liberation movement, which really meant that some safe struggles should be prosecuted to bring the US to its senses and force it from China's periphery. Improved relations with the United States depended on recognition of the legitimacy of Communist rule in China. Since the United States was not prepared to recognize Communist China, coexistence Soviet-style was impossible even if it had been considered desirable. Support of the national liberation movement was the only realistic main goal for the Chinese. It was suited to a state whose military establishment could not be effective far beyond its borders. In addition, as time has proved, the Chinese could control the dosage of support to national liberation movements so that it always remained below the threshhold of provocation of the United States. The war of words about the primacy of the national liberation movement very probably served as the public forum of a bitter private dispute over assistance to the National Liberation Front of South Vietnam.

The barely concealed differences of 1960 soon came into the open. In 1962 the Cuban missile crisis convinced the Chinese Communists that they had grossly overestimated the Soviet strength in intercontinental nuclear weapons. Since the Soviet leaders are particularly secretive about weakness, the Chinese had to judge the size of the Soviet intercontinental forces on the basis of Khrushchev's boastful speeches and the defensive US reaction, which took the form of talk about a missile gap. Unlike Eisenhower, Mao had no U-2 photographs to give him a sound basis for estimating the military balance. Hence, the Soviet defeat in the missile crisis came as an unpleasant surprise that confirmed the worst Chinese suspicions about Soviet recklessness. The Chinese charge also found muted expression within the Soviet

Union. Khrushchev could not match the United States's strength in a short time, and he recovered his position somewhat by reaching an agreement with the United States not to test nuclear weapons in the atmosphere, on the surface of the earth, or in the oceans. The Chinese could adhere to this agreement only by renouncing the possibility of becoming a nuclear power. Khrushchev, in order to salvage his own weakened internal political position, had put the Chinese in a position where they had to accept either permanent second-class status or diplomatic isolation.

When Khrushchev was deposed in October 1964, the Chinese hailed it as a victory. In all probability dissatisfaction with Khrushchev's handling of the China problem was one of the factors that combined to produce his dismissal. Khrushchev's successors tried to improve relations with the Chinese, but the effort foundered, partly because of the power struggle within China.

Khrushchev had carefully avoided giving aid to the North Vietnamese or to the National Liberation Front in South Vietnam (Laos was an exception), differing with the Chinese on that score. However, in the early part of 1965, when the United States started to bomb North Vietnam and assumed the major burden of military operations in South Vietnam, the Soviet Union radically changed its policy toward Vietnam. The USSR made extensive military and economic aid available to North Vietnam and exhorted the Chinese to participate in a program of joint action and assistance to North Vietnam.

Peking refused to bow to these pressures. She preferred a system of separate Chinese aid to North Vietnam and rebuffed all Soviet overtures to joint action. Such action would have meant the restoration to positions of influence of the professionals in the army and the bureaucratic group whose leader was Liu Shao-chi. The bureaucrats, although good Chinese patriots, needed Soviet assistance in the kind of domestic program they were competent and eager to execute. Mao, then preparing a Great Cultural Revolution roughly similar to Stalin's transformation of the CPSU between 1934 and 1938, found that US policy suited his domestic political needs. He realized, or decided to assume, that US plans did not go beyond what he called "special warfare" in Vietnam, that is, a local war. China issued many statements that an invasion of North Vietnam by American troops or an attack on China would provoke a Chinese response. Thus Mao clearly implied that he could tolerate the American war in South Vietnam and the bombing in North Vietnam. In taking this position, Mao furnished ammunition to the Soviets who, taking a leaf from the Chinese book, started to accuse the Chinese of collaborating with the Americans.

Mao might have refused the Soviet offer for joint action in Vietnam even if the refusal had not suited his domestic political purposes. But the fact remains that hostility to the Soviet Union was advantageous domestically.

Some Conclusions

This reconstruction of Sino-Soviet relations is incomplete and uncertain. Nevertheless, enough emerges to allow some conclusions about the nature of the relationship. The key to its deterioration is the weakness of the ruling coalition in each country. On the Soviet side that weakness dates from the death of Stalin. The fragility of the Chinese coalition probably dates from Mao's attempt to regain power in 1957, after the failure of the Hundred Flowers campaign. In the Soviet Union defeat in the political struggle has meant complete eclipse. (Since Stalin, death is no longer the frequent consequence of political defeat.) In China the losers have been disgraced and put on the shelf, and although comebacks have thus far been more frequent than in the Soviet Union, the costs of political defeat are severe enough to make avoiding them essential. Thus factions sacrifice the long-range interests of the Communist movement to intraparty necessities. The coalition on which Khrushchev's power rested required détente or at least the prospect of détente with the United States. If this meant damaging Chinese interests, the worse for Chinese interests. Similarly, if Mao's internal party needs required a continuation of hostility toward the Soviet Union, then the North Vietnamese had to make the best of an uncoordinated Sino-Soviet support of their struggle with the United States.

In the Soviet Union and China the faction in power, when challenged, has sought to consolidate itself by appeals to ideologies with wider mass appeal than communism. In the Soviet Union, nationalism is many centuries old, and Soviet leaders have revived the memories of Genghis Khan and identified the Chinese with the Mongol invaders of the thirteenth century. The present Soviet leadership, not noted for delicacy either of sentiment or of language, has employed racial appeals. Its talk of the yellow peril is closer to Kaiser Wilhelm II and William Randolph Hearst than to Lenin. The Chinese factional leadership, on the other hand, exploits traditional hatred of foreigners. The cries against the long-nosed barbarian and the appeals to Chinese nationalism are very difficult for Mao's opponents to rebuff.

Such chauvinism is not peculiar to the Communist alliance system. In Latin America a leader in difficulty with his own elites or anxious to buttress a shaky position often gains mass support by being more anti-North American than anyone else. This tactic is not confined to radicals but is also employed by quite conservative elements. But the North-South American relationship is much less damaging to the interests of either of the parties than the Chinese-Soviet relationship. North Americans can afford to ignore or paper over differences with their South American allies, and in any case the possibility of North American economic sanctions is taken seriously by South Americans. This does not mean that every conflict in which Latin American leaders want to exploit anti-North American sentiments will be successfully resolved. But the comparison illustrates the much worse position of the Soviet Union.

In the American alliance system the United States still offers significant economic support—that is, access to superior technology and markets—so that Latin American leaders must reckon the cost when they seek to exploit domestic anti-American sentiment. By contrast, the Soviet policy of trying to punish the Chinese and bring them to book has systematically deprived the Soviet Union of every instrument of leverage. Each time the Soviets have employed a sanction against the Chinese, causing the Chinese to learn how to make do without that particular bit of Soviet economic or foreign-policy assistance, the Russians have deprived themselves of a useful weapon. Now practically the only contact between the two countries is ideological.

And ideological conflicts, without the leaven of concrete state interests, are exceedingly difficult to resolve. As long as the Sino-Soviet alliance had territorial, economic, and foreign policy aspects, relative advantage could inhibit pure ideological hostility. Chinese hopes of economic or industrial aid could cause the sense of humiliation to be suppressed. But once the traditional bargaining counters are gone, only ideology remains. Since the positions of internal factions are rationalized in terms of the "correct" communist ideology or in terms of more traditional nationalism, resolution of the differences between the two states is not sufficient for a détente. The combination of genuine differences of interest and, in each country, political advantage for a faction that exploits the differences has made the quarrel so intractable. For example, if either the United States or France had been willing or able to play a significant role in the internal politics of the other, it is unlikely that relations would have improved after de Gaulle's retirement.

Some Soviet writers express the hope that after Mao passes from the scene, relations can be restored to roughly the situation of the early 1950s. But others argue that the Communist party of China is not merely a deformed Communist party but a non-Communist party.

Under the Brezhnev doctrine which justified the invasion of Czecho-slovakia on the ground that the Communist party was being destroyed, such analyses of the state of the Chinese party imply that intervention is necessary. Perhaps these suggestions of invasion are merely threats calculated to compel a measure of Chinese compliance, but it is possible that the Soviet controversy about the nature of the Chinese Communist party is the surface of an internal argument about the promotion of separatism in the border regions or even Soviet occupation of some of the border provinces. Before the Chinese agreed to border talks in the fall of 1969, the Soviet press carried open threats of the destruction of Chinese nuclear facilities.

The Chinese employ the weapon of the weak in a peculiarly effective way against the Soviet leadership. When the Chinese become provocative and insulting, the Soviets must either punish them or accept the humiliation of repeated Chinese affronts. The Chinese dare the Soviet Union to invade and occupy parts of China. If they don't, they appear craven. If they do, the argument may run, they will not get much further than the Japanese, they will consolidate Chinese unity against the foreign invader, and the most effective deterrent to such an action—the Soviet Union—will suffer a mortal ideological wound. This last needs amplification.

Although ideology plays a diminishing role in Soviet relations with nonsocialist powers, it continues to play a powerful role in relations among socialist states and within the Soviet Union itself. The Soviet leadership has demanded and extracted sacrifices from its own population in the name of an eschatological outcome. Socialism was not simply another form of government for the Russian lands; it was to produce a millennium on earth. Not only Russia but the world would be saved. Although few Soviet citizens still have such a simple faith, although large elements of the Soviet population are disillusioned, although many are increasingly cynical and more resigned, perhaps the great majority of the people believe that socialism is inherently superior to other systems. It is admitted that socialist leadership has been bad, and that Stalin committed crimes, but few are willing to believe that the terrible sacrifices were to a false god. The Soviet leadership risks being repudiated if socialism as an international system is repudiated, and a war between the socialist states would be the final denial of the universality of socialism. A non-Communist may see international socialism as a myth, but for the Soviet leaders it is an indispensable myth. If this set of beliefs is to be retired, a new raison d'être must be supplied for the Soviet system. The present Soviet leaders seem unlikely candidates for bold new innovations in any field and particularly in theory. Thus, the weaker Chinese possess a formidable weapon when they dare the Soviet Union to attack.

It would be foolhardy to predict that the Soviet Union would never be so destructive of its own interests as to engage in a war with China. Analysts of Sino-Soviet relations only half a dozen years ago predicted that relations could get no worse because it would be too damaging to the interests of both parties. The parties concerned obviously had a different rationale, for they accepted heavy damage to each other. But if we exclude a Sino-Soviet war and examine the probability of a restoration of relationships, the conclusion emerges, as usual, that the past cannot be restored. The waning of the cold war makes it impossible for the Sino-Soviet alliance to be restored as it was.

A useful definition of cold war is a state in which opponents who differ ideologically expect tension to mount steadily and possibly to culminate in war. When tension waxes and wanes and rapprochement and détente are conceivable, "cold war" no longer describes the situation. This definition of cold war applies equally well to Sino-American and to Sino-Soviet relations. Sino-American relations are very limited at present and may continue so, but the general expectation is that they will improve somewhat, not that they will inexorably worsen. The Soviet Union fears modest improvements because only old-fashioned cold war between the United States and China can force the Chinese back into the same relationship with the Soviet Union that obtained during and immediately after the Korean war. Active US-Chinese hostility obviously pushes the Chinese toward rapprochement. Distant, if not friendly, relations with the United States either make it unnecessary for the Chinese to accept Soviet terms or permit them to bargain on a better basis. As the familiar binding elements of alliances, the common enemy, becomes effaced, a possible Sino-Soviet rapprochement has to be on a different basis. If one assumes that the Vietnamese war will end and that some moderate regularization of Sino-American relations will occur, then it is difficult to posit the restoration of the status quo ante in Sino-Soviet relations.

Only simultaneously stable, firm coalitions within the Soviet Union and China will permit the allies to negotiate in terms of their state interests without appeals to mass support in each country and without letting factional party interests in each country dominate the relationship. Chinese and Soviet internal affairs are unpredictable, and it is difficult to discern a point at which each is headed by a stable coalition. Until then, the Soviet Union and China will quarrel in ideological terms, to the detriment of their common interest.

Part Two

Hegemonic Conflicts

Chapter 4

Conflicts Within Hegemony

The United States and the Dominican Republic

ABRAHAM F. LOWENTHAL

I

On April 28, 1965, more than 500 US Marines landed
at Santo Domingo in the Dominican Republic in the
midst of a bloody clash among Dominican civilian
and military factions. Armed and authorized to return
fire, the Marines were the first combat-ready US forces
to move into a Latin American country in close to
40 years. Within a week, a rapid buildup had put
nearly 23,000 US soldiers ashore, almost half the
number then fighting in Vietnam. Another 10,000 troops
stood ready just off the Dominican coast, and thousands
more were on alert at bases in the United States.

The massive American military intervention in the
Dominican Republic surprised, even shocked, most
students of US policy in Latin America. After almost
a century of repeated American military intervention
in this hemisphere, particularly in the Caribbean area,
the United States had forsworn this practice in Latin
America and had even joined the other members of
the Organization of American States in formalizing
the proscription against unilateral intervention. But
now US forces had been sent into Santo Domingo
without specific consultation in the OAS, much less
the members' prior approval. Observers of American
policy began at once to ask whether President Lyndon
B. Johnson was formulating a new "doctrine," one
that would justify again the use of American troops in
this hemisphere. Soon President Johnson himself
seemed to confirm this interpretation, declaring that
"what is important is that we know, and that they know,
and that everybody knows, that we don't propose to sit

This essay draws largely on the author's previously published article,
"The Dominican Intervention in Retrospect," *Public Policy*, 18
(Fall 1969), 137–148, and on other articles cited in the text.

here in our rocking chair—and let the Communists set up any government in the Western Hemisphere."[1]

If the military intervention of April 1965 raised questions about the course of US policy, the events of the next few weeks underlined these questions and provoked many more. At first the United States government announced that it was landing its troops at the request of Dominican authorities to protect the lives of Americans and other foreign nationals, although not a single American or other foreign citizen had been hurt. It was later revealed, however, that the Dominican "authority" which asked for American troops was a junta established at the suggestion of US officials and that the formal invitation from this junta had actually been solicited by the US government.

American authorities then added that the intervention was being undertaken not only to save lives but also to preserve the Dominican people's right to a free choice of government. Soon it appeared, however, that American troops were actually aligning themselves with Dominican forces who were taking lives, even commiting atrocities, who had deprived the Dominican people of their freely chosen government by overthrowing it in 1963, and whose determination to thwart the attempted restoration of the elected regime accounted for the 1965 crisis.

The political stance the US government adopted was particularly baffling. The US seemed to back first one faction and then another, while proclaiming its continuing neutrality, and to call one group "rebels" and another "loyalists," while professing not to favor either. Having created one "loyalist" junta, the US refused to extend it diplomatic recognition, rather seeking to have it replaced by a second "loyalist" junta. No sooner had the second junta been announced than Washington was involved in detailed negotiations with the opposing faction, looking toward the formation of a "pro-rebel" regime. Yet at the very point when formation of a US-backed, "rebel"-dominated government seemed imminent, the US government suspended negotiations, withdrew its negotiators, and sent in new diplomats with orders to establish yet another government, unconnected with either of the groups with whom the United States had up to then been dealing.

The impression of overwhelming confusion which American policy conveyed during the first few weeks of the Dominican crisis was heightened by the proliferation of efforts to deal with the situation. Having sent in its forces without prior consultation, the US government sought then to consult widely and to associate as many entities

[1] Lyndon B. Johnson, quoted in Philip L. Geyelin, *Lyndon B. Johnson and the World* (New York: Praeger, 1966), p. 238.

as possible with its attempt to solve the Dominican problem. The military task of patrolling Santo Domingo was shared with forces from Brazil, Paraguay, Nicaragua, Honduras, and Costa Rica and the search for peace was joined by the OAS secretary-general, a five-man OAS special committee, a special observer from the United Nations and his military and political advisers, and the papal nuncio.

After some weeks, the Dominican imbroglio finally settled down into a more or less structured series of negotiations. United States ambassador to the OAS, Ellsworth Bunker, and other OAS representatives from Brazil and El Salvador worked with a Dominican diplomat, Dr. Héctor García Godoy, to design a provisional regime that could oversee national elections and prepare the way for the withdrawal of American troops. National elections were held in June 1966, all American troops were officially withdrawn by the end of September, and the Dominican Republic disappeared from US newspaper headlines. United States commitments to the OAS and to nonintervention were reaffirmed, but President Johnson's statements about the American government's determination to prevent the establishment of another Communist regime in the Western hemisphere were never qualified. Questions remained, therefore, about what the United States might do in future situations, such as the uncertainty likely to be faced at the end of Duvalier's regime in Haiti.

The United States sent its troops into the Dominican Republic in April 1965. The Soviet Union invaded Czechoslovakia in August 1968. In each case, one of the two great powers of the contemporary world, discarding its pledges and confounding expert appraisals of its supposedly established foreign policies, deployed massive forces in the territory of a nearby friendly state, a fellow participant in the great power's regional organization. In each case, the great power claimed that its forces had been invited by legitimate national authorities in the invaded country, but it turned out that the formal "invitations" were prompted and the supposed "authority's" claim to legitimacy doubtful. In neither case was the great power unquestionably acting to defend its security in an immediate sense; the powers seem to have acted on the basis of longer-range calculations, as embodied in axiom, and because of extraordinary sensitivity in a particular geographic area, stemming partly from recent adverse experiences. Both great powers accompanied their actions by vague pronouncements that seemed to portend new "doctrines," but later seemed to back away from these statements without retracting them.

In each case, the great power—having committed itself militarily—sought then to gain the legitimizing participation of members of the regional organization. In both instances, some members of the regional organization agreed to participate and even to contribute troops to the occupation operation, but with differing motivations and degrees of enthusiasm. The participation of allies in the military intervention tended to legitimize the initial act somewhat, to delegitimize the regional organization, to exacerbate strains within the alliance and political tensions within member states, and probably also to constrain the acts and policies of the great power toward the invaded state.

In each case, the great power followed up its military intervention quickly by taking steps aimed at achieving a political solution to the crisis. First the great power fortified its own clients; then it seemed to move (unexpectedly) toward reinstating precisely the faction it distrusted and had at first sought to weaken. But the apparent attempts to compromise with the distrusted group gave way, after a confusing series of twists and turns, to measures that tended to consolidate the hold of the power's clients.

In both cases, too, the military occupations gradually gave way to less overt forms of hegemonic control, including revised economic and diplomatic relations. As time passed and the invasions themselves faded into memory, opinions differed as to the interventions' consequences. The great powers' immediate objectives, at least those stated, had apparently been achieved, but the costs—within the great power, within the invaded country, and within the region—were high, although hard to calculate.

Why did the great powers intervene? What were the effects of the interventions, their consequences and costs? What lessons can be derived from these episodes? This essay discusses these questions with reference to the Dominican intervention; Professor Rothschild's essay deals with the Soviet intervention in Czechoslovakia.

II

This is not the place for a detailed analysis of the US government's decision to send troops to Santo Domingo or for an extended examination of the confusing process by which the Dominican intervention was finally ended.[2] Something may be said, however, about the

[2] My Harvard doctoral dissertation (and forthcoming book) on the Dominican intervention analyzes the decision to intervene in detail. It draws on extensive interviews with some 150 Dominican, American, and other participants in the 1965 crisis, on review of the State Department's cable traffic for this period, and on other pertinent documents, many of them still highly classified. See Abraham F. Lowenthal, "The Dominican Intervention of 1965: A Study of United States Policy," doctoral dissertation submitted to the Department of Government, Harvard University, 1970. Jerome Slater's *Intervention and Negotiation: The United States*

historical and political context of the intervention, in order to help explain how such a surprising action, seemingly precluded by inter-American agreements, was still possible in 1965.

First, the long-standing and extraordinary involvement of the United States in Dominican affairs should be underlined.[3] Three times in the twentieth century the United States has landed troops on Dominican soil, and even these are but the most dramatic episodes in a continuous history of US interference in Dominican politics. Events in the Dominican Republic, for instance, occasioned the "Roosevelt Corollary" to the Monroe Doctrine, the initial American interest in customs receiverships, and undisguised efforts by Washington to dictate public policies to the Dominican government—all occurring before the US military occupation of 1916–1924. More recently, in the five years before the 1965 intervention, the US government undertook a wide variety of activities in the Dominican Republic: implementing OAS-approved sanctions against the brutal Trujillo dictatorship; using the threat of military force to stabilize a volatile situation after the dictatorship's sudden end; expending foreign aid for immediate political purposes; and assisting various Dominican regimes in many ways, even by training Dominican police and by providing tactical political advice.

The US has also played a predominant role in the Dominican Republic's economy. From 1916 until 1947, US currency was actually the legal tender of Dominican commerce, and for years before 1916, US officials had been collecting the customs revenues in Dominican ports on behalf of Dominican authorities and foreign bond-holders. The Dominican Republic's foreign commerce has long been mainly with the United States; in 1918 over 80 percent of Dominican trade was already with the United States, and by the 1960s the Dominican Republic did a larger percentage of its trade with the United States than did any other country. The export sector of the Dominican economy—sugar, fruit, and, more recently, bauxite—has been controlled primarily by American investment.

The United States, in short, has been and still is a major and continuing presence in Dominican affairs. Although nominally sovereign and independent since 1844, the Dominican Republic has never been able to escape the shadow of the United States; it has suffered the

<hr>

and the Dominican Revolution (New York: Harper & Row, 1970) provides a useful account of American policy in the Dominican Republic from the intervention through the eventual withdrawal of US forces in 1966.

[3] The following paragraphs draw largely on Abraham F. Lowenthal, "The United States and the Dominican Republic to 1965: Background to Intervention," *Caribbean Studies* (July 1970) and "Foreign Aid as a Political Instrument: The Case of the Dominican Republic," *Public Policy*, 14 (1965), 141–160.

positive disadvantage of dependence without gaining the possible advantages that annexation might have brought.

It should not have been surprising, therefore, when American troops began to land in Santo Domingo. Earlier and extensive American involvements in the area did not make the 1965 intervention inevitable, but they did help to shape the attitude of American officials, thus making the 1965 episode more likely. For decades the United States government had approached the Dominican Republic and the Caribbean generally as an area, vital to American security, from which any potentially hostile influence should be excluded. This historic approach, reinforced by the experience of Castro's takeover in Cuba and the consequent introduction of Soviet power into the Caribbean, caused American officials during the early 1960s to focus on Santo Domingo with special attention and apprehension. Events and circumstances that might have passed unnoticed elsewhere became instead the background to intervention.

Political instability has characterized the Dominican Republic since the assassination of Rafael Trujillo in 1961.[4] Political parties, labor unions, student groups, and military factions have formed, split, realigned, and split again. Constant turnover has occurred at top levels of every government department, even in the supposedly autonomous agencies established to insulate development administration from political turmoil. Shifting groups of "outs" have arrayed against equally temporary alignments of "ins" in a continuous political kaleidoscope. There has been almost no institutional continuity, very little consistency with regard to program or ideology, and not even much loyalty to personal *caudillos*.

Perhaps the key characteristic of recent Dominican politics has been the predominance of direct confrontations among groups in conflict. Contending forces in the Dominican Republic have increasingly employed undisguised and unrefined displays of power, directed more often at replacing the government than at forcing it to take specific actions. Students and university politicians have organized, rioted, marched on the National Palace, and clashed with police and army units. Labor unions have demonstrated, gone out on strikes—including several nationwide general strikes—disrupted traffic, and even engaged in sabotage. Businessmen have staged general strikes of their own and have organized paramilitary groups for self-defense and for terrorism. Even the Church has often exerted its political power, directly

---

[4] The following paragraphs are taken from Abraham F. Lowenthal, "The Dominican Republic: The Politics of Chaos," in Arpad von Lazar and Robert R. Kaufman (eds.), *Reform and Revolution: Readings in Latin American Politics* (Boston: Allyn & Bacon, 1969), pp. 34–58.

through pastoral letters and other public appeals and indirectly through the personal influence of individual priests.

Since Trujillo's death, competing Dominican factions have also engaged almost incessantly in conspiracy and subversion, encouraging their military counterparts to coup and counter-coup. Various military cliques have suppressed opposition, prevented governments from executing specific policies, overthrown regimes and established others. Even before the 1965 crisis, internal struggles within the Dominican armed forces led to strafings and less violent demonstrations of strength—troop movements, tank deployments, and airplane maneuvers —by one side against another. The violent conflict of April 1965, pitting army troops and armed irregulars against other army units and the Dominican air force, was the ultimate denouement of years of political chaos.

This rampant disorder had its roots deep in Dominican history, but it owed much in particular to the special effects of Trujillo's reign and its aftermath. The traditional instability of *caudillo* politics gave way after Trujillo's death to unprecedented strife. The Dominican Republic came to face in extreme form the classic problem of "praetorian politics": the expansion of political participation outpaced the creation of political institutions.[5]

It would have been difficult, under the best of circumstances, for American officials to understand and cope with the Dominican politics of chaos. What further constrained American effectiveness was the approach US officials took to the Dominican problem. Unprepared to understand what was happening in the Dominican Republic in terms of Santo Domingo's past, US observers attempted to interpret the complicated swirl of Dominican events by referring to the experience of nearby Cuba, with which they were more familiar and which was salient in their minds. The Dominican Republic came to be regarded as a potential "second Cuba"; differences between the two countries, each with very distinct histories and problems, were overlooked.

The US government's preoccupation with avoiding a "second Cuba" structured the way American officials looked at the Dominican Republic during the 1960s, influencing what they noted and what they regarded as significant. Politicians of various types were reported on with reference to their supposed place in the ideological spectrum, without recognition of the fragility of ideological and even personal commitments in contemporary Dominican politics. The Dominican armed forces were conceived, not primarily as rival bands of plunder,

---

[5] See Samuel P. Huntington, *Political Order in Changing Societies* (New Haven: Yale University Press, 1968), especially pp. 192–263.

but as an institution opposed to instability and to Communist advance. Generally, Dominican politics were interpreted not in terms of praetorian disorder but largely in terms of "Castro-Communist" attempts to gain power. What was asked about Dominican politics, time after time, was how a given set of circumstances would affect Communist strength. Organizational responses were predictable; the US government prepared itself to generate information and reports on the activities of all known or suspected Dominican Communists, but with a very inadequate understanding of the context in which they were acting.

The distorting effect of this insistent focus on the "Castro-Communist" threat became most sharply evident, of course, during the April 1965 crisis. From the very outset of the crisis, both Washington officials and the US embassy in Santo Domingo keyed their questions and reports to the need to avoid a "second Cuba." Constrained by poor information on most aspects of the crisis but supplied with voluminous reports on Communist activities, American officials consistently exaggerated the strength of Communist elements. By the time President Johnson faced the decision whether to authorize armed intervention in Santo Domingo, he felt he had no choice but to do so or risk an imminent "Communist takeover."

The President acted, therefore, to prevent the anticipated domestic and international consequences of a "second Cuba," although this "threat" was not really the one being faced. That the Dominican Republic lacked an intensely dedicated, skillful, and attractive political leader like Castro; that no popularly based guerrilla movement existed there; that Dominican Communists were weak, fragmented, and wholly lacking in rural support; that Dominican society was diffuse, with power nowhere centralized or susceptible to overnight seizure—all these facts were forgotten, if they were ever known, by the President and his chief aides as they briefly discussed how to respond to the American Ambassador's request for a Marine landing. The power of misplaced analogies and bureaucratically reinforced rhetoric to determine foreign-policy perceptions and actions was dramatically illustrated.

III

The Dominican intervention and the confusing American statements and actions immediately thereafter appeared initially to mark a severe setback for US diplomacy. Neutrals, adversaries, and allies condemned various aspects of American policy, emphasizing particularly its departure from established US declarations and its violation of inter-American accords. Public protest welled up in almost every country of Latin

America, and in many countries outside the hemisphere. Suspicions and fears were aroused or revived, and the concepts of inter-American cooperation were severely tested. Relations among the members of the Organization of American States and between the OAS and the United Nations seemed to cloud.

Within the United States, the Dominican episode at first provoked strong adverse reactions. Although mass public opinion, as reflected in the major polls, expressed confidence in the administration's handling of the Dominican affair, significant sectors strenuously opposed the government. The five newspapers then most widely read in Washington policy-making circles—the *New York Times,* the *New York Herald Tribune,* the *Washington Post,* the *Wall Street Journal,* and the *Christian Science Monitor*—published reports and editorials so critical of the administration as to become themselves major factors in the crisis. Later, several leading public figures, most of them from the administration's own party, attacked specific aspects of American policy.

As time passed, however, what loomed at first as a major disaster came to be regarded, by many in Washington at least, as a remarkable success for American policy, apparently producing desired results at little cost. Viewing the Dominican intervention in retrospect, some observers have argued that all four announced objectives of US policy were attained: to protect American and other foreign citizens, to halt violence, to prevent a Communist takeover, and to restore constitutional processes to the Dominican people. Except for relatively minor matters, such as admitted inadequacies in US public information activities and perhaps the failure to inform members of the OAS in advance of the US decision to intervene, these analysts look back on the Dominican episode as a successful exercise of American power.[6] A State Department publication has noted, for instance, that "when we confronted the Communists promptly and vigorously in our own hemisphere, as in the Dominican crisis, they were halted; when we failed to recognize and confront them, as in Cuba, the tumor took root and grew."[7]

Such a statement may perhaps be dismissed as simplistic propaganda, but its premise—that the Dominican intervention turned out well from the standpoint of US objectives—is very widely accepted. As Samuel Huntington has remarked:

...the dominant tendency is to view [the Dominican] intervention as a

[6] See, for example, Center for Strategic Studies, Georgetown University, *Dominican Action: Intervention or Cooperation?*, Special Study Report #2 (Washington, D.C., 1966).

[7] *Foreign Policy Briefs,* June 5, 1967.

success. Whether or not there was a threat of a Communist takeover on the island, we were able to go in, restore order, negotiate a truce among conflicting parties, hold reasonably honest elections which the right man won, withdraw our troops, and promote a very considerable amount of social and economic reform. For those of us who thought in 1965 that there were good political and moral grounds for escalation in Vietnam but none whatsoever for intervening in the Dominican Republic, the apparent results of the two operations are a useful reminder that results are all that count.[8]

Among some in Washington there is even a tendency, in a period when Americans are preoccupied by the failure of US power in Vietnam, to review the Dominican experience in search of lessons for successful intervention.

The view that US policy in the Dominican crisis was ultimately successful tends, however, to be based on an incomplete and misleading reckoning of the costs of the Dominican intervention. It may still be too early to reach a final and conclusive judgment on whether the Dominican intervention provided benefits ultimately "worth" all its costs, but it is certainly not premature to think about its total price, beyond its tragic but incalculable toll in casualties and consequent human agony.

The financial cost of the Dominican intervention has been considerable, for instance. Besides the expense of the military operation itself, emergency relief and assistance during 1965 and 1966 came to over $100 million. The events of 1965 also resulted in the assumption by the United States of an extraordinarily large aid program; by the late 1960s the AID mission resident in Santo Domingo was the largest assigned in Spanish America. The cost of maintaining this massive aid program has been compounded, moreover, as general US aid appropriations have been reduced and funds have consequently become unavailable elsewhere in the hemisphere.

The intangible costs of the Dominican intervention—in the hemisphere generally, in the United States, and particularly in the Dominican Republic—are difficult to estimate, but the impossibility of precise quantification should not preclude consideration of these consequences. Public opinion polls and regional summit conferences, for instance, should not obscure the fact that some sectors of Latin American and world opinion found their faith shattered or their fears confirmed by the Dominican intervention. Disagreement is possible about the extent to which the Good Neighbor policy had succeeded in erasing the legacy of interventionism or about the extent to which the Alliance for

8 Samuel P. Huntington in Richard M. Pfeffer (ed.), *No More Vietnams?* (New York: Harper & Row, 1968), p. 2. Professor Huntington dissociates himself from the dominant view.

Progress had improved the US image in Latin America, but none can dispute that the Dominican intervention set these efforts back. Many students of the Alliance, indeed, attribute its loss of mystique in large part to the Dominican episode, which seemed to align the United States with reactionary forces against those who favored change.

The Dominican experience also hurt the Organization of American States. Although the OAS may have lent some legitimacy to US actions during the crisis, it undoubtedly lost standing in the hemisphere; the OEA seemed, to many Latin Americans, just *otro engaño americano*, another American trick.[9] Some apparent costs of the Dominican crisis within the OAS, such as the sharp division into blocs which characterized the 1965 debates, now seem not to have been permanent, but other consequences have been lasting. The morale of the permanent secretariat of the OAS was undermined by the Dominican operation. The carefully cultivated efforts to build support for basic reforms of the organization's charter and to strengthen the mechanism of the Inter-American Peace Committee lost much of their effectiveness as a result of the Dominican crisis. The idea of an inter-American force composed of units from the democratic countries in the hemisphere seems to have died as a result of its premature birth and distortion in the Dominican context.

The Dominican intervention may also have decreased the chances for the kind of peaceful change which the United States claims to support in Latin America. The Dominican crisis had the immediate consequence in several countries of heightening frictions between opposing political groups and between local military establishments and popular parties. Longer-term effects arose from perceptions of the Dominican intervention as part of a pattern of US policy. Some Latin American conservatives—particularly in Central America—drew the conclusion from the Dominican crisis that the United States will not allow nationalist reform movements to succeed and that therefore conservatives need not accommodate themselves to proposed changes. Other Latin Americans committed to change, including Juan Bosch himself, concluded from the American intervention in Santo Domingo that the United States is unalterably opposed to democratic revolution in Latin America, or that the American preoccupation with anti-Communism makes US officials incapable of distinguishing reformers from Communists.[10] For Latin American university students, particularly, the Dominican intervention confirmed their impression that the Bay of

9 See Jerome Slater, "The Limits of Legitimization in International Organizations: The Organization of American States and the Dominican Crisis," *International Organization*, 23 (Winter 1969), 48–72.

10 See Juan Bosch, *Pentagonism: A Substitute for Imperialism* (New York: Grove Press, 1968).

Pigs invasion was no aberration but rather represented the main thrust of US foreign policy.

The Dominican intervention also had serious consequences in the United States itself. It is difficult, in retrospect, to separate the Dominican crisis from the almost simultaneous escalation of the war in Vietnam, which has overshadowed all other foreign-policy issues since 1965, but the Dominican episode surely helped cause the deepening malaise about American policy. The Dominican crisis, particularly the seeming twists and turns of US policy during its first weeks and the administration's obvious lack of candor, heightened the sense of marked distrust and even hostility between the administration and many leading journalists, scholars, and other informed opinion-shapers. For many Americans, the "crisis of credibility" began with the Dominican intervention.

The intangible costs of the American intervention of 1965 may well have been most serious in the Dominican Republic itself. No one can state with certainty what would have happened in that country had its amorphous "revolution" not been interrupted by the introduction of American forces. Nor can anyone know what might have happened had the United States been willing and able to use the opportunity afforded by its armed intervention to build closer ties with Dominican non-Communists on the left and to cooperate with them in restructuring the Dominican military and police establishment—then more vulnerable than at any time in recent years. It is clear, however, that the crisis of 1965 heightened the fragmentation of Dominican politics, further decreasing the already slender chances that the Dominican Republic can soon develop effective political institutions.[11] Families, social and economic groups, political parties, the armed forces, even the Catholic Church were divided by the crisis and the US intervention, and capable individuals were "burned" politically because of their participation on one side or the other, or in efforts to resolve the crisis. And although it is too early to know what lasting effects the US intervention will have had on the Dominican polity, one can certainly not be confident about its long-term results. Five years after the 1965 intervention, the Dominican Republic appeared again to be sliding toward intensified violence. Demonstrations, disturbances, assassinations, and repression scarred the 1970 election campaign, and continued into President Balaguer's second term without any sign of an early end.

Among all the uncertain consequences of the 1965 intervention, two

11 See Howard J. Wiarda, "From Fragmentation to Disintegration: The Social and Political Effects of the Dominican Revolution," America Latina, 11 (April–June 1967), 55–71.

results are all too sure: the intervention further entangled the US government in the Dominican morass, and it reinforced the dependence of Dominicans on the United States. Just as the US imposition of sanctions voted by the OAS against Trujillo involved the United States deeply in the post-Trujillo Dominican political struggle, so the 1965 intervention and its aftermath forced the US Government to play an even more central role in Dominican affairs. This intense involvement may decrease in time, but the long-term prospects for establishing normal diplomatic relations between the United States and the Dominican Republic and the rest of the Caribbean territories were undoubtedly diminished by the events of 1965. The political, economic, and psychological effects of renewed intervention have further undermined the possibilities for independent development in the Caribbean, while increasing the likelihood that, if development does occur there, it will be based—as in Cuba—on virulent anti-Americanism.

IV

Some observers conclude, even after weighing all the costs here enumerated, that the 1965 intervention in Santo Domingo was well advised from the standpoint of US foreign-policy objectives. They stress the importance of the advantages they believe were produced by the intervention: preventing a bloodbath perhaps even worse than that which occurred; precluding the possible takeover of the Dominican Republic either by Communists or by a right-wing military dictatorship; and perhaps even discouraging radical uprisings elsewhere in Latin America. Since the Dominican intervention was limited in time and extent, they argue, it did not entail the more permanent costs that might have arisen had hostile power been introduced into the Dominican vacuum.

To contest fully the judgment that the Dominican intervention was well advised from the US standpoint would require evaluating some fundamental assumptions about the nature of American interests in the Caribbean, analyzing in detail the extent of "Castro-Communist" strength and the degree of violence and potential violence during the Dominican crisis, and examining carefully the various alternatives for US policy. Much less is required, however, to show that the Dominican intervention should not be considered a model for future US actions, for *even if* the Dominican operation is *assumed* to have been "successful," it should be stressed that unique aspects of the Dominican case helped account for its outcome.

Military intervention in the Caribbean bears fewer costs and risks for the United States than it would in any other area. For instance, in no other region are US capabilities so overwhelming as in the island nations of the Caribbean, heavily dependent on US trade and susceptible to naval blockade and other exercises of American power. And US intervention in a Caribbean island entails far less political cost than would follow a landing of US forces on the South American continent or even on the mainland of central America. South Americans tend to distinguish themselves from the peoples of the Caribbean on racial, cultural, and historical grounds, and many South Americans consider the Caribbean a US "sphere of interest." The apparent decline in evident South American concern about the US intervention, after the initial outbursts and demonstrations had subsided, may be due partly to the Dominican Republic's distance—geographically and in terms of self-image—from the countries of South America.

Even within the Caribbean, the United States found it easier to intervene in and to extricate itself from the Dominican Republic than it would elsewhere. Nationalist consciousness in the Dominican Republic is (or was until the 1965 intervention, at least) less fully developed than in most Latin American countries—a fact that accounts partly for the lack of effective armed opposition to the US military presence. The background of extensive US participation in their politics made Dominicans more receptive to American efforts to establish a new Dominican government during the 1965 crisis than most Latin Americans would be. Moreover, certain key US officials gained, from the unusually active embassy role during this period, sufficient understanding of the personalities and dynamics of Dominican politics to perform the difficult task of helping to devise a political solution for the Dominican crisis. And when the Provisional Government formula was finally achieved, its success depended largely upon the compatible abilities of two individuals, US Ambassador (to the OAS) Ellsworth Bunker and Dominican President Héctor García Godoy. Each displayed gifts of patience and judgment that probably averted the resumption of open hostilities at several stages, and each was vindicated in several instances when his policies were questioned within the US government. Should the United States again be faced with ending an intervention, it might not be so fortunate as to have a diplomat of Ambassador Bunker's capacity available for the assignment and to find a statesman of Dr. García Godoy's caliber willing to assume the difficult task of political leadership in an occupied country.

It should also be pointed out that official exaggerations of the dangers faced in the Dominican crisis may obscure the perils the United States would face if it intervened elsewhere in circumstances more like those it originally perceived in the Dominican Republic.

The United States government, for instance, greatly overestimated the coherence, strength, and political influence of Dominican Communist groups when the massive intervention began. Dominican Communists proved to be few in number, almost totally lacking in rural support, and relatively untrained in the techniques of urban violence. Their role within the "constitutionalist" movement was not difficult to determine or to limit, for they proved relatively easy to isolate. The United States might find elsewhere that the real strength of local Communist organizations would preclude the rapid disengagement of American forces once they had intervened.

United States officials also exaggerated the extent to which Dominican society had disintegrated at the end of April 1965. After US troops imposed an uneasy peace in Santo Domingo, it turned out that the nation, while shaken, had not been so thoroughly torn as some American observers had initially feared. Most of the country outside the capital city was little affected by the violent struggle in Santo Domingo, and it soon proved possible to maintain nearly normal economic activity throughout the countryside. As weeks passed, the US learned that there were still fairly well-organized groups in the Dominican Republic with which it could deal. The US entered into aid agreements with members of the permanent Dominican national bureaucracy and also with established municipal governments and private development associations. United States officials negotiated with recognized political parties and encouraged existing business, labor, and professional associations to put forth their views on how to resolve the political impasse. When the time came in 1966, the feasibility of orderly and meaningful elections depended on competition between two well-known political groupings, each headed by a former Dominican president with a substantial following in the country. That the Dominican people were familiar with the electoral process and had reason to trust the honesty of elections held under OAS auspices because of the 1962 experience was also helpful.[12]

In considering the problems that might arise in Haiti—the country most likely to cause the United States to consider another intervention —it is worth noting that precisely those factors that facilitated early US withdrawal from the Dominican Republic would be lacking. If the United States were to send its forces into a country such as Haiti— without clearly established institutions and groupings, without political figures of obvious stature, influence, and popular appeal, without ex-

[12] See Henry Wells, "The OAS and the Dominican Elections," *Orbis*, 7 (Spring 1963), 150–163.

perience at meaningful elections, even without a functioning bureaucracy, and about which the United States has relatively little knowledge or experience—it might be very difficult to pull the troops back out.

Finally, it may be worth reflecting on a possibility that some administration officials mentioned at the time—that a number of insurrections might occur at once. The Dominican intervention, which occurred when the United States had but 50,000 men in Vietnam, strained the standing-force capabilities of the United States in the hemisphere. Over 35,000 troops were engaged in the Dominican operation at its height, almost 23,000 of them on shore in an area of only a few square miles. The consequences of this overwhelming type of response for the capability of the United States to deal simultaneously with a perceived security threat elsewhere should be examined.

V

Review of the 1965 Dominican crisis, therefore, does not provide the United States with a manual for successful intervention. What it shows, on the contrary, is the very high price of military intervention and the uncertainty of its consequences, even under conditions relatively favorable to the exercise of American power. Analysis of the Dominican case suggests, in fact, that a future American intervention, even in the Caribbean area, might well be more costly and less effective as a means of achieving US objectives than was the Dominican operation of 1965.

The chief lesson of the Dominican intervention, therefore, is the need for the United States to reexamine traditional hegemonic policies and practices in the light of a changing international environment. Historic axiom, unchallenged premises, bureaucratic procedures and momentum all made it easy for the US government to land troops in Santo Domingo in 1965 and, almost simultaneously, to escalate a limited military involvement in Vietnam into a war of tragic proportions. The consequences of these military interventions were varied and mainly painful, but one of the most important (and most hopeful) results may have been to force the American people and their government to reconsider the nature and extent of US interests abroad and the appropriate instruments for protecting them. Conflict within the hegemonic sphere of the United States will doubtless continue, but it is less likely now than in 1965 to take the form of unilateral military intervention.

The Soviet Union and Czechoslovakia

JOSEPH ROTHSCHILD

"The principle of peaceful coexistence applies only to relations among states with contrasting social systems."—0. Pavlov in *Mezhdunarodnaya Zhizn* (October 1968)

Four international and intrabloc Communist conferences —at Dresden, Warsaw, Cierna, and Bratislava—came and went in the spring and summer of 1968 before the Soviet leaders managed to steel themselves for armed intervention in Czechoslovakia. Thereafter, it required two threats of further invasion, an abortive coup, repeated warnings, elaborate intrigues, and backstair maneuvers to achieve the deposition from Communist party leadership of the national hero of Czechoslovakia's exhilirating "spring" of 1968, Alexander Dubcek, eight months after the original military intrusion of August 20–21, 1968. Such contortions reflect both the difficulty of the problem confronting the Soviet rulers and their want of political skill. Lenin's and Stalin's lessons on the need to divide the opposition and to provide plausible justification for political policy appear to have been lost on their current successors.

The victims of these clumsy developments are the people and the Communist party of Czechoslovakia, the liberal intelligentsia of the Soviet Union, the residual hopes and expectations of the international Communist movement, and a series of Western and east central European assumptions about the evolution of the Soviet system and the operative "rules of the game" governing Soviet behavior. In the light of the purpose and design of this book, we had best turn our attention first to the last of these victims.

The Presumed Rules of the Game

During the decade after the Soviet crushing of the Hungarian revolution of 1956, a number of inferences and generalizations about Soviet policy had gained the consensus of Western specialists and diplomats as well as the hopeful assent of east-central Europeans all too aware that the fulfillment of their own political and social aspirations depended on the validity of these assumptions. They pertained to:

1. The predictability and rationality of Soviet behavior
2. The relative weights of ideology and national interest in Soviet policy-making
3. The nature and quality of Soviet decision-making under conditions of collective responsibility
4. The priority-value assigned by Soviet leaders to achieving a stable détente with the United States
5. The possibilities of bridge-building
6. The importance to the Soviet leadership of international (especially west European) Communist support for Soviet policies in the context of the Sino-Soviet rift
7. The degree of Soviet detachment from domestic developments in the states of east-central Europe, provided these remained within the following elementary and known perimeters of permissibility: (*a*) no unilateral defection from the Warsaw Pact, the Council of Economic Mutual Assistance (CEMA), or the bilateral alliance with the Soviet Union; (*b*) maintenance of the sovereignty of the Communist party and prohibition of opposition parties outside the cosmetic framework of the "national front"; (*c*) no repudiation of collectivized agriculture where it has been achieved or of the nationalization of the industrial sector's commanding economic heights.

These several "post-Hungary" assumptions about Soviet behavior appeared to be confirmed during the early and mid-1960s by Moscow's toleration of Romania's daring deviations within the supposed perimeter-rules. As Western analysts thus became increasingly confident about the validity of their assumptions, they tended gradually to lose sight of certain limiting factors and unexamined premises.

1. Romania's Communist regime has not lost control of its policies to popular spontaneity. Ideologically, therefore, it neither undermines the Soviet image of structural-political orthodoxy nor interests dissident Soviet intellectuals.

2. Romania has no common border with either of the two Germanies, it is of secondary strategic significance, and is far less industrialized and hence economically less significant to her neighbors than Czechoslovakia. (The same applies, *a fortiori*, to defected Albania.)

3. The supposedly political-analytical assumptions rested on the ideological-historical wish that the Soviet leaders might grow less "paranoiac" about east-central Europe as the Soviet Union became more prosperous and stronger and developed a viable détente with the United States. Indeed, it was even hoped that precisely east-central Europe would draw the Soviet Union into greater liberalization. These wishes overlooked the Soviet *apparatchiki's* conservatism, rigidity, and fear of the future, as well as the tendency for resurgent nationalism to replace decaying Marxism as their operational political reflex.

Not only was Czechoslovakia invaded despite her adherence to the supposed rules of the game, and despite the Dubcek government's repeated professions of loyalty to all its intrabloc Communist obligations, but the timing and manner of that invasion shattered yet another Western assumption about the general environment of international relations,—the rhythmicity of crises. For the invasion occurred in the absence of any domestic unrest in Czechoslovakia and *after* the climax of intrabloc political tensions had apparently been benignly eased at the Cierna and Bratislava conferences (July 29–August 1 and August 3) in the course of which all the protagonists—Czechoslovakia, the Soviet Union, East Germany, Poland, Hungary, and Bulgaria—had solemnly, albeit conditionally, pledged not to interfere in each other's domestic affairs. During the three-week interlude between these pledges and the invasion, the Soviet Union made no effort to prepare world or domestic public opinion for a radical reescalation of tension. Thanks to this sequence, the Soviet leaders incurred the "surplus" charge of cynicism on top of the inevitable one of brutality. Finally, there were certain other anomalies about the invasion:

1. It appears not to have been followed by the conventional endorsing and confirming plenary session of the Central Committee of the Soviet Communist party.

2. It was followed by the loud silence of all members of the Soviet Politburo, none of whom identified himself at the time with the invasion. (Even the so-called Brezhnev Doctrine of limited sovereignty and the right of Soviet intervention within the Communist bloc was first

articulated on September 26, 1968, by a relatively minor *Pravda* commentator, Sergei Kovalev.)

3. It was immediately accompanied by an obbligato of rumors to the effect that Kosygin, Suslov, even Brezhnev and other senior Politburo members had opposed the invasion but had their hands forced by those of lesser rank and by marshals of the armed forces.

4. It was surrounded by peculiarly spasmodic Soviet behavior toward the person of Dubcek—he was first embraced, then successively warned, denounced, imprisoned, slugged, reaccepted, restored, isolated, ousted, and humiliated.

In the aftermath of these events, our understanding of Soviet decision-making in crisis situations is even more tentative than heretofore. At the very least, we have been taught that "collective responsibility" does not necessarily entail greater restraint and more steadiness than the allegedly "harebrained schemes" of a single strong leader. Indeed, when the need to preserve the collectivity becomes more important than the identification of an optimal strategy, the resulting pressures are conducive to "collective irresponsibility" (that is, initial irresolution dissolving into eventual stampede) in the absence of either a purposive hand at the tiller (the Stalin era) or effective counterpressures (pluralism-democracy-constitutionalism). Although it might be presumed that these facts and considerations would prompt a searching Western scrutiny of the credibility, content, and nature of détente with the Soviet Union—though perhaps not of its desirability—it appears now that "August 1968" will prove a weaker catalyst of policy reviews in the non-Communist world than the three other recent international crises that focused on Czechoslovakia: September 1938—the experiment in appeasement of aggressors; March 1939—the reversal toward resistance; February 1948—the crystallization of NATO. The Czechoslovak events of August 1968 were also a lower-level crisis in the sense that at no time did they threaten to ignite a general war, however much they may have contaminated the international atmosphere. Finally, it would appear that all who were involved in this last crisis lost—the Czechosloslovak people, the Soviet rulers, the other Warsaw Pact members, the Americans, the French, the West Germans. The rules of the game have become uncertain in east-central Europe, and in consequence, the continent's general stability has been rendered more fragile.

The Challenge of Bonn's Ostpolitik

In one sense, of course, the invasion of Czechoslovakia was but a particularly chilling episode in the chronic crisis that has plagued the

Soviet system, the Soviet bloc, and the world Communist movement since Stalin's death in March 1953. The very omnipotence of his personal authority seduced Stalin into neglecting to build a solid international organizational structure that would routinely guarantee Soviet hegemony in east-central Europe. Khrushchev sought to compensate for Stalin's lapse by energetically developing the Warsaw Pact, CEMA, and periodic international Communist conferences as integrating institutions—devices preferable to Stalin's "administrative" intervention via the KGB in the domestic affairs of other Communist states and parties. But Khrushchev (and his successors) failed to develop legitimate political mechanisms to enforce acceptance of majoritarian international Communist decisions on recalcitrant minorities (for instance, the Chinese, the Albanians, the Romanians, and eventually the Czechoslovakians, not to mention several nonruling Communist parties) to whom a particular issue in dispute was even more a matter of principle than was the organizational unity of the movement. And with each successful defection, the Soviet Union's ideological prestige slipped another notch. In August 1968, the heirs of Stalin and of Khrushchev decided to compensate for their declining *authority* by an assertion of their *power*; for their loss of *respect* by a demonstration of their *capability*. That Czechoslovakia was destined to be both the operating table and the victim in this Soviet surgical scenario was the consequence of a fortuitous synchronization of her domestic developments with West Germany's renascent *Ostpolitik* of détente and engagement —a parallelism thoroughly alarming to the defensive and conservative rulers of East Germany, Poland, and the USSR.

Soviet attitudes toward West Germany appear to combine, on one hand, a rash desire to drive her into such a state of frustration as to bring to power a right-radical reaction that would isolate her morally from her NATO allies and prepare her politically for a bilateral accommodation with the USSR to achieve some of her national aspirations. On the other hand, the Soviets genuinely fear that a politically dynamic and economically powerful West Germany would penetrate and subvert the Soviet Union's own east-central European sphere of hegemony. Both the wish and the fear are historically well grounded —Tauroggen, Rapallo, the Hitler-Stalin Pact, and the several partitions of Poland in the first case, and two world wars culminating in the devastation of the Russian motherland in the second.

Bonn's *Grosse Koalition,* formed in December 1966, achieved an early breakthrough for its new *Ostpolitik* on January 31, 1967, when Bucharest agreed to establish diplomatic relations without insisting on preliminary conditions that included Bonn's acknowledging the Oder-Neisse line (as Warsaw demanded), recognizing the DDR (as Pankow insisted), or renouncing eventual control over nuclear weapons (as Moscow wished). In effect, this Romanian refusal to regard West Germany as either an enemy or a threat initiated the general Warsaw Pact-Soviet bloc crisis which culminated in the invasion of Czechoslovakia by five of her pact allies 19 months later. For West Germany's economic attractiveness to the Danubian states of the bloc neatly balanced the political anxiety that she inspired in the northern ones. Czechoslovakia was here in the middle. In the meantime, Romania's violation of the bloc's general diplomatic quarantine of West Germany went unpunished. In 1967 the Soviet leaders were particularly anxious not to offend de Gaulle, whose interest in that "fellow nation of Latin culture" on the Danube was well known. Furthermore, Romania is geographically so remote from Germany and militarily so accessible to the Soviet army that there was no need for haste in disposing of her. In any event, the Romanians indulged in no tampering with the "leading role of the party" or dismantling of "democratic centralism" within it and thus presented no revisionist challenges to the Soviet image of political legitimacy.

By 1967–1968, Czechoslovakia's political fears of West Germany, based on Munich, wartime occupation, and the revanchism of Sudeten expellees, had abated, whereas her economic fascination with the possibility of obtaining West German assistance in modernizing her obsolescent productive plant was growing. (The average age of Czechoslovak textile machinery was 40 years.) An orderly, prospering West Germany, anchored to NATO and EEC, with her expellee population well integrated, no longer appeared a plausible threat to Czechoslovak security—certainly not a threat great enough to warrant the continued high price for counterprotection that Czechoslovakia had been paying the Soviet Union, ever since the end of World War II, in the form of diplomatic dependence, political synchronization, and economic vassalage. The Czechoslovaks were, of course, aware that under the known rules of the game, they could not repudiate their ties to the USSR, the Warsaw Pact, or CEMA, but they hoped to reinterpret the terms so as to gain some freedom to maneuver toward West Germany's new readiness to invest her technical and financial power in east-central Europe.

Bonn's hopes of eventually isolating East Germany through such economic engagement with the other countries of the Soviet bloc were, however, no secret. Precisely because of these hopes, it was imperative for Ulbricht and, by extension, Gomulka to cleave to the image of a Nazified, war-bent West Germany that must be kept in strict quarantine until she came to recognize the DDR and the Oder-Neisse frontier. Pankow and Warsaw were, indeed, far more allergic to Bonn than was Moscow itself, which sporadically appeared to appreciate the benefits that might accrue from some accommodation. In any event, West Germany's *Ostpolitik* was confronting the Soviet Union with a triangular challenge: to hold her several clients in line; to avoid being paralyzed by the two most conservative ones; and to redefine her own stance so as not to let the West German initiative erode the Soviet stakes in east-central Europe. Czechoslovakia, whose economy was by 1967–1968 in desperate need of the kind of capital equipment and long-term, government-backed, hard-currency loans that only West Germany appeared able and willing to supply, loomed as the acid test of the Soviet Union's capacity to handle the *Ostpolitik's* challenge. Were Prague to go the way of Bucharest, there would be no restraining the other Danubian clients, and Soviet hegemony might yield to a virtual German-Soviet economic condominium over east-central Europe.

Already, toward the end of the otherwise ultra-orthodox Novotny regime, Czechoslovakia had been cautiously edging toward some maneuverability by verbally differentiating between normalizing political relations with West Germany—which was conceded to be still impermissible—and merely establishing diplomatic ties with her—which Bonn's recent repudiation of the Munich agreement had allegedly now rendered feasible. The Czechoslovaks also pointed out that despite their total political hostility, East Germany and Poland were intensifying their economic relations with West Germany. In August 1967 Prague agreed to exchange trade missions with Bonn—making Czechoslovakia the last bloc state to take this step. Half a year later, already under Dubcek, she requested Moscow to advance a hard-currency loan of $440 million—five times greater than any previous hard-currency loan ever granted by the Soviet Union—to retool Czechoslovak industry with Western capital equipment. Prague's implication seemed clear: unless Moscow proved vastly generous, which was unlikely, Bonn would be approached.

Fall of Novotny—Rise of Dubcek

The economic recession of the 1960s, however important, was but one of several landslides undermining Czechoslovakia's political topography. Economists, demanding radical structural and policy reforms—which the regime verbally endorsed but practically sabotaged—were joined in protest by the nation's cultural intelligentsia, now reverting under the oppressive but palsied rule of Novotny to the historic national tradition that in times of repression, the intelligentsia serves as the surrogate for prohibited political opposition. Finally, the Slovaks —Communist and non-Communist—determined to end and to revenge Novotny for cheating them of their region's promised political autonomies and economic expectations. This coalition succeeded in breaking the regime after four corrosive incidents in 1967:

1. The spectacular popularity of Israel during and after the Six-Day War, in the teeth of the Czechoslovak regime's adherence to the Soviet Union's pro-Arab policy. Analogies were drawn to Czechoslovakia's own position at the time of Munich, and Israel was applauded for fighting instead of abdicating.

2. The regime's clumsy, abortive, and ultimately counterproductive attempt to curb and punish the intelligentsia for making eloquent attacks on censorship and repression, official anti-Semitism, and betrayal of the national interest and of true socialism—attacks that were voiced at the Fourth Czechoslovak Writer's Congress, June 27–29, 1967. Precisely because the rebellious writers were Communists speaking in disillusionment and alarm, their protest was the most effective heard in east-central Europe since that of their Hungarian colleagues in 1956.

3. The public's derisive reaction to massive police brutality directed at the October 31 student protest against inadequate utilities ("We want light!") and general inefficiency and bureaucratism, followed by the government's unprecedented retreat and quasi-apology to the students on December 4.

4. Novotny's irascible denunciation of critical Slovak Communists as "bourgeois nationalists" at the Central Committee Plenum of October 31. Such a charge could not but evoke ominous memories of the bloody purges of the early 1950s, for which Novotny shared personal responsibility. It elicited the prompt solidarity of conservative, moderate, and liberal Slovak Communists.

It was thus manifest by the end of 1967 that no substantial economic recovery could be expected without radical political reforms, and that such reforms could not be secured without the ouster of the increasingly spasmodic Novotny from the first secretaryship of the Communist party of Czechoslovakia (CPCS). Formally, this took the form of a proposal to separate the offices of party first secretary and state president—Novotny being the incumbent of both.

Novotny sought to avert his fate with a preemptive military coup, accompanied by the preparation of mass arrest-lists, in December or January. But the egregious police violence of October against the students had alerted his enemies, and the military agents on whom he relied proved to be weak reeds. The plot unraveled. The hard-line Soviet ambassador Chervonenko endorsed a plea by Novotny that he be saved through Soviet political intervention. Brezhnev duly came to Prague but, reconnoitering the situation, quickly decided not to hitch his prestige to a falling star and confined his intervention to a demand that any leadership changes be arranged without scandal or recriminations so as not to rock the party's public boat. In any event, the current crop of Soviet leaders—and Brezhnev in particular—had little reason to be tender to Novotny, who had criticized their ouster of Khrushchev in 1964 and, by implication, Brezhnev's succession to Khrushchev's post. It might also be argued that these Soviet leaders had inadvertently undermined Novotny by prohibiting his acceptance of massive and rapid West German economic assistance, by committing him to the unpopular pro-Arab stance, and by conducting witchhunts of liberal Soviet intellectuals. On January 5, the CPCS Central Committee, in almost continuous session since mid-December, finally replaced Novotny with Dubcek as first secretary after a stalemate had developed between the competing candidacies of Josef Lenart (conservative) and Oldrich Cernik (moderate). Dubcek, at 46 the youngest man and the first Slovak to lead the party (Gustav Husak is the second), thus emerged as the least divisive common denominator. Having lived for 13 years of his youth in the USSR (1925–1938) and spent another three (1955–1958) as an adult student at the Soviet Communist party's Academy of Social Sciences in Moscow, which graduated him with honors, Dubcek was eminently persona grata to the Soviet leaders. Ignoring Ulbricht's and Gomulka's cool responses to the leadership change in Prague, Brezhnev and other Soviet leaders (and Romania's Ceausescu) were cordial to Dubcek's succession.

In addition to Soviet benevolence, Dubcek's other initial assets were his record as protector of critical Slovak intellectuals against Novotny's malevolence during his term as leader of the Slovak subsection of the CPCS (1963–1968) and his freedom from moral taint for the purges of the early 1950s. Pledging loyalty to Marxism-Leninism and to the Soviet Union, Dubcek simultaneously made clear his commitment to reform and renovation through debate and criticism. In a New Year's message issued a few days before his elevation, he had warned:

The Party does not live outside or above society, but is an integral part of it. . . . We must resist attempts to assert the Party's influence by means which society will necessarily regard as authoritarian or forcible.

And upon returning early in February 1968 from his initial visit as first secretary to Moscow—where his reception had been warm—he again mused:

Real democracy anticipates discipline, and loyal discipline is proportional to the amount of democracy in the decision-making process. So in this sense, there will never be enough democracy.

Finally, at the end of March, in an interview with the Italian Communist paper *L'Unita,* he philosophized:

The leading role of the Party is not given once and for all. It must go on being renewed. The Party must continually keep winning the trust and support of public opinion.[1]

Strange rhetoric, indeed, from a veteran Communist.

Dubcek soon staked his leadership on a balanced and difficult triangular policy:

1. Renovate the economic structure and enliven the political order of the country through the Communist party's own initiative (the famous "Action Program").
2. Contain the resulting effervescence from spilling over the "post-Hungary" perimeter of permissibility.
3. Obtain public confidence in the reality of the coming reforms by institutionalizing them beyond reversal, including the emancipation of state and economic institutions from smothering party supervision.

The lever of this policy would be disciplined but massive participation in free discussion. This would elicit the public's confidence while simultaneously isolating the conservatives, whose most discredited representatives were soon driven to apologies for their dark deeds of the 1950s and to recriminations against each other. Though Dubcek himself always professed his commitment to Marxism-Leninism, to the

---

[1] The first two quotations are from Deryck Viney, "Alexander Dubcek," *Studies in Comparative Communism,* I, 1–2 (July–October 1968), 27–28. The third quotation is from Vera Blackwell, "Czechoslovakia at the Crossroads," *Survey,* 68 (July 1968), 75.

"leading role" of the party (which had, however, to be earned), and to Czechoslovakia's intrabloc obligations, the general debate that he licensed soon enveloped many doctrinal sacred cows and political shibboleths in a cloud of skepticism and criticism. One after another public institutions and governmental agencies—even the Defense and Interior Ministries—fell to the control of liberals. Officials mixed with the people and made themselves available for authentic interviews and probing discussions. Interest-group politics burgeoned as the "transmission-belt" tradition of darker years distintegrated. By the end of February 1968 censorship had tacitly been abandoned. (It was formally abolished in June.) Given the intrabloc circulation of newspapers and multilingual broadcasting, the abolition of censorship in one Communist country erodes it in all. But nothing in the content of the Czechoslovak press or in the euphoric behavior of the society was as yet substantively or formally directed against the Communist party as such. Hence, despite the alarmed urgings of their East German and Polish clients, the Soviet leaders for long remained remarkably patient with the Czechoslovak experiment in responsive democratization. The March 30 election of General Ludvik Svoboda, who had fought on the Russian side in two world wars, as president to succeed the discredited Novotny was quite satisfactory to Moscow. Even the CPCS's famous "Action Program" of early April, with its ambiguous affirmation of the party's leading role linked to a repudiation of monoplistic *apparat* rule and toleration of an independent political line for the trade unions and other constituents of the National Front, and its commitment to socialist legality, was initially treated in the Soviet press as an imperfect but tolerable program for the Czechoslovak party's self-renewal. Having earlier placed their confidence in the now increasingly popular Dubcek as a pragmatic man of the middle, the Soviet leaders were long reluctant to withdraw it and face the resulting polarization. Indeed, their eventual decision to destroy him is less surprising than their extended patience with him.

Not until the end of April—a full month after East Germany and Poland had launched a full hue and cry against the Czechoslovak developments—were the first Soviet reservations expressed. But even now they still took the form of concern lest the well-intentioned Dubcek become the captive of "anti-party elements." At the same meeting of the Soviet Central Committee at which Brezhnev is said to have expressed this anxiety, General Alexander Yepishev, chief of the Soviet armed forces' Main Political Directorate, is alleged to have emphasized the Soviet army's readiness to come to the aid of "real" and "faithful"

Communists (that is, against "revisionists") in Czechoslovakia (*Le Monde,* May 6, 1968; Yepishev denied the story on May 17). Moscow was perhaps disturbed more by the manner than by the substance of a recent shakeup of the CPCS Central Committee, which not only had reduced the conservatives to half the membership (still substantial) but had done so *in public*—an implied concession to pressure from below suggesting that the people, rather than the party, were sovereign.

The Kremlin, of course, was also sensitive to the increasingly shrill cries from its East German and Polish clients that the Czechoslovak abscess was dangerously contagious to their own societies—witness the Polish student riots—and must be lanced. In each of these two states an aging leader, a factious elite, and an unpopular regime composed a situation where either the risk of subversive contagion from Czechoslovakia was genuine or the very allegation to that effect could serve as a convenient device to stifle local discussion and hamper movement. Finally, the long string of international defeats which the Soviet leaders had suffered during the decade—Cuban missile crisis, anti-Communist victories in the Congo, Ghana, and Indonesia, Sino-Soviet rift, Albanian and Romanian defections, Six-Day War—now made it relatively easy to arouse their political "paranoia" over the Czechoslovak effervescence and the West German *Ostpolitik.*

A series of intrabloc conferences and bilateral exchanges of visits ensued, in the course of which the Soviet stance toward Czechoslovakia oscillated nervously between pressure and understanding. Indeed, this Soviet irresolution may well have led the Czechoslovak leaders to misjudge how far they might ultimately go. Interestingly enough, the bouts of Soviet pressure tended to be either political (editorial and oratorical warnings) or military (maneuvers and troop movements), but not economic—presumably to avoid pushing Prague even more rapidly toward Bonn.

While the very convolutedness of Soviet policy may have deluded Dubcek into miscalculating his freedom of maneuver, the fact that it did entail periodic (and gradually escalating) pressure served to arouse Czechoslovak public opinion into applying its own counterpressures on him to demonstrate ever more vividly his patriotic and democratic commitments. By the high summer, Dubcek was trapped in a tightening vise where each reassurance given by him to one side only increased the misgivings of the other. On specific points of fact, of course, Dubcek was always able to demonstrate to his Soviet interlocutors that Czechoslovakia was doing nothing that either was not being done by another bloc country or could not somehow be subsumed by the canons of

Marxist-Leninist orthodoxy. But such logical and rhetorical adroitness carried diminishing conviction with the Soviet leaders, who were increasingly fearful of the spontaneous style of the Czechoslovak development and apprehensive lest all their other regional dominos be toppled. Czechoslovakia was, after all, their most western, industrialized, and strategic domino—the only one sharing borders with both Germanies as well as the USSR.

In justice to Dubcek, it must be stated that so far as is known publicly, at no time during these contorted maneuverings in a narrowing arena did he betray his people's trust.

Soviet Assessments Harden

Why did the Soviet leaders finally steel themselves to the invasion of August 20–21 after prevaricating for so long? And how did external and domestic factors interact to account for both that earlier prevarication and the ultimate invasion?

Precisely as a result of those interlocking overreactions, to which I have referred, on the part of neighboring leaders and the Czechoslovak public, the pace of developments accelerated during the last two months before the invasion. The Soviet leaders appear to have taken their first severe alarm over the "Two Thousand Words" statement issued by a number of Czechoslovak intellectuals on June 27. Immediately disavowed by Dubcek, it rapidly acquired general popularity. A stinging indictment of two decades of party dictatorship, a ringing demand for accelerated democratization—to be enforced, if need be, through strikes, boycotts, and demonstrations—this statement juxtaposed its endorsement of the Dubcek regime with stern insistence that all external pressures be resisted, if necessary with arms. Moscow denounced it as clearly counterrevolutionary and delayed the withdrawal from Czechoslovakia of Soviet troops who had recently participated in Warsaw Pact maneuvers there—maneuvers which, resented as a form of pressure, had themselves provoked the publication of the "Two Thousand Words." Undoubtedly compounding the Kremlin's anxiety was the disappointing failure of the supposedly untainted Czechoslovak proletariat to "unmask" these "dirty intrigues" of the intellectuals or to resist the liberalization program in general. On July 3 Brezhnev warned, "We cannot remain indifferent to the fate of socialism in a neighboring country," and by July 11, *Pravda* was ominously comparing the current situation in Czechoslovakia with that of Hungary in the autumn of 1956. A week later it was publishing sinister canards about West German arms caches in Bohemia (which were, in fact, a "planted" provocation).

The Dubcek government declined, on July 9, to attend a general Warsaw Pact conference to discuss the situation in its country. All the other Pact members except Romania nevertheless met on July 14–15 in Warsaw, where they formally announced their "deep disturbance" over Czechoslovak developments and put forward a severely worded bill of indictment: the censorship must be reimposed, the intellectuals curbed, West Germany rebuffed, and liberal trends reversed. Prague's July 18 rebuttal of this ultimatum was dignified and firm, and—surprisingly—elicited one more Soviet invitation to bilateral talks. The Kremlin's collective leadership was having manifest difficulties in collectively bracing itself to cross its rubicon.

Nevertheless, Dubcek was scarcely back on square one, for a number of other frictions had further tightened the pressures on him, and even his now vastly enhanced popularity ironically served to entrap him. A Communist leader who can reply on television to the Warsaw Ultimatum with the candid observation, "In the past the masses were not satisfied with the Party's policies; obviously the Party cannot replace the masses; so it must change the policies,"[2] offers himself as hostage to the expectations of these masses while simultaneously signaling the other side that he does not truly appreciate the Leninist evaluation of control over spontaneity.

Next, Dubcek's dexterous but ambiguous handling of the Prchlik affair probably troubled Moscow. Responding to multiple Soviet deceptions and evasions connected with the recent Warsaw Pact maneuvers on Czechoslovak soil, Lieutenant-General Vaclav Prchlik, chief of the CPCS's State Administrative Department, on July 15 publicly advocated that the pact's command structure be revised so as to give greater weight to its non-Soviet partners. Moscow took offense, and on July 25 Dubcek duly transferred the errant general but simultaneously used the occasion to eliminate his entire bureau—the party's traditional watchdog over the armed forces. In Leninist terms, this was surely organizational heresy.

Very serious, too, and perhaps ultimately decisive was the Kremlin's concern with the spillover of Czechoslovak effervescence into the Soviet Ukraine, where uncensored Ukrainian-language broadcasts emanating from Slovakia appear to have proven subversively stimulating. The threatened "boss" of the Soviet Ukraine, Pyotr Shelest, eventually

2 Quotation from Viney, "Alexander Dubcek," p. 34.

emerged as perhaps the most insistent Kremlin advocate of ruthless intervention in Czechoslovakia. Soviet intellectuals in general were also intrigued by the Prague experiments. Thus, Ulbricht's and Gomulka's early cries of alarm notwithstanding, the Czechoslovak "disease" may have been more contagious eastward than northward.

This increasingly fast-paced sequence of crises culminated in the bilateral discussions at Cierna-nad-Tisou in eastern Slovakia on July 29–August 1; they were held to the accompaniment of massive Soviet maneuvers in the neighboring western Ukraine. Superficially, Cierna marked another defensive success for the Czechoslovaks, who had refused to attend a multilateral Warsaw Pact conference or to leave their country for a Soviet city. But by now both sides were the prisoners of their respective constituencies. Czechoslovak public opinion prohibited Dubcek's offering any serious public concessions while the Soviet Communist party's *apparatchiki* were taking an increasingly stern view of their leaders' hesitations. Hence, the resulting agreement had to be extremely vague—which meant, in fact, that its political interpretation promptly slipped from Dubcek's hands into those of his own public and of the Soviet *apparat*.

Nevertheless, the Soviet decision to go to Cierna and grant Dubcek one last reprieve, instead of invading immediately on the heels of their Warsaw Ultimatum of mid-July, remains something of a mystery. It was unprecedented for 13 (out of 15) members of the Politburo to leave the territory of the Soviet Union in the midst of such a deep crisis. Presumably Brezhnev, who had blithely allowed the Pandora's box to be opened with Novotny's ouster early in January, and Kosygin, who had vainly sought to play an ameliorative role while vacationing in Czechoslovakia in mid-May, could no longer be trusted to handle the Czechoslovaks alone. Presumably, too, the Soviets hoped that the conservatives in the Czechoslovak party Presidium—still about half its membership—might yet recover control. That this was not an idle fancy is indirectly confirmed from the other side by the eve-of-Cierna warning by Dubcek's ally Smrkovsky that "the nation and the Party will sit in judgment" on any Czechoslovak waverers at Cierna.[3] The Soviet ambassador to Prague, Chervonenko, is also alleged to have exaggerated the strength of the conservatives in his reports. Beyond these and other tactical explanations, however, stands the more intrigu-

---

[3] Quotation from Fritz Ermarth, *Internationalism, Security and Legitimacy: The Challenge to Soviet Interests in East Europe, 1964–1968*, RAND Memorandum RM–5909–PR (March 1969), p. 95.

ing possibility that the Soviet leadership was at the time gripped by a serious crisis of confidence, self-confidence, and general authority, of which indecision over Czechoslovakia was but the most acute external expression.

The likelihood of such an internal Soviet crisis is supported by certain discrepancies in the invasion when it finally came on August 20–21. Contrast, for example, its professional military competence with its inept political improvisations. Contrast further the false *Pravda* and *Izvestia* reports, to the effect that the invading armies were happily welcomed, with the valid concessions in *Trud* (close to the KGB) that they met with universal hostility. Note, finally, the inconsistent treatment of Dubcek during and after the invasion. Indeed, grounds exist for suspecting that attacks on Dubcek by some Soviet organs were actually screened attacks on Kosygin, a would-be reformer in his own context. The internal Soviet crisis may have had vertical as well as horizontal dimensions. In other words, the lines of disagreement possibly ran not only *within* the Politburo but also *between* it and subordinate institutions such as the Central Committee, the *apparat* at large, and the the military establishment. On the basis of this hypothesis, the final decision to invade was largely forced by these lower bodies and hence tantamount to a kind of constitutional upheaval in a nonconstitutional political system.

Some doubt is thrown on this hypothesis by the absence of any subsequent personnel shakeup within the supposedly humbled Politburo. (It should, however, be remembered that two full years elapsed after his Cuban missile fiasco before Khrushchev's head rolled.) Alternatively and more simply, the Politburo's own consensual judgment of the Czechoslovak situation may finally have hardened during the first half of August. In this latter scenario, the Czechoslovaks perhaps tipped the Kremlin scales against themselves by staging such ostentatious welcomes to Tito and Ceausescu on August 9 and 15 and —even more fatally—by publishing, on August 10, a draft of the new party statutes to be formalized at their party congress scheduled for September 9. Under the terms of these statutes, all party officials would thereafter be elected by secret ballot for limited terms of office and—a quite devastating revision of Leninist orthodoxy—minority views might henceforth be recorded, defended, maintained, and proposed for reassessment within the party, even after formal votes, without fear of penalties. Hereafter the Soviet leadership could conclusively persuade itself that it had a legitimate ideological warrant to invade a Communist neighbor so blatantly slipping into apostasy—a conviction neatly complemented by the expectation that the invasion would catalyze a rising of the orthodox faithful against the false prophets of liberalization in this about-to-be redeemed neighbor country.

An Interim Balance Sheet

Having done their best to prod Soviet leaders toward the invasion decision, Gomulka and Ulbricht were now appropriately summoned to share responsibility for its execution—but so were Hungary's Kadar, who had hoped to avert it, and Bulgaria's Zhivkov, who had all along simply tacked with the Moscow wind. The largest military operation launched in Europe since the close of World War II, the invasion also marked the third occasion since 1945 on which the Soviet army went into action—each time against "fraternal" workers, never yet against "imperialist" enemies: East Berlin (1953), Budapest (1956), Prague (1968). On Czechoslovak soil, the invaders were met with—and initially rather demoralized by—massive nonviolent civil resistance and unprecedented national solidarity spanning all ethnic and class categories. Over time, however, the sheer weight of Soviet power has prevailed despite its blundering application, and in the long run, it is—alas—quite possible that the Czechoslovak masses may genuinely repudiate the liberalizers of 1968 who "got us into this mess." So far, however, these masses have kept the faith and only acquiesced in, but not morally accepted, their current fate.

Similar chronological considerations complicate the task of calculating the Soviet leaders' costs and gains. Immediately after the invasion, their costs appeared prohibitive; two years later the balance would seem to have shifted toward a net gain; but they may yet incur long-run costs still hidden from view. Hence, the following tabulation is inevitably an interim one.

GAINS

1. A political experiment perceived in Moscow as ideologically dangerous and potentially contagious has been halted.

2. The Soviet Union's power-credibility in its own area of hegemony has been vividly reasserted.

3. The errant Romanian leaders were somewhat intimidated and the self-important Yugoslavs deflated.

4. The West German *Ostpolitiker* and the American bridge-builders were knocked off balance, and west European confidence in Washington's political wisdom and dexterity was shaken.

5. The reliable Ulbricht and Gomulka were braced.

6. NATO's notion of "political warning time" preparatory to military action has been punctured by the sequence (1) Cierna (2) invasion.

7. The Kremlin's reputation for unpredictability has been enhanced —a useful bargaining asset tactically (but compare with cost 14, below).

8. And all this has been achieved *without* (1) provoking a Hungary-like upheaval in Czechoslovakia or dangerous unrest in her neighbors, (2) rupturing America's continued interest in détente with the Soviet Union, or (3) triggering any impressive reconsolidation of NATO.

COSTS

1. The traditionally (but no longer) Russophile population of a strategically and economically important Soviet client has been alienated, its 14-division army demoralized, its Communist party disoriented, its economy crippled.

2. The Czechoslovak industrial proletariat, far from allowing itself to be "played off" against the critical intelligentsia, has been politicized into solidarity with it and opposition to the Soviet occupation. Work slowdowns and "inspired" lowering of productivity have become pervasive.

3. A 30-year-old Czechoslovak assumption, dating from the Munich calamity, to the effect that national independence is linked to alliance with the USSR, has been shattered.

4. The residual hopes of their east-central European dependents that Soviet leaders might permit the transformation of the "socialist community" into a genuine partnership have been blighted and now yield to general fatigue. The ideologically bankrupt "Brezhnev Doctrine," with its implication that the smaller Communist states are less sovereign than non-Communist ones, is acutely embarrassing to the regimes of the non-Soviet members of the Warsaw Pact.

5. The disarray into which the world Communist movement outside eastern Europe has been thrown is even more severe than that which arose over the Hitler-Stalin Pact of 1939 or the suppression of Hungary in 1956. The ideologically sophisticated west European Communist parties, in particular, who had recently invested much energy in a major effort to project an image of a more democratic and responsive Communism among their respective national publics, have been profoundly offended and are no longer automatically available to endorse Soviet policy vis-à-vis China—whose dignity and respect have been enhanced at Soviet expense.

6. In consequence, an unhealthy and possibly dangerous encirclement psychosis, analogous to the pre-1914 German one, is seizing the
Russian public. Not only are the Americans, West Germans, and
Chinese feared as dangerous—and even as colluding with each other
against the Soviet Union—but the east-central Europeans have again
shown themselves unreliable and even some of the non-Russian peoples
of the USSR—the Balts, Caucasians, Jews, Moslems, Ukrainians, etc.—
are now suspect. History suggests that such anxiety is readily transmut-
able both into truculent chauvinism and into bitter revulsion against
leaders whose political ineptness has "saddled us with enemies" on so
many fronts.

7. Yugoslav (and Albanian) Adriatic ports will not be available to
the Soviet Mediterranean fleet for bunkering and shore leaves; the
fleet has to rely exclusively on home (Black Sea) and Arab facilities.

8. The Soviet army will be obliged to extend itself to compensate
for the near-neutralization of the Czechoslovak and Romanian armies
and the apparent demoralization of the Hungarian one.

9. The Soviet military elite, comparing its own reasonably capable
performance in Czechoslovakia with the political leadership's deficient
fumblings, concludes that it alone is a competent protector of Russia's
power and interests. Marshals Grechko and Yakubovsky now operate in
east-central Europe like virtually autonomous satraps.

10. The repudiation of a genuine effort at building "socialism in one
country"—but a country other than the USSR—has exposed the post-
revolutionary ossification of the USSR's political system, its incapacity
to comprehend or handle nationalism, liberalism, modernism, democratization, or social development in general and "Marxist humanism"
in particular.

11. None of the underlying problems that prompted the Czechoslovak developments have been solved by the invasion. Indeed, their
solution has thereby been postponed and possibly foreclosed. The
Soviet leaders have advanced no feasible long-range policy solutions
other than the traumatic but barren application of force.

12. Reforms, including economic and technological reforms, are a
blocwide casualty of the invasion—and yet remain an urgent necessity.
In the words of a Polish proverb, "pears do not grow on willow trees."

13. It is problematical whether the Soviets have helped themselves
in the long run by encouraging "social-fascist" ruling types in Poland
and East Germany at the expense of liberal-humanists in Czechoslovakia.

14. All in all, by assaulting a Communist neighbor who had scru-

pulously observed every known requirement of international legality
and all formal intrabloc perimeters of permissibility, the Soviet leaders
seriously damaged their erstwhile reputation—fairly widespread in the
West as well as in the third world—for reasonableness and composure.
Strategically, they may have struck a poor bargain in exchanging that
image for one of unpredictability and irascibility. Nor will the non-
Communist world show much sympathy for their protest—albeit valid
—that Alexander Dubcek's adroit manipulation of the bloc's internal
taboos was just as dangerous as Imre Nagy's explicit violations had
been in 1956.

15. The invasion imposed a—possibly fatal—postponement of fif-
teen months upon the crucial SALT (Strategic Arms Limitation Talks)
negotiations between the USA and the USSR. Should it eventually
prove to be the case that this delay, with the intervening development
of American MIRV capability, has rendered unavoidable another
round in the arms race, the Soviets may well find their invasion of
Czechoslovakia to have been extremely costly.

Between January and August 1968 Soviet policies toward Czechoslovakia had run the gamut of all politically possible options—hopeful
abstention for the first four months of the year, cajoling pressure over
the next three, ultimate intervention in the eighth. Critical Czechoslovaks, in turn, are reluctant to concede that their country's own
decisions and stances played any role at all in prompting these several
Soviet shifts. They tend, rather, to believe that internal Soviet frustrations and the backlash from earlier diplomatic defeats worked themselves out over an epiphenomenal Czechoslovak scapegoat. This
interpretation is, of course, half true—but only that. Czechoslovakia
in 1968 did present the post-Khrushchev Soviet leadership with its most
searing test yet, and the manner in which it met that test was certainly
conditioned not only by several recent international reverses but also
by the kind of domestic system over which that leadership presides
and of which it is a product. In turn, the Soviet response to the Czechoslovak test both answers and begs a number of questions about the
current Kremlin leadership. For one thing, its rationale that intervention was rendered necessary by a "silent counterrevolution" in Czechoslovakia is operationally too vague to serve as a new, knowable
perimeter of permissibility and hence is itself conducive to future difficulties. Since, after all, virtually any political development can be
interpreted as silent counterrevolution, the content of the Soviet Union's

relations with its east-central European regional clients and the scope of its eventual détente with the United States have been rendered gratuitously uncertain by this particular justification of the invasion. In that sense, the invasion has changed rather than restored an earlier status quo and mystified rather than clarified others' perceptions of Soviet policy.

A corollary problem concerns the role of the Warsaw Pact in Soviet relations with east-central Europe. On one hand, the pact's main function is clearly to serve as Moscow's chief tool for policing its clients (despite Article VIII, which guarantees mutual noninterference in the members' internal affairs). On the other hand, the pact is manifestly an inadequate device for ensuring ongoing stability in these relations between the hegemonial power and its clients, or even among the several clients—witness the Czechoslovak-East German-Polish imbroglio of 1968. Finally, the pact's recent enforcement upon Czechoslovakia provoked the nemesis of disciplined massive civilian resistance with which the pact is evidently unable to cope, and whose initial spontaneous appearance discomfited and scared the Soviet rulers. What if this mode of resistance were to be perfected and repeated in this or another client state?

It can, on the other hand, be argued that the sequential Soviet armed interventions in East Germany (1953), Hungary (1956), and Czechoslovakia (1968) demonstrate the futility of clients' challenging this particular hegemonial power and suggest that the only revolution that conceivably could succeed against it would necessarily have to be one internal to the Soviet Union, though not necessarily a violent one. While conceding that such a contingency may indeed appear remote and unlikely, we must nevertheless note that the Kremlin's invasion of Czechoslovakia provoked widespread dismay within the Soviet intelligentsia—both scientific and literary—and exposed the rulers as conservative, defensive, and—most devastating—unsure and unskilled political men. They lack Lenin's insights into the dialectics of revolution, Stalin's commitment to dynamic social change, and Khrushchev's readiness to risk institutional experiments. Too young to have shared in the exhilaration of the civil-war era and too old to be able to deny complicity in the Great Terror, these stagnant, conformist bureaucrats personify a systemic commitment to the status quo, a fear of transforming reality. Under their leadership, the Soviet Union rapidly approaches the conditions identified by Marx as those of a prerevolutionary situation: a congealed political superstructure fetters a developing technical-economic substructure. The Actual impedes the Potential.

Some questions are still open:

1. Should Czechoslovakia have offered armed resistance to the invasion? Given her distinctly nonmilitant, "Schweikian" political behavior before, during, and after World War II, would an anticipatory *threat* to resist have conveyed conviction and credibility? Might actual resistance have elicited new factors—for instance, a regime upheaval in Moscow? Would the Russians have desisted or simply been confirmed in their suspicion that fascism had seized power in Czechoslovakia? Would military resistance supplementing the civilian resistance have brought the Czechoslovaks even greater and more lasting moral solidarity and pride at the price of immediate physical and biological injury? Per contra, will the failure to fight entail the eventual cracking of national morale and descent into the morass of casual collaboration and pervasive mistrust?

2. Would more US governmental interest in Czechoslovakia before the invasion have had a cautioning or an aggravating effect on the Soviet leaders? Can the international circumstances surrounding the invasion be interpreted as a Soviet signal of willingness to liquidate its interest in some revolutionary movements of the third world—for example, in Latin America—in return for American acquiescence in Soviet regional hegemony in east-central Europe? Will the aftermath of the invasion bring a secular erosion of west European confidence in America, initially in the form of a separate West German accommodation with the Soviet Union and ultimately of a *sauve qui peut* disintegration of NATO? Or will the West be jolted into modernizing its European structures and policies? Can the United States pursue its dialogue *à deux* with the Soviet Union over Vietnam, the Middle East, arms control, and the like, without further provoking the desertion worries of its allies?

3. Will "Prague" prompt Washington and Peking into some tacit understanding of a mutual interest in containing Soviet hegemonial urges? Or will the desired détente with Moscow retain American priority? In the pursuit of such a détente ought the United States to show silent "understanding" over the invasion of Czechoslovakia—and thereby risk encouraging the Soviet hawks in their apparent impression that they can "get away with" any adventure? Or should the United States somehow "punish" the perpetrators of the invasion—but thus risk clipping the Kremlin doves (if any) and grounding the very idea of the détente? Indeed, what really are the proper inferences to be

drawn from the invasion of Czechoslovakia for the strategy of seeking détente?

Since the days of their martyred fifteenth-century hero Jan Hus, the Czechs have taken as their national motto his assurance that "the truth prevails." In the light of their fate in 1968, one may well wonder whether this aphorism, intended as a beacon of hope, is not also an unhistorical myth.

Chapter 5

Conflicts Muted by Hegemony

France and Germany

ROY C. MACRIDIS

From the French revolution to World War II, the
Franco-German rivalry has dominated European and
world politics.[1] The two most devastating wars of
our century were triggered by this rivalry and left bitter
memories and resentments in their wake. At the end
of World War II, the demands of French
foreign-policy-makers were more punitive than
those made in what the Germans had called the
Diktat of Versailles. They now asked for the division
of Germany and its prolonged occupation, for the
eventual "decentralization" of the Reich, for the
economic and political annexation of the Saar, for the
"internationalization" of the Ruhr, and for heavy
reparations in the form of the transfer of capital goods
from Germany and even in the form of requisitions
from current production. On the diplomatic front
and in the best tradition of French diplomacy, an
elaborate network of treaties was erected aimed at the
defeated and occupied country—the Franco-Soviet
Treaty (1944), the Dunkirk Treaty (1947) with
England, and the Brussels Treaty (1948) forming the
Western European Union. As late as 1954, the debate
in the French National Assembly over the ratification of
the European Defense Community provided an
opportunity for the expression of strong nationalist and
anti-German themes driving home one of the cardinal
reasons for which the treaty was finally rejected
by the French—their opposition to the creation of a
German army and the fear that Germany might again
assume a dominant role in Europe.

---

[1] Good background material appears in relevant sections of
The New Cambridge Modern History, vol. 12, *The Era of
Violence, 1898–1945* (Cambridge: Cambridge University Press,
1964).

It is premature to say that this long rivalry has come to an end. This chapter will discuss some of the underlying factors that have muted it and some that may cause it to be transformed or even to flare up again. It is difficult, however, to do more than speculate. French foreign policy and the direction it imparted to Franco-German relations have been stated clearly, eloquently, and independently by French leaders and notably by de Gaulle.[2] As yet, however, there has been no free and unfettered formulation of the foreign policy of the German Federal Republic—or for that matter of the German People's Republic. The authoritative and independent voice of either part of Germany has yet to be heard. The reasons are quite obvious. The need for protection, given the proximity of Soviet forces to the Federal Republic, the status of Berlin, and, until very recently, the unwavering commitment to the reunification of Germany mortgaged the foreign policy of the Federal Republic to the West and to the United States as the only power that could provide protection, preserve the Berlin status quo, and, hopefully, force reunification. This objective situation alone accounted for the subordination of the Federal Republic to its Western allies and, above all, to its American partner. And it is only now that changing conditions permit the two Germanies, and more particularly the Federal Republic, with which this chapter is concerned, to exercise a certain freedom of expression and independence of action that will reveal answers to many questions, including that of the future of Franco-German relations.

The End of Rivalry?

For a number of reasons the rivalry between France and the German Federal Republic appears to have muted and transformed gradually into close, cooperative relations that exclude military confrontation. Some of these reasons stem from the particular situation in which the two countries found themselves right after the end of World War II. Others relate to the predicament of the whole of Europe as it was fashioned at Yalta and Potsdam—notably Russian control over eastern Europe, particularly East Germany, and the division of Europe into two blocs. Yet other reasons—the most significant ones, I shall argue—relate to the drastic transformation of the balance of forces in the world. World War II left both countries diminished in power and status. Reviewing the aspirations of France to play a role in the postwar

[2] Most of the citations from de Gaulle come from Roy Macridis (ed.), *De Gaulle: Implacable Ally* (New York: Harper & Row, 1966), where the reader will find de Gaulle's major speeches with introductory comments.

settlement in a manner that might restore the status quo ante, even de Gaulle had to admit that the sword of France was blunted. As developments were quickly to show, the sword was also borrowed. For the first time in Europe's history, the settlement of European affairs eluded France. Talleyrand had more to offer at the Congress of Vienna than de Gaulle could have produced at Yalta and Potsdam. At the same time, the only concern of the German populations—east and west—was survival. Until 1949 the overwhelming consideration of German leaders was to avert the destruction of their people and, once this had been accomplished, to seek some degree of internal autonomy and self-government upon terms that the victors were willing to grant. The western zone—representing some 65 percent of the German population and containing its highly industrialized sector—developed its own political institutions and gained internal sovereignty in 1949, but only after the cold war had brought it and the whole of western Europe under the military protection of the United States and only after massive American aid began to lay the foundation sfor economic recovery. Only after 1955, when West Germany became a part of NATO and began to build its own conventional army, did it assume a certain degree of independence. But the composition of its forces and their overall deployment and strategy were tailored to American designs and strategic goals. The French were not in an appreciably different position. Their economy began to recover only after massive American aid was made available to them, and their efforts to maintain their colonial possessions taxed their political system and wasted their resources. They too came within NATO, and despite their desperate efforts to develop independence, they too had to use the same fabric in fashioning their strategy and security. Rivalry between France and West Germany would have further weakened both countries. Cooperation was the condition for the maintenance of the little power each of them had; it was also a prerequisite for the potential increase of the power of both. The situation required that the rivalry which existed in the feelings and memories of these two peoples be deferred, muted, eradicated.

Cooperation began in earnest with the organization for European Economic Cooperation (1948) and with the Schuman plan that brought coal and steel production and trading of the Six under a European body. Whatever the loopholes in the Coal and Steel Treaty, and however restricted the supranational power of its authority, the accent was on cooperation. In May 1950 the French foreign minister, Robert Schuman, declared, "The union of European states imposes the elimination of the secular rivalry of France and Germany. . . ." Referring to the Coal and Steel Community, he added, "The intimate link in production thus formed between the two would be open proof that any Franco-German war has become not only inconceivable but a material impossibility."[3] Four years later, despite the agonizing soul-searching of the French and their rejection of the European Defense Community, West Germany became a member of NATO. In 1956 the deliberations that were to lead to the formation of the European Economic Community began; the ensuing treaties were prepared and ratified rapidly; and one of the most successful experiments in our times was launched on January 1, 1959. Again, despite many criticisms and despite the waning spirit of Europeanism and the lack of supranational powers in the hands of the Commission, cooperation between Germany and France became the rule. In order to maintain the Community, each side was forced to make difficult political and economic decisions with regard to many of its national constituencies—especially agricultural interests. The gradual recovery of the French economy, coupled with the beginnings of decolonization in Africa—and ultimately the withdrawal from Algeria—together with remarkable recovery of the economy of West Germany seemed to support the thesis of those who saw cooperation as the only possible way for the two nations to recover and for a modicum of power to be restored to each.

The situation of western Europe as a whole reinforced the need for cooperation. With or without outside support, the survival of each and all political communities depended upon the suspension of old rivalries and the fashioning of cooperative arrangements. In the development of atomic energy, in the growth of economic cooperation through the OEEC and the Schuman plan, in the gradual elimination of tariffs, in the progressive erosion of national frontiers the accent was on desirability of cooperation if the European states were to have a chance of resisting the colossus of the East. The fact that the United States gave protection and provided economic support was a powerful contributing factor, though some have claimed that it lessened the incentive of the European nations to integrate their military resources in order to assume responsibility for their own defense.

But the end of Franco-German rivalry stemmed above all from the new distribution of power in the world. Even if there had been no cold war, even if there had been no division of Germany and no internal difficulties in France, even if NATO and the Warsaw Pact had not come into being, simple power considerations would have compelled French and German leaders to put an end to their secular rivalry. To put the matter very simply, the overwhelming concentration of power had shifted, perhaps irreversibly, from Germany and France to the

[3] *Année Politique* (Paris: Presses Universitaires de France, 1950), pp. 102–103.

United States and the Soviet Union. By no conceivable stretch of the imagination could the continuation of the rivalry between Germany and France add an iota of power to one or the other. Even if we were to think of the unthinkable—a war between the two—a victory of one over the other in the classic sense of the term would not have appreciably increased the power of the victor. To speculate about a Franco-German war in the 1950s or 1960s is just as boring as it would have been to contemplate a war between Sparta and Athens under the Roman Empire. Under only one hypothesis could Franco-German rivalry have emerged—the attachment of each to one of the two antagonistic centers of power. But both France and Germany had strong reasons to resist such an outcome for fear that it would lead to their total subordination.

This, of course, did not come to pass. The divergences between the two superpowers and the fact that West Germany and France were, for a number of reasons, parts of the American power complex made rivalry between the two extremely unlikely. Cooperation was necessary in order to profit from American support and aid, in order to continue to receive protection, in order to develop some modicum of power that might enhance their respective positions vis-à-vis the United States, and finally, in order to lay the foundations for a future independent position.

Thus the internal condition in the two countries, coupled with the situation of post-World War II Europe and the distribution of power on a worldwide basis, accounted for the muting of the Franco-German rivalry. The Germans and the French were forced in to the same power bloc—something that had never happened before. As long as American power and leadership promoted the common interests of West Germany and France, and as long as Russia appeared as a menace, renewed Franco-German rivalry was impossible and their cooperation necessary. Only in a situation in which dependence on America failed to maximize the interests of the two and the Soviet threat diminished could a certain freedom emerge for the two countries to reexamine the conditions of their cooperation, even at the risk of renewing submerged rivalries.

The Divergence of Motives

Until roughly 1961, the emphasis was on cooperation under American leadership within NATO and within the various organizations of western Europe. The requirements of common defense, the prospects of attaining a certain degree of autonomy within the American complex, and the possibility of being able in the future to qualify American hegemony all called for cooperation. The first signs of Franco-German rivalry appeared when General de Gaulle outlined his project for intimate Franco-German cooperation in 1962–1963 in order to reduce America's influence. In other words, dissension arose over questions of the extent, intensity, and purpose of cooperation!

For a given period of time, objective conditions often determine a course of action and force a choice in foreign policy. Leaders who submit to them often do so with the hope that they may regain their freedom of action when these conditions change. Franco-German cooperation might be only the child of necessity masking latent conflicts. One side may, while obeying the irresistible objective conditions that call for cooperation, construe cooperation in such a manner and work for it in such a way as to gain the upper hand in the end. "What I want to consider," said de Gaulle in rejecting the notion that ideology is a source of conflict, "are the deep-rooted realities which are human, national and consequently international." Like ideology, cooperation may cover only "power and ambitions."[4] What, then, were the underlying motives behind Franco-German cooperation?

The French design, unfolded by de Gaulle and widely supported by the French, has been clear. France, with its small nuclear force, would assume the leadership of western Europe. The European base would give de Gaulle added leverage and would allow France to formulate the strategy and the foreign policy for the whole. In return, France seemed to be willing to work for a reunified Germany with the Oder-Neisse as its eastern frontier, without setting a time or elaborating on the particular arrangements. As for the manner in which French leadership would be exercised, de Gaulle proposed periodic consultations among the heads of state or the foreign ministers of the Six, first on the basis of the Fouchet plan and later through the Franco-German treaty of cooperation of 1963. In both cases, the existing institutions of the Common Market were to be bypassed.

In addition to her *force de frappe,* France's claims for leadership derived from her historical role, her "victory" in World War II, and her special ties with some of the European countries other than the Six. She also had special bargaining powers that were not available to West Germany, notably the threat of turning the flank of western Europe by special military and diplomatic arrangements with the Soviet Union and of subordinating German reunification to other ends. For French aspirations to be realized, it would have been necessary to weaken both NATO and the Warsaw Pact, to provide for a gradual

---

[4] Macridis, *De Gaulle: Implacable Ally,* p. 6.

withdrawal of American and Russian power from western and eastern Europe, to maintain the economic infrastructure of the Common Market, and to make the overall design acceptable to the Six and particularly to the German Federal Republic. Franco-German cooperation became the cornerstone of the design. In 1967, in a remarkable speech, de Gaulle put his aspirations in a nutshell:

> ...*There is one fact that seems to dominate everything. It is the enormous power of the United States....The United States has become the greatest power...and have automatically attempted to enlarge their power and extend it....So there are two alternatives. One is to accept the situation as it is, that is to say to become part of a whole dominated by American power. This is the easiest way out. But there is a second alternative—it is to preserve our national personality. But to do this there are some indispensable conditions. The first is that France and Germany stay together; if not they will not be able to avoid American preponderance; the second is to maintain what we have built among the Six in the economic realm and not allow it to be dislocated....The third is that in eastern Europe we move in the direction of détente and cooperation so that something other than the two blocs emerge in world politics....* [5]

The Gaullist prescription for 1967 differed fundamentally from the one he had outlined before the end of World War II and had reported in his memoirs, which many of the German leaders had read. At that time de Gaulle argued that the abolition of "a centralized Reich" was indispensable for the security of France and for a viable European settlement. He suggested a "federation of German states," international control of the Ruhr, and independence for the Saar territory but with special and privileged trade relations with France. "This conception of tomorrow's Germany," he concluded, "related to my image of Europe." With the dismantling of the Reich, the Soviet annexation of eastern Europe would lose its raison d'être. The vassal states would liberate themselves because the masters of the Kremlin, as he put it, would be unable to maintain their control over eastern Europe once it was clear that Germany was no longer a threat. Thus, "the unity of Europe," he concluded, "could be established in the form of an association including its peoples from Iceland to Istanbul, from Gibraltar to the Urals." [6]

---

5 The address was delivered on the occasion of the meeting between the French and German heads of state on July 12–13, 1967 (*Année Politique* [1967], p. 207).

6 For de Gaulle's views on the settlement of European problems and the dismantling of Germany, see *The War Memoirs of Charles de Gaulle* (New York: Simon & Schuster, 1960), vol. 3, pp. 50–54, 204–205.

The heart of the Gaullist design for Europe was the substitution of French for American leadership. Elevated to the role of spokesman for western Europe, France would at once claim American support and protection and seek Russian friendship and collaboration. In other words, de Gaulle was resolved either to accomplish the hard way what he had proposed to the United States and England in 1958—joint leadership with the Anglo-Saxons—or to resurrect and implement the Franco-Soviet Treaty of 1944, provided, of course, that the Russians would prove amenable to some liberalization in eastern Europe. By forcing the United States to support him in order to impede his pro-Russian schemes and by inciting the Soviets to help him in order to weaken Europe's ties with the United States, de Gaulle hoped to manage to fulfill his major aspiration—developing a power center that would "mediate between the two Empires."

That was his scheme. It was ultimately embodied in the Franco-German Treaty of 1963—which represents the high mark in cooperation between the two countries but also the beginning of its decline. The background of the treaty is just as significant as the treaty itself. De Gaulle had said no to England's joining the Common Market despite German objections; he had refused Polaris missiles from the United States on terms similar to those presented to the British and accepted by them at Nassau. The MLF had been received with hostility by the French and with varying degrees of indifference by most other members of NATO except the Germans. The McNamara strategy had been developed and the United States had unilaterally decided to withdraw some of its forces from West Germany. British and, at least apparently, American willingness to talk with the Russians about modifications in the status of West Berlin had been noted. German leaders appeared disillusioned over American strategy and began to express doubts about American determination to maintain its position in Europe. De Gaulle's prophecy, a part and parcel of his strategy, seemed to be coming true. The weakening of American resolution together with the growth of western European power strengthened the German Gaullists for whom Adenauer had become one of the most vocal exponents. The time had come for a Franco-German condominium of western Europe.

The treaty[7] provided for meetings of heads of state, for meetings of ministers of foreign affairs to be held at least four times a year, and for meetings of ministers of defense and chiefs of staff at least five times a year. The purpose was to arrive at common policies through consultation on problems related to the European commu-

[7] The text appears in *De Gaulle: Implacable Ally*, pp. 184–191.

nities, on East-West relations, on matters dealing with the North Atlantic Treaty Organization, on the harmonization of strategy and tactics, and on the exchange of personnel between the armed forces and joint armament projects. In addition, the treaty provided for cultural exchanges of young people, joint information and educational arrangements, and the establishment of joint research institutes. On its face the agreement was far more extensive and binding than the Franco-British entente before World War I or the Franco-Soviet treaty of the thirties or that of 1944. It was speedily ratified by the legislative bodies of the two countries—the National Assembly in June and the Bundestag in May 1963—in the first by 325 votes against 107, with 42 abstentions, and in the second unanimously. But the Bundestag refused to ratify the treaty until it had passed over the bitter opposition of Konrad Adenauer, a clarifying preamble that became an integral part of the treaty. The preamble provided that nothing in the treaty could modify or qualify the "rights and obligations of the Federal Republic stemming from multilateral treaties." In fact, the treaty was to be applied only "in conformity with the broad goals that determine German policy." They were stated as being "the maintenance and the reinforcement of the alliance of the free peoples and particularly the close association between Europe and the United States," the reunification of Germany "on the basis of the right of self-determination," the "integration of the armed forces of the NATO members," the "unification" of Europe with the institutions of the Common Market serving as a model, and England's entry into the Common Market.

The contradiction between the body of the treaty and its preamble clearly indicated how far apart the two countries were in their motives and in their goals. As the Gaullist scheme unfolded, the differences between the two countries were even more sharply delineated. What de Gaulle proposed to do began to frighten the Germans. Their fear became apparent in the year immediately following the signing of the treaty. In order to maintain his freedom and independence of action, de Gaulle refused to accept the implementation of the Rome treaty— that is, he refused to allow majority voting in the Council of Ministers of the Common Market or to give to the Commission the authority to initiate policies and to speak on behalf of the Six. By emphasizing the need of making special consultative arrangements for the formulation of policies instead of using the existing institution of the Common Market, he was denying the Common Market the prospects of growing and developing in the political sphere. By assigning a special extra-European role to France and by simultaneously reopening the prospects of Franco-Soviet collaboration, he was denying to the Germans and to the other members of the Common Market the very consultative procedures he had advocated. Finally, by subordinating the Six to France's designs and aspirations, he was serving notice that he would be ready to sacrifice the interests of others if it suited France's purpose. He was slowly forcing those who agreed that Europe could not be made without France to an alternative that they were bound to reject—that Europe could be made only under France.

Both the design and the means of bringing it about were unacceptable to the German Federal Republic. The aims of German leaders, and specifically of Adenauer, in entering into cooperation had been formulated immediately after the war and were different from those of the French.[8] First, for the Federal Republic the European entanglement meant protection against two possible dangers: Soviet military intervention and a return to a militant German nationalism. European organization was both a shield and a safeguard. Second, Europe was not to be conceived without NATO—which meant integration of military policy and strategy *under* the United States. Third, reunification was to be pursued through NATO and in the context of European and Franco-German cooperation. Fourth, the Federal Republic—with or without the eastern part of Germany—was to become an equal partner within a western Europe that would generate common leadership and reach common decisions. As the Gaullist design unfolded, German lines hardened. De Gaulle did not consult with the leaders of the Federal Republic when he visited the Soviet Union, and they were left in the dark when Kosygin visited France in 1966. They were not consulted when the French removed themselves from the integrated military structures of NATO. The Franco-Soviet contacts caused concern; the withdrawal of France from NATO produced dismay. If NATO were to disintegrate, Germany would be left to the mercy of the Russians with only the protection of the French to fall back on. Finally, the continued opposition to England's entering the Common Market, the constant effort to weaken the political institutions of the Market, and the pronounced anti-American gestures of the French leader became a source of irritation. Even German "Gaullists"—who had been advocating close strategic and foreign-policy cooperation with France—found that de Gaulle was setting his price too high. The preamble came to life while the body of the treaty began to decay. Closer ties with the United States were stressed. When de Gaulle proposed that the German problem was primarily a European problem to be solved by

8 For a discussion of the background factors of West Germany's foreign policy, see Alfred Grosser, *Western Germany: From Defeat to Rearmament* (London: George Allen & Unwin, 1955), and K. W. Deutsch and L. Edinger, *Germany Rejoins the Powers* (Stanford: Stanford University Press, 1959).

Europeans (including the Russians but presumably excluding the United States), a cold Siberian wind swept through the chilled bodies of the German leaders in Berlin and in Bonn. The basis of cooperation seemed to give way to the stark realization that rivalry over such scarce international commodities as influence, power, and security was far from muted. Potsdam was bad enough, but a new Potsdam engineered by de Gaulle might be worse!

Thus for more than 20 years we have witnessed what appeared to be the muting of the secular Franco-German conflict under conditions—domestic, regional, and international—that made cooperation virtually mandatory. The motives, however, and with them the goals shared by French and German leaders in giving shape and direction to cooperation, differed significantly. As the objective conditions that called for cooperation lost the urgency they had from the inception of the cold war up to the early 1960s, a certain degree of freedom and initiative was restored to the leaders of both countries. De Gaulle's embrace of the Federal Republic and the treaty of 1963 concealed the traditional French design for the attainment of European leadership and the rank of a world power by subordinating Germany to France's ambitions. It was an embrace from which both the most ardent Europeans—who saw clearly what the Gaullist motives were—and the German Gaullists quickly extricated themselves.[9] The Franco-Soviet rapprochement used by de Gaulle to threaten and cajole the Germans had the opposite effect. But at the very same time the failure of the French design and the nonimplementation of the treaty gave to the Federal Republic the first genuine opportunity to pursue its own goals and to seek the realization of its own ambitions in terms of consultations and bilateral arrangements with eastern European countries and with the Soviet Union. At least potentially, these moves may carry the Federal Republic away from the European entanglement that her leaders had sought and championed for so long. Such a shift, if successful, could restore to West Germany some of the independence and influence that had been denied it for so long. Such a change is not likely to be compatible with French interests and aspirations. The two countries are likely to vie with each other for the assumption of European leadership and influence, if not domination.

The period of what Roy Willis calls "organized disagreement,"[10] covering roughly the time from the signing of the treaty to the with-

---

[9] The contradiction of French foreign-policy motives with German ones is well brought out in Roy Willis, *France, Germany and Western Europe, 1945–1967* (Stanford: Stanford University Press, 1968), particularly chap. 11.

[10] *Ibid.*

drawal of French troops from NATO, may well give place to that of organized rivalry. The stakes can never be quite what they were in the past, and the two superpowers will have every reason to seek to control the contest. But if the Germans succeed where de Gaulle was destined to fail, if they are able to find an opening to the East, the prospects both of some form of unification and of increased power and status will be brighter than ever before. The Gaullist legacy may be the direct road to a new Rapallo and to the revival of the rivalry that the last 20 years appeared to have put to rest.

Prospects and Limits of Rivalry

General Hans von Seeckt, who then headed the German army, is reputed to have described German goals bluntly right after World War I: "We must regain our power...and as soon as we do we naturally will take back everything we have lost."[11] It is difficult to imagine a German general making this statement after the end of World War II or even a generation later. The reason, of course, is that Germany's defeat in World War II drastically altered the distribution of power in the world, something that had not happened after the Treaty of Versailles. It would be idle to assume, however, that either Germans or Frenchmen have lost their drive for power and their aspiration for high rank. Their mode of expression has simply changed so as to accommodate international realities immediately after World War II. De Gaulle and many other leaders and members of the French elite have rightly seen the condition of the restoration of French power to be the modification of the international system, and more specifically the elimination of the two blocs led by the two superpowers. With even greater realism, de Gaulle underscored the dominant position of the United States and drew the conclusion that only its weakening could provide for a western European power center, based on Franco-German cooperation and led by France. Had his assessment of the Soviet Union's power been different, de Gaulle would have been more anti-Russian than anti-American. The position and motives of the German Federal Republic were different from those of France. In their efforts to regain lost power and status, German leaders accepted the inevitability, perhaps even the desirability, of the two blocs and committed themselves to the Atlantic one. For a long time it provided them with protection and with the hope that reunification could be attained from a position of strength. Until the very early sixties, both French and German aspirations could find

11 Hans W. Gatzke, *Stresemann and the Rearmament of Germany* (New York: W. W. Norton, 1954), p. 12.

room within the European community and NATO. For the French, they had been a necessary stage on the way to establishing the basis for fully independent action. For the Federal Republic, they had seemed to be indispensable instruments for the attainment of their two major goals—protection and reunification. Once the latter had been achieved, everything would have to be reconsidered—not only the Bonn Constitution but foreign policy as well.

The first signs of Franco-German rivalry appeared when the conditions that brought about cooperation lost some of their potency.[12] First, both France and the Federal Republic have recovered some of their strength. Second, the two superpowers, either because of internal difficulties or because their attention is drawn elsewhere, appear to be less committed to the preservation of control over western and eastern Europe, Czechoslovakia to the contrary notwithstanding. Third, a direct confrontation between them appears to be less and less likely in Europe. Two courses were therefore open to the French and the Germans. They might have forged ahead jointly with a European political arrangement based upon the equality, if not of all participants, at least of Germany and France, in order to seek a settlement in the heart of Europe and fashion new defense arrangements. France's aspiration to assume leadership and subordinate the Federal Republic to its own designs arrested this development. The second course was to seek their allies and determine their policies independently of each other. Under de Gaulle, the French followed this course when they withdrew from NATO and sought to reinforce their ties with the Soviet Union at the expense both of NATO and of the Franco-German Treaty. The Federal Republic responded first by reinforcing its ties with the United States and subsequently, under Willy Brandt, by pressing for a new eastern European policy calculated to appease the Soviet Union and to prepare the terrain for bilateral talks not only with the Soviet Union and some of the eastern European satellites but with East Germany as well.

The Rapallo "hypothesis" alluded to above is, of course, one among many others. It reflects a possible current trend and nothing more. In the last analysis the future of Franco-German relations is functionally related to the future of the international system in which they live, but which they can no longer control or even very greatly affect. Relations between the two superpowers and perhaps the ultimate trifurcation of power in the world will determine the nature of Franco-German relations and account for their fluctuations. For the foresee-

---

12 For some indications of rivalry as expressed by the German and French elites, see K. W. Deutsch, L. Edinger, R. Macridis, and R. Merritt, *France, Germany and the Western Alliance* (New York: Scribner's, 1967).

able future it would be idle to assume the demise of either of the two superpowers. It is, on the contrary, quite plausible to assume that the status quo will continue and that it will be modified only by fluctuations in the respective power of the United States and Russia. It is also difficult to assume that either the Soviet Union or the United States will withdraw completely from its respective sphere of influence and control in Europe. We must rather think of gradual or limited withdrawals and incremental changes in their power on the continent.

The weakening of American power or its withdrawal from Europe —difficult as it may be to envisage—would put both Germany and France at the mercy of Russian power. In such circumstances, it would be hard to imagine any renewed Franco-German rivalry. The weakening of Russian power, on the other hand, or its withdrawal from eastern Europe—also hard to envisage—leads us to a different perspective. The Soviet threat has kept the Federal Republic under the harness of American power and has led it to develop its commitment to Europe. The weakening of Soviet power would at once remove the ground for West Germany's commitment to Europe and the incentive for America to use its power to control Germany's policy. To be sure, even a hard-pressed Soviet Union would not readily relinquish the power it holds in eastern Europe, but each and every concession to Germany contributes to the growth of German influence and power in Europe until the moment may come when Germany emerges as a threat to France once more. Ironically, under these circumstances Germany could claim the leadership of Europe from the Atlantic to the Urals and adopt the Gaullist design for a new power center that would rival the Americans! With de Gaulle's exit from the political scene and with the weakening of the European integrative spirit—partly due to de Gaulle's own efforts—Germany finds herself for the first time in a position to pursue for her own sake some of the objectives de Gaulle pursued in the name of French leadership and power.

Under the new leadership of Willy Brandt, West Germany is now ready to live side by side with an East German state, to renounce the use of force, to take the risk of signing the Nuclear Nonproliferation Treaty, to abandon the Hallstein doctrine, to seek agreements in eastern Europe and with the Soviet Union, and to accept the Oder-Neisse line as the eastern boundary of the "German nation."[13] These

13 Many of the current trends can be gauged from Willy Brandt, *A Peace Policy for Europe* (New York: Holt, Rinehart & Winston, 1968). See also his "German Policy Toward the East," in *Foreign Affairs* (April 1968), and Karl Kaiser, *German Foreign Policy in Transition* (Oxford: Oxford University Press, 1968), particularly chaps. 6, 7, and 8, where the new trends are discussed especially with regard to the policy toward the East.

changes do not correspond to any significant change of power; they may nevertheless put an end to the French design. If coupled with Soviet concessions with regard to the future of the two German states and with minor reciprocal changes in the deployment of NATO and Warsaw Pact forces in West and East Germany, the prospect of reunification will become brighter and the prospect of European unity will dim. Wishing to forestall such developments, France may well become the champion of European unity and the advocate of British entry!

It is possible, therefore, that the rivalry between the two nations will be renewed, though it will not attain its previous scope and intensity. Its limits are set by the international system; the system defines the parameters of the possible rivalry and the manner in which it is likely to express itself. The power of America and Russia makes it impossible for any other country to displace them in their respective spheres and alliances. In the face of their power it becomes precarious for the nations within the two blocs to shift from one to the other. The examples of Hungary, Czechoslovakia, and even Romania, and also of Latin American countries and Greece, are fairly convincing.

Despite some of the more grandiloquent statements of de Gaulle and other French leaders, and despite French efforts to open up areas of influence in the Middle East, in Biafra, in Canada, in Latin America, and in eastern Europe, it is virtually impossible to conceive of a situation in which Franco-German rivalry can again manifest itself through military action and territorial expansion in areas outside western Europe. The so-called third world enjoys a subordinate independent status on condition that it remain noncommitted. Neither France nor Germany can hope to gain power over the other through colonial or "neocolonial" expansion. The third world will not accept it, and the superpowers will not permit it.

Thus the geographic setting of a Franco-German rivalry is limited; the form such a rivalry can take and the manner of its expression are even more seriously circumscribed. The contest is primarily for the political leadership of western Europe and possibly for influence in some of the eastern European states. In the latter sphere, it will primarily take the form of diplomatic conflict over spheres of trade and over the jockeying for advantageous bilateral agreements and understandings—with the Germans following in the footsteps of the French. But above all, rivalry will revolve around the leadership of the Six, again through the use of diplomacy and persuasion and through the use of economic capability and trade.

Rivalry, then, over the leadership of western Europe and assumption of an independent position in Europe are realistic prospects. But renewed cooperation, coupled with a rebirth of the European integrative spirit, also continues to remain a distinct possibility. The conditions for such a development are present, for the institutions of the Common Market are intact and the French resistance to the exercise of their powers may not last. Nor is the Franco-German Treaty dead. Its provisions may be revived and implemented so as to provide a genuine and equal cooperation between the two countries in matters of foreign policy and defense. A possible redirection of French strategy toward closer cooperation with NATO against the most likely enemy—"from the East"[14]—coupled with the economic difficulties that have seriously affected the ambitious schemes to develop nuclear capabilities, point also in the direction of collaboration. The treaty may after all become part of the Gaullist legacy—but only because it will have served a purpose other than the one that inspired de Gaulle.

The basic conditions that emerged after World War II and led to cooperation have not been seriously altered. Both countries are immeasurably stronger, economically and militarily, than in the years after World War II. Yet in relative terms—that is, when compared to the two superpowers—they are just as weak as they were then. Their strength, even if combined, is no danger either to America or to Russia. The prospect of military conflict between the two remains remote. But so is the prospect of intimate cooperation, as envisaged by the Franco-German Treaty, if such cooperation is established for the purpose of creating a new center of power under *either* French *or* German leadership.

A realistic perception of this situation on the part of both French and German leaders may still lead to cooperation. If the French divest themselves of de Gaulle's ambitious design, and if German leaders do not claim it as their own, a European arrangement based upon genuine and equal Franco-German collaboration in the context of the institutions of the Common Market is a prospect open to both countries. It may put an end to their secular rivalry and create a stable regional organization in line with the hopes of those who unfolded the dream of European political unity and worked so hard to bring it about. But in international as in domestic politics, "reason" does not always lead policy-makers to the making of covenants of peace. The future is uncertain and with it the stability of western Europe and of the Atlantic alliance.

14 These hypotheses and many others must be discussed with the possible alternative courses open to Western Europe in mind; see Alastair Buchan, *Europe's Futures, Europe's Choices* (New York: Columbia University Press, 1969).

Argentina and Chile

ROBERT N. BURR

Chilean tourists take pleasure in shopping in Argentine cities, and Argentine tourists enjoy the delights of Chile's Pacific Coast resorts. But even as such contacts take place, both groups of tourists and their compatriots who remain at home personally and strongly sense and frequently share the antagonism between their nations. That antagonism is the expression of a rivalry which manifests itself in repeated rumors of invasions, the nagging fear of armaments races and their effects, and numerous diplomatic crises over disputed areas along the extensive Argentine-Chilean frontier.

Judged by the gross criteria of international power, Argentina and Chile appear to be unequal rivals. Argentina's territory of over one million square miles is nearly four times larger than Chile's. Argentina's population of 23 million is more than two and one-half times as great as Chile's. The per capita gross national product of Argentina is 40 percent larger than that of Chile. And the total personnel of the Argentine armed forces is more than double that of Chile's military establishment.[1] Yet certain factors operate to enable Chile effectively to rival Argentina. Geography is on Chile's side. The subsystem of power politics in which Argentina and Chile operate provides Chile with leverage. And the hegemony of the United States over Latin America occasionally mutes the rivalry between the two nations.

Geographical aspects that make it difficult for Argentina to bring the full force of its power to bear upon Chile include the distance of Argentina's center

---

[1] See University of California, Los Angeles, Latin American Center, *Statistical Abstract of Latin America, 1967* (1968), for this and other comparative statistical data.

of population and wealth—the city and province of Buenos Aires—from the Chilean frontier, the natural fortress of the towering and rugged Andes mountains, which lie between the two nations, and the fact that Argentina has no territory on the Pacific and lacks adequate bases for naval operations against Chile.

The mitigating action of the South American subsystem of power politics of which Argentina and Chile are members is far more subtle and complex. Both the roots of the existing rivalry between Chile and Argentina and the factors that compensate for Chile's present relative weakness must be sought in the historical development of that South American system.[2]

In the half-century after Argentina and Chile achieved independence in the early nineteenth century, it became apparent that the states of South America had both the inclination and the opportunity to play power politics among themselves. Products of a culture essentially derivative of Europe's, South American leaders tended to imitate the European system of power politics, using as models the European great powers. Their own weakness prevented the South American states from competing with the great powers, but similar impediments did not exist to competition with each other.

The dynamics for a system of power politics were provided by intense rivalries which developed among the new South American states as they sought to define their unsettled boundaries and to regularize their relations with one another. These rivalries revolved around such vital matters as the control of strategic land areas and waterways, development of commerce, ownership of resources, territorial integrity, and political independence.

Moreover, the South American states had the opportunity to shape their political relationships with each other without excessive outside influence. Had they been close to Europe, the weak South American states might have been drawn into the vortex of European power politics, where their interests would have been substantially subordinated to those of the great powers. But vast expanses of ocean kept the South American states out of easy reach of the great powers. Moreover, as long as they could protect and advance their commercial and economic interests in South America, the great powers were not

2 For the history of the development of a South American (sub)system of power politics see Robert N. Burr, "The Balance of Power in Nineteenth-Century South America, An Exploratory Essay," *Hispanic American Historical Review*, 35 (February 1955), 37–60; Robert N. Burr, *The Stillborn Panama Congress* (Berkeley and Los Angeles, 1962); and Robert N. Burr, *By Reason or Force: Chile and the Balancing of Power in South America, 1830–1905* (Berkeley and Los Angeles, 1965).

really interested in dominating such remote, chaotic states or in interfering in conflicts among them. The policy of the European nations, therefore, particularly that of Great Britain with its predominant naval power, was the essentially negative policy of preventing the extension of rival political influence. As a result, the South American states were relatively free to concentrate on one another and to develop their own system of power politics.

The South American system evolved, in two phases, in the nineteenth and early twentieth centuries. In the first phase, which spanned the half-century following independence, none of the South American states acted on a continent-wide scale. Inadequate economic and technical resources, small populations, and domestic political instability made it extremely difficult to bridge the formidable Andean system and the jungle-choked Amazon basin which separated the east and west coasts of South America. The South American states therefore at first tended to confine their international political activities to areas linked by waterways and to form regional systems of power politics. In the second phase these regional systems became fused to produce a South American system.

During the first phase Argentina was a major actor in one regional system, Chile in another. When the two nations came into conflict in the 1870s their respective regional systems began to fuse together, and thereafter Argentine-Chilean rivalry was to be the major fulcrum of the South American system of power politics.

Argentina was a member of the Río de la Plata regional system, where its major rival was Brazil. The origins of Brazilian-Argentina antagonism lay in the imperial struggles of their predecessor states, Portugal and Spain, for control of the Paraguay-Paraná-Uruguay river systems which flow into the Río de la Plata estuary and thence into the Atlantic ocean, providing communications with the outside world for vast interior regions of the South American continent. In 1776 Spain, to contain Portuguese expansion, consolidated its Platine holdings into an impressive power block—the Viceroyalty of the Río de la Plata—which encompasses the present territories of Argentina, Uruguay, Paraguay, and Bolivia. That large administrative unit was dominated economically and politically by its capital city and only major port, Buenos Aires. Beginning in 1810 the leadership in Buenos Aires sought to transform the Viceroyalty into the independent nation of Argentina, which these leaders planned to dominate as they had the Viceroyalty. But provincial leaders rejected domination by the city of Buenos Aires and in the ensuing strife Brazil was able to crack the structure which had contained Portuguese expansion. By 1870, in the course of four international wars, Uruguay and Paraguay had broken away from the control of Buenos Aires and had become independent buffer states in the Platine regional system. The maintenance of Uruguayan and Paraguayan independence was now considered essential to an equilibrium between the system's two major members—Brazil and Argentina. Each of these two major powers sought unremittingly to extend its own influence over Paraguay and Uruguay and to prevent its rival from doing so. The buffer states sought to maintain their precarious independence and to advance their interests by playing upon the rivalries of the major powers in their system.

While Argentina was involved in the formation of the Platine regional system, Chile was playing the major role in the establishment of a complex system of power politics on the Pacific coast. During the long colonial period, Chile had been a small, impoverished frontier colony, subordinate for all but a few years to the Viceroyalty of Peru. But in the 1830s, while its neighbor states continued to be plagued with domestic turmoil, Chile achieved remarkable political stability. And, aided by the discovery of vast silver deposits and by the expanding commerce of Valparaíso, the first major port of call for Atlantic-Pacific trade, Chile began to experience steady, substantial economic growth.

Chile's major international problem then lay with Peru, which not only resented the commercial vitality of Valparaíso at the expense of its own port of Callao, but which as former center of viceregal power felt entitled to play the leading role on the Pacific coast. A crisis occurred in 1836 when Peru and Bolivia united to form a single nation and at the same time Peru abrogated a recently ratified commercial treaty with Chile, favorable to Chile's interests. Chile, charging that the unification of Peru and Bolivia upset the South American equilibrium, declared war. The mutual independence of Peru and Bolivia was restored after a Chilean victory, and Chile assumed hegemony on the Pacific coast, dedicated to a policy of maintaining a balance of power in that area, a balance which favored Chilean hegemony.

Beginning in the late 1840s Chile's position was challenged by Peru, which was strengthened by greater internal political stability and increasingly larger revenues from a national guano monopoly. No direct conflict then developed, but Chileans watched carefully the growth of their rival, remaining particularly wary of its growing naval power. In the 1850s, when rumors circulated that Peru was planning to annex the Ecuadorian port of Guayaquil, Chile made it clear that it would resist any change in the territorial status quo. Now, because Ecuador was a buffer state between Colombia and Peru, the extension of Chilean interests to Ecuador linked all of the involved nations into one Pacific coast system of power politics. In this system Chile and Peru were major rivals for hegemony. The independence of Bolivia and Ecuador was essential for the equilibrium between them. And Colombia was involved because of its interests in Ecuador and its rivalry with Peru.

Throughout the 1860s Argentina and Chile were primarily concerned with the power politics of their own regional systems, but beginning in the 1870s these two regional systems fused into a continental South American system of power politics and now the two nations confronted one another. That development was largely a response to the accelerated economic development of the South American states after 1850. That development was in part the result of the mounting world demand for South American raw materials and foodstuffs: rubber, nitrates, guano, wheat, beef. It was also pushed by increasing European investment in South America and augmented by immigration and by technological innovations such as the railroad, steamships, and the telegraph system.

From the viewpoint of relations within South America, three results of this economic development were especially noteworthy. First, increasing world demand for particular South American products centered attention on certain disputed territories that had previously been considered of little importance. Two such areas were the Amazon basin, the world's major source of rubber, and the Atacama desert, which possessed guano and nitrates as well as silver. The ownership of the Amazon was contested among Brazil and four Pacific coast states, and the resulting conflict contributed both to an intensification of rivalries among the Pacific coast nations and to the integration of the Platine and Pacific coast regional systems.

The economic promise of the Atacama desert caused Bolivia and Chile hotly to contest its control. A boundary treaty of 1866, intended to solve the problem, failed because it permitted Chileans to exploit the Bolivian sector of the desert on a basis of equality with Bolivians. As aggressive and efficient Chilean enterprise developed the area, which was far removed from the center of Bolivian authority, the Bolivian government began to fear that Chile might attempt to incorporate it politically. Peru was also interested in the nitrate region and, always suspicious of its traditional rival, made it clear that it would oppose Chilean seizure of the territory and in 1873 negotiated a secret anti-Chilean alliance with Bolivia.

The economic expansion of South America also, and importantly, had the effect of contributing to the differentiation of the South American states into small and great powers. Those states owning resources in world demand, or able to offer favorable conditions to foreign capital or immigration, developed more rapidly than others. "These nations profited most from technological innovation, and attracted the largest amounts of foreign capital. Their foreign commerce and government revenues increased most rapidly. When these nations also possessed sizeable territory and population they became the great powers of South America in comparison with less fortunate states. . . ."[3] These "great powers" not only adopted a more sophisticated continental view but they also acquired financial resources which enabled them to buy the modern war matériel to support a larger role in South American affairs.

Although Chile, Peru, and Brazil were emerging as great powers in the 1840s and 1850s, into the 1860s they remained primarily concerned with regional affairs. It was their continued growth, combined with the emergence of Argentina as the fourth great South American power and the consequent expansion of the spheres of interest of the first three South American great powers, that led to the formation of a continental system of power politics.

Argentina's rise to great-power status became possible when, beginning in the 1860s, after a half-century of internal chaos, it achieved political stability. At about the same time Argentina began a period of population growth and economic expansion more rapid than that of any other South American state. As Argentina prospered, it became increasingly interested in the development of remote, hitherto unpopulated areas to the south and west of its settled territory. Because some of these areas were claimed by Chile, which was also expanding, a serious conflict between the two developed in the 1870s. This conflict forged the link between the Platine and Pacific regional systems and became the major fulcrum of the South American system of power politics.

Involved in the Argentine-Chilean boundary dispute were three areas: the fertile plateaus between the eastern and western heights of the Andes; Patagonia; and the Strait of Magellan and Tierra del Fuego. The most important of these for Chile was the strait, for its possession by a potential enemy would seriously threaten Chile's Atlantic commerce and its military security. To Argentina, Patagonia was important as a natural extension of its territory into which its expanding population might pour. Tension mounted in the early 1870s when Argentina pressed for control of a part of the Strait already occupied by Chile, and when Chile decided to make good its claim to Patagonia. The resulting conflict prompted Brazil and Peru to seek

3 *Ibid.*, pp. 110–111.

assistance for the solution of their special problems with Chile and Argentina beyond the confines of their regional systems.

Between 1865 and 1870 Argentina and Brazil had been reluctant allies in a costly war against Paraguay. During that war their traditional rivalry had impeded effective cooperation, and after it was won they came into such serious conflict over the peace settlement that war between them threatened. Aware of the tension in Argentine-Chilean relations, Brazil looked across the Andes to Chile for support in its conflict with Argentina. In response, the Chilean government assured Brazil of its benevolent neutrality in any war between Brazil and Argentina and suggested that Chile and Brazil explore further the problems Argentina posed for both of them.

Peru, seeing an opportunity to exploit the Argentine-Chilean conflict, invited Argentina to join in its 1873 anti-Chilean alliance with Bolivia. The Argentine government agreed, and called its congress into secret session to ratify the treaty. While congress was giving lengthy consideration to the secret document, menacing rumors concerning its nature circulated in South America. Brazil now demanded assurances from both Argentina and Peru that the matter being secretly considered was not adverse to its interests. Chile responded to the rumors by requesting an alliance with Brazil.

In the end Argentina did not join the alliance of Peru and Bolivia, nor was a formal treaty reached by Chile and Brazil. The Argentine congress feared that ratification would precipitate an alliance between Chile and Brazil. Peru's enthusiasm for bringing Argentina into the Peruvian-Bolivian alliance waned because it did not wish to antagonize Brazil. It was important to Peru to retain Brazilian good will for two reasons: to prevent a Brazilian-Chilean alliance that would strengthen Peru's west coast rival; and to obtain Brazil's support in Peru's conflicts with Colombia and Ecuador over disputed Amazon territories. Brazil was reluctant to enter into an alliance with Chile because it feared that such action might precipitate war with Argentina.

The moves and countermoves of the early 1870s demonstrated that a continental system of power politics was replacing the regional systems. From the perspective of the Argentine-Chilean conflict, henceforth Chile would seek Brazil's assistance in dealing with Argentina, while Argentina would attempt to make use of Chile's west coast rivals.

This pattern of power politics became clear during the War of the Pacific, which from 1879 raged between Chile and the Peruvian-Bolivian alliance, as a result of continued friction over control of the nitrate and mineral resources of the Atacama desert. While within its own regional system Chile sought to attach Ecuador to its side and to neutralize Colombia, which was permitting the transshipment of war matériel to Peru over the Isthmus of Panama, Chile's main concern was to prevent Argentina from helping the enemy forces. A Chilean mission to Buenos Aires tried unsuccessfully to settle pending boundary questions, while a Chilean mission to Rio de Janeiro sought Brazilian cooperation in the event of trouble with Argentina. Brazil remained officially neutral, but its government gave sufficient assurances of sympathy to make Chile feel a formal alliance was unnecessary.

Argentina's technical neutrality during the entire war did not prevent it from acts that Chile considered hostile. Argentine troops occupied territory in Patagonia claimed by Chile, and Buenos Aires permitted war matériel destined for Bolivia to pass through Argentine territory. Moreover, when it seemed that Chile would win the war and demand territorial concessions that would greatly increase its strength, Argentina undertook a tenacious diplomatic campaign to convince Brazil, Colombia, and Venezuela to participate in a joint mediation to prevent Chile from acquiring the territory it was demanding from vanquished Peru and Bolivia. The campaign was unsuccessful, largely because Brazil refused to cooperate, but Argentina's efforts kept alive hopes of outside assistance in Peru and Bolivia, unduly prolonging their fruitless resistance.

In 1881, after Chile had knocked Bolivia out of the war and occupied Lima, both Argentina and Chile found reasons for settling their border dispute. Argentina realized that further delay would force it to deal with a Chile strengthened by consolidated conquests. Chile, for its part, wanted to be free to deal with the serious problems it expected to have with its defeated enemies. Therefore, the two nations took advantage of a United States mediation offer to conclude a comprehensive boundary treaty in 1881. Argentina received all of Patagonia, and Chilean sovereignty over the Strait of Magellan was recognized. Chile accepted the neutralization of the strait in return for Argentina's pledge not to block the Strait's Atlantic mouth. Tierra del Fuego was divided between the two, and the Andean frontier was stated to lie along the "highest peaks which divide the waters." All disagreements concerning the treaty's implementation were to be submitted to arbitration.

With the Argentine problem apparently solved, Chile proceeded to bring its northern enemies to terms. In the Treaty of Ancón (1883) Peru ceded to Chile the valuable mineral-producing province of Tarapacá. Chile was also authorized to occupy the Peruvian provinces of Tacna and Arica, north of Tarapacá, for ten years, after which a plebiscite would be held to determine their permanent ownership. Bolivia refused to sign a peace treaty acceptable to Chile, but an indefinite armistice was agreed upon in 1884 which for all practical purposes gave Chile what it wanted. Chile was to occupy and govern the entire Bolivian seacoast pending a final peace treaty.

Chile's conquests in the War of the Pacific enormously increased both its territory and its economic resources, enabling it to play an even more forceful role as a South American great power. Particularly important to Chilean strength was the nitrate industry, whose rapid expansion was reflected in the doubling of Chilean government revenues in the postwar decade. Chile, having reduced Peru to a third-rate power, now had unchallenged hegemony on the Pacific coast, and except for a friendly Brazil, Chile was the strongest nation in South America and would remain so until the early 1890s. During this period of Chile's hegemony, Argentine-Chilean problems lay quiescent.

Beginning in the 1890s, however, changes began to take place which threatened Chile's dominant position and led to a revival of the Argentine-Chilean conflict. Peru commenced to recover from its prostration and demanded the return of Tacna and Arica—provinces that Chile was by now determined to retain at any cost. Landlocked Bolivia continued to insist that Chile provide it with a seaport, and when its demand was not met, Bolivia turned toward the Plata, threatening to move into the Argentine orbit. But the most serious threat to Chile's position came from renewal of the conflict with Argentina.

The focal point of this conflict was disagreement over the interpretation of the boundary treaty of 1881, which stated that the Andean boundary would follow "the highest peaks which divide the waters." When the actual boundary demarcation was undertaken, however, Argentina insisted that the boundary should follow the line between the highest peaks of the principal chain of the Andes, while Chile demanded that the boundary follow the line between the highest peaks on the *divortium aquarum*—a line that lay well to the east of the one proposed by Argentina. Between these two lines lay an area the size of present-day Hungary. If the Chilean line were accepted, a part of Patagonia would go to Chile. If the Argentine position were accepted, Argentina would win control over the mouths of certain rivers emptying into the Pacific and thereby might became a Pacific power, threatening Chile's hegemony in its own sphere.

But the boundary dispute involved more than real estate, for it became a symbol in the struggle of Chile and Argentina for supremacy in all of Spanish-speaking South America. Argentina's remarkable prosperity had by now permitted it to surpass Chile in several respects. Whereas in the mid-1870s the two countries had been roughly equal in population and government revenues, by the mid-1890s there were three Argentinians for every two Chileans and the revenues of Buenos Aires were nearly twice those of Santiago. Argentinians, proud of their achievements and aware of their growing power, now believed that their nation must be recognized as the leader. Chileans, accustomed since the War of the Pacific to being the great Spanish-speaking power, were not ready to relinquish their position to the upstart nation across the Andes.

Surrounded by and infused with highly nationalistic feelings, the Argentine-Chilean conflict became increasingly intense in the 1890s. Although a protocol of 1893 agreed that Argentina would have no territory on the Pacific and Chile none on the Atlantic, relations continued to deteriorate. Argentina and Chile plunged into a race to build up their military and naval establishments. Argentina sought to drag Bolivia into its orbit and showed an increasing tendency to side with Peru and Bolivia in their troubles with Chile. Chile, faced with potential enemies on all fronts, sought to create a counterpoise to Peru by strengthening ties with Colombia and Ecuador, at the same time courting Brazilian support against Argentina. Chile even invaded Argentina's diplomatic sphere of influence by, among other things, encouraging Paraguayan cadets to study at Chile's outstanding military academy. In the midst of this maneuvering, several incidents nearly led to war between Chile and Argentina.

Finally, at the turn of the century, Argentina and Chile, faced with financial exhaustion because of the cost of their armaments race, moved to come to terms. In 1899 they submitted their boundary dispute to the arbitration of Great Britain. Then, in 1902, to remove more basic sources of conflict, they reached several agreements that provided for compulsory arbitration of all future disputes and, more important, established a power structure that satisfied the real interests of both powers. Argentine fears of future Chilean expansion were assuaged by an explicit Chilean renunciation of future territorial conquests. Chilean fears that their hegemony on the Pacific might be threatened by Argentine cooperation with Peru and Bolivia were removed by the implicit establishment of spheres of influence, which also provided Argentina with some assurance against a Chilean-Brazilian alliance. In effect, Argentina agreed not to intervene in the affairs of the Pacific, while Chile promised to keep out of the Atlantic and the Plata. Naval rivalry was to be eliminated by an agreement to maintain equivalence in naval power for five years.

The treaties of 1902 put an end to the threat of war between Argentina and Chile and led to improved relations. Although disagreements arose over the ownership of several islands in Beagle Channel in Tierra del Fuego and over the Antarctic region, these disagreements produced no diplomatic crises or threats of war. This was partly because the major causes of controversy between the two powers had been removed and partly because each nation had more serious problems on its hands. Chile was primarily concerned with settling its outstanding differences with Peru and Bolivia and legitimizing its hegemony on the Pacific, and in 1904 it succeeded in obtaining a treaty that ended its war with Bolivia and gave Chile sovereignty over the former Bolivian seacoast. But Chile's efforts to settle the Tacna and Arica matter with Peru led only to increased tension between the two nations.

For Argentina, the main problem was now Brazil. Not only did Brazil improve its relative power position by an "unwritten alliance with the United States,"[4] but it also embarked upon a naval building program that included a plan to purchase two dreadnoughts. Moreover, to the irritation of Argentina, Brazil injected itself into a dispute between Argentina and Uruguay over the jurisdiction of waters in the Plata river system. Argentina responded by ordering two dreadnoughts for its own fleet. In addition it suggested a defensive alliance with Chile.[5]

Chile's reaction to the suggestion of a treaty with Argentina indicated that despite improvement in its relations with Argentina, the attitudes of rivalry and the patterns of power politics that had prevailed before the 1902 pacts still affected the thinking of Chileans. Faced with an unresolved problem with Peru, and still suspicious of Argentina, Chile welcomed the growing power of a Brazil, which had given clear evidence of wanting Chile's friendship.[6] Chile therefore rejected the Argentine proposal by suggesting that Brazil be included in it. Chile also sought to improve its own power position by ordering two dreadnoughts.

After the outbreak of World War I, rivalry among the three great South American powers abated sufficiently to allow them to take tentative steps toward cooperation in what became known as the "ABC entente." The entente was manifested chiefly in a joint media-

---

[4] See E. Bradford Burns, *The Unwritten Alliance: Rio Branco and Brazilian-American Relations* (New York, 1966).

[5] Oscar Espinos Moraga, *El precio de la paz chileno-argentina (1810–1969)*, 3 vols. (Santiago de Chile, 1969), III, 204–205.

[6] Burns, *Unwritten Alliance*, pp. 191–193.

tion by the three nations in a dispute between the United States and Mexico and in the signing of an agreement to settle their own disagreements peacefully. In addition, Argentina and Chile signed a convention agreeing to submit their dispute over the Beagle Channel islands to the arbitration of Great Britain.

The ABC entente aroused suspicions in neighboring states that the three nations were planning to cooperate to ensure their hegemony over South America. But such suspicions were short-lived, for the already feeble basis for Argentine-Brazilian-Chilean cooperation was further weakened when Brazil entered World War I on the side of the United States while Argentina and Chile remained neutral. The consequent expansion of Brazil's military power once again precipitated a naval race with Argentina which intensified their traditional rivalry.

Following World War I, two major changes in the South American power structure came to influence Argentine-Chilean relations and initiated trends which have increased in importance from that time until the present. In the first place, the United States, with immense naval power and a position unchallenged by Europe's war-ravaged states, assumed hegemony in the western hemisphere and rapidly expanded its economic and political power. Moreover, United States interests, previously concentrated in the Caribbean, began to reach into South America. For South America, the protection its weak powers had received from rivalry among the great powers had ceased to exist. The South American nations were now faced with an expanding great power, which had already established a series of protectorates in the Caribbean, to which there was no counterpoise, and upon which they were increasingly dependent for the trade and investment essential for their developing economies. The challenge, from the South American viewpoint, was to find a policy that would enable it to benefit from increasing economic relations with the United States and at the same time prevent United States interference in its political affairs, or the domination of the United States.

The second major change in the power structure of South America after World War II was the relative decline of Chile's power. Although Chile's population and government revenues had been inferior to Argentina's in the prewar period, nevertheless Chile had possessed sufficient prestige, experience, and resources to maintain its position as a South American great power. After the war it became increasingly difficult for Chile to uphold that position. The gap between the size of the populations of Argentina and Chile continued to widen, and the Argentine economy expanded while Chile experienced mounting economic difficulties. Particularly damaging was the discovery and marketing of synthetic nitrates, which destroyed the nitrate monopoly that had been the major source of Chilean government revenues.

Chile attempted to improve its relative position by initiating a movement for the limitation of the naval armaments of Argentina, Brazil, and Chile. At the same time it sought to settle the Tacna and Arica question with Peru in order to restore friendly relations with that country and remove a potential enemy to the north. With respect to naval limitations, Chile was unsuccessful, but continued rivalry between Argentina and Brazil had the effect of strengthening Chile's own situation. The solution of the problem with Peru consumed most of the 1920s, and Chile, in its deteriorated position, found it necessary to cede two vital points in order to resolve their differences. First, although Chile had stubbornly insisted that the Tacna-Arica question must be solved by the two nations involved without outside intervention, it accepted the good offices of the United States. Second, Chile had been resolved to retain all of Tacna and Arica, but in 1929 it accepted a compromise in which Peru received Tacna and Chile got Arica. This compromise restored satisfactory relations between Chile and Peru.

Chile also responded to the changing power structure with efforts to develop a policy designed to hold the United States at bay. Now, because Argentina had a similar foreign-policy objective, an opportunity for cooperation presented itself, one that might mute Argentine-Chilean rivalry. They were initially unable to cooperate. Chilean policy was to accept the fact of the United States's dominant position and to work through the inter-American system to contain the expansion of US influence. Specifically, Chile sought to promote the unity of the Latin American states in order to force the United States to accept as a principle of American international law the doctrine that no nation has the right to intervene in the domestic or foreign affairs of another.[7] Argentina, which had close economic ties with Europe and whose improving power position encouraged it to aspire to a greater role, opposed strengthening the inter-American system and sought directly to challenge the leadership of the United States in Latin America.

Nevertheless, after the Tacna and Arica dispute had been settled and the extent of United States economic penetration in Chile became apparent, Chile moved toward cooperation with Argentina as a first step toward creating a Latin American bloc to contain the United States. At a 1933 meeting in Mendoza, Argentina, the foreign ministers

[7] For Chilean policy in the 1920s and 1930s see Frederick B. Pike, *Chile and the United States, 1880–1962* (Notre Dame, Indiana, 1963), pp. 214–242.

of Argentina and Chile reached a series of agreements. Not only did they resolve to deal with commercial problems and to settle their dispute over the islands in the Beagle Channel but they also adopted two resolutions designed to contain US influence. The first was an agreement to cooperate in order to end the Chaco war between Bolivia and Paraguay—a move aimed at providing an exclusively South American solution to a conflict the United States was already seeking to end. Second, Argentina was planning to confront the United States, at an inter-American conference later that year, with the Saavedra Lamas Anti-War Pact, which contained a strong nonintervention clause. At Mendoza Chile agreed to support that pact.

But the cooperation between Argentina and Chile, expressed at Mendoza, did not prosper. A major basis for the entente decreased in importance after 1933, when the United States accepted the doctrine of nonintervention and proceeded to implement a good-neighbor policy toward Latin America. Moreover, Argentine-Chilean relations seemed to deteriorate on their own. In spite of the Mendoza commitment, Argentina proposed that the Chaco war be settled by an Argentine-Brazilian-United States commission that left Chile out in the cold.[8] President Alessandri of Chile reflected growing irritation with Argentina in his response to a proposal that Argentina's president visit Santiago. Alessandri bluntly stated that as long as problems like those of the Chaco and the Beagle Channel were not solved, there would be no presidential visits.[9] Even the foreign minister of Chile, who had been an advocate of an entente with Argentina, began to have doubts. At a secret session of the Chilean senate in 1936, he indicated that he believed the real problem in Argentine-Chilean relations was the growing ambition and power of Argentina. "The Argentine Republic has ambitions to be a world power and recently has begun arming," the foreign minister said at one point in his testimony. And at another point he claimed that "the great growth of Argentina and its spirit of superiority has created in some sectors of that fellow nation a somewhat imperialist idea, in which one notes the aim of assuming the leadership of American international politics."[10] The foreign minister suggested that Chile intensify its diplomatic activity throughout America and especially in Brazil.

During the succeeding two decades, despite occasional efforts at

8 Bryce Wood, *The United States and Latin American Wars, 1932–1942* (New York, 1966), p. 68.

9 Ricardo Donoso, *Alessandri, agitador y demoledor; cincuenta años de historia política de Chile*, 2 vols. (Mexico City, 1952–1954), II, 333.

10 *Ibid.*, p. 340.

cooperation between the two nations, Chilean fears grew that Argentina was seeking to be the dominant power in South America and that its aspirations threatened not only Chilean interests but also, possibly, its security. These fears were a reaction to the policies of the military group which seized power in Argentina in 1943 and from which emerged the dictatorship of Juan Perón. The Argentine military took over the government partly for reasons of domestic politics, but they were also motivated by grave concern over the growing military power of Brazil. Not only was Brazil far larger than Argentina, in both population and territory, but it had entered World War II and was rapidly building up its military power with assistance from the United States. The Argentine military wanted to control the government so that they could build up a counterpoise to Brazil. They set out to build up Argentina's heavy industry, augment its armed forces, and increase its international diplomatic clout through the formation of a bloc of South American nations, to include Paraguay, Uruguay, Bolivia, and Chile, under Argentine tutelage.

Chilean leaders were seriously concerned by exposure of a secret Argentine military memorandum outlining this plan, by evidence that Argentina was inciting the Chilean military to seize the Chilean government, and join forces with Argentina, and by aspects of the "third position" policy adopted by Perón—a policy that would challenge US hemispheric leadership by uniting Latin America ideologically under Perón's leadership. Chilean officials were particularly disturbed and irritated by propagandizing on behalf of Perón's populist doctrine of *justicialismo* carried on by Buenos Aires' labor attaché in Santiago.[11]

Chile resisted Argentina's drive for hegemony in many ways, two of which are especially relevant here. First, in the years after World War II the Chilean government sought protection from the United States by cooperating with it in developing the inter-American security system. The key to this system was the Inter-American Treaty of Reciprocal Assistance signed at Rio de Janeiro in 1947. This treaty provided for automatic collective sanctions against aggression either from outside the western hemisphere or from the signers of the pact. Argentina aroused Chilean suspicion during the negotiations at Rio by unsuccessfully proposing that the collective action envisaged in the treaty be confined to aggression from nations outside the hemisphere, and that it not apply to inter-American conflicts. Chile was not enthusiastic about any treaty that might involve it in a great power war without assuring Chile and the other Latin American nations of the assistance they were demanding from the United States

[11] See Alejandro Magnet, *Nuestros vecinos justicialistas* (Santiago, 1953).

for their economic development. Nevertheless, Chile felt the need for protection against Argentina and accepted the Inter-American Treaty of Reciprocal Assistance, which provided that protection. Since that time Chile's security with respect to Argentina has rested heavily on the guarantee of the inter-American system, which in effect means the guarantee of the United States.[12]

A second Chilean reaction to Argentina's drive for hegemony was Chile's refusal to enter into agreements with that nation for complementary economic development. In fact, economic cooperation with Argentina would have been extremely useful to Chile in carrying out its programs of industrialization, economic diversification, and social improvement. Chile was well endowed with resources for industrialization, but it lacked a sufficiently large domestic market for the products of large-scale industry and suffered from food shortages; Argentina could have helped to fulfill both these needs. Yet when Argentina and Chile negotiated a customs treaty in 1946, providing for a reduction in tariff barriers and for joint Argentine-Chilean participation in development activities, the Chilean congress rejected it, chiefly because it feared that the treaty might bring Chile under the political domination of Argentina. The same thing happened in 1953 after Presidents Perón and Ibáñez announced at a joint meeting in Santiago that they had agreed upon a treaty of economic union.

The fall of Perón in 1955 momentarily relieved tension between Chile and Argentina, but incidents soon began to occur that not only revived Chilean suspicions but also convinced many Chileans that Argentina was committed to a policy of depriving Chile of territory and, at Chile's expense, achieving a dominant position over the southern tip of the continent, giving Argentina free access to the Pacific and control over the southern Shetland islands and parts of Antarctica, both of which are claimed by Chile. The achievements of such objectives, according to Chileans, would give Argentina control of the waterway between the Atlantic and the Pacific and thereby enable it to play a greater role as a world power. Argentinians, in a superior power position, have been less concerned with a threat from Chile, but Argentine nationalists, including members of the armed forces, have pointed to the large numbers of Chileans living in the Argentine sector of Tierra del Fuego and parts of Patagonia, charging that Chile has aggressive intentions in those places.

Since the fall of Perón, incidents have occurred at three points: the

---

12 Alejandro Magnet, *Nuestros vecinos argentinos* (Santiago, 1956), pp. 418–421.

Palena district; the Laguna del Desierto region along the southern Andean frontier between the two nations; and in the waterways surrounding Tierra del Fuego and particularly in the Beagle Channel which separates that island from a group of small islands stretching south to Cape Horn. The dispute of greatest importance concerns the Beagle Channel and particularly three small islands—Lennox, Picton, and Nueva. The boundary treaty of 1881 clearly divided the mainland of Tierra del Fuego between Argentina and Chile from its northern tip to the Beagle Channel. The treaty stated that the islands to the south of the Beagle Channel and to the west of Tierra del Fuego belonged to Chile. The dispute between Argentina and Chile, which has been active since the early twentieth century, revolves around two points: the location of the Beagle Channel and whether the Argentine-Chilean protocol of 1893, which stated that Argentina would have no Pacific coast territory and Chile none on the Atlantic, applies to the question. If the Chilean view on these points prevails, Lennox, Picton, and Nueva belong to Chile. If Argentina's position is accepted, the islands will belong to Argentina and, more important, precedents might be established that would fortify Argentina's claim to other islands and to territory down into Antarctica.

Because of the traditional rivalry between Argentina and Chile and the persistence of mutually suspicious attitudes, incidents in the Beagle Channel and in the other trouble spots assumed great importance to the nationalistic peoples of both nations after the fall of Perón, and led to heightened tension. In 1958 Chile established a lighthouse on Snipe Island in the Beagle Channel area. The Argentine navy destroyed it. When Chile protested and reestablished the signal, Argentina destroyed it again, and its naval forces occupied the island. Chile then recalled its ambassador from Buenos Aires, and more serious consequences appeared likely to follow. But the two powers managed to reach agreement to restore the status quo ante. In the same year jurisdictional conflicts flared between Argentine and Chilean police in the Palena district. The next year Chile protested what it claimed was a violation of its territorial waters by Argentine naval vessels and took steps to augment its naval power. But in 1960, although another jurisdictional dispute arose in the Palena district, the two governments negotiated a series of protocols arranging for the settlement of the Palena and Beagle disputes and providing regulations concerning the use of territorial waters. But these protocols aroused opposition in the Chilean congress, where it was charged that they constituted acceptance of the Argentine position in the disputes and gave Argentina too much freedom to use Chile's territorial waters. After three years the Chilean government withdrew the protocols.[13] Then in 1964 another jurisdictional dispute occurred in the Palena district.[14] Once again the two governments reached agreement. The Palena question was to be submitted to the arbitration of Great Britain, and the Beagle Channel dispute was to be turned over to The Hague Court, after Argentina and Chile agreed on the matters to be considered by that tribunal. Negotiations for submitting the Beagle case to the Hague were continued after 1965 by the new Christian Democrat government of Eduardo Frei, but were disturbed by a clash in the Laguna del Desierto region in which a Chilean policeman was killed. So serious was this dispute that the ministers of defense of both nations participated personally in a meeting to define the boundary in the area. The Palena dispute was ultimately settled by British arbitration but no progress whatsoever was made on the Beagle question.

Relations between Argentina and Chile deteriorated further after 1966 when the military once again seized power in Argentina and installed General Juan Carlos Onganía as president. The military had already seized power in Brazil in 1964, and a military dictator ruled Bolivia. Democratically governed Chile, embarked upon a program of social reform, now began to feel isolated and threatened by a possible coalition of military governments hostile to its system. Rumors began to circulate that an Argentine-Brazilian axis was being formed to assert the hegemony of the two powers throughout South America. Moreover, Bolivia had severed relations with Chile over a river-water-rights dispute and was stridently demanding that Chile provide it with a port on the Pacific. Chile was convinced that the Argentine government was supplying Bolivia with arms and encouraging its claim to a port. Chile's suspicions of Argentina were further enhanced at the meeting of American presidents held at Punta del Este in April 1967, where Argentina opposed a Chilean plan to limit the purchase of costly offensive armaments by the Latin American nations.

While relations with Argentina had been deteriorating, Chile had begun to develop a new policy which had implications for its position with respect to Argentina. In 1960 the South American nations had formed the "Latin American Free Trade Association." That association was designed to create a common market through the gradual elimination of tariff barriers. Chile had been a strong supporter of the movement, for it seemed to offer opportunities to further

---

[13] Rafael Santibáñez Escobar, *Los derechos de Chile en el Beagle* (Santiago, 1969), pp. 150–157.

[14] Guillermo Lagos Carmona, *Las fronteras de Chile* (Santiago, 1966), p. 200.

Chilean economic development. President Frei of Chile also saw political possibilities. If the Latin American nations could form a solid economic bloc, he believed this coalition would give them greater bargaining power in dealing with the United States. By 1965, however, it became clear that the Latin American Free Trade Association movement faced serious problems chiefly because of differences between the interests of the more highly industrialized nations and the less developed ones. Chile continued to support the integration of Latin America as a whole, but it moved also in a new direction by advocating the development of regional integration as a step toward total integration. In 1966 the presidents of Chile, Colombia, and Venezuela, along with representatives of Ecuador and Peru, issued a joint statement in Bogotá announcing formation of an Andean Group to cooperate for the integration of their economies. The concept of regional integration was accepted by the American presidents meeting in April 1967, and the Andean nations moved rapidly toward achieving their goal. Although the chief purpose of the Andean group was economic development, its establishment had obvious implications for Chile's position with respect to Argentina. If the Andean nations succeeded in cooperating economically, they would be disposed to be neutral in any conflict between Chile and Argentina. Chile would therefore be relieved of the threat of hostile powers to its north and could devote its full energies to dealing with Argentina in the event of trouble. It was also possible that the Andean group might ultimately find advantages in acting as a political bloc that would further strengthen Chile's position. It was significant, therefore, that in August 1967 Bolivia joined the Andean group.

But then another incident occurred to create tension between Argentina and Chile. At the end of August 1967 a Chilean warship and an Argentine fishing boat came into conflict over the boundary in the Beagle Channel and produced a flareup of the old controversy. In the midst of efforts to settle the question, the conservative Chilean Nationalist party accused the government of failing to provide the armed forces with armaments adequate to uphold the nation's rights. It was simultaneously being widely rumored that the nationalists were involved in intrigues to establish a military regime in Chile, possibly with foreign assistance. The Chilean government reacted by arresting party leaders for sedition, charging that their attacks on Chile's military strength invited enemy aggression.[15] The Chilean government also now began to take the offensive to settle the Beagle Channel question.

The general arbitration treaty of 1902 between Argentina and Chile

15 *New York Times*, September 8, 1967, p. 2.

provided that either party could ask Great Britain to arbitrate any dispute which could not be settle directly, and that the other party was obligated to submit to such arbitration. In December 1967 the Chilean government formally submitted its case to Great Britain. During the next few months Argentina failed to respond. The moderate *El Mercurio* of Santiago reflected growing Chilean concern, in April 1968, in a strong editorial describing the buildup of Argentine armaments and pointing out the seriousness of this escalation for Chile at a time when Argentina appeared to be resisting a peaceful settlement of the Beagle dispute.[16]

When Argentina finally rejected British arbitration and suggested submitting the case to The Hague Court, *El Mercurio* accused Argentina of failing to abide by the 1902 treaty, and the Chilean government rejected jurisdiction of The Hague, pointing out that the matter had been discussed for many years without success. Chilean fears mounted when Argentina announced that it was strengthening its naval base in Tierra del Fuego and that the annual training maneuvers for the Argentine fleet would take place in the south Atlantic. While Chilean anxiety heightened, Argentine newspapers charged that Chile had aggressive plans, and the governor of the Argentine naval base on the Beagle Channel was reported to be expecting a Chilean attack at any moment.[17]

Amid this tension the Chilean government once again undertook a diplomatic offensive. While continuing to promote its relations with the Andean group, Chile also invaded Argentina's sphere of influence. In July 1968 the Chilean foreign minister visited Uruguay, where several economic and cultural agreements were reached and arrangements were made for Uruguay's chief executive to visit Chile. Within a few days of his return to Chile, the foreign minister again departed, this time to Asunción to attend the inauguration of the president of Paraguay. While in Paraguay, a nation that depends on Argentina for a commercial outlet to the sea, the Chilean foreign minister negotiated a treaty of economic complementation that provided Paraguay with a tax-free zone for its commerce in the Chilean port of Antofagasta. Finally, in September President Frei made an eight-day visit to Brazil. There he and the president of Brazil issued a joint statement in which, among other things, they affirmed their support of the pacific settlement of international conflicts and their approval of regional integration, demonstrating that the traditional friendship between Brazil and Chile was still alive and flourishing.

[16] *El Mercurio* (Santiago, Chile), April 2, 1968.
[17] *New York Times*, May 8, 1968, p. 18.

Chile, through diplomatic maneuvering in the South American system of power politics, had compensated for its inferior power position by isolating Argentina. Chile's growing sense of security was evident when, in February 1969, the Chilean government expelled 14 Argentine professors teaching at the University of Chile without offering any explanations. Yet as long as the Beagle Channel dispute remains unsettled and nationalistic passions continue to run high, the possibility of armed conflict remains between the two nations.

Nevertheless, a number of factors mute the rivalry between Argentina and Chile and tend to diminish the possibilities of an explosion. One is the strong current of responsible opinion in each nation which holds that war would devastate development programs aimed at solving serious domestic problems. The influence of this opinion sector has long been evidenced in the fact that during a century of rivalry, punctuated by periods of great tension, aggravated by violent incidents and war scares, Argentina and Chile have not gone to war, despite the loud cries of hawks in one country and the other. In recent years the strength of the antiwar elements has been reflected in the numerous protocols, declarations, and agreements which, although they have not produced long-term solutions because one side or the other has refused to recede from fixed positions, have indicated a desire to avoid the use of force.

A further factor tending to lessen the possibility of war between Chile and Argentina is the South American system of power politics. That system has had, and still has, the paradoxical effect of intensifying rivalry between them and at the same time contributing to the maintenance of peace. Rivalry has been heightened by the efforts of each nation to play a leading role in the system; peace has been maintained by the balancing of power in South America in such a way that neither nation would be sufficiently strong to risk war with the other.

Finally, the hegemony of the United States over Latin America has in recent years probably played a subtle role in preserving peace between Chile and Argentina. The United States, officially committed to a policy of nonintervention and aware of the growing sensitivity of two leading Latin American nations to the display of United States power, has not openly and directly sought to curb Argentine-Chilean rivalry. However, the United States has forcefully used its influence to maintain peace in Latin America by actively supporting the inter-American system in resolving conflicts among other nations in Latin America and attempting to discourage armaments races in the area. Moreover, it has indirectly favored Chile, the weaker of the two contending powers, by providing it with economic assistance out of pro-

Robert N. Burr: Argentina and Chile

portion to its size. However, if these subtle pressures, combined with the function of the South American system of power politics and antiwar sentiment in Argentina and Chile, are not sufficient to prevent an open conflict, the United States may be called upon to live up to its obligations under the Inter-American Treaty of Reciprocal Assistance and to take action against the aggressor.

Part Three

Violent Conflicts

Chapter 6

Divided Countries

East and West Germany

ELKE FRANK

If German history and politics have a dominant element, it is conflict. A study of contemporary Germany involves an examination of conflict on three levels: (1) the intricate issues in the pattern of relations between the Federal Republic of Germany (FRG) and the German Democratic Republic (GDR); (2) the place each of the two German states has carved out for itself among its neighbors in eastern and western Europe; (3) the role each of the two Germanies plays as a pawn of the two great powers that initially acted as sponsors in their struggles to regain statehood.

The Role of Conflict in German History

The division of Germany is doubtless the most emotionally loaded issue of conflict in contemporary Germany; yet it goes back to the seventeenth century. The Thirty Years' War (1618–1648), a classic in religious and political conflict, was largely fought on German soil, and German princes were its main antagonists. The peace settlement at Westphalia in 1648 carried with it the seeds of further conflict and continuing particularism since the subjects of every prince were required to accept their sovereign's religious affiliation. The Westphalian settlement encompassed more than 300 states—all German and all either Protestant or Catholic—whose subjects were bound to their rulers by ties of religion, even though they might have been closely aligned with their neighbors by language, custom, and social status. Thus, religious division became one of the main obstacles to German unification, even though, through language and customs, German nationalism has roots that reach into the Middle Ages.

The close religious identification between ruler and ruled that came out of the conclusion of the Thirty Years' War led to strong ties between ruling families and subjects. After the French Revolution and the Napoleonic wars, different German ruling houses responded in a variety of ways to the demands for constitutions and popular participation in government. Both these elements—political diversity and religious identification—added up to strong particularism.

German unification during the nineteenth century was accomplished largely through conflict carried to its extreme—war. Although Chancellor Otto von Bismarck was a master practitioner of the art of diplomacy, three main wars—the Danish War (1864), the Seven Weeks' War (1866), and the Franco-Prussian War (1870–1871)—were decisive in the unification of Germany under Prussian hegemony. The Seven Weeks' War excluded Austria from the German Reich, and Prussian rulership resulted in Protestant dominance of the unified Germany. Protestant dominance, in turn, deepened alienation and friction between the predominantly Protestant northern Germans and the mostly Catholic southern Germans.

Even Bismarck, the "Iron Chancellor" who finally enabled his Prussian king to wear the crown of German emperor in 1871, could not deliver a truly unified Reich to his monarch. The Reich was a federation rather than a unitary state. In the German parliament, the Reichsrat (upper house) represented the princely states: particularism in its dynastic and religious manifestations. The Reichstag (lower house) was the assembly of political parties (which crossed state boundaries) but it acted as an advisory rather than a truly legislative body.

After the defeat of the Reich in 1918, Germany became a republic. Despite a constitutional prescription that appeared to give greater powers to the central government,[1] particularism continued. The religious cleavages and the pro- and anti-Prussian sentiments in the north and south were not resolved. Moreover, worldwide depression was intensified in Germany because of the high reparation costs that accompanied the peace of Versailles, and the prolonged depression helped to perpetuate Germany's uneven economic development. Southern Germany, the poorest section, was essentially an agrarian

[1] The Weimar Constitution gave to the central government authority over foreign affairs, currency, customs, communications, national defense, citizenship. Joint powers with the states were: civil rights, civil and criminal law, public health, trade, transportation, industry. The national government was empowered to set fundamental principles guiding the states in matters of taxation, education, religion and major social matters. In case of conflict, the national government was supreme.

economy based on small farms. The west had the resources for heavy industry, but some of the crucial territories had been ceded to France by the Treaty of Versailles. The north had a mixed economy of farming and manufacturing. Eastern Germany had the resources for heavy industry, a well-developed manufacturing industry, and an agricultural system based on large-scale farming.

Hitler's Third Reich, meant to be an example par excellence of total centralization of authority, control, and national identification, did not succeed in overcoming the cleavages between Bavarians and Prussians, Saxonians and Rhinelanders. Personal feuds between National Socialist party leaders continued the conflicts that had existed between princes in earlier days. The party recognized German particularism by organizing itself according to *Gaue*. A party *Gau* (district, headed by a *Gauleiter*, district leader) was the equivalent of a German region, and often the *Gau* borders duplicated the old principalities—Schleswig-Holstein, Saxony, Upper Frankonia, Bavaria, and so on. Even when German nationalism was carried to the extreme of racism, the forces marshaled in favor of unity were not strong enough to overcome the traditional patterns of conflict: religious cleavage, particularism, and regional concern for economic well-being.

German nationalism was based on a common language shared by Germans ever since Martin Luther had translated the Bible into the vernacular. German nationalism was rooted in the memories of a shared past closely identified with the Holy Roman Empire and steeped in the hatred of "outsiders" who, in the absence of natural boundaries, early invaded German territories. Nevertheless, German nationalism was not strong enough to overcome religious, political, and economic conflict. In all of German history since the Middle Ages, a united German state had existed for only 74 years, from 1871 to 1945. Those years encompassed two bloody total wars, a disastrous experiment with representative government (1918–1933), and the Third Reich (1933–1945), which marked the all-time low in German history.

Two German States: the Federal Republic of Germany and the German Democratic Republic

In the period after 1945, a new element of conflict appeared among the historically divisive factors of religion, particularism, and uneven economic development: military occupation and the emergence of two German states, each sponsored by one of the factions in the cold war. The Federal Republic of Germany and the German Democratic Republic grew out of an arbitrary division in 1945 of what was left of the Third Reich by the four main victorious allies of World War II. Under the influence of cold-war politics, what started out as four separate zones of occupation gradually turned into two political systems between 1945 and 1949. The Federal Republic, a merger of the three zones occupied by Western powers, was created under the tutelage of the United States, Great Britain, and the Fourth French Republic. The German Democratic Republic was the Soviet Union's answer to the formation of the Federal Republic. Both "zones" adopted constitutions and elected governments in 1949, and were granted formal sovereign status, in 1954 the FRG, and 1955 the GDR.[2]

To a student of the cold war it is immediately clear that any states formed at the height of the cold war and sponsored by the main protagonists in that war were bound to be a continuous source of conflict. In looking at relations between the two Germanies, however, we perceive a range of conflicts many of which had their origin in the cold war—but many of them would be found among any neighboring states. Conflict between the two Germanies has continued largely for three main reasons: (1) differing capacities; (2) differing ideological and political systems; and (3) differing attitudes toward the settlement of problems in the wake of World War II (borderline adjustments).

The Federal Republic and the Democratic Republic share a common border, marked by barbed-wire fencing. Berlin, an island in the German Democratic Republic, is divided by a reinforced concrete wall, which makes most major thoroughfares in the city dead-end streets. And the memories of common history are now overshadowed by what a scholar refers to as "front line" mentality. The German Democratic Republic is *the* east European state controlled by the Communist party whose borders are farthest west.[3] Aside from Austria (which accepted a four-power-endorsed neutrality status when its peace treaty was concluded), the Federal Republic is the easternmost country of western Europe. Slogans like "bulwark of democracy" have

---

[2] For a documentary record, see US Department of State, *Germany, 1947–49: The Story in Documents* (Washington: US Government Printing Office, 1950). For general background consult Frederick H. Hartmann, *Germany Between East and West* (Englewood Cliffs, N.J.: Prentice-Hall, 1965), chaps. 2 and 3; Peter H. Merkl, *The Origin of the West German Republic* (New York: Oxford University Press, 1963); Arnold J. Heidenheimer, *The Governments of Germany* (2nd ed.; New York: Thomas Y. Crowell, 1966), chaps. 1, 2, 3, 9, 11.

[3] Arthur M. Hanhardt, Jr., *The German Democratic Republic* (Baltimore: Johns Hopkins Press, 1968), p. 5.

characterized the ideological foreign-policy stance of the FRG government and the role of West Berlin; and similarly the government of the GDR considers itself the last outpost of peoples' democracy in Europe. The consciousness of being an ideological outpost facing a staunch, unrelenting opponent is found among the citizens of both Germanies and places their leaders in the front line of battle in the ideological conflict.

The ideological issues—(political representation and a mixed economic system versus an authoritarian one-party system and a state-planned and state-controlled economy)—although they serve as ammunition for the leadership of each state to justify the existence of the political system, are not the main sources of conflict. When separation occurred, each state found itself forced to build a separate economy, a separate identity, a separate security network, and a separate set of relationships with its neighboring states. As each state succeeded in doing these things, its separate identity became more distinct. But by no means did the two states develop equally, and the difference in development has contributed probably more than any other factor to continued conflict between the two Germanies.

The FRG and the GDR are not equal in size, population, natural resources, or industrial capability. The territory of the German Democratic Republic today consists of about 23 percent of the Third Reich, and it is less than half the size of the Federal Republic. This disparity in size has been much less a source of friction than the movement of the population between the two states—or rather the exodus from the east to the west—mostly of highly skilled and well trained labor. Between 1947 and 1965, the population of the German Democratic Republic dropped from over 19 million to a bare 17 million.[4] More than two million people moved westward.

This mass migration from the GDR was one of the reasons behind the construction of the Wall in Berlin in August 1961. The Wall was intended to close the main gate of entry into the Federal Republic of Germany. It was built not so much to cover up the appeal of West Berlin as a "showcase of the West," as Westerners often maintain, as to plug up a leak into the West, since West Berlin functioned as a receiving and processing station for refugees into the Federal Republic. The FGR stressed its willingness to welcome East German

---

4 For population density and migration figures (which are slightly divergent), compare Helmut Arntz, *Facts About Germany* (Federal Government Press and Information Service, 1968), pp. 23, 24, 25; United States Department of State, *Background Notes, Soviet Zone of Germany*, Department of State Publication 7957 (Washington: US Government Printing Office, 1965); *Statesman's Yearbook* (New York: St. Martin's Press, 1965), p. 1061.

refugees with open arms, and within the context of the cold war it gained much propaganda mileage from stories of families being reunited or whole villages and towns being resettled in the Federal Republic at great expense and sacrifice from the taxpayer and the government. In reality, those refugees, most of them able, well-trained, and hard-working people, contributed significantly to the reconstruction of the economy of the Federal Republic of Germany[5] and left behind a corresponding gap in the economy of the German Democratic Republic.

As I have mentioned, the different regions of Germany had quite different economic bases and, to use a concept now popular in political science, had reached very different levels of economic development. The various resources and levels of development would fit into one economy, and, given political union, the economic transactions among the German regions were complementary. Table 1 indicates that while the East had the lion's share of copper ore and brown coal mining,

Table 1 : **East Germany's Share of Production of Raw Materials, Energy, and Manufactures in 1936 Germany**[a]

Iron ore mining	5.1 %
Copper ore mining	92.8
Coal mining	2.3
Brown coal mining	64.1
Oil production	0.02
Chemical-technical industry[b]	24.0
Electro-energy[c]	33.8
Machine construction[d]	31.3
Including: Machine tools[e]	37.9
Textile machinery	54.3
Agricultural machinery	22.2
Vehicle construction	27.5
Precision tool manufacturing and optical industry	33.1
Clothing industry	44.9
Consumer goods and luxuries industry	31.9

[a] Territorial status of 1957, including the Saarland. [b]Without Berlin. [c]1939 without Berlin. [d]Including vehicle construction, shipbuilding, and airplane industry. [e]Without Berlin.

Source: Gerhard Schmidt-Renner (ed.), *Wirtschaftsterritorium Deutsche Demokratische Republik* (East Berlin: Verlag die Wirtschaft, 1961), p. 23; quoted in Hanhardt, *The German Democratic Republic*, p. 115.

[5] For a detailed account of the role played by refugees during the critical phases of Economics Minister Ludwig Erhard's "Economic Miracle," see Henry C. Wallich, *Mainsprings of the German Revival* (New Haven: Yale University Press, 1955).

many of its major industries were by no means self-sufficient. The table also implies the percentage of contribution to the economic productivity of the region made by the rest of Germany (most of which later became the Federal Republic of Germany).

After the division into two Germanies in the era after World War II, neither state could be self-sufficient, and each was forced to seek closer economic ties and new markets outside the newly created borders. The Federal Republic, which had been one of the major recipients of Marshall Plan aid (some of which began to arrive while the FRG was still divided into three zones occupied by the three Western allies), built closer trade relationships with her Western neighbor-states and with the Western allies, under whose supervision the FRG emerged as an economic and political entity. After the signing of the Treaty of Rome in 1957, the FRG played a major role in the European Economic Community and became completely integrated into the economy of her neighbors.

The GDR, on the other hand, linked up with the economic systems of the USSR and other eastern European Communist states; this tie was strengthened by the fact that her economy had been severely depleted by high reparations paid to the USSR in the late 1940s and early 1950s. In the GDR the greatest deficiency in raw materials for heavy industry is the lack of iron ore and hard coal, the basis for a steel industry (see Table 1). However, manufacturing, especially of machine tools, textiles and textile machinery, consumer goods, and precision instruments makes the German Democratic Republic a valuable trading partner as the producer of diversified goods needed in an industrialized society.

A recent study of the German Democratic Republic outlines the economic development of the GDR and divides overall economic policy into four stages:

1. Autarky from 1949 to 1954. During this stage concentration was on internal economic development and readjustment to the changes in raw material supplies due to the division.

2. COMECON from 1954 to the early 1960s. With the end of the reparations came the integration into the economic system of Communist states.

3. World market from the early to the middle 1960s. The "New Economic System," as this phase was called by its planners, sought, in its initial stages, to trade with both East and West.

4. COMECON-Soviet Union from 1966 to present.[6]

[6] *Ibid.*, p. 99.

Despite attempts of GDR planners during the early 1960s to stimulate worldwide trade, the USSR, Czechoslovakia, and Poland are still its most important trading partners. About 50 percent of the GDR trade is with the USSR, 75 percent with the USSR and eastern European states as a whole. More and more the manufacturing industries of the German Democratic Republic have made it a competitive economic entity within the eastern European economic structure, just as the FRG has emerged as one of the industrial giants of western Europe. When the USSR insisted on the conclusion of a new trade agreement with the GDR in the fall of 1965, it found itself subject to extensive bargaining and wrangling by the GDR negotiating team, and the new trade agreement was not signed until December of that year.

During the same years, the Federal Republic of Germany has become fully integrated into the European Communities (encompassing the European Coal and Steel Community, the European Atomic Energy Community, and the European Economic Community). Its economic policies are much more controlled by the plans of the EEC as a whole than the policies of the German Democratic Republic are determined by COMECON, since the EEC is a much more closely integrated community than COMECON. Recording exports of $28.6 billion and imports of $23.6 billion in 1969, the Federal Republic ranked as the second most important trading nation of the world (after the United States).[7] The Federal Republic's currency, the Deutsche Mark (DM) is one of the strongest currencies in the money market. It is backed by considerable reserves in gold and foreign exchange, which in 1969 totaled about $7 billion. To any American economist deeply concerned about the flow of gold out of the United States and the lack of balance of payments in the US economy, the most enviable factor in the economy of the Federal Republic of Germany is the balance of trade, which in 1969 added up to a tidy surplus of $5 billion. In the *World Bank Atlas* of population and per-capita productivity, the Federal Republic of Germany ranks tenth in gross national product per capita, with $1,750. The German Democratic Republic ranks fifteenth, with a per-capita GNP of $1,300.[8]

Each of the two German states, as we have seen, has a "frontline

---

[7] US Department of State, *Background Notes*, Department of State Publication 7834 (Washington: US Government Printing Office, 1970). The *Background Notes* indicate that the FRG gross national product grew by 11.8 percent in 1969 to $156 billion (fourth largest in the world).

[8] International Bank for Reconstruction and Development, *World Bank Atlas*, 1969.

mentality," and there is no doubt that the different ideologies dominating each of the two Germanies are crucial obstacles in the way of establishing meaningful dialogue. The Federal Republic of Germany is based on concepts of representative government, majority rule, and minority rights. Although the FRG has moved from a multiparty system to what amounts to a two-party system, it has preserved and strengthened the most important element in representative government—the element of choice for the voter, choice not only of candidate but also of party. In contrast, the German Democratic Republic is a one-party state. Although about ten parties and interest groups operate in the GDR and run candidates in elections, all these parties are part of the National Front. The National Front is a cover organization totally run by the Socialist Unity party (SED), the ruling party of the GDR and the East German counterpart of the Communist party. There is very little difference between the collectivist ideology of the SED and the belief-systems and practices of the Communist parties in the USSR and other eastern European states.

The ideological split between the two Germanies is illustrated by the different paths taken by Walter Ulbricht, president of the German Democratic Republic and head of the Socialist Unity party, and Herbert Wehner, leader in the Social Democratic Party of Germany, presently the leading partner in the country's coalition government. These two men started out as comrades-at-arms, fighting the National Socialists and the Third Reich together, and they shared concentration camps and exiles. They broke their long-time association on the question of what political shape, what economic structure, Germany should take after World War II. Their break symbolizes the ideological conflict between the Federal Republic and the Democratic Republic.

Both men cut their political teeth in the Communist party of the Weimar Republic. Walter Ulbricht, exiled in Moscow, survived not only National Socialism but also the various Great Purges of the Stalin era, and he became postwar Germany's most loyal advocate of Moscow's policies. He was among the first of exiled German political leaders to return to Germany after the war. He never waivered in his determination to create a new Germany in the image of the USSR as he had known it during his exile. Among eastern European leaders, he has retained the most Stalinist image for himself and his government, even despite experimentation with the New Economic System, by which the GDR moved beyond trade agreements with eastern European states and the USSR and entered the world market.

Herbert Wehner, then a member of the German Communist party, also left the Third Reich for exile in the USSR. In 1937, however, caught in the intraparty struggle and purges in the USSR, he moved to Sweden. In 1946, he broke with the Communists and joined the Social Democratic party in Germany. Like many of his former communist and Socialist comrades, he firmly opposed the Communist party's takeover of political affairs in the eastern occupied zone of Germany. When the enforced merger of the Social Democratic party and the Communist party into the Socialist Unity party took place in the Soviet-occupied zone of Germany in April 1946, many German Social Democrats fled to the western zones of Germany. Like Wehner, they became bitterly hostile to the political and economic goals of the eastern ruling elite, which to them continued totalitarian rule under a new name.

Although the Social Democrats in the Federal Republic are among the bitterest opponents of the policies of the Socialist Unity party in the Democratic Republic, the Social Democratic party has consistently advocated opening a dialogue not only with the German Democratic Republic but also with the eastern European states.

Opening the dialogue with the GDR and especially with the Polish government has called for clarification of the issue of the Oder-Neisse line. In 1945 the Allies declared that the division of Germany would be temporary.[9] The Potsdam conference, although it stressed the temporary nature of the German division, did not modify statements of the Yalta conference specifying the Oder and the Neisse rivers as the new borders between Germany and Poland. Territories beyond the Oder and Neisse had been settled by Germans and Poles for centuries and had been battlegrounds between Poland and Germany. The Yalta conference gave the land beyond the Oder and the Neisse to Poland as compensation for territories the USSR had claimed from eastern Poland. In order to assure Poland of the newly ceded territories, the Allies agreed to evacuate the Germans living in the area and to resettle the territory with Poles. When the two new German republics came into existence, one of the main conflicts between them arose over the permanence of that border. The German Democratic Republic accepted the Oder-Neisse line as its eastern frontier with Poland; the Federal Republic, whose government had won the first election with the help of many refugees and evacuees from the territory ceded to Poland, vowed never to accept the Yalta borders as permanent.

Since then, citizens of the Federal Republic of Germany who oppose recognition of the GDR have maintained that such recognition

[9] The Potsdam Conference (July 17–August 2, 1945) referred to the "eventual reconstruction of German political life on a democratic basis and for eventual peaceful cooperation in international life in Germany." See Potsdam Agreement, US Senate, Committee on Foreign Relations, *Documents on Germany 1944–1959* (Washington: U.S. Government Printing Office, 1959).

would be tantamount to acceptance of the Oder-Neisse line. The government of the GDR, however, must continue to accept the Oder-Neisse line in order to maintain friendly relations with neighboring eastern states, into whose policies and patterns it has become as closely integrated as the FRG has in those of western Europe.

The Consolidation of Each State

Over 20 years, as each of the two Germanies built its own economy, developed quite divergent political institutions, and embraced an ideology that seemed appropriate to its own economic and political structures, each has insisted that the other is just a temporary aberration. Each maintains that the other is a puppet of the eastern or the western superpower who uses its sphere of control over Germany to station troops, to subvert the Germans to its own ideology, to create a new sociopolitical order in its own image, and to increase the rift and conflict between new generations of young Germans. Each side has maintained its intention to reunify Germany under its own way of life.[10]

Citizens of the Federal Republic of Germany have been constantly assured that their counterparts in the east are solidly opposed to "the regime" and want nothing more than to be reunited with the west. Given a free choice, western editorial writers and politicians argue, the inhabitants of the GDR would overwhelmingly reject their system in favor of integration into the Federal Republic. Hans Apel, a West German analyst of public opinion, decided to test the recurring assertion that 90 percent of the people in "the zone" are against the regime (see Table 2).

Although the samples are small, there is a clear indication of an increasing identification with and support of the government on the part of GDR citizens. The percentage of outright opposition was cut in half between 1962 and 1966. Even taking into account that opponents may have classified themselves as ambivalent, or that some opponents may have pretended out of fear to be supporters of the system, the figures indicate an increasing sense of support, which is no doubt related in part to improvements in the economy and the

10 The West German weekly newsmagazine *Der Spiegel*, Vol. 23, No. 53 (December 29, 1969), however, refers to a survey taken by the Allensbach Public Opinion poll in November 1969 in which 51 percent of the respondents considered the recognition of the GDR by the FRG as inevitable, and one-third would accept recognition of the GDR under international law in exchange for a guaranteed status of West Berlin (p. 23).

living standard and to the coming of age of a new generation to whom the GDR is the most familiar and "natural" political and socioeconomic system. The Berlin Wall and the government-controlled mass media, which isolate the population of the GDR from the Western world, probably have contributed considerably to the identification of the people with the system.

Table 2: Support for and Opposition to the Goverment of the German Democratic Republic, 1962–1966

Posture Toward Regime	1962	1964	1966
Loyal	37%	51%	71%
Opponent	28	23	14
Ambivalent "going along"	35	26	15
	(N = 70)	(N = 220)	(N = 365)

Source: Hans Apel, "Bericht über das 'Staatsgefühl' der DDR-Bevölkerung," *Frankfurter Hefte,* XXII, No. 3 (March 1967), p. 171.

If participation in free parliamentary elections can be used as an indicator of support for a political system, the citizens of the Federal Republic are quite firmly committed to their way of life. Election turnouts for the 1961 parliamentary elections were 87.7 percent of eligible voters. The figure declined slightly in 1965 to 86.8 percent, and 1969 saw 86.7 percent of the electorate going to the polls. The election results indicate that the voters of the Federal Republic are not inclined to give their mandates to extremist parties whose ideological outlook and party platforms run contrary to a representative political system, even if those parties included demands for reunification among their campaign slogans.

The German party (DP) had been vociferously demanding reunification of "German soil" in language reminiscent of the Third Reich. It failed to gain the necessary five percent of the popular vote in the 1961 elections and has ceased to be a statewide party. A newcomer, the National Democratic party (NDP), which made virtually no attempt to hide its ties to National Socialist ideology and placed much emphasis on reunification and denunciation of the Oder-Neisse line in its campaign, failed to get the five percent of voter support in both the 1965 and the 1969 elections. The Communist party, outlawed in 1956 by a decision of the Constitutional Court, has been supporting candidates in various front organizations, especially in peace movements and reunification groups. It, too, failed to seat any deputies in the parliamentary elections.

Since political parties in a representative system provide the link between public opinion and government policy, we need to examine party views. On the issue of reunification, the larger political parties in the Federal Republic of Germany have taken quite different stands. The Christian Democratic Union, although it maintained the ultimate need for reunification, pursued as its immediate goal a complete and irrevocable tie-in of the Federal Republic of Germany with the European Economic Community. West Germany was to become an equal social, political, economic, cultural, and military partner of the West. Therefore, during much of the time when the cold war was intense, the establishment of a dialogue with East Germany was not advisable. Even though the FRG established diplomatic relations with the USSR in 1956, and trade missions provided contact between East and West Germany, the CDU/CSU, leadership made no decisive political and diplomatic moves to bring the two states closer together. The Free Democrats (FDP), even when they were the smaller coalition partners of the CDU/CSU until 1956 and from 1961 to 1967 espoused unification, but not to the point where they would withdraw their support of the coalition's overall foreign-policy program, which the CDU/CSU, the senior partner of the coalition, defined as the closest possible integration into the Western alliance.

On the other hand, the Social Democratic party, since the establishment of the FRG, has been deeply committed to reunification, despite the bitter opposition of its leading members to the policies of the GDR's Socialist Unity party. Its commitment to dialogue and to ultimate reunification stemmed essentially from two motives. Traditionally, its stronghold had been in the eastern parts of Germany; many of the SPD's postwar leaders had fled the east, which made for more roots in the east than among the CDU leadership. Further, the SPD was very reluctant to accept the CDU/CSU's exclusively western foreign-policy orientation. The SPD leadership, beginning with Kurt Schumacher and including Erich Ollenhauer, Willy Brandt, and Herbert Wehner, wanted a German foreign policy designed to ease the east-west polarization. Both German states, so the SPD leadership suggested, could do their share to help reduce east-west tensions. On one issue, however, the SPD leaders remained firm; they rejected any form of dialogue based on renunciation of West Berlin's status as one of the states of the Federal Republic of Germany. Such a renunciation, together with a demand for recognition of the GDR, was one of the basic conditions raised by the GDR for the inauguration of talks between the two Germanies.[11]

[11] For a penetrating discussion of the domestic attitudes toward reunification in the Federal Republic of Germany, see Wolfram Hanrieder, *West German Foreign Policy, 1949–1963: International Pressures and Domestic Responses* (Stanford: Stanford University Press, 1967).

Berlin, the capital of imperial Germany, ironically has continued to be a symbol of a unified Germany at a time when both Germanies have disavowed imperialism and monarchy. Both states claim Berlin as the capital city. The GDR actually has its government located in the eastern part of the city, and the FRG makes sure that major ceremonial occasions such as the election of its president take place in West Berlin. Probably the most important role Berlin plays is beyond the control of either Germany. Berlin is an outpost for the military forces of the US and the USSR, both of which maintain garrisons in Berlin. Berlin is a symbol of a political fact—the East-West German conflict is not simply a conflict between the GDR and the FRG.

In its preamble, the Basic Law of the Federal Republic states that its purpose is "to give a new order to political life for a transitional period." The framers of the Basic Law "also acted on behalf of those Germans to whom participation was denied. The entire German people is called upon to achieve, by free self-determination, the unity and freedom of Germany." No matter what diverse views the political parties of the Federal Republic of Germany hold toward reunification, however, neither they nor the SED in the German Democratic Republic can settle their conflicting demands as purely German issues. Until Willy Brandt became chancellor of the FRG in the fall of 1969, neither state was willing to acknowledge that two German states could exist side by side. The GDR had built the wall in Berlin and was maintaining a barbed-wire boundary line the entire length of her western frontier, while the politics of CDU/CSU domination had prevented any grand initiatives on the part of the FRG.

The Two Germanies and the Great Powers

On the world scene, every state acts as an individual and as a member of a variety of regional and functional groupings. What makes the situation between the two Germanies different from the usual pattern of international politics is the special relationship that each German state maintains with its respective cold-war sponsor.

The Western allies in the London and Paris agreements of 1954 recognized the sovereignty of the Federal Republic of Germany, opening the way for its full-fledged membership in the North Atlantic Treaty Organization and the Western European Union. Similarly, the USSR and other eastern European governments recognized the German Democratic Republic and accorded it member status in the Warsaw Pact in 1954. The Federal Republic of Germany has become one of the mainstays of NATO, especially since the French Fifth

Republic under President Charles de Gaulle disengaged itself. Militarily speaking, the two Germanies are completely integrated into their respective military alliances. This integration ranges all the way from the training of recruits and officers to the sharing of weapons and equipment.

Despite assertions of independence, sovereignty, and autonomy by the two Germanies and the two superpowers, special ties remain between the Federal Republic and the United States and between the German Democratic Republic and the Soviet Union. These ties are most visible in the presence in the Federal Republic of 228,000 US troops (the largest US troop contingent stationed abroad outside Vietnam) and of 250,000 to 300,000 Soviet troops in the German Democratic Republic. All these troops are stationed in the two Germanies under the auspices of regional defense agreements (NATO and Warsaw Pact), yet each set of troops has been called up for maneuvers whenever the superpowers have tried to impress each other with their respective strength in Europe, or whenever a crisis situation has arisen in the sphere of influence of the eastern or the western superpower. A recent example is the participation of Warsaw Pact troops (including Soviet troops stationed in the German Democratic Republic) during and after the Soviet intervention in Prague in 1968. Both the Federal Republic and the German Democratic Republic still play the role of pawns in the hands of the superpowers, and that role influences their interactions with each other and increases the potential for conflict between the two German Republics.

The New Eastern Policy

As we enter the 1970s, leaders and citizens of the two Germanies face another conflict. For the first time, the issue of reunification is confronted with the very real alternative solution of the permanent establishment of the two republics. Chancellor Willy Brandt's figure of speech—"two German states in a German nation"—certainly abrogates the insistence of previous German governments that the "other side" is a temporary aberration. From political rhetoric to operational reality, however, is a long way, even though Chancellor Brandt has emphasized his government's intention to pursue a "new eastern policy" (*Neue Ostpolitik*). Direct communications between the heads of government in the two German Republics were established for the first time in 1970, and even though they produced no dramatic communiqués, they opened up dialogue and the possibilities for continued consultation.

Eastern and western Europe appear receptive to increased diplomatic and economic interaction between the FRG and the GDR, and between each of the two and the rest of Europe. The "new eastern policy" of the Brandt government has resulted in increased economic relations between the FRG and Rumania, Poland, and Yugoslavia especially, and in the upgrading of diplomatic relations. The GDR has increased her trade relations with France in particular.

Each of the two superpowers, the US and the USSR, although anxious to maintain its military establishment in what it considers a European frontier outpost of its way of life, seems to encourage a normalization of political processes in Europe. Neither is anxious to spur the other to extend its military commitment in terms of troops and weapons in Europe, least of all in the two Germanies. United States involvement in Indochina and in the Near East is no doubt a contributing factor in the desire not to "rock the boat" in Europe. Similarly, the Soviet Union's uneasy relations with China and its involvement in the Near East give it an interest in a "quiet" East-West German pattern of relationships.

However, even though the United States and the Soviet Union give tacit approval to the top-level meetings between leaders of the two Germanies, both sides keep critical watch on further developments. Chancellor Brandt's "new eastern policy" represents a new wave in Western foreign policy. The Federal Republic's industrial strength is a trump card in negotiations with western as well as eastern countries (including the German Democratic Republic), and Brandt overlooks no chance to use it. To the east, increased trade with West Germany is useful, and the posture of the West German government—pursuing new goals with east European countries and the USSR, independent of US foreign-policy aims—is no doubt viewed positively in the east. It also rates enough attention in the United States to welcome Brandt on a state visit to Washington in 1970, shortly after his government held increased negotiations with Moscow.

The United States, which has openly encouraged the east European states to break away from "eastern-bloc" mentality, welcomes a similar assertion of independence on the part of the GDR, although the experiences of the Dubcek government in Czechoslovakia during 1968 have served as warning signals to prevent an overenthusiastic response by western powers to east European advances toward the West.

What will happen if the dialogue between the two Germanies results in closer ties between the two states? Two powerful German states seem unlikely candidates for the role of pawn between the superpowers. The separatist policies of France within NATO during the presidency of Charles de Gaulle provided the United States (and France's European neighbors) with endless problems. Too independent a foreign policy by the Federal Republic of Germany, especially on the European scene, is not in the interest of the United States as perceived by American policy-makers, whether Democrats or Republicans. American resentment toward overly independent FRG moves runs especially high if those moves are coupled with demands that the United States continue to provide a protective military "umbrella" that will enable the German Federal Republic to carry out its foreign-policy objectives, including policy innovations toward the east.

Too much experimentation on the part of East Germany creates similar fears and suspicions in the USSR. The events in Hungary in 1956 and in Czechoslovakia in 1968 indicated that the USSR is not about to risk loosing its pawn. Willi Stoph, despite his willingness to meet with his West German counterpart, cannot afford to overlook Alexander Dubcek's experiences, if indeed he was ever willing to initiate as much change as Dubcek had aimed for.

The question has been raised why the German conflict has become so much more muted than the conflicts existing between the two Chinas, divided Korea, and Vietnam. It is by no means easy to judge the "mutedness" of conflict in these diverse situations. Perhaps the two Germanies differ most significantly from the two Koreas, the two Chinas, and the two Vietnams in that the two Germanies are Western. Eastern Europe and East Germany are still part and parcel of most of Western history, and their historical experiences are similar to and shared with the states around them and with the two superpowers. The Federal Republic of Germany and the German Democratic Republic have their roots in many common conflicts, wars, alliances, and aspirations that have shaped the histories of their neighbors and of the two superpowers to whom they primarily owe their present structure. They do not have the weapons and the military resources of the two superpowers, but they do know the same rules of diplomacy. They were never colonies, and they did not experience a lengthy political tutelage by large outside forces, as the two Koreas and the two Vietnams did. They have not been as secluded from Western military and political affairs as the Chinese. This shared Western history has no doubt been an important factor in enabling both the GDR and the FRG to turn the role of pawn into a position of diplomatic bargaining power wherever possible. Whether the tools of diplomacy can ultimately offset military strength is at this point a matter of speculation, but certainly the current indications are that the FRG and the GDR stress diplomacy and economic policy in their contacts with each other.

The initial meetings between the two German chancellors in the spring of 1970 were held for the avowed purpose of opening a dialogue between the two Germanies. Hopefully, dialogue between the chancellors and their staffs will open up increased opportunities for contact between citizens of the two Germanies, many of whom are members of the same families and have long been separated by political events. Economic contacts and trade will be improved, and each German state, as a member of the part of Europe in which it is situated, may contribute to increased linkages between the two Europes. Chancellor Brandt has maintained that the two German states have a great deal of catching up to do before they reach the degree of interaction between themselves and with other European states which most European states have been able to achieve, at least in bilateral relations, in the years since 1945.

Ultimately, dialogue will not be enough, however, and the question of either formal recognition of two German states in one German nation or some form of reunification will have to be faced. A long-range settlement of the East-West German question and the various ideological, legal, military and economic conflicts related to it can be resolved only if men in positions of leadership at all levels of the problem—East and West Germany, eastern and western Europe, the USSR and the US—are agreed on forms of settlement. No matter who rules in East Berlin and Bonn, and no matter how broad the base of support for their rule, the ultimate decisions do not lie in their hands, although they can do a great deal in paving a way toward solution.

North and South Korea

GREGORY HENDERSON

It is the practical men, not the idealists, who ever since the dawn of history have, by their practical policies, produced the unending series of disasters, the catalogue of miseries, which we call human history.— LEONARD WOOLF

The Problem

The framework of international conflict contains few settings more striking or stranger than Korea.

National rivalry, diverse cultural entities within one nation, and diverse historical experience provide conflict's most familiar territory. Korea's conflict has never stood on this ground. To the contrary, it is hard to think of a more homogeneous national or cultural entity anywhere than the Korean peninsula; no other has been divided with a more mindless artificiality by purely external powers; in none are communications so utterly ruptured or conflict positions more implacable.

Korea shares some conflict elements with the two Germanies, the two Vietnams, the two Chinas, even with India-Pakistan. Yet the Korean case sheds over both its own conflict and others so icy and disturbing a clarity that one is led to ponder whether we are not facing some deep and cruel law of nature and its selection process. The power released by splitting nature's homogeneous element, the atom, is most intense. Does the splitting of the most homogeneous nations automatically enhance conflict? Is the energy released intensified by some natural process?

Korea's importance as a conflict case does not end with a hypothesis of natural law. The conclusions we derive from its situation are also greatly practical. Korea not only demonstrates the violence and implacability that division supported by hostile patrons can quickly implant; it also tends to demonstrate that the surgery of division, however extreme and artificial, is remarkably easy and the prognosis for each sundered entity unexpectedly favorable in almost every respect except, perhaps, reconciliation. Ancient—or modern—unity can, as with Germany, split and sire viable states whose reasons for reuniting ebb as the success of each part surges. This lesson is not unimportant. It has served to some degree as a model for Vietnam, where many policy-makers have brought experience in Korea to bear on the attempted American solution; this solution in effect seeks two viable states where the Communists have, as in Korea, sought one.

Korean division also demonstrates the power of psychological forces, which, when separate loyalties are created, reinforce each new fealty with the iron bonds of hostile norms and vocabulary. Here, not in history, the conflict concentrates. Behind, in a more obvious and less subtle sense, the larger, parent cold-war hostilities work their own tidal history and capacities to deepen conflict or to nudge their clients toward unification by externally aided means. The external carriers of conflict disease are subject to shallower and more erratic motivations where their interests inhere less deeply: Korea, Vietnam and Germany all lacked powerful internal arguments for disunity, but Korea and Vietnam are without those persuasive and historically deep-rooted external pretexts and fears of aggression that forced the rending of Germany. Relative to its neighbors, Korea inspires aggressive fears far less than Vietnam.

The Internal Background of Unity

The personality of Korea as a conflict situation is sharp. Almost no national communities have operated nearly so anciently as one political, linguistic, and economic unit as has Korea, which, from A.D. 668 until 1945 filled most—later all—of the Korean peninsula south of the Yalu-Tumen line. Even including China-Taiwan (or, of course, Laos or India-Pakistan) as well as Germany and Vietnam, no presently divided country had been previously united so continuously or so long. Throughout two millenia of historical times, Korea has been united ethnically and linguistically; the country has lived under the same rule and ideologies and never from A.D. 668 to 1945 has in any significant way been cleft.[1] Colonialism, strengthening north-south

1 For further detail and for minor qualifications to this point, see Gregory Henderson, *Korea: The Politics of the Vortex* (Cambridge: Harvard University Press, 1968), pp. 13–35.

communications and operating with a centralism far more powerfully tooled than the old dynasties', added to rather than detracted from this unity.

Potential for the present conflict in or over Korea began to be generated by modern political forces in the era after World War I. These forces worked chiefly outside the country and were largely limited to some thousands of persons engaged in the independence movement. The chief new divisive factor was Communism which, from 1918 on, operated effectively on the large Korean communities in eastern Siberia and Manchuria and, to a numerically smaller extent, on Koreans in north China.[2] A small Korean Communist party started within Korea in 1925, but went underground during the period of Japanese militarism (1931–1945); it had perhaps 4,000 or fewer members organized in strong cells by the time liberation came. From 1920 on, there were constant political clashes, and a few military ones, between Korean Communists, some supported by the Comintern, and the many conservatives in the independence movement—some of whom, like Syngman Rhee, lived in the United States. By 1945 a second generation of expatriate Koreans, trained in schools that were Communist, democratic, colonial or Japanese, or even anti-Communist, were ready to play their roles. Potential divisiveness there was, but no relevance for a north-south Korea split; Communism was if anything stronger in some cities and a few rural areas in the south than in the north.

Division by Occupation

In 1945 the United States 24th Corps and units of the First Soviet Far Eastern Front entered and occupied Korea, conforming to the terms of General Order No. 1 which General Douglas MacArthur, Supreme Commander for the Allied Powers, caused the Japanese government to issue to all its armed forces on September 2, 1945. MacArthur followed it with a Proclamation to the People of Korea, based on the order and issued on September 7, 1945.

The country had only small ground for left-right conflict. Handled within the framework of one government, such potential conflict would have proved to have considerably shallower roots and a narrower social base than left-right divisions in other occupied states

[2] By at least 1922, Koreans were the third largest ethnic group in the Soviet Far Eastern Republic, numbering some 200,000–300,000. See Suh Dae-sook, *The Korean Communist Movement, 1918–1948* (Princeton: Princeton University Press, 1967); Chong-Sik Lee, *The Politics of Korean Nationalism* (Berkeley: University of California Press, 1963); and Xenia J. Eudin and R. C. North, *Soviet Russia and the Far East, 1920–1927* (Stanford: Stanford University Press, 1957).

Gregory Henderson: North and South Korea

such as Austria. In August 1945 no normal development seemed likely to make conflict in Korea uncontainable within normal political development, let alone a threat to the country's unity.

A below-the-surface power struggle for US–USSR spheres of influence, more implicit than explicit in 1945, plus a governmental horror story for the ages performed for Korea what its own internal forces could not do. For this development, no policy reason sufficed. Unlike Germany, a united Korea offered no threat to the interests of any of the victorious powers. Nor was Korea a vanquished state to be punished; it was considered a liberated country. There is no sign in the US–USSR discussions at Cairo, Teheran, Yalta, or Potsdam that division was intended, and no surface indication of conflict over Korea.[3] Roosevelt proposed a Soviet-American-Chinese trusteeship of 20 to 30 years in Korea to prepare Koreans for self-government. Stalin merely commented that the period should be as short as possible and that the British should be invited. Both agreed that foreign troops should not be stationed in Korea.[4]

Despite occasional urging from both War and State Department aides, neither Roosevelt at Yalta nor Truman at Potsdam pushed the matter to a viable trusteeship arrangement or to a committee that would present concrete proposals. When at Potsdam, first Molotov and then Stalin raised Korea in a trusteeship context, Churchill cut them off and Truman said nothing.[5] Stalin "fully agreed with the desirability of a four-power trusteeship for Korea" when Harry Hopkins raised the question in the Kremlin on May 28, 1945. Although the State Department had provided him with a fairly detailed plan for four-power administration of civil affairs, followed by a five-year trusteeship in Korea, Hopkins did not choose to obtain anything but a general

---

[3] At Potsdam, Harriman privately expressed fear that the Soviets would utilize trusteeship in Korea as a means of asking for trusteeship over Hong Kong and Indochina. Stimson urged minimal US troops during trusteeship on the ground that the Soviets had one or two divisions of Soviet-Korean troops which they were likely to use to "Polandize" Korea. Such fears, however, were expressed in internal American documents only. *Foreign Relations of the United States: Conference of Berlin (Potsdam)*, II (Washington: Department of State, 1960), 260, 631.

[4] *Foreign Relations: The Conferences at Malta and Yalta, 1945* (Washington: Department of State, 1955), p. 770. The trusteeship idea was based on Roosevelt's underestimation of Korean abilities at self-government and was opposed by Koreans after the war. It would, however, have provided an initial framework for leaving the peninsula united.

[5] *Conference of Berlin*, II, 253, 606. Churchill's motives are not known to have been related to Korea. He evidently feared that a Korean trusteeship would open the door to Soviet participation in trusteeships over the former Italian colonies, thus bringing Soviet power to the Mediterranean.

trusteeship agreement from Stalin.[6] Perhaps because of an oral agreement at Yalta not to station troops in Korea, the question of the occupation of Korea, whether joint or separate, was never raised. The Soviets actually invited joint US–USSR military action in Korea, which American policy also favored.[7]

Meanwhile, internal American planning generated the idea, contrary to the oral agreement at Yalta, that Korea would be occupied and that trusteeship would follow. Joint Allied (or US–USSR) occupation was intended, or at least implied, but when Soviet troops entered Korea, on a schedule known to the Americans, the sleaziness of previous planning was revealed, the situation declared "unforeseen," and a hasty *ad hoc* solution devised in the Pentagon and cleared with the State Department. It authorized the USSR to receive the Japanese surrender north of the 38th parallel, the US to receive it south of the parallel; until the surrender was complete, "the administration of civil affairs" was to be "the responsibility of the respective commanders of the two zones in Korea."[8] General Order No. 1 and its successive directives then divided Korea according to this "policy." American planners operating in the face of both knowledge and warnings enabled the Soviets to achieve in Korea what they had denied them in Japan: a separate occupation zone in which they could, unhindered, work their separate will.[9] Practical, good-willed American officials of

---

6 *Conference of Berlin*, I, 47; *Foreign Relations: 1945*, VII, 882–883. Ambassador Harriman has recently stated, in answer to a question, that "it would have been folly to push the Korea trusteeship idea further," since he knew that Stalin and Molotov would have tried to use it to acquire a Soviet occupation zone in Hokkaido. Molotov had recognized that four-power trusteeship, as an unusual device, would require "a detailed understanding" (*ibid.*, p. 914).

7 General Antonov at Potsdam, *Conference of Berlin*, II, 351. Even State's briefing paper for Hopkins on Korea did not mention "occupation" but only "joint civil affairs administration."

8 *Foreign Relations: 1945*, Vol. VI, *The British Commonwealth and the Far East* (Washington: Department of State, 1969), 1037–1040. James C. Dunn signed the crucial State memorandum—clearly a political decision by the agency concerned—and Dunn, Assistant Secretary of War John J. McCloy, and Assistant Navy Secretary Bard presided over the 38th-parallel decision, which was proposed by Colonel Dean Rusk and Colonel (later General and UN Commander in Korea) C. II. Bonesteel III. The State Department briefing papers prepared for Yalta as far back as late 1944 and January 1945 contained stern warnings about the dangers of divided zones of operation or occupation in Korea (*The Conferences at Malta and Yalta*, pp. 358–361).

9 Behind this planning lay, of course, views of comparative military capabilities. The War Department believed that "Russia is militarily capable of defeating the Japanese and occupying Karafuto, Manchuria, Korea, and Northern China before it would be possible for the US military forces to occupy these areas" (*Foreign Relations: 1945*, VII, 876–877).

high reputation, pursuing practical solutions, had thus shaped a catastrophe for Korea, the United States, and all mankind.

Having created occupations, Washington and Moscow were both diverted to the even larger problems of Germany, liberated Europe, and Japan. The problem of Korea was in effect handed to the occupying commands for several months. Neither was a refined political instrument. The US 24th Corps, in particular, had been hastily chosen because of the short time needed to bring it from Okinawa. The corps and its commander, General John R. Hodge, were totally unprepared for the problems of Korea. Lacking Washington directives, they relied heavily on field civil affairs manuals and "Blacklist," a plan for MacArthur in which Korean operations were insufficiently differentiated from those planned for Japan. The occupying units of the First Soviet Far Eastern Front were probably likewise cut off from detailed instruction from Moscow, but Communism provided considerably more effective local operating procedures than did manuals. The Communists had cadres, at least some of which appear to have been specially trained for the Korean situation. They also had standard Communist procedure for political takeover and its organizational components. In addition, they came armed with up-to-date information supplied by the Soviet consulate-general in Seoul.[10] The two commands had had no contact; no feeling of alliance had developed, as it had in Europe; each was wound up for an imminent major attack and tended to cast the other in the role of the enemy.

"There is a limited time within which an occupying power has optimal chances of successfully launching major reforms."[11] In Korea, that time passed. Despite urgent and timely pleas from Seoul to contact the Soviets on a higher level, SWNCC was sluggish and no move was made toward trusteeship in Korea until the Moscow Conference of late December 1945. No useful overall political directive reached General Hodge from Washington until January 29, 1946.[12] The Soviet

[10] Since the USSR declared war on Japan only on August 8, a large Soviet consulate-general operated in Seoul throughout the war. The Comintern school at Ula in the Bashkir Republic secretly trained Koreans for the struggle against Japan and an eventual takeover in Korea. Wolfgang Leonhard, *Child of the Revolution* (Chicago: H. Regnery Co., 1964), pp. 214–215.

[11] Robert E. Ward, Social Science Research Council "Items," Vol. 21, No. 3 (September 1967), *Military Occupations and Political Change,* a Conference held in New York, April 20–22, 1967.

[12] A SWNCC directive (176/8), initially drafted September 1, was released and finally forwarded to Tokyo on October 17. There is some question whether it reached Seoul promptly; its political provisions were in any case long outdated by that time. Originally useful for planning, SWNCC proved far too cumbersome a mechanism for Seoul's urgent needs and volatile developments (*Foreign Relations: 1945,* VI, 1073–1091).

occupiers, Korea policy or no, had cadres and programs for political power. The US Army, operating with far less sophisticated procedures out of the army manuals, no cadres, and no policy, carried out its occupation in a largely undirected, instinctive manner.[13] For both commands, post-Moscow conference instructions envisioning trusteeship and a joint government came too late. Americans greatly underestimated the power of occupations to influence attitudes and group formation. In the 15 weeks till the end of 1945, each of the two commands intentionally or unintentionally created in each zone a group cast in—or caricaturing—its own image, a group so hostile to the other that no later directives or policies could bring them together. The brief opportunity to implement policy had been allowed to pass without policy's having been introduced; thereafter, the Korean political forces supported by each command dedicated themselves to stands even more extreme than those held by the Americans and Soviets. Nor was the conflict thus invoked even enclosed within the peninsula; it spread at once to Korean communities abroad, especially to the more than 600,000 Koreans who form the community in Japan, which even today remains irreparably sundered.

Formation of Hostile Groups

The effect of 15 weeks' work presents conflict analysis with a dramatic phenomenon and problem. How could the strong, unifying, and homogenizing work of 13 centuries be reversed in so brief a time and chiefly by foreign influences? Even if language and basic culture survived, how could ideology and the aims and organization of politics be so quickly reshaped, and loyalties shattered and reconstructed? How can brothers in a closely knit culture be recast so quickly into enemies?

History does not answer this dilemma. Korea's division is antihistorical. Even the splits of the independence movement play a fairly small role for a few thousand Korean residents. Ideology is important, though more for the Communists than for their opponents, and even so its role is less than that played by Catholicism and Protestantism in dividing Czechs or Germans in the 16th century There are overtones of power politics, but they appear to be only partly intentional and are largely inexplicit in policy; they go part of the way toward explaining US-USSR hostility. But these factors are the backdrop to Korean conflict, not the conflict itself. What force worked among

[13] Not even civil affairs teams landed with Hodge; the first, trained for the Philippines, arrived only after five weeks. Meanwhile, the occupation was implemented by tactical troops (Henderson, *Korea,* p. 124).

Koreans from September to December 1945, so advancing hostility that South Koreans began to undercut any attempt by the US to negotiate for reunification with more divisive demands than the US wished to make? None of the factors mentioned adequately explains how the occupying powers communicated their hostilities to the Koreans so rapidly, and in the US case so largely unintentionally, as to pulverize the unifying forces built up over centuries.

The answer appears to lie chiefly in the nature of group formation and in the psychology that operates when groups form. That no trusteeship, and above all no central government, either foreign or domestic, was provided for in the first 15 weeks deprived the occupations of the forces of merger and compromise. Largely unintentionally, the organized military forces of both sides were given *carte blanche* to create their own systems. The policy *carte* was *blanche*, but not the culture with which the occupations operated. Large armed forces by their very movement and daily action, directed or undirected, stamped their zone with their image. Strengthened by the organization of war and the prestige of victory, the two administrations rapidly forged two Korean groups with incompatible political, economic, and international orientations and openly hostile intentions toward each other. These groups quickly graded themselves in terms of fidelity or hostility to Communism instead of by linguistic, historical, or ethnic ties; such cultural ties suddenly became no more a barrier to hostility than were ancient ethnic, linguistic, and historical ties to the hostilities between American Tories and revolutionaries in 1775.

True, if Korea had had the communication system of, say, Ethiopia and had never known, even remotely, modern political systems or a rightist-leftist split, the result would certainly have come far more slowly and probably been very different. The nature of the communication system within Korean society permitted the imposed systems to be internalized with such sensational rapidity. So, perhaps, did the fact that the environment was malleable and had previously contained no basic cleavages. Korean social process gave unseen support to the divisive forces of the occupation and helped to undermine the resistance that the unifying historical centuries might have thrown up against them. Such factors, as part of the communication of hostility, need explanation; for the communication of hostility is a basic component of conflict.

HISTORY

Korea's history made her open to the leads of foreign powers. A small country next to the world's most commanding civilization, she accepted much of her religious, philosophical, and sociopolitical culture from China. The tradition continued when the West impinged on the Orient. She even successfully internalized much that Japan forced on her. The overnight removal of the Japanese model brought vacuum: the country had been swept beyond traditional ways and sought and needed from the victors new models for modernization. Traditionally isolated from all contact except with China and, intermittently, Japan, only a few Communists and the Christian community of a few hundred thousand had any very strong preconceptions of what kind of direction they should seek, and from whom.

SOCIETY

The society's vulnerability to messages from the capital also had sociohistorical roots. Korea had long been a peculiar and extreme society: a relatively homogeneous environment in which a paucity of interest groups and local power was capped by a highly developed centralism that neither had nor tolerated rivals. This central power had long been the instrument for transmitting foreign systems. The central structure also outweighed all others by incorporating organization and techniques of selection and administration designed for China's gigantic needs. The overwhelming strength of the center had several implications. Once central power in Pyongyang or Seoul had been captured, its messages could be broadcast—and amplified—downward. Receptivity to the broadcasts of centralism was great: nothing competed with government, or blocked, compromised, or qualified its terms. Such unopposed power created its own dynamic and mass society, summoning in atomic form, like iron filings, all social members toward it in a regimen of imperious magnetic power.[14] Such atomic beings, lacking the experience of unity in intermediate groups, tended to incorporate rivalry, jealousy, and hostility more easily than solidarity and mutual cooperation; the structure of society showed a lack of connection among the parts that hindered their coagulation into interest expression or opposition, even opposition to foreign occupiers.

In 1945, atomization happened to be at its most patent level. The Japanese government's always stern centralization had by then been greatly enhanced. Since the Manchurian incident of 1931, Japan had rapidly industrialized and urbanized Korea as a base for penetration of the continent. War had necessitated mass mobilizations. Koreans by the hundreds of thousands were knocked from their rural niches and their social settings and herded into new environments in urban centers in both Korea and, through forced labor, Japan. Rootless, they

14 See Henderson, *Korea*, pp. 195–224.

were prey to the mass "populist" movements of workers, contributors, volunteers, and "patriots" of Japan's later militarist days, much as rootless Korean emigrants had been prey to communism in Irkutsk and Khabarovsk. When Soviet and American occupiers suddenly stood in the still-warm Japanese boots, most Koreans unconsciously looked to them and expected mobilization. This the Russians gave them. So, in the south, did the new politicians and their youth groups. Mass mobilization provided instant mass communication.[15] Even the anticipation of mobilization prepared people to listen.

COLONIALISM

Finally, the nature of the Korean colonial experience made an important contribution to the heat and divisiveness of the situation in 1945. The intensity of Japan's rule and controls was unequaled by any other colonial power. Korea, an ancient kingdom with a highly developed court, culture, and sense of identity, felt inner superiority to its colonial master and outrage at the heavy-handed efforts to "Japanicize" her. These feelings were goads, more powerful than for most colonial peoples, to prove through rapid modernization that underdeveloped Korea was still as good as Japan, developed but historically despised. Each occupation power loomed as the instrument through which Koreans could catch up; in their desire not to be marginal in the struggle, much criticism of foreign methods was muted.

THE LURE OF BUREAUCRACIES

Separated until 1945 by a thick layer of 700,000 Japanese from that access to rule which they considered their Confucian birthright, aspiring Koreans perceived the evaporation of the Japanese presence as a chance to reenter the old dynastic race for access to power. Tens of thousands of government jobs suddenly opened.[16] Under the circumstances, these jobs gave each occupation government enormous leverage on the society of its half of Korea, and the substitution of new systems for old received automatic impetus. The awarding of jobs was also a basis for rift. The Communists expelled thousands of

[15] See William Kornhauser, *The Politics of Mass Society* (Glencoe, Ill.: Free Press, 1959), for a memorable exposition of this phenomenon which has classic application to Korea's situation in 1945.

[16] Japan had used 95,385 officials for the entire peninsula as late as 1938, somewhat more by the end of the war, the upper 50% being almost entirely Japanese. By 1953, the bureaucracy in the Republic of Korea alone had swelled to over 300,000.

Koreans who had accepted jobs in the colonial government, and turned the population against them. These people fled to the South, which then became the "traitorous heir to colonialism."

Finally, though Korea in 1945 was underdeveloped in some economic and organizational respects, Koreans already lived in a relatively developed environment of communications; they enjoyed many newspapers, journals, and radio stations and a rising literacy rate. The Communists, with their effective cadres, commandeered and effectively utilized these media. They were even able to publish their own newspaper for many weeks in Seoul before General Hodge closed it. The Americans, with neither policy nor cadres, never operated any of the newspapers of Korea, though most, as Japanese-owned property forfeit to the occupation, were handed to the US commander on a silver platter. The US command did, however, use the radio, and the press carried its statements, the newly appointed media managers being indebted to the American authorities. Conservative landlord elements controlled Korea's chief newspaper and influenced others, becoming important instigators of a campaign opposing the Communists and trusteeship and supporting a separate government. The role of the communications media was vital in highlighting the differences between the two systems, in criticizing what was deemed hostile, and in rallying support for demonstrations or campaigns.

Refugees. The Soviet occupation immediately brought a swelling mass movement of refugees south. Some movement arose from instinctive fear: the Japanese had indoctrinated Koreans against Communism. Many refugees, especially the large Christian population of the northwest, reached for a future with a "Christian democracy." Others were targets of the communist system. The intense organization in the North of "people's committees," "social organizations," the Communist party, leading by early 1946 to a "people's democracy" under a Red Army officer, Kim Il-song, spread strong propaganda and activity everywhere against property-holders, former officials, and independent-minded students. Some 17 percent of the North Korean population, or by mid-1947 approximately 1,800,000 persons, fled south. Part of this group remained very briefly in refugee camps: the Korean extended family plus the many abandoned Japanese properties provided opportunity for rapid integration into South Korean communities. This rapid integration created an important communication system, spreading the hostilities of the refugees and their adverse experiences in the North through most of the society, especially in Seoul and other opinion centers. The departure of this large body of people from the North and its incorporation into society in the South constituted an immense force for hostility and polarization.

These factors are crucial in explaining the rapidity with which the American and Soviet systems, once introduced at the top, could spread, the thoroughness with which they and their ideologies could permeate the society, and the dynamism behind the extremeness and hostility that replaced the ancient unity of the peninsula.

The Communist Message. The Communists magnified all these communications instruments with a holistic ideology, with cadres, and with previously planned operating procedures. The cadre articulated communism on a local level and taught new converts in a fluid situation, including loyalty to Communism and the Soviet Union. Denunciation, threat, and expulsion constituted actions that in themselves increased the solidarity, the interaction, and the image of the new groups. The language of Communism provided a new reference through which the eager young men of village and town could view what were rapidly emerging as new friends, new enemies. Groups, with their actions, their constant indoctrination sessions, and their vocabulary, rapidly accumulated new social norms and values. For the predominantly young population, Communism offered a strong ideological explanation that seemed a firm anchor in a critical and uncertain time, a dynamic substitute for Confucianism's worn but impressive holism. The initial groups were small, permitting intense and intimate interaction, rapid involvement of the individual in a group, and inculcation of internalized discipline, norms, and expectations. These were then rapidly woven into a hierarchy and structured to bring further conformity. Communism's hierarchy served also as a new form of the ancient culture's bridge to the capital's heady and mysterious "big time." In August and early September almost nothing opposed this process. Few intermediary organizations existed, for the Japanese had allowed no politics for a decade; in the Soviet zone, communism's detractors, conservatives and Christians, soon fled. Rapid and ruthless Communist politicization in the north was a major stimulant for South Korea to evolve its own hostile political system.

The American Message. In the South communication of the new was unplanned, slower, more informal, less defined. Hodge rebuffed the existing local committees and the "People's Republic" they had just elected. In destroying these groups he destroyed the only organized political activity in existence. On the local level, there was nothing to take its place: Hodge had no trained cadres. His inadvertent influence on group formation began, four days after he landed, with the announcement that he would "consult" only with "organized political groups." Dozens, finally hundreds, of such groups answered what they perceived as an invitation to enter the ancient game of access to power. Though even communism was far from outlawed, the party stance likely to be best received was clearly implied: the Christian, English-speaking Koreans whom Hodge chose as advisers and his treatment of the "People's Republic" soon conveyed a beckoning message to rightist groups.[17] These small, transitory "parties" served as seed beds for a vague but generally noncommunist training and posture. As refugees came in, without homes or occupations but already implanted with hostility to communism and the Russians, they formed influential new social, religious, and political groups that spread their feelings. The collapse of colonial government and the defenselessness of Japanese property brought crime and (rightist) police buildup. Rightist-leftist splits, from October 1945 on, brought fights. An age of youth groups dawned. Each major rightist independence leader, each major "political party" assembled a youth group. Hundreds of thousands of young hopefuls also joined Communist or leftist youth groups and "fronts" in South Korea.

Within days or weeks, quarrels between right and left became endemic, affecting youth groups and all colleges and schools of middle-school level or above, down to the rural level. Groups on both sides hardened around these splits, compromise was seen as disloyalty to the group, and leadership developed, much of it gained by those making the most extreme appeals. Suddenly these confrontations substituted, emotionally, for those between Koreans and Japanese that had vanished with repatriation. In a world waiting between a disarmed Japanese army and the arriving Soviet and American divisions, weapons were quick to hand; street violence and the October 1946 uprising in the South further hardened the divisions and hostilities. The leadership of Rhee and the independence leaders had force as well as skill: many had formed tough anticommunist forces in pre-World War II days and formed them now. Especially after the Moscow conference, opposition to trusteeship provided a popular rallying point and was seized upon by the rightists. When, about New Year's Day 1946, the Communists abruptly reversed their stand against trusteeship, the split widened. Thereafter it grew constantly as the US–USSR joint commissions sought to establish groups to consult in the formation of a provisional government. "Democratic process" thus contributed to hectic rivalry in group formation. The acrimony of this

17 William R. Langdon, acting political adviser in Seoul, admitted that "it is quite probable that at the beginning we may have picked out a disproportionate number of rich and conservative persons" (dispatch of November 26, 1945, *Foreign Relations: 1945*, VI, 1135).

rivalry eroded neutralism and moderation. Those pleading unity more urgently than anticommunism were reduced to a thin few whom not even belated official American support (1946–1947) could forge into a viable political force. As so often at this stage of conflict formation, nativistic movements dominated the social atmosphere.

The Road since 1946

Since 1946–1947 Korea has been visited by a dramatic and often told history of UN involvement, war, armistice, and 16 years of negotiations at Panmunjon. Despite escalation, internationalization, and notoriety, however, the conflict's less-known original terms survive surprisingly intact.

Division and hostility soon—in 1948—crystalized into two Korean governments. The United States brought the unresolved issue to the United Nations, which did not defuse it. Refused entry to the North, the UN commission observed the 1948 elections in the South that resulted in the Rhee government of the Republic of Korea (ROK). The new government cast aside even the few restraints of US military government: the Communist party was made illegal; mail exchange at the 38th parallel was ended; moderates standing for peaceful unification were persecuted and, in the case of some National Assembly members, jailed on charges of Communism after farcical trials; the police and the army were further strengthened; a vague and comprehensive National Security Law was passed. Anticommunism became the touchstone of the regime's outlook and actions.

The North, now formed as an independent" "Democratic People's Republic of Korea" (DPRK) under Kim Il-song, under Soviet guidance had already pursued Communist measures of even more drastic ilk. These efforts were now increased. The armed forces were built up to at least 150,000 men, compared to the South's 100,000, with considerably better equipment, provided by the Russians, and seasoned Korean units. The occupations had never claimed each other's territory; now both ROK and DPRK stridently voiced a claim to all Korea. The states became the macrocosms of the smaller political groups each had formed in the wake of the divisions of 1945.

The 1950–1953 Korean war climaxed this process of constant escalation in divisiveness. Since North Korea continued to be closely bound to the Soviet Union, which, it is now known, ordered the Chinese forces to support the North Koreans in late 1950, one aspect of the war clearly represents culmination of a constant and rapid accelaration of Soviet troops, might, success, and ambition in the Far East since 1944.[18] Kim Il-song's ambitions are another cause. The precise mix behind the Communist invasion of 1950 remains a mystery.

The Effects of War

INTERNATIONALIZATION

War's effects were many and they broadened the issue beyond the peninsula. In 1948–1949, each super-power, following its occupation, sought to disentangle itself from the hostilities it had created by withdrawing its troops from the peninsula.

War again made international a conflict previously confined to the peninsula: the troops of 17 foreign nations, the relief and aid activities of many more, and the United Nations itself descended upon the crisis. This breadth of international involvement has since slowly but greatly contracted: no similar UN commitment has been repeated, and UN political involvement in Korea for at least a decade has been reduced to ritual. Except for the United States, the UN members who contributed troops to the Korean conflict have long ago withdrawn them. Their signed statement of July 27, 1952, affirms "that if there is a renewal of armed attack . . . we should again be united and prompt to resist. The consequences of such a breach of the armistice would be so grave that, in all probability, it would not be possible to confine hostilities within the frontiers of Korea. . . ." The statement stands, but the will, though untested, has presumably ebbed with the years: trade and diplomacy are the limits of the ties today, and these activities, for both Koreas but especially for the South, have grown greatly. The war affected NATO, European and Japanese economic growth, the concept of collective security, Soviet tactics, US-ROK relations, Sino-American relations, the issue of Taiwan, the maintenance of US forces in Vietnam and their further involvement there, the whole issue of war and defense. Clearly, the conflict still has an international dimension, but in a broad UN framework it is recessive.

The focus of Korea as an international problem lies in the four great powers within the arena of whose influence Korea's geographical position and her history of contact isolate her. The war and its aftermath have enlivened the interest of these four powers in Korea's conflict situation. The Chinese Communists emerged, perhaps for the first time, as a major international power capable, in effect, of inflicting partial defeat on the United States. The external threat of the

---

[18] See, among others, Harrison E. Salisbury, *War Between Russia and China* (New York: Norton, 1969).

Korean conflict became a major cement for Peking's internal control of its masses; the Chinese military system was considerably enhanced and perfected; Red China formed close and, for a while, dominant ties with the DPRK, exerting broad influence on Korea in collectivization and much else. The United States was violently reinserted, now more lastingly, into Korean affairs, signing a mutual security pact with the ROK just after the armistice, continuing to maintain 50,000 troops in Korea, and pumping billions in economic and military aid into its economy.[19] Japan was given great impetus on her road to economic recovery by the Korean war, and threat from Korea has certainly operated to increase Japan's military power. These two factors have fueled Japan's resumption of active relations with the ROK in 1965 and Japan's gradual return to her natural position of importance in the affairs of her neighbor. The Soviet Union's position is the least changed: it was forced to launch a massive—and successful—reconstruction effort for the DPRK, but China's powerful position in Korea, the Sino-Soviet split, and the DPRK's markedly increasing nationalism have worked to counter the increase in influence this might have given. The restoration of primarily four-power interest in Korea is probably fortunate, for if a solution to the Korean conflict situation is to be found, four-power agreement is most likely to be its instrument.

INTERNAL ESCALATION

Internally, the Korean war inflicted casualties never counted but believed to amount to a million civilians on each side, more than half a million North Korean soldiers, and more than 300,000 ROK military casualties. Nearly two million refugees fled South in the wake of the UN forces' occupation of most of North Korea; all told, one-third or more of North Korea's population has fled since 1945. Moreover, abnormal savagery marked the war's first six months; there were mass executions of civilians not only by opposing sides but also within each side as those suspected—often wrongly—of collaboration were disposed of.

The hated Communist occupation of three-quarters of South Korea from July–September 1950 greatly increased and personalized the anticommunist, anti-DPRK sentiment of South Koreans. Blood and cruelty spread personal hatreds and fears still deeper through the

[19] The Library of Congress Legislative Reference Service estimated that by 1956 the Korean war cost the United States about $83 billion, second only at that time in cost to World War II. Walter G. Hermes, *Truce Tent and Fighting Front* (Washington: Office of the Chief of Military History, Department of the Army, 1966), p. 501.

two societies. The acts of the foreign Chinese Communist occupation in the opening weeks of 1951 were almost always reported to have been far milder than the acts of North Koreans during the 1950 occupation, and the worst acts of the earlier occupation were often perpetrated by Communists of South Korean origin. Clearly, conflict was not simply between Communists and anticommunists but carried the added implication of intra-Korean resentment against rival groups and loyalties.

The war brought to a climax the steady buildup in North-South group hostility. Almost all Communists remaining in the South, and many leftists and sympathizers, came out of hiding and into responsible positions during the Communist occupation of the South; then the tide turned, and these people either were killed or fled. Discontents from the North came south as refugees or were accused and killed by the North; likewise, thousands of innocents in both Koreas perished. In addition, war eliminated moderates as a political force in the South for many years to come, and foreclosed the slim chance that they might grow in the North. Oppression, intolerance, and extremism luxuriated in the political, social, and economic life of each part of the country. Assemblymen and a former minister in the South and ministers and senior leaders in the North did not escape condemnation, jail, and even death on charges, often implausible, of collaboration with the other side.

Finally, war turned a land for centuries averse to the military into one of the most militarized enclaves of the present world. Soon after the armistice, ROK armed forces reached a level of 655,000 men and those in North Korea nearly 400,000, all far better trained and equipped than in 1950. Though the ROK armed forces today may have come down to the 600,000 level, a "home guard" of 2,000,000 men has been built in response to the North Korean "People's militia" of 1,000,000 men. Discounting paramilitary forces, the 85,000-square-mile peninsula has 1,000,000 armed men, far more than all Africa, with its wars, 11.5 million square miles, and 41 nations; nearly 50 percent more than in all Latin America; more than one-third the standing army of Communist China with 20 times Korea's 43 million population; more than twice the armed strength of the two Germanies with nearly twice Korea's population. More recently, armaments on both sides have been still further modernized: rockets, modern tanks, jet planes, torpedo boats, and improved artillery have been introduced by both super-sponsors. The instruments of conflict have multiplied.

The dynamics around the crisis are also high and rising. South Korea has 62 or more college-level institutions with some 100,000 college students. North Korea, with a 13–14 million population, has some 98 colleges and universities, and about one-third of her population is in schools of some sort. Throughout Korea literacy and newspaper-reading are very high. North Korea has about 1,600,000 Communist party members, some 12 percent of her population. (Only five percent of Russians belonged to the Soviet Communist party in Stalin's day.) Urbanization has grown rapidly in both states. One-third of South Korea's population now lives in cities, a proportion greater than Belgium's urban population and almost as large as that of the Soviet Union. The capacity of the two states to reach, activate, and dicipline their citizens is thus tremendously high, perhaps higher than for many developed countries.

INTERNAL DEESCALATION

There are also cooling factors. The four-kilometer-wide demilitarized zone, continued guarantees of security by the United States, the pledges of the 16 former allies, and the fact that the US, not the ROK, is signatory to the armistice and "represents" the South at Panmunjom, while the Chinese continue beside the North Koreans, tend somewhat to reduce feelings of direct Korean responsibility for the peninsula's conflict situation and to limit—without eliminating—daily hostile contact. Despite the recurrence of occasional "spy" cases in the courts and, more particularly, the rise in 1968 of serious North Korean armed infiltrations in the South,[20] the Communist issue is almost entirely eliminated internally and only occasionally refired, in 1969 and 1970 by incidents of limited size; more commonly it lapses and has less of that relevance and intimacy of personal feeling it had in 1945–1947 and 1950–1951. The endless acrimony of Panmunjom has turned into as ritualistic a hostility as that of a Pueblo Indian dance; the Korean propaganda on either side is hardly less stultified. Inevitably young men and women are growing up, hopefully in the North, certainly in the South, who no longer share the intensity of feeling that animates their parents and their present governments. The economic buildups

---

[20] The ROK-UN Command side reports 1,082 armistice violation incidents by the North between January 1968 and August 1969, leaving 221 killed and 351 wounded among UN Command personnel, 96 ROK civilians killed and 160 wounded and some 600 North Korean infiltrators killed south of the DMZ. A total of 6,561 violations have occurred from 1953–1969. UNGA, Committee document Alc. 1/985, 15 October 1969, letter of 11 October 1969 from the ROK Ministry of Foreign Affairs to the UN Secretary-General pp. 21–23. The DPRK similarly charged "the U.S. imperialist aggressors" with over 7,570 violations of the Armistice Agreement between January and September, 1969. UNGA 1st Committee Doc-A/C. 1/987, 17 October 1969, letter dated Oct. 8, 1969, from the DPRK Ministry of Foreign Affairs to the Secretary-General and to the President of the General Assembly, p. 7.

that have raised both nations from the ashes to successful modern economies of medium power have dampening as well as escalating effects: economic concerns increasingly edge out political issues in the minds of the North and South Koreans. This gradual depoliticization retains a force, usually unexpressed, even though political problems remain forever unresolved—the Geneva conference efforts in 1954 to solve the Korean political problem were as ineffectual as those of the earlier joint commissions.

RECENT DEVELOPMENTS

Here the Korean conflict essentially rests: aggravated, institutionalized in two independent nations, and partly internationalized at Panmunjom and the United Nations, yet probably not essentially changed since early 1946. The war in Vietnam has produced further aggravation by engaging some 50,000 ROK soldiers and 15,000 civilians in fighting and support activities there, inviting North Korean response within Korea in the form of hostile infiltration, ambush, and other armed action that reached a climax in the January 1968 Pueblo capture and the large—and outrageous—armed commando attack of 31 well-trained men on President Chung Hee Park. In 1968, 15 American soldiers, 149 South Koreans, and some 321 North Korean soldiers and agents were killed in Korea's "cold" war.[21] Underneath, the more personal and political schisms that caused the original cleavage have long been internalized and frozen. The weak but united peninsula of the era before 1945 has shown a worm's capacity to be divided in two, each side crawling away to form its own organism, amazingly stronger and completely separate. Far from weakening the country fatally, as all feared in 1945 and 1946, division, rivalry, hostility, even war itself seem to have resulted in endowing each side with a power that a united country might scarcely have achieved. Each new country has discovered an amazing capacity to supplement or find internally what used to come from the country's other half, sabotaging and slandering, subverting and warring on each other as if they had been traditional *archfoes* of ten thousand years. The rallying points of this hostility, the ideologies needed to sustain it, the weekly rehearsals of hostility at Panmunjom and the annual ones at the UN, international aid, the concerted ministrations of the cold war: all of these have given unrivaled focus, support, and strength to each Korea. Each side uses its hostility as a lightning rod for internal dissension;

---

21 Philip Shabecoff, *New York Times*, April 27, 1969. The restrained response of the United States to the Pueblo and the EC-121 plane-shooting incident clearly show US disinclination to raise the stakes in Korea.

each uses it as a constant spur to greater effort and greater legitimacy; both rejoice in their "frontier" position and psychology.

SCOPE OF THE PRESENT DANGER

The danger does not abate. Korea's armies today have five times the men they had in 1950; their training and equipment have mounted by far higher multiples. In a microcosm of the nuclear rivalry, both sides build up strength designed not to be used, in a force-level gamesmanship replete with hostility and opportunity for misunderstanding. Half unseen by the world, Korea threatens world peace today more than on the eve of the 1950 war.

Outside the peninsula's borders too are possible aggravations. Where North Korea would stand in an aggravated Sino-Soviet dispute has not been calculated. With the rise of Japan, risks could escalate still further. It should not be forgotten that one of the twin causes of World War II lay in Japanese expansion whose first step was her determination that the Korean peninsula fall to no foreign power's domination. In 1950 Japan was still occupied by the United States, was forbidden armaments of her own, and was in no psychological state to use them in any case. These conditions no longer exist in 1971. Prime Minister Sato has declared the security of Korea "essential" to Japan. Should a severe threat arise in a Korea located next to a conservatively led, independent, and increasingly armed Japan that would stand to lose incalculable gains in her living standards, the effect on Japan's armament and direction as a state might well be decisive. By rough calculation, if she considered conditions in Korea threatening, Japan might be five times as justified in taking action there as the United States was in acting during the Cuban missile crisis. Such action would invite dangerous response from China and, perhaps, the Soviet Union. No major state besides China is so irretrievably involved in Southeast Asia as Japan, China, the Soviet Union, and probably the United States are in Korea. Following the end or diminution of the Vietnamese war, therefore, Korea's conflict situation could conceivably be a greater threat to world peace than is Vietnam today. It is also possible—and, we hope, more probable—that a conservative and strong Japan, increasingly committed to the ROK, may stabilize the present situation in the peninsula and gradually, in more nonmilitary ways, take over American responsibilities there, without reasserting control.

Possible Solutions

The disarray of the means to assuage this conflict is one of its most baleful aspects. The greatest impediment, of course, is that each side prates of peaceful unification while actually fearing it and feeling no pressing need for it. Neither would in any way give up what it has achieved. So long as this remains true, no solution to the conflict appears very probable. This condition excepted, there are possible steps toward solution, but these steps now seem unlikely to be taken.

Normally, the UN would have been a natural vehicle for unification. The US choice of the UN as the instrument for unification in 1948 and the UN role as belligerent in 1950, almost universally applauded by noncommunists at the time, has tragically blocked this avenue. Presently there is no expectation that either Communists in general or the DPRK in particular will come to regard the UN as a legitimate instrument for political compromise on an issue in which it took violent sides and still retains a residual role as the formal antagonist to North Korea. The activities of UNCURK, the UN Commission for the Unification and Reconstruction of Korea, are not only useless but counterproductive: by continuing to commit the UN, they obstruct any possibility of its intermediary role. The ritual acrimony of the Panmunjom meetings of the Military Armistice Commission increase rather than decrease hostility and render a point of contact meaningless for serious negotiation. In addition, the growing strength of both Koreas, the ROK's aid to the US in Vietnam, the general loosening of satellite ties, and the Sino-Soviet rift have weakened the control of both the Soviet Union and the United States over their Korean clients. Conservative powers eschewing armed conflict have less influence; the two regimes, one the most extreme type of narrow Stalinist regime, the other less aggressive but still rigid, both with vested interests in instability to excite more aid, increasingly dominate and endanger the conflict situation.[22]

The threshold of action is difficult. Each side so relies on hostility for its existence that it cannot take or respond to initiative for negotiations or even contact as envisaged in the current Soviet-backed North Korean stand that the question "should be solved by the Korean people themselves independently and by peaceful means on democratic principles without interference of any outside forces."[23] The United States and the Soviet Union have prime responsibility for perpetuating

---

[22] There is no question, however, of the greater aggressiveness of the DPRK. No recent ROK statements can be compared with Kim Il-song's reported threats of "liberating South Korea," "a war of revolution may come at any time," the attainment of victory "only by a forcible method" and of other high officials' boasts of "turning the whole country into a fortress" (A/C.1/985, pp. 26–27).

[23] Kim Il-song, interview with the Delegation of Democratic Youth League of Finland, *Pyongyang Times*, No. 39 (237), September 12, 1969 (and many other similar statements). The principle has an odd similarity to the stand of Israel.

Gregory Henderson: North and South Korea

a division that could not have occurred without them and for initiating action thereon.

Such action cannot initially be political: no political solution can be imposed from the outside, nor is any now feasible. It can only take the form of reducing the armed instruments of both sides, encouraging restoration of at least the mail contact which the two zones once had, and trying to encourage the formation on both sides of asymmetrical, partial, superordinate goals involving some contact. This is manifestly in US–USSR interests: both would like to reduce conflict danger in the peninsula, see their clients economically prosper with less aid, and reduce their own expenditures in the spirit of the SALT negotiations. The US and the USSR can at least make it prohibitively expensive for the ROK and the DPRK to maintain their armed forces at present levels. Even such action will come hard so long as the ROK's claim on arms help is increased by her contributions in Vietnam, and so long as the USSR must eschew alienating the DPRK in the Sino-Soviet dispute. It should, however, be done if anyone wants to reduce conflict.

The United Nations could also help reduce conflict in Korea, clearly not, as now, as the protagonist of one side, but in the role of neutral intermediary, as in Cyprus and the Middle East. Assumption of this role will involve dissolution of UNCURK and an invitation to both Koreas to take part in any UN debate involving the peninsula's future. Both sides should become members of international technical and scientific groups. It will be understandably difficult for the ROK thus to cede the international priority it has enjoyed; yet in its own long-range interests it must do so for the sake of a larger, safer, and more prosperous Korea. Occasions where the two sides can be brought together for the discussion of comparatively noncontroversial technical, scientific, banking, and developmental problems are not only steps toward peace; they are needed therapy for the group-psychological conflict now so deep-seated for Koreans who have never met in any environment let alone a peaceful one. The Human Rights Commission should also take initiative to restore at least communication by postal forms between the two Koreas on the ground that the inability of divided families to obtain basic information about their members violates human rights. (The DPRK has long proposed mail exchange.) Such communication should progressively be broadened to regular mail and other material, as between the two Germanies, and eventually to cultural and athletic exchanges.

Taking such steps might lead to conditions enabling reconsideration of the unification issue itself in a decade or more, probably more fruitfully in the context of the four powers intimately concerned than of the United Nations.[24] Such reconsideration would require the entry of mainland China into the United Nations system and into formal relations with the United States, considerably more detente in US–USSR relations, and the creation, largely through advanced education and broadened contact with world opinion, of relatively large numbers of educated North and South Koreans who are more independent of tight, centralized government control and less committed than their governments to continuation of the conflict stasis. While such conditions may not come about, none is inconceivable within the next two decades. Japan might take increasingly helpful initiatives to create them as her power in Asia grows. The growing electronic revolution may also be helpful in bringing both Koreas, especially the North, nearer the main currents of world opinion.

The ultimate goal of a disarmed, neutralized, independent, and united Korea guaranteed by China, Japan, the US, and the USSR seems today a distant dream. It is probably the only conceivable solution to the Korean conflict by peaceful means. The conflict is both too serious, too unnecessary, and too mindless in origin to permit forgoing such a solution. Korea remains one of the world's most serious conflicts. It calls in the next decades for constant and imaginative attention of a kind the world has yet to give it.[25]

---

[24] DPRK Foreign Minister Nam Il proposed at the Havana Conference on 27 April, 1954, that "those nations who are most concerned with maintenance of peace in the Far East should guarantee the peaceful development of Korea and thereby create favourable conditions for the rapid solution of the task of accomplishing peaceful unification of Korea as a single, independent nation."

[25] Since the drafting of this Chapter, the US announced in the summer of 1970 that it would reduce its forces in Korea by 20,000 men to the 40,000–44,000 level by June 1971. Plans to withdraw all U.S. troops from Korea by 1975 have been unofficially reported. The latter, as fulfilling the DPRK's conditions, would almost certainly spur reconsideration of unification. Meanwhile, U.S. Phantom jets have been shifted to Korea and a program of U.S.-financed modernization of ROK armed forces at reported probable costs of $1.5 billion has been initiated. Such steps are unlikely to reduce tensions. Rising ROK contributions to the costs of her own armed forces and high debt-servicing costs in the '70s may, however, force some ROK army reductions. On August 15, 1970, President Park announced that if the north desisted from military provocations and renounced intention of communizing Korea by force, he would suggest "epochal and realistic measures" to remove "artificial barriers...between the south and the north" and would, if the north recognized the authority and competence of the UN, drop opposition to the north's presence in the UN deliberations on Korea. The 1971 opposition party platform for some exchange and communication with North Korea has been less conditional. While these stands do not yet bring the two sides much closer, they do presage far more discussion of the issue which may, within the 1970s, result in some communication, exchange and reduction of tension between North and South Korea.

Chapter 7

Ethno-National Confrontations

Israel and the Arab Countries

DAVID VITAL

I

The identity and purposes of the parties to the conflict between Arabs and Jews in the Middle East can be discussed, in principle, on at least four levels: first, at the quasi-objective level of active and potential *material* involvement; second, at the level of the terms in which each side sees itself; third, at the level of the terms in which each side sees the other; and fourth, at the level of behavior in concrete and, above all, critical situations. All levels are significant. None can be usefully seen as exclusively so. It is, indeed, the intricate and irregular relationship between them that must be grasped before all else.

At the initial level of analysis, matters are relatively straightforward. There have been shifts and changes from time to time, some of them of the greatest importance. But it is not impossible by the normal means of historical and political inquiry to set out those placed in the inner circle of direct conflict and those in the outer circles who offer no more than political and material support in one degree or another, or who, at the very least, are capable of rocking the boat, but may equally refrain from doing so.

Fifty years ago the Jewish settler community in Palestine and the Zionist movement that promoted and backed it could by no stretch of the imagination be seen as representative of more than a minority of world Jewry. The Zionists were intent upon a colossal restructuring of the Jewish people along entirely fresh social and economic lines. The fundamental item of their analysis and program was the absolute necessity of reestablishing the Jews as a nation with political capabilities—in other words, a state—and of promoting and defending Jewish national interests first and

221

foremost through independent political and, if necessary, military instrumentalities, rather than by the age-old techniques of lobbying, remonstrance, and the rendering of services in exchange for immediate or future protection. Like all revolutionaries with a serious and therefore disturbing case to argue, they were for the most part resisted or ignored for a very long time. But today their position in Jewry as a whole is transformed. On the one hand, the State of Israel exists and acts and is equipped with independent instruments of policy beyond the wildest dreams of its forerunners. And on other hand, opposition to the State—that is, to the Zionist program—has practically disappeared among Jews and is limited to veritable fringe groups. These groups are, broadly, of two varieties: the hyper–religious and the adepts of universalistic, usually ultra–leftist, creeds. The one offers retreat to the Middle Ages. The other offers release from the dilemmas of Jewish identity altogether. Thus neither is in a position to appeal to, let alone act for, the bulk of Jewry.

The origins of this great change amount to too broad a subject to be dealt with here. But it may be pertinent to recall that few Jews, regardless of their circumstances, could remain indifferent to four major events of our period: the physical liquidation of almost the whole of central and eastern European Jewry by the Germans; the establishment of Israel itself; the rise of the Jewish population of Israel through the Ingathering of the Exiles and through natural increase to the point where it constitutes the third (possibly the second) largest Jewish community and is for a host of reasons the natural focus of all Jewish cultural and religious activity; and finally, the trauma of May-June 1967. At all events, the immediate consequence of this great shift in the central currents of Jewish opinion has been to reduce almost to a nullity the old distinction between Zionist and non-Zionist Jews. For a Jew, to be anti-Zionist today is to be, in a profound sense, retrograde, self-contradictory, apostatical, and, in the extreme case, disloyal. In a word, it is to cut oneself off from what has become the central Jewish cause. It is not difficult to find individuals, members of the western European and North American intellectual communities in particular, who have done just that. But they carry little political or economic weight and are too remote from the vital arena of the conflict to affect it seriously beyond providing a measure of moral comfort to the other side. The really crucial contemporary distinction among Jews is rather between those who are directly involved in the Middle East conflict—that is, the nationals and inhabitants of Israel—and those who are not and whose attitudes are therefore free to range all the way from complete emotional and intellectual identification with the former to polite indifference to their fate.

The Arab camp has experienced a parallel and in some ways still more intense drawing of lines and acceptance of the conflict as a central national issue in the sense that for an Arab *qua* Arab to fail to support the cause is to be profoundly disloyal to his people. This has long been the case, but it was not always so. In 1919 the most considerable spokesman for the Arab world of the time, the Emir Feisal of Hejaz, was prepared to tell the Paris Peace Conference that Palestine "for its universal character should be left on one side for the mutual consideration of all parties interested"—among whom the Jews obviously figured. Moreover, Feisal specifically agreed with the Zionists in a written memorandum that "in the establishment of the Constitution and Administration of Palestine, all such measures shall be adopted as will afford the fullest guarantees for carrying into effect the British Government's Declaration of November 2, 1917" (the Balfour Declaration), and that "all necessary measures shall be taken to encourage and stimulate immigration of Jews into Palestine on a large scale, and as quickly as possible to settle Jewish immigrants on the land through closer settlement and intensive cultivation of the soil."[1]

Feisal's purpose was evidently to recruit Jewish support for his independent Greater Syria project and he added a proviso to the effect that the Agreement would be void if his major plans were incapable of fulfilment. It remains that in his eyes Palestine was a special case and that Arab political interests in it could be properly subordinated to the general purpose of achieving independence for the Arab heartland.

Today the Weizmann-Feisal Agreement cannot but be rated a curiosity of history, an aberration. Palestine is very far from being seen as a special case to which other Arab interests may properly be subordinated. And as the question of formal political independence for Arab lands as a whole has long been solved, Palestine necessarily remains in Arab eyes the one lone—and therefore great and unacceptable—exception. As for the Palestine Arabs themselves, it was clear by the early 1920s that they were unalterably opposed to the establishment first of a Jewish majority in the country and then of a Jewish state. And the closer the Jews appeared to come to their goal, the sharper became the general resistance to them.

Here and there in the Arab parts of the Middle East there are some small, informal pockets of skepticism and less than wholehearted support for the general crusade against Israel seen as a cause in which all Arabs are concerned. In Egypt and Lebanon notably, but also in the Maghreb, there has always been a current of what might be

---

[1] Weizmann-Feisal Agreement, January 3, 1919, paragraphs 3 and 4.

David Vital: Israel and the Arab Countries

termed local nationalist or particularist opinion running contrary to the now preponderant pan-Arab trend. It is still alive.[2] But such dissent from pan-Arabism does not necessarily—in fact, very rarely—mean explicit dissent on the specific issue of Israel. And where it does, it is neither organized nor institutionalized. On this subject it is the official policies and ideologies alone that are supported and voiced and that have general social respectability. And they are such as will admit no real deviation. State and society are for all practical purposes at one here, and thus, as in the Jewish world, what really matters is the extent and intensity of positive support for the cause which may, indeed, vary from mere lip service to the most ardent participation at the front.

The basic difference between the Jewish and Arab camps in this context is a structural one. The Arab people are overwhelmingly subjects of Arab governments. The Jews are overwhelmingly subjects of non-Jewish governments. To put it differently, membership in the Jewish camp, not only for purposes connected with the Arab-Israel conflict but for many if not all others as well, is predominantly voluntary. Membership in the Arab camp is not. This difference has the consequence that in strict and concrete terms the human and material resources available to Israel and under its unquestioned authority and therefore, by extension, the diplomatic and military resources on which it can count at all times, have always been and no doubt will always be substantially inferior to those available to the Arab governments. The quantitative disparity is marked even where the minority of Arab governments actively involved in significant military conflict is compared with Israel.[3] But against this must be set Israel's advan-

---

[2] On the revival of Egyptian (as opposed to Arab) nationalism in the wake of the 1967 war see, for example, Ibn al Asal (pseud.), "Return to Cairo," *Encounter*, August 1969.

[3] On the basis of figures published by the Institute for Strategic Studies in 1969, the following typical comparison may be made:

	Population	GNP (millions)	Armed manpower	Combat aircraft
Algeria, Egypt, Iraq, Jordan, Saudi Arabia and Syria combined	67,800,000	$14,740	501,000	982
Israel	2,800,000	$ 3,900	290,000[a]	275

[a] Regular cadres *and* reservists.

Note: None of these figures is stationary and all should be treated with care. According to Mohammed Hassanein Heikal, Egypt's armed forces have already passed the half-million mark and "will probably become one million strong by the time of the anticipated battle" (*Al Ahram*, 12, December 1969).

tages: qualitatively superior military manpower, interior lines of communication, a more effective command structure, and so forth.

What both sides have in common, however, is the fact that each consists of a multitude of independent participants placed, as it were, in a series of concentric circles such that active involvement in any given case will vary more or less with distance from the center; and that it is those centrally placed whose behavior and interaction give the conflict its underlying dynamic and its essential structure. The centrally placed participants—Israel on the Jewish side, Egypt and, in a rough descending order of political and military importance, Syria, Jordan, Iraq, Algeria, Saudi Arabia, Lebanon and Libya—are not oblivious to, nor can they fully depend upon, their allies—the various Jewish communities outside Israel and the other Arab governments, respectively. But it is they and not their allies who determine at the margin how each camp will act as a whole and it is on them that the attention of all concerned, whether within the broad circle of the conflict itself or outside it altogether, is rightly focused.

The exceptional case is that of the Palestine Arabs themselves. The end of the first Arab-Jewish war (1947–1949) found the Palestinians in almost total political and social disarray. They themselves had taken very little part in the war: the major fighting was between the Jews and the regular Arab armies of Egypt, Syria, Iraq, and Jordan that had moved into Palestine to forestall and, failing that, to destroy the newly proclaimed Israel.[4] The Arab Palestinian state, which the United Nations partition resolution of 1947 had provided for along with the Jewish state, was lost in the ensuing shuffle. Most of the territory set apart for it was annexed by Jordan (with British encouragement, but over the violent protests of all the other Arab states); part was annexed by Israel; and a third part (the Gaza Strip) was occupied and ruled, although never formally annexed, by Egypt. Individually, many of the Palestinian Arabs became refugees and most of these have lived thereafter in a state of great hardship. Some stayed put and became citizens of Israel; a greater proportion became citizens of Jordan; and the rest became and have remained, in effect, stateless persons variously under the control of the Egyptians, the Syrians and the Lebanese. Jordan apart, the Palestinians were thus in no position anywhere to exert a measure of real influence over the governments under whose authority they had come and, even in Jordan, many years passed before they began to play a significant role. Such

---

4 "This will be a momentous war of extermination which will be spoken of in history like the Mongolian massacres and the Crusades" (Abd al-Rahman Azzam, Secretary-General of the Arab League, BBC, 15 May 1948).

political and military organizations as were set up from time to time and purported to represent them were by and large initiated and manipulated, or alternatively repressed, by their protectors.

The second Arab-Jewish war (1956) was one to the precipitation of which small groups of Palestine Arab marauders and saboteurs, inspired and largely organized by the Egyptians, certainly contributed. But it was fought as a war between Egypt and Israel and the defeat of Egypt, and the subsequent interposition of United Nations forces between the two countries served to underline the well-nigh complete dependence of the Palestine Arabs on the major Arab states, and on Egypt before all others. If the Arab world was divided (Egypt had fought alone in 1956) and its greatest army incapable of crushing Israel, what remained but to work for union and build up the collective forces in anticipation of the ultimate, victorious confrontation? In the meantime, it was for the Palestine Arabs to continue as wards of the Arab states.

At first the third Arab-Jewish war (1967) appeared likely to evolve somewhat more along the lines of 1948 than of 1956: Arab unity was largely preserved and the Arab forces, collectively, were clearly greater than those of Israel. The defeat inflicted on the Arabs in the Six-Day War was therefore all the more shattering, but hostility toward Israel was, if anything, intensified by the humiliation. And so far as the Arab camp was concerned, the effects were in one significant respect the reverse of those of 1948. The Palestine Arabs emerged as a fairly independent political factor on their own account. Ironically, their reentry on the scene was greatly facilitated by Israel's occupation of all of the former British mandated territory, "Palestine," by which means the bulk of the Palestine Arabs was largely freed from the tutelage of the Egyptians and the Jordanians. But possibly of greater import still was the fact that the war and the events leading up to it had discredited both the Arab governments and their leading Palestinian clients. In its aftermath the incapacity of all concerned to reverse the events by conventional military and diplomatic means was fully manifest. The field was thus free for new men to act out new and fashionable ideas, and these opportunities were rapidly seized by a host of fresh personalities and movements. The broad result has been that the Palestinians now figure once more as a considerable, if still imperfectly definable, political-military factor in their own right, with complex, yet uncertain, consequences for the evolution of the conflict as a whole. In real terms, they amount to hardly more than an adjunct to the main Arab forces. If they were denied the safe bases offered them with varying degrees of good will by the Arab states, they would be unable to operate at all. But politically and psychologically their impact on Arab-Israeli relations is that of prime catalysts and symbols of the conflict. And therefore the fact that they have attained a high degree of independence of action means that for the first time since 1948 an organizational divergence within the Arab camp is at least possible.

II

A summary identification of the parties to the conflict in real terms —that is, in terms of actual and potential material, especially military participation—thus suggests that involved in it are two untidy and uncertain coalitions of communities. One is to all intents and purposes identical with the state members of the Arab League and the associated military and political organizations of the Palestine Arabs. The other is composed of a firm center—Israel—and a soft penumbra of Jewish communal and ecclesiastical institutions and individual well-wishers in the Jewish Diaspora around it. A discussion of the parties and their purposes on the secondary and tertiary levels of analysis— namely, the terms in which they see themselves and the terms in which they see their opponents—is a much more difficult undertaking. Nevertheless, it is on these levels alone that the cement that binds these coalitions together is to be found and the immensely powerful drives that fuel and perpetuate the conflict are to be detected.

One key to the Arab perception of the conflict—and indeed to their involvement in it—is the view that the Arabs constitute a single people or nation which was, and by rights should be once more, united. The Arab nation is seen as being endowed with unique attributes, such as a language which is inherently superior to all others and, its members being preponderantly Muslims, a pervasive and collective sense of spiritual values which distinguish it from the nations and nationalism of the West. Moreover, where

internal divisions exist, such as sects or tribes, [they] are but the result of ignorance or of foreign interference. Add to this the claim, made with varying degrees of conviction, that the most outstanding features of civilization in the West have their origin in the Arab-Muslim tradition and the peculiar feeling of being a chosen people derived from their central position in Islam, and you have all the elements from which historical constructs are constantly being devised and revised, all designed to justify aspiration and hope for the future in terms of past achievement.[5]

What matters in practice is that Arab leaders are impelled by this view to maintain a posture of unity and mutual trust, even where neither really obtain, and to accept that the familiar norms of international behavior with respect to nonintervention by one state in the internal affairs of another do not apply and cannot be held to apply in the Arab world.[6] On the contrary, mutual involvement and mutual responsibility are the norms, and they can always be invoked, often to great effect, by those who claim to be the most catholic in their pan-Arab policies. The Syrians, for example, have made frequent use of this tactic, often to the embarrassment of other Arab governments caught in the contradictions that simultaneous, if uncertain, pursuit of both particularist and universalist goals often entail.

For all these reasons it is an established and noncontentious item of the Arab position that the Palestine issue—meaning both the fate of the Palestinian Arabs *and* the fate of the former British mandated territory "Palestine"—is the concern of all Arabs qua Arabs, and, contrariwise, that the Palestinian Arabs are entitled to call upon all other Arabs for assistance. So although the immediate matter of the contemporary conflict between Jews and Arabs in the Middle East is the Palestinian territory and its government—entirely so up until the occupation of Egyptian and Syrian areas in 1967, but still essentially so to this day—the issues cannot but be seen as affecting all Arabs. Moreover, were the loss of Palestine, once it had been identified as Arab in the Arab mind, to be final, it could not but be judged a blow, perhaps a mortal blow, certainly a very cruel blow, to the resurgent Arab nation. In alternative terms, acquiescence in the establishment of Israel, and *a fortiori* the maintenance of amicable relations with it could only begin to be conceivable on the basis that pan-Arabism be radically amended in content or entirely abandoned and that the

---

[5] G. E. von Grunebaum, *Modern Islam, the Search for Cultural Identity* (New York: Vintage Books, 1964), pp. 284–285.

[6] An example: The Egyptians were very heavily involved in the Yemeni civil war which broke out at the end of 1962 and has still not entirely ended. As its peak the Egyptian expeditionary force numbered 68,000 men   (*The* London *Times*, December 21, 1966, p. 9). Smaller bodies of Egyptian troops have been sent at various times to Syria, to Iraq, Algeria and, more recently, Libya. In each case, the object of the exercise was purely domestic or inter-Arab, i.e., to support a ruling faction against competitors or to assist one Arab state against others (specifically, Algeria against Morocco). What matters is that, from a pan-Arab point of view, there is nothing fundamentally illegitimate about such intervention.

existing division of the Arab world into 14 fully sovereign states accepted as permanent.

Against such a background of what is both right *and* politic for Arab leaders the third Jewish Commonwealth takes on a distinctly sinister aspect. First, because it is Jewish; second, because it is a Commonwealth, i.e., an independent political entity; third, because the continuing failure of the vastly more numerous and militarily and politically better-endowed Arabs to suppress it calls into question the practicability of the one great idea or creed which offers them at least a vision of something better than the present unstable and petty *kleinstaaterei*, inefficient and corrupt government, and technological and economic underdevelopment.

Despite occasional protestations to the contrary, some sincerely meant, some not, there can hardly be any question that the Arabs, as Muslims, approach Jews as Jews from a profoundly anti-Semitic standpoint.[7] Whereas the Arab as such does not really enter into the Jewish historic past except in the environmental sense, the Jews, as the progenitors of all monotheists, played a minor but critical role in the origins of Islam. And as with Christianity, it is a role that is generally resented.

The Muslim tradition has it, for example, that while the Jews recognized the authenticity of Mohammed's mission, their pride and will to dominate impelled them to reject the faith. Moreover, they deceived the Prophet and attempted to frustrate him and his followers by eliminating all mention of him in their Bible. Altogether, they are a perfidious, malevolent, and contemptible people, and, as is specifically foretold in the *Hadith*, their destruction will necessarily precede the Resurrection and the Last Judgment.[8] The proper attitude for Muslims to take toward the Jews is therefore one of cautious toleration—to put it at its best. But certainly there is no room here for their being accepted as in any sense equals, least of all politically. Thus

[7] Strictly speaking, the term is an absurd one, doubly so in this case as it is improbable that more than a minority of modern Jews are Semites and entirely likely that a great many Arabs are. Nevertheless, a glance at, say, political cartoons in the Arab press (hook-nosed, humpbacked Jews, and all the rest) should suffice to justify the use of the term in its accepted, contemporary sense. "Anti-Jewish" would be a piece of pedantry.

[8] Georges Vajda, "Juifs et Musulmans selon le Hadit," *Journal Asiatique,* 229 (January-March 1937), 112-113: "The Jews will be among the supporters of the *Dajjal,* the Muslims' Antichrist. When he is vanquished his companions will be slaughtered; and should a Jew then seek refuge under a tree or a stone the object itself will speak up, saying to the Muslim, 'There is a Jew here hiding beneath me, kill him!'" For a general account see S.D. Goitein, *Jews and Arabs: Their Contacts Through the Ages* (New York: Schocken Books, 1964).

the emergence of a Jewish polity in their midst would have been very difficult for the Muslims to accept in the best of circumstances. That it should have been acquired to the accompaniment of great failures of Arab arms and the displacement, through panic flight, of a great many of their brethren goes a long way to account for the urge not merely to proclaim Israel an embodiment of injustice, but to explain the catastrophe in terms of Jewish perfidy and malevolence, rather than anything else.

In short, the Jewish character of Israel has served to intensify very greatly both the hurt its establishment has caused the Arabs and the great and somewhat self-righteous fervor which many of them devote to the conflict and to the underlying claim that the State of Israel is an abomination that may be legitimately, indeed must be, destroyed. As the then first vice-president of the United Arab Republic explained during a visit to Pakistan in 1966, "the aggressive Israeli existence is the clear embodiment of a depraved humanity which must be up-rooted."[9] It is to be noted that this has in fact been the major line of propaganda and argument in the Arab world on the present subject for a great many years—particularly, but not exclusively, in the domestic sphere. It is supported by all possible technical means and it tends to rely on any material that comes to hand, not excluding that ancient forgery, the *Protocols* of the Elders of Zion (which has been disseminated in recent years on a massive scale).[10]

Whether and to what extent the bulk of Arab leaders and the Arab intelligentsia actually subscribe to this view of their opponent it is impossible to say. It is evident that many do, that the machinery of government fosters this view in most Arab states and denies it in none, that it is staple diet in schools and the armed forces, in the press and on the radio, and that there is abundant evidence that it falls on highly receptive ears. What matters is that it is fundamental to the climate in which the conflict is waged. Indeed it may well be thought the keystone of its present structure: it is to this quasi-demonological view of Israel as an evil and an aberration that must be liquidated,

[9] Field Marshal Amer, quoted by Cairo Radio, December 8, 1966. There is a very full discussion of the subject in Yehoshafat Harkabi, *Emdat ha-Aravim be-Sikhsukh Israel-Arav* (The Arab Position in the Israel-Arab Conflict) (Tel Aviv: Dvir, 1968).

[10] Harkabi identifies at least seven different translations of the *Protocols* into Arabic in ten editions published in Beirut, Cairo, and Damascus (pp. 487–488). Only one is earlier than 1951. A further 37 works published between 1947 and 1967, but mostly in the sixties, either quote the *Protocols* extensively or else explicitly rely on them. Some of these works were issued by official bodies, including the Jordan Ministry of Education.

that the Arab leadership—Palestinian and non-Palestinian alike—have now committed themselves.[11] There is no public dissent, and little that is private. There are large political and military organizations founded upon this view and a great deal of money changes hands in the interests of implementing it.[12] In a word, the conflict with Israel has been thoroughly institutionalized on an ideology-intensive basis. There are thus strong grounds for believing that a resolution of the conflict on any terms other than those now predicated on all sides about its nature would amount to a political catastrophe for almost the entire gamut of the military and civil leadership, and first and foremost the leaders of the militant Palestinians themselves.

III

The Jewish side is placed very differently. Both the situation of Israel and its "case" require and rest on a preference for the status quo over all other conceivable situations—with many of the considerable political and psychological handicaps that tend to accrue in such instances.

The cardinal tenet of Zionism has long been fulfilled: the Jewish State has been reestablished in the historic fatherland of the Jewish people. The great majority of Jewish communities in distress—all those, in fact for whom Zionism constituted a practical as well as an ideologically attractive, or at any rate meaningful, solution to their problem (with the one great exception of Russian Jewry)—have been taken in and settled. Over 43 percent of the Jewish population of Israel is now native born and the proportion of native born is, of course, rising all the time.[13] In brief, Zionism has ceased to be an issue except for individual *non*-Israelis in the very narrow and marginal context of the opportunity Israel provides the Jew to identify himself fully and unreservedly with an ancestral culture.

[11] Not merely in statements of policy, but in constitutional instruments as well. For example, Article 10 of the National Charter of the United Arab Republic (Egypt) provides for the liquidation of Israel—described as "a dangerous pocket of imperialist resistance to the peoples' struggle."

[12] According to a Kuwait Government source (December 28, 1969) $156 million, or a quarter of the Kuwait budget, is allocated for assistance to Egypt and Jordan. The guerrilla organizations would be getting £24 million in the same year. All told, according to the same source, Kuwaiti, Saudi, and Libyan contributions to the war against Israel would amount to £175 million ($420 million).

[13] 1967 figures: no less than 88 percent of Jewish children up to the age of 14 are native born. It may also be worth noting that 16 percent of the native born are of native parentage and a further 46 percent are of African and Asian parentage.

It is on practical and instrumental issues of public, social, economic and foreign policy, not those of ideology, justice in the abstract, and the nature of their enemies, that the attention of policy-makers and public alike is riveted. Indeed were it not for the military threat which the Arabs pose to the Israeli state and its citizens, Arab opposition would by and large be ignored, or at the very least treated as an unpleasant irritant or embarrassment to which some adjustment must reluctantly be made.

The fact is, of course, that the military pressure and threat have consistently been substantial, and have taken a great variety of forms all the way from primitive, pogrom-like attacks on Jewish communities in the 1920s to repeated attempts to wage both total, technically sophisticated war and systematic, irregular warfare from 1948 on. Thus the fairly persistent employment of armed violence against the Yishuv (or Jewish community in Palestine) and Israel has amounted to the one really effective mode whereby the Arabs have made an impact on the Jews; and naturally enough it is by these means above all that the Arabs have participated in the erection of the essential framework of ideas within which the Jewish interpretation of the conflict and their setting of ways and means of coping with it are pursued. As Arab pressure has mounted in recent years and as the difficulty of ascribing to the opponent any operational goal other than the physical liquidation of Israel and the majority, if not all, of its inhabitants has grown to the point of being insurmountable, the Israeli approach to the conflict in its totality has been steadily pared of all base lines and criteria, adding up to an ever more simple (if not simplistic) pragmatism.

One consequence of this approach to the opponent is that there has been nothing in Israel remotely like the massive political and institutional commitment to the conflict—still less to its perpetuation in the present form—that is to be observed on the Arab side. No leaders are bound to it. There are no organizations whose *raison d'être* is rooted in it. The nationalist ideologues who argue the historic and legal rights of the Jews to all of the former British mandated territories of Palestine and Transjordan have not, in fact, made the slightest material effort to effect those rights since the state was established a generation ago. And today the nub of the argument they address to all but the initiated is essentially instrumental: security is best ensured by hanging on to the territories occupied in 1967. The armed forces themselves are, as is well known, composed preponderantly of reservist officers and men; furthermore, as the events of 1967 amply demonstrated, military leaders have only the barest influence on major policy (as opposed to tactical military) decisions. All in all, it is entirely typical that in the difficult period following the 1967 war, when military service and military expenditure have had to be greatly extended, both official policy and popular attitudes have been directed toward maintaining economic and social life on a level as close to the normal and the socially desirable as possible.

Another, and politically much more important, consequence of this well-nigh exclusive preoccupation with what is and what is not conducive to social and physical survival is the inability of the Israeli policy-making machinery to operate efficaciously in any but critical situations, indeed in any but the extreme situation of impending war. The origins of this weakness are partly institutional and partly conceptual. As already suggested, there is no significant dissent on what, for Jewish purposes, is the key issue of the conflict: survival in viable form. Disagreement (and hence dissent) occurs on the instrumental level, namely, what policies are best calculated to strengthen Israel's capabilities as opposed to weakening them. Since there can never be any simple and unequivocal answer to this kind of question except in purely military terms, and since Israel is an open society and is governed according to parliamentary rules—and the rules of proportional representation at that—policy-making tends to be reduced to, or even replaced by, a search for the lowest common denominator of the ruling party coalition. The propensity to settle for a combination of defensive military activism and diplomatic immobility, or, at the very least, to eschew political initiative is thus very great. It is certainly in marked contrast to the Arab posture which is founded on a narrow but very specific and therefore operationally superior principle of action: the integration of Israel-Palestine into the Arab sphere.

It remains to discuss the parties to the conflict at this latter, operational level.

IV

It was suggested that the parties to the conflict can be seen as adding up to two great, geographically widespread, somewhat unsteady, and, in some important respects, heterogeneous coalitions. In each case, the differences and contradictions within each group tend to be offset in one degree or another by powerful, but again unequal and unsteady, ties of identity. The question in what circumstances the common ties will operate—or can be made to operate—most powerfully is therefore critical to an assessment of how the coalitions may be expected to act against each other, above all in crisis.

The short answer to this question is that the Arab coalition holds together best over the long haul while the Jewish coalition is only fully effective at the brink of impending catastrophe. This would appear to follow quite naturally both from the respective situations in which each is placed and from the views of the conflict which predominate on each side. The Arab coalition, being almost identical with the member states of the Arab League, is able to function authoritatively through the machinery of the governments concerned. Moreover, as indicated, there are ample political constraints against deviation. So long, then, as the costs of involvement in the conflict are relatively small, or thought to be small (as they were thought to be even on the eve of war in 1967), the coalition is capable of acting with a marked degree of unity. It will be particularly effective in the international diplomatic context where the emphasis is necessarily on a common verbal front. But it will be capable of cooperation and coordination on the military plan as well. It is when the anticipated and assessed costs of involvement begin to rise too rapidly that the effectiveness of the coalition is in doubt. The more concrete the issues and the greater their consequent amenability to hard assessment, the greater will be the general propensity to take stock and reconsider where particularist interests lie. Where military defeat clearly threatens, say, the loss of oil revenues, or the loss of territory, or a serious weakening of the regime, there will almost invariably be (or rather, there always has been) some fading out from the operative coalition and a reduction in its effective membership, at any rate where such a fading out is possible. It is not always possible. The weaker the regime, for example, the less it can withstand nationalist pressure to remain in the van against Israel. Where high material and political costs have already been suffered—as by Jordan and Egypt after the June War—the broad anti-Israel drive will, on the contrary, be reinforced by the specific (and particularist) political and emotional need to restore the status quo ante.

The logic of these familiar dilemmas requires the Arab side, if it is to hold together in crisis at approximately the level of its nominal membership, to seek to build up the greatest military establishment of which it is capable and, simultaneously, subject Israel to whatever pressures seem likely to sap the latter's strength in the meantime. In this way it may hope to reduce the costs of ultimate confrontation to an acceptable minimum, and thus open the way to achievement of the common goal. For if it cannot act in concert it cannot really act at all.

The Jewish coalition presents a very different aspect. Jews in Israel and Jews elsewhere live under different political authorities and the ability of the Israeli Government to lead the Diaspora is limited in kind to a measure of vague moral pressure and limited in extent to the conscious adepts of the Israel cause. Beyond the latter lies the broad band of individual Jews who go about their business with very little thought to these questions apart from an occasional twinge of sympathy when events in the Middle East are prominently reported in the mass media. In what proportions the various Jewish communities divide into adepts, sympathisers and to those entirely indifferent or even hostile, is quite impossible to assess. But there is the evidence of Jewish behavior in June 1967 to indicate that support and sympathy are at their widest and deepest, which is to say the Jewish coalition tends to be at its highest operational level, at precisely those times when the Arab coalition is itself at its most coherent, effective, and promising. So if to this is added the fact noted earlier that Israeli policy-makers are at *their* most effective in crisis, it will be seen that the closer the Arab coalition approaches, or is thought by either side to approach, its goal, the more it tends to strengthen and unite its opponent. At the same time, as crisis looms and Jews in and outside Israel pull together, the more strongly are the Arabs confirmed in their unrelenting view of Israel and the firmer becomes their determination to destroy it. It is, perhaps, in this curious symbiotic relationship between the disputants that the main elements of the tragedy lie.

But this is not all. The duality of Arab interests encourages Israel to seek to deter pressure and disrupt the coalition by maximizing the actual or potential costs of conflict to the individual Arab states and organizations. Like the Arabs, Israel must therefore seek to build up as large and efficacious a military establishment as possible. But in fact, Israel's ability to deter the Arab coalition is very uncertain. Judged in the light of the first, quasi-objective level of analysis suggested here, the Israeli military potential cannot but seem small when set against the vast human and financial resources and great military buildup available to the Arabs. And the more powerful the members of the Arab coalition grow—and therefore the more effectively the coalition may be expected to operate—the greater must the imbalance appear. Israel is therefore constrained to attempt to deter not merely by amassing and parading its military capabilities, but by repeatedly demonstrating their effectiveness in the field. And when the level of arms on the opposing side appears to be rising too fast relative to that of Israel's, the balance of advantage for Israel will always lie in preemptive war. But here again, each one of Israel's military successes; each attempt to deter or disrupt or incapacitate the coalition, serves equally to confirm and intensify the Arab tendency, however unsteady, to act in unison and to see in Israel a threat to the pan-Arab cause as a whole, and in its very presence in the Levant a painful and open wound in the Arab body politic. That military encounters should occur against a background of repeated insistence by Israel that it wishes for no more than peace and security, is generally held on the Arab side to constitute so much evidence of Israel's essential perfidy and malevolence. For their part, the Arabs can argue that they, at any rate, never have, and do not now proclaim their aims to be peace and coexistence. To which the ever more conscious and explicit response of the Israelis is to discount the expectation of an eventual resolution of the conflict in terms of peace and security for all and to accept a prospect of interminable minor warfare punctuated from time to time by major clashes.

Each side is thus either committed or constrained to see in the other an opponent to be confronted by nothing less than unremitting hostility. The goals are in each case such that the closer they are to attainment the more strongly the parties are impelled to pursue them. In these circumstances it is not surprising that the chronology of the Arab-Israel conflict should be one of spiralling violence. Nor, for all these reasons, is it possible to envisage a radical change in the structure of the conflict, still less in its climate, without prior and equally radical change in the identity and goals of the parties to it.

In practice, this could only mean one or more of the following: the abandonment of pan-Arabism, i.e., the concept of the common interests and identity of all Arabs; the establishment of Israel's military security on so firm a basis that the realization of Arab goals would manifestly have to be postponed to the Greek calends; the successful liquidation of Israel and the death and dispersal of its Jewish inhabitants; or the successful imposition of a settlement by the great powers. Of none of these four possibilities is there today the slightest prospect; but each may be very briefly considered.

An attempt has already been made to indicate how profound are the roots of the pan-Arab ideology in the contemporary Arab world and why the conflict between Arabs and Jews is far from being a mere territorial dispute between the two major ethnic groups which inhabit "Palestine." The position is that *any* concession to the Jewish national movement, which is to say any measure of acquiescence in the perpetuation of a Jewish state of any dimension whatsoever, is held to be a betrayal of a constituent member of the family of Arab peoples, the Palestinians. Accordingly, the settlement which from the Jewish point of view is least desirable but still conceivably acceptable —say, a fresh partition of Palestine—would still entail either the abandonment of the Palestinians by the other Arabs or else a resolve by the Palestinians to make their own peace with the Jews and go it alone.

Neither possibility is in prospect. No Arab government will dare undertake the former and few have any real need to; and such feeble attempts by Palestinians to negotiate independently with Israel as occurred after the end of the Six Day War rapidly withered. They neither wished nor dared to cut themselves off from their neighbors in so unpopular a cause and they have never been influential enough even in their own areas to make it worth Israel's while to negotiate with them. In the meantime, the entirely intransigent Palestine Liberation Organization, which groups about a dozen of the principal guerrilla organizations and is fully in key with the conventional Arab approach to the problem, is making all the running. So while the freeing of the Palestinians from the tutelage of the other Arabs did indeed open up the possibility of a direct settlement between them and the Jews *in theory*, in practice the dominant Palestinian party is pressing the other way. Alternatively, if a direct Israeli-Palestinian settlement were arrived at, it would spell a moral defeat of the first order for the general Arab cause. It may, therefore, be wiser to suppose that a weakening of the general pan-Arab movement would have to come *before* any such settlement were within reach.

The three remaining possibilities all involve the powers that are external to the region—first and foremost the United States and the Soviet Union. Israel's human and material resources are clearly too limited for it to establish itself in Arab minds as invulnerable. So, short of a still unimaginably profound breakthrough in military technology, it is hard to see how the Arab world could be persuaded to give up the struggle, unless a lasting and credible military link were established between Israel and one of the great powers. On the other hand, the Arab states, for all their overwhelmingly greater military potential, are unlikely to achieve the straightforward victory over Israel to which they are committed unless they are aided by one of the powers in ways that go substantially beyond the forms of assistance (supplies, technical advisers, and limited combat personnel) with which the Soviet Union provides them at present.

Neither of these two possibilities is inconceivable. The latter, as things stand at the time of this writing, is marginally more likely than the former, but neither is really easy to envisage. The reasons are complex, and an adequate discussion of great-power policy would be well beyond the scope of this chapter. But certain points may be made in passing. The first is that while it was partly through exploitation of the Arab-Israel conflict that the Soviet Union has been able to replace the western powers as the preponderant power in the Middle East in the period since 1955, the particular engine of this penetration was, and remains, a somewhat shaky alliance with the principal Arab states. An end to the conflict through the liquidation of Israel, or ossification of the conflict as a result of Arab despair at ever achieving that liquidation, would only reduce Arab dependence on the Soviets and place many of the Russian achievements in jeopardy. The interests of the Soviet Union are better served, at least for the present, by keeping the conflict at a temperature just short of the boiling point.

Second, any substantial tipping of the balance of forces between Jews and Arabs in favor of the Jews—and an alliance between Israel and any extra regional power, would clearly tip the balance that way—would tend either to vitiate the uses of the Arab–Soviet link in the eyes of the Arabs or impel the Soviets, for that very reason, to make much more substantial moves in their favor. Since neither for Russia nor for the United States are Middle East interests quite at the top of their global priorities, and both sides are reluctant to risk a major clash between themselves over matters of secondary (although not negligible) importance, no really binding commitment to Israel by the United States or any other western power is very likely to be undertaken. And since the United States, Britain and France are all concerned with lubricating their relations with the Arabs, no such commitment is even likely to be seriously considered.

The third point is, simply, that—as has been argued in some detail, albeit indirectly—the structure and dynamics of the Arab-Israeli conflict owe nothing of substance to external factors. In all significant respects it constitutes an autonomous system, the members of which are able and willing to draw upon the political and material resources of the extra regional powers only to the extent that these powers can serve their own internal purposes. Thus, while the conflict attained its mature phase, so to speak, well over two decades ago and has persisted in broadly identical form ever since, all the great powers have thought it politic to change sides at least once.[14]

For all these reasons, the last of the four ways in which the conflict might terminate is inherently the least likely. The great powers can

---

[14] In 1948 the Soviet Union favored the establishment of Israel and supported it against the Arabs. Britain strongly supported the Arabs. The United States opposed the establishment of the state and only reversed its position after the Israelis defied Secretary Marshall's dire warnings and presented the Americans with a *fait accompli*. Nevertheless, even after the formal point had been conceded, a severe embargo on arms was maintained. As the Arabs were well provided with (British) arms, the American embargo had the same effect as the one imposed by the French 20 years later. The bulk of Israel's arms came then from the Soviet side.

Part Three: Violent Conflicts

probably enforce a temporary cessation of hostilities for a while. They may even succeed—although this is more doubtful—in imposing a territorial settlement of their own devising. But the motor forces driving the Arab and Jewish national movements are so powerful, and the attachment of each side to its respective position so fervent, that no settlement could be expected to endure very long. A large and fully viable Israel would continue to serve as a goad to Arab revanchism; a moderately reduced Israel would encourage the Arabs to persevere; a greatly reduced Israel would both encourage the Arabs and impel the Jews to reverse the process. So unless the great powers were prepared to impose full control over the region in forms that might well be reminiscent of classic nineteenth-century imperialism, it would not be too long before the status quo ante was restored.

India and Pakistan

WAYNE WILCOX

Human conflict is a complex social process, and
requires of those who would understand it a very broad
range of perspectives. The social problems that erupt
into political violence are themselves clusters of
conditions, attitudes, and opportunities, each capable
of different interpretations. How much more complicated
is war that springs from social conflict and spills
over state frontiers! And the intergroup violence
of war that persists over decades, alternating between
conditions of armistice and belligerency, requires an
understanding both of the roots of the conflict and
of its evolution as a political process constantly adapting
to, and shaping, historical change.

Convincing theories of persistent intergroup conflict
are few, because the requirements for rigorous analysis
are so demanding and the evidence so ambiguous.
This gap in the study of conflict is serious because
persistent conflict is relatively typical of nation-state
systems and has become widely prevalent in the
post-World War II world. In Africa and Asia, the bad
fit between traditional social group boundaries and the
frontiers inherited from European empires provokes
the same kinds of tension as those associated with
the cold-war partition of peoples who were once united
in Korea, China, Vietnam, and Germany. The problem
is made worse in the Third World by the need of
new governments to build effective political authority
while attempting to align ancient group loyalties
with a modern national patriotism. In this attempt,
neighboring governments will be bidding against one
another for the same potential citizens without
themselves possessing an effective political base. The
undemarcated frontiers of European empires become
the irredentist causes of new nations, and national
loyalties are forged in the heat of wars of self-definition.

Thus, most of Afro-Asia seems destined to repeat Europe's turbulent Age of Nationalism.

Two recent developments, however, make this forecast doubtful. The first is the impressive growth of international organizations concerned with peace-keeping and regional cooperation, and the second is the unprecedented concentration of military power in the United States and the Soviet Union. These developments have led to new forms of conflict management in which local disputes rarely remain localized. The world community, led by rival superpowers, rapidly internationalizes "threats to world peace" and imposes conditions on the belligerents that are crucial to the outcome of their competition.

While this form of interference may lead to the reduction of conflict, it may also have the opposite effect. In the European system, war facilitated and enforced political change. In the contemporary world, however, the entry of global powers introduces very great uncertainty into the calculations of warring smaller powers and may deny a potential victor the fruits of a nation's sacrifice. Local conflict may, therefore, become indecisive and perhaps persistent. This chapter examines the conflict between India and Pakistan from this perspective.

An analysis of five aspects of conflict in south Asia helps to explain its depth, complexity, and persistence. First, the roots of the conflict lie entangled in the pattern and consequences of political change and communal competition in the last two decades of British rule. Second, the conflict was made less manageable as part of the process by which what had been a colonially balanced system of group competition was transformed by independence into an unmanaged and unstable interstate relationship. Third, the conflict was embedded in the public life of both countries in the formative period of their domestic and foreign policies. Fourth, the historic roots of the conflict were constantly renewed and reinforced by the interstate violence that flowed from political separation, and by unresolved group tension within both states. Fifth, the impact of the cold war and the international system on the region tended to preserve the freedom of local elites to undertake hostile actions without creating conditions that would lead to their resolution.

Incunabula: Differential Rates and Patterns of Group Mobilization

Group competition, motivated and symbolized by different religious, ethnic, tribal, or cultural loyalties, is a historical phenomenon in south Asia, as it is elsewhere in the world. Ancient Hindu society accommodated the subcontinent's diversity by establishing a society of "mutually repulsing" castes with very decentralized structures of authority. Empires in India were transitory coalitions led by minority groups ruling a society of inattentive sects. Most colonial governments, whether Mogul, Afghan, or British, welcomed the lack of unified organization in the society and found group conflict an imperial convenience as long as it did not become "unmanageable."

The British inherited this kind of empire from the collapse of Muslim rule in India and found themselves with embittered ex-rulers, divided Hindus, and enormous continental diversity. Until social change and economic development began to produce a measure of functional unity in India, the British managed their empire by balancing its struggling groups, and they managed it with great parsimony.[1]

As education, urbanization, and the unifying aspects of the new Western culture came to be important in India, it was the Hindu upper classes that benefited most. The Muslims continued to nurse the wounds of a fall from imperial power and found themselves severely punished for participation in the 1857 mutiny against the new raj. Thus while the British and a new class of urban Hindus were fashioning a new society in the last half of the 19th century, the Muslims were only beginning to stir as an organized community.

By 1906 the Muslim elite recognized that a new world was upon India and that the Muslims were not reaping any of its advantages. They organized the All-India Muslim League, following, by a generation, the organization of the Indian National Congress in 1885, along the lines of a communal trade union. When the British attacked the Muslim Ottoman Empire at the end of World War I, even the non-political religious divines of the Muslim community were brought into the modern political system then being revolutionized by Gandhi. Government reforms in 1919 and 1935 opened opportunities in representative government for Indian politicians, and the rapid expansion of education and urban employment in the professions increased the access of "modern" Indians to power, wealth, and status in British India. The weak new Muslim professional classes, the concerned religious leadership, the landholding elite, and the young came together in a revitalized Muslim League to demand "quotas" to protect them from the better-trained elite of the majority community. The

[1] As late as 1939 the British ruled undivided India with only 1,299 members of the elite Indian Civil Service. While they were supported by subordinate services, the police and the army, the British component of the government was extremely small. See Philip Woodruff, *The Men Who Ruled India: The Guardians* (London: Jonathan Cape, 1954).

British were accommodating, and although the rules of balancing groups were ancient, the scale of the effort was dramatically new.

In the interwar period, 1919–1939, Indians of all castes and communities were asked to choose a political identity relevant to the twentieth century. The Indian National Congress stood for *swaraj*—freedom—with Gandhi championing a Hindu populism and Nehru speaking for a progressive secular India of the future. The Muslim leadership was divided by situation and dream.

The Muslim rural aristocracy faced hostile Hindu urban leaders intent upon "socialist reforms" that would end their position of privilege in landholding. Pious Muslims found themselves threatened by the prospects of a Hindu state legislating against Muslim conscience or adopting heathen ways of organizing an irreligious society. Muslim professional classes found themselves outnumbered, outranked, and outschooled by Hindus who had taken to British ways a generation earlier and as a consequence dominated the lower rungs of the professions, the universities, and the government services. Muslim traders, new to the bourgeois ways of British India, found themselves between large British managing agencies and experienced networks of Hindu business and banking groups. And Muslim politicians, representing a one-in-five minority, were uncomfortable with the thought that majoritarianism was the post-British prospect for Indian politics.[2]

These separate but parallel "conflict sets" existed in the context of intensified social and economic change in the last two decades of British rule. The depression of the 1930s reduced opportunities for newly mobilized Muslims and Hindus; the war years of the 1940s increased mobilization while radicalizing it in an environment of wartime inflation.[3] Throughout this period social violence grew enormously at all levels of society, and it often tended to focus on communally defined issues. Rural violence frequently pitted Muslim against Hindu. Language enthusiasts in north India struggled for Hindi or Urdu, despite their similarity, because they were written in the scripts,

[2] The politicians reflected their community's anxieties to a great degree because the British electoral rolls were not territorial but communal. Muslims ran for office in Muslim-only constituencies, limited by property requirements. Only in Punjab, Bengal, and Northwest Frontier Province were the Muslims strong enough in numbers and organization to find coalition politics attractive. In northern and western India, the experience with the 1937 elections was disastrous to the cause of communal coalition-building in politics. See especially Maulana Abul Kalam Azad, *India Wins Freedom* (New York: Longmans Green, 1960), pp. 15–27.

[3] The cost of living index (1939 equals 100) stood at 270.1 in 1945 and 310.4 in 1946, rising further in the year of partition and independence.

of Hindu and Muslim elites. Businessmen blamed economic problems on members of the other community, and factions within the professions and military and civil services competed with rival groups from the other community.[4]

The British colonial system was one of "imperial counterpoise," the use of colonial authority to balance intergroup conflict and limit its expression. But the radical change produced by war, increasing popular participation in the nationalist movements, the increasing multiplier effects of the nationalist, vernacular, and partitionist press, more open access to institutions of authority, and an increasing scale of conflict meant that the imperial counterpoise required more resources. Yet the British will and capacity to intervene decisively was slipping rapidly in World War II and its aftermath. Once the British announced that they would leave at war's end, all Indian parties knew that their absence would leave no "balancer." The issue was then clear. The leaders of the Indian National Congress intended to replace the British as the authoritative managers of multigroup competition in south Asia; the Muslim elites and especially the leaders of the Muslim League sought to withdraw from that particular system of multigroup competition and establish their own system of authority.[5] Pitted against both the Congress party and the Muslim League were provincialists who feared "nationalization" of political power regardless of the communal composition of the superordinate elite. The departing British were forced to meet this three-cornered competition by granting independence and the partition of British India; their successors were forced to accept a federal form of government.

Metamorphosis:
From Intramural Competition
to Interstate Conflict

During the process of their political mobilization, various Muslim elites had externalized their several dissatisfactions, imputed them to the British and Hindus, and cumulated them in the platform of the

---

[4] Communal conflict has rarely been studied in a comprehensive manner. For a case study of early violence, see Clifford Manshardt, *The Hindu-Muslim Problem in India* (London: Allen and Unwin, 1936). The period just before independence has been described by Nirad Chaudhuri, *The Autobiography of an Unknown Indian* (London: Macmillan, 1951). The continuation of communal tension in independent India is described in detail for one Indian town in Richard G. Fox, *From Zamindar to Ballot Box* (Ithaca, N.Y.: Cornell University Press, 1969).

[5] Almost all the groups in India realized that the state was central to the relation-

Muslim League. Every disparate segment of the Indian Muslim community could add its "points" to the charge sheet against non-Muslims, and therefore cultural, linguistic, economic, and social *differences* became political *problems*. This was neatly summarized at one point by Mohammad Ali Jinnah, the leader of the Muslim League, when he accused the British of originating the deprivation of India's Muslims, and the Hindus of sustaining it. He could not reduce the grossness of the charge without strengthening his two rivals, provincialists favoring multicommunal coalitions and federal autonomy, and Muslim collaborationists supporting a united India led by the Indian National Congress elite. The only viable policy for the Muslim League "nationalists" was to champion a separate state—Pakistan.

The idea of Pakistan had been in the air since the middle 1930s, popularized in the poetics of north Indian culture and bitterly attacked by the Congress party, many Muslim groups, and almost all provincial leaders. As Jawaharlal Nehru wrote in his 1936 *Autobiography*, "The Muslim nation in India—a nation within a nation, and not even compact but vague, spread out, indeterminate—politically the idea is absurd."[6] But within a decade the absurd idea was about to become a reality, and Nehru would accept it as less onerous than a federal India in which the central government would be no more than a weak mediator between warring provinces and communities.

Moreover, the creation of Pakistan seemed to be the only way to avoid an open civil war. In 1945–1946, more than a million men were demobilized from military service, there were cases of mutiny in the services, government expenditures and employment rolls were cut back, and inflation continued to spiral. The Muslim League at this juncture called for direct action to topple coalition governments in provinces having Muslim majorities; all political parties made a maximal organizational effort to take "post position" when the British withdrew; and the British themselves added to the uncertainty by announcing their impending withdrawal but not the terms under which it would take place.

In these tense circumstances, as in the decade before, communal violence tended to bring the minority communities throughout the subcontinent together through a common sense of insecurity and a common expectation of violence. The cycle therefore became one in

---

ship of groups and communities, and had been even before British rule. See D. R. Gadgil, *Poona: A Socioeconomic Study*, II (Poona: Gokhale Institute, 1945). For south Indian confirmation, see Robert L. Hardgrave, Jr., *The Nadars of Tamilnad* (Berkeley and Los Angeles: University of California Press, 1969).
6 London: Macmillan, 1936, p. 469.

which social differences led to anticipated or real violence; such violence led to increasing minority integration and organization, which in turn led to an identity-reinforcement that heightened difference and further provoked insecurity, anxiety, and violence.[7]

In 1947, therefore, intergroup conflict could no longer be managed by colonial authority, and intergroup distrust and tension did not allow cooperative, political steps toward conflict resolution. Moreover, an "Islamic state" promised something to almost all Muslims: public piety and support for religion for the traditionalists, conservative economic policy for the landholders and businessmen, open opportunities for the professional middle classes, great autonomy for the politicians, and increased opportunities for the young.

The difficulty was that once Pakistan was created, the disparate Muslim elites could no longer externalize, cumulate, and transfer their grievances to Hindus or British, and the struggle between Muslim elites produced tension and conflict, not unity and security. Hindu-Muslim elite conflict was "internationalized," but it was not ended, and the scale and cost of conflict increased. What Muslim leaders might have wanted, according to one Indian expert, was "the destruction of south Asia and the reconstruction of West Asia," that is, the Muslim world.[8] What they inherited, however, was a vulnerable position on either side of an increasingly hostile and powerful India. As Maulana Abul Kalam Azad wrote, sadly,

Can anyone deny that the creation of Pakistan has not solved the communal problem, but made it more intense and harmful? The basis of partition was enmity between Hindus and Moslems. The creation of Pakistan gave it a permanent constitutional form and made it much more difficult of solution.[9]

Indian national leadership was in a much better position. As the representative of the "majority," the Congress party did not have to fear the coming of representative government and indeed would ride such a development to the heights of power. Moreover, with the

---

[7] This apparently is a general social process found in much social conflict. A group's identity is in large part a function of external definitions of it, brought home by violence affecting all members of the groups, and therefore "integrating" them. See Lewis A. Croser, *The Functions of Social Conflict* (New York: The Free Press, 1956).

[8] S. P. Varma, "Foreign Policies of South Asian States," in S. P. Varma and K. P. Misra (eds.), *Foreign Policies in South Asia* (Bombay: Asia, 1969), p. 5.

[9] *India Wins Freedom,* p. 259.

Muslim majority provinces gone, the Congress party could centralize authority much more rapidly. Moreover, since Indian society is explicitly pluralist in orientation, there was no imperative need to find a consensus on policy when a nationalist coalition served the same purpose for the Congress party.

Yet the top leadership of the Congress party was badly divided. Over 500 princely states had to be integrated into the union, the praetorian civil and military services had to be brought under political control, the Indian national state had to be built and strengthened, and the poorest large country in the world had to be launched on the voyage to economic growth and industrialization. On the surface, India in 1947 appeared to be a relatively secure country, full of optimism and faith in its leadership—but the realities were quite different. The fact that both the Indian and the Pakistani governments lacked the confidence and capacity to govern coherently had much to do with the disasters of the first three years of independent foreign relations.

Crystallization: Insecure Elites and Embedded Conflicts

When in the spring of 1947 the British found themselves with rapidly declining authority and two intransigent nationalist elites, Lord Mountbatten interpreted the cabinet's decision to "grant" Pakistan as needing to be implemented with the greatest haste. Seventy-two days after the announcement, the British withdrew. In the same period, officials from "India" and "Pakistan" catalogued, negotiated, divided, and transferred the governmental assets of more than a century of British rule. They did so in the midst of unprecedented social violence, political contention, personal anguish, economic chaos, and governmental confusion.

It might have happened that the subcontinent's partition would have been territorially unambiguous, that its governments would early have evolved a sense of secure maturity, and that Indian-Pakistani relations might over time have developed as mutually accommodating. Two events in the summer of 1947, in the midst of the undeclared civil war, ended that prospect for at least a generation: an unplanned population exchange of perhaps 13 million people accompanied by the death of perhaps half a million more, and a war for the princely state of Jammu and Kashmir.

While the figures are rough, most experts believe that about 13 million people became refugees in 1947 and 1948, most of them in northern India and west Pakistan.[10] Figures vary more considerably about the number of dead and missing, but the range is between 200,000[11] and the government of Pakistan's official estimate of 500,000.[12] For the elite fleeing Delhi, Lahore, Dacca, or Calcutta, there were the memories of whole city wards on fire; for the Punjabi peasants moving both ways across the killing grounds they once farmed, death, violence, and deprivation had an immediacy which personalized the symbols of politics that had been abstractly mooted by leaders a month before.

The fury of the mobs in both India and Pakistan frightened and depressed elites in both countries, and there was considerable courage shown by both new governments in protecting the lives of minorities. The example of Gandhi's fasts and travels for communal peace were well known; hundreds of others set for themselves the same task. Nonetheless, the worst possible aspersions, made in the heat of political polemics, appear to have been validated in the atrocities of 1947 and 1948. While it seems clear that some of the killing was the work of organized terrorist groups championing their work in communal slogans, most of the violence resulted from the breakdown of authority in the midst of widespread population movements. It was a time to settle old scores, and the victims were more vulnerable than they would have been in their villages or towns, where protection was more available.

Nonetheless, the leaders responsible for partition had to accept the responsibility for the conditions leading to the carnage, and they could not bring themselves to consider that partition might not have been necessary. For the wavering and the unsure, the violence of partition forced commitment; for the committed and the responsible, violence sealed the choice.[13]

[10] The Indian government's census organization estimated 4,400,000 refugees from West Pakistan in 1948 and 1,600,000 from East Pakistan in 1949. The estimate of Muslims who had migrated to Pakistan was 5,800,000. Richard Symonds, *The Making of Pakistan* (London: Faber, 1950), pp. 83–84. Many observers consider these figures to be low. The most recent and complete attempt to survey and analyze the post-partition population flow is Pravin M. Visaria, "Migration Between India and Pakistan, 1951–1961" *Demography*, 6, 3 (August 1969), esp. 323–334.

[11] Penderel Moon, *Divide and Quit* (Berkeley and Los Angeles: University of California Press, 1962), p. 293.

[12] Symonds, *The Making of Pakistan*, p. 83.

[13] One would be hard pressed to describe a better political example of Leon Festinger's hypothesis of postdecisional attitude change and reinforcement, which

That a war for Kashmir developed simultaneously with the civil war in the Indian plains made matters worse because it tended to fuse the communal riots and anarchic violence with Indian-Pakistani war. While the roots of widespread social violence were embedded in subcontinental society, the Kashmir war was, at least in part, the result of elite indecision and chance.

Jammu and Kashmir state, ruled somewhat irresolutely by a Hindu Maharaja and his retainers at the expense of the governed, most of whom were Muslim, had witnessed the same sorts of social mobilization and political participation, though not at the same levels, as the rest of northwestern India. Because it was a princely state, however, the ruler could be more arbitrary. Sheikh Abdullah, the leader of the state's largest political movement, was a democratic socialist and a Muslim. In order to wrest control of the state's government from the autocratic prince and his agents, Sheikh Abdullah concluded an informal agreement with the Indian National Congress and especially Jawaharlal Nehru. As independence approached, the Muslim League sought to move the Muslim popular forces in Kashmir into the Pakistan movement, if necessary at the expense of Sheikh Abdullah. The Maharaja attempted to remain free of an independent and democratic India, which would end his autocratic rule, and an independent and Muslim Pakistan, which would end his non-Muslim rule. To do so, he had to suspend political activity and weaken all popular parties.

In 1947, Sheikh Abdullah was in prison and the state police and army repressed efforts to organize political parties. In Poonch district, a rebellion led by former servicemen broke out, and as violence spread throughout northern India, conditions also deteriorated within the state. Lord Mountbatten, Gandhi, and Jinnah all attempted to get the Maharaja to declare which country Jammu and Kashmir state would join, but he refused. At that point, Pathan tribesmen from the Northwest Frontier Province of Pakistan and from the contiguous tribal zones in Afghanistan invaded the state, looting and raping their way to the gates of Srinagar, the state capital. The Maharaja released Sheikh Abdullah from jail and made him prime minister, signed an instrument of accession to India, and witnessed the dispatch of Indian troops to Srinagar, which they held. Lord Mountbatten accepted the accession of the Maharaja "subject to a reference to the people." As

---

suggests that a reevaluation of attitudes occurs after a decision in order to make "relevant cognitions" consistent with choice of behavior. See *A Theory of Cognitive Dissonance* (Stanford, Calif.: Stanford University Press, 1957).

the war in Kashmir developed, the tribesmen fell back, the government of Pakistan committed regular units to battle, and the war was "internationalized."[14]

Once Pakistan was "officially" in the war and responsible for the non-Indian forces fighting in it, it was possible to think of the war as organized between states and hence a conflict that could be terminated in the UN-arranged armistice of January 1, 1949. Pakistan anticipated that the UN would play the role once reserved for the British, the management of intergroup competition in south Asia. The government of India anticipated that its national power would have to be recognized by Pakistan, and that any settlement in Kashmir must recognize India's strategic superiority.

Even without the refugee influx and the Kashmir war, many factors made for tension between India and Pakistan. The government of Pakistan was the insecure government of an insecure community, and it was hypersensitive to its weakness. Having attempted to establish a government in slightly more than two months, coping with destroyed cities and seven million refugees in the first year, witnessing the entire disruption of the economy and the breakdown of civil order throughout the country, attempting to make real a state divided by 1,000 miles of hostile Indian territory, fighting the Indian army for Kashmir, and somehow surmounting the national trauma of the death of Mohammad Ali Jinnah, the *Quaid-i-Azam* (Great Leader) within 15 months of independence, the few people managing the government of Pakistan might reasonably have broken under the strains.

To these problems were added those of an Indian semiblockade, the hostility of some members of the Indian government to transferring to Pakistan the share of goods and supplies previously agreed to, the Indian threat to divert or withhold headwaters from the upper reaches of the Indus canals, and the difficulties of operating semi-

---

[14] No brief summary of this dispute does justice to its baroque complications and the fine points of legal, military, clandestine, diplomatic, and moral practice which it witnesses. Most good arguments develop from three points: (1) Why did the British permit the princes to choose their dominion of choice, and why was the Maharaja of Jammu and Kashmir "immune" to the blandishments of Lord Mountbatten? (2) How much did Pakistan's government have to do with organizing, arming, and transporting the tribes to Kashmir, and how much collusion was there with the Poonch forces? (3) What was the nature of Gandhi's mission to Srinagar in the spring of 1947, and what covert Indian strategy was being pursued to encourage the Maharaja to join India without violating political ties to Sheikh Abdullah? A good comprehensive study is Sisir Gupta, *Kashmir: A Study in India-Pakistan Relations* (Bombay: Asia, 1966), which has a 20-page bibliography.

integrated taxation, currency, and foreign exchange systems.[15] While these were severe problems, even greater ones were presented: establishing a national identity; creating a sense of political legitimacy; developing instruments of national authority; and creating social institutions of command and control. No Indian National Congress organization existed to see to the needy. These fundamental political weaknesses within Pakistan made its government even more insecure in its struggles with India.

The Indian leadership also seems to have been badly divided in the aftermath of partition, especially on policies toward Pakistan. The president of the Congress party, Maulana Abul Kalam Azad, was for reconciliation, as was Gandhi; Nehru as prime minister was struggling with Sardar Vallabhai Patel, the deputy prime minister, for control of the government, and Patel stood for a hard line toward Pakistan. Lord Mountbatten, the residual British guarantor of the partition, had a special voice with Nehru in his role as governor-general of India. Thus, what appeared to Pakistan's tenuous political elite as willful sabotage and unremitting hostility was the product of a complex, confused interplay, within the Indian government, of competing leaders and priorities.[16]

In the face of his weakness, Liaquat Ali Khan, Pakistan's first prime minister, accepted the role of peaceful supplicant in India-Pakistan relations, pursued a strategy of seeking a UN settlement of the Kashmir question, and attempted to centralize political authority within his government. He was unsuccessful in all three quests.

Without losing a degree of its independence, India could not allow the UN or any foreign power to reassume the British role of balancer in India-Pakistan relations, and therefore would not willingly witness the internationalization of the Kashmir dispute. Similarly, the only way Pakistan could be made to accept India's regional hegemony and leadership was for it to have no alternatives. Thus, in 1950–1951 when the UN actively sponsored a plebiscite in the state, the Indian government refused its cooperation and, moreover, moved troops from its overwhelmingly larger army to the Pakistan frontier to remind its leaders of their vulnerability and of the absence of any external

[15] These are discussed in helpful detail by G. W. Choudhury in his bristling *Pakistan's Relations with India, 1947–1966* (New York: Praeger, 1968).

[16] This process reconfirms the reality of images, projected insecurities, and the expectancy of violence as more important than "objective reality." For a wide range of insights on this aspect of conflict, see the contributions in Leon Bramson and George Goethals (eds.), *War: Studies from Psychology, Sociology, Anthropology* (New York: Basic Books, 1964).

"counterpoise." As Nirad Chaudhuri, one of India's closest observers of security policy, has written:

India held the pistol at the head of Pakistan, until, in 1954, the American alliance delivered the country from that nightmare. . . . at least twice, if not three times, between 1947 and 1954, India intended to invade Pakistan and was deterred only by American and British remonstrances.[17]

Thus Liaquat's policy of negotiation with India and reliance upon the United Nations did not yield either security or Kashmir. For his moderacy he faced an abortive coup d'état in 1950, and, probably for his attempts to centralize authority in Pakistan, he was assassinated in 1951. In almost a decade thereafter, Pakistan's governments were extremely tenuous, efforts to find an international solution to the Kashmir dispute were unsuccessful, and India-Pakistan relations have corresponded to Hobbes's definition of war:

As the nature of foul weather lieth not in a shower or two of rain but in an inclination thereto of many days together; so that the nature of war consisteth not in actual fighting but the known disposition thereto during all the time there is no assurance to the contrary.[18]

Reinforcement: The Residual Civil War

Serious as were the early disputes between India and Pakistan, and determining as they were for the course of early interstate conflict, their immediate roots were unique to a generation. Refugees become citizens in the second generation; the carnage of partition might be forgotten over time; the mundane quarrels over resource disposition fade, and the passions of one era and one social experience tend to have a short half-life. The problem was that many of the factors making for intergroup conflict before partition *continued* in both India and Pakistan and constantly reinforced interstate tension.

Indian power and status in the international community seemed to leaders in Karachi to threaten Pakistan's *existence*. As the late Keith Callard noted:

Many political leaders and most of the articulate section of the population have reacted with emotional intensity to any suggestion of Indian superiority

17 *The Continent of Circe* (New York: Oxford University Press, 1966), p. 244.

18 *Leviathan,* chap. 11, cited in Alastair Buchan, *War in Modern Society* (London, 1966).

in any field. . . . the degree of passion has been heightened by the feeling, largely justified, that on every matter on which the real interests of the two nations have come into conflict, India has contrived to emerge victorious.[19]

The relationship, therefore, embodied the civil-war notion that what one side won, the other automatically lost.

While it would appear that India was the confident regional power isolating Pakistan and consolidating its position, many members of the Indian political elite viewed Pakistan and the western approaches to the subcontinent with alarm. Thus V. P. Menon, one of the most powerful and articulate civil servants in the Indian government, wrote:

Ever since the time of Mahmud Ghazni, that is to say, for nearly eight centuries. . . India has been subjected to periodic invasions from the northwest. . . . Within less than ten weeks of the establishment of the new state of Pakistan, its very first act was to let loose a tribal invasion through the northwest. Srinigar today, Delhi tomorrow. A nation that forgets its history or its geography does so at its peril.[20]

Pakistan, therefore, was the "jackal" at the door which in the past had so often swung open to admit India's enemies.

As the government of Pakistan searched for allies and psychological support for its Muslim identity, India moved to isolate it. In 1950 India and Afghanistan signed a five-year treaty of peace and friendship at a time when Afghanistan was sponsoring an irredentist claim to "Pukhtunistan," the Northwest Frontier Province of Pakistan. While the religious ardor of Pakistani diplomats was sometimes making them unwelcome in countries like Turkey, the Indians were aligning with Cairo in what to become the Nasser-Nehru-Tito neutralist axis. As late as 1969 and the Rabat conference of the heads of Islamic countries, India and Pakistan were struggling over Pakistan's *exclusive* right to politically represent south Asian Islam.[21]

Another aspect of this problem is that in both India and Pakistan about 11 percent of the population still constitutes "residual" minority

[19] *Pakistan: A Political Study* (New York: Macmillan, 1957), p. 304.

[20] *The Integration of the Indian States* (New York: Macmillan, 1956), p. 413.

[21] India was forced to withdraw its delegation under embarrassing circumstances, and Pakistan's truculent attitude certainly made it no new Arab friends. See the report in *Far Eastern Economic Review*, October 16, 1969, p. 158, for a summary. The point is that Islam is central to the political legitimacy and identity of Pakistan's leaders, and therefore it cannot be shared with India in any visible political circumstance.

communities. There was no "clean break," as happened in the Greek-Turkish population exchange in the interwar period, and the absolute magnitudes involved offer no such prospect. Thirteen million Hindus in Pakistan are concentrated in the eastern wing and would debouch upon Calcutta's already swollen hinterland. But 55 million Indian Muslims would increase Pakistan's population by 50 percent!

Without such an exchange in prospect, however, the tense history of group and state conflict testifies to the potential for pogroms in both countries. A demonstration effect unfortunately takes hold when rioting breaks out in one country; frequently, disturbances then occur in the other. This tends to perpetuate and reinforce the hostile stereotypes of the other community or state in the minds of both Hindu Indians and Muslim Pakistanis, and leads to expectations of further violence. Thus, a symbiosis occurs between political and communal contexts that constantly leads to embittered interstate relations.

The scant evidence on communal riots tends to show that they arise from local frictions, have almost nothing to do with international politics, and take place generally in cities in which local authorities are lax or permissive.[22] Thus, the Ahmedabad Muslims and Dacca Hindus of 1969 were attacked not because they were thought to be "fifth columnists" or traitors, but because they were competitors for resources, jobs, and space, and because they had less protection from social violence than they might have had if they had belonged to the majority community. It goes without saying that most social violence in both India and Pakistan is directed at members of the same community on noncommunal grounds. What makes the communal riot so important is that it has an "international effect" independent of the public policy of either government.

In conditions of periodic war, continual distrust, interstate rivalry, expectations of violence, and group insecurity, communal rioting adds a reinforcing support. The handling of such conflict by the press exaggerates it and universalizes the feeling of threat. Thus the Urdu

[22] This seems to be the uniform pattern reported in the Indian press from the investigations of riots. The government of Pakistan report on communal rioting in India, issued in 1964, cataloged riots between 1947 and 1964 and reported 655 of them, with 713 Muslims dead and 4,393 injured. Since then, the number of riots has increased appreciably. For many reasons, including their almost total concentration in East Pakistan where they are not insignificant or vulnerable, the Hindus have witnessed communal violence on a large scale only in 1950, 1964, and 1969. Report, Amt of Pak to Report of the Commission of Human Rights, May. 20, 1970, UN.

daily *Hurriyet* (Karachi) reported on October 23, 1969, that it had an "exclusive eye-witness account that 8,000 Muslims were killed, 45,000 made homeless, in the Ahmedabad riots" and that 43 mosques and 13 shrines were destroyed. This sort of news tends to confirm the accepted conviction that *India* is out to "undo" Pakistan, that the *Hindus* aim to convert or destroy the Muslims, and that every evidence of the Muslim community is to be uprooted and destroyed. This proves the necessity of the creation (and persistence) of Pakistan.

Some observers charge that Pakistan's unity is a product of a pathological fear and hatred of India, and that its insecure leaders play upon that fear to maintain their position of power. Large defense expenditures and General Mohammad Ayub Khan's rise to power are therefore explained by the high value placed on (anti-Indian) security in Pakistan. While it may be argued that Ayub's government *after 1965* needed conflict with India for its domestic popularity, it seems more convincing that the existing popular hostility to India was the only available issue by which the government could increase its support. In short, latent public hostility, though less visible than elite rivalry, is less its creature than its master. But it is also true that elites remake reality to agree with their private images and social roles and that a government like the one Pakistan inherited has seldom been able to see reality as much more than active Indian-Hindu hostility.

This is not strictly a psychological-communal phenomenon. India and Pakistan are not established nation-states, and the provincialist forces present at their beginnings remain and have grown in strength. East and West Pakistan, for example, are separated not only by a thousand miles but by language, culture, and outlook. East Pakistan and West Bengal state in India share a comon language and, to a degree, a common set of social preferences. The possibilities of an "independent Bengal" or an Indian-inspired "United Bengal within the Indian Union" have concerned every Pakistani government since independence.

Kashmir, on the other hand, is held by India, but the Plebiscite Front party appears to entertain pro-Pakistani inclinations that might compromise Indian sovereignty within the state. Similarly, Pakistani opportunities to compromise Indian rule exist in the Naga and Mizo hills, in Assam, and elsewhere in northeastern India. But India has the opportunity of encouraging Afghanistan to push the Pukhtunistan dispute. It would appear that the mutual vulnerability of the states keeps these opportunities from being fully exploited, much as the mutual "hostage" situation of the communal minorities allows neither government much latitude where their protection is concerned.[23]

The rivalry structure between India and Pakistan also exists in nonstrategic, noncommunal areas. Both compete for the world jute market and for cotton quotas in the developed countries. Both seek air travelers bound for south Asia; both seek the same high levels of economic assistance. They have the world's two most accomplished field hockey teams, and they vie for the same committee chairmanships in the UN. The partition line gives India the headwaters of shared rivers necessary for agriculture in both East and West Pakistan, while Pakistan controls the continental routes necessary for Indian security and trade in middle Asia.

In most of these relationships, India and Pakistan almost always have only a "conflict set" of positions in which the minimal positions of the opposed states do not overlap, and agreements are thus impossible. Since "trade-offs" or overlapping positions are present in few areas, "package settlements" are not possible. All disputes demand the "grand settlement" so characteristic of bargaining positions since 1947.[24]

Agreements found outside areas of clear mutual advantage require leadership on one side or the other to pay a considerable price (Gandhi on the finances transfer crisis of 1947–1948, Liaquat Ali Khan on the Kashmir armistice settlement of 1949), or for third parties to separate issues in contention and create extraregional incentives for settlement (Indus waters). Otherwise, contention between India and Pakistan appears to be resolvable only in a subordination-superordination relationship.

Externalization: Foreign Multipliers, Brokers, Balancers

Pakistan has responded to its insecurity by making heavy allocations of resources to defense and foreign affairs. Always ready to find in

[23] This assessment of the civility of both governments is probably too Machiavellian (or, to keep the South Asian idiom, Kautilyan). I have heard both Indian and Pakistani officials say that they welcomed the "hostage" problem because it allowed a humane public policy that could be justified on a hard, "quid pro quo" basis rather than on high principle. Mutual noninterference in territorial disputes is less consistently honored, perhaps, but neither state has emphasized it to the degree possible.

[24] Kenneth Boulding's notion of three possible bargaining outcomes—conflict, sole

Indian capabilities and initiatives a threat to identity, authority, or territory, Pakistan's governments have reacted by redoubling their hostility, their diplomatic activity, and their security expenditures.

India sees Pakistan as its major *diplomatic* antagonist, much as it sees China as its major security threat, and as a troublesome neighbor intent upon "spoiling" India's world role by constantly pursuing an irredentist policy toward Kashmir at almost any risk and cost. India holds Kashmir, and its army outnumbers that of Pakistan five to one, as does its population and industrial capability. India can forecast in the near future a nuclear weapons capability, a major weapons production capability and some measure of freedom from dependence upon military suppliers. Pakistan's prospects are those of a smaller country that is largely agricultural and is short of the minerals and industrial base necessary for a weapons industry. India may, by 1980, count mostly on itself; Pakistan must depend on others if it is to compete in south Asia—and it has defined itself as a competitor.

Most India-Pakistan interstate conflict since 1947 has been generated by Pakistan. The weak party in this situation is also the revisionist power, and at times it has pursued what Boulding could characterize as "rational aggression," "the deliberate, planned conflict or game of ruin" against India, in the calculated hope of *relative* benefit.[25] India's posture, at least until 1962, was that of a satisfied power. Since 1962 and the Chinese border war, India's security choices and investments have yielded not only a potent defensive force against China, but also an offensive capability sufficient to establish regional hegemony in the absence of great power involvement on Pakistan's behalf. President Ayub Khan in his biography noted that "if a big country like India has the capability to attack Pakistan, intentions can change, pact or no pact."[26]

Pakistan is left in the difficult—almost impossible—position of holding assumptions of permanent, implacable Indian hostility and facing a clear capability trend, the implications of which are an unending and ruinous arms race in which India finally wins. Since this set of assumptions leads to the conclusion that Pakistan's fate is sealed, it is necessary to "maximize under the constraints" by pursuing an active alliance policy invoking external balancers to keep India from asserting its

---

bargain, and acceptable alternative—is a useful structure for this analysis. See his *Conflict and Defense: A General Theory* (New York: Harper & Row, 1962).

[25] *Ibid.*, pp. 88–89 (my italics).

[26] *Friends Not Masters: A Political Biography* (New York: Oxford University Press, 1967), p. 121.

paramountcy.[27] These defensive alliances, coupled with a postulated (hoped for) disintegration of the Indian Union, give Pakistani leaders the hope that they can maintain "theater parity" until the propitious moment in Indian (Kashmiri) history.

The nature of the strategic environment in south Asia since independence has been a function of: (1) the quality and quantity of transferred economic and military resources and the policies of external security managers (first, the British, followed by the United States and, more recently, the USSR and China); (2) Pakistan's relative weakness under conditions of its relative commitment to revision of the territorial boundaries of the present south Asian states; (3) Indian commitment to the status quo, accompanied by lack of enough power to independently guarantee it.

As Indian capabilities increase, the cost to external security managers or manipulators increases, if they intend to intervene decisively in south Asian regional relationships. Pakistan's situation vis-à-vis India calls for *major* support from a would-be ally and leaves Pakistan with the support only of countries willing to compromise their relations with India. The only major country that fits this calculus in 1970 is the Chinese People's Republic, with which Pakistan has good relations. Pakistan's relations with both the US and the USSR are conditioned by their support for India and their poor relations with China. With both, Pakistan aims at a diplomacy conducive to "balance" between India and Pakistan on such vital issues as Kashmir, economic assistance, and military sales.

The strategic paradox in south Asia is that all Pakistani strategies in the end are based upon a diminution of Indian unity, will, or relative power, whereas India must count upon Pakistan's being relatively able to manage its own territories but not having the strength necessary to challenge India in Kashmir. Pakistan's leaders appreciate the fact that China is weak compared to India's patrons, and therefore a Sino-Pakistan relationship is merely a stalling diplomacy. If Pakistan can stall, its diplomats can hope that internal strains within India will progressively weaken the central government and finally lead to a fragmentation that will make it possible for a united Pakistan to seize its opportunities. India, on the other hand, fears the disintegration of Pakistan, which might involve foreign powers in the resulting "vacuum" and would open the subcontinent's flanks to external powers,

---

[27] This, of course, justifies Pakistan's policy of cordial relations with China, the rationale of which is spelled out polemically by former foreign minister Zulfikar Ali Bhutto, *The Myth of Independence* (London: Oxford University Press, 1969).

possibly involving India in a conflict for which it has neither the capacity nor the vital interests to fight.

Curiously, American policy from 1953 to 1965 accommodated this strategic paradox. US arms assistance to Pakistan provided it with an excellent small army equipped with weapons, superior to those of India. Pakistan's insecurity vis-à-vis India was thereby diminished. Washington's support for Pakistan at the UN and in the international community kept its hopes for a favorable Kashmir solution alive. Coincidently, US economic assistance strengthened the Indian national government, while the effect of US aid to Pakistan was to build Pakistan's ability to manage its own affairs without being able to take the successful initiative in Kashmir.

For a decade, American policy made possible very low arms budgets, facilitated quite high levels of economic growth, led to some imaginative international initiatives with problems like the Indus waters, and (contrary to the conventional wisdom) led to better rather than worse India-Pakistan relations. When the rhetoric is discounted, the fact is that India-Pakistan relations were at their best in the period (1954–1962) when the US was the dominant security manager for south Asia.

The Indian arms buildup after the 1962 Sino-Indian border war ended this decade of stability and, coupled with decreased US interest in an alliance with Pakistan, provided an entirely new diplomatic situation in south Asia. The India-Pakistan war of 1965 was a product of the unstable regional political environment.[28] The Tashkent agreement of 1965 was the charter of a *Pax Russica* for south Asia, with Moscow stepping into the former US role of arms supplier to both countries and benevolent neutral in the Kashmir dispute. China remains the "spoiler," just as Pakistan continues to be the state with the greatest interest in the destruction of the status quo, no matter who is its guarantor.

As India prepares to meet a militarily superior China, its increasing level of defense preparations constitutes an immediate threat to Pakistan, which attempts to offset the Indian position of hegemony in south Asia. Once both US and USSR became anti-Chinese while remaining pro-Indian, Pakistan's only "great power" support in a possible Indian conflict was China. This contingent plan brings China into Pakistan, which comprises India's flanking areas, on concessional

[28] I have attempted to analyze the domestic factors in Pakistan responsible for this war in *Asian Survey*, 9, 2 (February 1969), 87–93. For a very detailed assessment of the war and its antecedents, see Russell Brines, *The Indo-Pakistan Conflict* (London: Pall Mall, 1969).

and invitational terms, making Indian defense expenditures all the more necessary. Thus is generated the spiral of "threat–defense expenditures–enhanced threat."

On balance, therefore, the interest of the world powers in south Asian "peace" has not yielded a stable strategic environment, nor have crosscutting global power relationships offered great flexibility to the south Asian states. Rather, external intervention has had the effect not of moderating the conflicts in the region, but has rather escalated their cost and absolute scale.

Summary:
Groups, States, and the World of Conflict

Even so brief an analysis will certainly demonstrate that at the root of the India-Pakistan conflict, and before it the Hindu-Muslim conflict, was the desire of Muslim elites to move out of a system of constraints imposed by a "different" society and authority pattern and to create opportunities for autonomy and assertiveness. Social violence in British India had the effect of integrating the Muslims to a surprising degree, considering both their social disorganization and their physical separation on the eve of independence. The pattern of integration, however, created an elite structure and ethos that defined Pakistan as the antithesis of Hinduism, the Indian National Congress party, and India.

The "play of the game" after partition and independence witnessed the sealing of national fortunes in the refugee flow and in the Kashmir war. The reinforcement of these trends flowed from communal riots, insecurity of the political elite, and introduction of paralleling foreign inputs. This pattern suggests that the initiatives for conflict and its resolution still fundamentally stem from local factors and actors. Neither the US nor the USSR has the interest or the capacity to be the Asian "regulator." Therefore it is difficult to avoid sharing Russell Brines judgment that "the initiative for conflict has passed [from the great powers] to the majority of ill-assorted legal nations created from the wreckage of European colonialism."[29]

---

[29] *The Indo-Pakistan Conflict* (London: Pall Mall, 1969) p. 16.

Chapter 8

Internal Conflicts

South Vietnam

SAMUEL L. POPKIN

Villages Under Diem

In 1955, after the Geneva conference, the government of Ngo Dinh Diem was placed in a position of power in South Vietnam by the departing French. Although the new regime may have been legitimate in the international sense, it still faced the arduous task of actually winning domestic control and legitimacy within a divided and fragmented country. Twenty years later, the problem has not significantly changed.

The problems of Diem's regime would have been little different even without the Viet Minh.[1] Policies had to be enforced, villages pacified and won over to the regime; overcoming peasant apathies and the rigidity of village traditions was inevitably as difficult as combatting the physical Viet Minh threat itself. The new government had to make itself acceptable to the peasants.

The central problem for Saigon and its allies had always been the translation of economic resources and military force into village control; but clearly neither force nor money was enough to ensure the development of a political organization that could meet the needs of war. Such organizations could have been created only by developing links of trust between peasant and government through local village leadership acceptable to both. But the dealings of central authorities with the village have consistently reflected the days of the mandarins, when the peasant was simply an object to be ruled.

When Ngo Dinh Diem assumed power, South Vietnam

---

[1] "Viet Minh" is used for the period before 1954 and "Viet Cong" for the period after 1954. Use of "Viet Cong" instead of the more proper "National Liberation Front" follows common usage.

was religiously, ethnically, and politically fragmented. Building a coherent and viable nation meant developing a political system to unite diverse elements of the population. But to a man like Diem, who combined the militant Catholicism of a Grand Inquisitor and the insensitivity to change of a tradition-bound mandarin,[2] government meant personal rule, not a meaningful political system with participation by religious and ethnic minorities other than Catholics. As he stated to a reporter from *Le Figaro* in 1959, "The political regime of Vietnam has always been founded on State management, not by the people's representatives, but by a sovereign and a few experienced ministers. Formerly, this conception yielded excellent results."[3]

Diem brought his style of personal rule to a country characterized by ethnic and cultural diversity.[4] After Geneva the population of Vietnam was 10 percent Chinese, 6 percent Montagnard tribesmen, and 3 percent Cambodian. Among the 80 percent who were ethnically Vietnamese were three well-organized religious movements, each containing about 10 percent of the population: the Catholics, who were well established in Vietnam before 1800; and the Hoa Hao and the Cao Dai, two twentieth-century millenarian peasant movements. The rest of the country—about 50 percent—was nominally Buddhist, but organized Buddhism probably attracted no more than 15–20 percent of the population.

In the countryside, the key minority groups were the Montagnards, Hoa Hao, and Cao Dai. The Montagnards controlled the geopolitically crucial highlands, and the great cohesion of Hoa Hao and Cao Dai had been the main reason that the Viet Minh had done less well in the Meking Delta than in any other region of the country. Although both the Hoa Hao and Cao Dai were laughed off as feudal by most Western observers, they were in fact nationalistic, concerned with peasant welfare and mass participation, and they both had widespread support among the peasants.[5]

Diem's method of dealing with these groups was to try to destroy all organization and enforce individual rather than group assimilation to the national system. After Geneva, when the US backed Diem, the

[2] Bernard Fall, *The Two Vietnams* (New York: Praeger, 1963), p. 236.

[3] *Le Figaro*, March 23, 1959.

[4] See Guenther Roth, "Personal Rulership, Patrimonialism, and Empire Building in the New States" *World Politics*, 20, no. 2 (January 1968), 194–206.

[5] Francis Hill, "Millenarian Machines in South Vietnam" in *Contemporary Studies in Society and History* (forthcoming).

Hoa Hao and Cao Dai, backed by the French, had made a direct military challenge which Diem crushed. Afterward, he made little attempt to integrate the two religious sects into national life. In short, Diem transformed Vietnam's diversity into an inflexible pluralism.

In addition to all this, of course, large areas of the countryside had been controlled by the Viet Minh continuously for nine years. These liberated areas, mainly central Vietnam and the eastern and southern fringes of the Mekong Delta, contained about 30 percent of the population, and even the most fervent anti-Communists were impressed by conditions there. As Joseph Alsop wrote in 1954:

The thing that impressed me most, in fact, was not the Communists' extraordinary feat of organizing, maintaining, and expanding an independent state in southern Indochina without exterior support and in the teeth of French power. What impressed me most, alas, was the moral fervor they had inspired among non-Communist Viet Minh cadres and the stout support they obtained from the peasantry.[6]

Former Viet Minh cadres were an obvious threat to Diem because they had great prestige among the peasants. Many of these cadres, however, disillusioned by events taking place in the north and by a resistance movement that was becoming more and more Communist in nature, had become inactive. But only random and infrequent attempts were made to recruit such men to the new government. In fact, Diem's officials who had supported the French took the "Denunciation of Communism" campaign as a chance to exact revenge throughout the countryside on the men who had discredited their colonial rule among the peasants. The final toll was comparable to the much more widely publicized killings in the North.

Diem's model for society was no more successful in parts of the country relatively untouched by movements such as the Hoa Hao, Cao Dai, and Viet Minh. His basic assumption was that "village traditions, if once reinstated, would of themselves expel the Viet Cong... like natural antibiotics."[7] But the strength of the traditional village had declined drastically as the French developed a strong central government and urban areas. As Paul Mus noted in 1949, it was necessary

[6] Joseph Alsop, *New York Herald Tribune*, December 31, 1954.

[7] Dennis Duncanson, *Government and Revolution in Vietnam* (New York: Oxford University Press, 1968), p. 259.

to desist from efforts to pacify the country by re-establishing traditional village institutions as part of a political and military security network—a concept which...is economically and socially obsolete.[8]

Diem assumed that pacification could be accomplished by returning to the pre-French situation in the villages—but a country that had started to modernize could not be unified by a return to the past.

Diem fell back on a sentimentalized picture of an ideal "village" Vietnam and made himself its guardian. He extolled the virtues of a Vietnam that probably never was. While the Viet Cong assumed the task of forming a nation, Diem and his successors seemed to be walking backward into the future.

It has become fashionable to talk of the "breakdown of the village" and the loss of the qualities and virtues it once possessed. This is romanticism—this is the "myth of the village." Ways of life that may have survived only because no alternatives existed are extolled as virtuous. Peasants who have nothing to wear and who go hungry are thought to have a rich spiritual life. A son who sticks to his father for the sake of survival is an example of "filial piety." People in one village who do not talk to their neighbors in another are praised for their "village solidarity." The necessities and oppressions of one era somehow become the traditional values of the next.

The participation of the masses as a style of politics was anathema to traditional Vietnam. Village government was mandarin, elite, and passive. The village council's function was to do the administrative work of government, not to make its decisions.[9] Its members, the village elders, were more concerned with their status in the village than with prospects for dynamic change; activism within the council might have threatened their status by breaking down village parochialism.

Diem did not understand how village traditions were being affected by changes taking place elsewhere in the country. He regarded the village unit wholly as an expression of the system and values of the mandarin era. His statements about the peasants, in fact, sounded like those of an old plantation owner explaining that all his darkies wanted was to be left alone. This paternalism was obviously conducive neither to integrating the various social strata nor to establishing

---

[8] Paul Mus, "The Role of the Village in Vietnamese Politics," *Pacific Affairs* (September 1949), p. 271.

[9] A village is roughly equivalent to an American town, district and province to county and state. See Gerald Hickey, *Village in Vietnam* (New Haven: Yale University Press, 1964), and James Hendry, *The Small World of Khanh Hau* (Chicago: Aldine, 1966).

modern political system. By clinging to his traditional view of the peasant as a passive, nonpolitical creature, Diem eliminated the possibility of establishing viable relations between the central government and the villages. To compound its problems, the government of Vietnam (GVN) tried to win legitimacy and support from peasants through a state apparatus consisting of men who were bound to treat them with contempt. To Diem integration meant penetration of the countryside by urban bureaucrats and soldiers. Linking the village with the national government always meant sending men from the city into the countryside, not drawing men in from the villages and training them for rural administration. Cities produced an educated, urban, middle class eager to fill administrative jobs and to become army officers, but reluctant to accept the peasant as a citizen.

Political Judo

In revolution, as in any political struggle, successful strategy is based on maneuvering into a situation where the opposition, no matter what it does, strengthens your position. This is political judo, the art of turning the opponent's force against himself. For 40 years Vietnamese Communism has been able to gain through political judo, because of the established government's inept leadership and clumsy use of force to combat revolution.

Viet Cong success has always been at least partially attributable to its ability to enforce and carry out GVN proclamations. Ironically, often only an "illegal" group had this capability. The execution of Diem's land reform provides an example. The Viet Cong no doubt profited from the land problem,[10] but not simply because Diem was a reactionary or an oppressive ruler. It was able to use land reform by transforming into a political issue a seemingly arbitrary set of decisions which peasants did not feel morally obligated to accept.

The Vietnamese system of land tenure could be exploited in many ways even without large-scale redistribution of land: rent levels, market prices, interest rates, and fertilizer prices all could be manipulated to improve the welfare of an individual farmer. Diem's policies for dealing with these vagaries were often sound: set rent ceilings, provide for displaced persons, institute loan programs. But because he lacked effective organizations for reaching into the villages, Diem was unable to implement his programs. Only the Viet Cong had the

[10] See Robert Sansom, *The Economics of Insurgency in the Mekong Delta* (Cambridge: M.I.T. Press, 1970).

necessary links with the peasantry. Thus, for many peasants the Viet Cong easily emerged as the champion of the just cause simply by carrying out the government's promises. The dynamics of insurgency seem to be such that any government not consciously trying to expand participation will find the base of popular support constantly narrowing.

In the civil sphere, the distance between the central government and the peasant, and the rigid conception of administration permitted by this distance, opened an easy route by which the Viet Cong could establish its own authority in the villagers' minds in place of governmental authority. Men who shared Viet Cong views on even a single issue were treated as potential enemies by the government. District chiefs, in order to guarantee that they would not be personally betrayed by village officials—consciously or unconsciously—tended to rely more and more on men whose loyalty to the GVN, or incompatibility with the Viet Cong, was certain. But men absolutely guaranteed to be unacceptable to the Viet Cong—and hence least likely to be traitors to Saigon—were the men least likely to be trusted by the lower bases of peasant society and least likely to try to overcome distrust. During the period of appointed local officials (until 1967), these officials became more and more isolated from the peasantry.

Viet Cong recruitment techniques vividly illustrate the impossible bind of a government that has neither accurate intelligence nor personal intermediaries trusted by both government and peasants. The Viet Cong could easily place peasants in a position where they felt compelled to join. For example, Viet Cong would come to a village and renew contacts with old friends, make new friends, or simply treat a young man they wanted as if he were already on their side. Given the government's arbitrary and often brutal treatment of suspected Viet Cong, the peasant often literally begged the Viet Cong to take and protect him.

In more recent years, the Viet Cong have been helped in drafting soldiers by being able to exploit peasant fear of the government. For example, the Viet Cong have frequently destroyed the identification papers of a youth who refused to join them. The peasant then had to choose among asking for new papers, joining the Viet Cong, and facing arrest as a Viet Cong because he had no papers. If new papers were always politely issued on request, the Viet Cong would have an easy way of obtaining identification papers; they could simply buy or steal them. And if the government always refused to issue new papers, the Viet Cong could gain a recruit just by stealing a man's papers.

Territorial Forces vs. the Viet Cong

Until the Tet offensive of 1968, Vietnam was divided like a wheel with Saigon as the hub. Although the government controlled most of the population, the Viet Cong controlled villages forming the rim and spokes of the wheel and the government controlled the areas in between. Hence, although the GVN occupied most of the villages, a person could still go almost anywhere in Vietnam and never leave Viet Cong territory. Even though the government had a force superiority of better than ten to one in most districts in Vietnam, the Viet Cong still could move everywhere at will simply by staying within the villages and hamlets they controlled.

The territorial troops—the Regional Forces and Popular Forces (RF and PF)—were the main military presence in most of the countryside and constituted half the total military strength. Nearly every village had at least one PF platoon, and each district had one or more RF companies. In theory, the territorial forces were to be the last line of defense in the countryside, with the regular Army of the Republic of Vietnam (ARVN) doing most of the fighting. In practice the situation was nearly reversed. Instead of moving all over the countryside to break up large Viet Cong units, most ARVN units, especially in the Mekong Delta and around Saigon, were relatively immobile. Their commanders were more concerned with political maneuvers, avoidance of casualties, and corruption than with effective combat. In 1966, for example, one ARVN division lost more soldiers in traffic accidents than in battle, even though the Viet Cong were exerting very heavy pressure on the RF and PF in the same area.[11]

Village soldiers were usually poorly armed and had no source of reinforcement if attacked. In the early 1960s, the Viet Cong depended for nearly all their armament on what they could capture. This made it dangerous to arm the village soldiers adequately, for in any area the Viet Cong could mobilize a unit large enough to overwhelm any single village unit. The alternative to arming the PF adequately would have been to ensure very good communications between PF and ARVN. But this course was even more dangerous, because radios were real prizes for guerrillas, immensely increasing their combat capability. Hence, the village, on its own, was pitted against coordinated efforts of the Viet Cong. Through 1962 nearly all casualties in the war were village soldiers,[12] and until 1964 these RF and PF casualties were

[11] William Corson, *The Betrayal* (New York: Norton, 1968), p. 98.

[12] Duncanson, *Government and Revolution in Vietnam,* pp. 305–306.

rarely admitted to ARVN hospitals.[13] Military commanders treated local soldiers no better than government officials treated peasants.

The RF and PF cared more about defense—protecting themselves and their families—than about preventing the Viet Cong from moving through their areas. The soldiers, recruited mainly from the areas where they served, were usually treated with contempt by the city-born district and province chiefs under whom they served. A PF soldier, after his 30-man platoon had tried to defend a hamlet against 350 Viet Cong, described the situation:

When the Viet Cong attacked this hamlet, the reinforcement forces came so late that our platoon was encircled. The assistant platoon leader, Huong, was hit by four bullets in the chest; and though the wound was serious, he tried to take care of Xuan, a comrade in arms who was very seriously wounded. But toward the end Huong was too weak to do anything for him and so he let him die and left his own rifle as well as Xuan's behind. Yet when we got back to the district we were bawled out for leaving the dead and the weapons behind. Well, I know that the duty of a soldier is to fight off the enemy, but if by bad luck you get run over not only are you not comforted but you are scolded; it really is disheartening. In the family you have the wife to comfort you; in the services there are the leaders. They do not encourage our spirits. They do not comfort us. They chew us out. It really is sad.[14]

Instead of patrolling their areas and making it difficult for the Viet Cong to move, the territorial forces before the 1968 Tet offensive were virtually immobilized by lack of reinforcements, poor training, and governmental neglect.

The Viet Cong succeeded not only by using the ways of the countryside to foil the strength of the government forces, but also—and just as important—by learning how to put that same rural understanding at the service of their own wider purposes. They learned how to bring about changes in the rural order while working within it. They made themselves attractive to the disenfranchised peasantry. In contrast to a government that wanted the peasant to learn his place and stay there, the Viet Cong emphasized that the poor did not have to be poor forever, that people did not have to accept arbitrary rule and remain in low social stations forever. Simply by interesting youth in careers and in their own advancement, the Viet Cong undermined a village

[13] *Ibid.*, p. 301.

[14] Quotations are from the author's interviews in 1966–1967 and summer of 1969, unless otherwise noted.

political system based on acceptance of the status quo and rule by elders. As one Viet Cong prisoner remarked:

In the past the rich and the bourgeois used to tell us that the poor were simply those not blessed by heaven. But the Viet Cong worked very hard to change this. They said the people were poor because they didn't have any land to till; heaven had nothing to do with economics. So people listened and decided that if heaven did not affect their economic life they did not have to go to the shrine and pray for a better life, and they stopped going. . . .[15]

The Viet Cong alone offered both status and psychological security to the peasants. The youth were offered excitment, adventure, security, and a chance to advance. They may have faced regimentation within the Viet Cong, but they were "freed from the freedom to perish in neglected and harassed social isolation." As one youth described his "recruitment" to the revolution:

The Viet Cong taught me to sing songs. I enjoyed being with the Viet Cong at night because at night they had a group that would sing. It was a group of young people my age, about 12 years old. They would go to the temple. There a Viet Cong teacher would teach us to sing. They would sing a phrase and then the people would sing a phrase. . . .

The Viet Cong, then, were virtually unopposed in the countryside. Passive village government could not challenge them politically, and military attempts to crush them could not succeed when village soldiers were weak and lacked reinforcements. By 1965, had it not been for the US decision to commit ground troops to battle, the Viet Cong would have won within the year. Search-and-destroy operations generally did not affect the Viet Cong infrastructure because the large units employed in these missions often stayed in a particular hamlet or village for only a day or less before moving on. Viet Cong cadres could hide nearby for that short a period and then return when the soldiers left, or they could stay in a tunnel whose location no one else knew or dared to disclose.

Furthermore, the American military system emphasized destruction and attrition of main enemy forces—body counts and kill ratios—and

[15] Quoted in David Halberstam, "Voice of the Viet Cong," *Harper's*, January 1968, p. 48. Harry J. Benda, "Reflections on Asian Communism," *Yale Review*, LVI, no. 1 (October 1966), 1–16.

often completely ignored the political-administrative functions of the Viet Cong infrastructure and military units.[16] The pressures put on US commanders took the form of three major dicta from a frenzied and panicked Washington: (1) make progress, go fast; (2) keep US casualties as low as possible; (3) keep the civilian toll as low as possible. Only two of the three constraints could be followed at a time. To stay clean and keep US casualties low, it would have been necessary to go slow; to keep the civilian toll low and show progress, it would have been necessary to tolerate much higher US casualties; and if the first priority was to show progress and keep United States casualties low, civilian suffering was inevitable.

Before Tet

After 1965, the character of the war changed entirely with the influx of men and materials from Hanoi and Washington. In the public eye the guerrilla war began to be eclipsed by the ever mounting number of deaths, casualties, and refugees that resulted from search-and-destroy missions and from bombing and defoliation.[17]

As the scale of US intervention grew, it became clear that the Viet Cong would not be able to win a military victory against the huge military machine. Yet the period 1965–1968 showed no significant increase in the areas brought under GVN control. The exodus of refugees left the Viet Cong with a smaller population base in 1968 than they had in 1965, but they still retained the intelligence network and connections necessary for planning and executing strikes at major cities and provincial capitals.

By 1965, when US troops began engaging in major battles with PAVN[18] units, the Viet Cong already controlled or at least had extensive influence in the vast majority of South Vietnam's villages and had a well-developed cadre system and infrastructure. The Viet Cong's strength in the countryside made it possible for them to "receive, conceal, feed and deploy" reinforcements from the North.[19] Although

[16] Lt. Cols. W. J. Buchanan and R. A. Hyatt, *Counter-guerrilla Operations* (Washington, D.C.: National War College, 1968), pp. 1–27.

[17] See especially Frank Harvey, *Air War: Vietnam* (New York: Bantam Books, 1967); Katsuichi Honda, *Vietnam: A Voice From the Villages* (Tokyo: Asahi Shimbun, 1967); Daniel Lang, *Casualties of War* (New York: Random House, 1969); Jonathan Schell, *The Military Half* (New York: Random House, 1968); and *The Village of Ben Suc* (New York: Random House, 1967).

[18] People's Army of Viet Nam—the North Vietnamese army.

[19] Duncanson, *Government and Revolution in Vietnam*, p. 367.

the civilian toll of casualties and refugees was enormous, less than two percent of all US offensive operations produced any contact with the Viet Cong.[20] Thus, as Brigadier General Richard M. Lee noted, hit-or-miss efforts "only operate to make the entire VC infrastructure stronger" in the areas of such military operations.[21]

The major result of the large-scale search-and-destroy war was the dislocation of between two and four million peasants. Few of these displaced persons were voluntary refugees; policy deliberately encouraged moving large numbers of people from Viet Cong areas in order to deny the Viet Cong their labor. This drove to the Viet Cong some people who otherwise might have supported the government. They sometimes went out of hatred stemming from the bombing, but more often they went simply because a very poorly run refugee program was unappealing, and no jobs were available. One peasant, for example, stayed with the Viet Cong when they took over his hamlet because, as a refugee,

I could not earn my living. In order to work for the Americans I would have needed some powerful man to help me. Since my children are so many I have to stay here to live on agriculture.

At the same time, the simple fact that the government had to move people was interpreted as a sign of weakness and generated great hostility. As an official US study of refugees in Phy Yen Province found:

For a people as pragmatic as Vietnamese peasants, the message implicit in refugee movement is a clear one—the GVN is not able to protect even its supporters from the insurgents so one had best withhold making any over-commitment to the government.[22]

Except for such deeply entrenched Viet Cong strongholds as Quang Ngai, Quang Nam, Binh Dinh, and Phu Yen provinces in central Vietnam, and war zones C and D, a lot less heavy fighting occurred in most areas than the popular image of the war conveyed. Through 1967, for example, only 5,000 US soldiers were positioned in the entire Mekong Delta, where half the peasant population lived. Although

---

[20] Corson, *The Betrayal*, p. 147.

[21] Brig Gen. Richard M. Lee, "A Program Against the VC Infrastructure" July 27, 1967, quoted in Buchanan and Hyatt, *Counter-guerrilla Operations*, pp. 1–31.

[22] A. Terry Rambo, Jerry M. Tinker, and John D. Lenoir, *The Refugee Situation in Phu Yen Province, Viet Nam*, abridged version (McLean, Va.: Human Science Research, 1967).

90 percent of the population lives on 20 percent of the land, most of the heavy fighting took place in the very sparsely populated highlands. In effect, North Vietnamese divisions largely acted as a bullfighter's cape to keep US troops floundering in unimportant areas.

While search-and-destroy operations were a military and moral disaster, the government's economic programs—despite enormous corruption—had a more harmful effect on the Viet Cong. Before the Tet offensive, the Viet Cong were losing military effectiveness only very slowly, but their popularity was dwindling rapidly. They imposed very heavy taxes, higher than under the landlords, and regimentation in their villages was very strict; both these necessities of the war effort made revolutionary communities, even where there was no bombing, less desirable places to live than government villages. The contrast between living conditions in Viet Cong villages and government villages began to increase in 1967 and to hurt the Viet Cong badly. It was no longer true that dedicated and virtuous cadres could improve living conditions as much as corrupt cadres backed by US money. Under the pressures of war the Viet Cong were no longer able to deliver social benefits to the population.

Meanwhile, the GVN, living on American money, was able to begin supplying the countryside with massive quantities of fertilizer, Hondas, infirmaries, schools, and hundreds of thousands of nonagricultural jobs. A captured Viet Cong village official expressed the ways in which the economic programs affected the "liberated" Viet Cong areas:

> ...the most vicious, dangerous scheme was their aid to the people. They distributed fertilizer to the people because fertilizer was the thing that was of utmost importance to the people. The fertilizer was contained in bags bearing GVN flags and anti-Communist slogans. In the liberated areas, anyone who carried a GVN flag was condemned as a traitor to the fatherland and was executed. But now, we could see right in the liberated areas two villagers carrying a bag with a GVN flag and vicious anti-Communist propaganda. ... for political reasons the Front couldn't forbid the people to accept fertilizer to increase their production rate.[23]

Liberation by the Viet Cong had meant good clean government, protection from landlords, and wider sharing of power, but living in liberated areas began to take on negative connotations—less access to booming markets, schools, fertilizer, and medicine.

None of the GVN economic advantages drew the population to-

[23] "Studies of the National Liberation Front," Interview no. DT–154 (Santa Monica, Calif.: RAND).

gether or created the much needed links between peasant and government, village, and state. The majority of peasants preferred the GVN for its corruption. Freedom without justice was satisfying for the peasants, but it was no principle with which to draw the peasants closer to government cadres and encourage cooperation and active support. As one peasant stated in 1967:

The Viet Cong collect higher taxes but they know how to please the people; they behave politely so people feel that they are more favored. They behave politely and nicely to the people in order to make people like them. They do not thunder at the people like the government soldiers.

People like the government because of freedom, but there is not equality even though the taxes are lower than the Viet Cong's. The thing the people don't like in the government is its behavior. For example, the soldiers often arrest and oppress the people only for revenge—in short, it is banditry.

What was happening, then, was that peasants were adjusting to the war by avoiding the Viet Cong. Life under Viet Cong control meant a commitment to the struggle—willing or not. Politically, living in a government area simply meant a peasant was not living under Viet Cong control—no more, no less.

Except for the Hoa Hao, Cao Dai, and Catholics, peasants who sought moral purity, a strong sense of virtue, and clean government identified with the Viet Cong; the GVN had no way in the world of competing with the Viet Cong on those terms. What the GVN did have to offer were the attractions of the city, markets, media, medicine —in short, a modern economy.

After Tet

The 1968 Tet offensive, which threw Washington and Saigon into shock and contributed to Lyndon Johnson's decision not to seek another term in office, showed in the most vivid terms the transparency of US claims that the war was approaching its end. Inside Vietnam, in contrast, the final effect of the offensive was far more complex. A Viet Cong defector who had been on the district committee of an old Viet Cong stronghold in the Delta gave a clear indication of the effect of the Tet offensive on popular expectations and Viet Cong credibility:

When there was an order to start the fighting...the morale of the cadres and population was extremely high; people were very enthusiastic...they thought that after 15 years...the General Offensive Insurrection in the whole country should bring about a happy end to their efforts. They did not have any fear of death and were very enthusiastic, and faithful to their "insurrection" duties. . . . [Now] the population have lost confidence in the Front cadres living in their areas. Before the Tet events, the Front said that they only needed seven days to achieve the revolution...but after the anticipated seven days, they said that this was only a first stage, the first wave. When came the second stage, on the seventh of May [1968], they said there was then an almost complete destruction of the enemy, and soon the third stage would come, in August 1968, which was also to be the final stage; but, as a matter of fact, there has been since then no final stage at all;...these facts have accounted for the cadres and the general population losing confidence in the success of the Revolution by the Front.

Instead of an end to the war, the Tet offensive brought two major changes in Vietnam that placed the chances of a total Viet Cong victory more in doubt than ever before. The first of these changes was the replacement of a discredited General William Westmoreland with General Creighton Abrams. Abrams placed much more emphasis than Westmoreland on rural security and pacification. In the aftermath of Tet, Abrams encouraged President Thieu to increase support of the territorial forces responsible for rural security, almost doubling their number, improving their armament, and placing more emphasis on backing them in battle. This upgrading of the army actually began for the first time to hamper Viet Cong mobility in the countryside. By early 1970 the Viet Cong controlled less than 40 percent of their pre-Tet villages, and more than half the combined Viet Cong-PAVN soldiers were based in Cambodia or Laos, not in South Vietnam.

Second, and more important, the events of 1968 finally forced President Thieu to give serious and sincere consideration to the problem of rural government and security. For the first time, it became clear that the Viet Cong would still be around after the withdrawal of foreign troops, and that the United States was not going to destroy a movement whose roots went back 40 years. Thieu's course after Tet was predicated on the assumption that in a choice between his right-wing government and left-wing Communism, he would be able to survive. Hence, he followed a policy designed to maximize the polarization of society. While trying simultaneously to eradicate the Viet Cong infrastructure and to repress any political groups that could offer a middle position politically, Thieu set about trying to make the government's rule more tolerable to the masses.

One of his new policies was an emphasis on village government.[24]

[24] There had always been some emphasis on village government, but it was comparatively minor. See Samuel L. Popkin, "The Myth of the Village: Revolution and Reaction in Vietnam" (unpublished Ph.D. dissertation, M.I.T., 1969).

Local elections had been held in a few areas in 1967, but now they were extended and the elected officials were given new status. The pressures of war had made village and hamlet officials terribly important to the peasants. These officials were responsible for countless papers and permits and handled numerous AID programs, including those for fertilizer and rice seeds. Whether or not peasants liked the GVN or wanted it to win the war, a friendly local official was a definite asset. For this reason alone, the elections generated great interest.[25] Most peasants knew the names of candidates and the number running and had definite ideas about what they expected of the new officials. (One thing they expected was more justice and a slower hand on the gun. The peasants' main concern in insecure areas was overfast guns and bad justice).

The elections brought forth candidates who had resources no outsider could ever supply: long years of contact with the community and close knowledge of its affairs. Even where the same officials were reelected (the majority of cases), peasants expressed optimism over having participated in the process of selection, a participation that signaled their right to approach the officials. The local authorities were beginning to belong to the peasants. Yet the links of trust that had been missing between Saigon and the peasant population were only partly forged. Whereas under Diem the principal gap had been between the village chief and the peasant, under Thieu the village official was joined with the peasant, but integration at higher levels did not take place.

Besides developing to popularize his government, Thieu instituted reforms meant to cut the strength of the Viet Cong. After Tet the GVN began in desperation to arm hundreds of thousands of peasants in People's Self-Defense Forces (PSDF) in an attempt to stop Viet Cong recruiting, taxing, propagandizing, and terrorizing. These local, night-time security men were put under the direction of the village chief.

The Phoenix program, designed to destroy the Viet Cong infrastructure, was instituted by the CIA in 1967 and officially acknowledged by Thieu after Tet. It was intended to coordinate the many fragmented intelligence services and to provide an intensive effort to kill, capture, or cause the defection of as many Viet Cong political leaders and agents as possible. It had limited success at best.[26] The word of a village chief was often ignored. This damaged the cause of civil justice

25 Interest strong enough to truly shock my interviewers, particularly when compared to the apathy or disgust displayed by peasants toward most government programs.

26 James P. Sterba, "The Controversial Operation Phoenix: How It Roots Out Viet Cong Suspects," New York Times, February 18, 1970, p. 2.

in the villages and widened the gap between village officials and the central government. Quotas of Viet Cong to be neutralized were established. To fill these quotas police agents arrested many peasants who had committed minor "crimes." The program gave corrupt police and intelligence officers many opportunities for extortion.

With Phoenix unsuccessful, the GVN was vulnerable whether it tried to hold the country by military means and deal with PAVN and the Viet Cong without American troops or whether it was willing to risk political competition. Trying to deal militarily with the Viet Cong required ARVN, after many years of uneven performance, to match one of the most effective armies in the world and to develop the ability to work in the countryside without acting like an army of occupation.

If Saigon wanted to risk electoral competition with the Viet Cong, the hazards were just as great. Over the years Saigon, expecting total military victory, had failed to develop workable political organizations and had tolerated only the most conservative and reactionary groups. The army and its American allies, moreover, had been the major cause of misery and deprivation in the countryside. After years of a regime that aimed to kill Viet Cong without regard for the civilian toll, it was unlikely, in an open election, that many people would vote for a military candidate. Even though the peasants were not really attracted by the Viet Cong, it was risky to expect them to support men who had unleashed the US Army—to say nothing of the Koreans—on the countryside.

All of Thieu's attempts to make his government popular with the peasantry were hampered by an army concerned with its own position. Clearly, giving control to local officials was incompatible with maintaining the army's power; after years of search-and-destroy missions, rape, and pillage, few popularly elected leaders would side with a military government. In 1970 Thieu found himself in the position of not being able to build a popular political base without sacrificing the political backing of the army.

Conclusion

Victory in war is not merely a matter of who has the greatest military strength. Potential support can be mismanaged. Force without intelligence is inefficient and self-defeating, and even good information is not very useful without an understanding of society and an empathy for its people.

War does not of itself draw a people together. Sometimes when massive force is applied to a population, there are increases in solidarity, cohesion, and the ability to perform complicated communal tasks—but only where citizens can rally around accepted and trusted leaders. Organizations are needed, and they can be created only by developing links of trust from peasant to government through local leadership acceptable to both.

The experience of war can be profoundly disorganizing. A Londoner, leaving a bomb shelter during the Battle of Britain, could turn to a trusted figure for advice and consolation. A Vietnamese peasant whose village has just been bombed has no one to whom he can turn. He might have found, as indeed happened in Hue, the doctors he expected to help him fleeing with their families and the provincial authorities in hiding. The experience of war can unify only if someone is able to organize the means of dealing with its horrors, someone who can rally the people, someone whom they can trust.

If a military threat alone cannot weld a people together and gain their cooperation, neither can the strategy of the carrot. Economic "bribery" can make a state somewhat more tolerable, or more acceptable than any alternative states, but still someone must have the authority behind him to risk local enforcement of necessary but unpopular decisions and, more important, to provide the protection essential to economic activity.

It is reasonable to expect the Saigon government to survive, if only because it has somehow survived so many earlier crises. In 1954–1956 the Hoa Hao and Cao Dai challenged Diem; in 1960 the Viet Cong arose in earnest; in 1963 the Buddhists and students brought about Diem's fall; in 1965 the war would have ended if the United States had not intervened; in 1966 the Buddhists challenged Nguyen Cao Ky; and in 1968 the Tet offensive stunned the regime. To survive all of these crises, of course, required massive United States aid, which is not likely to be cut off any time soon.

It is just as reasonable to expect the Viet Cong to survive. Although they are not the enormous mass movement of earlier years, they are still a perceptive and talented political party with solid support, making up perhaps 10 to 20 percent of the peasantry; and they are still able to operate nearly everywhere in the country.

Optimistic supporters of Saigon draw analogies to Korea and hope that a militarized society with huge amounts of US aid will be able to hold together. They ignore the fact that Vietnam is a fragmented country governed mainly by an elitist group of generals.

Optimistic supporters of the Viet Cong, remembering their earlier popularity and the military prowess of PAVN, expect the "Thieu-Ky clique" to fall immediately after a United States pullout. They forget that fundamental changes in the economy and the society have deprived the Viet Cong of much of its support and that, even though PAVN was far superior to ARVN, defeating an ARVN backed by US air power could be extraordinarily costly.

Optimistic Vietnamese, meanwhile, keep hoping for the emergence of a third force comprising leftists in Saigon and rightists in the Viet Cong. They forget that the far right and the far left control most of the guns. Their only hope is the possibility of gaining control of the territorial forces and People's Self-Defense Forces in order to counterbalance ARVN.

It may well be that the realists are those Vietnamese who see no reason to expect a viable solution, who look to Indonesia under Sukarno for their model of the next decade, and who foresee a long period of struggle even after American withdrawal.

Nigeria and Biafra

CHARLES R. NIXON

Wars are unique events. Yet the contexts in which they occur may have parallels to situations elsewhere. It is this parallelism that gives hope that wars can be explained and that theories can be constructed about them. It is this parallelism that provides the imperatives for understanding them so that similar contexts will not produce similar tragedies elsewhere.

The war between Nigeria and Biafra was not inevitable. Its occurrence, however, demands that we seek to understand, first, the factors that heightened the probability of open conflict in the Nigerian scene and, second, the factors that shaped the conduct and the outcome of the conflict. The first two sections of this chapter examine the basic sources of stress and the factors that led to the final breakdown of the system. The third and fourth sections examine the internal and external factors that shaped the conduct and outcome of the conflict.

Why Was the Problem of Natural Unity So Difficult in Nigeria

Nigeria became an independent state on October 1, 1960. It did not exist as a distinct, identifiable entity before the gradual subjugation of its various peoples by Great Britain in the late nineteenth century. Before the British took control, Nigeria's various peoples lived in a variety of separate political systems with long and varied political histories, and none called themselves Nigerians. Thus, Nigeria is a postcolonial state, a state created by the colonial powers that drew territorial boundaries to mark off their respective areas of control, a state whose very existence is a product of the colonial control from which it gained its freedom in 1960.

Nigeria has the largest and most diverse population of any African state, with more than 400 identifiable linguistic and ethnic groups included in its population of more than 40 million.[1] The matter of sheer numbers, whether of total population or of identifiable ethnic and linguistic groups, is not very important. What is important—indeed, crucial—in understanding the collapse of the Nigerian political system into a state of war is the size, the territorial distribution, and the nature of the differences and relations among these various groups. If each of Nigeria's 400 ethnic groups had been of about equal size, 100,000 each, with relatively minor cultural differences between them, this diversity would not have been nearly so disruptive. Or if the pattern had been one of a major core group of about 40 million surrounded by a great number of small, diverse groups, Nigeria would probably have gained national unity by means of the large core group's clearly exercising predominant power and the other groups' accommodating themselves to it.

In actuality, however, Nigeria's groups were divided between a number of relatively large groups territorially separated from each other by a variety of smaller groups, and the problem of creating a single Nigerian state posed complex problems of relating both major and minor groups to each other. In addition, patterns of culture were characterized by sharp and fundamental differences, and these cultural differences—especially differences in conceptions of political authority and legitimacy, accepted patterns of social status, and responses to western education, technical skills, and economic activities —were central to the political problems out of which the war developed.

Three basic types of political culture existed in Nigeria, and they shaped the precolonial character of political institutions, influenced the patterns of colonial administration under British rule, and determined the character of political organization and activity that developed as colonial control was withdrawn. These three types are epitomized by the large-scale emirate structures of the far north, the Yoruba kingdoms of the west, and the decentralized and fragmented town polities

---

[1] G. P. Murdock, *Africa: Its Peoples and Their Culture History* (New York: McGraw-Hill, 1959), identifies about 430 groups of which, in 1921, only six had a million or more members and another 12 had over 100,000. The 1963 federal census identifies, out of a total population of 55 million, eight groups with over a million members and another 27 groups with over 100,000 each. The official figure of 55 million is considered by most scholars to be a gross exaggeration. A more reasonable estimate for 1967 would be 40–45 million.

of the east.[2] A brief characterization of each should suggest how the differences between them could serve as a basis for critical tensions that eventually disrupted national political unity.

The emirates of the far north functioned in a highly stratified class structure in which political authority rested with a few aristocratic families, access to political office depended largely on family position, and substantial authority rested with the emirs and their counselors. At times this authority could be exercised in a fairly autocratic way; southerners, depicting the undemocratic nature of the system, often (though incorrectly) called it feudal. The communities governed by this system usually had an Islamic religious culture, showed a sharp social division between upper classes and peasantry, and held a rather fatalistic attitude-pattern that contrasted with the more aggressive, achievement-oriented outlook that prevailed in the south. It was highly protective of the traditional Islamic outlook and behavior and was thus strongly resistant to Western education and slow in acquiring Western technical skills. Thus the northern culture was characterized by the acceptance of hierarchical political authority, ascriptive claims to office, sharp class divisions, a strong emphasis on traditional values and behavior patterns, and the absence of a strong orientation toward achievement, which elsewhere provided the basis for a modernizing ethos.

The sharpest contrast with the large-scale emirates of the far north is found in the decentralized and fragmented town polities of the Ibos of eastern Nigeria. Here, indigenous political systems did not recognize chiefs with extensive executive powers over large jurisdictions. Rather, authority was frequently exercised by councils in which there was wide participation. The greatest authority often lay not in the largest or highest unit of the structure but in the lower units, particularly the *umunna,* the extended family group to which each individual belonged, to which he owed his greatest loyalty and obligations, and from which he could draw the greatest support. No recognized authority stood above that of the town council, in which several family and village groups would participate. At all levels, broad participation in discussion of problems requiring community action led to a strong egalitarian and participatory tradition in political life and to traditionally strong resistance to external, superimposed author-

[2] Descriptions of basic political culture patterns are found in Murdock, *Africa,* chaps. 13, 17, 31, and J. L. Gibbs, Jr., *et al., Peoples of Africa* (New York: Holt, Rinehart & Winston, 1965), chapters on the Ibo, Hausa, Fulani, Tiv, and Yoruba.

ity. These political patterns operated in the context of a generally egalitarian society in which status was gained by outstanding achievements often represented by the accumulation of wealth, by education and professional standing, and by outstanding service to the community. In these societies motivation toward achievement was very strong, leading to intense internal competition between members of the societies within the framework of their own communities, a strong commitment to acquiring Western education and technical skills and using them for both personal and community advancement, and an extensive involvement in modern economic activity. Christianity—especially Roman Catholicism—predominated except where traditional African religious practices still held sway.

The Yoruba kingdoms of the west showed clear patterns of executive authority held by various offices within the state, but these patterns were much less hierarchical than those in the north. Authority was distributed among various office-holders, providing a rudimentary check-and-balance system in political affairs. Yet offices with authority and substantial jurisdictions clearly existed, and thus the state structure was more clear-cut than that of the east. Social class lines were also more recognizable and prevalent than in much of the east, but they were less rigid and more strongly influenced by wealth and education than class lines in the far north. The religious culture was divided between Muslim and Christian. These communities thus were more democratic than those in the north though somewhat less egalitarian than those in the east.

The distribution of these cultural patterns never closely fit the larger administrative and political division of either colonial or independent Nigeria.[3] In northern Nigeria, the emirate patterns characterized the Hause-Fulani and Kanuri cultures of the far north, but the fragmented town polities and kingship patterns predominated in the middle belt. In southern Nigeria, which was eventually divided into the west, midwest, and east, the west and Lagos were both predominantly Yoruba in culture; the midwest was divided between the kingship patterns of the Edo (Benin) and Urhobo and the town

---

[3] Treatments of the political and constitutional developments leading to independence are found in J. S. Coleman, *Nigeria: Background to Nationalism* (Berkeley and Los Angeles: University of California Press, 1958), and K. Ezera, *Constitutional Developments in Nigeria*, (Cambridge: Cambridge University Press, 1960). The character of the political parties and electoral processes at independence are treated in R. L. Sklar, *Nigerian Political Parties* (Princeton: Princeton University Press, 1963).

Part Three: Violent Conflicts

polities of the midwestern Ibo; and in the east the town polity that characterized the culture of the dominant Ibo group also characterized the political cultures of the Ibibios and Efiks of the southeast, including Calabar, but the kingship patterns were followed by the Ijaws of the Rivers area.

These different patterns could coexist fairly harmoniously during much of the period of British control because the various peoples were not contending with each other for either jobs or political control. However, once economic modernization stimulated substantial internal migration of southerners—especially Ibos from the east—into the jobs offered by the expanding commercial and technical economy of the north, the basis for serious friction was established. And when independence placed ultimate and central political power in the hands of Nigerians, these fundamental differences led to intense controversy. When the electoral processes were controlled to fit the traditional norms of the northern group, they inevitably violated the traditional democratic and constitutional norms of the south. When appointments to office were managed by the north in ways that seemed legitimate to them, these appointments struck the southerners as violations of the legitimate criteria of achievement. And when the northerners resisted policies promoted by the south for rapid political, social, and economic change, the southerners viewed this resistance as a way of holding Nigeria back.

When the constitutional arrangements for independence were being worked out in the period 1950–1957, there was acute awareness of ethnic and cultural differences; minority-group leaders in the middle belt, as well as in the west and the east, asked for their own regions free from Hausa-Fulani, Yoruba, or Ibo control. However, the leadership of the far north insisted that the north be held together as a unit, and the British finally supported the far north's position. Once the decision had been made to leave the north a single unit, the existing divisions (drawn in 1939) between western and eastern Nigeria were also retained. Thus, what had been the basic British colonial administrative divisions between the north, west, and east now became the political divisions for a federal system. In its ethnic and cultural composition each region had a predominant ethnic group and a collection of minority tribes attached to it. Each region was viable in terms of public finance, and in many respects constituted a viable economic unit for purposes of development. Thus each region could pursue its own policies of development at its own pace, pushing its program largely on the basis of its own resources and interests.

Why did the Nigerian System Break Down?

The disintegration of the Nigerian political system, including the collapse of the political community itself, may be understood by examining: (1) the breakdown of constitutional arrangements; (2) the collapse of the army as a national unifying force; and (3) the failure to provide a new framework of national authority through negotiation.[4]

THE BREAKDOWN OF CONSTITUTIONAL ARRANGEMENTS

The presupposition underlying the constitutional arrangements, and an essential condition for their success, was that each region, with its own predominant political culture, would have internal political autonomy. No region would dominate another, and no one region would have sole control of the central government in Lagos, which would presumably represent a balance of regional interests.

The collapse of this constitutional system occurred when the fundamental presumptions—internal political autonomy within the regions, and regional balance at the center—were undermined. In the period 1962–1965 the political forces in the north gained effective control of the federal government in Lagos and made the western regional government dependent on northern support.

With control thus obtained, the north was able to undermine the democratic character of electoral procedures and to control critical positions in the federal government. The culmination of this process was the continuation of the Akintola government in power in the western region following what was widely considered to be a rigged election in October 1965. Leaders in the east, as well as Akintola's opponents in the west, viewed this event as final proof that democratic processes were no longer available to protect southerners against northern domination. Hence, the southerners not already allied with

[4] Treatments of various steps in the breakdown of the constitutional system prior to the military coup of January 15, 1966, are presented in P. Mackintosh, *Nigerian Government and Politics* (Evanston: Northwestern University Press, 1966); F.A.O. Schwartz, Jr., *Nigeria: The Tribes, the Nation, or the Race* (Cambridge, Massachusetts: M.I.T. Press, 1965), and W. Schwarz, *Nigeria* (New York: Praeger, 1968). A Biafran view of developments leading to secession is presented in A. A. Nwankwo and S. U. Ifejika, *The Making of a Nation: Biafra* (London: C. Hurst, 1969). The speeches, journals and statements of the Biafran leader, C. O. Ojukwo, are presented in C. O. Ojukwu, *Biafra*, 2 vols. (New York: Harper & Row, 1969).

The Federal view is presented in "Government Statement on the Current Nigerian Situation," Federal Ministry of Information, Lagos, 1966. A Northern view is presented in *The Nigerian Situation: Facts and Background* (Zaria: Gaskiya Corporation, 1966).

the north turned in revolt, first through a process of widespread disorders in the western region and, second in the military coup of January 15, 1966. That coup marked the end of the civilian political system established in 1960 and placed the immediate future of Nigeria in the hands of a military government.

THE COLLAPSE OF ARMY UNITY

The military regime established in January 1966 was not the regime planned by the young officers who staged the coup. Rather, control went to a man who had been marked for elimination by the coup— Major General Aguyi-Ironsi, commander of the Nigerian army, who rallied loyal troops in Lagos to prevent the organizers of the coup from taking over. Ironsi was installed as supreme commander in Lagos, and military governors were appointed for each of the regions.

This military regime lasted only six and a half months. Like the civilian government before it, it failed because it did not realize the depth and vitality of the fear the people of each region had of being dominated by people from another region. In this case, however, it was the fears of the north that were stimulated by government actions. On May 24, 1966, the government issued a series of decrees abolishing the regions and asserting federal control over certain high-level positions in the regional governments. These changes were made without waiting for a previously appointed constitutional reform committee to complete its work and without getting (or apparently even seeking) the informal consent of leaders of thought in the north. Coming as they did from a supreme commander who was an Ibo, on what was assumed to be the advice of a small group of Ibo advisers in Lagos, these decrees appeared to conservative leaders in the north to provide a critical instrument for Ibo domination of the country.

The northern response was twofold. It sought to drive out of the north the easterners who predominated in skilled jobs, and to destroy the Ironsi regime and the eastern influence in the army. The move to drive the easterners out of the north began with a series of riots against easterners on May 29, 1966; these riots occurred sporadically through June, were intensified at the time of the overthrow of the Ironsi regime on July 29, and then took the massive form of a pogrom in late September 1966, when attacks on easterners, both those in their homes and those fleeing to the east, took a toll variously estimated at 10,000 to 30,000 killed and untold numbers injured, and produced an exodus from the north of hundreds of thousands of persons. The brutality and horror of these events, the most horrible of which occurred after northerners had assumed control of the army and of the government in Lagos in August, gave popular credence to the eastern and later Biafran charges of genocide. Certainly nothing could have been more calculated to destroy the idea of one Nigeria for people in the east, and this may have been the underlying intent of the moves.

The destruction of the Ironsi government came with the mutiny of northern army personnel on July 29; in addition to the assassination of General Ironsi, there was a systematic elimination of about 200 officers and men of eastern origin stationed with northern troops at various points outside the eastern region. This uprising brought Lieutenant Colonel Yakuba Gowan, the ranking northern officer, to the fore as the top officer who could control northern troops. It also led to the August 9 agreement to station all military personnel in the region of their origin. This decision was partly implemented by the return of all army personnel of eastern origin to the east, the withdrawal of all noneastern army personnel from the east, and return of western and midwestern army personnel to their respective regions. Northern troops, however, were not withdrawn to the north but remained stationed in Lagos, the west, and the midwest. Lieutenant Colonel Ojukwu, military commander of eastern Nigeria and a strong supporter of General Ironsi and his program, refused to recognize the authority of Lieutenant Colonel Gowan as new supreme commander. Thus the army itself became divided along ethnic, territorial, and political lines, and in early August 1966 Nigeria was left without that essential ingredient—a unified military command—that can provide ultimate assurance of internal peace when normal political processes have collapsed.

THE FAILURE OF NEGOTIATIONS

Open warfare might have been avoided if it had been possible to reach peaceful agreement on a structure that would keep Nigeria one and that could be recognized as legitimate by leaders in all regions. Alternatively, war might have been avoided if there had been a peaceful agreement to divide the country into two or more independent states or if there had been a willingness to acquiesce in the Biafran secession. The failure to reach such agreements reflected not only the tensions between the east and the rest of Nigeria but also other conflicts in the Nigerian political community.

The various proposals for a new political structure that might hold Nigeria together were finally crystallized into two fundamentally conflicting alternatives. One position envisioned holding the existing regions in a very loose confederation in which regional powers would be even greater and federal powers even weaker than they had been. The other position envisioned dividing the old regions, especially the north and the east, into a number of new regions, giving the larger minority groups of the north and east their own regions and eliminating the political imbalance of the old system in which one region, the north, held half the seats in the federal parliament. A corollary of this proposal was a stronger central government, needed because the new, smaller regions would be weaker, less viable financially, and less effective as units for economic development planning.

The confederal pattern appeared to most eastern leaders to be the only tolerable condition for remaining in Nigeria. The attack on eastern personnel in the army during the July coup, and the massacres and forced exodus of easterners from the north in the period May–October 1966 convinced them that their elemental needs for personal safety could be met only if the major authority, including police and military authority, lay in their own regional government. The power of the federal government had to be sufficiently restricted that it could not directly control life and property in the east or interfere with its economic development.

During the traumatic days following the July coup much sympathy for the confederal view was voiced in both north and west. Fears of Ibo domination had led to strong secessionist feelings in the north before the July uprisings, and proposals from the north, as well as the west and the east, presented to the ad hoc constitutional conference in September, advocated a right of secession for states joined on a confederal basis. In time, however, forces opposed to the confederal view gained the upper hand among northern leaders, and in conjunction with leaders in the midwest and Lagos these forces developed the alternative, multiple-region position.

Two lines of thought prompted intense opposition to a loose confederation. The first view reflected the interests of a variety of ethnic groups which under the old system of large regions found themselves subject to what they called the political domination of the larger tribal groups constituting the central core of each region's population. In particular this line of thought was important among the various smaller groups who inhabited the north's "middle belt" and whose appeal for separate regional identity in 1956–1957 had been turned down. General Gowan and a substantial portion of northern troops did in fact come from this middle-belt area, and they saw the opportunity for making basic changes in the political system of Nigeria as an opportunity through which they could be separated from the far north and from the political control the NPC had exercised over them during civilian rule. A loose confederation of strong regions would have meant their staying with the north. And as these middle-belt leaders became aware that their personnel were in significant control of the military in Lagos and had significant representation in the top levels of the civil service, they envisioned a new structure for Nigeria that could free them from the far north.

This minority line of thinking was easily compatible with another line of thinking by those concerned with building an even stronger central government in order to create what they felt was a better political framework for the economic development of the country. This group viewed the rivalries of the earlier regions as being obstructions to the rapid economic development which they felt Nigeria's resources warranted. Centralization of these resources and a reduction of the force of "regional, parochial interests" in development policy was central to their view of what was necessary if Nigeria was to regain its strength. In addition, the newly developed oil fields in the coastal areas of the eastern region promised a great new source of wealth—wealth that would be available for national programs and shared by the whole nation under a centralized governmental scheme, but that would go largely to the east and the midwest under a confederal scheme.[5]

One of the ironies of the situation is that this centralist pattern of thought had earlier been held by Ibo advisers of General Ironsi, and by others in Lagos, and had led to the May 24 decrees that had so disturbed the north and that had brought about the collapse of the Ironsi regime. Now, however, this line of thought did not involve the threat of an Ibo takeover; it could therefore be pursued under northern direction and thus become more acceptable to Hausa-Fulani, as well as minority groups in the north.

Inasmuch as the centralizing forces were in control in Lagos, they were able to veto moves in the direction of a confederation—the proposals generated both by the ad hoc conference of September 1966 and by the meetings of the Supreme Military Council, including Ojukwu, at Aburi, Ghana, in January 1967. Yet, at the same time, Lagos was unable to produce the framework of an agreement with the east that would ensure eastern security and yet provide a unified authority for the country. Finally—and without the agreement of the government in the east, although with the support of some minority group leaders from the Calabar and Rivers areas of the east—the federal government formally proclaimed its multiple-region proposal on May 26, 1967, and divided Nigeria into 12 states, six in the north, three in the east, and three composed of the west, the midwest, and

[5] In 1969 M. Diallo estimated Nigeria's oil reserves: proven reserves, 200 million tons; probable reserves, 600 million tons, possible reserves, 1,200 million tons ("The Power and Energy Resources and Utilization of Nigeria," a paper presented at the Conference on National Reconstruction and Development in Nigeria, Ibadan, March 24–29, 1969).

Lagos. Almost immediately afterward, on May 30, 1967, Biafra proclaimed its independence.

The failure to agree on secession, or even to acquiesce peacefully, is explainable in part by the same pattern of forces that opposed a loose confederation. When Biafran secession was proclaimed, however, the critical problem was not whether the east—that is, Biafra—would be politically and economically viable. This it certainly could have been. The really critical problem was the absence of any agreement about what the character of the rest of Nigeria would be and about the consequences of Biafran secession for the rest of the country.

The Biafrans assumed that the rest of the country would also break up, probably with the west and the midwest becoming a separate state and leaving the north on its own. But the very reasons that had led to abandonment of the concept of northern secession in early August 1966 were still operative—perhaps even more so—by May 1967. Important forces in the north saw its position as threatened by the prospect of being cut off from the sea, both from Port Harcourt and from Lagos. Moreover, minority groups in the north did not wish to be permanently caught in an independent northern state where they would still be subject to the Hausa-Fulani group that had ruled the northern region in the period of Nigerian civilian rule. Thus, if Biafra seceded and the west also sought to secede, pressures in the north would feel it important to maintain their route to Lagos and thus to hold the West and the North together.

All this was very uncertain, however, and ultimately the leaders in Lagos, in the middle-belt minority groups, in the far north, and in the west found it better to try to keep Nigeria united and thus prevent the secession than to sort out the conflicing alternatives for the rest of Nigeria if the eastern region were allowed to go its own way. The alternatives for the rest of Nigeria seemed no more likely to provide the basis for a peaceful agreement than the alternatives for keeping Nigeria one state.

Thus, Nigerians were unable to agree on a new pattern for political unity; at the same time they could not agree on the bases for a peaceful division.

Many of the factors that operated in these discussions had also been present in the early discussions in the 1950s. But one critical factor that had led to a peaceful resolution in the 1950s was not present in the 1960s. In the 1950s the British government still provided a single unifying authority for the whole country, and the discussions took place within the framework of that authority. The desire of Nigerians in all three regions to get rid of that authority had provided the impetus for compromise and the basis for agreement. In 1966–1967 however, no single unifying authority held sway over the country. The collapse of army unity had destroyed the final overriding shell that might have provided a framework within which civilian leaders could have been forced to find a compromise for their competing viewpoints. Now, in 1966–1967, the army had itself become divided and a partisan in the discussions. And the conflicting parties finally turned to military means to resolve their conflicting points of view.

The War and the Internal Politics of Nigeria and Biafra

Once the decision to secede was made, and once the federal government had committed troops to defeat that secession, the problem of future relations between the east and the rest of Nigeria was posed in clear–cut but intractable terms. Either Biafra would be allowed to exist as an independent sovereign state, free to organize its own pattern of political life and free to exploit its own economic resources in its own way and for its own benefit, or it would remain an integral part of Nigeria but be divided into three regions and be subject to federal authority in Lagos.

It is unlikely that either side saw the full consequences of its decisions—a war of 30 months' duration in which the death toll of civilians and combatants together may have reached two million people. Yet throughout the 30 months of war each side clung tenaciously to its position, and there seemed no area for compromise between them on the basis of which hostilities could be halted and peaceful negotiations resumed. With the issues cast in these all-or-nothing terms, the outcome of the conflict depended on two fundamental factors: the nature of the internal politics of each side, and the nature of the international politics in which they were involved. Both are relevant to the character and conduct of the war and to its eventual outcome in the unconditional surrender of Biafra on January 14, 1970.

One basic conception on which Biafran hopes were built was that the cultural diversities that had disrupted the Nigerian political system would operate in such a way that Biafran secession would be followed by a secession of the western region and thus the collapse of the federal regime.[6] This conception of internal disunity in federal Nigeria

[6] A "Memorandum on Future Association Between Biafra and the Rest of the Former Federation of Nigeria," issued by the Biafran government in August 1967, states as its basic political assumption: "In this exercise, an overall view of the rest of Nigeria breaking up into independent and sovereign units has been taken."

was the foundation both for the initial military offensive undertaken by the Biafrans and for their dogged determination to carry on once that offensive failed. In August 1967 the Biafrans launched a military thrust through the midwest to cut Lagos off from the north, hoping that once this connection was severed, the west and the midwest would join Biafra in the secessionist move, creating either a common southern state entirely separate from the north or possibly two southern states that would coexist in a friendly relationship.

This strategic concept very nearly succeeded. The takeover of the midwest came suddenly and quickly with the cooperation of the midwest's Ibo population and the Ibo personnel in the midwestern component of the federal army. Within a week Biafran forces had penetrated to the borders of the western region and seemed to be within striking distance of Lagos. However, the thinness of the Biafran spearhead and the stiffening resistance of federal troops brought the Biafran forward thrust to a halt at Ore, where, after two weeks of standoff skirmishing, federal forces gained the upper hand and began a gradual roll-back of Biafran forces. By the end of September Benin had been returned to federal control, an event Biafrans attributed to the treachery of their military commander, who, when tried for treason by the Biafrans, was charged with planning a countercoup against Ojukwu and the Biafran leadership. By the end of October the federal troops had pushed the Biafrans out of the non-Ibo sections of the midwest, and from this point on the military history of the war was one of nearly continuous federal advances and of Biafran retreats into smaller and smaller areas.

Once its midwest campaign had failed, Biafran hopes lay in the prospect of international recognition and international pressure on Nigeria to halt the war, and in the possibility that the western region would become increasingly discontented with military rule, with the strains of war, and with what Biafrans viewed as northern domination of the federal government, and that an internal political disintegration in federal Nigeria would bring the federal war effort to a halt. This hope that if Biafra could hold out, the federal cause might collapse, the hope that international pressure might force Nigeria to negotiate with Biafra and give it some recognition, and the intense fear that the real federal objective was the absolute and complete destruction of the Ibo people led the Biafrans to maintain very strong internal unity and an extraordinary display of determination and persistence despite an obviously inferior military position and conditions of acute suffering among civilians.[7] In the end its own exhaustion was more acute

---

[7] See *Africa Research Bulletin*, September 1–30, 1967.

than any dissension that may have occurred within the federal side, and renewed federal military action in December 1969 met only the brittle resistance of a people already exhausted.

Whatever the discontent within federal Nigeria—and there was considerable uneasiness over a variety of issues—it did not lead to the political disintegration of the country and the collapse of its war effort. Whatever reluctance may have existed in the western region for the prosecution of the war in the beginning was greatly diminished by the threat of Biafran penetration and control of that region in August 1967. The campaign designed to divide Nigeria served in fact to unite it. It stimulated a more substantial mobilization of Nigerian resources than had yet occurred. The war became easier to view not simply as a question of whether Nigeria should let Biafra go, but one of the potential threat that an independent and successful Biafra might hold for the rest of Nigeria.

Federal unity, however, had a more substantial basis than simple fear of Biafran success. General Gowan succeeded in transforming the nature of internal political relationships in federal Nigeria so that what had previously been dissident minority ethnic groups in the north, now assured of their own separate states, were prepared to support federal Nigeria and its unity, knowing that their own internal autonomy depended on that unity. General Gowan also involved western leaders in the federal effort to the extent that they too would share the responsibility if it failed. Though to the Biafrans he remained a spokesman for the north, in federal Nigeria he clearly established himself as a leader with moderate views and an all-Nigerian concern. Beyond Gowan's effectiveness in accommodating the diverse interests of the federal areas, it was possible to conduct the war on the federal side with relatively little strain on the economy because returns from oil resources provided the essential financing for the war effort. Hence, for both political and economic reasons, the strains of the war did not produce the dissensions counted on by the Biafrans, and Nigeria did hold together long enough for its vastly greater resources to finally weigh in the balance of the military struggle.

In this realm of resources, however, the international politics of both Nigeria and Biafra played a major role in the war.

International Involvement in the War

How internal is an internal war? In a fundamental sense—in its basic roots and in the conditions under which it erupted—the Nigeria–Biafra war was an internal war. But in its conduct and in the factors determining its outcome, it depended on very substantial international involvement.

The most substantial support for the federal side came in the supply of arms from Great Britain and the Soviet Union. Because Great Britain, the colonial power that had created the entity of Nigeria in the first place, had substantial involvements with Nigeria long antedating the development of this particular conflict, it watched closely and painfully the disintegration of the Nigerian political system and exercised what influence it had to hold Nigeria together. However, when the final break came with the declaration of secession and the federal decision to reassert its authority in the east by military means, the initial response of the British government was to stay aloof. London announced that it would not continue the supply of arms to the federal side, nor would it supply arms to the Biafrans, and the United States assumed a similar position of neutrality.[8]

During August 1967, however, Britain reversed its position, first by agreeing to deliver arms that had already been ordered by the federal government, and later by becoming the primary supplier of the arms and equipment necessary to expand the federal army from its initial complement of seven or eight thousand men to the more than 100,000 men in uniform by the end of the war. Various statements by Prime Minister Wilson and other British officials expressed the view that, in becoming the primary arms supplier to the federal government, their position was determined as much by the pattern of involvement of other foreign powers in the Nigerian conflict as by their own concern for maintaining Nigerian unity. In particular, the Russian commitment in August to supply arms to Nigeria was seen by the British as the kind of offer that would render ineffective any policy of seeking to withhold arms from both sides in order to minimize the character of military operations in the conflict. It seemed to pose for Britain a choice either of maintaining the close relationships with Nigerians that it had always enjoyed and continued to enjoy after independence, or of abandoning that relationship to the Russians by virtue of their more positive support to the federal government under the stress of conflict. Even near the end of the war, when the pro-Biafran pressures in Britain had mounted to a very sizeable lobby, the British rejection of the view that cutting off arms supply could bring the war to an end was based on the proposition that this possibility had been explored with the Russians and that the Russians would refuse to co-

[8] Basic information on international involvements, including diplomatic recognition, arms, relief supplies, and peace conferences, appears in the monthly issues of the *Africa Research Bulletin*.

operate with it; therefore, such an alternative was not open to Britain as a realistic way of bringing a cessation of hostilities.

This extensive British involvement in the supplying of arms and equipment to the federal side was set against a historical background of tension and conflict between Britain the colonial ruler and the eastern region's Ibo population—who had proved the most intractable of the various Nigerian subjects during the colonial period. Given, too, the role of eastern personnel in the nationalist movement to drive Britain out of Nigeria and achieve independence, Britain's involvement appeared to the Biafrans to be simply an extension of a long British tradition of hostility to the Ibos and a desire to see control of Nigeria vested firmly in northern hands.[9]

After Great Britain, Russia provided the most substantial active support to the federal side. Very early in the conflict Russia declared itself a supporter of the federal position, supplied Russian planes with Egyptian pilots, and in the last months of the war provided long-range howitzers which, it was assumed, would give the federal forces final control and a capacity to break the Uli airstrip, Biafra's last link with the outside world. Following Biafra's surrender, the Nigerian ambassador to Moscow said in a news conference that the federal victory could be attributed "more than any other thing—more than all other things put together" to Soviet aid.[10]

Russian planes, Russian howitzers, British armored cars, and vast quantities of munitions and other supplies provided through British and Soviet sources undoubtedly gave the federal troops an overwhelming superiority of matèriel that weighed heavily in the federal military victory. This military aid, however, came through Britain's and Russia's willingness to *sell* arms to Nigeria, not through loans of money or gifts of arms. The Nigerians financed their own war effort, largely by revenues from the oil fields of the midwest and the federally controlled areas of the former eastern region.

Biafra also had access to military supplies from outside, and though these were much smaller in amount, and limited essentially to small arms, these supplies, plus the food and medicines flown in by relief agencies, played a critical role in Biafra's ability to sustain itself for

9 Following the breakdown of the Kampala talks (May 1968), the Biafran leader Ojukwu, in a speech to a joint meeting of the Consultative Assembly and the Council of Chiefs and Elders (June 30, 1968), stated, "We have consistently said that the British Government is our real enemy. It is the British Government which goaded Nigeria into the current war of genocide, and it is the British Government which has sustained Nigeria with arms and ammunition to carry out the massacre of Biafrans" (Ojukwu, *Biafra*, 1, 281).

10 *Los Angeles Times*, January 21, 1970; Associated Press dispatch from Moscow.

the last 18 months of the war. Biafra's first real external support come from Portugal; though not formally recognizing Biafra, that country let the Biafrans use Portuguese territory as a critical supply route and as a way of maintaining communications with the outside world. Lisbon became the center of the initial Biafran effort to purchase and ship arms from Europe, and San Tome, a Portuguese island off the coast of Nigeria, became a main base of operations for flights designed to break the Nigerian blockade. This blockade, a crucial factor in Biafra's defeat, barred from Biafra all external supplies except the food and medical supplies that Nigeria allowed to be flown in until May 1969, when permission was withdrawn because the flights served also as a cover for bringing in arms supplies. Particularly from May 1968 onward, however, the major military supplies came from France and from the French-speaking West African states, Gabon and the Ivory Coast, that recognized Biafra in that month. In addition to these major sources of supplies and cooperation, pilots for the Biafran airlift were recruited from South Africa, and the Swedish Count Gustaf von Rosen, who had earlier been involved in relief support to Biafra, secured a small group of pilots and light planes to support Biafra's military operations. A strong Nigerian conviction is that the relief and arms which Biafra received beginning in April 1968 served to prolong Biafran resistance an additional 20 months.

Differences in the amount and character of supplies, both military and relief, that came from the outside world were closely related to differences in the diplomatic positions which the two governments occupied vis-à-vis the international community. During the two and a half years of its existence, Biafra received formal recognition from only five nations—Tanzania in April 1968, Gabon, the Ivory Coast, and Zambia in May 1968, and Haiti in 1969. Although it received substantial aid from France, Portugal, and South Africa, these countries did not extend formal diplomatic recognition. All other countries continued to recognize Nigeria, and Nigeria broke off diplomatic relations only with those countries that recognized Biafra. This difference in the international position of the conflicting parties is a critical factor in the conflict. Nigeria could maintain normal relations with the outside world; it could buy and sell arms and oil, food and clothes, medicines and drugs; and all nations that might have been in a position to challenge the blockade in fact recognized and accepted it.

Biafra, on the other hand, was cut off from normal relations with the outside world; all its dealings had to be treated as clandestine operations, and it had no international platform that could be claimed as a matter of right. Though Biafran emissaries did in fact move rather freely around the world and could come and go from Biafra through the Lisbon-San Tome-Biafra route, it was in the corridors, not on the platforms of international bodies, in which they had to plead their cause. A major factor in Biafra's relative diplomatic isolation was the Nigerians' success in winning and holding a commitment from the Organization of African Unity to the maintenance of the territorial integrity of Nigeria.[11] In a diplomatic sense, the Nigeria-Biafra conflict was viewed first as an internal affair of Nigeria and second as an African affair. Unless Biafra obtained broader support from African states, non-African states did not feel free to provide formal recognition, despite the broad sympathy for the Biafran cause felt by various non-African peoples and states. The attitude of the African states was thus central to the diplomatic position of the conflict, and some examination of African attitudes is essential.

Africans were deeply disturbed and divided by the Nigeria-Biafra conflict. Many African states share some of the underlying problems of Nigeria. They are products of a period of colonial rule; their boundaries were shaped by colonial agreements; and they faced the problems of building national states from culturally and ethnically diverse peoples. Thus many states feel that they hold within themselves similar roots of conflicts, their own potential Biafras. The prospect that a successful secessionist movement could occur, that a people could break away from a central government, thus weakening the power of the nation, brought visions of a fragmentation of present African states into smaller units and a further weakening of African power in the world, a moving away from the goal of a stronger African voice in the international community, rather than toward it. At the same time, the picture of African peoples caught in deadly combat against each other was a horrifying one, and African leaders were anxious to erase it. Julius Nyerere expressed the concern of Biafran sympathizers in his statement on the occasion of Tanzania's recognition of Biafra: "Unity can only be based on a general consent of the people involved."[12] It was not that Tanzania wished to see Biafra an independent state; rather, it wished to see the war brought to a close, an end to the killing and the suffering, and it believed that its act of recognition could put pressure on the federal forces to be more compromising in their approach to the problems of peaceful discussion and negotiation. But the fear of future secessions weighed more heavily throughout the continent than the fear that such issues of conflict

---

[11] The original OAU resolution condemning secession and supporting Nigerian unity was passed at Kinshasa in September 1967, and all subsequent OAU efforts at mediation were conducted within the framework of this resolution.

[12] *Africa Report*, June 1968, p. 27.

might be settled by force of arms. The result was that the OAU continued with its formula that a settlement should take place within the concept of maintaining Nigerian unity and territorial integrity, and its efforts to create peace talks based on this presumption failed so long as Biafra continued to view this condition as an abandonment of its own position before the talks began.

Though several peace conferences were organized by the OAU, the closest the Biafrans and the Nigerians came to real negotiations was at Kampala, Uganda, in May 1968, under the auspices of the Commonwealth Secretariat. Neither side was willing to make concessions on the critical points of Nigerian unity or Biafran recognition, however, and the talks broke down, a failure which federal supporters attributed to the new hope given a collapsing Biafra by stepped-up aid from French sources.

It is worth noting that with the OAU having assumed a responsibility for attempting to bring peace talks between the competing parties, the issue of the Nigeria-Biafra war never came before the United Nations. U Thant himself indicated that it was an African problem, and so long as the OAU was assuming responsibility, the UN could not properly make a formal entry into the dispute.[13]

The patterns of international involvement suggest several aspects about the relationship of African states to the world community at the present time. First, the idea that internal conflicts might be isolated from international involvement, that internal issues might be cordoned off so that competing parties might fight it out among themselves, proved to be fallacious. This idea was perhaps the initial one with which both the US and Great Britain would have liked to approach the conflict. But these two powers are clearly not the only ones that may have interests in Africa, or be concerned with developing interests there. And the parties to a major conflict are not reluctant to seek help elsewhere if those with whom they have traditionally had close relationships impose restrictions on the amount of help that would be given in times of crisis and conflict. Thus the Russian entry into the scene on the federal side quickly moved Great Britain from the stance of a concerned bystander to that of an active supplier of the federal government. And in time France saw that a Biafra which succeeded in sustaining itself through a year of war might indeed have potentialities for survival and might thus change the patterns among African states so as to decrease the influence of the former British colonial areas. Despite these international involvements, however, the responsibility for decisions still rested with the Nigerians and the Biafrans,

13 UN press release SG/SM/1062, New York, January 28, 1969.

not with outside powers that may have been sources of supply and support. In this sense, the war between Nigeria and Biafra was an internal war. Yet the fact remains that the character, length, and conduct of the war depended upon resources which the international community made available to Nigeria and Biafra. And recognition of the Nigerian blockade of Biafra was a decisive factor in determining the eventual outcome.

Conclusions

In a conflict as complex and tragic as the Nigeria-Biafra war, many factors play roles in generating conflict and determining its outcome. As the major postcolonial war in Africa it will be examined for a long time for the lessons others may glean from it. From this vantage point—shortly after the final surrender—several general observations seem warranted.

First, postcolonial states created by "uniting" peoples who have radically diverse cultures, or who belong to traditionally hostile ethnic groups, must seek and maintain rules to accommodate the vital interests of the major powerful and independently viable groups, if national unity is to be maintained on a consensual basis. This rule applies to military and civilian regimes alike, for in the Nigerian case at least the Ironsi regime's sensitivity to the fears of the north and the civilian regime's disregard of the concerns of the south contributed to the collapse of the political community.

Second, the internal unity of the military is the last thread by which an otherwise divided state may be held together. When this thread is broken and the army itself is divided both ethnically and territorially, a move for secession will follow a failure to restore unified command.

Third, secession—even when those who are seceding are feared, disliked, and have been driven from much of the rest of the country—will be opposed when (1) those who are left behind do not see clear and attractive political alternatives for themselves and (2) the seceding group appears to take with it the major mineral wealth which the rest of the country sees as critical to its own future economic development.

Caught in the tensions of rapid political, economic, and social change, postcolonial states face extraordinary problems of conflicts of interest. Peaceful change requires the search for solutions in which various and changing vital interests can be accommodated. The cost of the failure to find such solutions is what the Nigeria-Biafra conflict has shown.

Part Four

Muted Conflicts

Chapter 9

Three-Sided Conflicts

Malaysia, the Philippines, and Indonesia

PETER LYON

The states of maritime southeast Asia, which are sometimes called the Malay world, are now inextricably involved in world politics. And yet full involvement in the international system of independent states is still a novelty for this part of the world. The Philippines achieved independence from the United States in 1946, and the Indonesians from the Dutch in 1949; and the federation of Malaysia (an expanded version of the Federation of Malaya, which first gained independence in 1957) became an independent state only in September 1963.

The relations between the Philippines, Indonesia, and Malaysia are far more complicated than might at first be implied by the rubric "three-sided conflicts." For in the last century, whenever conflict has threatened or erupted in maritime southeast Asia, it has tended to remain internal to one country, and only occasionally has it engaged the close attention of two of the three "Malay" powers or of several more parties. Only for a brief period from 1963 to 1965 was it accurate and appropriate to characterize conflict affecting these three countries as basically triangular; and even this triangularity was overlaid with other connections. Nevertheless, the actions of each of these countries are intimately affected by what happens in the others.

In order to illustrate the fluid configurations of relations in the Malay world, it is necessary to sketch some of the basic and persisting regional features, and then also to set out, rather summarily, some of the basic constitutive features of these three countries. Then I shall turn to a series of issues around which both cooperation and conflict focused among these three states, issues mostly arising directly or indirectly from concern about the constitutive features of their nation-statehood. These issues amply illustrate the rich complexities of local history, politics, and society that shape the international relations of these three embryonic nation-states.

The Regional Environment

Maritime southeast Asia has been an important cultural and commercial crossroads for several thousand years. For centuries large numbers of people have migrated throughout the area. Furthermore, considerable immigration into the area from outside has taken place, especially by Chinese (the so-called Nanyang Chinese, the Chinese of the Southern Seas) but also by Arabs, Persians, Indians (especially in the late 19th century and early 20th centuries into Malaya), and successive European traders and colonizers (Portuguese, Spanish, Dutch, British), as well as Americans and Japanese.

Two indirect consequences of these many migrations—these minglings or, more often, compresences, of peoples—have been the heightening of communal and local consciousness and conflict, and rapid growth and overpopulation of primate cities (especially Djakarta and greater Manila, but also Singapore and Kuala Lumpur), so that capital cities have populations at least four or five times larger than the next largest cities. Urban unrest is more easily combustible than agrarian unrest; both are to be found in present–day Malaysia, Indonesia, and the Philippines.

The generally difficult terrain has meant that the main and easiest form of communication throughout maritime southeast Asia has been by water—by sea, river, or stream. Control of the chief waterways, especially the narrow seas and the main straits, has therefore always been the key to political predominance, whether indigenous or alien. Until the early-20th-century rise of large-estate agriculture (especially rice farms and rubber plantations) and large-scale mining (especially tin), the political roles of the Spanish, Dutch, and British were expressed very patchily, and did not differ much from those of earlier ascendancies. Rivalries between these coastal powers were cardinal features of almost a thousand years of history before 1900, with supremacy shifting from Sri Vijaya (8th-10th centuries) to Mojapahit and its forerunners (12th-15th centuries), Malacca (16th century), Atjeh, Banten, and Batavia (17th century), Batavia (18th century), Batavia and Singapore (19th century), and finally Singapore (and to a lesser extent Penang) in the 20th century. The rivalries between Spanish (later American), Dutch, and British imperialism were in many ways expressions of traditional economic and geographic factors. These rivalries operate to the present day and undoubtedly affect the contemporary relations between Malaysia, Indonesia, and the Philippines.

Historically, divisive factors in this area have been intermeshed with unifying features that traditionally have been not so much locational or political as commercial, ethnolinguistic, and cultural. Most of the major ethnic groups throughout the archipelago—especially the Malays but also the Atjehnese, Javanese, Sudanese, Minangkbau, Buginese, and Makasarese—belong to the so-called Proto- and Deutero-Malay peoples and have many obvious physiological and cultural traits in common. Each large ethnic group has its distinct language, but most are based on a Malayo-Polynesian foundation, and for centuries a flexible and simple form of market Malay has served as a *lingua franca* for traders from Sumatra to Sulu and from Malacca to Mindanao.

Religion is sometimes a unifying factor, but more often its effect is divisive among peoples within maritime southeast Asia. The character of adherence to Islam varies considerably, from a largely traditionalist orthodoxy in rural Malaya and in parts of Indonesia's Sumatra and west Java, to a subtle mélange of Buddhism, Hinduism, and Islam in central and east Java. The Philippines is principally Roman Catholic. But in all three countries ethnic or other minorities are often further differentiated by their religious beliefs and practices from other members of "their nation-state": some obvious examples are Buddhists in northern Malaya, Christians in the Moluccas of Indonesia, and Moros (Muslims) in the southern Philippines.

Many common cultural influences and roughly similar patterns of subsistence, shared throughout maritime southeast Asia from late prehistoric times, were never entirely obliterated either by mass migrations of newcomers or by European incursions, as happened in parts of mainland southeast Asia. In the absence of sharp human differentiation or of large-scale displacements of peoples, the precolonial political and human geography is at once more persistently relevant to the present and more plastic than that of mainland southeast Asia. The colonial impact undoubtedly wrought decisive and irreversible changes; but more remote traditions—and in a sense that is at least contemporaneously fashionable, more "indigenous" traditions—are now reasserting themselves. Perhaps only now, when the transfer of power from colonial to independent nation-state status is virtually complete, can the case for perceiving an underlying and persisting Malay unity be plausibly made and sometimes believed. This is despite the plentiful, often obvious and recurrent signs of discord.

Why some notion of Malay unity persists, despite diversities and discords, was explained well by a leading British political geographer, Charles A. Fisher, in 1963:

Hitherto it has been . . . profound differences of political outlook which have provided the decisive obstacle to closer association between the three countries and, while it is true that Indonesia competes with Malaya in tin and rubber, with Brunei in oil, and with the Philippines in coconut products, the purely economic advantages of mutual co-operation would certainly outweigh any of its disadvantages. . . . Yet, despite their current differences, there is an important element of unity even behind the political thinking of the three powers, amounting to something more than a vague sense of Malaysian kinship. For while they assess its significance differently, each is seeking a solution to the transcendental problem posed by the obscure relationships which exist, or may come to exist, between the three great dynamic forces of messianic communism, the demographic and military strength of Communist China, and the activities of the vigorous ethnic Chinese minorities within their own borders. And, while this problem is one which all three share with the rest of South-east Asia, their own prospects of collectively withstanding possible future pressure from China would seem to be significantly better than those of the mainland States to their north, thanks both to their greater geographical detachment and related capacity for being supported by the maritime powers, and also to the fact that their products, unlike those of the rice-exporting mainland States, will continue to find their main export markets outside the Communist bloc.[1]

The Domestic Environment

The themes that recur throughout the history and contemporary politics of maritime southeast Asia are thus trade and economic matters, ethnic affinities and differences, the role of ethnic minorities, especially the Chinese minorities, and the various and varying involvements of outside power. These elements may be viewed more clearly with reference to the domestic environment. Awareness of the territory, populace, and government of each of these states, together with some knowledge of their economic resources and potential, goes a long way toward explaining their conflict situations and why internal conflict

[1] Charles A. Fisher, "The Malaysian Federation, Indonesia, and the Philippines: A Study in Political Geography," *Geographical Journal*, 129 (1963), 327. By 1970, with the Soviet Union now Malaysia's biggest single customer for her natural rubber, Professor Fisher's final sentence already looked a little odd, and serves as a reminder of the difficulty of precise prediction.

management is a more continuous and absorbing task than their involvement in international conflict.

THE PHILIPPINES

The archipelago republic of the Philippines comprises 7,100 islands, of which only about 800 are inhabited. The two largest, Luzon in the north and Mindanao in the south, account for two-thirds of the total land area. The large, fertile, central plan of Luzon dominates the political, social, and economic life of the country.

Ferdinand Magellan landed on a northern island of the Philippine group in 1521. Toward the end of the same century successive expeditions from Spain and what is now Mexico slowly strengthened Spanish influence over the northern Philippines, though the Muslims (Moros) of the south resisted strongly until about 1850 and were never completely subdued or brought fully within the Spanish administrative pale. In the late 19th century a proto-Philippine nationalism rapidly developed, and resistance to Spanish rule erupted, culminating in the declaration of independence by Emilio Aguinaldo on June 12, 1898, now celebrated as Independence Day. The United States defeated Spain in the short Spanish-American War and brought Spanish rule to an end simultaneously in the Philippines and in Cuba. Many leading Filipinos, who had first welcomed the Americans as liberators, fought against them fiercely when they discovered that the United States was about to fill Spain's recent governmental role. But American colonial rule was imposed and maintained until Japan invaded and occupied the islands from 1942 to 1945. After a brief restoration of US rule, the Republic of the Philippines was proclaimed on July 4, 1946. Terms of independence ensured close continuing ties with the United States, especially in military and economic matters. Although the Philippines joined SEATO in 1954 and sent troops to Vietnam, recently the Filipino government has initiated efforts to reduce the symbols of continuing American dominance in the military and economic fields, while not breaking all major connections with the US.

A high rate of population growth and pockets of extreme population density pose many problems for this country. Of an estimated 37 million people in 1969, almost 50 percent were under 15 years of age. In addition, underemployment and unemployment are serious problems; in the late 1960s about one in ten was unemployed—and many new would-be workers were flooding the labor market.

Population growth thus throws lengthening shadows of a Malthusian nightmare over the Philippines—rural overpopulation, drift from the countryside to the capital, strains on food supplies and on social and educational resources. The greater Manila-Quezon City area has one of the highest ratios of students to total population of any capital city area in the world. The pressures, ambitions, and frustrations of youth are thus felt to be particularly strong—and are perhaps becoming more desperate—in this politically inflammable region.

Both Quezon City and Manila are located on the central plain of Luzon, the turbulent political and social heartland of the Philippines, which contains one-eighth of the national population. Here unemployment and underemployment are more acute than anywhere else in the country. Ownership of land in the central plain is very heavily concentrated in the hands of a small class of large landowners, many of whom reside in Manila and back the political, social, and economic status quo. It is thus not surprising that this region has been a center of peasant unrest at least since 1920. The year 1931 saw the Tayug uprising, and during World War II the Communist-led Hukbalahap movement launched recurrent guerrilla attacks against both the Japanese conquerors and the Filipino landowners. Hukbalahap opposition to landowners reached a peak in the late 1940s and early 1950s (and was only suppressed, not entirely extinguished, by the energetic counterinsurgency efforts mounted by Secretary of Defense Ramon Magsaysay, later president of the Republic) and has continued sporadically ever since, though in the 1970s the Huks seem more like gangsters than guerrillas, operating their own "protection" rackets and systems of taxation.[2]

INDONESIA

Indonesia, where about half the people of southeast Asia live, is the world's most geographically fragmented major state. Because of its population's size (115–120 million in 1970, making it the world's fifth most populous country), its areal sweep (extending 3,000 miles, broadly athwart the Equator, from the Andaman Sea almost to Australia), its natural resources and strategic importance, this country is indubitably of considerable importance not only in southeast Asia but also in world politics.

---

[2] For an eloquent nationalist history by a leading Filipino historian, see Tesdoro A. Agoncillo, A Short History of the Philippines (New York: New American Library, Mentor Books, 1969); see also Dante C. Simbulan, "A Study of the Social Economic Elite in Philippine Politics and Government 1946–1963" (unpublished doctoral dissertation, The Australian National University, Canberra, 1965); Jean-Luc Vellut, "Asian Policy of the Philippines 1935–1963" (unpublished doctoral dissertation, The Australian National University, Canberra, July 1964); Peter Lyon, "The Foreign Policy of the Philippines," The World Today, December 1964; Michael Leifer, "The Philippines and Sabah-Irredenta," The World Today, October 1968.

The islands of Indonesia (together with those of the Philippines) form an extensive series of stepping stones between the Indian and Pacific oceans, making the main straits between the islands strategically important sea lanes, even though they are narrow and shallow. The Indonesian republic shares land borders with Malaysia (on the large island of Kalimantan, formerly Borneo), with Portuguese Timor, and with the Australian territories of Papua and New Guinea. Java, the political heartland of modern Indonesia, is one of the world's most densely populated areas; in 1970 its population numbered 70 million, in an area roughly the size of New York State. Java is thus the overcrowded political power base for the whole Indonesian archipelago, with about two-thirds of the nation's population living together on less than a tenth of the country's territory. This density gives a great prominence and potential explosiveness to Javanese politics. The other main islands of Java are Sumatra, Celebes (Sulawesi), and the southern part of Kalimantan.

The Indonesian independence movement seriously began during the first decade of this century and grew rapidly between the two world wars. At a youth congress in October 1928, the pledge, "One People, One Country, One Language," was first made publicly. Indonesia's nationalist leaders were drawn from a small group of young, educated men and students, many of whom were from that even smaller group which had been educated in The Netherlands. A number of these people were imprisoned for long periods because of their political activities. Indonesian nationalism grew rapidly and was quickened during the three-year occupation of the Indies by the Japanese in World War II. Some Indonesian political leaders went "underground," others were appointed to positions in civil administration that had been closed to them under the Dutch, a few achieved nationwide recognition and reputations—Sukarno, certainly, among them. On August 17, 1945, three days after the Japanese surrendered, a small group of Indonesians prompted Sukarno and his associate, Hatta, to proclaim independence and establish the Republic of Indonesia.

Indonesia was proclaimed one nation, but from the beginning it has suffered serious divisions. In 1948 the Indonesian Communists (PKI) staged an armed uprising in east Java, which was quickly crushed by the army. In 1950 self-proclaimed "Federalists" revolted in several local areas. In 1956–1958 large-scale rebellions again were mounted in certain regions; they received support from abroad, including help from Malaya, Singapore, and the Philippines.

In addition to dealing with these serious revolts and expressions of regional discontent, the central government had to wage continual campaigns against bandits and religious dissidents (especially the

Darul Islam), and the army acted as principal instrument for law and order operations and for attempts to forge national unity. Furthermore, the anticolonial struggle against the Dutch lasted from 1949 to 1963, because Indonesia's new leaders aspired to rule the whole of the former Dutch realms in southeast Asia. The Dutch clung stubbornly to west New Guinea, even after reluctantly abandoning their colonial rule elsewhere in the archipelago. (They did not give up their rule, however, until some guerrilla warfare, expropriation of property, and acrimonious diplomacy-cum-propaganda by the Indonesians, and pressure from their sympathizers, most notably from the United States, had "persuaded" the Dutch.) Eventually, in 1962, the Dutch did cede west New Guinea (then renamed West Irian) first to an United Nations administration and then, after May 1, 1963, to an Indonesian administration.

The combination of acute internal unrest and instability, involvement in small-scale warfare, and diplomacy that utilized various forms of pressure recurred several times in Indonesia soon after independence. The combination was evident while the nation was achieving independence, while it was gaining West Irian, and then again, but less successfully, during the "confrontation" with Malaysia, which virtually culminated in the bloody Gestapu affair of September 1965.

In this affair, which apparently involved the complicity of President Sukarno, the PKI murdered six leading Indonesian generals and, with the assistance of some army and air force dissidents, tried unsuccessfully to effect a coup d'état. The immediate consequence of this abortive coup was a prolonged and bloody series of reprisals launched against the PKI and their alleged supporters and sympathizers. Whether innocent or guilty of complicity with the PKI, the overseas Chinese, especially in Java and Bali, suffered greatly in this grisly settling of scores. Though estimates vary considerably, it seems that several hundred thousand Indonesians were massacred in the months immediately following the attempted coup.

President Sukarno gradually lost power, and since 1966 Suharto, one of two leading generals who survived, has headed a military regime oriented primarily toward economic and administrative reform.

The tasks facing the new regime have not been easy. One of Indonesia's major problems is that economic growth has not kept pace with rapid population increase, which now amounts to an addition of 2.5 million people every year. Keeping pace would require a yearly net investment of at least 15 percent of Indonesia's national income. But as one of the country's leading intellectuals and diplomats has stated,

When one considers that the annual rate of investment, including imputed investments in the rural areas, did not rise higher than 5–6 percent in the years before 1966, it becomes clear that a really dramatic effort and considerable structural changes are necessary if per capita income is not to continue to fall. [Observe] the nature and magnitude of the stresses under which Indonesian society is labouring. . . . no political system, whatever its ideological colouring, democratic, communist or militarist, has a chance of surviving unless it is capable of a vigorous attack on these problems. In fact, political stability is only possible on the basis of a rapidly expanding economy. The problem is aggravated by the economic shambles left behind by the Sukarno regime.[3]

Although Indonesia possesses untapped resources—tin, nickel, bauxite, iron ore, timber, fish, and especially petroleum—the new regime has been forced to start from the basic fact that Indonesia's present economy is fundamentally agricultural and depends heavily on a few primary exports. More than 70 percent of Indonesia's people earn their living in the agricultural sector, and more than 70 percent of its foreign exchange in 1965–1970 was earned by agricultural products. Four items—rubber, coffee, copra, and tobacco—provide more than half this total. The industrial sector contributed only about 12 percent of the nation's GNP in the late 1960s, compared with considerably more than half from agriculture. The average income per capita is only about $85 (US), an amount that is, of course, a perilously small base from which to restructure an economy.

The policies pursued by the Suharto regime have generally been regarded as satisfactory by the Western powers most concerned—meaning especially the United States and Japan, but also several European states that are members of the aid consortium for Indonesia established in 1967. Since 1966 the Djakarta-Peking axis, which Sukarno had encouraged, has disintegrated; confrontation with Malaysia has ended; earnest efforts are being made to deal with the economic situation along lines approved by the Western powers. There is some talk of a "return" to constitutional government, a quiet constructive interest is being shown in nonmilitary regionalist organizations (especially ASEAN), and a cautious policy of nonalignment has been reaffirmed and resumed in foreign affairs.

The immediate future of Indonesia depends very much on the role of the army, and eventually on whether the transition from military to civilian rule, always difficult to make, will be tried fully and will

[3] Soedjatmoko, "Indonesia: The Dyason Lectures," *Australian Outlook*, 21, No. 3 (December 1967).

succeed. To date, Suharto's "new order" has adopted much the same governing style as did the Dutch when they were colonial rulers, emphasizing efficiency and technocratic skills, and government by administrators rather than by politicians.[4]

MALAYSIA

"Malaysia" first became the official name of a distinct political entity in 1963, but it had been used as a loose descriptive label, roughly synonymous with the Malay world, for decades. Malaysia is thus the newest nation-state of the three states considered here, and in some respects it is politically the most diverse and fragmented.

Malaysia is a federation of the 11 states of the former Federation of Malaya, located along the whole lower portion of the Malay peninsula; these federated states gained their independence from the British in 1957. They were joined by Sarawak and Sabah (formerly called British Borneo, now eastern Malaysia), more than 400 miles across the South China Sea on the island of Borneo.[5] The Federation of Malaysia first came into existence in September 1963 and then included Singapore as a constituent state.[6] But Singapore separated from the Malaysian federation and became a fully independent state in August 1965. Malaysia had grown smaller within two years of its formal launching.

The complex demographic pattern of Malaysia is also the complex central clue to Malaysian politics, the prime cause of most of the country's internal turbulence, and the main difficulty that stands in the way of realizing national unity in a genuinely multiracial country. The population of Malaysia in 1970 was approximately 12 million

[4] See Ruth T. McVey (ed.), *Indonesia* (New Haven: Yale University Press, 1963). I want to acknowledge a general intellectual debt to Ruth McVey for her conversation and her writings, published and unpublished, which have helped my understanding of Indonesia. See also Soedjatmoko, "Indonesia"; Robert Curtis (pseud.), "Malaysia and Indonesia," *New Left Review*, 28 (November–December 1964); George McT. Kahin, "Malaysia and Indonesia," *Pacific Affairs*, Fall 1964; L. H. Palmier, *Indonesia* (London: Hudson, 1965).

[5] The Federation does not include the small, oil-rich Sultanate of Brunei, which is surrounded on three sides by Sarawak and on the fourth by the sea, even though both the British and the Malayan government had hoped that Brunei would join.

[6] See Wang Gung-wu (ed.), *Malaysia* (London: Pall Mall, 1964); J. M. Gullick, *Malaysia* (London: Benn, 1969), and *Malaysia and Its Neighbours* (London: Routledge & Kegan Paul, 1967); Rupert Emerson, *Malaysia* (London: Macmillan, 1937; University of Malaya Press, 1964); and J. P. Ongkili, *The Borneo Response to Malaysia, 1961–1963* (Singapore: Moore, 1967).

people. The ethnic composition of this population was roughly in the following proportions: Chinese 36 percent, Malays 48 percent, Indians and Pakistanis 9 percent, and non-Malay indigenous peoples about 7 percent; but these proportions vary considerably from area to area, and political, economic, and ethnic patterns must be related to smaller units of the national mosaic in order to throw real light on their interactions. In peninsular Malaya (West Malaysia, as it is now officially called) the Chinese are more heavily concentrated in the prosperous west-coast states, and particularly though by no means entirely in the towns and industrial areas, while the Malays predominate in the east coast's poorer states and in rural areas. The Indians are for the most part either town-dwellers or workers on rubber estates. The Chinese make up 31 percent of the population in Sarawak and 23 percent in Sabah, and as a whole they tend to be concentrated in the towns or in the more developed rural areas. The Malays live in kampongs (villages) in the settled areas near the towns, whereas the other indigenous peoples are found mostly in the interior.

The Malays are Muslims, almost without exception, and they speak the Malay language, whereas most of the rest of the population is distinct from them ethnically, linguistically, and religiously. About one-third of the Malays in western Malaysia[7] are first- or second-generation immigrants from Indonesia, and thus contemporary representatives of the age-old movement of Malay and other peoples across the local seas. The Chinese of Malaysia came mainly from south China originally, though many Chinese families have now lived several generations in Malaya, which is longer than many Malay immigrants from Indonesia. The Indians came mainly from south India and speak Tamil; most are Hindus, but some are Buddhists and Muslims. The indigenous tribal people in Sarawak and Sabah generally are animists (although some have a veneer of Christianity or of Islam) with their own language or dialect and customs. Undoubtedly, East Malaysia has been catapulted more swiftly and with less preparation than West Malaysia into the modern world.

When we remember, too, that the Malays monopolize federal and most state political power, that the Chinese exercise economic power considerably greater than their numerical strength suggests, and that geographical separation and very difficult colonial and recent experience and political patterns complicate relations between East and

---

[7] But it should not be thought that the Malays of Borneo are the same as those of the peninsula. See, for example, Tom Harrison, *The Malays of South-West Sarawak Before Malaysia* (London: Macmillan, 1970).

West Malaysia, then we can begin to appreciate the complexities of contemporary Malaysia.

Combating insurgency (especially the emergency of 1948–1960, which was caused by an unsuccessful communist guerrilla movement, and the confrontation with Indonesia 1963–1966), encouraging and enjoying economic growth, and governing (some would say merely administering) the country have been the continuous experience of virtually the same small group of leading Malays ever since the middle 1950s. The Malay predominance in key posts of the federal government and administration, in the army and in the police, expresses and symbolizes the Malay character of the regime. The Malay community had a special part in the key administrative service (and in some other nontechnical roles) even in the days of British colonial rule, for the British colonial bureaucrats went into partnership with the traditional rulers and recruited the sons of Malay sultans and other aristocrats into their services. After Malaya became independent in 1957 some 2,000 British colonial officials were gradually replaced. The Malays moved into the seats of power in government and the administration; the technical services were filled up mainly by Malayan Chinese and Indian professional men. There remained the colonial and traditional legacies of social distance between the educated men in authority and the mass of peasantry and workers. Malaya, and then Malaysia, remained a plural society (or, more strictly, a segmented one), with vertical communalist stratification now further complicated by new horizontal stratifications through occupational specialization. Social and political change, though occurring in contemporary Malaysia, lags behind economic change.

Unlike the Philippines and Indonesia, Malaysia has achieved and sustained impressive economic growth and financial stability over the past decade. Its economy is based on the production and trade of primary commodities, particularly rubber, tin, and timber. In addition, Malaysia already has reached a high stage in per capita production and standard of living relative to other newly independent countries.

The major clouds shrouding Malaysia's future are not economic but political. The main question is whether communalist prejudices and conflict will further disturb and disrupt national life. (Such an event occurred in Kuala Lumpur in the post-election race riots of May 1969, which resulted in the proclamation of a state of emergency, the suspension of Parliament, and rule by a Malay-dominated National Operations Council.) Communalism is still the main key to Malaysian politics, the basis for cooperative efforts, and the prime source of internal conflict.

In maritime southeast Asia, foreign affairs are the close and continuing concern of only a small, educated elite, nearly all of whom live in capital cities and belong to what Hildred Geertz has termed a "metropolitan superculture." Almost by definition foreign affairs have seldom really affected the daily lives of the vast majority of the three national populaces during the past two decades. These people are fairly well insulated from international conflict, but as my discussion of the domestic environment has suggested, they are not insulated from internal conflicts, both economic and communal. As a consequence, recent international conflicts in maritime southeast Asia have not arisen from profound causes but very often from such trivia as personal prestige, pride, or pique have played a precipitating part. Because international conflicts have not been based on deep-rooted interests, throughout the Malay world cooperation and conflict are not polar opposites but coexist within the same situation; which theme is dominant at a particular time has changed very rapidly. In order to demonstrate this coexistence, we must deal here with past examples of both conflict and cooperation among these states—with confrontation and the Sabah dispute, on one hand, and with the Maphilindo proposal and ASEAN, on the other.[8]

CONFRONTATION

Confrontation was the name the Indonesians gave to their campaign against the Federation of Malaysia. This confrontation had an economic, a military, and a political-diplomatic character.

Indonesia's economic actions against Britain and Malaysia began in September 1963 with the seizure of British and Malaysian properties and other assets within Indonesia and with the complete severance of trade. Despite the severe dislocations caused to its trade by Indonesian action, the overall trade of Malaysia expanded throughout con-

[8] Richard Allen, *A Short Introduction to the History and Politics of Southeast Asia* (New York: Oup, 1970); Arnold C. Brackman, *Southeast Asia's Second Front: The Power Struggle in the Malay Archipelago* (New York: Praeger, 1966); Richard Butwell, *Southeast Asia Today—and Tomorrow: Problems of Political Development*, 2nd edn., rev. (London: Pall Mall, 1969); Bernard K. Gordon, *The Dimensions of Conflict in Southeast Asia* (Englewood Cliffs, N.J.: Prentice-Hall, 1966); General Sir Walter Walker, "How Borneo Was Won: The Untold Story of an Asian Victory," *Round Table*, 233 (January 1969); General Walker was commander of British Forces in Borneo and later director of operations from December 1962 to March 1965.

frontation. Singapore suffered more in economic terms than did the Malaysian peninsula, but even so, the net effects were far from disastrous. By contrast, the Indonesian economy slumped further downward.

Militarily, confrontation was a peculiar affair. Indonesia's military buildup was tentative and gradual, and domestic politics within Indonesia (within the armed forces and between the armed forces, the PKI, and Sukarno) played a significant part at each stage. Indonesian action was mounted in two places—in Borneo, and later on against mainland Malaya—and consisted of sabotage and small-scale guerrilla forays. But the small groups of pathetically undertrained Indonesian infiltrators, never more than 40 at a time, proved to be no match for the well-trained and armed men in the Malaysian police forces, many of them veterans of the earlier counterinsurgency operations during the "emergency" of the 1950s. Furthermore, the local population showed no noticeable disposition to welcome the Indonesian infiltrators as "liberators."

The political and diplomatic factors prompting Indonesia's confrontation were many and interwoven, and a full explanation would involve a study of the whole domestic and international position of the country. Any adequate account would have to weigh the significance of President Sukarno's unique political position and his overweening ambition and confidence in the destiny of his country. Proper emphasis would also have to be given the extensive maneuvering and bitter rivalries of the Indonesian Communist party, by now apparently very strong, and the armed forces; the tragic and prolonged mismanagement of economic matters; the general resentment of Javanese rule by the non-Javanese; and the peculiar triangularities of Indonesia's relations with the Soviet Union (from whom she had recently obtained extensive and sometimes remarkably up-to-date items of military hardware) and with Communist China (expressed in many gestures of mutual regard and apparently constituting the most significant expression of Sukarno's doctrine of the fraternity of the New Emerging Forces).

Indonesian spokesmen repeatedly and insistently described the establishment of Malaysia as a "neo-colonialist" plot designed by the British to perpetuate their power in southeast Asia while they pretended to decolonize the area. Even if the British had handed over political power, they had also, it was alleged, maintained financial and military power, the sinews of effective control.

During the three years of armed skirmishes that were part of confrontation, it was estimated, almost 2,000 casualties had occurred on both sides. It is an indication of the greater importance of internal politics in this area that these casualties were relatively few, in human terms, when compared to the Gestapu affair. But the cost to Indonesia (and to a lesser extent to Malaysia and Singapore) in political and other terms was immeasurable. The cost to Britain was high in terms of money, manpower, and matériel.[9]

Confrontation was ended formally in 1966 by the new government which came to power in Indonesia after the Gestapu affair. Malaysia demonstrated patience and poise in the pursuit of that peace, and the new Indonesian government managed the end of confrontation gracefully. Since 1966 the blossoming of Malaysian-Indonesian cordiality has been officially encouraged; it has found expression in border agreements, comembership in ASEAN, state visits, Indonesian provision of many teachers of Malay for Malaysia, and the signing of a treaty of friendship.

But the end of confrontation, paradoxically enough, also saw a change of direction in British-Malaysian relations. During confrontation Malaysia was dependent on Britain and sustained at first by substantial support from that country and, to a lesser extent, from Australia and New Zealand. By 1970 officially cordial relations with Britain, though still continuing, had lessened considerably, particularly after the British refused in May 1966 to grant increased military assistance, which the Malaysian government felt had been promised. Anglo-Malaysian relations cooled further as the British Labor government decided not to keep any British troops permanently based in Malaysia after 1971. The victory of the Conservative party in Britain's general elections in June 1970 perhaps has arrested this growing estrangement, at least pending further decisions concerning British involvement in Commonwealth five-power arrangements (for Australia, New Zealand, Britain, Malaysia, and Singapore) after 1971. Anglo-Malaysian relations are thus now in a state of mutually suspicious uncertainty, moderated in part by memories of close cooperation, the size of British investments in Malaysia, and a disposition on the part of both present governments to maintain as good relations as possible.

SABAH

Filipinos increasingly claim that they must assert, or reassert, their identity with Asia, particularly with Indonesia and Malaysia. One unexpected course taken in this quest began in 1962 and was heightened in 1963 as the Malaysia project was being launched. The gov-

[9] Peter Boyce, "Malaysia and Singapore in International Diplomacy," *Documents and Commentaries* (Sydney: Sydney University Press, 1968), pp. 133, 141, 143–144.

ernment of the Philippines claimed a large but still unclearly defined portion of Sabah on the avowed grounds, among others, that the government had become the reversionary heir of the sultans of Sulu and thus had inherited the sultan's rights of suzerainty over Sabah.

The whole question is very complex and tangled when seen from the Philippines. For the Malaysian government the issue is very simple: Malaysia does not "claim" Sabah but possesses it by sovereignty *de jure* and *de facto;* thus the Philippines is trying to aggrandize itself by territorial expansion, or at least by serious trouble-making, at Malaysia's expense.

Part of the Philippine claim, actively prosecuted in the years 1963–1965 and again from 1968 until now, revolves around an interpretation of the nature of an agreement made by the sultan of Sulu in 1878. Did the sultan make a lease, a grant, or a cession? Did the sultan actually rule or control the area in question? The answer to the second question is almost certainly no. But the first question is more difficult. Terms such as "lease," "cession," and "grant" were used interchangeably in the nineteenth century and today they cannot stand up under precise definition. But whether the crucial term is properly translated as "lease" or "cession," there is no doubt that the act was made "in perpetuity." It is difficult to see what possible international advantage the Philippines derives from this claim.

Relations between Malaya and the Philippines were officially cordial but never really close between 1957 and 1961. Since the onset of the Philippine effort to gain Sabah, diplomatic, commercial, and all other relations between the two countries have oscillated between mutual animosity and rather stiff, formally correct relations, depending mostly on the degree to which Manila has insisted on publicly advertising its claim. For Malaysia, Sabah is unquestionably a piece of national territory, and under no condition is Malaysia prepared to concede or even to pay serious heed to Filipino demands.

This dispute remains in limbo; whether the Filipinos will attempt to save face while dropping their territorial claims or whether they will prosecute the dispute further remains unclear. But both Sabah and confrontation point up the seemingly inescapable dilemma of Malaysia's nation-statehood: "The more it strengthens its efficiency, the more it offends its neighbours, the more it appeases its neighbours, the more it exposes itself to foreign intrigue and internal collapse, or at best disruption."[10] As the Maphilindo proposal further suggests, the controversies over the existence of Malaysia and its boundaries

[10] Dennis J. Duncanson, "Malaysia as a Nation-State," *International Journal* (Toronto), Winter 1968–9, p. 165.

have created the issues around which relations in the Malay triangle have since revolved.

MAPHILINDO

Maphilindo is an acronym coined by Dr. Subandrio in July 1963, when he was Indonesia's foreign minister, to express ideas originally propounded by Filipino President Macapagal; the word was formed from the names of its three potential members, Malaysia (or Malaya), the Philippines, and Indonesia. Maphilindo never, in fact, passed the political blueprint stage, and was only serious practical politics for a few weeks in the middle months of 1963. This period spanned the two conferences in Manila, just before Malaysia was formally launched, a time when the heady wine of pan-Malay sentiment and solidarity was served with great gusto by Presidents Macapagal and Sukarno and with somewhat less ebullient enthusiasm by Tunku Abdul Rahman of Malaysia. What in substance was intended by Maphilindo was never made entirely clear. Doubtless each of the three main participants envisaged different benefits; this difference of viewpoint was made apparent in the final speeches of the talks among Maphilindo heads of state that ended in Manila on August 5, 1963.[11]

President Macapagal, having proclaimed that this agreement marked the reunion of the trinity of Malay peoples, which he said had been separated by the imperialists, went on to claim that the Manila meetings pointed toward the ultimate fulfilment of his boyhood dreams of Malaya irredenta. What was never made clear was precisely how the Sabah issue fitted into this scheme of things, or exactly whose irredentist urges were to be satisfied, in what ways, and at whose expense.

President Sukarno probably saw Maphilindo as a rallying cry for the expression and projection of Indonesia's leadership throughout the whole Malay world, the carrot to the stick of confrontation, and another chance for his country and himself to act as lodestars for newly emerging forces against colonialist powers and their allies. The Tunku probably regarded Maphilindo at best as merely a formula— possibly convenient so long as suitably innocuous—that would enable him to settle his immediate disputes with his two neighbors and perhaps to lay a new foundation for their future cooperation.

Behind these obviously individual—or, rather, national—motives, pressures, calculations, and ambitions lurked an unspoken common denominator: Maphilindo was implicitly anti-Chinese. But even this

[11] These points are taken from the texts of the final speeches as given in Filipino press releases on August 5, 1963.

implicit commonality was ambiguous. It was one thing to be vaguely agreed in sharing suspicions about the Chinese. It was quite another matter to agree who, where, and exactly what were these Chinese enemies, these "threats," and what should be done about or to them. Were they the Nanyang Chinese, or those of Taiwan or those of mainland China? In 1963 this Maphilindo bias against the Chinese probably did not mean mainland China for Sukarno, though it could well have meant the mainland for Macapagal, or for the Tunku, or for both of them. Only Sukarno may have meant to make a gratuitous gibe against Taiwan. If it meant a common front against the Nanyang Chinese, then this was an expensive but bearable luxury for the Philippines and Indonesia, which had relatively small Chinese minorities, however valuable these minorities may have been for running their "national economies"; anti-Chinese pogroms had been recurrent convulsions in the histories of both countries. But for the Malayan government any newly active discrimination against the Chinese in their country would strike at the very basis of the stability and prosperity of the state, given the size, importance, and diffusion of the Chinese in Malaya. However, in 1963 Maphilindo was stillborn, a victim of the overlapping disputes within the Malay triangle.

Since the Gestapu affair in Indonesia there has been a good deal of quiet speculation from several capital cities in southeast Asia that Maphilindo, or something rather like it, might have to be revived. But if this were to be so, it would have to operate in a rather different context from that of 1963. A principal difference is that Singapore since August 1965 has become an independent state and is very anxious not to be treated as the common irritant of all three larger "Malay" countries: a kind of Israel of southeast Asia. Ever since 1963 governmental leaders in Kuala Lumpur, except for the communal chauvinists, have recognized very clearly that in their long-term interest Maphilindo, if it is to be reactivated, should not be merely a club for fanning communalist passions and prosecuting anti-Chinese campaigns. And since ASPAC, the Asian and Pacific Council, and ASEAN have been launched, a revival of the Maphilindo idea seems unlikely.

ASA-ASEAN

Both Thai and Malay leaders claimed parentage of ASA, the Association of Southeast Asian states, which was launched in 1961 with Malaya, Thailand, and the Philippines as founding members. ASA was begun with high hopes and expectations of promoting greater cooperation among the members in a wide range of fields, and also with a view of the organization as the nucleus of a much broader southeast Asian organization. In fact, practical difficulties prevented the implementation of some of the initial schemes (such as the establishment of a joint ASA airline), and the association in effect soon had to settle for very modest ambitions, such as promoting cultural and educational cooperation—and even these projects were halted when the Philippines pressed its claim to some of Sabah's territory. Only in 1966 was ASA tentatively being revived. By early 1967 its members were holding meetings to discuss the liberalization of trade and the promotion of commerce and industry, and were planning joint consideration of problems of higher education.

With the end of confrontation ASA was absorbed in a new organization, ASEAN, the Association of Southeast Asian Nations, which was formally established in Bangkok in August 1967 by five founding members: Malaysia, Thailand, the Philippines, Singapore, and Indonesia.

A seven-point declaration signed by the leaders of the delegations of the five participating nations said that the five countries would cooperate to accelerate the region's economic growth, social progress, and cultural development. They were also determined, according to this communiqué, to ensure the stability and security of the area from external interference, and they affirmed that foreign bases were temporary expedients. A standing committee of the organization was envisaged to operate at the ambassadorial level. Subsequently a small national secretariat was set up in each member country to carry out the work of the association for the member concerned.

Though Thailand has been active in ASEAN, this project is significant mainly for having Indonesia as a founding member and thereby indicating the change in relations among Malaysia, the Philippines, and Indonesia since the end of confrontation. It remains to be seen what further significance ASEAN can achieve, and whether it can survive recurrent strains imposed by such local conflicts as the Philippines' claim to Sabah.

ASA and ASEAN's mostly consultative activities so far have not produced dramatic changes, and probably will not do so of themselves. But they may properly be seen as publicizing cherished ideas, as providing forums, and supplying means for launching pilot schemes that might possibly lead to future political collaboration as well as economic cooperation among the members, and perhaps to wider groupings, of a kind the Indonesians were actively showing some interest in late in the 1960s. Certainly, ASEAN represents a potential for future achievement rather than a sign that complex forms of cooperation have been achieved.

In addition to ASEAN, Indonesia, the Philippines, and Malaysia have common memberships in several large regional organizations: the Economic Commission for Asia and the Far East (ECAFE), the Columbo Plan, the Asian and Pacific Council (ASPAC), and the Asian Development Bank. These overlapping memberships however, do not appear to play a prominent role in the relations between the three states.

To date no real interpenetration or even close, substantial, and continuing cooperation has existed among the ruling elites of the different countries of the Malay world. International stratification into separate nation-states mostly still inhibits, even if it does not entirely impede, substantive transnational cooperative endeavors between governmental and nongovernmental associations (e.g., religious, cultural, and educational) in the area. ASEAN and even the broader international associations represent signs that the situation is now changing, and transnational transactions increasing, but it is still too early to proclaim that these embryos are capable of more growth.

Conclusion

The recent history and present prospects of maritime southeast Asia demonstrate that conflict is more often internal to the states concerned—not international, and covert rather than overt. One must beware of regarding the international politics of maritime southeast Asia exclusively as a states-system, a set of states where each government is in full control of all territory, men, and resources within the state's boundaries. Any moderately adequate account of the international politics of this part of the world has to pay due regard to overlapping authorities, divided or indecisive loyalties, and uncertain sovereignties. Repeatedly, we encounter fundamental ambivalences about international status and position, inevitably involving questions about the content and meaning of independence.

The Malay triangle is not at present, and is most unlikely to become in the next decade, (if at all) an area characterized by absence of military preparation for mutual hostilities or low expectations of violent mutual conflicts. Rather, the present mixture of cooperation and conflict is likely to continue indefinitely. Which of the two will prevail in any particular period will depend, as in the past, on the personalities and strength of leaders in power, on the relations between the various indigenous groups that compose each state, and on the effect of events and conditions beyond the control of individual governments in an area where domestic turbulence is endemic.

Somalia and Its Neighbors

SAADIA TOUVAL

One of the most striking features of the conflict between Somalia and its neighbors is the fluctuation in its course. Like many other conflicts, it started with diplomatic exchanges and later escalated to guerrilla warfare and occasional clashes between regular armies. Then, in 1967, a dramatic change occurred, as within a few weeks the antagonists concluded a series of agreements leading to a détente and to the normalization of relations between them.

In this chapter, I shall suggest some explanations for this course of development. What are the issues over which the parties have been quarreling, and how do the parties perceive these issues? What main environmental elements seem to have influenced the conflict? What factors have contributed to decision-making at two crucial turning points—escalation and disengagement—and influenced their implementation? And finally, what are the prospects for the future?

What Is The Conflict About?

Within a broad historical perspective, the contemporary dispute can be viewed as merely the modern expression of conflicts that have accompanied the migrations and expansion of the Somali tribes, the beginnings of which lie obscured in the mist of history.[1] It is currently believed that the nomadic

[1] For background see A. A. Castagno, "Somalia," *International Conciliation*, no. 522 (March 1959); S. Touval, *Somali Nationalism* (Cambridge: Harvard University Press, 1963); J. Drysdale, *The Somali Dispute* (London and Dunmow: Pall Mall Press, 1964); I. M. Lewis, *The Modern History of Somaliland* (London: Weidenfeld and Nicolson, 1965); V. Thompson and R. Adloff, *Djibouti and the Horn of Africa* (Stanford: Stanford University Press, 1968).

Somalis began expanding their habitat, originally confined to the shore of the Gulf of Aden, in the tenth century. Over the centuries they gained possession of new lands, and today they occupy the bulk of the triangular area known as the Horn of Africa, from Djibouti in the north to the Tana river in the south. In the process, the Muslim Somalis clashed repeatedly with (among others) the Christian Amhara people of Ethiopia, who were pressing to extend their domain southward and eastward, and with Bantu-speaking peoples who withdrew southward, under Somali pressure, into the area that is now Kenya.

The contemporary conflict also stems from the development of Somali nationalism under the impact of colonial rule. Since the 1940s the principal and overriding objective of the Somali nationalist movement has been to unify all Somalis within a Somali nation-state. The fulfilment of this aspiration would require that about a fifth of Ethiopia and a large chunk of Kenya, which are inhabited by Somalis, be annexed to the Somali Republic. It would further require the attachment to Somalia of all or parts of the French territory of Afars and Issas (formerly known as French Somaliland). Two justifications are advanced for these claims: one is of European, democratic-liberal lineage—the right to national self-determination. Modern political consciousness among the Somalis has indeed resembled European forms of nationalism—in the sense of claiming independent statehood for a large ethnic group that possesses considerable cultural cohesion and is conscious of a common historical destiny. The second justification is anticolonial: the borders between Somalia and its neighbors, which were drawn by the colonial powers, are part of the colonial order that the new states should aim to overthrow.

When British Somaliland and the Italian-administered territory of Somalia attained independence in 1960, they immediately united to form the Somali Republic. The establishment of the republic was seen by nationalists as a step toward the realization of "Greater Somalia." Henceforth, the resources of the Somali state were put at the service of the nationalist struggle.

The Somali claim was viewed by Ethiopia and Kenya as more than merely threatening the loss of territory or population. The two states viewed the claim as a challenge to their very existence. Like most African states, Ethiopia and Kenya are multitribal; granting the right to self-determination or secession to any tribe or region would threaten these two countries by creating a dangerous precedent. Both Ethiopia and Kenya are particularly sensitive to such a threat. Since the early 1950s Ethiopia has been faced with the problem of separatism in the north, in Eritrea. From time to time, unrest has been reported among another important ethnic group in Ethiopia, the Gallas. Among the Christian Amharas, the dominant ethnic group in Ethiopia, all three problems evoke memories of the age-old conflict between the Christian Ethiopian state and neighboring Muslim peoples. Kenya, although not burdened by similar historical memories, is equally sensitive to the Somali challenge and concerned that any gains by the Somalis might encourage other tribes to put forth political claims of their own.

Beyond the fundamental issue—that is, the Somali challenge to Ethiopia's and Kenya's integrity as states—several additional factors have contributed to the dispute between Somalia and its neighbors. Periodic clashes between local Ethiopian and Kenyan authorities and nomadic Somali tribesmen, who cross from the Somali Republic into Ethiopia and Kenya in search of water and grazing areas, have contributed to the vehemence of Somali demands. Conversely, the belief that the disputed territories contain valuable mineral deposits has strengthened Ethiopian and Kenyan opposition to Somali claims. Yet, these factors merely helped to heighten feelings on both sides. They are not root causes.

The conflict is rooted in the incompatible self-images of the parties and concerns what Kenneth Boulding has termed "core values."[2] The self-image of Somali nationalism—of the Somali tribes constituting a Somali nation entitled to form its own nation-state—cannot be realized without inflicting severe injury on both Ethiopia and Kenya. The viability of these two states is contingent upon the acceptance of the legitimacy of their present boundaries by all tribes presently incorporated within them. And conversely, as long as Ethiopia and Kenya continue to exist within their present boundaries, the Somali aspiration for national unity within a nation-state cannot be realized. Thus, the conflict arises out of the incompatibility of the most fundamental values of the parties concerned—the essence of their national existence.

The conflict over Somali claims to the French territory of Afars and Issas, although involving vital interests, concerns values that are essentially different in level of importance. Several disputes are interwoven in this problem. One is between Somali nationalism and France, which retains control over this territory. Another is the parochial competition between the Issas, a Somali tribe, and the Afars, who are not of Somali stock. Each group constitutes a little over 40 percent of the territory's population, and the two compete for dominant status in the territory. But the most significant conflict is between Somali and Ethiopian claims for succession to the territory in the event of French

---

[2] K. Boulding, *Conflict and Defense* (New York: Harper & Row, 1963), pp. 311–312.

withdrawal. The port of Djibouti is Ethiopia's most important outlet to the sea. On this ground, as well as on the ground of affinity between Ethiopian tribes and the Afars, Ethiopia has claimed the territory. In the Somali view, on the other hand, the territory is part of the national homeland. Yet, notwithstanding the importance both sides attach to this territory, the Ethiopian-Somali conflict over Djibouti is altogether different in nature from the fundamental clash between Somali nationalism and Ethiopia's integrity as a state.

The Environment

In analyzing the environmental factors that have influenced the course of the dispute, we may conveniently use the distinction between factors within the domestic environment and those external to it. However, instead of making a comprehensive inventory of the environment, we shall focus on those elements that appear to have influenced the course of the dispute: from "pure" diplomacy to the introduction of force, and the subsequent de-escalation and détente. Most important among the domestic elements were the aridity of the country and the Somalis' nomadic way of life, the military capabilities of the parties, and the character of their internal politics. The principal external influences stemmed from the African environment and from the great powers.

THE DOMESTIC ENVIRONMENT

The arid nature of the country and the pastoral economy of the nomadic Somalis are undoubtedly the most imposing environmental features. To a considerable extent they condition Somali behavior in the conflict, for the livelihood of many influential tribes depends on seasonal migrations across the border into Ethiopia.

This dependence on water and grazing areas in Ethiopia has often led to clashes between Somalis and the Ethiopian authorities, for the nomadic tribes resented Ethiopian attempts to control and regulate their movements. It added fuel to the *shifta* (guerrilla) war and served to mobilize popular support for nationalist goals. Yet this situation also held other political potentialities. From time immemorial, Somali tribes have been competing among themselves for the scarce resources necessary for basic subsistence, a competition leading to much intertribal strife. As a result, Somali national solidarity has suffered, and some tribal groups have sought to secure access to water and grazing areas by cooperating with the Ethiopian and Kenyan authorities. Somali dependence on water and grazing areas in Ethiopia also holds out a potential possibility of cooperation in joint development of these vital resources.

The relatively undeveloped economies of the three states had multifarious consequences that in some respects restricted their capabilities to wage the conflict but extended them in others. One such consequence was that none of the three states has been capable of building and maintaining a large military establishment from its own resources. Yet this lack did not much affect Somalia's capacity to direct and sustain the *shifta* campaigns against Ethiopia and Kenya. The financial cost of the guerrilla war was relatively low, and the weapons and human resources were easily available. Yet, to the extent that the Somalis considered the possibility that Ethiopia or Kenya might react by attacking the Somali Republic, Somalia's military weakness may have acted to restrain Somali offensive action.

With respect to Ethiopia and Kenya, underdevelopment tended—paradoxically—both to restrict and to extend their defensive capacity. The restriction stemmed from the requirements of waging anti–guerrilla warfare: large forces, efficient and sizable transport capabilities, and concomitant support units. Thus, such warfare both costs more and requires a more developed economic and technological infrastructure than is necessary for organizing and sustaining guerrilla harassment. In these respects, the low level of development tended to restrict Ethiopian and Kenyan capacity to wage an anti–guerrilla war. On the other hand, the unintegrated state of economy and society tended to increase the level of tolerance to damage inflicted by the external enemy. Fighting in the Ogaden did not affect life, economic activity, or politics, either in Addis Ababa or in Ethiopia as a whole. Neither did the turmoil in the Northern Frontier District (NFD) have any influence on life in other parts of Kenya. Thus, the relatively unintegrated state of the economic and social systems in Ethiopia and Kenya has helped to increase their endurance.

Domestic politics seem to have exerted greater influence on Somali conduct than on Ethiopian or Kenyan behavior. Popular participation in politics in Somalia was quite extensive under its democratic system of government. The unification issue was a fundamental tenet of a nationalist ideology that had penetrated to the most distant parts of the republic. The widespread participation in politics and the high priority accorded to the unification issue made it necessary for Somali governments to appear to be pursuing a vigorous unificationist policy. Governments were pushed toward activist positions, toward escalating the conflict, and their freedom of action in negotiations was restricted. The governments' desire to increase their popularity, or to win an election, may indeed have been responsible for several incidents and flareups.[3] Yet, if this was the general pattern of the influence of domestic politics upon the behavior of the Somali Republic in the dispute, then the success of Prime Minister Egal in initiating and pursuing a policy of disengagement and détente, contrary to the apparent dynamics of Somali politics, raises a question which requires explanation; we shall return to it.

In trying to assess the influence of domestic politics on Ethiopia's and Kenya's behavior in the conflict, we may distinguish between two kinds of influence. In both Ethiopia and Kenya, the basic posture of uncompromising opposition to any secessionist movement or irredentist claims is dictated, of course, by the sociopolitical structure of the two states, which made it incumbent upon them to react sharply to any separatist challenge. Beyond this basic concern, however, the behavior of Ethiopian and Kenyan governments in the conflict seems not to have been much influenced by considerations of domestic politics. Ethiopia has little popular participation in politics; hence, the question of popular pressures influencing government policies did not arise. There is, of course, considerable politicking among the insiders within the establishment; yet there is no evidence that policy on the Somali problem was an issue in these political contests. Popular participation in politics is more widespread in Kenya than in Ethiopia, and an organized opposition had been relentless in attacking government policies. Significantly, however, the government's Somali policy was not criticized. Apparently, both government and opposition groups felt that popular interests and concerns could be aroused more easily by such issues as unemployment, landlessness, tribal favoritism, and neocolonialism than by the question of Somali secession.

It is difficult to assess to what extent idiosyncratic factors affected government policies. In Ethiopia and Kenya the same personalities have remained in power since the onset of the conflict. In Somalia several changes have taken place. The phase of diplomatic prelude to the conflict coincided roughly with Abdillahi Issa's tenure as prime minister (1956–1960). Indeed, Prime Minister Issa was occasionally criticized for his moderation, and this criticism may have contributed to his replacement. In 1960 the premiership was assumed by Abdirashid Ali Shermarke; launching of the Somali guerrilla campaigns in Ethiopia and Kenya is associated with his tenure as prime minister. In 1964 Shermarke was replaced by Abdirazaq Haji Hussein. While Hussein continued to support the guerrilla movements, he was more selective than his predecessor in extending support, and thus he suc-

---

[3] A. A. Castagno, "The Political Party System in the Somali Republic," in J. S. Coleman and C. Rosberg (eds.), *Political Parties and National Integration in Tropical Africa* (Berkeley and Los Angeles: University of California Press, 1964), p. 548 and *passim*.

ceeded in establishing tight governmental control over the activities of the Somali *shiftas* in Ethiopia and Kenya. In 1967 Shermarke was elected president of Somalia. Shortly afterward, Prime Minister Hussein was replaced by Mohammed Haji Ibrahim Egal. The initiative for disengagement and détente, marking a major shift in Somali policies, was to a significant extent Egal's personal accomplishment. Thus, the record suggests that the personality of the Somali prime minister has made a great deal of difference to policy-making.

THE EXTERNAL ENVIRONMENT

Among the elements of the external environment, Pan-African ideology was probably the most pervasive. Yet Pan-Africanism contains many ideas and is open to different interpretations. One cardinal principle of Pan-Africanism is African solidarity. No doubt the desire to demonstrate solidarity with other African states has affected the policies of all three governments and has generally had a restraining influence upon them. Pan-African solidarity was reflected, for example, in Somali propaganda and in official justifications of Somalia's irredentist policy, placing the main burden of responsibility for the conflict on Britain, and on colonialism in general, and ascribing only a secondary role to the Ethiopian and Kenyan leadership. Self-restraint was also evident in Ethiopia's policy: Ethiopia had the capacity to inflict heavy punishment on Somalia, in retaliation for Somali support of the *shiftas*. That Ethiopia refrained from doing so can be attributed in part to self-restraint stemming from the desire to conform to the norm of solidarity and thus become eligible for a leading role in the Pan-African movement.

Yet the dedication of the three governments to Pan-African solidarity was not enough to prevent escalation of the conflict. In fact, several ideals of Pan-Africanism provided weapons in the struggle. The Somalis argued that their campaign for self-determination for the Somali inhabitants of Ethiopia and Kenya, and for the revision of colonial boundaries, was in accord with Pan-African ideals. On the other side, Ethiopia and Kenya invoked Pan-Africanism in support of the status quo. They criticized the Somali government for violating African solidarity by raising an issue that was bound to cause bitter conflict between Somalia and its neighbors and might threaten peace in Africa in general by stimulating boundary claims elsewhere as well.

The parties exerted considerable efforts in trying to win the support of inter-African organizations and conferences for their policies.[4] In

---

[4] For further details see S. Touval, "The Organization of African Unity and African Borders," *International Organization*, 21, no. 1 (1967). See also S. Touval, *The International Politics of African Boundaries* (forthcoming), chaps. 5 and 6.

the diplomacy of conferences and organizations, Somalia had few successes. Pronouncements expressing support for Somali aspirations came mainly from nongovernmental meetings, such as the Second All-African People's Conference at Tunis, in January 1960, and the Moshi Conference of the Afro-Asian Peoples Solidarity Organization, in February 1963.

Ethiopia and Kenya were more successful. Their interests apparently coincided with the interests of the majority of African states, which sought to strengthen their security and stability by establishing a general norm that existing boundaries must be respected. This common interest enabled Ethiopia and Kenya to bring about the adoption of the resolution by the Organization of African Unity (OAU) Summit in Cairo in July 1964, pledging African states "to respect the borders existing on their achievement of national independence." A similar call was issued by the summit of non-aligned states in Cairo in October 1964. Yet, significantly, because of the reluctance of African states to become engaged, the conferences refrained from expressing themselves on the merits of the specific dispute.

The OAU also made some feeble gestures aimed at reconciling Somalia with its neighbors. However, the member-states' fear of involvement, and, paradoxically, their desire not to hinder the OAU's capacity to promote solidarity, inhibited the organization in its peace-making efforts. The OAU confined itself to adopting resolutions calling on the parties to settle their dispute peacefully.

In assessing the effect of the OAU on the Somali dispute, it is useful to distinguish between the organization's formal acts and its other effects. The formal acts had very little impact. The most that could be said about the resolutions is that they probably gave the Somali government a sense of isolation, and in the long run this sense of isolation may have influenced Somali policies. A more important effect of the organization on the dispute was that it provided a place where representatives of the states involved could meet informally and explore each other's attitudes.

The same policies that were followed by the African states within the framework of the OAU were followed by them in bilateral contacts with the three states involved in the dispute. Generally, they sought to avoid any involvement or commitment and to preserve their neutrality.[5] There were a few exceptions. Among the states that frequently lent diplomatic support to Somalia, and that supplied some military aid, was Egypt, which has also been an important source of technical and

[5] For a more detailed discussion see Touval, *The International Politics of African Boundaries*, chaps. 8 and 9.

educational assistance to Somalia. Diplomatic support occasionally was rendered to Somalia also by Sudan (after 1964), Tanzania (after 1965), and Ghana (until 1966). Yet the support lent by these states was sporadic and reflected periodic convergence of interests rather than support of Somali territorial claims. Egypt's support of Somalia served to promote Egyptian influence in an area that has traditionally attracted Egyptian interest: the sources of the Nile and the southern entrance to the Red Sea. Egyptian support helped to promote Egyptian influence in Somalia, and it prompted Ethiopia and Kenya to lend an attentive ear to Egyptian views. Sudan's cooperation with Somalia was the consequence of tensions between Sudan and Ethiopia over Sudanese suspicions that Ethiopia was helping the southern Sudan rebels and Ethiopian suspicions that Sudan was helping the Eritrean secessionists. Tanzania lent support to Somalia following a period of gradual estrangement between Tanzania and Kenya. Ghanaian support for Somalia was limited to the few situations where it appeared that the Somali position coincided with Nkrumah's conceptions of African unity.

Ethiopia and Kenya received in 1963 and 1964 support from Kenya's east African neighbors, Tanzania and Uganda. This support stemmed from their long-term association with Kenya, dating from the independence struggle. Ethiopia's position on the question of the French territory of Afars and Issas was generally supported by the French-speaking African states. But their support probably stemmed more from their closeness to France than from any identification with Ethiopian interests in Djibouti. (For Ethiopia's and Kenya's capacity to wage the conflict, more important than the political support of various African states was their mutual defense alliance. The alliance, concluded in 1963, served to coordinate anti–guerrilla measures as well as political moves.)

States outside of Africa adopted neutral policies and generally adhered to them, particularly at moments of crisis. Thus, at the height of Somali-Ethiopian fighting in January and February 1964, the Soviet Union sent deputy foreign minister Jacob Malik to Addis Ababa and Mogadishu; he called on the Ethiopian and Somali governments to solve their dispute peacefully. The Chinese prime minister, Chou En-lai, happened to visit the area at the same time, and he also proclaimed his country's neutrality. The Soviet and Chinese refusal to take a stand on the merits of the dispute was repeated on subsequent occasions. Similarly, the Western powers refrained from taking a stand and adhered to a neutral policy.

The effect of the proclaimed neutrality of the Soviet Union, the United States, and Britain was greatly diminished by their involvement as suppliers of military and economic assistance to the parties.[6] (Chinese aid to Somalia, besides arousing Ethiopian and Kenyan suspicions, did not affect the dispute to any significant extent.) Since the early 1950s the United States has been the principal source of both economic and military aid to Ethiopia. Kenya concluded a defense agreement with Britain after it attained independence, and within the framework of this agreement Britain supplied substantial military assistance to the country. Britain was also a major source of economic aid to Kenya. Somalia's initial sources of economic and military assistance were Italy, Britain, and the United States. In 1963 Somalia decided to accept a Soviet offer of military assistance, which enabled it to greatly expand its armed forces, preferring the Soviet offer to a smaller one made jointly by the United States, Italy, and West Germany. Since then the Soviet Union has assumed the role of main supplier of assistance to the Somali army, while the United States has continued to aid the police force.

The assistance received by Somalia, Ethiopia, and Kenya from external powers led to substantial increases in their military power and their endurance in waging the conflict. To be sure, Somalia required no great resources to support the guerrilla campaign in the Ogaden and the NFD. However, the external aid Somalia received greatly strengthened the defensive capability of its army, increasing Somalia's self-confidence and assuaging Somali concern over possible consequences of Ethiopian retaliation. On the other hand, Ethiopia and Kenya were greatly assisted in bearing the heavy burden of the anti-*shifta* war. Thus, external assistance encouraged Somali daring, on the one hand, and provided the means for Ethiopian and Kenyan successes, on the other.

The economic and military aid flowing to the three parties also had political consequences. These were asymmetric. In Somalia a feeling grew that the Soviet Union was an ally, actively supporting Somali aspirations, despite the USSR's formal neutrality. In Ethiopia and in Kenya, however, no parallel feelings developed about the United States and Britain. While their assistance was acknowledged and appreciated, no confidence developed in the long-term reliability of their aid or in the stability of their policies.

[6] M. J. V. Bell, *Military Assistance to Independent African States;* D. Wood, *The Armed Forces of African States;* J. L. Sutton and G. Kemp, *Arms to Developing Countries, 1945–1965* (all published by the Institute for Strategic Studies, London, as Adelphi Papers, no. 15 [December 1964], no. 27 [April 1966], and no. 28 [October 1966] respectively). For some further information on British aid to Kenya see Great Britain, House of Commons, *Parliamentary Debates,* 695, cols. 176–178 (written answers), June 3, 1964.

The United Nations was relatively passive in the conflict. The UN refrained from intervening because African states asked it not to; they wanted African disputes to be handled within the African family.

Escalation and Disengagement

The influences of the environment are more apparent in the process of disengagement than in the escalation of the conflict. Escalation may have been more a consequence of the dynamics of interaction among the parties and of internal psychological stimulants than a result of environmental influences. Since the initiative for both escalation and deescalation came from the Somali side, we shall direct our attention to the factors influencing changes in Somali policies, and limit our examination of Ethiopian and Kenyan policies to an assessment of their responses to the Somali initiatives.

The evolution of the conflict can be divided into three main phases: diplomatic prelude, confrontation, and disengagement. The diplomatic prelude began in 1943 with the formulation of the unification goal by the Somali Youth League (SYL), the principal nationalist party in Somalia. Somali diplomatic efforts were pursued by means of two parallel approaches. One aimed at obtaining partial satisfaction of Somali goals through the instrumentality of the former colonial powers, Italy and Britain. The other sought to engage Ethiopian and Kenyan leaders in a direct debate, aimed at softening their opposition to Somali goals.[7]

Both diplomatic approaches were disappointing. Talks between Italy and Ethiopia concerning the long-disputed Somali-Ethiopian boundary ended in a stalemate in 1960. Somali attempts to obtain Kenya's Northern Frontier District from Britain, before Kenya's independence, also failed, and as a result Somalia severed diplomatic relations with Britain in 1963. Contacts between Somali leaders and the Ethiopian emperor, and between Somali and Kenyan leaders, also failed to advance the Somali cause.

The second phase in the conflict saw direct confrontation between the parties. The confrontation was marked by the launching of guerrilla campaigns in the Ogaden region of Ethiopia and in the NFD. The military confrontation was accompanied by a diplomatic campaign in which both sides tried to win the support of African states

[7] For further details see Drysdale, *The Somali Dispute,* pp. 100–158; Lewis, *The Modern History of Somaliland,* pp. 183–193; Touval, *The International Politics of African Boundaries,* chap. 10.

and African conferences and thus create an environment favorable to their viewpoints and objectives.

It seems reasonable to assume, although no proof is available, that the guerrilla campaigns were initiated as a result of deliberate decisions made at the highest level of the Somali government. Both guerrilla campaigns were launched following the failure of attempts to exact concessions from Ethiopia and Kenya by diplomatic means. Guerrilla action against Ethiopia began in 1960, with Somalia's independence, and against Kenya in 1963, on the eve of Kenya's independence. Thus, the decisions to initiate guerrilla activity can be regarded as identifiable turning points or thresholds of escalation.

Both decisions were influenced by emotions. But to the extent that the decisions reflected a rational calculation of ends and means, they were motivated by the desire to improve Somalia's bargaining position. Somalia hoped that the guerrilla activity would serve to awaken doubts in Ethiopia and Kenya about their ability to retain effective control of the Ogaden and the NFD, and indicate to them that their uncompromising stand entailed both risks and heavy costs. In addition to the direct pressure Somalia wished to exercise, the Somalis hoped that the insurrections in the Ogaden and in the NFD would attract international attention, which would amount to indirect pressure on Ethiopia and Kenya.

It was probably not difficult for the Somali government to reach the decision to initiate guerrilla action. Commitment to the goal of national unification was strong among both the leading politicians and the population at large. The international atmosphere of the early 1960s, which was marked by a general upsurge of radicalism, was in accord with the Somali mood. Somali self-confidence was reinforced by the image of Ethiopia as suffering from severe internal weaknesses. The Emperor was believed to be unpopular among the elite because of his autocratic methods, and separatist sentiments were thought to be ripe not only in Eritrea but also in other parts of Ethiopia. In these circumstances the failure to obtain satisfaction by pure diplomacy led to the resort to force. The attempted coup against the Emperor in December 1960 tended to confirm the Somali image of their adversary and encouraged them to persevere in the new policy they adopted.

Once the Somali government adopted the policy of guerrilla action against Ethiopia, the extension of this policy to Kenya followed quite naturally. The escalation was no doubt stimulated by disillusionment over Britain's refusal to satisfy Somali claims for the NFD. In addition, the policy was motivated by expectations of gain, similar to those which motivated Somali policy with respect to Ethiopia. The Somali image of Kenya as torn by tribal strife encouraged the policy of guerrilla warfare. Somalia was further emboldened by the conclusion of the military aid agreement with the Soviet Union.

Somalia's decision in 1967 to disengage from the conflict, terminate guerrilla activity, and normalize relations with Ethiopia and Kenya was probably much more difficult to make. It amounted to a major reversal of previous policies.[8] Somalia, to be sure, denied that that policy had been reversed. The declaration of respect for the territorial integrity of its neighbors was represented as nothing really new, since Somalia had accepted this principle by adhering to the charters of the United Nations and the OAU. Furthermore, Somalia never admitted that it was aiding the *shiftas*. Thus, it did not have to explain the cessation of *shifta* action. But even if the view is accepted that no reversal of policies occurred, priorities seem to have been reordered, and the means by which the Somali government pursued its objectives seem to have been modified.

What brought about these changes? The Somali initiative for disengagement and normalization of relations with its neighbors seems to have resulted partly from cumulative processes and partly from the Arab-Israeli war of 1967. The cumulative processes were both negative and positive. On the negative side, the cumulative effects of attrition became increasingly more pressing. The Somali populations of the Ogaden and the NFD began to break under pressure of Ethiopian and Kenyan anti–guerrilla measures and gradually ceased to provide the *shifta* with the local support they required. Furthermore, the Somalis of the territory of Afars and Issas began to pay a heavy price for their support of Somali nationalism. Diplomatically, Somali policies did not evoke sympathy from other states, but rather tended to isolate Somalia. The economic burden of the policy of confrontation also pressed heavily, despite massive foreign assistance, because it necessitated continuing diversion of resources to the maintenance of a greatly expanded army. In addition, the closing of the Ethiopian and Kenyan borders began to hurt; it interfered with seasonal migrations of nomadic tribes in search of water and grazing areas. The border closing also reduced trade drastically between Somalia and its neighbors; this trade, although relatively small in monetary value, affected the livelihood of additional groups in the population. In these circumstances, frustration began to set in. Suspension of the conflict and normalization of relations promised to relieve Somalia of the difficulties brought about by the confrontation policy.

[8] For a detailed discussion see R. Thurston, "Détente in the Horn," *Africa Report*, 14, no. 2 (February 1969); Touval, *The International Politics of African Boundaries*, chap. 12.

Collaboration with Ethiopia and Kenya also promised some positive advantages to Somalia. Normalization of relations with Kenya was believed to be the key to Somalia's association with east African regional organizations for joint services and economic cooperation. Somalia's air communications would also be greatly facilitated by linking Mogadishu to Nairobi, thus adding this major intersection of air routes to the Cairo and Aden lines.

The Somali initiative for a détente can be attributed partly to the effect of the Arab-Israeli war of 1967. The war shook Somalia's self-confidence. The ineffectiveness of Soviet support for Egypt, and the Soviet Union's failure to intervene on Egypt's behalf, cast doubt on the reliability of the implicit alliance that many Somalis believed to exist between the Soviet Union and Somalia. The outbreak of the war, which exemplified a process of escalation resulting from guerrilla warfare, also invited reflection. Finally, the closing of the Suez canal brought about a worsening in Somalia's economic position and made it more difficult for the USSR to supply assistance.

Gradual changes on the Somali side and the sudden impact of the Six-Day War explain why a policy of détente now appeared advantageous to the Somalis—but these factors do not account for the facility with which this policy was put into effect. It is usually assumed that détente is greatly hindered by domestic pressures, which restrict the leaders' freedom of action. Underlying this assumption is the idea that détente is more vulnerable to criticism than policies of firmness toward the adversary. Indeed, in the Somali case, the political structure, the intense and widespread commitment to nationalist and irredentist ideology, and the wide participation of the population in politics tended to restrict the government's freedom of action.

The government gained the necessary room for maneuver by a combination of circumstances. In June 1967 elections took place in Somalia and Dr. Abdirashid Ali Shermarke was elected president. A new government headed by Mohammed Haji Ibrahim Egal, was formed. It was disposed to demonstrate its newness and freshness by breaking with policies and practices of its predecessor. President Shermarke's impeccable nationalist-radical reputation, won by concluding the military-aid agreement with the Soviet Union in 1963, reflected on Prime Minister Egal's government. Furthermore, Egal's government was based on broader parliamentary support than had ever been enjoyed by a Somali cabinet: it was confirmed by a majority of 119 out of 124 members of the National Assembly. To be sure, the policy of détente led to a revolt within the ruling Somali Youth League (SYL). This internal struggle within the SYL was the significant contest, and it ended by squashing the prospect of any opposition to détente. Opposition parties, because of their narrow tribal base, were not powerful. Even so, the two most important opposition groups in the National Assembly supported the government's policy of détente.

The government's freedom of action was greatly increased by its ability to control the guerrillas in the Ogaden and the NFD. The effectiveness of the government's control is reflected in the decline of guerrilla activity timed to precede the Somali diplomatic initiative in September 1967 and the tapering off of subsequent activity. Announcements by the guerrilla movement supporting the government's policy of détente and condemning those opposed to it are other indications of the close control exercised by the government.

The success of the policy of détente was made possible by the support given it, and the new Somali government, by the great powers. The US was at various times actively involved in attempts to reconcile Somalia with Kenya and with Britain. Since the dispute had served to introduce Soviet influence into Somalia, through the Soviet-Somali military-aid agreement, the US probably expected a détente to help diminish Soviet influence. Britain, for its part, hoped that following the normalization of Somali-Kenyan relations, diplomatic relations between Britain and Somalia would be restored. Indeed, agreement on the resumption of relations was reached in December 1967.

From the Communist side, the Soviet Union also seems to have favored a détente. Since the Soviet connection was regarded in Somalia as an implicit alliance, the Soviet Union preferred the tension to subside so it would not again be placed in an embarrassing situation, as it had been with respect to the Arab-Israeli war of June 1967. It seems significant that the Soviet Union came to the defense of Egal and his policy when détente encountered criticism in Somalia. At this critical moment, the Soviet Union issued a statement praising the new government's policy and criticizing former Prime Minister Hussein's government for "squandering" 30 percent of the national income "on dead-end policies in violation of OAU decisions."

The Somali initiative could have failed had it not been conducted with exceptional diplomatic skill. Analysis of the Somali initiative suggests that the scenario and the tactics were very carefully planned. In launching their new policy, the Somalis made skillful use of intermediaries. Prime Minister Egal took advantage of opportunities for personal contact provided by the OAU Summit Conference at Kinshasa in September 1967 to approach Ethiopian emperor Haile Selassie and the leader of the Kenyan delegation, Vice-President Daniel arap Moi. Thus, the OAU performed an important function by providing an opportunity for the parties to meet. When Somali-Kenyan talks reached a deadlock, Prime Minister Egal asked President Kaunda of

Zambia to intervene. Kaunda was indeed successful in persuading the Kenyan leaders to moderate their position, and agreement was reached on the Kinshasa Declaration, which expressed the two governments' "desire to respect each other's sovereignty and territorial integrity" and undertook to resolve their differences by negotiation. Kaunda performed similar services through later stages of Somali-Kenyan negotiations.

Yet the détente was made possible not by President Kaunda's talents as mediator, nor by any "breakthrough" in formulating a declaration acceptable to both sides. The parties were not far from a similar formula at an abortive conference in 1965. But in 1965 suspicion and total lack of confidence among the adversaries were major obstacles. In 1967 Somalia made a special effort to overcome this obstacle and to convince its adversaries of the sincerity of its intentions. A most important signal was the marked diminution of guerrilla activity, and the suspension of anti-Ethiopian and anti-Kenyan propaganda over Mogadishu radio, *before* the Kinshasa conference. Somalia indicated the seriousness of its intentions also by pushing aside a three-year-old controversy about the venue of Ethiopian-Somali talks and making the gesture of sending a high-level delegation to Addis Ababa. Furthermore, in order to avoid the suspicion that it was trying to disrupt the Ethiopian-Kenyan alliance, Somalia approached Ethiopia and Kenya simultaneously. The Somali endeavor to make parallel progress with both adversaries was a lesson drawn from Somalia's failure to reach an agreement with Kenya in 1965, when Ethiopia acted as a brake, hindering the Kenyan-Somali negotiations.

The détente in Somali-French relations over the Afar and Issa territory was a necessary corollary of the Somali détente with Ethiopia. Indeed, it was a condition for the success of the whole détente policy, for a continuation of activist Somali policies on Djibouti would have undermined the understanding with Ethiopia. This, in turn, would have endangered the détente with Kenya. The disputes were interrelated, and to be successful the policy of détente had to embrace all three of Somalia's neighbors.

Somalia was probably encouraged to mend its relations with France by the prospect of additional benefits likely to follow from such a policy: the abatement of anti-Somali measures in the Afar and Issa territory, French economic aid, and French good will in the EEC, of which Somalia was an associate member.

The personalities of the main actors seem to have facilitated negotiations. This is suggested by the differences in the personalities involved in these successful negotiations as compared with those who took part in the abortive 1965 Somali-Kenyan talks. On the Somali side, the negotiations were conducted by Prime Minister Egal, whose British cultural background probably helped him to establish rapport with the Kenyan leaders. (His predecessors in 1965 hailed from Italian Somaliland.) The principal Kenyan negotiator was Vice-President Daniel arap Moi, whose judgment on the Somali problem Kenyatta seemed to trust more than that of his predecessor, who was sometimes suspected of being too much influenced by the Somalis. As for the mediator, President Kaunda enjoyed an advantage over President Nyerere of Tanzania, who performed this role in 1965, and whose relations with Kenyatta were not always smooth.

The Somali initiative would not have succeeded, however, had Ethiopia and Kenya not cooperated. Since disengagement meant, in fact, that Somalia was suspending its efforts to change the status quo, it did not require modification in Ethiopian and Kenyan basic attitudes. Kenya, however, made a minor concession; it stopped insisting that Somalia explicitly recognize the NFD as "an integral and *de jure* part of the Kenya Republic." Furthermore, since disengagement promised to relieve Ethiopia and Kenya from the burdens of the anti-guerrilla warfare, they had good reason to respond favorably to the Somali initiative and, indeed, to help the Somali government to overcome domestic opposition to the new policy.

For reasons of domestic politics, Somalia claimed that the agreements contained two major gains. First, Kenya and Ethiopia "now explicitly recognize the existence of a dispute and both have expressed willingness to try to find ways of solving it." Second, Somalia now "had a say" by way of "consultation" in the affairs and administration of the NFD and the Ogaden. That Ethiopia and Kenya refrained from challenging these interpretations should be attributed not to their agreement with them but to their desire not to hinder acceptance of the new policy in Somalia. Kenya's cooperative attitude and understanding for the domestic political needs of the Somali government was also indicated by Kenya's lifting the state of emergency in its northeastern province on March 15, 1969, a change timed to occur ten days before the Somali general election. Since the Somali Prime Minister had earlier justified his policy by claiming that it helped alleviate the plight of Somali populations in Ethiopia and Kenya, the timing of the Kenyan move seems significant.

The Instability of Détente

It would probably be overoptimistic to hope that the détente which began in 1967 marks the effective termination of conflict between

Somalia and its neighbors. The détente created conditions under which cooperation between the parties could develop. One can even imagine the growth of an intricate network of cooperative relations and the development of vested interests in continued collaboration. Unfortunately, however, circumstances exist that may disrupt this process and cause relations between Somalia and its neighbors to revert to their previous state of conflict.

The conflict might be renewed because the basic incompatibility of the parties' fundamental goals and national self-images remains unabated. In Somalia, the nationalist ideology which envisages the ultimate unification of the Somali people within a Somali nation-state continues to reign supreme. Ethiopia and Kenya regard the realization of this goal as entailing an unacceptable injury to their national selves; they consider Somali aspirations to be a challenge to the very existence of their respective states. Ideologies and self-images may change on both sides, but such changes are gradual and slow.

If processes of change are underway, they are in danger of being disrupted by a number of factors. Probably the greatest danger to the stability of détente lies in the volatility of Somali politics. In a way, Prime Minister Egal invited pressures for the resumption of irredentist policies by raising the expectation that progress toward the realization of Somali unity can be made by the policy of détente. The coup that toppled his government in October 1969 does not appear to have been aimed at the détente with Ethiopia and Kenya. But his successors, to the extent that they continue to adhere to the policy of détente, face the danger of being accused of betraying the national interest.

A potential problem likely to put the suspension of the Somali conflict (if it lasts) to a severe test is the future of the French territory of the Afars and Issas. If France decides, for whatever reasons, to disengage from its commitments in the territory, then the Somali-Ethiopian conflict over succession to Djibouti is likely to be resumed with great fervor. And if the conflict over Djibouti is resumed, it is likely to spread to the Ogaden and to cause a chain reaction leading to the renewal of the Somali-Kenyan conflict.

The conflict may also be revived by accident. Clashes among nomadic tribesmen are part of the Somali nomads' way of life. Such a clash among Somali tribes might involve the Ethiopian or Kenyan authorities, and escalate, contributing to other pressures for the resumption of the conflict between the states.

Thus, in view of its instability, the détente might appropriately be viewed not as an event marking the termination of the conflict, but rather as a phase—a most interesting phase, perhaps—in a continuous relationship between the Somalis and their neighbors. This continuous relationship between neighbors contains elements making both for conflict and for collaboration. The particular mix of these two elements may change, and their relationships may fluctuate between different degrees of collaboration and conflict. Yet, unfortunately, for the foreseeable future the elements making for conflict are likely to predominate.

Chapter 10

Intercontinental Cooperation and Potential Conflict

Portugal and South Africa

LARRY W. BOWMAN

Portugal and South Africa have a long history of amicable but limited relations. Although many thousands of miles apart, they established substantial and important contacts in the late nineteenth century. The crucial reason that these two countries have interacted with one another for so long is, of course, Portugal's control over Angola and Mozambique—her two "overseas provinces" or colonies. Because these territories are contiguous with South Africa (or, in Angola's case, with South West Africa, which South Africa controls), it is within the southern African context that most important South African-Portuguese interaction has taken place. It is largely within this African framework that I will discuss the background and evolution of these relations.

Portuguese explorers were the first Europeans to touch the coast of South Africa and to round the Cape of Good Hope. Portugal's permanent trading and resting stations were established on the east and west coasts, thereby leaving the southern tip of the continent for later white penetration by Dutch and English settlers. The first extensive interaction between Portuguese and white South Africans came during the scramble for Africa in the 1880s and 1890s, when considerable disagreement arose over borders, especially in Mozambique. These differences, however, were largely resolved over European bargaining tables; the much more active and lasting local intercourse took a quite different form.

Gold was discovered on the Witswatersrand toward the end of the nineteenth century. From then until today, the Rand has been a lodestone for African workers seeking employment. Heavy migration from southern Mozambique to the Rand began soon after the mineral discoveries, and just after the end of the

Boer War in 1902 a Portuguese-South African convention was adopted (it has been revised several times since) that granted the Witswatersrand Native Labor Association permission to recruit an annual maximum average of 100,000 Mozambique Africans from south of 22° latitude for work in the mines. This concession was made in exchange for a South African guarantee that 47.5 percent of the sea-borne import traffic to the Rand would pass through the Portuguese port of Lourenço Marques. This pattern of labor migration has continued unchanged to the present day. It is likely, in fact, that well over 200,-000 Mozambique Africans enter South Africa each year, and their earnings have been estimated at over $50 million a year.[1]

Until the end of World War II, Portuguese-South African relations were largely limited to administering the labor agreement between South Africa and Mozambique. South Africa had few contacts with either Angola or continental Portugal. Economic development in the Portuguese colonies was almost entirely closed to non-Portuguese, and South Africa's economy was linked externally to the British empire. Politically, each country had gone its own way during World War II, and as yet little world pressure had been mounted against either country for their African policies.

In the last 25 years, and even more markedly in the decade of the sixties, this pattern of limited South African-Portuguese relations has been sharply altered, and there seems little reason to doubt that the coming years will see an intensification and broadening of their relations. The reason for this sharp break with the past is the much altered context of international politics in southern Africa. The growth of African nationalism and the movement to independence for most African countries, coupled with the fierce resistance to such trends by Portugal and South Africa, have highlighted the polarized racial situation in this part of the world. Pressure against the two countries has mounted in nearly all international bodies and has left South Africa and Portugal diplomatically (if not economically) isolated at the United Nations and in much of the world community.

---

[1] The work of Marvin Harris is crucial for an understanding of South African-Portuguese labor migration patterns. See his *Portugal's African "Wards"* (New York: American Committee on Africa, 1958) and "Labour Emigration Among the Mocambique Thonga: Cultural and Political Factors," *Africa*, 20 (January 1959), 50–66. Also of value are two South African studies: Ken Owen, *Foreign Africans: Summary of the Report of Froneman Committee* (Johannesburg: South African Institute of Race Relations, 1963), and G. M. E. Leistner, "Foreign Bantu Workers in South Africa: Their Present Position in the Economy," *South African Journal of Economics*, 35, 1 (March 1967), 30–56. The earning estimates are for the year 1964–1965 and are in the *Africa Institute Bulletin* (Pretoria), 5, 5 (June 1967), 143.

At the same time, guerrilla wars of liberation have opened in both Mozambique and Angola and no doubt will move to South Africa in time. Largely in reaction to these developments, South Africa and Portugal now find themselves intimately involved in defense and security arrangements, undertaking widely expanded trade and investment relations, and increasingly linked together in the diplomatic world. Far from guaranteeing ever closer relations between the two countries, however, the pressures upon them and the expanding relations between them may well carry not the promise of unending friendship under a situation of duress but the seeds of much potential conflict. This chapter examines the complexity of current Portuguese-South African relations and suggests possible patterns of evolution and change that may grow out of present and prospective future circumstances.

The Common Foe

The determination to maintain white supremacy and the consequences that flow from this decision provide both the most serious problem faced by Portugal and South Africa and the primary contemporary reason for their close relations. The nature of their internal policies is too well known to require analysis here. South Africa's apartheid and the theoretical nonracialism in Portugal's colonies—a nonracialism that ensures European domination—have incurred the enmity of most of the world. Within Mozambique, Angola, and South Africa, increasingly repressive measures have been used to crush internal dissent and resistance.

For more than a decade, both governments have been under pressure (from internal and external sources) to alter their supremacist policies. At the United Nations, for instance, much of the attention of the world body during the 1960s was directed toward questions of decolonization and racism. Numerous special committees, as well as the General Assembly and Security Council, annually consider resolutions and reports on the Portuguese colonies and South Africa. This pressure has been carried over to such other bodies as the International Labor Organization, the Economic Commission for Africa, and the World Olympic Committee. Where South Africa and Portugal have not voluntarily withdrawn from such organizations, they are under constant pressure to reform or leave.

In a related development, which should be briefly noted because of its immediate and long-range relevance to both South Africa and Portugal, the United Nations in May 1968 imposed full mandatory sanctions against Rhodesia's rebelling white government. Neither South Africa nor Portugal supports trade boycotts or sanctions against Rhodesia, and their assistance has been instrumental in maintaining that country's white government. Fearing that sanctions eventually might be extended to include themselves, both governments are determined to show the world that trade sanctions are an ineffective weapon for inducing political change, and for this reason they are unlikely to assist UN actions against Rhodesia.

With regard to their own position within the UN, both Portugal and South Africa follow a strict interpretation of article 2(7) of the UN charter, which states that "nothing contained in the present Charter shall authorize the United Nations to intervene in matters which are essentially within the domestic jurisdiction of any state." (Portugal insists that Mozambique and Angola are "overseas provinces" of a single, integral Portuguese state.) Since Britain asked the organization to implement sanctions against Rhodesia (not a UN member), it was not very difficult to get the UN to act in these unique circumstances. Presumably it will be much harder for foes of South Africa and Portugal to get the UN to act against a member state. For this reason, among others, both South Africa and Portugal seem committed for the present to staying within the UN. Still, the climate for both countries in most international organizations is very hostile and, barring substantial and unexpected changes in the policies of both states, this hostility seems unlikely to lessen.

United Nations pressure has been given more explicit assistance by the regional African association—the Organization of African Unity. Formed in 1963, the OAU has constantly inveighed against the continuing colonial presence of the Portuguese and the white supremacist policies of South Africa. The OAU has formed a Liberation Committee, which is supposed to raise money from member states and channel assistance to the nationalist movements operating against the southern African white states. Even though I. William Zartman has suggested that "the antagonistic relations between the system [independent black Africa] and the fringe area [white southern Africa] are one of the elements that help keep the system together," the Liberation Committee has had only limited success in raising money or achieving military aims.[2]

Other more informal regional groupings such as the April 1969 meeting of a "Summit Conference of East and Central African States on Southern Africa" have helped to sustain pressure against South

[2] I. William Zartman, "Africa as a Subordinate State System in International Relations," *International Organization*, 21, 3 (Summer 1967), 547.

Africa and Portugal. In a manifesto adopted at the end of this conference in Lusaka, Zambia, the African states put forward their basic case against the white regimes:

It is on the basis of our commitment to human equality and human dignity, not on the basis of achieved perfection, that we take our stand of hostility towards the colonialism and racial discrimination which is being practised in Southern Africa. . . . Our objectives in Southern Africa stem from our commitment to this principle of human equality. We are not hostile to the Administrations of these States because they are manned and controlled by white people. We are hostile to them because they are systems of minority control which exist as a result of, and in the pursuance of, doctrines of human inequality. . . . To talk of the liberation of Africa is thus to say two things. First, that the peoples in the territories still under colonial rule shall be free to determine for themselves their own institutions of self-government. Secondly, that the individuals in Southern Africa shall be freed from an environment poised [poisoned?] by the propaganda of racialism, and given an opportunity to be men—not white men, brown men, yellow men, or black men.[3]

Despite the intensity of the pressure and the consistency with which it is expressed in many world forums, it has clearly made little impact on the internal policies of South Africa and Portugal. Some even argue that by expressing hostility to racism, organizations and individuals only serve to harden southern African white attitudes and make matters worse for those they seek to assist.[4] In reaction to continued white defiance, the decade of the 1960s saw the development of broad-scale guerrilla wars in both Angola and Mozambique, and South African nationalists in exile have turned to assisting Rhodesian guerrillas while awaiting the opportunity to liberate their own country.

The emergence of guerrilla warfare has altered considerably the political situation in southern Africa and forced both South Africa and Portugal to reevaluate their policies. Because this reevaluation is still going on (indeed, it is at the very heart of all political speculation about the area), what the future will bring is not yet clear. It

---

[3] "Manifesto Adopted by the Fifth Summit Conference of East and Central African States on Southern Africa," (Lusaka, Zambia, April 1969); Full text published in *The Review* (Geneva), 2 (June 1969), 56–61. *The Review* is published by the International Commission of Jurists.

[4] See G. A. Mudge, "Domestic Policies and United Nations Activities: The Cases of Rhodesia and the Republic of South Africa," *International Organization*, 21, 1 (Winter 1967), 55–78. A similar argument is generally used by those who oppose the use of sanctions. Neither case is convincing.

seems apparent, however, that the emergence of sustained guerrilla conflict poses a substantial threat not only to white rule in all of southern Africa but also to South African-Portuguese relations. It is to a more careful analysis of why this apparent common threat to white rule should pose the possibility of disagreement within South African-Portuguese relations that we now turn.

Portugal's Position in Africa

The war in Angola began in 1961 and the war in Mozambique in 1964. At the beginning of 1970 both wars were still in progress, with a Portuguese expeditionary force of 100,000 troops committed to the two wars (plus 30,000 more in Guinea-Bissau). The Institute of Strategic Studies estimated the Portuguese defense budget in 1969 at $420 million (versus $305 million in 1968). These figures represent about half of the government's total budget; in 1967 Portuguese defense expenditures were 6.7 percent of her gross national product, the highest percentage of any western European nation.

Portugal is thus faced with wars that are extremely costly, by her standards, and that represent a relentless drain on her economy and citizenry (men generally serve four years of military service, and up to 25 percent emigrate to western Europe to avoid the draft). These wars show no sign of ebbing. Aside from one published lament by Salazar in the January 11, 1968, *Manchester Guardian Weekly* that "if the troubles continue very much longer, they will diminish our ability to carry on," there has been virtually no official Portuguese suggestion that the costs could not be borne or that colonial policies would have to change. The Portuguese determination to stay in Africa has been reconfirmed many times by the new prime minister, Marcelo Caetano. Those who think Caetano is likely to change Portugal's Africa policy should remember that his early career and reputation were made as a theorist of and apologist for Salazar's "New State" policies in Africa.[5]

The Portuguese have, however, made one substantial policy change that reflects their concern over the financial drain produced by the wars. They have opened the colonies to foreign economic investment. This decision was not taken lightly or happily by the Portuguese leaders. They had long run Mozambique and Angola as classical colonies—as places to unload continental Portugal's exports and as

[5] See his *Colonizing Traditions, Principles and Methods of the Portuguese* (Lisbon, 1951) and *Os natives na economia africana* (Coimbra, 1954).

suppliers of the foreign exchange necessary to make up Lisbon's chronic balance-of-payments deficit. Not until April 28, 1965, did the Portuguese do away with investment regulations (primarily that Portuguese financial interests must hold majority control in any investment venture) that had left Mozambique and Angola very undeveloped. That this decree providing "a maximum degree of security for foreign capital" and guaranteeing the "repatriation of foreign capital invested in Portugal irrespective of the date on which the investment was made" came only after four years of warfare in Angola is testimony not only to Salazar's fiscal orthodoxy but also to the fear felt that investment policy, as clearly as military setbacks, could lead to a diminution of Portugal's control over the colonies.

The dilemma felt in Lisbon was well put in an article by Austin Coates in a Johannesburg business journal:

If Portugal is to survive in Africa, she can no longer go it alone; unless she goes it alone, she may not survive. . . . Angola and Mozambique are not afraid of losing their Portuguese identity; it is Portugal who needs to be afraid of losing her identity in them.[6]

Despite the risk, Portugal took this fiscal step in the hope that Western financial interests would come into her colonies, become financially involved, and then work either indirectly or directly to support the political status quo. This policy seems to be working with considerable success. Large amounts of American and West German capital have gone into the colonies. Portugal's fears, however, have not been unjustified, and they are most often voiced with respect to the growing South African financial involvement in the two colonies.

South African economic penetration of the Portuguese colonies is extensive and growing rapidly in all economic sectors. South African companies and financial groups are moving into mining ventures (copper in Angola, iron in Mozambique), fishing industries in both colonies, citrus and agricultural projects, and into the manufacturing sector. South Africa has largely financed a natural-gas pipeline from Moambo, Mozambique, to the Rand. Most recent attention, however, has been paid to the South African involvement in two hydroelectric projects (Cunene in Angola near the South West African border and Cabora Bassa on the Zambezi above Tete, Mozambique) and to the

[6] Austin Coates, "Portuguese Roots in Africa," *Optima*, 15, 1 (March 1965), 12–13. On the Portuguese economy see Paul Chabrier and Julius Rosenblatt, "Recent Economic Developments in Portugal," *International Monetary Fund Staff Papers*, 13, 2 (July 1966), 283–353.

proposed use of foreign capital to finance the new six-year (1968–1973) development plan for Angola and Mozambique.

The Cunene scheme, half of it financed by South Africa, is a project costing over $200 million that will provide power and irrigation for much of southern Angola and northern South West Africa—an area of increasing importance to both countries because of expanding guerrilla incursions in eastern and southern Angola. Apparently South Africa is building a base and may provide manpower, supplies, and equipment to protect the Cunene site.

The Cabora Bassa scheme is one of the most ambitious and expensive single development projects in the world. It is scheduled to be the fifth largest hydroelectric dam in the world, and the largest in Africa. Construction contracts (totaling over $350 million) have been granted to ZAMCO, an international consortium consisting of West German, French, and South African interests. (A Swedish firm that had originally been included has recently dropped out because of protests over the political implications of participation.) The chairman of the consortium is E. T. S. Brown, a director of South Africa's Anglo-American Corporation, the premier financial group in all of southern Africa. Barring unforeseen circumstances, of which there may be many, Cabora Bassa is due to be completed by 1975. The entire Tete area is now a primary guerrilla target, and South Africa has recently sent troops to guard the dam site. The project itself would never have been undertaken without solid South African guarantees that she would purchase about half of the proposed 18 billion kilowatt hours of power to be produced annually (roughly twice the output of the Aswan dam).

The development plan for 1968–1973 proposes not only sharply higher expenditures in the colonies but also a far higher degree of foreign economic investment than ever before. For instance, the sources of external financing for the new plan are projected at 42.7 percent for Angola and 26 percent for Mozambique. A high percentage of this foreign investment is expected to come from South Africa. (The Cabora Bassa scheme is not included in the Mozambique figures, for its financing is entirely external.) In comparison, foreign investment in the development plans of the 1950s was on the order of five percent.

Portugal has every right to fear the growing South African involvement in Mozambique and Angola. There is reputed to be considerable unease in Lisbon over the pouring of so much capital into a single project like Cabora Bassa that will largely serve South Africa. *New York Times* correspondent Marvine Howe, writing from Lisbon, has reported that Portuguese liberals argue that the West must lend Portugal more military support in its fight against the guerrillas, if for no other reason than to keep South Africa out.[7] (Whether South Africa in fact wants to come in will be discussed momentarily.)

South Africa's strength vis-à-vis Lisbon is considerable. South Africa's gross national product is three times that of Portugal, including the Portuguese colonies. South Africa has contiguous borders with these colonies, and her own military strength is the greatest in Africa. South Africa's whites have a standard of living greater than that possible for most Portuguese in either Portugal or the colonies. Portugal has in fact become a leading source of South African white immigrants. In important respects, southern Mozambique is little more than a South African labor reservoir, port, and tourist playground. A broad economic study of Angola is presently being undertaken by an official South African delegation. Although there is much passing of official visits and many vows of mutual respect, it is interesting to note Salazar's speech of November 30, 1967, in which he dealt with relations between the Portuguese and their neighbors without even considering South Africa. There was much press speculation that Salazar was fearful that in time Mozambique and Angola would drift out of Portugal's sphere of influence and into that of South Africa.[8] Despite apparently close relations, latent tensions are deep. The tensions will become more apparent as we turn to a discussion of South Africa's foreign-policy options.

South Africa's Foreign Policy

The late 1960s saw marked changes in South Africa's foreign policy. Rebounding from the isolation felt after the Sharpeville massacre in 1960 and the withdrawal from the Commonwealth in 1961, South Africa has embarked on an aggressive outward policy particularly designed to woo neighboring black-governed states with trade and aid. South Africa has entered into full diplomatic ties with Malawi and Lesotho, and close relations exist between South Africa, Botswana, and Swaziland. "Diplomatic suburbs" are being established in

[7] Marvine Howe, "Portugal at War: Hawks, Doves and Owls," *Africa Report*, 14, 7 (November 1969), 21. On the development plan see Portugal, *Projecto do III Plano de Fomento para 1968–73* (Lisbon), esp. vol. 3. Also see the *South African Financial Gazette* (Johannesburg), Feb. 9, 1968, and *Boletim Geral do Ultramar* (Lisbon), nos. 509/510 (November-December 1967) and 511/512 (January-February 1968).

[8] The text of Salazar's speech is in *Boletim Geral do Ultramar* (Lisbon), no. 509/510 (November-December 1967), pp. 3–17. See also the *New York Times*, December 1, 1967, and the *Johannesburg Star*, December 2, 1967.

Pretoria and Cape Town so that black African diplomats can live among whites rather than in the outer-city locations reserved for resident black Africans. South Africa's trade with Zambia has expanded considerably in the aftermath of Rhodesia's unilateral declaration of independence, and South Africa is seeking increased trade and closer political links with the Malagasy Republic and with other African countries whenever the opportunity presents itself.

In light of the profound political differences between South Africa and all black-ruled states, these developments may seem astounding. Both pressures and inducements, however, are driving neighboring black states into closer, rather than more distant, political and economic relations with South Africa. Transport and labor link the internal economies of several neighboring states directly to South Africa. For her part, South Africa is willing, even anxious, to promote trade, provide capital, and make developmental loans to African countries. When South African willingness to help (the only cost being political neutrality toward South Africa's internal policy) is juxtaposed with the steady decline in American assistance to black Africa and the obvious decline of British influence and interest in the area (except in South Africa), the limited options available to African states are evident. It may well be that Western nations are deliberately abdicating responsibility for the development and growth of black-governed states in the southern part of Africa in the expectation that the burden of aid to these countries will be picked up by South Africa.

At the same time that these changes are occurring, South Africa is becoming involved in supporting neighboring white governments. She and Portugal support Rhodesia in her struggle to circumvent sanctions, and since August 1967 South Africa has had troops in Rhodesia to help combat guerrilla attacks. As I have noted, South Africa is ever more deeply involved financially in Angola and Mozambique; South African troops are known to be in Mozambique, and they may also be in southern Angola. The *London Times* of March 12, 1968, reported that regular monthly meetings are held between the military high commands of South Africa, Portugal, and Rhodesia to map out joint security planning. The Portuguese and South African defense ministers have recently exchanged visits.

Several questions obviously arise. Can South Africa anticipate continuing success in promoting *both* black friendship and white resistance to black rule in neighboring countries? If the situation in the region or the world were to change so that South Africa were forced to choose between these two policies, which would she choose? And, more narrowly, how does Portugal fit into South Africa's long-term security plans? Or—and here is a danger that Lisbon must face—can we foresee South Africa considering separate political arrangements with Angola and Mozambique essentially without reference to continental Portugal's presumed authority?

To take the last question first, at the heart of South Africa's relations with Portugal is this question: to what extent and at what cost is Portugal really committed to staying in Africa? Even with Portugal's emotional commitment, will she have the manpower and resources to stick it out if the military situation deteriorates or domestic pressure against the endless drain grows?

If Portugal's resolve wanes or her capabilities are stretched too thin, what will South Africa's reaction be? Portugal has some reason to anticipate South African support. She has fought the wars alone since 1961 and in her tenacity has given South Africa many years to develop her security forces. (South Africa's defense budget in the 1960s rose from about $50 million a year to over $400 million a year; the latter figure equals Portugal's annual outlay, and Portugal is paying for three wars.) The colonies also have two things that many South Africans desire—oil and space. The new Angolan oil fields give South Africa potential protection against worldwide petroleum sanctions, which she fears may one day come. The size of Mozambique and Angola keeps the guerrillas, for the present, hundreds of miles from South Africa. Portugal also holds out to South Africa the promise (yet to be fulfilled) that the Cunene and Cabora Bassa schemes together will lead to the emigration of up to 1.5 million white Portuguese to Africa.

There is no unanimity in South Africa, however, that the white-governed border states should be defended if their military situation deteriorates. The *Economist* of May 10, 1969, reported a current joke in South Africa: "South Africa should defend Mozambique, Angola, and Rhodesia to the last Pommie and Portugoos." [9] The implication of the joke was clear and pointed—they were worth defending only with troops from their own countries.

There is much political speculation that South Africa might be prepared to seek accommodation in the borderlands, rather than commit herself heavily to their defense. Several options are conceivable. Many local settlers in Mozambique and Angola would not be averse to making their own declaration of independence (à la Rhodesia) if they were assured of South African backing. The prospect of such backing would surely alienate Lisbon from Pretoria even if it did not do much to alter the character of the local regime. It is also suggested

[9] "Pommie" is a derogatory term for anyone of English descent, i.e., most white Rhodesians.

that the Portuguese expeditionary army might be prepared to join the settlers in a move toward independence, again outside of Lisbon's direct control.[10] If either of these possibilities were to develop, it is hard to imagine an alternative white elite in Portuguese Africa that would move to break from Lisbon without first garnering South African support. When Marcelo Caetano visited the colonies in 1969 (something Salazar never did during his 40 years in Portuguese leadership positions), he promised greater administrative autonomy for the colonies—a promise perhaps intended to cool the fires of prospective white separatism.

South Africa's recent successes in enticing neighboring black states may also lead her to think of the possibility of trying to install and support similar African moderates in Angola and Mozambique. South Africa could, for instance, promise investment at the current level in exchange for border security and the promise that guerrillas would not be allowed to operate against her borders. South Africa's economic hold within her neighboring states, and her military superiority over all of them, is so substantial that an African government would have to think a long time before declining such an offer, and an even longer time before sponsoring military incursions against South Africa. This too would leave Portugal out in the cold though South Africa might well continue to wield much of her present influence in Angola and Mozambique.

But are any of these choices likely to arise? The questions posed earlier must now be considered.

The Future

I have argued in another paper that the countries of southern Africa are linked together in an international subsystem that is most prominently characterized by the dominance of South Africa over all neighboring states and by the white-governed states' relative freedom to pursue deviant racial practices because of the inability or unwillingness of outside forces (whether the great powers, the United Nations, or even the rest of the African states) to agree on a course of action designed to alter the present situation.[11] This analysis still seems to me to be accurate and, in and of itself, provides the strongest argument for expecting that the status quo will continue.

[10] Douglas L. Wheeler, "The Portuguese Army in Angola," *Journal of Modern African Studies*, 7, 3 (1969), 425–439.

[11] "The Subordinate State System of Southern Africa," *International Studies Quarterly*, 12, 3 (September 1968), 231–261.

The present low level of Western concern for the political situation in southern Africa stems from a wide variety of causes—defense worries in the southern Atlantic and Indian Ocean regions, deep financial commitments in South Africa, South Africa's prominent position in the world gold market, Portugal's participation in NATO, inability to see international conflicts in racial terms. All these factors make it exceedingly unlikely that the Western nations will do much to alter the political situation in southern Africa. Unless the direction of coerced change can be closely controlled, it seems certain that, for the present, the Western nations would prefer to maintain the status quo.

Portugal's and South Africa's present strategies seem to be closely related to such a reading of the situation. Portugal continues to fight because NATO military aid is forthcoming and because there is no important external pressure on her to compromise. South Africa's decision to send South African white troops into the borderlands reveals a willingness to make commitments to the neighboring white countries that seems to contrast sharply with her traditional prudence in international relations. It is unlikely, however, that she would have taken this step unless she was confident that the West would not be dismayed by her external thrust. South Africa (all things being equal) clearly prefers to have white regimes on her borders, and if a few troops and a little aid will help, and no negative costs are apparent, South Africa will apparently decide to follow this course.

The guerrillas are the really important future variable in the southern African situation. They are presently active in Angola, Mozambique, and Rhodesia, with occasional sorties apparently even made into South West Africa.[12] Their presence has already had exceptional internal and external effects upon the white countries. Defense budgets have soared, Portugal has reluctantly consented to let South Africa and other states penetrate her colonies financially, and South Africa has been drawn into the defense of positions far from her own borders. These trends have clearly altered the political setting within Angola and Mozambique, where South African influence is on the rise.

It would nevertheless be rash to assume that South Africa is firmly committed to the defense of the white borderlands. The costs may be low to South Africa at the present, but the peril of a gradually

12 On the guerrilla movements see Russell Warren Howe, "War in Southern Africa," *Foreign Affairs*, 48, 1 (October 1969), 150–165; Eduardo Mondlane, *The Struggle for Mozambique* (Baltimore: Penguin, 1969), and Martin Legassick, "The Consequences of African Guerrilla Activity for South Africa's Relations with Her Neighbors" (mimeographed, 1967).

escalating, Vietnam-like commitment is present. It is possible that to avoid such a trap South Africa would pull back and look for another security stance along the lines of possible accommodations suggested earlier.

This chapter has suggested·that South Africa and Portugal face a common foe—all those who seek to supplant white supremacy. Yet far-reaching differences in military capability and economic strength, plus the advantages inherent in South Africa's geographical position, serve to make their options about the future quite different. South Africa's domination of the region, through her economic strength and her military superiority, gives her many options that Portugal does not possess. She can use the carrot of aid and development funds to buy political support (or at least political neutrality) from neighboring black states whose economic and military weakness (and lack of other options) gives them little room to maneuver. Portugal, on the other hand, has no such strength to fall back on. She has little to offer black Africa. She is already overextended; the internal conflicts in the colonies have reduced her capacity to control their future political development. It is hard to see how she will ever regain her control, which was once absolute. Indeed, Portugal is probably resigned to this fate but has chosen to fight (and to concede influence to South Africa and others) rather than seek a possible accommodation with nationalist forces that might allow her to retain long-term economic control, as Britain and France have done elsewhere.

Whether in the long run South Africa increasingly involves herself in the military defense of Angola and Mozambique or returns to a more insular policy and seeks a private accommodation with either blacks or whites in the borderlands depends upon South Africa's reading of the following factors: the potential or actual successes of the guerrillas; the West's interest, opposition, or indifference to South African expansion; and South Africa's own ability to elicit lasting good relations with neighboring black states. Although each of these factors is in a state of flux, the long-term trend for South African-Portuguese relations in the area seems clear. South Africa's influence in Mozambique and Angola is steadily growing, while Portugal can only look forward to gradual decline. In the long, long run South Africa may have to face internally the same decisions now being forced upon Portugal by the guerrillas. But speculation about this eventuality would be altogether premature. The conflicts of the 1970s will be in the borderlands, and, as we have seen, the trends here are by no means crystal clear. We will have to see how this works out before we can finally grapple with the international crisis that is South Africa alone.

The United States and Japan

DONALD C. HELLMANN

An era of close and special ties between the United States and Japan is ending. Since the conclusion of World War II, Japan has been a defense satellite of the United States, a distinctly junior economic partner, and a kind of protégé in free-enterprise democracy. In recent years, however, there has been a sharp rise in the intensity and frequency of conflict over specific issues such as military bases and trade, and new dilemmas have been posed for Japanese security by the uncertainty of future United States commitments in Asia. In consequence, delineation of Japanese-American relations has become a task reminiscent of the myth of Pandora, for the hitherto intimate and felicitous conditions of the recent past are now, and increasingly will be, tormented by the troubles of international politics in the nuclear age—for which the most appropriate cure may well be hope.

Until recently, the fundamental importance of the Japanese-American alliance was obscured by more dramatic events in east Asia and by the modest and passive role of Japan in international affairs. Two major wars on the Asian mainland, the rise of Communist China, the tensions attendant upon the liquidation of former colonial empires, and direct American military actions and commitments to contain Communism in Asia have overshadowed the infrequent conflicts between the United States and Japan and underscored the latter's almost complete security dependence. Three developments have radically changed this picture: (1) the sharply increased international weight of Japan; (2) changes in global strategy developing

An expanded version of this essay will appear in the author's forthcoming book *Japan and the New East Asian International System* to be published by Frederick A. Praeger.

357

with a more complex world order and in the wake of Vietnam; (3) rapidly growing claims by the Japanese for a more autonomous international role.

In economic terms, Japan has moved from being an impoverished and demilitarized international pariah to being the third most powerful nation in the world. Indeed, if past patterns of growth continue, by the mid-1970s Japan will have become the world's third economic superpower. In 1969 the approximate value of the GNPs of the four largest national economies were (in billions of US dollars): the United States, $932; the Soviet Union, $447; Japan, $168; West Germany, $142. According to the normally conservative estimates of the Japanese Economic Council, the main economic advisory body to the prime minister, after a 13.3 percent rise in 1970 the economy will expand in real terms at an annual rate of 10.6 percent (nominally, at 16 percent) from 1971–1975. There is general agreement that during this period the annual growth rates of the United States, the Soviet Union, and West Germany will approximate 3.5 percent, 4.5 percent, and 4.5 percent respectively. At the end of 1975 the GNPs for these countries would then be: the United States, $1,145 billion; the Soviet Union, $582 billion; Japan, $325 billion; West Germany, $185 billion. In five years the absolute size of the Japanese economy will exceed that of all of western Europe today and will have grown to almost three-fifths that of the Soviet Union. Most important, the gap between Japan and the next country, West Germany, will have become so large ($140 billion) that Japan will be more appropriately classified with the superpowers. Thus a world à trois, heretofore linked exclusively with the potential of a united Europe, will come into being in an economic sense—marking a fundamental change in the structure of the post-1945 world order. When and how this shift from economic bipolarity to tripolarity will bring corresponding increases in Japanese security capabilities is directly related to the changes that may occur in the American alliance.

Economic tripolarity will become even more pronounced if these rates of economic growth continue throughout the next decade, but the vastly superior military capabilities and concomitant global political commitments of the United States and Russia will render even a nuclear Japan a second-level power in international politics except in east Asia, where she will clearly be of the first rank. Although Japan will be able to afford both the material and the technical costs of superpower military status, her late start and the limited incentive for such a role make most improbable any effort beyond a concern for security problems in the Asian region. But even in Asia, where Japan is likely to be fully engaged in international politics, Communist China will ensure that the configuration is quadripolar rather than tripolar. Whatever the specific implications for global or regional politics, the sharply increased importance of Japan is a new feature on the international landscape to which the United States must accommodate itself.

In the Vietnam-spawned debate over American foreign policy, one of the few points on which all the participants agree is the central importance of Japan for future international stability in Asia. Japan is seen as strategically equivalent to Europe, and the extreme instability of international politics in Asia clearly creates problems for Japanese-American relations that vastly exceed those which have troubled the Western alliance during the past decade. Current security ties are mutually acknowledged to be unsatisfactory. The United States sees them as "unequal" in view of the modest scale of Japanese military commitments, and the Japanese see them as "unequal" in terms of the peculiarly dominant position held by America. The situation must change, and the risks are very high. As Herman Kahn has aptly said, "Japan, not China, will be the most important country in Asia during the next decade." Japanese-American relations may well prove to be the key for peace or war in this region.

Bilateral Relations

To an unusual degree, American policy toward Japan has given emphasis to bilateral, nonmilitary relations. Economic, cultural, and political contacts between the two countries have expanded enormously with a minimal amount of conflict. The very success of these policies has led to a curiously skewed but widely supported vision of the nature of Japanese-American relations. This vision gives scant attention to security policies (which have been predicated on quite different grounds), downplays the potential for conflict implicit in expanded patterns of interaction, and links the alliance with fulfillment of a moral (that is, democratic) potential regarding which the United States has a tutelary role. Japan's ties with the United States are in this sense very special indeed, and the basis for this relationship grows directly from the experience of the occupation.

The six-year occupation of Japan provided the United States with the opportunity to give concrete meaning to the liberal ideals for creating international peace in the name of which the war had been fought. "To insure that Japan would not again become a menace to the United States or to the peace and security of the world," the headquarters of General Douglas MacArthur instituted sweeping reforms on behalf of the objectives of demilitarization and democracy. Not only was the Japanese war machine dismantled, but Article IX of the new, American-drafted constitution renounced "war as a sovereign right of the nation and the threat or use of force in settling international disputes." With this gesture of utopian bravado, the occupation gave legal sanctity and symbolic dignity to pacifism and renounced what is acknowledged as the elemental requisite for a state's participation in international politics. Exemplifying his capacity for hyperbole and the profound idealism underlying American policy of that time, General MacArthur grandly announced, "Japan today understands as thoroughly as any nation that war does not pay. Her spiritual revolution has probably been the greatest the world has known."[1]

Concrete actions were taken to ensure that this spiritual rebirth was not chimerical. In keeping both with a New Deal style of reformist zeal characteristic of the early years of occupation and with the Wilsonian notion that defects in the internal political structure of states are the basic cause of war, a full-scale "democratization" of economic and social as well as governmental institutions was undertaken in ways that were "deemed likely to stress the peaceful disposition of the Japanese people."[2] To a degree without parallel in modern history, the United States directed a process of nation-rebuilding with the explicit aim of shaping a country's international behavior. From the outset, the American-Japanese alliance was placed on a unique level, standing as a kind of test of the most basic beliefs of the American diplomatic tradition.

America has served as a kind of political-cultural stepfather to Japan, and this role is evident in the scope and tone of American policy. Occupation reforms projected the United States so deeply into all aspects of Japanese society that most of the dramatic breaks with past political and social practices which have emerged in the postwar years are in some way seen (by Japanese as well as Americans) as "made in America." United States aid, trade, and technology have been major factors in Japan's spectacular prosperity. This development, in turn, has added meaning in that a basic theme in contemporary American diplomacy is the belief that sustained economic growth conduces to peaceful international behavior. Finally, the successful and self-conscious effort to broaden political and cultural contacts

---

[1] Supreme Command for the Allied Powers, Report of the Government Section, *Political Orientation of Japan: September 1945–September 1948* (Washington, D.C.: U.S. Government Printing Office, 1959), p. 765.

[2] John M. Maki, *Conflict and Tension in the Far East: Key Documents, 1894–1960* (Seattle: University of Washington Press, 1961), p. 129.

with the Japanese people as well as the government ("people-to-people" approach), a policy reaching its apogee during the tenure of Ambassador Edwin Reischauer, represents a diplomatic style in keeping with the occupation orientation and strengthens the paternalistic cast of bilateral relations. Like the father who rejoices in the self-image seen in a successful son, the United States has tended to see the alliance as ultimately resting on principles and political-economic conditions transcending narrow calculations of self-interest. This view has added a special glow to the successes of the past, but it has also served to place American relations with Japan on a uniquely moral plane—a position not unlike that which characterized our relations with China in the years prior to the triumph of the Communists. Any future conflicts with the Japanese will be colored by this posture, with its inherent potential for rigidity and sanctimonious overreaction that has on occasion characterized American cold-war policies.

The pervasive presence of the United States has profoundly influenced Japanese politics and the style and emphasis of foreign policy. Most basically, the greatly expanded scale of bilateral interaction has multiplied the occasions for conflict, a fact of increasing importance as Japan moves toward an international role that is politically more independent and economically more competitive. The shrill and unbroken anti-American campaigns by the Japanese Left, in which unarmed neutrality is offered as a substitute for the present policy, have ensured that every issue involving the alliance is given dramatic attention and have magnified the salience of American influence in all areas of policy. Although the Socialists have never posed a political threat to the ruling party, this obsessive concern has heightened the intensity and narrowed the focus of the Japanese foreign policy debate so that a kind of bilateral myopia regarding the United States has come to dominate. Conjunctively, the level of concern in this debate, both pro- and anti-American, has centered not so much on concrete conflicts of interest as on the grand issues of peace and democracy— matters of principle with strong emotional and ideological overlay. In a basic sense a mirror image of the American attitude toward Japan exists, for a strong moral cast underlies much of Japanese policy toward the United States—even if this policy has in fact coincided with calculated self-interest. Today, at the end of a prolonged period of intimacy during which Japan has emerged once again as a major world power, it is understandable but ironic that conservatives and leftists alike commonly measure international autonomy and nationalism in terms of movement away from the American axis.

The web of economic intercourse between the two countries places limits on any sharp change in relations and has important implications for possible political conflict.[3] On the one hand, Japan remains heavily dependent on trade with the United States. On the other, the Japanese are increasingly less dependent on international trade to maintain their economic well-being. Today Japan, like all industrial countries, has a smaller portion of its national product involved in trade than in the prewar period. In fact, Japan's imports now amount to only 8–10 percent of her GNP, a percentage well below that of most European countries. Among the basic reasons for this are the favorable downward trend of prices of primary goods that are her main imports and a shift in the economy to manufactures and services that require less import content per yen of product. This trend and the diversity in sources of import supply virtually free the Japanese from economic dependence on the much smaller states that make up east Asia—but, conversely, these nations have become increasingly dependent on Japan as their major trading partner. Decisions by the Japanese regarding trade with Asian countries cannot but have profound effects on them. Thus Japan can take a firm position toward those nations in which she has the greatest security interest.

Japan's relation with the United States is essentially the reverse of this position, which imposes an important qualification on the global trend toward tripolarity. In 1968, the United States took approximately 32 percent of Japanese exports, but this was only 12.2 percent of total American imports. Similarly, although the Japanese relied on the United States for 27.1 per cent of their imports, this constituted only ten percent of American exports. Although the volume of bilateral trade, $7.7 billion, is impressive, and Japan was our largest overseas trading partner, the asymmetry makes it inappropriate to describe this relation as one of "interdependence." A decision by the United States regarding trade may have a sizable impact on Japan without seriously disrupting the American economy. This situation provides the United States with substantial leverage for pressure on political as well as on economic matters, but it also raises the possibility of serious bilateral conflict generated by the successful lobbying of narrow interest groups in the United States, such as the textile industry. Japanese business is further tied to the United States through a large number of technical and licensing agreements, particularly in security-related industries. On the whole, however, Japan is far less affected by direct American investment than are European countries, both in

---

[3] For a general analysis covering the points that follow, see Kenneth N. Waltz, "The Myth of National Interdependence," in Charles P. Kindleberger (ed.), *The International Corporation* (Cambridge, Mass.: M.I.T. Press, 1970), pp. 207–214.

scale (totaling only slightly more than one billion dollars at the end of 1968) and in scope of control in basic industries, largely because of the highly restrictive policies of the Japanese government. Thus, despite a sharply greater capacity for independent international action as a result of economic growth, Japanese dependence on the United States market will constrain any radical *Realpolitik*. At the same time the potential for conflict will expand as Japan emerges as a major competitor of America in both international and domestic markets.

During the past two decades elaborate and highly effective channels of communication have been developed between the Japanese and American governments to deal with all aspects of their relations. For some time there have existed regularized procedures (for example, the annual consultative conferences at the cabinet level) and more irregular but long–established patterns of consultation on matters economic, military, and diplomatic. The past record of anticipating and diffusing potential conflicts constitutes a significant legacy for the future. Bilateral relations, however, have proceeded successfully not so much because of effective bargaining techniques, but because of an essential congruence of interests on matters of defense as well as nonsecurity issues. Indeed, if the past is a guide to the future, the question of security ultimately will define the nature of American-Japanese relations. This issue, of necessity, transcends direct relations between the two countries, encompassing the global commitments of the United States and the rapidly shifting tides of international politics in east Asia.

Japanese and American
Security Roles in Asia

The guidelines of past American security policy toward Japan cannot serve as the basis of the future alliance. Most basically, the strong commitment of the United States to active military support of non-Communist nations on the Asiatic mainland will no longer be tenable during the next decade. This is peculiarly significant for Japanese-American relations, for past security policy toward Japan has been determined not by bilateral considerations but by the general American policies toward containing Communism in east Asia. Consequently, any limitation on United States commitments in Asia raises fresh questions about the automatic identity of American-Japanese security interests and the continued abstention by Japan from all concerns of military *Realpolitik* in the region. The dimensions of the problem this poses for the Japanese-American alliance are clear from a review of

Donald C. Hellmann: The United States and Japan

the past record and an examination of the probable points of conflict over major security issues currently outstanding.

American security obligations regarding Japan and east Asia have developed in a piecemeal, *ad hoc* fashion in response to the specific needs involved in meeting the threat of Communist expansion and in liquidating the wars in Korea and Indochina. The first major change in policy toward Japan occurred in 1948. With the emergence of the cold war and the mounting triumphs of the Communists in China, the United States abruptly reversed course, dealing with Japan not as a defeated aggressor and primary threat to peace but as a major and essential ally. Occupation efforts that had stressed democratization and demilitarization now emphasized political stability and economic rehabilitation. Further change came with the outbreak of the Korean war, as a cautious step toward rearmament was made by the establishment of a small "police reserve" (later the Self-Defense Forces). The integral relationship between American security policy toward Japan and general strategy toward Asia was clearly manifested in the 1952 peace treaty in which the central objective came to be not settling issues related to the Pacific war, but securing an alliance with Japan to check Communist expansion in Asia.[4] A bilateral security treaty was made effective simultaneous with the peace treaty, and provision was made in it for continued deployment of the large numbers of troops already in the country as a result of the occupation and the logistical needs of the Korean war. Thus, the foundation of the American-Japanese security alliance, as well as the attendant specific military arrangements, grew out of the vastly expanded commitments of the United States in east Asia resulting from the cold war.

Drafted in the midst of the Korean war and in the shadow of the Treaty of Friendship, Alliance, and Mutual Assistance between Russia and Communist China, the American-Japanese Security Treaty of 1952 (and the accompanying Administrative Agreement) gave emphasis to the use of American forces in Japan to meet any military threats in the region. American troops could be used in any way that Washington felt would "contribute to the maintenance of international peace and security in the Far East." Japan was prohibited from granting military bases to a third power without United States consent, and despite a pledge against "territorial aggrandizement" in the Atlantic Charter, the United States insisted on retaining control of Okinawa and various smaller Pacific islands as "strategic territories."[5] Japan

[4] Frederick S. Dunn, *Peace-Making and the Settlement with Japan* (Princeton: Princeton University Press, 1963), pp. 45–52.

[5] Prime Minister Yoshida did reject the demand of Special Ambassador John Foster Dulles that Japan play an active military role in regional defenses—a position the Japanese still support.

returned to international politics totally committed to and dependent on the Western bloc, a logical if not indispensable position in view of the international milieu and her own demilitarized and weak economic condition. However, it was a position effectively chosen by the United States, not the Japanese, and it underscored the passive and dependent nature of the Japanese role in the alliance.

Revision of the Security Treaty in 1960 occurred before the Sino-Soviet split and was again predicated on cold-war assumptions that the Communist monolith posed the security threat in Asia and that the United States bore the full responsibility of meeting and containing that threat. Although this treaty remedied some of the more glaring infringements on Japanese sovereignty (for example, responsibility for internal security was returned), and although an explicit effort was made to emphasize reciprocity and partnership, Japan remained a military protectorate of the United States, and American troops stationed there were to continue to be used to maintain international security throughout the Far East. The Japanese did seek to avoid involvement in military operations beyond their territory, but the United States would consent only to "prior consultation" (not a veto) regarding combat deployment of Japan-based American troops and the introduction of nuclear weapons in emergency situations. Almost before the ink was dry on the treaty, the United States began to promote modifications in Japanese policy more in keeping with the rapidly changing strategic realities in Asia—changes that centered on China's development of nuclear weapons following the Soviet break and the profound impact of the war in Vietnam on all aspects of international politics in the region.

During the past decade, American policy has attempted to prod Japan more fully into east Asian international affairs, while the United States has continued to deal with all military conflicts. On the most general level, the aim has been to move the Japanese into a leadership role in Asian economic and political affairs under a military "partnership" featuring an American nuclear umbrella. This policy assumed that the United States would continue to remain deeply engaged militarily in the region, both on nuclear and conventional levels, that there was and would continue to be a basic identity of Japanese and American security interests, and that the economic and political dimensions of international politics could be effectively separated from security matters. All of these assumptions are already being subjected to serious challenge.

The war in Vietnam has had a number of effects on this policy. On the one hand, the enormous military and political investments of the United States in the war, *a reductio ad absurdum* of cold-war globalism in the eyes of many critics, has created the kind of implausibly exorbitant commitment to Asian security implied in our policy toward Japan. This has prolonged the Japanese withdrawal from all concerns of *Realpolitik* and has allowed the measured but steady expansion of their own conventional forces to occur free from any tangible security threats. On the other hand, the stalemate in the war has demonstrated that the United States, despite its vast diplomatic, economic, and military resources, lacks the capacity effectively to control international conflict in the region. It has also provoked bitter divisions within the United States, forced a general reassessment of American foreign policy, and made any military ventures in east Asia in the near future highly improbable. Thus, Vietnam at once ensured the short-term success of American policy toward Japan and demonstrated the infeasibility of America's general Asian policy which involved a policeman's obligation toward conflicts in the region. No matter what may be the final solution for ending the war or the ultimate content of the so-called Nixon Doctrine, the nature of future American involvement in conventional military action in east Asia will remain uncertain. This uncertainty raises the pressure for some sort of new, regionally centered security arrangements. How Japan will become further involved in international politics in Asia is likely to prove the crucial factor determining the future of the American alliance.

Just how deeply Japan already is engaged in Asia is not properly appreciated.[6] Japan stands as the first or second trading partner of every major non-Communist nation in east Asia and takes an average of more than one-third of the trade of each nation. This vastly exceeds the position of the United States (despite the massive and temporary expenditures connected with the Vietnam war), the next most important trader, and constitutes almost 25 percent of Japan's total trade. Similarly, Japanese economic aid to east Asia (excluding South Vietnam) currently exceeds that of the United States and there are plans to expand this threefold in the next few years at a time when American support will drop off. Moreover, in recent years Japan has been drawn deeply into regional affairs through active participation in numerous international agreements and organizations, both bilateral (for example, Indonesia and South Korea) and multilateral (Asian and Pacific Council, Asian Bank). Additionally, Japan has been the leading trading partner of Communist China since 1965 and, despite a lack of diplomatic relations, has maintained the most varied and extensive relations with Peking of any non-Communist nation. Indeed, the very

[6] For elaboration on this paragraph see Donald C. Hellmann, "The Emergence of an East Asian International Subsystem," *International Studies Quarterly*, 13, no. 4 (December 1969), 421–434.

success of the Japanese in attaining a "leading political and economic role" in east Asia makes it highly doubtful whether they can continue to remain insulated from political and military *Realpolitik* in the face of the chronic instability and war in the region and a diminished American security commitment.

Whether American and Japanese security interests will in fact always remain congruent in these circumstances is *prima facie* highly dubious, but there has been a notable reluctance to acknowledge and confront this development by American strategic experts. Expanded Japanese power and American frustration in Vietnam have prompted some (for instance George Ball and George Kennan) to suggest a strengthening of our link with Japan while effectively withdrawing from any military effort to "balance power" on the Asiatic mainland. Another widely supported position urges continued alliance with a Japan transformed into a more "responsible partner" through greatly augmented conventional military capabilities. Both positions imply continued acceptance by Japan of ultimate security dependence on America, presuppose that no security threat will confront the Japanese with which the United States could not and would not deal, and presume an active but nonmilitary foreign policy by Japan. On the most general level of response, we may note Robert Osgood's remark that "it would be one of the great anomalies of history if a state with the potential power, the extensive foreign interests, and the long run security problem . . . of Japan should indefinitely entrust the military protection of its interests to another state. . . ."[7] There are two fundamental alternatives: extension of the status quo, providing Japan with "a unique opportunity to prove that a nation can be great without possessing commensurate military force";[8] or a move toward an autonomous military posture. Which alternative is more probable, and the problems this may pose for conflict within the American alliance, is suggested by considering four basic security issues currently facing the Japanese: the threat of Communist China, the defense of South Korea, the status of American bases, and the problem of rearmament.

Communist China is viewed by both Japan and the United States as the greatest security threat in Asia, but the differences in the nature of this threat for Tokyo and Washington are so significant as to be the major potential source of conflict between the two countries. Two basic considerations have underlain American efforts to isolate and militarily

[7] Robert E. Osgood, *et al.*, *Japan and the United States in Asia* (Baltimore: Johns Hopkins, 1968), pp. 14–15.

[8] Thomas C. Schelling, "Peace and Security in Asia and the roles of Japan and the United States," paper presented at the Japan–US conference, Kyoto, January 1969, p. 1.

contain China during the past two decades: the global commitment to contain Communism, and specific policies pursued to stabilize the international situation in east Asia. Ten years of polycentrism and the broadening of the Sino-Soviet split have made imperative more flexible and muted policies of containment, and the stalemate in Vietnam has made all but inevitable a great reduction in future United States military commitments in Asia. Unless exaggerated emphasis is given to the still highly conjectural Chinese nuclear threat to the continental United States, the likelihood of conflict between America and China is destined to decrease. Conversely, for Asia, and especially for Japan, reduction of the American presence will heighten the concern over security from China.

What possible security threat can the Chinese pose for Japan?[9] If the Japanese continue to limit their security zone solely to their home islands and to accept *in toto* the American nuclear guarantee, there is not likely to be a clear or present military danger to them from China, or anyone, that could not be met by their own modest conventional defense forces. Yet the Japanese government has itself acknowledged since 1965 that China (not Russia) does post a security threat to Japan, and that this threat has a nuclear dimension. Moreover, a Chinese nuclear attack would certainly not be directed *in vacuo* against Japan, but would involve Sino-Japanese conflict over an "outside issue" or the conditions of alliance with the United States; that is, it would most likely take the form of nuclear blackmail.[10] Thus a Chinese threat is tied to Japanese engagement in Asia, either through autonomous commitments integrally involving security considerations or from alliance with America. The latter alternative is increasingly less probable in view of Japan's continued strong resistance to direct involvement in American military moves and America's increased reluctance to make them. The option of total withdrawal from Asian security problems ensured by the scope of past American actions cannot be held open much longer for the Japanese. Without isolation, a real or perceived threat from China could be avoided only in the highly improbable event that international conflict is purged from Asia or that the Chinese effectively withdraw from regional politics. A Japan engaged in Asia could not be expected to depend entirely on American security policy

[9] Assume that any direct attack by the Soviet Union would automatically provoke an American response and that the Soviets will move cautiously toward expanding military involvement in Asia.

[10] Notably, Japan was the first country against which Peking directed such threats. See Morton H. Halperin, "Chinese Nuclear Strategy: The Early Post-Detonation Period," *Adelphi Paper*, no. 18 (London: Institute for Strategic Studies, 1965), pp. 12–13.

in dealing with Peking, both because of the long-term unacceptability of such dependence to the Japanese and because the vicissitudes of international politics virtually proscribe an absolute identity of interests for the two nations. The pressures for an independent military posture may well prove irresistible.

In the November 1969 communiqué announcing the American return of the Ryukyu Islands, Japan explicitly acknowledged a "special security interest" in Korea (and Taiwan). This was the first formal public statement in the postwar era implying a broadened security role for Japan, and it elicited unusually strong reactions from both the Chinese and the North Koreans. Japanese security interests in Korea are rooted in compelling geographic, economic, and political reasons. American interests are also strong, but the reversion of Okinawa in 1972, the reduction of American bases in Japan, open government speculation on the withdrawal of United States troops now defending the 38th parallel, and the still uncertain implications of an impending general military cutback in Asia all point to a reduced capacity and commitment to defend South Korea. Conjecture about the Japanese replacing the United States has been categorically rejected by both Korea and Japan and is quite unfeasible in the immediate future. Yet the persistence of the Korean security problem illustrates in clear and specific terms the pressures for an autonomous military role for Japan and the dilemmas of expanded Japanese-American security collaboration in a post-Vietnam Asia.

A major check on the outbreak of war in Korea has been the deep involvement of the United States and the Soviet Union with the respective sides. The resulting cold-war type of confrontation has brought the usual constraints found when the superpowers directly face one another. This situation is changing. Even if the United States remains ultimately committed to defending Korea, after Vietnam it is very uncertain whether a full-scale "limited war," in the style of the 1950s, would or could be undertaken. Furthermore, even if the Russians were prompted by global strategic considerations to forestall or limit any outbreak of hostilities, it is far from clear that the Chinese, who have narrower strategic interests and a more immediate concern for the military importance of Korea, would be so constrained. In any open conflict of this sort, the critical pawn in the ensuing strategic game would be Japan, a nation essential to the effective conduct of a conventional war by the United States and immediately susceptible to a nuclear threat from China. Any Chinese effort to neutralize Japan in this way would directly test the credibility of the American nuclear umbrella and, whatever the result, bring the Japanese face to face with the realities of *Realpolitik* of contemporary east Asia. This scenario, or a similar and equally plausible one, would raise basic and difficult questions regarding the status of American bases and the nature and timing of rearmament—issues that have already served as sources of conflict in the Japanese-American alliance.

No matter what formal arrangements are devised, every military crisis in northeast Asia will almost surely lead to a domestic political crisis in Japan regarding the nature and use of American bases. Beyond their strategic value these bases have peculiar importance for the political foundations of the alliance. They will continue to serve as lightning rods for anti-American protest over a variety of issues. This aspect has been given much emphasis in the past and cannot be expected to diminish as the anti-Americanism of the Left persists and as nationalist sentiment grows. It is also important to recognize, however, that American military forces stand as a symbol of United States interest in defending Japan. Any serious cutback of these forces could be interpreted as a signal of a reduction in this commitment. As suggested by the response to the reversion of Okinawa with a drastically curtailed American military presence, further policy change in this direction is bound to precipitate strengthening of the Japanese Self-Defense Forces, leaving uncertain whether this will result simply in a broadened sharing of the defense burden or provide the impetus for developing a security capacity fully independent of the United States. American nuclear weapons currently are not allowed in Japan, nor are they likely to be, but the credibility of our nuclear umbrella is linked to the commitment implicit in the presence of conventional bases. A serious reduction of them will undoubtedly accelerate the trend, now evident, toward the establishment of a Japanese nuclear capacity. Thus, on the political plane, the bases leave the United States with an unfortunate choice: retain them at the risk of stoking anti-American and nationalist sentiments; reduce them and raise the pressure for an autonomous defense policy.

Strategically, the case for maintaining the bases is increasingly weak. With the development of high-speed air and sea transport, the need for the peacetime presence of American conventional forces has evaporated. If, in fact, the bases are cut back to skeletal proportions, as is widely expected by the mid 1970s, they would become useful only in emergencies—emergencies that will almost certainly be located on the Asiatic mainland or on Taiwan, not in Japan. From the viewpoint of Tokyo, the main effect of the American forces, apart from the hostage value regarding nuclear support, will be to implicate the Japanese in military actions in Asia at a time and place not exclusively of their choosing. Despite their limited and shrinking strategic value to the

United States, a serious conflict with Japan over the bases could well arise from their specific use in dealing with one of the region's chronic security problems in the region—Korea, for instance.

Japan must develop nuclear weapons to participate effectively in power politics in Asia with China as her main rival, especially in view of the cloud of uncertainty that will surround gradual American military disengagement from the area. In the foreseeable future, the only direct military threat to Japan will be nuclear. A conventional invasion is unthinkable and, in any event, would ensure American intervention in ways that a nuclear threat (linked to another military or political act) would not. A posture that would maximize the possibility for continued Japanese disengagement from Asia, avoid the uncertainties of American nuclear support, and meet immediate, narrow security needs would consist of nuclear weapons and limited conventional forces. By strongly promoting the Nuclear Nonproliferation Treaty, the United States is raising the one security issue on which Japan may ultimately be forced to break sharply and openly with American policy —an alternative clearly implicit in the long and sharply phrased statement issued by the Foreign Ministry when Japan signed the treaty. Emphasizing the inherent inequities for the non-nuclear powers, the government made clear that ratification by Japan was contingent, among other things, on "concrete measures of nuclear disarmament ... by *all* nuclear powers." The nuclear option, in short, will be kept open, and no serious technical or budgetary obstacles stand in the way. Japanese expansion of conventional capacities, strongly encouraged by the United States, is significant not so much in terms of the marginal increment provided for defense of the home islands, but in the positive effect on the national commitment to and the technical ability for sustaining a military establishment.

International conditions require that the basis of the American-Japanese alliance change. It is appalling that in the wake of the United States' greatest foreign-policy misadventure, which unequivocally demonstrates the intractability and instability of international politics in east Asia, basic and long-term security considerations are not accorded the overriding priority they deserve in Japanese-American relations. What in the past was effectively determined by statesmen will be increasingly beyond their reach in the future. Conflicts between the two nations now seem destined to be primarily defined by the maelstrom of international events in this region beyond the control of either country. This cannot but result in a divergence of American and Japanese policies in Asia, a change that will be further abetted by the continued growth of renascent nationalism within Japan.

At first glance, there is little new either in the Japanese political situation or in the government's policies to indicate a significant shift regarding the American alliance. It is almost a certainty that the pro-American conservative (Liberal-Democratic) party will remain in power for years to come. In addition, the political rhetoric of government leaders still defines Japan's national interest largely in moral and economic terms within the framework of the American security treaty. Furthermore, despite sporadic leftist outbursts, the public mood appears to endorse this direction and low-keyed approach to foreign affairs. Yet even a glimpse beneath the surface reveals profound alterations in the entire Japanese orientation toward international politics.

Within the elite that has dominated the making of postwar Japanese foreign policy, there is now almost unanimous recognition that an immediate effort must be made to bolster the nation's military capacities. This is manifested in the emphasis given to strengthening the Self-Defense Forces, in the insistence, previously noted, on keeping open the nuclear option, and in the explicit efforts to nurture an autonomous defense industry. Just five years ago it was all but inconceivable that responsible business and party leaders would openly advocate nuclear weapons or demand revision of Article IX to allow full-scale rearmament, but this is now a reality. In the past no real policy dialogue developed because of the split between the neutralist, anti-American Left and the ruling party. Now a debate over security has developed among the conservatives, and even more significant, there is a growing consensus among the public generally, with all but the extreme left-wing of the Socialist Party agreeing on the basic premise of this debate: in order to pursue a more independent foreign policy, Japan must consider ways to strengthen her defense capabilities. Among the public, the mood of pacifism has eroded to the point that now not only are the Self-Defense Forces accepted as necessary, but 45 percent of the people in a recent poll agreed that Japan should possess nuclear weapons under certain circumstances.[11] What is significant is not any concrete commitment to rearm but the acceptance that such a commitment is more or less inevitable and a broad consensus that will allow substantial latitude for policy development in this direction.

The process through which Japanese foreign policy is made virtually proscribes any Gaullist-style defiance of the United States, and ensures a passive and reactive role for Japan in international politics.

[11] *Mainichi Shimbun,* June 13, 1969.

The fragmented structure of the ruling Liberal-Democratic party, a style of authority that requires at least tacit consensus among all the responsible participants involved in decision-making (in this case, party faction leaders), and the extreme degree to which intraparty politics has been involved in all major foreign policy moves have produced a kind of policy *immobilisme*. Bold leadership by the prime minister on major issues is not possible, rendering Japan particularly susceptible to the shifting tides of international politics. Japan's active involvement in east Asia and her future relations with the United States are likely to proceed without the moderating control that strong policy leadership could provide, and the direction and content of her policies will be defined in narrow, circumstantial terms.

Like Pandora and Epimetheus, Japan has been living in a child's paradise free from danger and conflict, thanks to the American alliance and American commitments in east Asia. Continued trust in the United States cannot perpetuate this utopia, for America demonstrably lacks the capacity of the gods to ensure international harmony. The problems of war, revolution, and uncertainty are evils conspicuously evident in the international milieu in which the United States and Japan must live. The partnership in paradise has ended, and the hope can only be that conflict will not result in unbridled competition.

Chapter 11

Social-Economic Cooperation and Conflict

Canada and the United States

K. J. HOLSTI

Canadian-American relations have been characterized in numerous ways. To most statesmen, diplomats, and students of international politics, Canadian-American relations command little attention and are certainly no matter of concern as a possible source of international crisis. To the few Americans who are aware of Canada as more than a source of raw materials and hockey players, the relationship between their country and its northern neighbor is normally described as a model of friendly cooperation and "partnership" to be emulated by other nations. Many Canadians regard the relationship with general satisfaction, although they are not unaware of dangers to Canadian "independence" brought forth by the immense American economic and cultural presence in their country. Other Canadians, assuming that political power necessarily flows from economic investment, characterize the relationship as one of domination and dependence, in which Canada may not employ independent judgment on a wide range of foreign and domestic policy issues without facing possible economic retaliation or more subtle forms of interference from the southern giant.

While the United States could undoubtedly impose its will on Canada in almost any issue area, it does not in fact do so. One way to assess the validity of the domination model is to look at the *outcomes* of various conflicts. Does the great power always get its way? A review of various controversies

Information and opinions provided by 11 senior career officials of the Canadian Departments of Finance, External Affairs, and Industry, Trade and Commerce in interviews on October 14 and 15, 1969, have been helpful and have been taken into account by the author.

between Washington and Ottawa in recent years suggests that the model is inadequate in its descriptive, explanatory, and predictive capacity. The outcomes of various conflicts have been mostly (1) mutually acceptable, negotiated compromises, (2) avoidance or "passive settlements," where each government, after spelling out its position, ignored the obvious conflicts of interest, or (3) the granting of rather significant exemptions and favors by each country to the other. The outcomes, which have generally been as favorable to Canada as to the United States, must be understood as the result of a relationship that is much more complex than either the "partnership" or "domination" models portray.

Several considerations inhibit the United States from exploiting its potential for domination, including the fear of world opinion—other allies would immediately begin to look upon the United States with suspicion—and the recognition that in the long run an independent and friendly Canada is more valuable and reliable as an ally and trading source than one which is dominated and frustrated. Americans apparently are conscious of their potential for harm and go out of their way in most instances to treat Canadians as "respected partners." The peculiarities of the Canadian-American "diplomatic culture," to be discussed below, also inhibit certain types of behavior that would be found in many relationships between great powers and dependencies.

Yet one can also portray hypothetical situations where domination would replace the consultation, negotiation, and agreement that are typically employed in Canadian-American relations. For example, a direct military threat to the United States emanating through, or over, Canadian territory, where Canada did nothing to help in the defense of the United States, could very well encourage the United States to take unilateral defense action in violation of NORAD agreements, Canadian protests notwithstanding.

One must consider also the possibility of "nondecisions" as a major component of Canada's relations with the United States. Bachrach and Baratz have defined the "nondecision" as a situation where "A devotes his energies to creating and reinforcing social and political values and institutional practices that limit the scope of the political process to public consideration of only those issues which are comparatively innocuous to A. To the extent that A succeeds in doing this, B is prevented . . . from bringing to the fore any issues that might in their resolution be detrimental to A's set of preferences."[1] The possibility

---

[1] Peter Bachrach and Morton S. Baratz, "Two Faces of Power," *American Political Science Review*, 56 (December 1962), 948.

that Ottawa fails to press some issues against Washington because the latter "sets the agenda" should not be overlooked. What Canadian foreign policy proposals are *not* made because of fear of provoking strenuous American opposition? To be fair, however, we would have to ask the question of both governments in their mutual relations.

It is difficult to provide an empirically based answer to the question. Fear of unfriendly response, or deliberate avoidance of some issues, exists in both Washington and Ottawa, and observers on both sides of the border can cite cases of excessive timidity.[2] Until some method of identifying and measuring instances of "anticipated reactions" and "nondecisions" is developed, only impressions can be offered. In this case, the impression is that no great imbalance exists between Ottawa and Washington. If Canada's general orientation to the outside world has been similar or parallel to that of the United States, the explanation lies not in American domination, but in the structure of the international system, in the common Anglo-Saxon political and cultural heritage, and in common views of the major problems of international politics.

Our first tasks will be to identify the range of interests and problems that are common to both countries, to locate interests that are seemingly incompatible, and to describe the kinds of situations where conflicts and diplomatic irritations are most likely to occur. Once a conflict develops, what are the typical and exceptional means the governments use to achieve or defend the incompatible interests? This question leads us to examine next the bargaining procedures between Ottawa and Washington and the relevance of the great-power differentials between the two countries in that bargaining. Finally, we want to explore some of those social and cultural characteristics that form the basis of the diplomatic traditions of the two countries. Why, despite some conflicts of interest and occasional unsavory diplomatic episodes, has no distinctly hostile (that is, violent) act been undertaken between Ottawa and Washington since Canada began to exercise an independent foreign policy after World War I?

The Range of Interests and Interactions

Areas where American and Canadian interests overlap are multitudinous, extending from the mundane and technical to problems having

[2] See the round table discussion on this problem—with no agreement among the participants—in Stephen Clarkson (ed.), *An Independent Foreign Policy for Canada?* (Toronto and Montreal: McClelland and Stewart, 1968), pp. 43–56.

consequences throughout the world. In many areas, the interests of the two countries are perceived by policy-makers as essentially identical. Both have an interest in conserving fishing resources, developing raw materials, running the St. Lawrence Seaway, maintaining border monuments and freedom of travel, expanding bilateral trade, preventing the pollution of the Great Lakes and other common bodies of water, and, at least in the past, deterring a Soviet bomber attack against North American cities and the American nuclear deterrent. Other interests, while not identical, are at least compatible. Canadians have seen most of the problems connected with the cold war in terms similar to those of Americans. There have been differences on details of strategy (for example, Canadian opposition to American bombing in North Vietnam) but seldom on ultimate objectives. Canada's traditional interests in the Commonwealth, development of trade with the Pacific countries, or commitment of military and financial resources to United Nations peace-keeping efforts either coincide with, or are irrelevant to, American foreign-policy objectives.

In a few diplomatic-commercial areas involving third states, however, Canadian and American policies have been opposed. Despite the evident displeasure of Washington, Canada has maintained trade and diplomatic relations with Cuba; the United States has been more tolerant of Canada's trade and establishment of diplomatic relations with Communist China, but the policies here obviously differ.

Differences in the diplomatic-military field have also developed in recent years. Canada's changing views on Communist China's admission to the United Nations are incompatible with the American position on this issue. The impending reduction of Canadian troops in NATO runs counter to American policies in this area, and the Canadian government, despite strong urgings from the United States, is not at the present time prepared to join the Organization of American States.

Most irritations and conflicts between Ottawa and Washington arise, however, from extensive mutual economic interactions. The basic nature of the American-Canadian economic relationship in particular causes great concern among many Canadians about US threats to the country's independence, sovereignty, and identity.

Some figures will indicate this basic condition. Foreign interests, mostly American, own over 90 percent of the assets of all leading Canadian firms in petroleum products, tobacco, rubber, aircraft, and automobiles. In chemicals, mining and smelting, and electrical products, between 50 and 90 percent of the assets are owned by non-

Canadians, again mostly Americans.[3] Overall, 45 percent of Canadian manufacturing plants are owned by Americans, and the list of Canadian economic operations being purchased by American interests continues to grow. The American economic stake in Canada amounts to a $14 billion investment—a substantial sum when compared to the $12 billion American investment in western Europe, with its population more than ten times that of Canada.[4] In all economic activity, 45 percent of the Canadian GNP stems from American investment. In the area of Canadian-American trade the basic inequality persists, though an element of mutual dependence is more apparent than in the case of investment and manufacturing. Canadian exports to the United States constitute approximately 60 percent of total Canadian exports, while 70 percent of Canada's imports originate in the United States. While figures for the United States are much lower, they indicate that Canada is a market for American goods that must be considered a basic American interest to maintain. The United States sells more to Canada than to any other country in the world: 20 percent of the United States' exports go north. While this is not a large portion of the American GNP (about one percent), substantial American interests would be damaged by a diminution of Canadian markets.[5]

In a setting of such exceptionally high economic activity and impact, differences between the two parties are bound to arise.[6] In many circumstances, the advantages of one party can increase the gains of the other; in other commercial areas, however, the gain of one is seen as involving the loss of the other. To many Canadians, the short-run advantages of American trade and investment will not offset the long-run disadvantages to the country, namely the structuring of the economy to meet American needs, the loss of effective control over the pattern of economic development, and, through that means, the loss of meaningful political independence.

[3] Melville Watkins *et al., Foreign Ownership and the Structure of Canadian Industry,* Report of the Task Force on the Structure of Canadian Industry (Ottawa: Privy Council Office, 1968), p. 144.

[4] Figures cited in Stanley K. Tupper and Douglas L. Bailey, *Canada and the United States: The Second Hundred Years* (New York: Hawthorn Books, 1967), p. 99.

[5] Figures cited in Gerald M. Craig, *The United States and Canada* (Cambridge: Harvard University Press, 1968), p. 261.

[6] In many cases of course, the conflict is essentially between private interests in the two countries, which then prevail upon their governments to adjudicate or promote their claims for them. If somehow those claims can be portrayed as representing "national interests," then the conflict can be seen as one between the two governments as well.

We are concerned here, however, less with long-range possibilities in the overall structure of economic relationships between the two countries than with the handling of conflict between Ottawa and Washington. For us, then, a critical question is the extent to which this economic substructure is relevant to the handling of conflicts between the two governments, whether economic inequality leads in fact to diplomatic inequality.

The Actuation of Conflict

Given this setting of intricate, overlapping, competitive, and conflicting interests in the economic, technical, diplomatic, and military fields, what types of situations and fears are likely to give rise to conflict between Ottawa and Washington? Under what circumstances are forms of conflict behavior—warnings, threats, and protests—likely to be observed in their diplomatic relations?

A major fear of Canadian policy-makers is not American malevolence or threats of economic retaliation, but American ignorance of the consequences of its decisions and actions on the Canadian economy. The important problem as seen from Ottawa is one of faulty decision-making, in which officials in Washington occasionally fail to consider the consequences of their policies on other countries. Several times in recent years the American government, pressed by its internal economic or balance-of-payments problems, has initiated policies that would have had disastrous effects on Canadian interests had not special exemptions been granted after Ottawa made protests or tried vigorously to have the decisions reconsidered.

A second situation likely to give rise to warnings, protests, and various forms of "pressure" between the two countries occurs when American and Canadian views about how best to deal with Communist nations clash. A prominent example is the case of Canadian trade with Cuba. Since the effectiveness of American economic sanctions against the Castro government (based on the assumption that the best way to deal with Communist regimes is to isolate them diplomatically and economically) depended upon foreclosing alternative sources of supply for Cuba, strong pressures were placed on Canada to follow American policies—all the more so because many parts needed in Cuba to replace worn American machinery and automobiles could be purchased only in Canada. Aside from placing an embargo on strategic materials, the Canadian government did nothing to discourage its own citizens from trading with Cuba, and diplomatic relations were never severed. The extent and character of American pressures on Ottawa are not completely known, but the differences in perceptions and policies between the two governments were obvious.[7]

Conflict between Ottawa and Washington may appear to arise also when Canadian political groups attach symbolic importance to actions and transactions that are, from the official point of view, merely technical or commercial. Most Canadian policy-makers approach such questions as trade with China or American investment in Canada as "problems" involving rather specific economic gains or costs to the country. Some members of political parties, the academic community, and interest groups, on the other hand, often view these issues as symbolic of the entire Canadian-American relationship. They are particularly sensitive to any Canadian or American actions that, in their opinion, reflect adversely upon Canada's "independence" or "sovereignty." To them, for example, trade with Communist China is promoted not so much to bring benefits to the prairie farmers as to display to the world Canada's independence from the United States. Similarly, occasional cases of American subsidiary firms operating in Canada being warned by Washington not to conclude sales to Communist China (an application of the Trading with the Enemy Act in extraterritorial fashion) have been cited repeatedly as evidence, at worst, of American imperialism, or at least of Canada's subordination to the United States. Sensitivity to such problems means that many issues become "politicized" in Canada more readily than in the United States. A result may be strong domestic pressures on the Canadian government to make public statements of a hostile nature against the United States. In most such instances, however, the American government is generally aware of the sensitivity and, in order to avoid open conflict, shuns public rebuttals and prefers to work quietly through diplomatic channels.

American officials appear aware that occasional anti-American statements by Canadian politicians are made more for internal political advantage than for influencing Washington. During election campaigns in particular, themes abound that emphasize Canadian independence and criticize American interference in the country's internal affairs through subtle economic pressures. The casual reader of campaign speeches might easily conclude that Canadian-American relations are about to rupture irreparably, that a broad range of interests between the two countries are incompatible, and that Canadian independence and sovereignty can be maintained only through open

[7] See Denis Stairs, "Confronting Uncle Sam: Cuba and Korea," in Clarkson (ed.), An Independent Foreign Policy for Canada?, pp. 58–63. This conflict was perhaps more symbolic than actual since the total amount of Canadian trade with Cuba is very small. To many Canadians the trade symbolized the country's independence from the United States.

conflict with the United States. One should distinguish the appearance of conflict from its reality, however. Officials on both sides of the border who actually deal with the problems affecting both countries are essentially immune to the oratory.

Finally, we should note the frequent development of "irritations" between Washington and Ottawa, situations that arise not so much from differences in foreign policy or commercial objectives as from unique policy-making organizations, the personalities of top-level policy-makers, diplomatic blunders, varying domestic political situations, and the like. The diplomatic atmosphere between Ottawa and Washington was much less than cordial during the last two years of Prime Minister Diefenbaker's government. Some fundamental policy differences had arisen between the two countries, to be sure (for instance, trade with Cuba), but a number of little irritations piled upon each other to the point where commentators agreed that the Canadian-American relationship was at its lowest point in decades. For example, despite clear commitments, the Diefenbaker government could not decide for many months whether or not to accept American nuclear warheads for the Bomarc missiles in Quebec and the strike-reconnaissance aircraft stationed in Germany, because of cabinet disagreement on the issue and little consensus among Canadians. Frustrated at the indecision and at what it considered an inaccurate account of the nature of the commitments, as described by the Prime Minister, the US State Department released a curt statement correcting Mr. Diefenbaker, an unprecedented action in Canadian-American relations. This diplomatic maneuver aroused President Kennedy's ire and prompted Secretary of State Rusk to make a public apology; nevertheless, the episode led to the only instance in relations between the two countries when the Canadian ambassador in Washington was called home "under circumstances which clearly implied a strong diplomatic rebuke."[8]

Even in the most perfect relationships such irritations are inevitable. In the case of many pairs of states, such incidents might easily lead to full diplomatic breaches; in other cases, hostile actions involving threats and retaliations, possibly a low level of violence, might result. It is an important reflection on the basic character of the Canadian-American relationship that these irritations, while creating a bad "atmosphere," do not have much impact on the daily diplomatic and commercial dealings between the two governments.

[8] Peyton Lyon, *Canada in World Affairs, 1961–1963* (Toronto: Oxford University Press, 1968), p. 261.

Big Power Versus Small Power:
Attitudes, Bargaining, and Capabilities
in Handling Conflicts

Canadian and American policy-makers and officials hold several views and assumptions about the handling of their conflicts that would probably not be found in, let us say, relations between the United States and the Soviet Union. One is that conflicts of interest and diplomatic irritations are essentially "problems" to be solved rather than major confrontations to be won at all costs through campaigns and strategems of diplomacy and threats. Few issues arising out of the broad spectrum of Canadian-American interaction are irreconcilable, in their view, provided that tact and quiet diplomacy are employed in the process of "problem-solving." The short-run differences of interest will be offset by a common recognition of the overall interest of maintaining friendly relations. In negotiations, therefore, both sides commonly perceive definite limits beyond which they should not press their claims; at some point "victory" over the immediate issue, particularly if it involves private economic interests rather than "national interests," would so jeopardize the greater good as to make it hollow indeed.[9] Finally, approaching conflicting interests as problems rather than as confrontations suggests a willingness to learn from the other side. If an issue is portrayed as a problem, then presumably a solution requires maximum information, not only from one's own side, but also about the other's point of view. While understanding the other party's point of view does not make it correct or desirable, at least it helps to identify those areas of contention where there is room for trade-offs and concessions.

In cases where interests cannot be reconciled, the usual procedure is to present full explanations of the contending positions and then to accept the differences. Communiqués released at the end of Canadian-American joint cabinet committee meetings or other discussions occasionally refer to disagreements, where both sides have explained

[9] At the highest level, President Johnson, in transmitting a note to Congress asking for approval of the Canadian-American automotive parts agreement, a treaty which was not favorably received by all American automobile manufacturers, indicated a similar perception of limits. He pointed out that it was more important to the United States to maintain the "partnership" with Canada (thereby justifying important concessions to Canadian interests) than to protect the advantage of one group of manufacturers in the United States. For text of the note, see United States Embassy, Ottawa, United States Information Agency, *Canadian–American Relations, 1867–1967: A Compilation of Selected Documents*, 2 (1967), 128.

their views as thoroughly as possible with no reconciliation resulting from the exchanges. Both sides simply learn to live with the situation, a form of "passive" or avoidance behavior in conflict resolution.[10]

If most conflicts and irritations are approached with these views and assumptions, what kinds of bargaining techniques do the governments typically employ in negotiations? How, in other words, is the conflict prosecuted? How are conflicting objectives defended or extended? In most cases, Canadian and American negotiators rely heavily upon technical information (see below) to establish their bargaining positions. Their ability to make a persuasive case—to identify crucial needs (or at least to portray them as critical), to illustrate the favorable or detrimental consequences of policies, and to reveal how unsatisfactory economic, political, or military matters presently stand —is important to the ultimate outcome. In some cases, such as the negotiations over extending commercial airline routes between the two countries, which dragged on more than five years, the bargaining can become extremely hard and even cut-throat, but even in such cases the essential process is the same: extending technical information, evaluating this information from both points of view, outlining needs, calculating consequences, and proposing bargains.

Some bargaining ploys should also be mentioned. Canadian negotiators frequently emphasize the nature of the Americans' *own* long-range interests. They appeal to the opposition's self-interest, but from a time perspective that may be different from that of the American negotiators. In the economic issue areas in particular, Canadian officials often successfully contend that American initiatives to protect their domestic producers against Canadian imports can severely affect the overall pattern of Canadian-American trade, whose structure and large volume it is definitely in the American long-range interest to preserve.

Canadian negotiators can also cite the state of domestic public opinion to strengthen their position. Matters that may be of only peripheral interest to the average American can have the greatest significance, symbolic or actual, to Canadians. In these circumstances Canadian officials can often expedite the handling of a problem or

---

[10] See Kenneth Boulding, *Conflict and Defense: A General Theory* (New York: Harper & Row, 1962), chap. 15. One wonders, however, what would happen if the irreconcilable interests involved basic national values: for example, if the United States in a moment of economic distress cut off all investment in Canada, or if Canada allowed the Soviet Union to build a submarine base in Halifax. Presumably, in such circumstances few of the comments about typical attitudes and assumptions surrounding Canadian-American conflict would hold.

even gain important concessions by referring to the extent to which they are "locked into" a position by public clamor at home. United States officials may not be greatly concerned about a problem, or they may drag their feet on it until they are led to see that the matter is indeed being taken seriously in Canada. The American counterpart to this proposition is to invoke Congress: certain Canadian interests cannot be satisfied, or further concessions cannot be granted to Canada, it is claimed, because they would never be approved by Congress.

Canadian officials agree that threats are extremely rare among Canadian and American actions to protect or advance their respective interests. A few denied that threats were ever made; others took exception to the word "threat." To them it implied a crude tactic or ploy that simply was not a part of the manner in which the two countries carried on their diplomatic relations, even in conflict situations. Most, however, could cite one or more cases of threat, when threat was defined as a communication from agent A to agent B: "If you do x, which is against our interests, we will do y, which will hurt you." This is a threat to retaliate. All who could cite such situations agreed that the instances were rare and were considered to represent drastic action. To buttress these views, one can scan the public record of Canadian-American relations in the past decade and find only a few instances of threats.

It is also highly exceptional for the two governments to make threats in one issue area in order to obtain concessions in another. This conclusion particularly challenges a view held by some Canadians that the United States can achieve diplomatic domination of Canada through its extensive stake in the Canadian economy. Not a single official interviewed could recall—and there is no public evidence to the contrary—any situation where one side in a conflict would threaten to use economic pressures in order to make its point of view prevail on some differences in foreign or defense policies. Canadian officials consider it highly improbable, for example, that the US would exploit Canada's economic vulnerability in order to achieve certain objectives on the problem of NORAD, or to prevent Canada from taking an independent position on the subject of Communist China's admission to the United Nations. When threats are made in Canadian-American conflicts, they are executed within a single issue area or domain. Naturally, in the economic sphere, the two governments are aware of facing possible trade restrictions from the other side in a broad range of commodities. A suggestion in the United States to restrict imports of Canadian lumber may be met with Ottawa's reminder that Canada represents a substantial market for certain American exports. Threats, then, can be made on different problems within the same general issue area, but they apparently never cross issue areas.

Just as threats are rare as a form of conflict and bargaining behavior, the official protest is also seldom employed in handling most Canadian-American problems. Protests may contain threats, but most do not. They merely point out that a government "cannot accept" the other's point of view or actions. Notes such as these are not to be found in profusion in Canadian-American diplomatic correspondence, though it must be assumed that for every official protest note there are many more oral and unofficial protests. Since 1958 there have been only five official protests made through notes; three of these originated in Ottawa.[11]

While Canadian policy-makers and officials are undoubtedly aware of the power differentials between the two countries, particularly in the sense that a variety of American foreign- and domestic-policy decisions, initiatives, and actions can have serious repercussions on Canada's domestic life and interests, they do not necessarily conclude that these disparities have much relevance to bargaining techniques or to the outcomes of conflict.

What, then, are the relevant capabilities of the two countries? What are the "equalizers" for Canada when confronting the superpower? Most of the relevant bases of "power" in the relationship have already been alluded to in describing the range of economic interests between the two countries and the typical bargaining techniques employed in conflict situations. Paradoxically, one important Canadian capability in handling conflicts arising out of economic problems is the extensive American trade and investment stake in Canada. It would be an exaggeration to argue that the $14 billion American investment to the north constitutes a hostage which Canada can threaten to nationalize in order to get concessions in other areas, or that the United States would suffer severe hardship from a cutting off of trade. There would be alternative sources of supply and markets. However, a significant element of mutual dependence exists in the economic relationship: some key industries in the United States rely extensively, even exclu-

---

[11] However, one of the formal protest notes from Ottawa was sent after the US State Department suggested that this action would be appropriate for getting the Canadian point of view across to Washington with more vigor. The protests surrounded conflicts over proposed oil quotas, the Mercantile Bank episode, and confusion over Canada's commitments to accept nuclear weapons. In 1969, the Department of External Affairs also sent a note to Washington holding the United States responsible for any damages to Canadian property resulting from the underground nuclear tests on Amchitka Island.

sively, upon Canadian raw materials or Canadian markets and can place very strong pressures on Congress and the Executive branch not to restrict the flow of imports from Canada or the flow of American capital to the north. Indeed, on some occasions, the Canadian government's closest allies in putting pressure on Washington to protect Canadian interests are American firms operating in Canada or American industries that rely on Canadian raw materials or markets. This interdependence and pressure help to explain in part the willingness of the American government to make special exemptions for Canadian interests in its foreign investment and balance-of-payments policies.

A second capability is information. In economic and commercial matters it appears that Canada has the advantage. With a smaller economy and fewer interests to identify and protect, Canadian officials have a better grasp of the overall interests of the country, make decisions more quickly, estimate the economic consequences of various foreign initiatives more easily, and present a more persuasive case of needs and anticipated repercussions based on extensive documentation. The complexity of the American economy, by comparison, means that American negotiators cannot build cases that are equally persuasive in breadth and depth. The intertwining of economic interests in the United States also helps to create bureaucratic and diplomatic paralysis. If American negotiators argue for tariff protection for some domestic industries, they are as likely to meet opposition from Congress and competing industries at home as they are from the negotiators of other countries. In general we can say that in many economic conflicts of interest, Canada has emerged with generally satisfactory results to an important extent because it could convince the United States, on the basis of extensive documentation, that its own needs, and the consequences of American policies, were indeed critical to the nation. Americans can seldom argue that what Canada does in its internal or external commercial policies is critical to the United States national interest.

In diplomatic and military affairs, however, the advantage derived from superior information would accrue decidedly to the United States. With its vast information-gathering and processing establishments, the American government is able to give its allies exceedingly persuasive "briefings." On most cold war problems, and on questions pertaining to NATO strategy, to the need for NORAD, or to the nature of the Soviet or Chinese military "threat," the American perception of reality and favored policies would normally prevail by virtue of a more extensive intelligence and diplomatic network and better documentation.

In addition to formal efforts by American authorities to persuade Ottawa to accept their views of the outside world, a more subtle American influence should be noted. The Canadian government regularly receives American (and British) intelligence digests and occasional special intelligence material. Most Canadian diplomats are also known to read the *New York Times* regularly. It is hard to gauge to what extent officials in Ottawa form their understanding (or misunderstanding) of political, economic, and military developments abroad from American sources of information, but the very great similarity of views between the two governments of the world outside North America must be accounted for at least in part by the similar sources of information.

We have already alluded to the role that public opinion plays in bargaining between the two countries. To the extent that such opinion can be invoked to help establish a bargaining position (from which one ostensibly dares not make concessions for fear of political reprisal at home), Canada would seem to have the advantage. Because of the sensitivity of many Canadians to American policies over a broad range of issues, it is easier to "politicize" problems in Canada than in the United States. This is not to suggest that officials in Canada deliberately whip up public enthusiasm; they would hardly need to do so since the press, opposition parties, pressure groups, and segments of the academic community are always alert to any hint of American malevolence or interference in Canadian affairs. Once the public is aroused, however, Canadian negotiators may be able to press for their points of view with great vigor against American officials. The latter can seldom reply that the general public in the United States requires them to adopt an inflexible bargaining strategy.

It is difficult to find a widespread outpouring of American sentiment against Canada, no matter what the issue. On some questions, such those involved in the Columbia River Treaty negotiations, interest groups of a local nature may work actively through the US government to make certain that their interests are defended or extended. But it is virtually inconceivable that the public in the southern or eastern United States could be concerned with what is going on in the Pacific Northwest, or that American steel manufacturers should concern themselves very much with the fortunes of American fishermen. Even on fairly broad differences in foreign policy, such as relations with Cuba, it is hard to find any America-wide sentiment against Canada. Compared to most foreign-policy issues that arouse interest in the United States, anything happening north of the border rates very low attention indeed. This fact has led some commentators on Canadian-American relations to point out that the usual banquet-speech panacea for improving those relations—to create more American "understanding" of Canada—may not be very wise. One puts it:

Would the situation improve if the American mass public were to become more aware of the fact that Canada is a haven for American draft-dodgers, that anti-Americanism exists in Canada, that Canada wants Red China in the United Nations, that Canada trades with both Cuba and Red China ... and that many Canadians oppose American policy in Vietnam? ... Before we accept the proposition that more knowledge will lead to less friction, we should ponder the ancient advice on how to treat sleeping dogs. Few people have ever been bitten by a sleeping dog.[12]

The relatively lower saliency of Canadian-American problems, as viewed from Washington, means less pressure on American officials to adhere rigidly to bargaining positions. Though the opposition of interest groups and some members of Congress can be invoked in some negotiations, an American threat to turn a problem into a nasty public confrontation is not credible.[13]

Factors That Mute Conflict Between Canada and the United States

The most satisfactory explanation of the relative lack of conflict between the two countries is the general compatibility or similarity of their interests. Officials in Washington and Ottawa tend to view the outside world in approximately the same way; their assessments of the major issues of world politics have not differed significantly in the past two decades, though notable differences arise about how to cope with some problems; and though the United States has a much higher level of involvement in world problems, Canadians have not in the past generally seen that involvement as inimical to their own external commitments and interests—particularly to the traditional involvement in the Commonwealth and British affairs. In short, the major foreign-policy interests of the two countries toward the rest of the world seldom clash.

[12] David Baldwin, "The Myths of the Special Relationship," in Clarkson (ed.), *An Independent Foreign Policy for Canada?*, p. 12.

[13] However, the Americans' lesser knowledge about Canadian interests and needs can work against Canada: American agencies may make decisions without being aware of their consequences for Canada, and American negotiators, even when faced with reams of Canadian information, may simply fail to be responsive to the reasoning behind Canadian proposals.

In the bilateral context, too, a broad range of interest is complementary, where both sides assume that the gain of one can bring advantage to the other. The number of situations that can be illustrated by the zero-sum metaphor, where the gain of one is necessarily the loss of the other, is not very large. Moreover, Canadians do not always agree among themselves on which situations *are* zero-sum. To many government officials, the vast American investment in their country brings important advantages, such as tax revenues, technology, higher employment, increased exports, and the like. To many others, including some prominent political figures, the nature and size of this investment presents a threat to Canadian independence. Despite considerable public concern over the issue, so far the more conservative and less nationalist point of view has prevailed in government policy, with the consequence that a narrower scope remains for serious economic conflict between the two countries.

Mutuality of interest is, however, not the only explanation for the generally favorable state of Canadian-American relations. Other factors, some unique to Canadian-American relations, help to mute conflict and prevent disagreements and irritations from reaching crisis or confrontation proportions. They produce, in the long run, a sense of mutual empathy and responsiveness between the two governments, and a propensity to limit conflict behavior to very low levels of intensity—occasional threats and official protests, but no violence. I will call these rather amorphous factors, taken together, a "diplomatic culture."

Most of the characteristics of the Canadian-American "diplomatic culture" (listed below) could be subsumed by two general categories: culture and communication. The two are, of course, closely linked. The vast, intricate, and open channels of communication within North America are in part a consequence of the cultural similarities of the two peoples and their extensive commercial interaction; at the same time, they are means of maintaining and extending the common values and outlooks of the two populations.

LANGUAGE

The common language used in Canadian-American contacts has often been noted as a factor that makes "mutual understanding" easy to achieve. Common idiom, slang, and intellectual assumptions or approaches to problem-solving help negotiators and policy-makers of the two countries to be extraordinarily frank with each other. Openness in diplomatic conversations and willingness to reveal all the facts, to interject personal views and interpretations into discussions, and to avoid diplomatic façades are to be found to such a great degree in the relations between only a few countries. This mutual feeling of ease and frankness apparently does not exist to nearly such an extent even in discussions and negotiations between Canada and Great Britain. The similarity of language, in the broad sense, also means that the two sides share intellectual assumptions, such as the need for pragmatism in problem-solving situations and the desirability of basing agreements on careful studies and extensive documentation.

EXCHANGE OF INFORMATION

The amount of technical and sensitive information that is freely passed between the officials of Washington and Ottawa, and between Canadian and American diplomats abroad, is also seldom found in relations between other states. It is the result less of planned policy than of habits that have grown over the years and of the high degree of trust and predictability between the two governments. Americans commonly extend official and unofficial briefings to Canadians, whether in Washington or in other nations' capitals, but not always to other governments.

As I have noted, the US provides intelligence materials to Ottawa. American policy-makers also like to "try out" ideas with Canadians first, to see what responses they can elicit before launching formal initiatives with other countries. At the more formal level, a tradition of consultation is well-established. Both sides assume, though they have not always carried out in practice, that important foreign and commercial policy decisions affecting the other should be taken only after consultations. The complex structure of consulting machinery between the two governments provides the setting for much of the discussion, but, as I shall emphasize below, frequent *ad hoc* consultations take place through informal means—usually direct telephone calls between agencies in Washington and Ottawa. Some of the most important postwar conflicts between the two governments have occurred when the consultative machinery was not employed, either through oversight or through fear of hostile response.

THE PROFESSIONAL DIPLOMATIC ETHIC

The professional diplomat's bias in favor of working through established channels, without wide publicity, must help to account for the low intensity of conflict behavior between the two countries. In 1964, at the behest of the American president and the Canadian prime minister, two distinguished diplomats, one from each country, wrote a report that set out ground rules for consultation and recommended that when conflicts between the two countries did develop, they be dealt with through "quiet diplomacy."[14] While parts of the report were extensively criticized in Canada because they implied that differences between the United States and Canada should not be aired publicly, Canadian diplomacy has in the past assumed that one gains more influence in Washington by employing quiet discussions than by raising all problems to the level of political debate in the country. Generally, it supports the use of consultative machinery for identifying and resolving conflicts before differences become highly "politicized." The natural inclination of the Canadian diplomat or government official dealing with American relations is "to take the heat out of a problem," to expend considerable energy to prevent the development of a crisis. And when conflict becomes widely publicized, the instinct of the Canadian official is to prevent its spilling over from one area into another. Judging by the virtual absence of threats or protests being made in one area, such as commercial relations, in order to achieve or defend objectives in another area, such as continental defense, action to isolate conflicts has been very effective.

EASE OF ACCESS

The volume and scope of Canadian-American interaction has required the development of a complicated formal and casual network of communication between Washington and Ottawa. Canadian and American officials in a variety of agencies normally work directly on their mutual problems, bypassing the formal diplomatic establishments. Direct telephone communication between the two countries is used extensively at all levels of government.

UNOFFICIAL UNDERSTANDINGS

A number of irritations and potential conflicts are avoided by the profusion of "understandings" and "unwritten laws" (both terms were employed by Canadian officials) that help to regulate transactions between the two countries. They are not written into treaties, but are nevertheless observed. When problems arise between the two governments, these understandings serve as points of reference and bases for decisions; the problems are resolved more by reference to the understandings than by diplomatic bargaining. Hence, many issues are taken care of at the administrative level.

[14] Livingston, T. Merchant and A. D. P. Heeney, *Canada and the United States: Principles for Partnership* (Ottawa: Queen's Printer, 1965); reproduced in USIA, *Canadian-American Relations, 1867–1967*, pp. 26–50.

In addition to extensive, informal, interagency communications, ten joint Canadian-American organizations are presently charged with the responsibility of policy-coordination, consultation, negotiation, and in some cases adjudication and regulation. Joint cabinet committees on defense and commerce meet occasionally for consultation, identification of problems, and explanation. The International Joint Commission, comprising an equal number of experts from both countries (significantly, there is no chairman with a deciding vote), has had an extraordinary career in handling various border and resource problems. It functions as a quasi-judicial and investigating agency, with no assumption that the members are serving their respective countries. They are experts whose primary task is to protect and advance common interests.

Institutions of this type, and the traditions of negotiation and problem-solving—the "diplomatic culture"—that operate within them, certainly help to prevent serious conflicts from arising between the two countries. Only occasionally do problems considered by the experts in many of these institutions become "politicized" to the extent that they are subjected to extensive political debate and official recrimination between Washington and Ottawa.

Some Consequences of the "Diplomatic Culture" on Canadian-American Relations

Mutual knowledge leads presumably to predictability of relationships, to empathy, and to expectations of "responsible" behavior. Each country knows generally what policies and actions to expect from the other; if policy changes are proposed, they are often discussed extensively between Ottawa and Washington before final decisions are made. Behavior is largely predictable; both governments appear reluctant to initiate certain self-serving actions and policies because they measure short-run gains against the value of the overall relationship; and the law of "anticipated reaction" apparently works extensively in both Ottawa and Washington: some things are not done because each side knows the other well enough to predict unfavorable responses easily. Even when sensitivity, knowledge, and anticipated reactions do not operate perfectly, and when interests and views conflict, the characteristics of the "diplomatic culture" incline both governments to suffer each other's actions with reasonable equanimity.

As long as there is no malevolence, conflicts of interests are normally either resolved or ignored. In relationships between other states, where no similar "diplomatic culture" exists, mistakes, problems, and conflicting objectives are more likely to lead to charges, threats, and protests than is the case in Canadian-American relations.

A second consequence of the "diplomatic culture" and the configuration of interests between the two countries is that government officials and private groups may become arrayed in peculiar coalitions. For example, an American agency may strongly support certain Canadian interests against policies proposed by another American governmental department. Though there have been cases where the US State Department itself was intransigent or unreceptive to Canadian policies, it has intervened frequently to protect the overall relationship from disruptive demands by American economic interests, Congress, or administrative agencies. Similarly, the Canadian Department of External Affairs occasionally puts pressure on other departments in Ottawa which are contemplating actions that might lead to conflict with the United States.

This willingness of the agencies of one government to act in the interests of another is, of course, by no means unique to Canadian-American relations; it is a normal pattern of diplomatic interaction among states that maintain reasonably friendly relations. It could be argued, however, that the degree of willingness of Canadian and American officials to exert themselves on each other's behalf is unique.

Another consequence of the Canadian-American "diplomatic culture" is the relative absence of "spillover" of conflict from one issue area into another. The extensive formal and informal communications network, bureaucratic specialization, and the sheer number of people working on Canadian-American problems help to reduce the probability that a conflict in one area will have much impact in other areas. If an issue is critical enough to reach cabinet level, disagreements between the two countries may have a cumulative effect, but at lower levels, where the majority of problems are studied and resolved, the issues remain mostly isolated. An impasse in negotiations over allocation of airline routes, for example, is not likely to have any appreciable effect on tariff negotiations or discussions about trade with Cuba. One cannot find in Canadian-American relations a situation comparable to the consequences of conflict between the Soviet Union and the United States. In these relations, when a crisis develops like over the invasion of Czechoslovakia, all types of transactions between the two countries are affected; trade discussions, cultural exchanges, and airline route negotiations are discontinued, and proposed arms control negotiations are "postponed."

The phenomenon of "spillover" is also rare in the vertical sense. If the personal relations of the Prime Minister and the President are not cordial, there are few appreciable results on dealings at lower levels. Indeed, it could be argued that Canadian-American relationships are so complex and extensive that a conflict of personalities at the highest level could seldom lead to estrangement at the bureaucratic levels. At most it could slow down consultations on global issues or make lower-level officials less desirous of expending the energy necessary to cope with some pressing problems. In brief, the Canadian-American relationship is essentially immune to the vagaries and personalities of the top political leadership in either country. When conflict or irritation develops at the top level, its impact on the total relationship seems to be effectively muted by the "diplomatic culture."

Conclusions

The future may see an increasing number of strains in Canadian-American relations, perhaps even serious conflict. Canadian views about the nature of Communism and how to cope with it differ increasingly from official American interpretations. Canada's approaches to Cuba and Communist China have been significantly different from those of the United States. The amount of public hostility in Canada regarding the United States' handling of the war in Vietnam may well be diverted into certain realms of Canadian-American relations. The public and governmental debate in Canada on the future and utility of NATO revealed widespread doubts about the official American interpretation of the "Soviet threat" to Europe; the Canadian public, if not its military experts, are not likely to be convinced that growing American expenditures on armaments and the ABM system bring security increments either to the United States or to Canada—indeed, in many quarters it is argued that certain trends in American military thinking are a direct threat to Canada. And if revolution breaks out in Latin America, there will likely be vigorous public pressures on the Canadian government to dissociate itself from any military intervention and to avoid providing any diplomatic support for the United States.

Different needs and interests in regard to water resources could also lead to controversy between Washington and Ottawa. Already the American government has made known its displeasure over Ottawa's decision to claim jurisdiction extending 100 miles into the Arctic Ocean for the purpose of controlling navigation of oil-bearing vessels which could pollute Canada's northern coast. The issue has so far been treated primarily in the context of legal language, through normal diplomatic channels, but Canada's determination to establish jurisdiction in the face of American objections might lead in the future to threats and other forms of hostile behavior. As the needs for fresh water increase in the United States, proposals by Americans to divert Canadian waters for American use will likely find sympathetic ears in Washington. Presently the Canadian public is divided on the issue of whether or not water resources should be "shared" or sold to the United States. But if the Canadian government takes a negative stand on the American proposals, and if the Americans are unable to clean up their own rivers, acute strains might develop between Washington and Ottawa. This prediction is made on the basis of the widespread phenomenon in international relations, where, if the acute needs of one society are frustrated by the actions of another, conflict is the likely result.

Finally, the prospects for increasing differences of view on world and Canadian-American problems must be assessed in terms of the changeover of Canada's diplomatic personnel. Lester Pearson and Paul Martin, both men of wide international experience and stature, strongly emphasized a quiet diplomatic style and maintained extraordinarily high confidence among officials in Washington. Both gained most of their diplomatic experience during the cold war, and their views of the world in general and of the Communist states in particular were quite orthodox. Within a decade or two, if the forces of Canadian nationalism coalesce around the issue of America's economic impact on the country, and as younger officials with less cold-war experience increasingly influence policy-making, divergences from the United States are likely to become more pronounced. It remains to be seen whether the unique Canadian-American diplomatic culture will operate to keep the differences from leading to more pronounced and hostile forms of conflict behavior.

Great Britain and France

LAWRENCE SCHEINMAN

Relations between France and Great Britain have rarely been free of some element of tension and conflict. The century and a half of hostilities, ending with England's orchestration of the defeat of Napoleonic France, slowly gave way to diplomatic negotiation of differences that related mainly to areas outside Europe. Germany's rise in the late 19th century forged a community of interest between the two nations, leading to alliance and culminating in Churchill's striking gesture to a dying France in June, 1940; he proposed the creation of an "indissoluble union" wherein "France and Great Britain shall no longer be two nations but a Franco-British Union." A scant five years later Charles de Gaulle, responding to British intervention between France and her mandated territories of Syria and Lebanon, nevertheless, found it possible to tell the British ambassador that although "we are not. . . in a position to open hostilities against you at the present time," Britain had "insulted France and betrayed the West. This cannot be forgotten."[1] This statement exemplifies what other events reveal—the seeds of a new era of Franco-British discord had been sown.

Three phenomena served to define and constrain both the nature of conflict and the means of its prosecution: the transformation of the international system in the postwar world; the emergence of a bipolar conflict between East and West; and the process of decolonization with the colonial powers' retreat to their European bases. The new system involved diminution of the position of Britain and France in the hierarchy of world powers although their mutual

[1] Charles de Gaulle, *War Memoirs*, translated by Richard Howard, III, "Salvation" (New York: Simon & Schuster, 1960), 221.

recognition of, and response to this situation, differed. Unlike the former great powers, Germany and Japan, Britain and France remained free to try to recover as much of their lost status as their material resources and diplomatic skills would allow, and to attempt to reassert themselves as major actors in world affairs. Their very determination to do so condemned them either to join together in seeking to create a third center of power between the two emergent superpowers or to pursue independent courses of action aimed at establishing their positions relative to the major powers, to each other, and to their potential long-range competitor in Europe—Germany. Traditional, independent courses of action prevailed.

The progressive loss of empire made Europe, and to a lesser extent the Atlantic, primary arenas of competition for leadership and for the assertion of influence. The full measure of this competition became evident as new forms of relationships emerged among European states (the phenomenon of integration, also a source of conflict) and as France found assertive, purposeful, and dynamic leadership under General de Gaulle. The sources of conflict preceded the return of de Gaulle to power, but their full manifestation depended largely on changes of international situation (the unfolding of the nuclear balance of terror, which opened a new range of possibilities for middle-range powers) and national condition (political and economic recovery and expansion)—changes that became evident only in the late 1950s.

Thus Europe was a fundamental if not an exclusive source of tension underlying postwar Franco-British relations—at first on the issue of its organization, but ultimately on the question of its political orientation. By "organization" we mean the structure of Europe: should that structure comprise cooperative relations based on loose intergovernmental organizations in which nations remain free to act according to their own judgments, or should it encompass supranational or quasifederal organizations resting on binding commitments and the circumscription of national sovereignty? Before de Gaulle, France, however ambiguous her attitude, was generally more sympathetic than Britain to the second kind of structure, and more willing to risk swimming with the supranational European tide.

"Political orientation" labels the question of the purposes to which European unity, once achieved, ought to be put: that is, what are the nature and objectives of a common European foreign policy? Is there a distinctive European purpose, and how is it to be defined? What is Europe's destiny?

The Franco-British conflict over European unity found its most dramatic expression in de Gaulle's historic press conference of January 14, 1963. The General, noting that Britain might "one day come round to transforming itself enough to belong to the European Community without restriction and without reservation," foreclosed Britain's bid to enter the Common Market. The French veto reflected a metamorphosis of basic positions for both countries. As Britain had grudgingly moved toward Europe, thus fulfilling earlier French hopes of a Franco-British partnership, France had moved purposefully toward a different posture, one in which Britain's presence in Europe was regarded not only as no longer necessary but even as inimical to French objectives. During this process questions of organization had given way to questions of political orientation, and attitudes toward the nature of European organization had been transformed on both sides, but especially in France.

Although the most dramatic episodes of Franco-British conflict occurred in the 1960s, they originated in the positions taken by the two countries in the early postwar years. France, aspiring to recover its great-power status and grandeur and in no way forsaking its overseas empire, which was still regarded as a source of power, nevertheless gave predominant attention to its situation in Europe. Colonial policy was a matter of status; European policy was a matter of security. Britain, in pursuit of fundamentally similar goals, chose a more global vocation. In the European context, Franco-British differences started with the question of the structure and institutions of the free states of Western Europe and gradually extended to the question of Western Europe's relation to the United States, on the one hand, and to Eastern Europe, on the other. Questions of European organization, of Europe's vocation, of trans–Atlantic and trans-European linkages, of the defense of the continent and the processes of détente are all part of a complex set of interdependencies. For the sake of convenience, however, questions of organization and political orientation will be treated separately.

Organization

Organizational issues predominated in the decade following the end of the war. France, obsessed with the problem of Germany, mapped out a policy based on disarmament, dismemberment, and decentralization of the hereditary enemy. The Rhineland was to be separated from Germany, the Ruhr detached and internationalized, the Saar brought under French control and linked to the French economy. Alliances to the East and West were to sustain this policy. The emergence of the cold war and the division of Germany ended what little support France had received from her wartime allies and put pain to this policy. In the late 1940s France faced the uncomfortable prospect of an emergent and increasingly unfettered West German state.

France had to seek alternative solutions to the problem of controlling and containing Germany; ultimately she chose the creation of a strongly organized west European system in which German recovery could be made compatible with French security interests. Within France this policy drew support from a broader circle than those concerned with the implications for France of a reborn Germany. On the one hand were those who shared concern about Germany but also believed that French capacity to operate independently of the two superpowers depended on the creation of a European power comprising states that could no longer act alone in international affairs. On the other hand were those less concerned about power and status, but who concluded that the peace and prosperity of western Europe, and the averting of another European civil war, compelled a policy designed to transcend the existing state system and to substitute reconstruction through integration for reconstruction through reassertion of national sovereignty. For those who cared about peace and prosperity, the question of Europe's relations with the superpowers was remote; for those concerned with power and status, it was not. Neither group, however, deemed the existing system satisfactory.

French leadership accepted as axiomatic that Britain should play a central role in forging European unity. De Gaulle, no less than his successors, had thought so. As president of the provisional French government, he had made an effort to reach agreement with Britain. "Confronting a new world ... our two old nations find themselves simultaneously weakened. If they remain divided as well, how much influence will either of them wield?" he asked Churchill. Considering their common interest in peace and in balance on the continent, he proposed that England and France "come to an agreement in order to uphold these interests. ... Thus, England and France will together create peace, as twice in thirty years they have together confronted war."[2]

Although Britain declined the offer, the concept of uniting Europe received one of its first endorsements from Churchill, then out of power, in 1946. Analyzing the failings of Europe in this century, Churchill concluded that "there is a remedy which ... would ... transform the whole scene. ... It is to recreate the European family ... and to provide it with a structure under which it can dwell in peace, in safety and in freedom. We must build a kind of United States of Europe."[3]

[2] *Ibid.*, pp. 58, 59.
[3] Speech at the University of Zurich, September 1946, cited in Carol Edler Baumann (ed.), *Western Europe: What Path to Integration?* (Boston: Heath, 1967), p. 13.

Later in his speech Churchill stressed that such a Europe must be based on "a partnership between France and Germany"—but many Europeans preferred to focus their attention on the clarion call to unity and to assume, or hope for, intensive British participation.

Efforts to translate the principle into practice quickly revealed that France faced a serious dilemma in seeking to create an organization that could simultaneously provide an adequate substitute for her former Germany policy and serve to entangle Britain on the continent. The first postwar European organizations—the Organization for European Economic Cooperation (OEEC) and the Council of Europe—satisfied neither French concern. Reluctant to merge sovereignty or to tie itself too closely to the continent, Britain argued successfully for loosely constructured organizations, and for intergovernmentalism and cooperation, neither of which allayed France's worries about containing Germany. Assessing the first five postwar years, Maurice Duverger commented in 1950 that "the entire history of the European idea since the war is the story of concessions made by its advocates to England in order to obtain its consent to participate. Thereby European organizations have been emptied of all content just for the pleasure of having England join."[4]

Disappointed in the outcome of the Council of Europe in particular but still confronted by the problems that had given rise to its creation, French diplomacy turned toward the integrative schemes embodied in today's European communities—the European Coal and Steel Community (ECSC), the European Economic Community (EEC), and the European Atomic Energy Community (EURATOM). The Schuman Plan of 1950 which organized a coal and steel community under supranational control, marked a watershed in French postwar diplomacy in two respects: first, a policy that assumed a mutual hostility gave way to a policy of reconciliation with Germany; second, France demonstrated a willingness to part ways with Great Britain as she sought to implement a European policy. The principle of reconciliation with Germany took precedence over the principle of securing British participation in European ventures. Participation in the ECSC was predicated on acceptance of the principle of supranational control. France welcomed British participation in the enterprise, but her own decision would not be governed by British conduct. France would not yield on the principle of supranationalism as the price of British participation. Britain chose to remain aloof; the ECSC was established without her among six continental west European states; and the division of free Europe took its first institutional form.

[4] Quoted in Edgar Furniss, Jr., *France: Troubled Ally* (New York: Praeger, 1960), p. 54.

The ECSC revealed the extent to which the two nations were prepared to pursue divergent paths in forging a European policy. The failure of France to adopt the European Defense Community (EDC), which had been spawned by France in response to American pressure to rearm West Germany, and which would have created a supranational European army in place of independent national armies, underscored the limits of that difference. The debate over EDC exposed the fragile nature of France's commitment to federal or prefederal formulas, revealed the depth of division of domestic French political forces on the issue of European organization and Franco-German relations, and indicated just how far France really was prepared to go without Britain at her side. The EDC was a clear test of commitment to supranationalism, and both Britain and France scored low. For France, a supranational army implied not only the end of national independence, something that Britain certainly never had been willing to accept, but also equality of status with Germany, its former enemy. This was far from satisfactory for it was equality with Britain, its ally in victory, to which France aspired. Indeed, Britain, not Germany, was the traditional alliance partner in the living memory of Frenchmen. Moreover, the theoretical equality of France and Britain within EDC might give way to a de facto superiority of Germany, and that could be offset only by the presence of Britain. France was committed to a policy of reconciliation with Germany and to European unity through integration. Reconciliation, however, had some real limits, and integration was to be taken in modest doses and still, in 1954, with some reference to Britain's role in the enterprise.

Transition

The year 1954 marked the end of an era. The defeat of EDC led to West Germany's admission to NATO through the creation of the West European Union (WEU), which linked the six members of ECSC with Great Britain. In this intergovernmental context Britain gave to France the guarantees that Paris had sought in the negotiations over the EDC—maintenance on the European mainland of the British Army of the Rhine. If such a commitment had been given when Paris asked for it, some of the French arguments against ratification would have been foreclosed—although even so France would not necessarily have acquiesced. (Some of the reasons for Britain's failure to make the commitment will be discussed below.) Resolving the German rearmament question and creating WEU opened the way to the resolution of remaining Franco-German differences, the status of the Saar in particular, and cleared the path toward a more profound Franco-German reconciliation.

In contrast, Franco-British relations, except for a brief moment of cooperation in 1956, took a turn for the worse. The conflict continued to be cast in terms of the organization of Europe, but it had more complex roots. France's European policy was based largely on the German problem. Another factor in the European equation was the desire to create a European entity that could take independent action on behalf of its participants—action that no one participant alone was capable of taking either with respect to its principal ally, the United States, or with respect to its principal antagonist, the Soviet Union. During the 1950s France's Atlantic relations, never fully satisfactory, had deteriorated progessively. Her colonial policy was implicitly challenged by the United States and Britain (e.g., both nations sold arms to Tunisia, affecting France's Algerian problem). Her meeting of alliance obligations was put into question by the drawing off of French troops for duty overseas. Her reluctance to ratify EDC was railed against in a blunt, open form epitomized by Secretary of State John Foster Dulles' threat that a failure to ratify would elicit an "agonizing reappraisal" of American policy toward France. Britain, if often ambivalent, appeared to be much more closely aligned with the United States than with France; and even when not favorably disposed toward American policy, Britain suppressed her negativism in deference to American wishes—on the whole question of European integration for example, and particularly with respect to EDC, which Washington vigorously supported but which Britain hoped would abort.

The implications of the defeat of EDC for future French support of the movement toward European unification were put to the test with the *relance européenne* initiated by the Benelux countries in 1955. At first cautiously and then with increasing conviction—nourished by an assessment of economic integration's value to developing the French economy and to maintaining a continued French presence in African territories—France again threw its weight behind creation of a strong west European organization. The Suez affair of 1956, in which an Anglo-French venture aimed at rampant Arab nationalism collapsed under American pressure, caused France to be increasingly concerned over being squeezed between the superpowers.

For France, correctly or incorrectly, Suez clarified a number of things. Its outcome seemed to compel the creation of a European bloc able to protect European interests against friend and foe alike, although no specific organizational form was linked to this conviction. It also gave justification to French nuclear aims and attested to the weakness of Britain's European commitment. That Britain had initially joined

France in the Suez venture without reference to the United States gave rise, briefly, to the hope that Britain had reevaluated its postwar European policy. In the wake of the Suez fiasco, however, Britain turned westward toward the United States, attempting to repair the breach in the "special" Anglo-American relationship, not eastward toward the continent. Within a year, the United States would be preparing amendments to its atomic energy law that would facilitate the granting of nuclear weapons assistance to Great Britain.

Open Rivalry

Whereas Britain had been indifferent to ECSC and had supported EDC only reluctantly, London responded with open hostility to the prospect of continental economic integration in the form of the European Economic Community. Britain sought to encapsulate the emerging EEC in a larger free-trade area whose ultimate impact might well have been to weaken the EEC fatally in economic and political terms —and from the moment Britain acted, a second and more profound divergence of Franco-British policy toward Europe and the West began to emerge. The conflict reached a first plateau in 1958 when France rejected the free-trade area concept and Britain, both as a defensive economic measure and as a potential political lever in future dealings with the EEC, responded with the creation of the European Free Trade Association (EFTA). A second, more serious plateau was reached in 1963 when de Gaulle vetoed Britain's application to join the EEC. During these years the question of the organization of western Europe was increasingly overtaken by the issue of the orientation of the emerging European communities. The question of what political purposes a continental bloc would pursue had always lurked in the background of France's European initiatives. France's first postwar impulse had been to act as arbiter between East and West. The bipolar nature of the international system and France's inherent weakness compelled her to adopt more modest policies. Now—as the international system evolved toward a nuclear balance of terror, as Europe recovered economically and politically from its wartime condition, and as French leadership turned in the direction of challenge and revisionism of the European, Atlantic and global systems—the question of orientation became more explicit and distinct. The merging of the organizational and orientational strands brought the sources of Britain's European policy to the surface and set the stage for a Franco-British "politics of confrontation" which, though muted at the beginning of the 1970s, continues to persist.

Great Britain emerged from the war reasonably well aware that "politics as usual" could not easily be practiced, but the force of tradition and the will to believe otherwise prevented her from turning her remarkable adaptive capacities to profit in her international relations. Traditional values tended to prevail in the aftermath of the war insofar as British policies toward the continent were concerned. According to a formula made famous by Churchill, Europe was but one of three communities to which Britain belonged. The other two, the Commonwealth and the Atlantic, really took priority. They conditioned Britain's European policy and created a chasm between her and the continental nations of western Europe.

Wartime circumstances and postwar conditions in Britain created a psychological condition that deepened and broadened this gap. Britain had been a major participant in the war effort and a victor in her own right. Unlike France, Britain had not succumbed in 1940; she had not been occupied and victory had not consisted of liberation by one's allies. Participation in the great postwar councils—the United Nations Security Council, the Allied Control Commission, and the Council of Foreign Ministers—was never in question, and Britain's presence did not depend initially on intervention by her allies. In no instance could the same be said for the only other major west European power inscribed in the columns of the victorious—France. Thus postwar British identity ran in directions other than toward the continent.

Still thinking in terms of traditional sources of power, Britain could not help but view her status at the head of the Commonwealth as providing a significant source of power and influence and a legitimation for her claim to great power status. That the Commonwealth could also be a source of weakness was not yet recognized. Its very heterogeneity—it spanned three continents, consisted of a vast, multiracial community, and represented many levels of economic development—prevented it from operating as a coherent and single-minded organization for the conduct of international politics. France would use its existence against Britain when London eventually turned toward the continent in its quest for a role.

The Atlantic link was predicated not only on history, language, and culture but also on the notion of a special relationship with the United States, the roots of which antedated World War II but the development and strengthening of which were largely products of that conflict. The claim to a special relationship with the United States had tangible foundations, particularly in the nuclear field. Three times in five years—the 1958 amendment to the Atomic Energy Act to facilitate transfer of nuclear information and material to Great Britain, the 1960 Skybolt offer to bolster the waning British delivery system, and the 1963 agreement to substitute Polaris for Skybolt—the United States gave Britain what it was not prepared to give to anyone else. These nuclear weapons developments made Britain increasingly dependent on the United States and came to haunt her when she eventually sought to gain entry to Europe. Another example of this special relationship is American encouragement of Britain's costly role "east of Suez." From Britain's viewpoint the costs of the special relationship were justified by the supposed value of tying American power to British objectives and of providing Britain with unique opportunities to influence American foreign-policy decisions. Two examples of this "influence" are frequently cited: the creation of NATO, whereby Britain secured an American commitment to continental defense, and the alleged restraining of American military action during the Korean conflict.

Commonwealth and Atlantic commitments prejudiced British responses to invitations to join organizations that sought to unify western Europe. Acceptance would have been inconsistent with her other relations—should Britain tie herself to a continental grouping, her freedom of action in the other two spheres would be diminished. Indeed, too close a linkage might even foreclose participation in the Atlantic or Commonwealth communities in any privileged way. At the least, little credibility would be left to British claims of capacity for independent action in spheres outside Europe.

Independence, or the question of sovereignty, was in fact another aspect of the problem of Britain's relations with Europe. In response to the ECSC concept, Macmillan had said, "We will allow no supranational authority to put large masses of our people out of work." Anthony Eden, referring to the suggestion, made frequently, that the United Kingdom should join a federation of the continent of Europe, remarked that this was "something which we know, in our bones, we cannot do." These statements succinctly express Britain's attitude toward the forging of constitutionally defined links between the nation-states of western Europe, an attitude that was much like General de Gaulle's. Speaking on the question of European cooperation at a press conference in September 1960, de Gaulle said:

To build Europe, that is to say, to unite it, is evidently something essential. . . . All that is necessary in such a domain is to proceed, not by following our dreams, but according to the realities. Now, what are the realities of

Europe? What are the pillars on which it can be built? The States ... are the only entities that have the right to order and the authority to act.

These sentiments could have emanated from Whitehall as easily as from the Elysée palace, for they echoed a firm belief, held by British statesmen, in the nature of authority in the international arena. Britain should have found it easier to come to terms with Europe once de Gaulle was in power, but questions of orientation were to prevail over questions of organization.

For reasons of commitments, policy, and ideology, Britain could not join the European enterprise. For some of the same reasons, she also could not allow it to materialize without her. Merging with traditional British continental policy was a practical consideration of the consequences for Britain if a powerful continental bloc were to materialize. Were the Europeans to succeed in creating a tight organization without Britain, she ran the risk of being economically damaged and of having to face a very powerful competitive voice in the dialogue with the superpowers. With respect to the United States, this could mean the displacement of Great Britain as the senior partner and principal European spokesman in the Atlantic triangle. The only alternative would be to join Europe, but the choice was not an acceptable one, for reasons already discussed. Britain's interest was defined in terms of having a Europe that was stable and cohesive enough to resist encroachment from the East, but not cohesive enough to dislodge Britain from its privileged status in the West.

Traditional British attitudes toward the continent also played a role. Historically, Britain had sought to prevent any one power from dominating the European continent, on the premise that only such a power could interfere with Britain's maritime and colonial interests or threaten security at home. The medium through which these interests were secured was summed up in the concept of "balance of power": Britain would throw her weight onto the weaker side of the scale if any state threatened to dominate the continent. This position entailed a policy of "free hands," of "no permanent friends, only permanent interests," and consequently no permanent alignments. Much of this lost relevance in the postwar period when the continent was divided in two, the eastern half coming under the domination of a hegemonic power and the western half turning into a political vacuum. Yet instinctive opposition to a western continental bloc prevailed in British policy, and London opted for injection of American power into the vacuum rather than creation of a European federation. Britain worked to prevent the emergence of strong institutions on the continent and to limit the effectiveness of those institutions that did emerge. In the case of the Council of Europe this meant limitations on both the power and the functions of the organization; in the case of EDC it resulted in a failure to make such timely commitments as might have changed the course of European history; in the case of EEC it led to a direct attempt to undercut the emergent community by absorbing it in a larger free-trade area limited to the industrial sector and devoid of the safeguards, guarantees, and commitments inscribed in the Treaty of Rome, largely at French insistence. In brief, from Britain's viewpoint, too coherent an organization on the continent could only reflect adversely on her postwar status and her privileged position.

And its Consequences

Speaking at West Point in December 1962, Dean Acheson evaluated Britain's situation:

Great Britain has lost an empire but it has not yet found a role. The attempt to play a separate power role—that is a role apart from Europe, a role based on being the head of a 'commonwealth' which has no political structure, unity or strength. . . .—this role is about played out.[5]

By the 1960s the British government appeared to be moving toward the same conclusion, though with great reluctance and little conviction, for in 1961 it made application for entry into EEC. The political value of the Commonwealth was becoming increasingly dubious. The pattern of British trade was steadily shifting toward Europe and the Atlantic. The Commonwealth still took more British exports than any of her other trading partners, but new trade was increasingly directed toward European and Atlantic markets. Thus, whereas British exports to the overseas sterling area rose from a monthly average of $310 million in 1958 to $322 million in 1964, during the same period exports to EEC countries rose from $108 million to $225 million, and exports to the United States from $69 million to $100 million.

The special relationship with the United States seemed less special under President Kennedy than it had under President Eisenhower, and Britain discovered that whether the time was one of crisis or of détente, London was less and less relevant in the dialogue between

[5] Quoted in George W. Ball, *The Discipline of Power* (Boston: Little, Brown, 1968), p. 75.

Moscow and Washington. Simultaneously, the EEC was moving toward a customs union at a more rapid pace than Britain had ever thought possible. And this progress was made largely because of the French government whose leader, before his return to power, had described the Treaty of Rome as a "mere scrap of paper." Furthermore, de Gaulle was taking initiatives in the political field. It was becoming increasingly clear to Britain that on the continent ferment was producing results that she could not cope with from the outside and from which she risked being permanently excluded.

Britain's bid did not fail because of a lack of common ground between herself and France on the question of organization (quite the contrary, for neither wanted a federated Europe). The British bid failed largely because of fundamental differences over the purposes of European organization, but also because the policy of Franco-German reconciliation had matured to the point where British participation in European development appeared to be less relevant to France than it once had been. By 1962, in any event, questions of form had given way to questions of substance and policy. The first British effort to gain access to Europe revealed that Britain had not yet "found a role." No real choice had been made between Europe and the Commonwealth or between Europe and the Atlantic. Britain sought to have her cake and eat it too—to participate in Europe without lessening her participation in the other two communities.

What had happened was this: Britain had recognized her situation for what it was—a condition of economic and political decline. She had perceived the reality of developments across the channel and had come to the view not only that the EEC might provide a viable framework for economic development but also that some of the ground lost in Commonwealth and Atlantic circles might be recovered in Europe. The European communities could become an instrument of British policy. In the view of France this raised an additional impediment to British entry—Britain could become a real threat to France's preeminent position in western Europe. Britain was free of the constraints that made Germany a noncompetitor to the French for the leadership of Europe, and Britain had a more global and active political view than did France's other continental partners. Britain would be able to challenge France for the role of spokesman for the European communities, and to compete with France for use of the European communities in support of policies that Britain was incapable of sustaining unaided. Unfortunately for Britain, de Gaulle had long recognized the value of Europe for French objectives and had no need of a competitor with resources, prestige, and political clout comparable to France's but with divergent objectives and goals.

DeGaulle's objective was the creation of a "European Europe," a "truly European entity,"—that is, a western Europe independent of the United States, capable of defining and implementing an autonomous diplomacy and of affording Europe a real influence in world affairs. This Europe—based politically on a Franco-German entente and structurally on the principle of organized cooperation among independent states—eventually would extend from "the Atlantic to the Urals." The division of Europe, imposed by the Yalta agreement would be overcome. Reconciliation and reunification of the continent and of Germany would result. The goal of making France an independent world power would be achieved. As the only western European nuclear power, France would speak on behalf of a western European entity over which she would exert a predominant influence. Ultimately she would be able to draw on the resources not only of an independent western Europe, but, also of a reunified continent.

To these ends, Europe had to be liberated from the "two hegemonies." The politics of bloc confrontation and the arrangements that tended to perpetuate both this confrontation and the continued presence of alien hegemonic forces had to be reversed. The challenge to the politics of bloc confrontation entailed the undoing of the Atlantic Alliance, which was predicated on the principle of integrated western defense and which blocked the way to European reconciliation. As long as the alliance remained intact, the system of blocs would be perpetuated and Europe would be incapable of asserting itself as an independent international force; its fate would remain the subject of bargaining between extracontinental powers. Only through the disengagement of American power from the continent, de Gaulle argued, could a European settlement be brought about, for only under these conditions could the Soviet Union be induced to revise the European status quo and accept continental reconciliation and German reunification. As long as Europe remained tied to the American colossus, little hope existed for anything more than continuation of a state of dependence and subservience for the European nations. The sum and substance of this Gaullist policy was the modification of the bipolar system and the overhauling of the existing alliance structure.

Britain's idea of Europe bore little resemblance to this "grand design." To be sure, Britain would not contest the notion of a "Europe of states," for such a formula coincided with her own organizational preferences. There also could be little disagreement with France on the desirability of overcoming the division of Europe or on the unspoken unacceptability of a nuclear Germany. But here the similarity ended. Never keen on seeing a powerful and cohesive political force emerge on the continent that could displace Britain from her privileged role as senior European member of the Atlantic Alliance, Britain maintained a determined opposition to the concept of "European Europe" and to its corollary of eliminating the American presence in Europe. Britain preferred, and continues to prefer, an "Atlantic Europe" politically linked to the United States (whose leadership London accepts) and interdependent with Washington in the fields of diplomacy and defense.

This commitment to a politico-military conception based on strong Atlantic ties is a persistent British theme. While paying increasingly warm respects to the concept of a united Europe and accepting the need to establish a distinct European entity vis-à-vis the United States in certain areas, Britain has continued to think in rigidly Atlantic terms insofar as defense is concerned. In a speech before the council of the WEU, a speech that hampered de Gaulle's efforts to establish a modest political union on the continent (the Fouchet plan) and that consequently may have influenced de Gaulle's decision to foreclose Britain's chances of admission into Europe in 1962, the Conservative leader and now Prime Minister Edward Heath stated:

We quite accept that the European political union, if it is to be effective will have a common concern for defence problems. . . . What is essential, however, is that any European point of view or policy on defence should be directly related to the Atlantic Alliance.[6]

The Labor party proved to be no different on this issue. Speaking of British aims in February 1965, Secretary of State for Foreign Affairs Stewart noted that Britain must,

have twin aims: to build a wider European unity; and to do so in such a way as not to weaken, but rather to strengthen the Atlantic partnership. There is no conflict between these aims. We do not have to choose between Europe and the Atlantic Alliance.[7]

The Conservative government elected to office in June 1970, while evincing greater interest in some kind of nuclear sharing arrangement

[6] Cited in Miriam Camps, *Britain and the European Community, 1955–1963* (Princeton: Princeton University Press, 1964), Appendix C, pp. 527–528.

[7] Western European Union, *The British Application for Membership of the European Communities, 1963–1968* (Paris: Western European Union, 1968), p. 35.

with France for Europe, has yet to take a truly dramatic step away from Britain's traditional Atlantic orientation.

De Gaulle tended to clothe his rejection of Britain in terms of the (legitimate) economic problems the British candidacy posed.[8] At the heart of the issue, however, were Britain's Atlantic commitment, the nature of Anglo-American relations, and the implications such a British presence in Europe would have for French objectives. The 1963 veto took place in the wake of events that, from de Gaulle's point of view, threatened the very foundations of his effort to forge and lead a "European Europe." President Kennedy's "declaration of interdependence" between a united Europe and the United States closely followed Heath's remarks on defense policy. These remarks had undermined possibilities for developing an independent defense base for Europe, and Kennedy's declaration threatened its economic and technological independence. Noting that Britain would be followed into Europe by other EFTA states, de Gaulle concluded that the likely effects would be:

the cohesion of all (EEC's) members . . . would not hold for long and . . . in the end there would appear a colossal Atlantic Community under American dependence and leadership which would soon completely swallow up the European Community.

However attractive this might be to some, he concluded, "it is not at all what France had wanted to do and what France is doing, which is a strictly European construction."

Another significant event was certainly the agreement made between Britain and the United States at Nassau in December 1962, in which Britain accepted nuclear dependence in exchange for American Polaris missiles. In de Gaulle's view Britain thus further distinguished herself from the continental members of EEC, none of whom was "linked on the outside by any special political or military agreement."

---

[8] Three problems would have plagued any French government of the day: the question of the Community's agricultural policy and British demands that the EEC accommodate not only Great Britain with its significantly different farm support system but some of its Commonwealth partners as well, all to the potential detriment of French interests; the weakness of British currency which served as an international trading and a reserve currency thus bearing burdens far beyond those borne by the currencies of the EEC countries. This currency could well have become a serious drain on the EEC as Britain's new-found partners bailed sterling out of difficulty. Third, Britain's abiding interest in free trade, if implemented (as it conceivably could be in some moderated form with German support) could create difficulties for French industry.

The theme of Anglo-American interdependence was to be constantly invoked against Britain by de Gaulle in the name of Europe. Reviewing the European situation in October 1966, de Gaulle reiterated that in 1963 Britain had not been "in a position to apply the common rules and . . . had just, in Nassau, sworn an allegiance outside of a Europe that would be a real Europe." Several months later, a few days after Britain's second application to join EEC, de Gaulle asked how continental and British policies in the political realm "could merge, unless the British assumed again, *particularly as regards defense,* complete command of themselves, or else if the continentals renounced forever a European Europe." The perception of Britain as America's "Trojan horse" in Europe never deserted de Gaulle. In his last public pronouncement on the subject in September 1968, he stressed that "our desire not to risk an Atlantic absorption is one of the reasons why, much to our regret, we have until now postponed Great Britain's entry into the present Community."

Britain remained firm throughout: de Gaulle's Europe was not her Europe; the strategy of revisionism was not her strategy. Although the extent of British Europeanism remains ambiguous, Britain has not been standing still. Aside from the amelioration of certain economic and monetary problems,[9] which even in a situation of abundant good will could be potential roadblocks to British entry, Britain has been reducing her extra-European commitments, most dramatically in her decision to withdraw forces east of Suez by 1971.[10] Such actions lend credence to British claims that she sees her future in Europe, though they have not appreciably improved Britain's image in France: the myth of "perfidious Albion" strikes deep in the French consciousness.

Britain parried France by using WEU to keep the European door ajar and attempts were made to entice France with visions of economic and technological independence from America—the most in the way of independence that Britain was prepared to concede. At the January

[9] Devaluation of the pound in November 1967 resulting in an eventual improvement of the balance of trade and of Britain's balance of payments met one of France's claimed concerns over the effects on EEC of British adhesion; however this still left the problem of sterling balances and the international status of sterling unresolved.

[10] The recently elected Conservative government under Mr. Heath has indicated its intention to retain some presence east of Suez, particularly in Singapore. This does not mean that London has revised its view on the future of Britain's relationship to the Continent, but it does open possibilities for those who would claim that Britain has not yet come to the point of identifying her future with that of Europe.

1967 meeting of the Consultative Assembly of the Council of Europe, Prime Minister Wilson in one breath proclaimed loyalty to the Atlantic Alliance and asserted that such loyalty must never mean subservience:

Still less must it mean an industrial helotry under which we in Europe produce only the conventional apparatus of a modern economy, while becoming increasingly dependent on American business for the sophisticated apparatus which will call the industrial tune in the '70s and '80s ... what we have to see is that the European industry of tomorrow does not become dependent on an outside technology, with all that can mean in terms of industrial power and independence.[11]

Such an appeal might be warmly received by a Servan-Schreiber who sees the American challenge in these terms but it would not satisfy a de Gaulle. Why should it? Was not France already engaged in bilateral technological projects with Britain, such as the Concorde project for a jointly developed commercial supersonic aircraft, and had the British not accepted a plan for a variable wing jet fighter—thus enabling France to draw on British aerospace technology in a classic cooperative pattern without having to share the leadership of Europe with her and without having to risk an "Atlantic absorption"? No matter that in practice bilateralism proved to have the defects of its virtues, and to be inadequate to the task of meeting the challenge of the trans–Atlantic "industrial helot." And in what measure could technological and industrial independence compensate for Britain's failure to offer its nuclear weaponry to Europe instead of to the United States —an act that would have demonstrated unreserved commitment to Europe in place of the special ties to the Atlantic colossus? Indeed, if the nuclear military components were to be reserved from technological cooperation, just how serviceable would the British offer of technological sharing be to the concept of a "European Europe"? To de Gaulle it must have appeared that Britain had not really moved very far from her position of 1943, when an agitated Churchill told de Gaulle: "This is something you ought to know: Each time we must choose between Europe and the open sea, we shall always choose the open sea. Each time I must choose between you and Roosevelt, I shall always choose Roosevelt."[12] The actors had changed, on one side at least, but had the play?

[11] Western European Union, *The British Application*, cited pp. 45, 46.
[12] Charles de Gaulle, *War Memoirs*, II, "Unity," p. 253.

Abatement of conflict came about not because differences were settled or objectives converged, but through the conspiracy of events. De Gaulle remained firm in his vision of a European Europe, and Britain continued to refuse her endorsement. For France, the American hegemony still had to be thwarted, the system of blocs undone; for Britain, the Atlantic connection remained the foundation of foreign policy. The internal crisis in France in May 1968, revealed the fragility of the French franc and the vulnerability of the economy; the Czechoslovakian crisis in the summer of that year put the concept of a Europe stretching from the Atlantic to the Urals at a very distant remove. These events, coupled with the rapidly developing Russian presence in the Mediterranean, an area of fundamental concern to French security, did not force a reversal of French policy, but they did contribute to the refurbishing of France's Atlantic links and to a Franco-American *rapprochement.*

How much could de Gaulle salvage? In February 1969 he apparently suggested to British Ambassador Christopher Soames that France might be prepared to consider British entry into Europe and the transformation of the EEC into something larger and more amorphous (and hence, less supranational). Such a transformation would involve creating a sort of European directorate consisting of France, Britain, Germany and Italy and presumably involving some kind of Franco-British nuclear arrangement. His suggestion indicated that Gaullist visions remained fixed in the grand lines but flexible in the modalities. Better an obscure form of independence and shared continental leadership than entrapment in a supranational structure. The outcome was not to be known. Britain refused, partly out of suspicion of de Gaulle, partly out of the ill-placed judgment that revealing the plan to France's continental partners could yield political profit on the continent. Three months later, having lost a referendum on constitutional reform, de Gaulle resigned from power.

Although the shape of post-Gaullist relations between France and Britain remains somewhat obscure, de Gaulle's departure has had a number of short-term effects. The Pompidou government lacks the visionary leadership that so dominated the Gaullist regime. This lack has meant the end of systematic, doctrinaire opposition to British entry into Europe. It has also meant the end of the grand design of a Europe stretching from the Atlantic to the Urals. The first signs of erosion of both of these policies were already evident under de Gaulle, as we have seen. With Pompidou the shift has been accelerated. Nevertheless, France maintains an abiding and widespread interest in reducing American influence in Europe, and French attitudes toward Britain will be to some degree conditioned by the depth and scope of British Atlanticism. Furthermore, Pompidou was elected to office on a platform of *continuité* as well as *ouverture* and he relies on a majority that contains many "orthodox" Gaullists. Consequently, no truly dramatic changes in French policy can be anticipated with respect to Franco-British relations.

Two other issues intervene in the matter of Franco-British relations after de Gaulle: the problem of Germany and the question of economic interests. Although they need not always do so, these issues tend to exert contradictory pulls on French policy: the Germany question pushes France toward closer links with Britain and the economic questions incline her toward a more vigorous anti-British posture.

Germany, we may recall, was the principal source of France's policy of European unification. Reconciliation in this context depended in no small measure on the willingness of Germany to follow the French lead and to refrain from challenging her leadership in the Communities. Deterioration of Franco-German relations under the Erhard administration was only partially offset by the more cordial attitudes that prevailed under the Kiesinger government. All through this period an obvious anomaly was dominant: West Germany was an economic giant and a political dwarf. Amelioration of France's economic problems, and especially of her monetary problems, in 1968 and 1969 depended largely on Germany's response (e.g., on Germany's willingness to revalue the mark relative to the franc). Germany's refusal to respond as France would have liked and the increased assertiveness of Bonn on these questions led many Frenchmen, de Gaulle among them, to consider the need for a British presence to help offset rising German power. De Gaulle could still think in terms of balancing Germany through bold and sweeping actions; his successors, Gaullist or otherwise, are more likely to seek support from Britain against Bonn. Hence, the Pompidou government is more responsive to British participation in Europe.

Economic interests, however, press in the opposite direction. One obvious concern in Paris is that Britain and Germany, sharing interests on agricultural questions, may ultimately be able to lead Europe toward policies antithetical to French interests. This is one reason France insisted on completing the Community's agricultural policy before opening negotiations with Britain. The general weakness of the EEC's agricultural policy, however, leaves the door open to future changes. What is significant in the passing of power from de Gaulle to Pompidou is that politics has ceased to prevail over economics. The idea of breaking up the Common Market and expanding it into a free-trade area, as suggested in de Gaulle's talk with Soames, is far less appealing to his Gaullist successors than it was to de Gaulle himself. In the defense of French economic interests, Pompidou is concerned with tightening and extending economic arrangements among the EEC members rather than with weakening them. Thus, the famous French triptych emanating from the Hague summit meeting of the Six in December 1969: "completion, strengthening, enlargement"—in that order.

As far as Franco-British relations on the continent are concerned, the transition from de Gaulle to Pompidou means that Britain will be judged less in terms of her Atlanticism and more in terms of the implications of her participation in the EEC for French agricultural, industrial, and commercial interests. In a sense this means a partial return to earlier French concerns about British entry, concerns that emerged in 1958 during negotiations for a free-trade area. Then, many French "Europeans," in the non-Gaullist sense of that term, and many who were sympathetic to the idea of an Anglo-French partnership stood firmly against British efforts to change the nature of the EEC or to diminish the agricultural, industrial, or trading advantages that French negotiators had won in the elaboration of the Treaty of Rome. As far as Britain is concerned, the difference between de Gaulle and his successors may well be only that the new French regime was at least willing to negotiate. Britain will be judged not on the basis of ethereal French vision but on the basis of bread-and-butter issues.

The muting of some of the more abrasive issues of political orientation does not mean the reassertion of questions of organization. In keeping with his commitment to the continuity of French policy, Pompidou defines his view of European union in the following way: "resolute advance toward a union devoid of dreams and surrenders but resting on trust, on realities, on close links between responsible governments ready to impose on themselves common disciplines."[13] This basically intergovernmental formula should prove attractive to British leadership and should facilitate negotiations. Alternatively, however, it may be a prelude to a new phase of Franco-British conflict. Today the two nations remain the only major European powers unfettered by political liabilities and both capable of and inclined toward playing an influential role in world politics. If the Gaullist grand design has been undermined by events, it in no way follows that France has forsaken a future political role in Europe. The scope of French vision has been narrowed, but this does not constitute ac-

[13] Quoted in *Economist*, December 20, 1969.

quiescence in British values and objectives. Atlantic interdependence may reassert itself, but questions would be left open: the shape of Europe, its role in the Western world, and the assertion of its leadership. On issues such as these the European Communities are likely to become stakes in a new era of rivalry between London and Paris, and probably also Bonn. This consolidation and extension of French economic interests may predominate in the short run, but in the long run the broader strategic and political issues are likely to prevail.

Retrospect

Despite the acerbity of General de Gaulle's statement quoted in our introductory paragraph, it is clear that no great dogmatic differences existed between France and Britain in the postwar era. Defined national interests and policies did clash on a number of highly important issues—political and economic integration, regional and global policy, the nature and direction of European organization, and nuclear strategy. Yet, in the presence of these differences the two nations could engage in cooperative ventures ranging from the Concorde project to the joint venture at Suez in 1956. One cannot easily visualize ideologically differentiated states engaging in these dimensions of cooperation. Furthermore one cannot discount the use of force to resolve political disputes when ideologically disparate states are involved unless one argues the case of the disuse of force between nuclear powers. Even as nuclear powers, neither France nor Britain regard each other as potential security threats against whom a deterrent or defensive posture must be maintained.

If cooperation in the context of conflict is one theme we can extract from an examination of postwar Franco-British relations, perhaps another is the idea that neither country really was of paramount concern to the other during this time. When Britain looked eastward toward the continent she tended to look beyond France to Germany and Russia. When France looked westward across the channel her view was inclined toward Washington rather than toward London. In this sense it might be argued that many of the policies each pursued toward the other were vicarious responses to more absorbing problems and more global objectives: de Gaulle's view of Britain as America's "Trojan horse" in Europe, or Britain's effort to gain entry into the European Communities as a means of controlling continental development and of securing a political springboard for British purposes, could be interpreted in this manner.

The perceived relative importance of each to the other must be seen, however, in dynamic and not static terms. In the first postwar decade Britain gave rhetorical encouragement, but remained behaviorally indifferent, to continental development, while France, operating from weakness and a sense of insecurity, sought to impose constraints on Germany through European structures and looked to Britain to support this policy. As Britain's inflated postwar status was progessively revealed and as France's weakness and instability were converted into dynamism and stability, the two nations reached a state of rough equipoise. From this point the two countries became more alike than different, and Britain's importance to France diminished correspondingly, while French policy loomed more relevant in British eyes. Perhaps it would be fair to say that it was their similarities rather than their differences that most separated them. Roughly equal in terms of demography, economic development, nuclear standing, and international status, and comparable as former great powers vying for international standing and position in a world transformed, they were potential rivals for leadership in western Europe. Their political differences circumscribed the scope of cooperative action although they did not preclude cooperation in highly sensitive political or strategic arenas. Harboring different visions and pursuing different objectives they could not turn their symmetry to constructive, progressive purpose by jointly transcending the classic pattern of interstate relations. The weight of tradition and the hope that the international situation was only temporary, or if not temporary then limited in its effects on middle-range powers, proved too strong for such a leap forward. At the very least, postwar Franco-British relations reveal the extent to which ideologically homogeneous powers can coexist in a state of conflict and cooperation, pursuing antagonistic national interests at one level while simultaneously cooperating in the same realm at a different level. Their relations also reveal, however, the limits imposed on each by clinging to traditional forms of cooperation in the technological age of the continental nation-states and highlight the paucity of what either can achieve alone.

Part Five

Policy Conflicts

Chapter 12

**Conflicts in Policy Formation
and Application**

American Policy: Southeast Asia

GEORGE MCT. KAHIN AND SAMUEL L. POPKIN

The political landscape in the United States is different from what it was when Richard Nixon campaigned for the Senate and the vice-presidency, and it is not just the Wallacites that make it so. New forces have arisen on the left as well, and they are articulately critical of the intervention in Vietnam and anxious to ensure that there be no even remotely comparable repetition of this experience elsewhere in southeast Asia. However overwhelming the political reaction from the right to the progressivism of the new student generation, the insistence on bringing moral and humanitarian values to bear on the conduct of foreign policy is likely to have a much greater influence than in the recent past.

Yet fear of the right still dominates much of the foreign-policy establishment, rendering still salient the slogan of not abandoning Asians to Communism. An administration that recalls the potency of the "loss of China" issue in the campaigns of 1950, 1952, and 1954 might temporarily favor this course, regarding it as useful in obviating attacks from the right, whether from George Wallace or from others. It must be acknowledged that a president—even an unpopular one—has great power to influence the public's perception of external realities. There is certainly presidential precedent for Mr. Nixon's finding it expedient to justify policies in terms of anti-Communist clichés and stereotypes, even though they may now have been discredited among many senior government officials and among intellectuals outside of government.

Much of the material in this essay is drawn from George McT. Kahin, "The Future of U.S. Policy in Southeast Asia," in Gerald L. Curtis (ed.), *Japanese-U.S. Relations in the 1970's* (New York: The American Assembly, Columbia Books, 1970).

If this reading of the past and the present shapes the premises upon which the United States bases its policies in the 1970s, those policies are not likely to be realistic.

Buying Time

An argument used increasingly by the Johnson administration during 1967 and 1968 to offset domestic criticism of its Vietnam policy, and still flourished by its apologists, is that the venture has at least bought time for the other states of southeast Asia. Thanks to the American intervention in Vietnam, so the argument runs, a shield has been provided behind which free nations have been able to rally their forces against Communism, address themselves to nation-building, and work out problems among themselves so that a foundation of regional, collective self-defense could be laid. According to this rationalization, for example, Indonesian generals, who might otherwise have wavered, were provided with an example that stiffened their backbones against the Indonesian Communist party and gave them the courage to move resolutely against it.

This false and misleading interpretation is a remarkable illustration of how far those seeking a publicly acceptable rationalization for a mistaken policy are prepared to distort history. Indonesia's international security and internal political situation have been little affected by American actions in Vietnam. Generals Suharto and Nasution and their colleagues needed no example of American anti-Communism to be persuaded that their own immediate and direct self-interest called for prompt measures against a hostile local Communist power which they believed threatened them. If American actions in Vietnam did have any significant effect on the political struggle in Indonesia, it was to enable the Indonesian Communist party to capitalize on the broadly based Indonesian opposition to the American intervention in Vietnam, an opposition manifest across the whole of the country's political spectrum.

If Indonesian military leaders had any reason at all to be grateful for the US intervention in Vietnam, it was that the magnitude of the involvement precluded any gratuitous American interference in Indonesia during the time General Suharto and his allies were consolidating their power in the struggle against Sukarno and the Communist party—a struggle wherein for some six months (1965–1966) the outcome was quite uncertain. American intervention in support of Suharto would almost certainly have turned nationalist sentiment against him and strengthened both Sukarno and the Indonesian Communist party.

Rather than buying time, in fact, the war has created new problems for all of southeast Asia. Not only have Laos and Cambodia suffered tremendous internal political disruption as a consequence of the Vietnam war, but, in addition, their relations with both parts of Vietnam have become much more strained.

The smouldering centuries-old traditional hostility between Cambodians and Vietnamese has been fanned into flame, and Cambodian fears have mounted that Thai and Vietnamese intervention will lead to further loss of territory to these neighboring states. Long-ingrained traditional animosities between the Thai and the Vietnamese have been enhanced as a result of Thailand's involvement in the war. By permitting the United States to establish air bases on its territory— bases that have played a major role in the bombing of both North and South Vietnam and of parts of Laos—the government in Bangkok has engendered bitterness and animosity among Vietnamese. Any normalization of Vietnamese-Thai relations after an end of the war will be all the more difficult if American bases are maintained in Thailand.

Among the southeast Asian states themselves, traditional animosities have a powerful and continuing dynamic that would remain operative whether or not there had been a Vietnamese war. These locally generated frictions are in themselves quite sufficient to develop serious threats to the region's stability. Among these states, competing claims to territory are still very much alive. Moreover, most of them are beset by problems of national integration, involving persisting tensions between majority groups and often large minorities, that generate problems which often affect neighboring states.

Nearly all the southeast Asian states emerged only recently from colonial straitjackets that had served to contain some of the major thrusts of their traditional foreign policies. Moreover, the boundaries imposed by the colonial powers often violated regional patterns of ethnic distribution and historically conditioned ethnic alignments. In few parts of southeast Asia can one say that present international borders do even rough justice to previous history or to the patterns of ethnic settlement.

The precolonial frontiers were not surveyed geographic boundaries, but were, in effect, something like broad "no-man's lands" where spheres of influence distant from the capitals converged or overlapped. The possibilities for international friction tended to be reduced by a situation wherein frontiers were not demarcated lines but broad peripheral territories that were either highly autonomous or virtually independent of the adjacent states. Consequently, these zones often served as buffers between the states.

These zones were usually upland or mountainous areas inhabited by ethnic minorities that frequently pursued modes of livelihood involving periodic shifting of village locale. The imposition of colonial rule established a new kind of fixed linear boundary that usually cut quite arbitrarily through tribal groupings of these upland minority ethnic groups. This was notably the case with frontiers between Thailand and Burma, northern Thailand and Laos, and Vietnam and Laos, with those shared by northwest Cambodia, Laos, and Vietnam, and with those between China and North Vietnam, Laos, and Burma.

Throughout the area, traditional rivalry between dominant lowland peoples and upland-dwelling minorities remains sharp and divisive, and either is already seriously disruptive (in Burma, Laos, Thailand, Cambodia, South Vietnam, and West Irian) or is potentially so (in Sarawak, Sabah, and Kalimantan). Because most of these minority groups straddle international boundaries, some of the lowland-upland conflicts cannot today be confined within existing frontiers.

The Vietnam war has had a generally destabilizing impact on many of the frontiers of continental southeast Asia. This effect is by no means confined to Vietnam's borders with Laos and Cambodia. It is also true of the Thai-Cambodian, Thai-Laotian and Cambodian-Laotian borders. The war has served to open up arbitrary, colonially determined boundaries, in a sense reconstituting some of the traditional frontiers, which were broad and fluid. Both the actual fighting and the unusual political and economic pulls arising from the war have caused upland tribal groups, particularly in Laos and the western reaches of Vietnam, to become dislodged from their old base areas so that they now move much more widely, frequently crossing political boundaries and thus altering local political balances and creating new economic problems. On Thailand's western border, this problem was already serious because of insurgencies by ethnic minorities in adjacent areas of Burma, often stimulated by their alliances with or supplies of arms from Kuomintang Chinese troops operating there. As a consequence of the fighting in Laos, hill-dwelling Meo and Yao tribesmen, who have been drawn into the conflict on both sides, have often been obliged to flee from their home areas, a significant number forcing their way across Thailand's northern borders.

Internal Forces

Partly because of the scale of US involvement in the Vietnam war, many observers tend to overemphasize the importance of external forces and underestimate that of internal factors in determining prospects for future stability in southeast Asia. The major force making for political instability during the next few decades undoubtedly will be socioeconomic. This factor will be related less to broad, distributive justice than to the frustration of hopes of a substantial educated or semieducated minority made increasingly restive because education has so outstripped the kind of economic growth that can utilize high school and university graduates. The number of people who have secondary or college education but are unable to find employment reasonably commensurate with their level of education (and thus with their expectations) is growing rapidly every year in all these countries. The political malaise stemming from this cannot easily be exaggerated. Throughout southeast Asia this increasingly widespread frustration is becoming sharper and can be expected to develop a political thrust with which even army-dominated governments must soon try to come to terms.

Violent political change, sometimes revolutionary in nature, is a normal political process in southeast Asia, and will remain so for a long time. Since the region's governments do not incorporate institutions that provide effectively for any significant measure of peaceful change in the socioeconomic or political status quo, such change is likely to occur only when physical power is brought to bear against status quo governments, either to force change or to replace them with new regimes.

Political violence is, after all, the basic means for maintaining the present socioeconomic orders and patterns of ethnic relationship in these states. In most cases the dominant political elites are unlikely to promote, or even acquiesce in, the kind of reform necessary to relieve social and economic inequities and ethnic discrimination before those who feel most aggrieved resort to violence.

But effective subversion of any of these governments can come only through indigenous forces. All variants of radical political change in southeast Asia will inevitably carry a heavy nationalist charge. Outside intervention in these processes—whether projected from the United States, China, the USSR, or Japan—is likely to have unpredictable consequences, and, at the military level, is almost certain to be counterproductive.

Conversely, if southeast Asian governments are going to be viable, they must be able to cope with local subversion on their own. In the long run the introduction of supportive foreign military power cannot save them and will progressively turn the force of nationalism against them.

Local military establishments, possessing the sophisticated military equipment offered by foreign powers, are now able to oppose political dissidence by means that permit greater physical distance between those applying the firepower and those they seek to control. But the more governments rely on such long-range means of repression, the less likely they are to appreciate the reasons for the dissidence and the less inclined they will be to seek political accommodation with those who have become active in the opposition. And because these means of suppression discriminate so little between the actual insurgents and others who live in the area, their use is likely to be politically counterproductive. They are likely either to create terror-stricken refugees (who evacuate to an adjacent area where they become an economic burden and cause friction with its settled population) or to stimulate local sympathy and even additional adherents for the insurgent group.

Throughout southeast Asia there is the danger that foreign economic aid will create artificial political situations in which governments become estranged from their people but are provided with a reprieve enabling them to rule for a time without having to maintain and develop a sufficient base of popular support. Heavy reliance on outside aid, economic as well as military, even if multilaterally channeled, can easily insulate a political leadership and reduce its sensitivity and responsiveness to socioeconomic problems and political discontent.

Status quo governments cannot be expected to support social and economic changes that appear likely to weaken their power base appreciably or to strengthen the power base of competing political elements, real or potential. Because foreign aid must be channeled primarily through existing governments, it is difficult, of course, to prevent them from using such aid to protect and strengthen their own power, even though this use tends to increase the socioeconomic inequities that provide the basis for the political appeal of dissident groups.

Where foreign economic assistance is provided on a multilateral basis, it is less likely to be used primarily to maintain a regime in power and more likely to benefit a significant part of the population, whether immediately or in the long run, by establishing some of the conditions prerequisite to economic development. The enlightened introduction of such outside economic and technical assistance can help to speed needed social reforms in southeast Asian countries. And where its application is in tune with local social and economic realities, outside assistance can sometimes temporarily reduce the likelihood of political malaise. But even where such aid is fully consonant with local developmental needs and is dispensed multilaterally, it may easily cause further distortion of socioeconomic patterns and thereby lead to an increase in political strains within the country, rather than a reduction of them.

The political stability of a recipient regime should be neither the overall objective of foreign economic aid nor a condition for continuing it. For at least a generation to come, intermittent political turbulence will be a natural phase in the political development of many countries. If outside economic assistance is to make any major contribution to their social welfare and economic growth, the donors should recognize that the improved political leadership necessary to bring about significant economic and social progress is likely to come to power only after an intervening period of political instability.

Regional Collective Security

It has become fashionable, particularly with the advent of the Nixon administration in Washington, to argue in favor of the establishment of a regional southeast Asian collective security arrangement. This idea was advanced during the last year or two of the Johnson administration and has received particular encouragement from the new administration, with several writers now referring to Nixon's October 1967 article in *Foreign Affairs*.[1] The idea of replacing an American military presence in southeast Asia with a collective defense arrangement among non-Communist southeast Asian states undoubtedly has considerable appeal for administration leaders and congressmen who, while they desire as much military disengagement from southeast Asia as possible, do not wish to be charged with abandoning the American mission of containing Asian Communism. This kind of arrangement can be presented as bespeaking a continuing responsibility toward anti-Communist southeast Asian governments, but being designed to avoid involvement of American ground forces while costing much less than bilateral defense arrangements between the United States and these countries.

China will always remain the major power most directly concerned with continental southeast Asia. Its primary strategic interests require that neither the United States nor the Soviet Union become predominant in this area or draw the area into an alignment directed against it. Peking will undoubtedly remain sensitive to the threat of American or Soviet bases and defense ties with Burma, Thailand, Laos, or Vietnam.

During the 1970s China can be expected to continue to attach more importance to preventing its southern neighbors from cooperating in

[1] See Richard M. Nixon, "Asia After Vietnam," *Foreign Affairs*, 46, no. 1 (October 1967), 111–125.

an American- or Soviet-supported containment belt than to fomenting or supporting subversive actions against their governments. Particularly with the tensions on its vast Soviet frontier, China will need all the more to avoid antagonizing the states on her southern border in ways that might induce them to accept American or Soviet military ties.

It appears unlikely that Leonid Brezhnev's call of June 7, 1969, for a Soviet-sponsored Asian security pact will lead to anything, but Russia's involvement in southeast Asia will apparently be greater after the Vietnam conflict is concluded than it was before. Against the background of the Soviet Union's antagonistic relationship with China and the tension over their long frontier, Moscow has taken an increased interest in the other states that border on southern China.

Because of Moscow's power and its much greater economic aid potential, it appears to exert a stronger long-term attraction for most Asian Communist leaders than does Peking. China's greater commitment to revolutionary struggle is appreciated by some non-governing parties, but is not enough to align them with China, particularly once they have achieved governmental power. Communization of additional states in the area—improbable as this prospect is in the next decade— would not necessarily be a promising development for China. In view of the Sino-Soviet conflict, it is unlikely that China would see either its security or its ideological-revolutionary objectives advanced by the overthrow of non-Communist or anti-Communist "bourgeois" states in southern Asia, for this would entail the risk of their being replaced by Communist allies of Moscow.

A common denominator among most of the countries likely to join a southeast Asian collective defense pact is antagonism toward and discrimination against their Chinese populations. A defense pact among Indonesia, Malaysia, and the Philippines could conceivably bring about collective action against the Chinese minority in one of those states, whether or not it came in the guise of "antisubversive" or "antiinsurgent" measures.

Collective action against overseas Chinese by southeast Asian countries would probably bring to ruin possibilities for good relations between them and either Taiwan or Peking. Unfortunately, the leaders of many southeast Asian countries are still not disabused of their quite erroneous assumption that a corollary of the United States's anti-Peking policy is antagonism toward overseas Chinese and a willingness to countenance and even encourage repressive measures against them.

The difficulties in organizing a mutual defense pact for suppression of insurgencies (Communist or otherwise) would be formidable because most southeast Asian states have frequently supported subversive insurgent activities against one another (this is true of insular and peninsular[2] as well as continental southeast Asia), and will probably continue to support such actions from time to time. It would not be inconceivable, however, particularly with the inducement of a considerable American financial contribution, for a number of these countries to join in organizing collective action against insurgent activity, whether or not it was Communist in nature. Collective military action might give a beleaguered member significant additional firepower in its efforts to suppress local insurgents. But though the host government might obtain temporary military advantages against the insurgents, nationalist sensitivities would almost certainly be aroused in a way that would further erode its base of popular support. And the social, economic and political conditions which generated the insurgency would remain. The political pressures that had been militarily contained would very likely build up to a greater intensity, to break through later with even greater force.

Protection from Whom?

Many Western writers, recently including some from the Soviet Union, have considerably exaggerated the extent of Peking's intervention in southeast Asia while they have minimized or disregarded that of the United States. In fact, quite apart from Vietnam, the record clearly shows that America's political and military intervention in southeast Asia has been far greater than China's and has had a much heavier political impact—for the most part destabilizing.

Vietnam is not an isolated case; it is simply the most recent in a series of American interventions, and, of course, by far the heaviest and most militarized. Nor is the Vietnam intervention unique in its futility and counterproductivity. Indeed, some of the lessons suggested by US involvement in Vietnam should have been appreciated through earlier American interventions in southeast Asia, that were equally fruitless or even counterproductive. But the formidable catalog of blunders has been largely unknown to Americans and to most of their representatives in Congress. Previous American military involvements and efforts at political subversion in southeast Asian countries have failed, and the consequences of these failures have a continuing life. In Burma, Cambodia, Indonesia, and Laos today, one can clearly

[2] "Insular and peninsular" southeast Asia subsumes Malaysia, Singapore, Brunei, Indonesia, and the Philippines.

see how the unfortunate residues of American political interventions during the 1950s still significantly affect the local political scene and circumscribe the possibilities for new and more enlightened American policies.

Difficulties plague any state that seeks to mold or maintain another country's political system, whether by the use of political, economic, or military means.[3] Since the obstacles to constructive accomplishment are high, one would think that a state's intervention could be justified only if its vital interests were at stake. Taking a wider view of America's entanglement in Vietnam, we must ask how American political and military leaders came to believe that the nation's interests required her to commit hundreds of thousands of men and billions of dollars to the support of a small and distant country. How could one believe that the stakes justified the measures undertaken?

Eight years ago it was written that "the West, instead of dealing with Russia in terms of a world policy, persists in the attempt to deal with the world in terms of a Russian policy, this being in essence the policy of containing Russia all over the world. The underlying orientation is faulty."[4] This is a fair description and a false judgment. The United States did fashion and follow a "Russian" foreign policy. We have been willing to act or to support the action of others in order to counter the outward thrust of the Soviet Union and associated states: for example, in Greece, Berlin, Korea, and Cuba. (We were not willing to support the Dutch in Indonesia in 1962 or the British and French in Suez in 1956.) American pursuit of a "Russian" foreign policy was not an error; it was instead the reversal of old and erroneous American habits. America's mistake before two world wars lay not in her failure to pay attention to little states but in her disregard of the course of great-power relations. Interests have to be guarded where they exist in greatest magnitude, as in western Europe; threats have to be met when they emanate from a state whose strength may endanger one's own security. By her military and other capabilities, the Soviet Union—and only the Soviet Union—has constituted such a threat. In sensible response, America pursued a "Russian" foreign policy; and the reverse can be said of the Soviet Union.

Throughout the 1950s, when it appeared to American policy-makers that Moscow controlled world Communist forces, a gain scored by any Communist state was presumed to add something to the strength of the Soviet Union. Russia was seen as directing the Communist

[3] Kenneth N. Waltz prepared the material through page 434, drawing heavily on his "The Politics of Peace," *International Studies Quarterly*, 6 (September 1967).
[4] Robert C. Tucker, *The Soviet Political Mind: Studies in Stalinism and Post-Stalin Change* (New York: Praeger, 1963), p. 183.

bloc, and the Russian danger and the threat of world Communism seemed to be one and the same. The term "bloc" has now fallen into desuetude; instead, the term "polycentrism" misleads us. Though the Communist movement is no longer effectively directed by the Soviet Union, many Americans still think in terms of an international conspiracy and talk as though interest and duty require us to counter its machinations. It can no longer be said, however, that a Communist government newly come to power in some minor state will enhance Russia's strength or somehow add to the power of a now mythical world Communist movement.

Spokesmen for recent administrations nevertheless have asserted the vital importance of showing that insurgencies are costly, damaging, and doomed to defeat; they have argued that one setback may lead to another; they have averred that China must be contained now as the Soviet Union was earlier. A strong case, however, cannot result from adding up weak reasons. The revolutionary guerrilla wins civil wars, not international ones, and no civil war can significantly change the balance of world power unless it takes place in America or Russia. In any event, the potency of irregular warfare and the ability of Communists to overthrow existing political orders, have been grossly exaggerated—as the record of events in Greece, Malaya, the Philippines, and Indonesia makes clear. Nor does one setback necessarily lead to another. We are misled by the vision of dominoes. States in the area of the fighting lack the solidity, shape, and cohesion that the image suggests. Externally ill-defined, internally fragile and chaotic, they more appropriately call to mind sponges; and sponges, whatever their other characteristics, do not from the transmission of impulses neatly fall down in a row. As for China, we have been mesmerized by the magic of mere numbers, and have led ourselves to believe that 800 million people must be able to do something highly damaging to somebody. They have in fact hardly been able to do anything at all; and any increase in Chinese strength would anyway be first and foremost a worry for the Soviet Union, not for the United States.

Because no realignment of national power in Vietnam could in itself affect the balance of power between the United States and the Soviet Union—or even noticeably alter the imbalance of power between the United States and China—the United States need not have intervened at all. We do not fight for our interest; not enough is at stake to bring important American interests into question. We must then be fighting for such abstractions as honor and anti-Communism and on behalf of somebody else's welfare as we see it. The perils of weakness are matched by the temptations of power. Good intentions, backed by great power, have often led to persecution, unnecessary violence, and widespread destruction. The pattern is uncomfortably common, whether in the relation of believers to infidels, of one race to another, or of nation to nation. A state that enjoys a margin of power in its favor is able to make choices. It can delude itself into trying to bring orderly government to those it believes are unable to govern themselves, it can kill people in the name of their liberty and seek to build a polity and shape a society by the use of B-52s. War is a blunt instrument. Once begun, it is hard to control. As more blood is spilled, more resounding reasons must be given for the carnage until finally unimportant wars fought for doubtful causes are justified in the name of high principle. The escalation of justifications in the war in Vietnam was as impressive as the escalation of force—and may have been ultimately as dangerous. The loftier the principles invoked, the more difficult it became to stop the war and disentangle the nation.

With no vital security interests at stake, America need not have committed its forces to battle. Because the war is an unnecessary one, contemplation of withdrawal without victory should not bring deep discomfort. The war, however, has become its own cause. How could the artificers of the policy and its supporters justify the war—politically, to the nation, and psychologically, to themselves—unless they believed that its purposes were somehow of an importance commensurate with the death toll. Thus President Nixon has coupled warnings that it is "our will and character that is being tested" with declarations that "the possibility of winning a just peace in Vietnam and in the Pacific is at stake." We will not, he insists, "be humiliated. We will not be defeated."[5]

The point of departure for most discussions of future American policy in southeast Asia is the prefatory remark: "Assuming some sort of honorable settlement in Vietnam . . ." or "on the assumption that the United States leaves Vietnam in a way that is not interpreted as a defeat. . . ." This foundation is an unrealistic one on which to build, and not merely because the nature of the war and of the American involvement preclude any honorable ending of it for the United States. Any realistic projection of American relations with southeast Asia must accept the fact that its Vietnam intervention will be widely regarded as a failure. Whatever the pattern and pace of the United States's withdrawal, the ultimate reckoning by Asians will be that American military and economic power, however massively applied, could not make up for a regime's lack of broad popular support or

[5] Text of President Nixon's speech, "The Cambodia Strike: Defensive Action for Peace," April 30, 1970, Department of State Publication, 8529, East Asian and Pacific Series 189 (Washington: U.S. Government Printing Office, 1970).

overcome indigenous revolutionaries who had secured that support. Nor will the lesson be lost on southeast Asians that American intervention in a civil war can be devastatingly destructive—so destructive as to bring the leaders of other governments that have security pacts with the United States to question whether in their own countries such intervention would be worthwhile. Quite apart from what the American public may countenance, the states of southeast Asia are in the future likely to be more circumspect about making arrangements with the United States that provide for its military intervention. The reluctance of Asians to suffer American protection is likely to be matched by the unwillingness of future administrations to extend it.

Southeast Asia is not an area of major importance to the security of the United States. It is not in the interest of the US to enter into commitments for the defense of these countries in any way that would significantly reduce its capacity to respond to outside threats to western Europe or Japan, both of which are much more important to American security than the whole of southeast Asia. Moreover, the overthrow of no government in southeast Asia would pose any real danger to American security. No matter what the US does, during the next decade a number of these governments will be overthrown. In some cases, their people may be better off as a consequence, although not necessarily. With the possible exceptions of Laos and now Cambodia,[6] it is improbable that during the next decade any southeast Asian government outside of Vietnam will become Communist. But if they do, the variety of Communism will almost certainly be highly nationalistic, with these states the satellites of neither Moscow nor Peking.

The United States must distinguish much more sharply than it has in the past between invasion and internal subversion. The meaning of "subversion" has become so twisted in popular American usage as to inhibit an objective view of political processes abroad. Subversion is not the monopoly of the Communists (after all, the YMCA was regarded as "subversive" by the imperial government of China), and it can be a healthy thing. It is as applicable to bad regimes as to good ones, to the overthrow of unrepresentative governments as to repre-

[6] Prior to the ousting of Sihanouk and the US invasion of Cambodia, the political prospects of the tiny Cambodian Communist party were insignificant—probably less promising than of any Communist party in southeast Asia. However, US support of the narrowly based group that ousted Sihanouk and the country-wide fighting and devastation widely regarded as set off by the US attack against the Vietnamese Communists' border bases has significantly increased the political potential of Cambodian Communists. They are now able to wrap themselves in the mantle of a politically legitimizing nationalism to an extent impossible for them before.

sentative ones. It should be recalled that the literal meaning of the word "subvert" is to "turn from beneath," and that its present primary definition is to "overturn or overthrow from the foundation." The majorities who constitute the social foundations of most southeast Asian countries are sometimes oppressed by governmental structures in which they are rarely represented effectively. A change in the structure of government may well be socially and politically beneficial for most of the people. The United States, in its relations with the present governments, should not seek to block such changes.

The United States should be guided by the fact that no insurgency in southeast Asia will be successful unless it reflects substantial popular support. If a government cannot cope with insurgents, then those insurgents do manifestly enjoy considerable popular backing—backing likely to be as great as or greater than that enjoyed by the government. The interposition of US firepower (whether directly or by proxy) on the side of a beleaguered government is more likely to prolong the fighting than to determine its outcome.

American Policy: Nuclear Proliferation

GEORGE H. QUESTER

The Nuclear Nonproliferation Treaty

A world in which many countries acquire nuclear weapons could be a much less pleasant one. Wars that today kill thousands might instead kill millions; wars that now are averted might instead be launched, simply because each side preemptively felt it had such powerful weapons that it dared not hesitate to use them. To prevent a further spread of nuclear weapons, the United States and the Soviet Union have offered for signature a treaty freezing the number of states possessing such weapons at the current five: the United States, the USSR, Great Britain, France, and Communist China.[1] These countries would pledge themselves under the treaty not to give away nuclear weapons or assist other nations to produce them. Countries not having such weapons would pledge themselves, under the same treaty, never to accept them and never to manufacture them. The non-nuclear states, moreover, would agree to accept inspection safeguards by the International Atomic Energy Agency (IAEA) for all their peaceful nuclear activities in order to ensure that such facilities and materials are not diverted to producing nuclear explosives.

At one time, American monopoly on the production of reactors, or of enriched uranium fuel for such reactors, supplied a natural control over most nations' cravings for atomic bombs.[2] Yet the great-power monopoly on

[1] For good basic discussions of the proliferation problem, see Leonard Beaton and John Maddox, *The Spread of Nuclear Weapons* (London: Chatto and Windus, 1962); Alastair Buchan (ed.), *A World of Nuclear Powers?* (Englewood Cliffs, N.J.: Prentice-Hall, 1966); and Leonard Beaton, *Must the Bomb Spread?* (London: Penquin Books, 1966).

[2] See William Bader, *The United States and the Spread of Nuclear Weapons* (New York: Pegasus, 1968), for an interesting discussion of general American policy on proliferation.

fuel or technology is now clearly threatened, and some countries (India and Israel, for example) have indeed always been careful not to be seduced into any full dependence on American enriched uranium. The problem of weapons spread thus may soon become urgent. The spread of electric-power-producing nuclear reactors *ipso facto* spreads the ability to produce plutonium A-bombs; progress in other civilian atomic fields can similarly spread production capacities for the enriched uranium used in A- and H-bombs. Little if any of this technological development will depend on military intent, for it is all profitable and justifiable in civilian terms. Yet the assurance can then hardly be given that the "cheap by-product" of nuclear weapons will not be produced wherever nations feel even the slightest tensions with their neighbors.

Under such circumstances, a nonproliferation treaty may serve some important purposes. For a start, it would strengthen the hand of domestic opponents of the bomb within every signatory state, for the legal status quo would then be on their side. If a great many states sign and ratify the treaty, making bombs will thereby have become a much less respectable thing to do, something a little beyond the pale. This kind of moral pressure may thereafter reassure states a little about their neighbors, with ensuing multiplier effects whereby all parties to a conflict discount the introduction of nuclear weapons into it. The addition of international inspectors may serve to detect any moves to make bombs before they can reach fruition. If the fast pace of technology makes this impossible, inspectors will still serve as a visible reminder of the state's international obligations, and thus dampen any indigenous tendencies to violate the treaty.

The treaty offers some definite advantages for the superpowers, and perhaps for the world as a whole; it may be less attractive, however, to the specific states that now must renounce the nuclear weapons that might have been within their grasp. Conflicts can appear here on whether such states will accept or reject the nonproliferation treaty; in light of this, conflict can still also appear on whether the super-powers will remain wholeheartedly committed to their treaty.

Conflicts of International Prestige

The nonproliferation treaty is thus an unusually stimulating issue for any traditional analyst of international politics, if only because it seems to present a "reversal of alliances," a refreshing new confrontation in which we all can have fun sorting out the ranks. When else have India, Germany, Brazil, Israel, and Japan been aligned against the US and the USSR? And where do we put Canada and Sweden, Rumania, Australia, and Egypt? While the American public has hardly become engrossed in the issue, some other publics have, and the new constellations of "countries like India" versus "the superpowers" have revitalized national-interest arguments in places where they had become stale. If many of us had come to see international politics as a largely bureaucratic phenomenon that simply played out intranational disputes on a bigger stage, the nonproliferation treaty has given a timely revival to the notion that it is nations, rather than bureaus, that have conflicts.

The treaty demands that all but five of the nations of the world renounce nuclear weapons: the authors of the treaty naturally are among the privileged five. Some invidious response from other states thus is not totally surprising. The Indian government at first wished to be quite cautious in its rejections of the treaty, but Mrs. Gandhi's statements in 1968 that India could not sign the treaty "under present circumstances" were greeted with such vehement enthusiasm that they retroactively have been recoded as a definitive rejection of the treaty. To a lesser extent, antitreaty sentiment also has been roused in Japan and Brazil; the indignity of being asked to submit to the "first unequal treaty of the twentieth century" can seem quite real wherever it is felt that the national prestige lately has been slighted.

It is interesting that commentators in many of these states fully expect all Americans to be enthusiastically for the treaty; after all, the US from its national interest, must be strongly attracted to a foreign renunciation of weapons that it is not required to match. The news that most Americans are somewhat indifferent to the nonproliferation treaty is greeted with polite disbelief in New Delhi and Rome.

It is thus all too easy to see a new line of political confrontation in the nonproliferation treaty, one that pits an alliance of near-nuclear states against the US, the USSR, and perhaps the United Kingdom. A third bloc of "underdeveloped" states sits on the sidelines, bored by the issue of proliferation, concerned that it not divert all the more developed states from channeling aid and assistance in their direction. China and France also play uncommitted or ambiguous roles, and a new age of diplomacy is upon us.

This picture may be severely challenged, however. For one, the old issues of the East-West conflict are hardly so dead that nuclear proliferation outweighs them entirely in the making of foreign-policy alignment. For a second, the internal impact of the treaty is hardly as clear as the discussion above suggested. None of the near-nuclear countries can really afford to be monolithically opposed to the treaty, just as the United States cannot be monolithically in favor. The cross-currents that beset the nations must be discussed in terms both of substantive issues and of bureaucratic factions. In the end, the treaty may be grist for the mills of the bureaucratic analysts as much as for the commentators on international politics.

There is indeed some truth to the raw "national-interest" or "foreign-policy" conflict between the superpowers and the near-nuclear nations. The experienced lawyers of the Italian or West German foreign ministries have always known that one does not concede a national prerogative without some *quid pro quo.* A long series of issues can thus be cited as stemming from the nonproliferation treaty. But the lists always run much too long, because these foreign offices instinctively begin to pad their arguments, and because these states have cooperated among themselves by swapping arguments against the treaty—however limited the arguments may truly be in their particular relevance. Thus one sees spokesmen for Bonn borrowing Indian terminology to demand that "vertical proliferation" (acquisition of new weapons by the superpowers) be halted along with horizontal proliferation. Since the German foreign ministry has tended to become extremely nervous at the very thought of Soviet-American disarmament talks—such talks can always lead to a thinning out of American conventional or nuclear forces in Europe—this German objection to the treaty hardly seemed the most serious. Indian scientists, conversely, can be induced to mention the risks of commercial espionage by IAEA inspectors, an argument first sounded in Bonn.

Almost as automatically, professional military men come to discover some military need for the atomic bomb. Nuclear land mines in the Himalayas become relevant for India; nuclear depth charges for the antisubmarine forces of the Japanese Self-Defense Forces. In every disarmament process of the past, nations were careful not to surrender a defense option too quickly; why should a Brazilian or Swedish military officer be untrue to his profession now?

Real issues arise out of the nonproliferation treaty. National prestige is itself a real issue, but a peculiar one in that it seizes upon and distorts other issues as surrogates and vehicles. It is not foolish for the Italian foreign office to echo Japanese complaints about the treaty —only misleadingly dishonest.

Political prestige is an important consideration in any nuclear weapons debate, and only the most disingenuous outsiders would deny it. Few Americans or Europeans today know that India is capable of making nuclear weapons; educated people should be aware of the scientific prowess India has shown, but they are not. It is useless to deny that the explosion of a rudimentary Indian bomb or peaceful explosive would make editorial writers and citizens all around the world sit up and take notice. The reaction of Afro-Asian countries to the Chinese explosion of 1964 was not to condemn but to show respect. Already it has been suggested that India be offered some substitute form of prestige—for instance, permanent membership in the UN Security Council—that presumably would remove India's psychological need to develop the bomb. Yet this all comes late; the lesson is clearly that if India had not moved this close to having a bomb, such suggestions would never have been made. One can ask, conversely, how much importance the outside world would attach to Communist China today if she had not entered the nuclear club. Would we not pass off Peking as an internationally insignificant conglomeration of feuding factions, its economic house not in order, greatly overrated as an international actor? Bombs do make a difference.

It is likely that the possibility of a severe American response already deters any Chinese use of nuclear weapons against New Delhi, as well as against Tokyo, Bangkok, or Sydney. Soviet responses here also probably deter China. Even for a conventional attack, American and Russian assistance for India are extremely likely. Indeed, Indian defense plans currently can be rationalized as assuming a great probability for such moral and material support from the outside world in the event of a Chinese attack.[3]

Only the more polemical Indian statements will deny this; yet only the more polemical Western statements will claim that this sums up the issue. The existence of even a rudimentary Indian bomb stockpile will inevitably change the expectations of both parties to any new confrontation in the Himalayas, and the balance of this psychological change might yet favor India. If the introduction of the superpowers' nuclear arsenals on behalf of India were not plausible and salient enough in the minds of all the publics that matter, Indian nuclear warheads would not be redundant. Any confrontation along a hostile frontier is something of a game of "chicken," a contest of whose resolve will come into question first. A visible addition of weapons of mass destruction to one side will not be without effect.

Economic Conflicts

One of the more serious arguments advanced against the treaty is that it will impose economic disadvantages on countries required to submit

[3] An illuminating discussion of Indian attitudes toward the strategic balance and nuclear weapons can be found in K. Suerahmanyam, *The Asian Balance of Power in the Seventies: An Indian View* (New Delhi: Institute for Defence Studies and Analysis, 1968).

to safeguards. Agitation on this point shows up among electrical power producers in Japan and Germany and to a lesser extent in Italy. Inspection will waste time and prevent profits, the argument goes, so that the treaty should be rejected; commercial espionage will carry off valuable trade secrets, and the whole future of the country's economic growth will be at stake.[4] Businessmen in similar positions in Sweden are surprisingly less prone to testify that Vienna will wreck their economy; the Swedish entrepreneur is considerably more under the thumb of state policy than his Japanese counterpart, and cannot as easily lobby for his private profits by pretending to defend the national interest.

Lest we debunk such claims of near-nuclear-nation businessmen too much, we should mention American sales representatives who have claimed (and perhaps hoped) that these forecasts are true. If one can beat Germany out of a reactor sale in Spain by claiming that the nonproliferation treaty will keep the Germans from supplying fuel, any energetic American firm would be derelict in its stockholder duties if it did not do so.

There is also an underlying issue of legal principle or nationalism here which will fester in any country contemplating adhering to the nonproliferation treaty. It is one thing to ask businessmen to accept international inspection of property delivered from some foreign country; a believer in property cannot deny that sellers have the right to place any conditions they please on how and what they sell. It is quite another thing to impose international inspection on what a nation has produced and will produce for itself. The nonproliferation treaty does not introduce the international inspector, except to some extent within the Euratom area. Rather, it introduces an entirely new justifying principle for inspection: international consensus by treaty rather than straightforward property rights. Property rights as an effective control on nuclear weapons proliferation might soon have collapsed, as the nuclear field becomes more and more a competitive buyers market. Yet signing away one's right never to truly "own" nuclear resources may seem a viscerally unpleasant requirement to impose on Japan, or on any country like Japan.

Yet some of the impact of businessmen in general may have been just the reverse all these years. If American business (together with the AEC) had not talked up the prospects of nuclear power so much,

---

[4] See Lawrence Scheinman, "Nuclear Safeguards, the Peaceful Atom, and the IAEA," *International Conciliation*, 572 (March 1969), for a comprehensive discussion of the role of IAEA on the NPT. See also Lawrence Scheinman, "Euratom: Nuclear Integration in Europe," *International Conciliation*, 563 (May 1967), for a basic description of decision-making in Euratom.

the implicit threat of proliferation might have been further over the horizon, giving the architects of the nonproliferation treaty more time. And if German and Japanese entrepreneurs had not maximized profits, these countries would be more able to defy the US on signing the treaty. For the moment, almost all reactors producing power in the world depend on cheaper enriched uranium from the United States, because selfish entrepreneurs put their profits ahead of the national independence achieved by use of natural uranium. India and Israel, of course, are exceptions to this pattern.

Apart from such inadvertent impacts on the political process, businessmen in near-nuclear countries can also have some rational reasons to favor the treaty. Standardization on IAEA safeguards, in lieu of the present mixture of IAEA, Euratom, ENEA, and national systems may make it easier to expand the nuclear electrical industry, since some sorts of fuel sales and equipment transfers are in effect now delayed or precluded by the incompatabilities of the various control systems. For a country selling uranium, such as South Africa, this standardization might expand a very profitable market; for a country excluded from "Europe," such as Sweden, the nonproliferation treaty, by killing off Euratom, might win a market entry that would otherwise have been denied. German nuclear industrialists criticize IAEA inspection practices for insufficient automation; this is an argument against accepting the treaty, but it is also a sales pitch to the IAEA to purchase German automation devices once the treaty indeed still goes into effect.

As "technological" a question as the nonproliferation treaty inevitably raises another internal conflict in all the states affected—that of scientist versus nonscientist. The scientist, predictably enough, sees his substantive advice being oversimplified and abused by less intelligent politicians and other laymen; he is in favor of free inquiry and full exploration of nuclear physics, but he also feels a moral responsibility that the products of all this effort be constricted to peaceful uses.

Hence, the impact of the scientific self-image on the political balance becomes interestingly unpredictable. Japanese physicists are normally left-wing, but alternate between distrusting foreign inspectors and distrusting their domestic government. German physicists were charged with designing bearable inspection apparatus, by use of automation techniques and "black boxes," to buttress their government's position that this will be very difficult; technological enthusiasm has led them to succeed much more than expected, thus to some extent undermining the German case against safeguards, but also promising sales to the IAEA of German-produced "black boxes." Sweden has accumulated prestige in being technologically proficient on questions of disarmament, to the degree that it is reluctant to walk away from the table even when the treaty's text is regarded as inadequate. India has sought prestige in the technology of nuclear physics, which stands in the way of accepting a treaty.

As more and more physicists are hired in the nuclear industry, their position shifts toward the businessman's distrust of safeguards, toward an "idealistic" "free pursuit of knowledge" without which science and national economic progress will be stifled. Until this happens, or until the IAEA inspector sets foot in the university research laboratories, the scientist (as in Italy) leans instead toward worldly "international co-operation" and peace, and favors the nonproliferation treaty.

Electoral Conflict

The businessman seeks to maximize profits; other citizens seek to hold elective or appointive political office, for the sheer fun of it, if for no other reason. The nonproliferation treaty is a confusing item for the profit-seeker to handle, but it is no less so for the office-seekers of the "nonnuclear" nations.

Depending on how it is made to appear in the popular press, a treaty like the nonproliferation treaty can be exploited for or against the incumbent political party in a country, with varying results for policy. If the treaty is unpopular, as in Japan, it may quickly become obvious that the government has been saddled with an albatross, as all the opposition parties rush to oppose it. The treaty is "Left" in the sense of being anti-armaments; but the Left in Japan can count on the United States to force the governing right-of-center Liberal Democrats to support the treaty (albeit many Liberals privately hope the Left's opposition will kill it), so that it makes more electoral sense to bend one's ideology against the treaty.

In Sweden, by comparison, the incumbent Social Democrats clearly have developed a vested interest in "working for peace"; any treaties thus make the incumbents' record look more productive, even though the team that negotiated at Geneva did not see Swedish amendments adopted and has private misgivings about the treaty. Opposition parties in Sweden resent the way in which disarmament negotiations were originally entered into on a multipartisan basis, only to produce an election issue that helped the Socialists retain power in 1968.

A disarmament treaty, which is what the nonproliferation treaty is in some sense, thus carries a lot of symbolic baggage within any internal debate. Regardless of direct substance, accepting such a treaty tends to reflect badly on the nation's military establishment, bringing into question both the practical need and the moral justification for such forces. Rejecting such a treaty, conversely, serves as a rebuke for the disarmers in one's political spectrum—typically, but not always, the socialist and other political leftists—and is a vote of confidence in the military defenders of the realm.

Thus the antiweapons factions of a number of parliaments become the natural allies of the US and the Soviet Union so long as the nonproliferation treaty is not discussed or understood in any great detail. A product of the Geneva disarmament conference, a "first step" toward disarmament, the treaty as portrayed by its sponsors attracts an emotional response in Italy, in Sweden, and to some extent in West Germany, simply because it is seen to have vindicated those who all along were opposed to weapons. Opponents of the treaty normally cannot dare to oppose the treaty on these terms; in Italy the Christian Democrats, the party of the pope, can hardly venture to become a pro-weapons party. And the Social Democrats in Sweden, despite their own disquiet over many aspects of the treaty, could hardly have thrown away their own considerable investment in peace as their issue. Opponents of the treaty must thus attack on relatively circular and elaborate paths in these contexts, and time and public interest may not then be great enough to block the treaty.

Russians and Americans had been sitting together in smoke-filled rooms polishing drafts of the nonproliferation treaty, and comparing notes on the bargaining strategy to be applied to states like West Germany, Rumania, and India. Such an experience might indeed have been justified purely by its novelty. For President Johnson, the treaty might thus have served somewhat to counter the Vietnam war in the 1968 election campaign, to prove that the Democratic administration could bring home peaceful products of cooperation with the Communist world.

If President Johnson had special reasons to favor the treaty, President Nixon has some to oppose it, and Nixon did express reservations throughout the 1968 election campaign. The treaty is, after all, co-sponsored by the Democratic party and by the Soviet Union. In the aftermath of Czechoslovakia, it may only have been fitting to slow down signs of cooperation with the USSR. The new Republican administration, moreover, was committed to shifting attention back to Europe from Asia, a shift that suggested more sympathy for West German and other forebodings about the treaty.

Not all the competition for public office revolves around elections. Holders of bureaucratic office attempt to get ahead by expanding their bureau's services, operations, and tables of organizations. Another treaty conflict thus has arisen, in advanced political communities, between the person whose political future is tied to the success of projects already launched and those who have not yet hitched their wagons to such stars. In India, the only serious support for signing the nonproliferation treaty came from senior civil service personnel who feared that rejection of the treaty might terminate American or Russian aid necessary to the smooth and successful operation of their bureaus. Younger and more detached Indians were much more willing to test the resolve of the superpowers, to run the risk that India might have to go it alone. Indian scientists wedded to the glamor of the atomic energy programs would, moreover, oppose any international commitment that seemed to take the edge off the nation's accomplishments here.

Law, Logic, and Reality

Societies advanced enough to have nuclear industries also have a system of law; therefore, they have a basic conflict between lawyer and layman that also confuses debate on the nonproliferation treaty.

The clearest example of a lawyer-dominated response comes in the West German arguments against the treaty, some of which are impossibly esoteric in form. The lawyer's dominance in Bonn can be explained variously as due to a surplus of such persons recruited by the foreign ministry or as due to a reaction to the "illegalism" of the Third Reich. At any rate, it rigorously demanded legal counterconcessions for every concession to the nonproliferation principle, even when other Germans thought a gratuitous concession here and there would have been politically more effective.

Yet a similar legalism might conversely be attributed to the Russian-American authors of the treaty, who produced progressively tighter drafts that in fact allow the treaty's critics to claim that earlier drafts were better. By insisting on inspection when the original Russian draft made no mention of it, the United States opened a question which may no longer be crucial to the halting of weapons spread, but which generates numerous opportunities for haggling and criticism. The treaty has similarly been visibly tightened from draft to draft with regard to peaceful explosives. A nonlawyer might have argued that a shorter and less elaborate treaty would have generated the necessary mandate against nuclear weapons at much less cost, perhaps omitting inspection, perhaps simply letting the test ban prohibit any peaceful explosive projects.

A different example of abstract legalism shows up in the policies of the United Kingdom. At an earlier stage, the British government seemed determined to behave exactly like the US and the USSR, since its privileged status as a nuclear-weapons state logically dictated that it do so. British statements favoring the treaty in Geneva were, if anything, more doctrinaire than those of the two superpowers. If part of this reflected embarrassment at the British exclusion from the drafting of the treaty, the rest simply stemmed from an assumption that all nuclear-weapons states "have an interest" in halting proliferation. At some point, however, a realization emerged that Britain's position might be special, given that she was suing for entry into Europe, which includes Euratom and Euratom's objections, real or imagined, to the treaty. If Germany is to be the principal partisan of British entry into the European communities, it will simply not do for Britain to act as if it regarded Germany as an "nth country."

It is difficult to assign priorities between arms control and the rest of foreign policy, but there is also a need to choose among methods of arms control, no matter what its priority. Stating an abstract aversion to "proliferation" may thus mask some other important trade-offs for policy, for the world may not consist of "sixth and seventh" countries, but rather of "Germany" and "India." To reduce the likelihood of one country's going nuclear may increase the likelihood of some other country's doing so, and this possibility raises a special need for choice.

It is not yet certain how the nonproliferation treaty will function here. It may serve to chain together all the prospective nuclear-weapons states, as abstract discussion of a problem makes the abstraction real. Thus a "sixth" nuclear-weapons state may open up the floodgates for the "seventh through fourteenth," but only because the great powers will have been successfully challenged and proven to be paper tigers. The first additional state to acquire nuclear weapons will have done so in the face of the well-articulated opposition of the United States and the Soviet Union; this was not true for Britain or for France, or for China. Sweden today must thus realize that its atomic bombs would be seen not simply as a Swedish military decision but as a precedent, and this should deter Sweden or any other erstwhile "sixth." The "sixth" is thus perhaps made less likely by American support for the nonproliferation treaty, and for the antiproliferation principle, but in part because the "seventh" would certainly follow closely on the sixth. Americans must decide whether this linkage is really a desirable balance.

It is also generally probable that any state that contemplates and then rejects the treaty will have thereby whetted its appetite for weapons. Although the treaty will have effectively inhibited states that sign and ratify, it may also accelerate decisions of others to produce weapons. Without a treaty, pressure against nuclear weapons could have been more closely tailored to each national case, without the implications of worldwide principle and precedent. The atomic-bomb question might never have come up in countries where political or technical circumstances otherwise would not have raised it. The implications of one more nation joining the nuclear club would also have been less earth-shaking.

If proliferation were indeed made into an abstract issue, Indian bombs would be as upsetting as German or Belgian bombs; yet the United States and the USSR have hardly seemed ready to deploy the resources required to persuade India to sign a nonproliferation treaty, and it is even possible that half-hearted pressures for the treaty have accelerated an Indian bomb decision.

Yet the picture should perhaps not be drawn quite so pessimistically. In a paradoxical way, the nonproliferation treaty may instead carve out a unique "sixth" slot for any nation that can cite special circumstances to opt out of it. If India now refuses to sign, and everyone else does sign, we all may start talking about "India's special strategic situation," with implicit resignation to India's joining the nuclear club whenever she gets around to it. The world will then consist of nuclear weapons states, weapons-renouncing states, and India. Preventing West German bombs may thus in the end have lowered the barrier to Indian bombs, and the US and USSR again will have to contemplate the character of the states on each side of the trade-off.

For a time, Indian diplomats kept referring to "countries like India" which also had to oppose the treaty. When signs emerged, however, that the US and the USSR might by default have to regard India as a special case (because of China, and because India was not on the losing side in World War II), the Indian government wisely decided to cease leading the pack in opposition to the treaty and to revert to stating its own position, which might have little relevance to other countries. If India indeed goes ahead and manufactures nuclear explosives, it will wish to deny that it has set a precedent, to deny that there are in fact any "countries like India."

Cold-War Conflicts

The cold war has been substantially modified in form and intensity, but it might be premature to describe it as "over," for American and Soviet interests will still conflict over the political future of some large and valuable pieces of real estate. The nonproliferation treaty was a vehicle of Soviet-American propaganda rivalry before it became a Soviet-American conspiracy, and the rivalry can still make either party have second thoughts about its commitment to the treaty.

It has always been possible that a nonproliferation treaty would limit American rights to deploy nuclear weapons abroad. Nonproliferation and nondeployment are psychologically linked, even if the current treaty distinguishes fairly clearly between the two. Citizens of a country in which American nuclear weapons have been located may resent this deployment, for example, but the resentment can be lessened by token exposure of local forces to nuclear armaments; the nonproliferation treaty may make this impossible.

Since the mid-1950s, the deterrent to Russian conquest of western Europe has depended heavily on the threat that any aggression would quickly escalate to all-out nuclear war. Reliance on the alternative of a purely conventional defense would have been more costly and would have required longer periods of military service for both Americans and Europeans. Stationing American nuclear weapons in Germany has been an effective way of making the threat of escalation credible, and this explains some of the Eisenhower administration's aversion to proposals for nonproliferation and denuclearization treaties. It is true that the Kennedy administration somewhat reduced the reliance on tactical nuclear weapons of its predecessor, but such weapons were deployed in even greater numbers to West Germany, and American theories of deterrence still required that they remain there. Any interpretation of this as proliferation, as banned by a nonproliferation treaty, thus is unacceptable to the United States, and precision and caution have been required in entering into negotiations on the subject.

With the bitter experiences of aid to Peking behind it, the USSR seems unlikely ever to have intended to offer nuclear weapons to its own satellites (to Hungary or to Czechoslovakia?). In the cold-war context, the nonproliferation treaty thus is a somewhat unilateral commitment by the United States and Britain, in exchange for a formalization of what was likely to be the Soviet position in any event. Perhaps more important, it is in exchange for a commitment from other states not to produce their own bombs. It has long been clear that the USSR wished Bonn to renounce nuclear weapons. Even if Bonn had no intention of ever exploiting the weapons option, it might have wished to retain the option until the Russians offered something in exchange —for example, progress toward German reunification. The nonproliferation treaty thus grants the USSR this demand without extracting any such counterconcession.

There is another unilateral aspect in the cold-war context, stemming from the extent to which Soviet propaganda has labeled the treaty an anti-Bonn treaty.[5] For Bonn to have accepted the treaty when Soviet propaganda was turned on full blast would have been an im-

[5] See Theo Sommer, "Germany's Reservations," *Survival*, May 1967, for a fuller discussion of German attitudes on the treaty.

plicit plea of guilty to the Soviet charges; the West German signature indeed was postponed until Soviet pressure had been considerably reduced. For the United States and Britain to have been so enthusiastically in favor of the nonproliferation treaty in the context of 1968 also served to lend credibility to Soviet propaganda against West Germany, and to alienate the West German regime. President Nixon's decision to deemphasize the treaty in 1969 thus also made the treaty easier for Bonn to accept.

Yet Germany is not the only former Axis power that has delayed accepting the treaty. Japan also has not yet signed.[6] The Japanese case is ironic, because American policy-makers have always been a little ambivalent on "non-proliferation" to Japan. Since 1945, the United States has been confronted with a Japanese "nuclear allergy," which logically might have been harnessed to winning quick acceptance for the nonproliferation treaty, an allergy which tends to disapprove of all things nuclear. The allergy has stood in the way of nuclear weapons for the Japanese Self-Defense Forces, as well as any deployment of American nuclear weapons to Japan, or even visits by nuclear-powered naval vessels. The United States has hardly done all it could to reinforce the allergy, and this has caused a general Japanese confusion about the nonproliferation treaty. Emergency access to bases in Japan would be helpful for the defense of Korea, if nothing else, and the issue of US respect for Japan as a nuclear-free zone has thus purposely been left somewhat obscure.

The Ryukyu Islands, of which Okinawa is by far the largest, have an ethnically Japanese population of almost one million people. These islands will be returned to Tokyo's sovereignty in 1972. Okinawa also supports a vast complex of American logistics bases and an important air base. It thus could not be handed back to Tokyo without weakening Japanese aversion to nuclear weapons or American plans for storing such weapons on the island. If Okinawa is the most valuable concession the United States can offer Japan, this bargaining point has hardly been cashed in primarily on behalf of the nonproliferation treaty. Instead, most of the haggling has arisen over the conditions under which the United States will be able to use military bases on the islands. Continued American attempts to retain an option to store nuclear weapons on Okinawa surely have weakened psychological pressures for the nonproliferation treaty.

In the late 1950s, nonproliferation proposals were thus viewed with suspicion in Washington because they threatened to erode American

---

[6] For Japanese views, see Ryukichi Imai, "The Non-Proliferation Treaty and Japan," *Bulletin of the Atomic Scientists*, May 1969.

commitments to West Germany and the NATO area in general. In the late 1960s the opposite concern may arise—that the treaty presupposes some new commitments to nations renouncing nuclear weapons, in order to restore their defensive security to what it might have been if they had become the sixth or seventh nuclear power. After Vietnam, few Americans will be inclined to defensive commitments in Asia or even in the Middle East. In the 1968 Senate Foreign Relations Committee hearings on ratification of the nonproliferation treaty, Secretary of State Rusk was quite explicit in denying that the treaty had imposed any additional defensive obligations on the United States, beyond those already imposed by the UN Charter.

One nation that has indeed been threatened with conventional attack in the past is Israel.[7] It might thus be foolish for the Israelis to renounce the nuclear weapons option if no guarantee of conventional support were forthcoming to take its place, or if no other concessions were made. As suggested above, however, the United States is hardly in the mood to extend formal commitments.

American support is thus bizarrely probabilistic. Israel commands the support of so many Americans that no American administration can ignore a well-advertised threat to that nation's existence. The classic problem, however, is that an Israeli military defeat, if it were ever to come, might be so sudden as to deny the United States time to decide to intervene effectively. Conventional assistance would come too slowly to save Tel Aviv and Haifa. US nuclear retaliation against Cairo and Damascus is neither promised nor likely. American tactical nuclear weapons already deployed in West Germany ensure that any Russian tactical victory in a ground war would induce escalation to nuclear war; nothing ensures this in the event of an Egyptian ground victory facilitated by the same model of Russian tank.

The cold war thus creates problems for an acceptance of the nonproliferation treaty in the Middle East, partly because the Arab-Israeli conflict has not been fully folded into the cold war. Israel does not want to become another NATO ally of the US or to have American troops and nuclear weapons stationed on her territory; if she did wish this, moreover, no American would suggest it. The United States wishes to retain links with Jordan and Lebanon, and indeed with any Arab state, and thus cannot give up pretenses at neutrality even when the Soviet Union has fully committed itself to the Arab position.

The nonproliferation treaty thus is hardly an attractive development for Israel. Given superior Israeli technical competence, an open

---

[7] A fuller discussion of Israeli attitudes can be found in George H. Quester, "Israel and the Nuclear Non-Proliferation Treaty," *Bulletin of the Atomic Scientists,* June 1969.

nuclear weapons option gives Israel more of a psychological lift than any of its Arab opponents. Russia would almost certainly not have given the Arabs nuclear weapons, and indeed may have to give them greater and greater shipments of conventional weapons to offset its explicit NPT denial of nuclear assistance. The United States will pressure Israel not to make nuclear weapons, and perhaps to formalize this by signing the treaty, but it could not credibly supply the security substitute if a substitute were needed.

For the moment the US will probably succeed in deterring Israel from manufacturing nuclear weapons. Yet if Washington can thus deter a bomb, it cannot similarly force Israel to accept the nonproliferation treaty or to forego inducing rumors that it is preparing to manufacture atomic bombs. A reliable, self-policing antiproliferation system is what the treaty is intended to bring to the Middle East. For the present the region must instead be policed by the United States in ways the Arab states may never find totally reliable.

The US perhaps will rest assured that the Israelis would not dare confirm the rumors of weapons manufacture. Yet no Arab state will ratify the nonproliferation treaty either, until Israel signs. An Israeli government, moreover, may decide to defy the US with a fait accompli at some point, especially if some other state has become the sixth. An Israeli legal obligation under the treaty would thus hardly be a negligible asset.

There will thus always be some doubt about whether the nonproliferation treaty was worth its costs and whether it might have been handled by the powers proposing it. Has proliferation not actually been encouraged in the internal debates the treaty has caused? Wouldn't a more subtle policy have been more effective? Aren't the assumptions of Soviet-American cooperation premature?

But the costs and conflict of the treaty have been obvious, whereas the hypothetically lower costs of the more subtle approach may be too easily underestimated. It was perhaps inevitable that the potential for nuclear weapons would produce some unpleasantness in the world. One form of unpleasantness is that bombs get produced and deployed. The alternative form is that constrictions be imposed to prevent this. Lamenting conflict and wasted effort is not always the most relevant exercise in political analysis. Some wasteful conflict may be inevitable, just as it is inevitable that 65 percent of the heat in a fireplace goes up the chimney and only 35 percent warms the room. If all heating systems are wasteful, still we do not elect to freeze.

It is thus far too early to say that the treaty has failed. Signatures and ratification are well behind the most optimistic schedules of its proponents, but the situation is not so immobilized that momentum for the treaty cannot be generated again. The stance of almost every nation regarding the nonproliferation treaty is necessarily complicated, and this complication makes premature much praise and criticism of the treaty. If the advantages of the treaty are far from unequivocable, this at least made the treaty an interesting rather than a dull political issue. The treaty in the end will probably turn out to have been neither very necessary nor very bad, but simply very debatable.

Chapter 13

Conflict in World Politics
by Kenneth N. Waltz

At least one form of conflict, war, has for centuries
been the central concern of those who brood over the
fate of men and nations. Yet few students of international relations have developed theories of conflict
worth mentioning. Sociologists, psychologists, social
psychologists, anthropologists, and economists have
dealt with the problem of conflict mainly at the level
of tensions within and among individuals and groups.
Even at this level, theorists have seldom established
criteria for distinguishing conflict from other phenomena.

Conflict is an elusive concept. Its chameleon quality
is usually explained by pointing out that conflicts are
so complex as always to be mixed in character, com-
pounded of cooperation, competition, and contention in
ever–changing and unspecifiable proportions. To be
sure, this statement has some validity; but it could be
applied to any set of continuing interactions. Successive
exchanges between parties certainly may, and often
do, yield not only changes in issues and interests but
also changes in the ways that the parties relate to
each other. The importance of developing some scheme
for identifying and classifying conflicts in international
relations is enhanced, moreover, by realizing that
without one we can hardly say which of the endless
differences among states actually constitute examples
of conflict. Without some formula for discrimination,
conflict becomes synonymous with international relations.

I am indebted to Ellyn J. Hessler, whose unpublished paper
on conflict was very helpful in the writing of this essay, and to
Helen E. Waltz, who suggested a number of substantive, organizational, and stylistic improvements.

Depending on perspective and definition, one may see conflict absolutely everywhere or almost nowhere. We have to ask which of an infinite number of collisions, which of the many instances in which contrary forces contend, we will in fact label "conflicts."

In order to develop means of identifying conflict, let us begin with a simple case. Pat and Mike have an argument, and finally Pat hits Mike in the nose. Is this a conflict? The answer is not so simple, for it depends upon what we choose to take as a focus. For which unit do we take the action as being significant—that is, as entailing a cost or providing a benefit? If we focus on Pat, we may conclude that she is *resolving* a conflict; in striking the blow she is lessening an inner tension.[1] At the level of the event, however, we can obviously say that the parties are in conflict. Some incompatibility has brought them to blows. The conflict is in the interaction.

Finally, the term "conflict" may be applied to struggles of wider effect—struggles that have important consequences for some larger organization. If the antagonists are placed within some wider order, then the blows exchanged can be evaluated in terms of their positive or negative effects for that order. Conflicts that promise damage, not only to the contenders but also to the system they are part of, are the most terrible and profound—whether of ego and id, of husband and wife, of sections, classes, and races within a country, or of world-shaking wars.

Strife may contribute to the creation and maintenance of an order, or it may become the means of its destruction. The tension of ego and id enlivens the individual, but the tension, if deepened, may drive him to self-destruction. Whether the unit observed is the person, the pair, the state, or the world of states, a distinction must be made between tensions and collisions that have little or no effect on the system within which they occur and those that contribute to the system's development, maintenance, or disruption. The distinction is difficult to make. Whether tension and struggle internal to the system will drive a person to suicide, dissolve a marriage, tear a country apart in civil war, or destroy an international order, depends not only on the units in contention and the intensity of their strife but also on the strength and resilience of the organizational framework.

Nevertheless, explanation of conflict usually proceeds by looking at the condition of each party. The cause of the conflict is found in the

[1] Cf. Lewis Coser, *The Functions of Social Conflict* (New York: Free Press, 1956), pp. 39–40.

properties of the separate units, as these typical questions suggest: Why did one party commit aggression? Why did the other party resist? The content of conflict, the aims and issues involved, are important; but from the answers to such questions one cannot know how content was transformed into conflict. The mechanisms for transforming the internal properties of parties into conflict between them lie not at their individual levels of organization but at a level of organization that comprehends both of them. Thus it was not Pat or Mike who produced the violent interaction but both of them together. In the absence of one, the other's tensions may have found release in his destroying an object or destroying himself. At the level of the unit, the conflict is seen as internal. When and how internal conflict finds external expression, if it does, cannot be explained in terms of either antagonist. To attempt explanation in unit terms is to commit an "ecological" fallacy—to reach conclusions about events at one level by drawing inferences from events, attributes, and interactions at a different level.[2] Attempted explanation at the unit level leads to the infinite proliferation of variables because at this level no one variable, or set of variables, is sufficient to produce the observed result. We must take the unit view and the organizational view simultaneously and ask what effects different organizational conditions may have on the processes of conflict and the prospects for its resolution.

The participants' perceptions of issues and causes will often diverge from the observer's. From the participants' standpoint, the struggle may not be interesting in terms of its generating or wrecking an order. The parties in conflict may care only about their own fates. To them the interesting and important questions then lie at the level of events, issues, motivations, actions, intensity of feeling, degree of bitterness, strength of will, amount of cost, magnitude of gain. The parties may see themselves only as actors—as personalities, so to speak, and not as parts of a system. At the same time, from the standpoint of the system, the contention among parts may appear to be only an uninteresting series of collisions. Fortunately, wars that shake the world order, or even a regional order, are rare. The systemic unimportance of most wars encourages students to treat wars as events to be understood simply in terms of the attributes and interactions of the contending units. Even so, from the standpoint of the observer, conflict

---

[2] For definitions and illustrations of ecological fallacies, see W. S. Robinson, "Ecological Correlations and the Behavior of Individuals," *American Sociological Review*, XV (June 1950), 351–357, and Erwin K. Scheuch, "Cross-National Comparisons Using Aggregate Data: Some Substantive and Methodological Problems," in Richard L. Merritt and Stein Rokkan (eds.), *Comparing Nations: The Use of Quantitative Data in Cross National Research* (New Haven: Yale University Press, 1966), pp. 131–167.

among units cannot be understood without including the organizational perspective.

This statement leads us to the important but difficult question of applying organizational concepts to international relations. Differentiation is a precondition of conflict, and differentiation implies organization, at least in the sense that the different parts stand in a specifiable relation to each other. We can use the term "organization" to cover this pre-institutional condition if we think of an organization simply as a constraint.[3] Because states constrain and limit each other, international relations can be viewed in rudimentary organizational terms. Each state arrives at policies and decides upon actions according to its own internal processes, but its decisions are shaped by the very presence of other states as well as by interactions with them. To make it clear that "organization" need not refer to concrete institutions, and in international relations ordinarily does not refer to them, we shall use the word "structure" and mean by it the relevant environment of states. Sometimes this will be a merely local or regional environment, but more often global structural effects will also come into play. Like a firm operating in a market, a state experiences structural effects whether or not the structure is correctly perceived; and, again like a firm, if the structure is correctly perceived, the strategy of a state can be more intelligently fashioned. Although states are independent, their perceptions of each other and their interactions create a structure to which they tend to adjust. As a consequence of their experience with one another, much of their action becomes habitual.

International Structure and National Behavior

One may look at conflict in terms of each of the units involved, in terms of the interactions of units, or in terms of an actual or postulated organization that overarches the units. The first perspective is appropriate only when the units are disconnected or near to being so. The second perspective is always insufficient for the reasons given above. The third perspective is ordinarily the appropriate one in cases of international conflict. If conflicts are viewed in terms of the effects of the environment on them and in terms of their effects on the environment, then the classification of conflicts will hinge on major differences in the structure of international politics. The following table sets forth such distinctions, indicates the modes of behavior

[3] W. Ross Ashby, *An Introduction to Cybernetics* (New York: Wiley, 1956), p. 131.

Kenneth N. Waltz: Conflict in World Politics

typical within the different structures, and distributes our 21 cases of conflict in an appropriate fashion among categories.[4]

STRUCTURE	TYPICAL MODES OF BEHAVIOR
A. *Loose association of states*	*Regression*

US and USSR
US and China
USSR and China
Argentina and Chile[a]
India and Pakistan[a]
Malaysia, Philippines, Indonesia
Somalia, Ethiopia, Kenya

B. *Close association of states: Opposition*	*Resolute contention*

East and West Germany
North and South Korea
Israel and the Arab Countries[a]
South Vietnam
Nigeria and Biafra
USSR and Czechoslovakia
US and Dominican Republic
US and Southeast Asia[a]

C. *Close association of states: Cooperation*	*Integration*

France and Germany[a]
US and Japan
US and Canada
Portugal and South Africa
Great Britain and France
Nuclear proliferation[a]

D. *Nonassociation of states*	*Withdrawal*

For an explanation of this empty
category, see pp. 469–470.

[a] The parts of three pairs fall into different categories. These essays were originally grouped for comparative purposes according to characteristics other than structure.

Before taking up each category separately, a few words should be said about the table's right-hand column. It derives from Kurt Singer's

[4] Although this book contains 22 separate essays, only 21 cases appear in the table. The discrepancy is accounted for by the fact that two essays were devoted to the Soviet-American case.

profound work on the theory of conflict. He has suggested that in response to situations of conflict:

four and only four basic types of meaningful behavior appear to be possible: renouncing one's objective by staying behind the barrier [regression]; attempting to remove or modify the barrier [integration]; leaving the whole obstructed field [withdrawal]; or resolving to destroy the barrier [resolute contention].

Singer argues persuasively that his classification is complete:

every conflict-solution involves two pairs of opposites, which allow for four and only four combinations: subjective and objective, positive and negative. The subject's attitude may be active or passive; and it may acknowledge the objective incompatibility or repudiate it.[5]

Both regression and withdrawal (A and D) are passive or negative approaches; both integration and fighting (C and B) are active or positive. Both in regressing and in fighting (A and B), the parties accept the presence of an objective incompatibility; both in seeking to integrate and in trying to withdraw (C and D), they refuse to accept their antagonism. "So long as we cling to the criteria of active and passive, positive and negative attitudes," Singer concludes, "the quadruplet of types can claim completeness and finality."[6]

Singer was writing of conflict in general, from psychic disturbance to war among states. When his categories of conflict are applied to international relations, his claim to completeness is validated. The four types of behavior cover both the strategies of states fending for themselves in an anarchic arena and the strategies of states who try to escape from that arena. A and B represent the traditional view of international politics, with states sometimes maneuvering to avoid war and at other times fighting fiercely. In A and C, states seek to avoid violence either by leaving each other alone or by making cooperative arrangements. In A, states concentrate their attention on their own fates, a tendency that is carried to an extreme in D. In B, C, and D, states seek to alter the organization of their affairs profoundly, though by radically different means in one category as compared to another; and if their aims are realized, international politics is brought to an end within the circle of states involved.

[5] Kurt Singer, "The Resolution of Conflict," *Social Research*, 6 (1949), 241. See also his "The Meaning of Conflict," *Australasian Journal of Philosophy*, 27 (December 1949) and *The Idea of Conflict* (Melbourne University Press, 1949).
[6] Singer, "The Resolution of Conflict," p. 242.

To link behavior with structure requires a careful examination of each category. This examination we now undertake.

Loose Association of States: Regression

Domestically, the force of a government is exercised in the name of right and justice; internationally, the force of a state is employed for the stake of its own protection and advantage. Rebels challenge a government's claim to authority; they question the rightfulness and justice of its rule. Wars among states cannot settle questions of authority and justice; they can only determine the allocation of gains and losses among contenders and settle for a time the question of who is the stronger. Domestically and internationally, relations of superordination and subordination are established; but internationally these are relations of strength, not of authority. The power of the strong may deter the weak from asserting their claims, not because the weak recognize a kind of rightfulness of rule on the part of the strong, but simply because it is not sensible to tangle with them. Conversely, the weak may enjoy considerable freedom of action and gain some tangible advantage if they are so far removed in their capabilities from the strong that the latter are not much bothered by their actions or much concerned by marginal increases in their capabilities.

In the unalloyed anarchy of international relations, each state provides the means for its self-preservation as best it can. Elements of conflict in the competition of states outweigh those of cooperation. When faced with the possibility of cooperative endeavor by which mutual gains may be scored, each state must ask how those gains will be divided. They are compelled to ask not "Will both of us gain?" but "Who will gain more?" If an expected gain is to be divided, say, in the ratio of two to one, one state may use its disproportionate gain to implement a policy intended to damage or destroy the other. Even the prospect of large absolute gains for both parties does not elicit their cooperation so long as each fears how the other will use its increased capabilities. Notice that the impediments to collaboration may not lie in the character and the immediate intention of either party. Instead, the condition of insecurity—at the least, the uncertainty of each about the other's future intentions and actions—works strongly against their cooperation.

The fate of each state depends on its responses to what other states do. Will these responses lead them to integrate their activities in order to improve their well-being, to contend resolutely, or to draw apart and watch each other with wariness and suspicion? The answer depends not only on the extent to which their fates are linked in terms of security but also on how closely they are entangled in other than military ways.

States are closely interdependent if they depend on each other for services and supplies that they cannot easily, if at all, provide for themselves. Out of a condition of mutual dependence is born the desire of each party to control whatever it is dependent upon. In such a condition, states cannot afford simply to leave each other alone. They have strong incentives to make one of two choices: either to use force in order to gain control or to build institutions in order to secure the benefits of cooperation. Their close interdependence leads them either to strive for dominance or to contrive institutions for the regulation of their intertwined affairs. In their daily lives, however, the states of category A are not closely entangled, whether one thinks of entanglement in terms of trade and investment or of cultural exchanges and tourism. Because these states are only loosely connected, they can afford to leave each other alone.

States of category A accept each other's continued existence, whether or not reluctantly. They seek neither to destroy the structure of their relations nor to change it drastically; rather, they contend for advantage within it. They do not use their political power to create enduring institutions and peaceful patterns of intercourse, but instead to maneuver and manipulate, to threaten and punish. They appear as both antagonists and partners, sometimes skirmishing in a test of wills, sometimes probing to expose weaknesses, sometimes moving toward agreement on specific issues, sometimes simply drawing apart. In the course of their conflicts, they may go to the brink in a sudden flaring of temper or testing of wills and then draw back. The option of drawing back is available, as is the possibility of occasional skirmishing and even of open warfare. But the structure, a loose one, is not broken either when the parties separate and become quiescent or when they confront each other directly. Their confrontations tend to be inconclusive. Their strategies are grounded on the principle that it is better to yield than to risk mutual destruction. The policy dilemma for states in this type of conflict is that both sides are unwilling to resolve differences completely and establish new patterns of coexistence, yet neither side is prepared to destroy the other.

In their relations with each other, the United States and the Soviet Union provide a nearly perfect example of this pattern. Some of their interests coincide: the prevention of nuclear war, the control of other states' weapons, the mutual limitation of defense budgets for the sake of their domestic economies. At the same time, they differ on a number of issues, notably in Europe, southeast Asia, and the Middle East.

Neither side is prepared to risk military weakness, but none of their disputes can be pushed to the point of war. Mutual opposition may require rather than preclude the adjustment of differences, and yet first steps toward agreement do not easily lead further. Instead, they mingle with other acts and events that keep the tension quite high. In the United States, for example, the 1963 test-ban treaty was described as possibly a first big step toward wider disarmament agreements. In almost the same breath it was also said that the United States could not lower her guard because the Soviet Union's aims had not changed.[7] Each country appears to the other as the only power in the world that can do it grievous harm, and each must worry about the other's use of this capability. Their mutual worry limits both the building up of tensions and the abatement of conflict. Incentives to collaborate, and temptations to fight, are limited by the framework of their action. The result is an ebb and flow of tensions as dramatic agreements are made (test ban, nonproliferation treaty) and as specific crises occur (Berlin, Cuba, the Middle East, Vietnam).

In each case within category A, the weaker party has been forced by its weakness to use military force cautiously, to cast about for allies, to resort to ideological warfare, or to readjust its aims. The conflicts between Somalia and Ethiopia/Kenya, and between Pakistan and India, are cases in point. Somalia and Pakistan, both considerably weaker than their adversaries, seek territorial gains at the expense of their neighbors in order to be united with a greater number of their compatriots. Neither of them can destroy its adversary, nor wishes to do so, but their ultimate objectives limit their cooperation. As a consequence, relations between Somalia and Ethiopia/Kenya and between Pakistan and India tend to be dormant when international and domestic conditions prevent the weaker party from pursuing adventurous policies. When the situation is temporarily altered, violence flares up, as in the brief war of 1965 between Pakistan and India and in the sporadic Somali guerrilla campaign that lasted from 1960 to 1967.

More than other cases in this category, Sino-Soviet and Sino-American relations are marked by intense antagonism; but the general patterns are similar. Territorial issues are a major irritant (Taiwan and the Sino-Soviet border area), although these issues are clearly not the sole causes of conflict. As the weaker party, China is unable to press its designs very far against either the United States or the Soviet Union and presents no important military threat to them. The strong parties are not prepared either to use major military force or to work to

[7] Cf. Kenneth N. Waltz, "The Stability of a Bipolar World," *Daedaelus*, 93 (Summer 1964), 903–904.

strengthen their relations with the weak one. Consequently the typical ebb-and-flow pattern prevails: China moves toward the brink over border incidents with the Soviet Union or in response to American actions in east or southeast Asia, while at the same time the Chinese talk sporadically with one of the superpowers in Warsaw or in Peking or Moscow.

In category A, regression is the dominant mode. Adventurous powers are forced to mold their intentions to contingencies, to let present goals await future opportunities, and to draw back from dangerous confrontations. As Singer suggests, regressive strategy represents the approach of a peasant—patient, shrewd, and persistent. This is a strategy of "dropping and drifting," but the weaker party is "secure in the knowledge that those who yield will . . . conquer in the end."[8] The policies of China, Pakistan, Somalia, Chile, of all of the Malay states, and even of the Soviet Union can often be viewed in these terms.

CLOSE ASSOCIATION OF STATES: RESOLUTE CONTENTION

In category A, the opposition of states raises the specter of possible warfare, but because opposition centers on particular issues, compromises and trade-offs can always be attempted. And even when states are fighting, they intermittently bargain and cajole.

In category B, the parties contend not simply over the difficult issue of who shall gain or lose. They struggle instead with the calamitous question: Who shall dominate whom? The answer to that question can satisfy only one of the parties. Politics, or political form, becomes the stake around which the conflict revolves. One of the parties in contention, and perhaps both of them, seeks to destroy the structure of their relations by undoing the other regime and, in some cases, by displacing its people. Structural struggles spawn strategies of resolute contention; at least one party decides that he will persist in the struggle even should this mean his own destruction. Bargaining becomes impossible, and the conflict becomes the communication.

As the cases of category B suggest, great-power interventions, civil wars, and contention among the dissimilar parts of states that were once united are characteristic instances of this type of struggle. In great-power interventions, conflict is resolved through the adjustment of goals by one party; the weaker state gives way in the face of the threats or the force of the stronger. In civil wars and in the struggle between the parts of a divided state, resolution comes, if it comes at all,

[8] Singer, "The Resolution of Conflict," p. 231.

through military triumph. Either these conflicts end definitely and abruptly as a result of military action, or they continue in crisis as long as the goal of destruction remains a part of the policy of one of the parties.

The Nigerian civil war was a typical conflict over structure. The conflict could not be resolved through compromise because the conflict involved nothing less than the question of whether one state or two would occupy the area known as Nigeria. As long as Biafra continued to exist, the aims of the Federal Government were thwarted. The defeat of Biafra transferred Ibo-Nigerian relations to another framework. In the Arab-Israeli conflict, the Israelis have managed to perpetuate their existence, but they have not managed to alter the aim of their Arab neighbors to destroy Israel. Their intense confrontation has furthered the integration of Israel and has produced some coherence among deeply divided Arab states. Unless at least one side drastically alters its definition of acceptable political arrangements, intense conflict will continue indefinitely.

Conflict within South Vietnam and between the two Germanies and the two Koreas turns on political and ideological differences, in contrast to the strong religious and ethnic divisions in the Middle East. In the German case, the prospect that force will be used to achieve reunification has receded in recent years. The most hopeful possibility in cases of this type is that, as the parties develop separate and viable regimes, the issue politics of category A will replace the structural struggles of category B. The parties may then discover, as the two Germanies show signs of doing, that they can cooperate on some matters without turning every issue into a test of the legitimacy of regimes. In the Korean case, close kinship has not led to reestablishment of social and economic contacts across a hostile frontier. The very intensity of hostility has promoted the tight political integration of both Koreas, a development that vividly illustrates the maxim that organizations are created by their enemies.[9] The political success of the two Koreas has at once lessened their need for each other and made them capable of vying fiercely for mastery.

At whatever level of intensity, the parties to these conflicts share a dissatisfaction with the status quo. They see their basic goals as being incompatible and define the question between them as being, who shall ultimately prevail?

The three cases of great-power intervention are like the others of this category in that the struggle is over the structure, but different

[9] Kenneth E. Boulding, *Conflict and Defense* (New York: Harper & Row, 1962), p. 162.

in that the parties are of grossly unequal power. These interventions represent forceful attempts to alter conditions within particular states or regions in order to bring client states into conformity with the superpowers' notions of proper political arrangements. In each instance, the superpower demonstrated concern over the integrity of its alliance system and, more profoundly, betrayed a fear that failure to maintain control in one area would weaken its control and lessen the credibility of its commitments elsewhere. In the Dominican Republic and in Czechoslovakia, solutions were swiftly and decisively achieved in central areas of the superpowers' concerns. In southeast Asia, the United States sought to reinforce her position at the periphery of her sphere of interest rather than at the core. She was unable to change conditions quickly and was also unwilling to yield. Prolonged conflict resulted. In South Vietnam, the American problem has not been merely to dissuade a government from taking certain actions and to compel it to perform others. Instead, America's self-appointed task has been to promote the establishment of a preferred political order, an immense undertaking that requires far more than military means. American aims, if achieved, would maintain the conditions for continued struggle among the new parts of the old Indochina. Any major part of Indochina that achieves strength will want to reunify the whole. That is the nature of structural struggles. The might of the superpowers allows them to determine the size and the intensity of such conflicts, but not always the outcome.

In structural strife, when the conflict is among unequals the stronger parties face difficult tasks. They wish to retain control or to maintain their friends in power, and such ends are difficult to achieve. In structural strife, when the conflict is among equals the struggles have continued interminably.

Close Association of States: Integration

What can bring two parties closer together than to be locked into a prolonged death-grip? The states of category B are closely associated; they are united in their antagonism. The states of category C are also closely associated, but in cooperative rather than hostile spirit. If states believe that violent conflict would destroy their common good, they may try to promote closer integration through the establishment of durable institutions and reliable patterns of behavior. What makes it possible for trust to replace hostility in the relations of sovereign states so that they may begin to benefit jointly from peaceful and cooperative endeavors? This question can best be answered by considering the change in the quality of the relations of western European states that took place after 1945. For centuries before that date, European great-power politics tended toward the model of a zero-sum game. One state viewed another's loss as its own gain and was constrained to do so by the very conditions of their mutual existence. Faced with the temptation to cooperate in order to secure joint benefits, each state became wary and was inclined to draw back. Category A described the condition of their precarious peacetime existence, a condition that made regression more appropriate than integration. When, on occasion, some European states did move toward cooperation, they did so in order to oppose other states more strongly. The fear that some states would contend resolutely in a structural struggle for dominance overwhelmed the possibilities of European integration. European states could not break the alternation from loose association and regressive behavior to close association and resolute contention as long as each state feared the damaging blows that other states could strike.

The emergence of the Russian and American superpowers created a situation that permitted wider ranging and more effective cooperation among the states of western Europe. They became consumers of security, to use an expression common in the days of the League of Nations. For the first time in modern history, the determinants of war and peace lay outside the arena of European states, and the means of their preservation were provided by others. These new circumstances made possible the famous "upgrading of the common interest," a phrase which conveys the thought that all should work together to improve everyone's lot rather than being obsessively concerned with the precise division of benefits. Not all impediments to cooperation were removed, but one important one was—the fear that the greater advantage of one would be translated into military force to be used against the others. Living in the superpowers' shadow, Britain, France, Germany, and Italy quickly saw that war among them would be fruitless and soon began to believe it impossible.

Once the possibility of war among states disappears, all of them can more freely run the risk of suffering a relative loss. Enterprises can be engaged in that are expected to benefit some parties more than others, partly in the hope for the latter that in other activities the balance of benefits will be reversed and partly in the belief that the overall enterprise itself is valuable. Economic gains may be granted by one state to another in exchange for expected political advantages, including the benefit of strengthening the structure of European cooperation. The removal of worries about security among the states of western Europe does not mean the termination of conflict; it does produce a change in its content. Hard bargaining within the EEC (by France over agricultural policies, for example) indicates that governments do not lose interest in who will gain more and who will gain less. Conflicts of interest remain, but not the expectation that someone will use force to resolve them.

International conditions permitted western European nations to work to upgrade their common interests. The self-interest of each nation encouraged it to join in, as is evident even in the policy of the most reluctant participant, Great Britain. Mutuality of involvement, and the intertwining of affairs, have drawn these states into common endeavors. They cannot easily, if at all, choose to leave each other alone. Because they cannot, the experience of conflict over interests and over purposes leads to efforts to create an apparatus that will reduce conflict or contain it. Politics—negotiation, log-rolling, compromise—becomes the means of achieving preferred arrangements. To manage conflict, a closer integration of activities is sought. The organization by which integration is to be promoted then becomes the object of struggle. How shall it be constructed, and what shall its purposes be? Once these become the most important questions, international relations begins to look like domestic politics.

Saying this makes it clear that some of the cases placed in category C may belong in category A, or may come to belong there. What placement is appropriate depends on how two questions are answered. Do the parties regard the framework of their relations as being so important that they are willing to compromise on particular military and economic issues in order to preserve and strengthen it? Are the parties free simply to leave each other alone? If the answers are first "yes" and then "no," category C is appropriate.

Contiguity, involvement in each other's affairs, mutual confidence built on common experiences—such factors lessen the possibility and the desirability of turning from cooperation and constructive competition and moving instead toward opposition and sharp contention on issues. The high interdependence of some states, as in the case of western Europe, locks them into a cooperative system, and so may the dependence of one state on another, as in the case of the United States and Canada. The close but asymmetric intermingling of their affairs affords the United States many ways of exerting influence.[10] The United States does not have to substitute force for persuasion. The

10 In 1965, for example, US residents owned 44 percent of the total capital invested in Canadian manufacturing firms. M. Watkins et al., Report of the Task Force on the Structure of Canadian Industry, *Foreign Ownership and the Structure of Canadian Industry* (Ottawa: The Queen's Printer, 1968), pp. 199–200.

imbalance of capabilities makes it unnecessary to do so. Each party, moreover, recognizes that its interests are better served by negotiating differences than by openly quarreling over them.

A state's perception of its own strength affects its definition of interest. In the six cases of category *C*, three types of weakness have encouraged behavior aimed at strengthening the structure:

1. The parties perceive themselves to be weak in relation to the great powers (West European states).
2. The parties fear potential weakness in relation to adversaries (Portugal and South Africa).
3. A marked difference in capabilities exists between the parties (US and Canada, US and Japan, the superpowers and potential nuclear states).

The nonproliferation treaty nicely shows how, on a particular issue, two countries may try to create a structure distinct from the general structure of their relations. Overall, American-Soviet relations fall into category *A*. The nonproliferation treaty appears, then, as a case of cooperation on a single issue born out of the desire of duopolists to preserve favored positions, a motivation clearly expressed by William C. Foster in 1965 when he was director of the Arms Control and Disarmament Agency:

When we consider the cost to us of trying to stop the spread of nuclear weapons, we should not lose sight of the fact that widespread nuclear proliferation would mean a substantial erosion in the margin of power which our great wealth and industrial base have long given us relative to much of the rest of the world.[11]

In order to maintain their advantages, strong states may wish to regulate the activities of weak states.

The case of the nonproliferation treaty also shows how different the same structure may look from the standpoint of different states. States that are reluctant to foreswear becoming nuclear powers indefinitely will see American-Soviet regulation not as a limited experiment in institution-building but instead as a simple case of contention. Disarmament efforts have been sponsored mainly by the United States and the Soviet Union. Not surprisingly, they have attempted primarily to regulate other people's armaments. "This has resulted," as a Japanese

[11] William C. Foster, "Arms Control and Disarmament," *Foreign Affairs,* 43 (July 1965), 591.

scholar points out, "in formulating regulations governing non-existent armaments—nuclear weapons of non-nuclear countries rather than governing existing armaments—nuclear weapons of nuclear powers."[12] Self-interest and common interest do not always diverge; the United States and the Soviet Union have tried to persuade other states to believe that a system of regulation will benefit all. Whether the treaty results in a durable system for effective regulation of course remains to be seen.

Nonassociation of States: Withdrawal

Category D is important, and yet it is devoid of cases. The explanation is obvious. "Conflict can occur," as Lewis Coser has said, "only in the interaction between subject and object; it always presupposes a relationship."[13] If effectively pursued, withdrawal strategies eliminate contact. The conflict of the parties may be deeply felt, but if the connection between them is broken, the conflict cannot find violent expression. There is then no case to write about.

In the absence of cases, we can nevertheless say a few words about withdrawal strategies both in aspiration and in reality. The ideal of most anarchists rests on the thought that lessening contacts reduces the possibility of conflict. They have dreamt of small communities of like-minded men living at peace with other such communities because all of them would be nearly self-sufficient and thus little involved in each other's business. The League of Nations' policy of plebiscites, which offered minority ethnic groups the chance to separate themselves from uncongenial nations, was in effect a strategy of preventing conflict by disentangling peoples. National strategies of withdrawal are usually pursued by countries that are especially weak or especially strong. The classic neutralist policies of Switzerland, Sweden, and Belgium, the aspirations of presently underdeveloped countries to remain "unaligned," Britain's traditional aloofness toward continental affairs, American isolationism—all of these fall into the category of withdrawal strategies. The possibility of withdrawing increases with distance. Withdrawal is an option available to the United States in southeast Asia, but not to Israel, Czechoslovakia, Biafra, and North and South Vietnam. The effects of withdrawal strategies are found not in cases of

---

[12] Hisashi Maeda, *The Nature of Disarmament Problems in the Nuclear Age*, unpublished ms. (Honolulu: East-West Center, 1970), p. i.
[13] Lewis Coser, *The Functions of Social Conflict*, p. 59.

conflict but in instances of conflict resolution, of which more will shortly be said.

Situations and Strategies

In each category of the table, a mode of behavior tends to dominate: regression, resolute contention, integration, or withdrawal. Rarely, however, does one of the four modes entirely prevail in the policies adopted by states. Several reasons for the mixture of modes are prominent.

First, the leaders of a state may fully understand the situation they face and may adopt corresponding policies. These leaders may, however, be displeased with the results of their policies and feel inclined to forsake or modify them. The two Koreas and the two Germanies, for example, seek to absorb each other in order to reunify their countries. But through a policy of resolute contention in which the legitimacy of the present structure is denied, a new order is inadvertently created. Each side develops new political, economic, and military ties with a different circle of states. A policy of withdrawal ensues that lessens contact between the two sides and decreases the likelihood of destructive conflict as well. Thus, a policy of resolute contention may foster the opponent's integration into a new order. The desire of the Brandt government to increase contacts with East Germany is based partly on the realization that by resolutely denying the legitimacy of the present structure, the West German government has actually strengthened it.

Second, even if the structure of its relations with others should strongly press a state to adopt a particular strategy, the leaders of the state may fail to understand just what the situation requires. Moreover, the pressures of global and regional structures may push in opposite directions. The complexity of most conflicts makes their placement in one category or another uncertain. We usually find mixed cases, not pure ones. The problem of proper placement becomes still more difficult when the policies of states produce changes, as in the German manner just mentioned, that move a case from one category to another or cause it to fluctuate among them. Even if situation determined strategy uniquely, the difficulties of defining situations precisely would still make for perplexity of choice among strategies.

Third, and most important in practice, the structural factor is only one causal force operating among many. Leaders may well appreciate the strength of the constraints upon them, but they may squirm at the thought of accepting them. China, for example, has pursued a strategy of regression in her actions, but a policy of resolute contention in her many defiant proclamations. The regressive strategy indicates her clear perception of limits; bold statements presumably express the frustrations felt. The vastly superior power of an opponent is a strong argument for adopting strategies of regression or withdrawal. Put starkly, if the superior power presses hard, the weak party should simply surrender. The Dubcek and Balaguer regimes quickly did so; Vietcong and Biafran leaders pursued policies of resolute contention instead. Structural constraints are barriers, but men can try to jump over them. Structure shapes and limits choices; it establishes behavioral tendencies without determining behavior.

Resolution of Conflict

Any one of the four modes of behavior, if formulated in an appropriate strategy and effectively carried through, resolves the conflict: actively, by integrating the parties through common institutions and procedures or by the conquest and absorption of one by the other; passively, by lessening their interactions or by breaking relations completely.

Active resolution seeks to manage conflict, or to end it, by strategies that increase conflict in the short run. The entanglement of states, in their economic affairs, in their physical fears, and in their ideological differences, draws them into conflict and violence. Many of the bitterest and bloodiest wars have been fought by peoples who were closely involved in each other's affairs and who, being most like each other, became obsessed with differences in interests and creeds that outsiders could not even understand.

Strategies of integration seek to promote closer mutual involvement. If successful, such strategies multiply the possibilities of conflict. These strategies are pursued, however, in the expectation that the experience of conflict will itself encourage the parties to seek means of regulation and management. To follow the integrative imperative means not to lessen tensions but to strengthen the order that contains them. The strategy is active and constructive; to the extent that it is successful, it takes the "international" out of international relations by subjecting the interactions of nations to a common control.

The imperative of resolute contention requires that one party struggle to prevail over its opponent, to break his will. The strategy is active, but destructive. The integration of the parties is once again the objective, but here by establishing a relation of dominator and dominated. The victor establishes a new imperium that places once independent states under his own protection and control. However achieved, integration ends international conflict by abolishing international relations.

Not conflict, but the insistence that conflicts be resolved, leads to the use of force. One way to manage a conflict is to refrain from using force in an attempt to resolve it. Using force may produce a settlement to the user's satisfaction; it may help to bring a more adequate organization into being; or it may end in mutual damage and destruction. One may decide to leave the benefits of integration aside in order to avoid risking the calamities of war. Passive modes of resolution avoid this risk. The parties potentially in conflict try to move backward to a looser organization, a simpler order, in which states interact less frequently and in less important ways, gain more autonomy, and become less interdependent. By regression, states reduce their contacts without ending them in the hope that yielding on issues will become easier. The final strategy for the passive resolution of conflict is withdrawal. If states had no relations, they could fight no wars.

As Georg Simmel has said in effect: no conflict, no movement.[14] In individual and in domestic political terms, the modern western mind associates movement with progress. Active strategies draw the parties together. They intensify conflict, and they offer the prospect of increased benefits through the development and management of collective enterprises. But in the relations of states the possibility of promoting progress through conflictive processes carries high costs. In order to evaluate active and passive strategies, we should look at the effects of those processes.

If force may be used by some states to weaken or destroy others, then all states live in fear and are likely to exaggerate the evil intentions and the dangers involved. The possibility that conflict will be conducted by force leads to competition in the arts and the instruments of force. Competition produces a tendency toward the sameness of the competitors, with those who are unable to keep up simply falling by the wayside. Thus Bismarck's startling victories over Austria in 1866 and France in 1870 quickly led the major continental powers (and Japan) to imitate the Prussian military staff system, and the failure of Britain and the United States to follow the pattern simply indicated that they were outside of the immediate arena of competition. Contending states imitate the military innovations contrived by the country of greatest capability and ingenuity. And so the weapons of major contenders, and even their strategies, begin to look much the same all over the world.

[14] Georg Simmel, *Conflict and the Web of Group Affiliation*, translated by Kurt H. Wolff and Reinhardt Bendix (New York: Free Press, 1955), pp. 14–16.

The effects of competition are not confined narrowly to the military realm. Something that might be called socialization to the international political system also occurs. Immediately after their revolution, for example, Bolsheviks appeared on the international scene as the hippies of their day. By his manner of speaking, his dress, and his life style, the hippy dramatically says, "I will not be socialized to *this* system." So the Bolsheviks in the early years of their power preached international revolution and flaunted the conventions of diplomacy. The attitude was well expressed by Trotsky, who, when asked what he would do as foreign minister, replied, "I will issue some revolutionary proclamations to the peoples and then close up the joint."[15] In a competitive arena, however, one party may need the assistance of others. Refusal to play the political game may risk one's own destruction. The pressures of competition were rapidly felt and reflected in the Soviet Union's diplomacy. Thus Lenin, sending foreign minister Chicherin to the Genoa Conference of 1922, bade him farewell with this caution: "Avoid big words."[16] Chicherin, who personified the carefully tailored traditional diplomat rather than the simply uniformed revolutionary, was to refrain from inflammatory rhetoric for the sake of working deals. These he successfully completed with that other pariah power and ideological enemy, Germany.

The close juxtaposition of states promotes their sameness through the disadvantages that arise from a failure to conform to accepted and successful practices. In the Darwinian view, the contending parties are carried to ever higher levels of accomplishment. But in international politics we may well wish that we could forego some of the movement in exchange for a reduction of conflict through the regression of states. And not only that. One may identify conflict with movement, and movement with progress, and applaud the gradual conformity of states to the patterns set by the most highly developed ones. Or one may view such conformity as a denial of national individuality and deplore the reduction of variety.

It has often been argued that benefits would accrue from passive strategies, not only in terms of the relations of states, but also in terms of those states themselves. Viewed internationally, withdrawal is a negative policy, its imperatives being "do less," "become passive," "acquiesce," "retreat." Viewed internally, the aims of the policy may be

---

[15] Leon Trotsky, quoted in Theodore H. Von Laue, "Soviet Diplomacy: G. V. Chicherin, Peoples' Commissar for Foreign Affairs 1918–1930," in Gordon A. Craig and Felix Gilbert (eds.), *The Diplomats 1919–1939*, 1 (New York: Atheneum, 1963), 235.

[16] V. I. Lenin, quoted in Barrington Moore Jr., *Soviet Politics: The Dilemma of Power* (Cambridge: Harvard University Press, 1950), p. 204.

positive: to perfect the society, to develop the economy, to strengthen the political order—in short, to become less involved in others' affairs in order to tend to one's own. Plato believed, and he has been echoed by a long line of utopian writers, that only the isolated state could realize its own individuality. Rousseau saw and deplored the homogenization of European culture that was developing from the close interplay of European states and their peoples. American isolationists prized and sought to preserve their nation's detachment from Europe so that a new world could be fashioned free of contamination from the old one. And many now deplore the Coca-Cola-ization of the world. These examples strongly support the argument that only the isolated state can preserve its distinctive personality and have the chance to develop that personality according to its own inner character.

Active strategies promise peace through the more adequate organization of closely interconnected activities. Passive strategies promise peace through lessening the contacts among contenders. Either way, international conflict is ultimately ended only by abolishing international relations. Kant's vision of perpetual peace through a voluntary union of republics competes with Rousseau's utopia of an isolated Corsica. Neither condition is attainable—hence the ubiquity of conflict and the recurrence of war among states.